THE WORLD'S
FEARLESSNESS TEACHINGS

A Critical Integral Approach to
Fear Management/Education for the 21st Century

R. Michael Fisher

University Press of America,® Inc.
Lanham · Boulder · New York · Toronto · Plymouth, UK

Copyright © 2010 by
University Press of America,® Inc.
4501 Forbes Boulevard
Suite 200
Lanham, Maryland 20706
UPA Acquisitions Department (301) 459-3366

Estover Road
Plymouth PL6 7PY
United Kingdom

Library of Congress Control Number: 2009935306
ISBN: 978-0-7618-4915-5 (paperback : alk. paper)
eISBN: 978-0-7618-4916-2

⊖™ The paper used in this publication meets the minimum
requirements of American National Standard for Information
Sciences—Permanence of Paper for Printed Library Materials,
ANSI Z39.48-1992

To all the world's fearlessness teachers

CONTENTS

FIGURES

FOREWORD

A culture's views and practices regarding something so fundamental to the human experience as education will naturally tell us a great deal about that culture itself. What counts as "important knowledge" and the ways in which that knowledge is supposed to be constructed and conveyed, especially to its young people, mirrors either the richness or paucity of a culture's values. This is why it is of more than just specialized, passing interest that in colleges of education across the United States today—and, indeed, in a growing number of educational sites generally in the post-industrial Western world—education is increasingly being reduced to a quasi-science, a "norm-referenced" and "statistically validated" body of impersonal, decontextualized techniques and tools whose basic purpose is to get students to score well on standardized tests.

These tests are designed to do one thing, and one thing only: to quantify how well a student can "master" (that is to say, "memorize") unrelated bits of information (which the student will promptly forget as soon as the test is over) in areas that have themselves been dissociated from each other (for "ease and efficiency of assessment"). In this manner, schooling becomes, as Joel Spring has so felicitously put it, a "sorting machine"—a way (indeed, *the* way) of institutionally determining which students will play what roles as "worker-citizens" in our brave new corporate society—that real-life dystopia that is now controlled by an increasingly select, powerful, and covert socioeconomic elite—what Paul Simon has portrayed in one of his songs as "a loose affiliation of millionaires and billionaires"; what Paul Friedman has called "the electronic herd" of venture-capitalists, armed with laptops, and ceaselessly in search of fresh politico-economic prey to dominate and devour; and what Peter Dale Scott has identified as the "deep political system" of covert military-fiscal interests that increasingly control the United States and other countries today. Powering this world-historical engine, from top to bottom is fear: a nation's fear of "falling behind" educationally and thus being "devoured" by other national military-industrial complexes; a corporation's fear of being "left behind" in the new world of transnational capitalism with its increasingly global control of markets; and the individual's fear of being downsized, out-skilled, or out-sourced.

What passes as "educational reform," whether of the neo-liberal or neo-conservative variety, is finally, as Michael Fisher skillfully points out in this important book, simply the insidious educational manifestation of these various forms of fear. We are educated into fear, he argues. We are taught, in various (mis-)educative sites (from television to malls to classrooms) and across the lifespan (cradle to grave, from kindergarten to adult education) that we have reason to "be afraid; be very afraid!" Fisher argues that this pathological view of reality—indeed, a view of reality *as* pathology—is educationally embedded in us at every level of our being, from the somatic to the spiritual, so that after pro-longed traumatic exposure a numbness and dumbness sets in, and it does not even remotely occur to us even to question the nightmarish notion that the uni-verse is a hostile place through and through, that universal nature is "red in tooth and claw" (as Tennyson averred), and that we are in an existential zero-sum game where one person's aggressive gain is, by definition, another's irreparable loss.

What makes this book especially consequential for the educator is Fisher's insistence that although this fear is toxic and often delivered educationally, edu-cation can, under his radical re-visioning of it according to his paradigm of fear-lessness, be homeopathically transformed from the toxin itself into an antidote. His pedagogy comes bearing the non-dualistic, Buddhistic good news that every impulse of fear that arises in us can be changed by us, *within* us, through skillful educational means, into an occasion for reconstructing our lives in mature opti-mism, sane empowerment, and loving creativity. This is what Buddhism calls "using the 'mind-weeds' of fear and doubt as compost to cultivate the delightful garden of liberation and empowerment." Fisher offers a vision of how this can be done educationally. And he wisely insists that because the terrible curriculum of fear has been implanted in us at every level of our being, it must be addressed in an integral, holistic manner that existentially transforms not only individuals but also their cultures. What Fisher offers us, at both the personal and collective level, are some preliminary theoretical ways and practical means to transcend the matrix of fear and step out (as is our birthright) onto the bright landscape of a teleological optimism—one that lies at the heart of Fisher's profound, and pro-foundly healing, educational vision.

Clifford Mayes
Professor, Educational Psychology
Brigham Young University
Provo, Utah, U.S.A.

PREFACE

[A]s [Pope] John XXIII pointed out, the 'Law of fear' is not the only law under which men [sic] can live, nor is it really the normal mark of the human condition. To live under the Law of fear and to deal with one another by 'the methods of beasts' will hardly help world events. . . . In order for us to realize this, we must remember that 'one of the profound requirements of nature is this: . . . it is not fear that should reign but love.' -Thomas Merton

Thomas Merton (1915-1968), internationally celebrated Trappist monk and scholar, was writing on faith and violence in the 1970s,[1] when he quoted the progressive late Pope John XXIII (1881-1963) on the ubiquitous problem of fear in our world. Merton also famously wrote, "At the root of all war is fear" and Buddhist monk Thich Nhat Hanh, wrote, "peace . . . means non-fear."[2] How might these truths shape how to teach peace and enact non-violence?[3]

Lamenting on this plague of fear, Merton further observed that it was not merely our fear of each other that stifled our progress but our fear of *everything*. Merton concluded that this pervasive force of fear stops us from even being able to trust and love our own self.[4] Whether one fully agrees with Merton's sentiments, I see enough universal truth in his claim to warrant opening this book with a somewhat sobering, yet realistic, view of our human condition and era.

However, in the chapter pages ahead I do not focus primarily on fear. Instead I attend to *fearlessness,* which typically receives far less discussion than fear (especially in the West). Therefore, I focus not on the cause of war, violence, self-hatred, dis-ease and mistrust but on the transformational[5] and emancipatory cause of just and democratic peace. In fearlessness, we experience an equally pervasive force which will enable great wisdom and selfless compassionate service through developing resilient trust and love for oneself and others.

What foundation can we build upon to enact 'great cause' toward what sociologist Elise Boulding calls a "culture of peace"[6] or what I'd call a "culture of fearlessness," instead of what sociologist Barry Glassner and others, like filmmaker Michael Moore,[7] call a "culture of fear"? The latter being a violent patriarchal "war culture" of "Empire," as described so well by cultural-environmental critic David C. Korten in *The Great Turning*[8] or by sociologist Benjamin Barber in *Fear's Empire*.[9] First and foremost, it will have to be supported by an ethical foundation that is not ruled by the "Law of Fear" and its various forms like "scarcity mentality," as business guru Stephen Covey called it.[10]

Motivation, especially at its deepest roots, intrigues me. I see myself as an educational architect, and one who pursues a philosophy and design resonating with what postmodern sacred architectural theorist Alberto Pérez-Gómez calls an architecture "built [motivated] upon love"[11] as opposed to what feminist architectural theorist Nan Ellin charges to be a violent "architecture of fear"[12] which is coming to dominate our contemporary urbanism and landscapes. Where would we look for historical and contemporary examples of such liberating structures, organizations,[13] or societies, not subsumed under the motivational Law of Fear but rather enveloped by the Law of Love? Who has been and could be adequate and qualified leaders to guide us beyond a *fear-based* law, paradigm and worldview? These questions motivate my fearlessness research and teaching and underlie everything in this book.

To focus on fearlessness and its many forms, however, is not wise if such focus denies or takes flight from the fear-based historical, economic, sociopolitical and cultural context in which most of humanity is living today. Though my in depth critical writings on fear are found elsewhere,[14] the introduction material of *The World's Fearlessness Teachings* gives fear its due credence. Clearly, fear and fearlessness are dialectical conceptions and phenomena, neither of which can be understood well without knowing the other.

For those of you who are critics, and part of the human potential movement and 'new age' communities, I challenge you to look beyond *only* the interior psycho-spiritual dimensions of fear. Rein in your quick diagnosis that "focusing on fear will bring only more fear." The partial truth therein is not what I deny; I merely ask readers and critics to embrace a wide context that includes but goes beyond the "mind creates everything" approaches, for a more critical holistic-integral approach to the Fear Problem and its solutions.

Many others, like myself, sense humanity's Fear Problem is growing ever more complex and embedded in the 'normal' and 'everyday.' In the early 1990s, postmodern literary and cultural critic Brian Massumi offered a chilling set of questions and a post-capitalist diagnosis that validates my academic observations today:[15]

> Fear is a staple of popular culture and politics. There is nothing new in that. In fact, a history of modern nation-states could be written following the regular ebb and flow of fear rippling their surface, punctuated by outbreaks of outright hysteria. . . . [The serious problem is in] the United States, where the tools of the organized fear trade seem to have undergone a particularly complex evolution adapting them to an ever-widening range of circumstances. . . . the social landscape of fear. . . . [The great concern is have] fear-producing mechanisms [i.e., "fear production," *via* mass media and its "technologies of fear"] become

so pervasive and invasive that we can no longer separate our selves from our fear. If they have, is fear still fundamentally an emotion, a personal experience, or is it part of what constitutes the collective ground of possible experience?. . . . in a sense we have become our fear, and if that becoming is tied up with movements of commodification carrying capital toward intensifying saturation of the same social space suffused by fear, does that mean that when we buy we are buying into fear. . . . There is . . . a general consensus that we cannot in fact separate ourselves from fear, thus it is necessary to reinvent resistance. . . . For if the enemy is us, analysis, however necessary, is not enough to found a practice of resistance. Fear, under conditions of complicity, can be neither analyzed nor opposed without at the same time being *enacted*.

Similar to Massumi's critique, one could read Naomi Kline's *The Shock Doctrine* (2007)[16] on the perils of "fear production" trauma of the masses, due to a hysteric war-making mentality in much of corporate media, management, and governing today. Fear's saturation of our social space and formation of our self/identity has led postmodern sociologist Zygmunt Bauman to write a revealing book on *Liquid Fear* (2006); a title which offers an apt metaphor for the insecurity of the excess 'fluids' and 'floods' caused by a structural globalization of capital (e.g., "fluidification," as Massumi called it[17]). How does one resist global liquid fear that floats, attaches to, and seeps through cracks in seemingly everything? How does one manage it when it is so ubiquitous we cannot even detect it most of the time—as it has become so normalized, and so how we think and behave, and who we are?

Yet, fearsome as all the media-exacerbated "Global Warnings" may be (e.g., "melt down of the economy" and social order or "killer viruses, killer waves, killer drugs, killer icebergs"[18] and "killer kids"), Bauman suggests humans are not mere victims but adapting (often unconsciously), and more than that they are transforming everyday liquid fear and themselves. Not all has been lost nor all been destructive. For Bauman sees an oblique and positive recurrent stream of near-immortal "resurrections." He wrote (in somewhat Zen-like tongue-and-cheek style),[19]

We can even come to *enjoy* the 'global warnings.' After all, living in a liquid modern world known to admit only one certainty—the certainty that tomorrow can't be, shouldn't be, won't be like it is today—means a daily rehearsal of disappearance, vanishing, effacement and dying; and so, obliquely, a rehearsal of the non-finality of death, of recurrent resurrections and perpetual reincarnations. . . . Like all other forms of human cohabitation, our liquid modern society is a contraption attempting to make life with fear liveable. . . . Our inventiveness knows no bounds.

No doubt, not everyone is able to stand back and take this privileged analysis as Bauman, myself and some others might. Perhaps humanity is maturing through these global "crises" and "rehearsals" of loss and death and "resurrection" as we carry on and repair the damage, cope, and sometimes reform, transform and heal. I argue in this book that we are being forced in the 21st century to learn new fear management/education strategies, and forced to re-vision our entire view of the nature of fear and its role in shaping humanity. Bring your experience and knowing, and simultaneously bring an open mind to your reading. Allow for a complete re-vision of your own biased lenses and knowledge about fear and how best to deal with it.

Evidence shows universally that the vast majority of humans have learned to organize their values, worldviews, their lives and institutions, largely around the Law of Fear instead of the Law of Love. Virtually every major religion of the world and the great secular philosophical wisdom traditions have made a similar claim as Merton's and the Pope's. The quest that drives me is to find the way *in between* the two "core emotions" *Love* and *fear*. Those are the two simplistic oppositional and ethical poles the 'great ones' often speak and write about. This paradigmatic theme returns time and again throughout this book.

Our daily challenge and choice-making, however, is an existence less purified and reified which weaves, wobbly at times, *in between* the motivational poles of Love and fear. I think the more useful concept, discovered in my studies, is the *path of fearlessness*. I share what I know now, and may we all add creatively to it. Let's build a better fear library for the world in order to help us learn and teach, and better discern when we are serving the wrong 'master.' This means we will have to really look at fear, as fearlessly as we can. Massumi quoted William S. Burroughs' appropriate (though limited) fear management approach to this task:[20] "Never fight fear head-on. That rot about pulling yourself together, and the harder you pull the worse it gets. Let it in and look at it. You will see it by what it does."

Good advice, perhaps for some—for Burroughs himself; but not everyone is interested, ready, or able to use the same fear management approach in all cases. Not everyone thinks about nor cares about the "global" situation (crises). Most people have other priorities with a focus on their own lives in their own psyche, or home or community. Generally, they care about immediate problems or crises and "local" fear(s). Their solutions are often short-sighted and short-term. Global liquid fear, for example, is not on their minds as a significant problem. This point is made throughout this book. One ought not try to get everyone perceiving, thinking and valuing the same way, with the same consciousness and concepts. It won't happen, because consciousness is expressed developmentally; and because people and their organizations embrace issues (problems) with various interpretations (worldviews); and thus, they differentially work to progress beyond them as they are ready and circumstances allow. Zealots of all ideological stripes, who perhaps lack patience and compassion for developmental realities, will be challenged with what I have to say. And I invite them to challenge me too.

My theory of fearlessness creates more room for customizing fear management/education in a postmodern sensitive, developmental and evolutionary framework. Yet, at some level, we are all called by pressing global circumstances to develop a new relationship with fear and ourselves. As an educator, I contend we need to develop a *critical literacy of fearlessness* that has rarely if ever been taught to us—certainly not in most schools or homes. And when it has been taught it is characteristically incomplete, misguided and distorted, even in the best intentions of the teachers and curriculum, be it from religious leaders, psychologists, business gurus, daycares, holistic health practitioners, popular cultures, or wherever people have been trying to help us manage fear.

As adults and children we have to learn to critically distinguish when we (or they) are following the Law of Fear and when we (or they) are not. Then we ought to act to intervene and change things if excessive fear is leading the way. "Skillful means" as the Buddhists say, is easier said than done. Good theory may help with devising the right means (motivations) but there are no "formulas" for success in all cases. We'll have to learn by our mistakes. One thing for sure is that we cannot leave it up to others (including authorities) to do that quality *fearwork* for us. Each of us has some degree of responsibility to better educate ourselves in fear management. I want to help.

The World's Fearlessness Teachings, timely for a world so obviously riddled with excessive fear, offers a plethora of teachings on fearlessness from sacred and secular traditions and new thinking. These teachings, some overt and some very subtle, are spoken and written as cultural artifacts and records through time and across sociocultural, political, geographic and disciplinary boundaries. They record how humans have come to know fear and promote fearlessness as a way of fear management and education. Having collected and studied tens of thousands of these records for the past 20 years, the pivotal questions for this book are: *How does one make sense of all the diversity of teachings?* Following that, *How can they be critiqued and improved? How can they be put to the best educational, if not therapeutic and transformative, use for the most people—even for whole societies and the global village?*

As the most basic definition of fearlessness I use in this text, *generic fearlessness* is a direction of intention and organization whereby less fear is desired rather than more. Such a fear management aim or direction is made individually and collectively. It is always going on, more or less hidden from our consciousness and choice-making. A foundational premise (and principle) from my research is that *when fear appears, so does fearlessness* to resist and counteract it—which means, a "natural" fear management capability is built-in to the success-focused Life-systems of Earth's evolution. I am talking about at least four billion years of 'Intelligence' already existing to back up the continuity of life forms on the planet. Of course, there is still risk of extinction, and always will be.

At the largest level of imagination one could argue and theorize that such a direction from *fear to fearlessness*, is ultimately the aim or *telos* of all development, consciousness, and evolution itself. I call that *historical fearlessness*. This principle is obliquely similar to Bauman's notion of "resurrection." The late R. Buckminster Fuller (1895-1983), world famous futurist, inventor and 'father' of the sustainability movement, knew also of this inherent cosmic spirit to be successful, when he wrote,[21]

[W]e are in an unprecedented crisis because cosmic evolution is also irrevocably intent upon making omni-integrated humanity omni-successful, able to live sustainably at an unprecedented higher standard of living for all Earthians. ...

Our crises have a great lesson to teach. Whether one agrees with Fuller or not, reality is not so simple as a principle or speculation. *Fearlessness* with its potential gift of resilience in crisis and fear, if one studies it deeply and widely, turns out to become a very exciting but extremely complex topic and phenomena, with at least 15 different meanings (like "definitions") offered in this text. Evidence shows different meanings sometimes contradict each other, and sometimes have overlapping similarities. They are also (mostly) in a discourse competition for who's truth is the *best* and *only* truth. My point is that various forms and interpretations of fearlessness by different people and organizations can counter and undermine the true effectiveness of good fear management/education. You may have noticed, Earthians have not all agreed on what direction to take to improve things, and probably never will. That said, my theory of fearlessness is an attempt in progress to find a more acceptable general truth, which more people can agree upon as the best way to go in managing fear and teaching about managing fear.

With all the conflict, injustice, wars, violence, suffering and environmental destruction that has also been recorded we may come to pause about any universal truth claim that human development has a trajectory toward fearlessness. This growing concern and fear is rampant in highly industrialized countries where many are becoming hyper-aware of environmental problems, since Al Gore's recent anti-Global Warming campaign. All of which raises not only pause but a souring doubt about progress as that of mastering human fear(s), as Modernity with its liberal science and capitalism (or even socialism or communism) often promised.

We, post-moderns, have indeed entered this "climate of fear," mood of doubt and often cynicism about such a defeat, and may question if such a thing as "fearlessness" is possible, desirable or even human. The sting of world wars, Hiroshima-Nagasaki, and the Holocaust, to name a few culturally traumatic events, remains often paralyzing to our vision of a better future. The vast majority struggle, especially those racked by poverty today, to have a positive and fear-less attitude toward healthy and sustainable progress, when more fear rather than less seems the consequence of time itself and especially modern development.

On the more conservative side (using that word in its widest sense) there is a large contingent in fact, who believe notions or actions of "fearlessness" are the very problem with humanity not the solution. They prescribe *more fear* to keep us and things in order. They may prescribe governments should be afraid of the people. I will argue against these types of fear-based prescriptions and instead pursue a model and theory which suggests we are progressing and very rapidly indeed and less fear not more is the way to go. Our means of fear management are, unfortunately, well behind the rate of change, evolution and fear-mongering going on. That is troublesome, if not despairing at times. Thus, the important timing of this book and our need to better understand fearlessness (and fear) in an evolutionary context.

The theory of fearlessness I put forth is optimistic and unique among the fear management literature humanity has produced. It is a *critical holistic-integral theory* that embraces and honors the better truths of Premodernity, Modernity and Postmodernity—and opens the door to a post-postmodern view of fear and fearlessness that I believe will 'blow your mind.' It does mine. At the same time, a postmodern perspective predominates where I situate myself as a curriculum theorist, fearologist, a "boomer" (lived as a 20s something through the Cold War) and as someone experiencing the reality of a post-9/11 era. As an academic living in Canada at the time, I handed in my dissertation comprehensive exams to my research committee six days before the 2001 attacks in the USA by "terrorists." The title of my dissertation is "Fearless Leadership In and Out of the 'Fear' Matrix." My future prediction of "Fear Wars" proved accurate. From then until now I have been working toward a praxis in order to put the 'rubber to the pavement'—step-by-step. This first, mostly theoretical book, offers my vision of a first step, not a complete applied answer.

The post-9/11 era has exacerbated our worst modernist fears perhaps, that the "century of fear" (i.e., the 20th, as the late Albert Camus called it[22]) is turning into the "century of terror" (21st). Most all of humanity is suffering in and/or witnessing suffering *via* the dramatization of something called the "War on Terror" as declared by the American G. W. Bush Jr. administration after September 11, 2001. This is a "War on Fear" (aka "War of Fear") by any other name.

One has to ask seriously whether such a war is increasing fear or lessening it? One could easily guess what Thomas Merton would reply, or millions more who are reflecting on this global problem that won't go away. What better *call* to awaken could there be? Our attention has been brought right front and center on the word "terror" (which is merely fear's extreme cousin) in order to force humankind to improve its fear management/education on this planet! May *The World's Fearlessness Teachings* enrich your vocabulary and discernment as the spirit of fearlessness emerges in and around you, step-by-step. As Yogic wisdom suggests "[A]waken my true nature of strength. . . . May the spirit of fearlessness possess me on my way through life, and may nothing but truth be the motive of my actions."[23]

R. Michael Fisher
Carbondale, IL
October 5, 2008

Notes

1. Thomas Merton, "Faith and Violence," in *Thomas Merton on Peace*, ed. G. C. Zahn (NY: McCall, 1971), 189.

2. Thich Nhat Hanh, *Anger: Wisdom for Cooling the Flames* (NY: Riverhead Books, 2001), 131.

3. Gandhi's approach sees fear and non-violence as incompatible, as well, the ancient ethical theories in South Asia (Buddhists, Jains, Hindus) also make this universal

point in terms of a concept and practice of "gift of fearlessness" (i.e., gift of non-violence, or no harm). See Maria Heim, *Theories of the Gift in South Asia* (NY: Routledge, 2004).

4. Thomas Merton, *New Seeds of Contemplation* (New Directions, 1972), 112.

5. Although I am interested in learning for the purposes of change, coping, healing, transformation, transmutation, and liberation; basically, I am a "transformer," by intention in my work and life. I prefer to focus on healing onward in this list. All these terms are addressed at some point in the text. Their meanings will depend on use. It would take too much space to delineate all of these learning processes in depth, and their controversial definitions. Suffice it to say for this text that "transformation" is drawn from many traditions as a "big change" (turn around, or maturation) in development, which can be applied to individuals or collectives. In the human potential movement/new age "Transferring energy from outer-dominance to inner-dominance, from ego to Essence [that is], is the work of transformation," according to Small. More often, I use the term transformation to mean shifting of development and identity (and actions, values, thinking) from fear-based to fearlessness. Educationally, I follow roughly the notion of "transformative learning" by Mezirow et al., although, there are more political (critical) views of this as well by other theorists (e.g., Giroux), which I also drawn on indirectly throughout. See Small, Jacquelyn, *Transformers: Personal Transformation: The Way Through* (Marina Del Ray, CA: DeVorss and Co., 1984), 111. Mezirow, Jack, *Fostering Critical Reflection in Adulthood: A Guide to Transformative and Emancipatory Learning* (San Francisco, CA: Jossey-Bass, 1990).

6. Elise M. Boulding, dubbed "The Mother of Peace Research" used the term "culture of peace" (in contrast to what she calls "war culture") in the late 1980s to early 1990s. It was taken up by UNESCO in 1989 and has remained as an important conceptual pivot for much of its programming since, according to Adams. David Adams, "Early History of the Culture of Peace: A Personal Memoire." Retrieved October 4, 2008 from http://www.culture-of-peace.info/history/introduction.html. Elise Boulding's agenda, although varied in her 40 year career in the Peace Movement, has recently focused on uncovering the hidden history of "cultures of peace" that have existed and been excluded from history books, the latter which focus on war and conflict not peace. See Elise Boulding, *Cultures of Peace: The Hidden Side of History* (NY: Syracuse University Press, 2000). Similarly, I have found a hidden (excluded) "history of fearlessness," especially in the Western world.

7. I highly recommend Moore's films *Bowling for Columbine* (2002) and *Fahrenheit 9/11* (2004).

8. David C. Korten, *The Great Turning: From Empire to Earth Community* (San Francisco, CA/Bloomfield, CT: Berrett-Koehler/Kumarian Press, 2005).

9. Benjamin R. Barber, *Fear's Empire: War, Terrorism, and Democracy* (NY: W. W. Norton, 2003).

10. Stephen R. Covey teaches a management approach based on "'abundance mentality' (as opposed to a scarcity mentality)." Cited in A. Nagle, and P. Pascareua, *Leveraging People and Profit: The Hard Work of Soft Management* (Elsevier, 1997), 128.

11. Alberto Pérez-Gómez, *Built Upon Love: Architectural Longing After Ethics and Aesthetics* (Cambridge, MA: The MIT Press, 2006). The main point of Pérez-Gómez is that both ethics and aesthetics (and "sustainability") in our postmodern world, if based on love, cannot alone be based on convention, science, and "rules." Goodness, Beauty (and Truth), are derived from much more subtle means and consciousness, as I pursue here under the guide of critical integral theory (cf. McIntosh, Wilber) and its application to a postmodern (ethical and aesthetic) theory of fearlessness.

12. Nan Ellin (ed.), *Architecture of Fear* (NY: Princeton Architectural Press, 1997).

13. Such structures/organizations are studied and defined by Bill Torbert (Boston College School of Management): "Continuous quality improvement requires a type of liberating organizational structure that maximizes productivity and inquiry—that maximizes accountability and the opportunity for developmental transformation toward self-balancing among peers." William R. Torbert, *The Power of Balance: Transforming Self, Society, and Scientific Inquiry* (Newbury Park, CA: Sage, 1991), 6.

14. See some of my writing on the Internet and/or my "CV" on my website http://www.feareducation.com.

15. Brian Massumi, "Preface," in *The Politics of Everyday Fear*, ed. B. Massumi (Minneapolis, MN: University of Minnesota Press, 1993), vii-x.

16. Naomi Kline, *The Shock Doctrine: The Rise of Disaster Capitalism* (NY: Metropolitan Books/Henry Holt, 2007).

17. Brian Massumi, "Everywhere You Want to Be," in *The Politics of Everyday Fear*, ed. B. Massumi (Minneapolis, MN: University of Minnesota Press, 1993), 15.

18. Bauman and I are excerpting a quote from Craig Brown in his witty chronicle of the 1990s. Quoted terms are from the edited extract in *Guardian Weekend*, 5 Nov., 2005, 73, cited in Zygmunt Bauman, *Liquid Fear* (Cambridge, UK: Polity Press, 2006), 5.

19. Ibid., 5, 6, 8.

20. Cited in Massumi, x.

21. R. Buckminster Fuller, *Critical Path* (NY: St. Martin's Press, 1981), xvii.

22. This iconic phrase was used by Camus in an essay "Neither Victim Nor Executioner" "two answers" which appeared in a 1946 edition of the French underground newspaper *Combat*. See http://www.ppu.org.uk/e_publications/camus1.html.

23. Selvarajan Yesudian, *Self-reliance Through Yoga: Aspects of Yogic Wisdom Collected and Commented on by the Author* (NY: Unwin Paperbacks, 1979), 134.

ACKNOWLEDGEMENTS

Voices from multiple experiences, times, and disciplines carry their way in this text. This is the first publication of mine, in a full-length book, that demanded such careful 'fitting' of so many. I trust the unity as well as the diversity holds the entire construction integrally, so as to do justice to the passionate voices herein. I am therefore deeply grateful to my "students" over the years, including: the public school teaching years, the work at Quest Ranch rehabilitation program for teens and their families in crisis (Cremona, Alberta, Canada), the adult learners in Continuing Education at the University of Calgary who braved their way through the radical course I taught on "Basics to the Path of Fearlessness," the hundreds of folks who came and went from the 'fear vaccine' program at the In Search of Fearlessness Centre (Calgary, Alberta), the class of a dozen undergraduates that traveled in the deadly heat of prairie summer through my latest exploratory course on "Addiction and Recovery as Fear Management," at the University of Lethbridge (Lethbridge, Alberta), and so many others, who have supported, critiqued, and otherwise engaged me and my work over the past two and a half decades in an educative quest for something profound and transformative. To those not mentioned specifically, you know who you are. I simply cannot mention everyone here. However, some are particularly outstanding in memory as ongoing full-risk life-time advocates from the lay public to academia (in no particular order): Chas Hale, Jan Sheppard, Normand Bergeron, Ken Markley, Dr. Gary Nixon, Gavin de Becker, and Dr. Sean Esbjörn-Hargens. Dr. Cliff Mayes, well, you were over-the-top as inspirator-compañero for me. And to Angela Prider, shaman-woman guide (and all otherworldly guides), I am grateful beyond rational measure, as the 'seed' for this book was planted from your magic 'soil.'

I cannot thank my daughters Leah (27) and Vanessa (25) enough for their unconditional spirit, but also challenging intellects. Your palpable belief in me and the vision of fearlessness carries me on your youthful 'wings.' Vanessa's sharp and compassionate editorial comments on the manuscript were a life-saver in the early stages of the ms. Some of what you read herein is crafted by a writer's hand more skillful than my own. I am grateful to Dinah Seibert, Mary Lee O'Hara, Greg Wendt and Barbara Bickel for valuable editorial comments to shape a more palatable book. I thank you all for letting me speak as I do, wildly and wobbily, as the curriculum of "R. Michael Fisher" isn't an easy straightforward one even for me. My life-partner and soul mate Barbara Bickel, as always, pointed to what was lacking in my work, and thus kept me humble. She led the way to encouraging me to complete this and financially supported the book. Her love in our 18 year relationship is truly a divine enigmatic source for me. Yet, it all began long ago with a short-lived soul mate, Catherine Sannuto.

Dare I neglect to mention the institutional academic support, variable as it was, to offer me the time, space, and resources in my late middle years, in order to put my experience into postmodern theoretical expressions. In particular, the grants and fellowships from The University of British Columbia and the Canadian government (Social Sciences and Humanities Council) were foundations that kept me and my family economically well, during the toughest of those graduate research years. To my publisher contact at UPA, Samantha Kirk, who was always generous and professionally responsible, I am indebted for reaching out and pulling me in to the 'legitimate' book publishing world. To UPA's Brian DeRocco and Victoria Koulakjian (Rowman & Littlefield), I send my praise for your patience in guiding me through all the technical details (nightmares) of preparing the camera-ready copy. And lastly, I thank all the world's fearlessness teachers who have led the way, making my task a whole lot simpler and less dangerous.

My acknowledgements include the following authors and publishers for permission to reprint excerpts:
"Fearlessness: The Last Organizational Change Strategy" (2007) by Art Kleiner with Margaret Wheatley, Reprinted with permission from *strategy+business*, published by Booz & Company, www.strategy-business.com; Website http://www.erickajackson.com and "The Fearless Revolution™" by Ericka D. Jackson, © 2008 by Ericka D. Jackson; and HuffingtonPost.com and Arianna Huffington, "Why We Need An Epidemic of Fearlessness to Counter The Fearmonger-in-Chief" by Arianna Huffington, © 2008 by HuffingtonPost.com.; and Judy Grahn excerpts from "Are Goddesses Metaformic Constructs?: An Application of Metaformic Theory to Menarche Celebrations and Goddess Rituals of Kerala and Contiguous States in South India" by Judy Grahn, unpublished dissertation. San Francisco, CA: California Institute of Integral Studies, © 1999 by Judy Grahn; and Beacon Press and Judy Grahn for excerpts from *Blood, Bread, and Roses: How Menstruation Created the World* by Judy Grahn, copyright © 1993 by Judy Grahn; and Anchor Press/Doubleday and Ken Wilber for excerpts from *Up From Eden: A Transpersonal View of Human Evolution* by Ken Wilber, © 1981 by Ken Wilber; and Random House, Inc. and Ken Wilber for excerpts from *The Marriage of Sense Soul: Integrating Science and Religion* by Ken Wilber, © 1998 by Ken Wilber; and Shambhala Publications, Inc. and Ken Wilber for excerpts from *A Theory of Everything: An Integral Vision for Business, Politics, Science, and Spirituality* by Ken Wilber, © 2000 by Ken Wilber; and Shambhala Publications, Inc. and Ken Wilber for excerpts from *Integral*

2000 by Ken Wilber; and Shambhala Publications, Inc. and Ken Wilber for excerpts from *No Boundary: Eastern and Western Approaches to Personal Growth* by Ken Wilber, © 1979 by Ken Wilber; and Shambhala Publications, Inc. and Ken Wilber for excerpts from *Grace and Grit: Spirituality and Healing in the Life and Death of Treya Killam Wilber* by Ken Wilber, © 1991 by Ken Wilber; and Shambhala Publications, Inc. and Ken Wilber for excerpts from *A Brief History of Everything* by Ken Wilber, © 1996 by Ken Wilber; and Shambhala Publications, Inc. and Ken Wilber for excerpts from *Integral Spirituality: A Startling New Role for Religion in the Modern and Postmodern World* by Ken Wilber, © 2006 by Ken Wilber; Shambhala Publications, Inc. and Ken Wilber for excerpts from *Boomeritis: A Novel That Will Set You Free* by Ken Wilber, © 2002 by Ken Wilber; and Shambhala Publications, Inc. and Ken Wilber for excerpts from *Sex, Ecology, and Spirituality: The Spirit in Evolution (Vol. 1)* by Ken Wilber, © 2005 by Ken Wilber; and Shambhala Publications, Inc. and Ken Wilber for excerpts from Shambhala's website "End Note 1 (Chapter 10)" in *Boomeritis* by Ken Wilber, © 2002 by Ken Wilber; and Sage Publications, Inc. and Ken Wilber for excerpts from "Odyssey: A Personal Inquiry into Humanistic and Transpersonal Psychology," *Journal of Humanistic Psychology* 22 (1982) by Ken Wilber, © 1982 by Ken Wilber; and Sounds True, Inc. and Ken Wilber for excerpts from *Kosmic Consciousness* by Ken Wilber, © 2003 by Ken Wilber; and excerpts reprinted from "Finding Courage," the Summer 2003 edition of *YES! Magazine*, 284 Madrona Way NE Ste 116, Bainbridge Island, WA 98110. Subscriptions: 800/937-4451 Web: www.yesmagazine.org.; and Paragon House and Steve McIntosh for excerpts from *Integral Consciousness and the Future of Evolution: How the Integral Worldview is Transforming Politics, Culture and Spirituality* by Steve McIntosh, © 2007 by Steve McIntosh; and "It Starts With Uncertainty," a dialogue between M. J. Wheatley and P. Chödrön, published in *Shambhala Sun* (magazine), November, 1999, © 1999 by Shambhala Sun; and Issa, for lyric excerpts from the song "When We Are Queen" from the CD *Dragon Dreams* by Issa, © 2008 by Issa, ww.IssaLight.com.

INTRODUCTION

Fearuality- the domain of animal and human experience related to fear and how it is managed (analogous to sexuality or spirituality).

Fearology- the transdisciplinary study of the interrelationship between humanity and fear(uality).

Fearuality, like fearology, is a very recent conceptualization of a field of knowledge for scholarly inquiry. They are unheard of and/or marginalized by the dominant fields of study in the academy. As an independent and public intellectual not deterred by the abjection of such terms, I have named and developed them myself.[1] Although others have developed reductionistic and/or less rigorous versions of the meaning for "fearology," which can be found by a simple search on the Internet, my version is quite complex.

Fearology is a legitimate new postmodern form of a larger domain I call 'Fear' Studies.[2] A whole new genre of 'ologies' have emerged in the past decade or so to study the most challenging, if not threatening, aspects of the human condition and our future sustainability. They have been looking for new ways to frame the worst problems and resolve them. I have been particularly intrigued with many that deal with the dark-side (i.e., shadow aspects, as Carl Jung might say) of human nature, its conditions, and its growth and pathologies.

You've all heard of "ponerology," right?—the study of the science of human evil. Although a new term, actually, that's a relatively old traditional field of study called "theodicy" (study of good vs. evil) in theology and philosophy. Also think of "criminology," a relatively recent field studying human criminal activity and how to best manage it. Somewhat more specifically relevant to fearology one could turn to the roots of modern dark-side genre research called "thanatology," as the study of humans' relationship to death and dying (of which much of existential philosophy and psychology has given a good deal of attention for a long time). On the other side of thanatology, of course, one ought not forget "sexology," in good Freudian fashion. More seriously, and particularly recent (i.e., with a postmodern mood of the last six decades), one can witness the rise of hybrid interdisciplinary and transdisciplinary branches from the roots in fields like "emotionology," "traumatology," "terrorology," "victimology," "kil-lology," "horrorology," and "panicology." Some more legitimate than others, perhaps. These are all symptomatic tropes of living in a postmodern "century of fear," as Albert Camus once wrote, or what postmodern literary critics like Shoshanna Felman described as our context in a "post-traumatic century"[3] and Kirby Farrell argued is a "post-traumatic culture."[4] However, despite the strangeness of the new 'ologies,' if one had to locate my research in one area that has substantial mainstream academic status today, it would be in the sub-domain of a "sociology of fear" (and risk) with a primary interest in studying the dynamics of the "culture of fear" (also called "climate of fear" or sometimes "politics of fear"). More on that later.

Yet, in many ways there is nothing new to what I am doing as an educator and fearologist. The late American adult educator/activist-poet, Bonaro Wilkins Overstreet (1902-1985), writing in the era of the American "Red Scare" (fear of communism), describes my own passion as well in her 1951 classic book *Understanding Fear in Ourselves and Others*:[5]

> Of all the emotional forces that pattern our individual and interpersonal behav-iors, fear has the most insidious power to make us do what we ought not to do and leave undone what we ought to do. Under its influence, and trying to es-cape its influence, we seem fated to give it a yet stronger hold upon us. . . . When Man's [sic] affairs are in a bad way, as they now are, every responsible person begins to feel that he [sic] must cut off some piece of the big problem and try to do something about it. The piece I have elected to cut off is the prob-lem of fear.

Her opening pages were stunning enough to me the first time I read them. Yet, her real eye-opener comes in Chapter Seven "Dangerous Disguises." Her crucial point, to me uncanny, is that humans, despite past respectable efforts, have failed to make a significant improvement upon fear and its management since very early historical times; the reason being that "We have [generally] responded to its disguises; not to that which is disguised." She continued her poignant critique, worthy of this lengthy quote:[6]

> It becomes, therefore, a matter of utmost practicality for us to know fear when we see it; for us to learn to penetrate at least its most common disguises. There is room for many of them within the general queerness of life. Certain dis-guises, however, are of destructive importance—chief among them *fear dis-guised as strength* [courage], *fear disguised as goodness*, and *fear disguised as love*. These are all dangerous because they are all exploitative: they all involve an effort on the part of the fear-ridden person [and organization, institution, so-ciety] to use other people as means to his [sic] own ends. They are all danger-ous, moreover, because they confuse us about the human qualities we most need to develop and trust. Our personal and common salvation [secular or relig-ious] may well depend upon the wide growth among us of strength, goodness,

and love; but we will not be saved either by honoring their limitations or by displacing to the genuine our dislike of the imitation.

The Greeks spoke for the Good, the True, and the Beautiful. Paul [in the Bible] declared 'And now abideth faith, hope, charity, these three'. . . . In our psychological age, we may want to state our confidence in strength [courage], goodness, and love—but [we only should] . . . if we can, in each case, have the genuine article, and not any one of the fear-born imitations that now confuse and harass our world.

There is one feature that these three disguises have in common. They are all, as we are discussing them here, *unconscious* forms of self-defense. They [also] have their conscious counterparts. . . . So far as destructiveness is concerned, however, these *conscious* disguises are harmless compared with those that are *unconscious* [shadow-repressed]. The most dangerous deceiver is the self-deceived.

It is not surprising that the distinguished American existential psychotherapist and theorist Rollo May (1909-1994), author of the classic *The Meaning of Anxiety* (1950), wrote "[Overstreet's] is the best book in print . . . for the general reading public on the exceedingly important problem of how to understand and overcome one's fears. . . . This is a book we have all been waiting for. . ." (from back jacket of her book). May's optimism aside, I am not convinced everyone was (or is) waiting for the stealthy bite and disarming truth of Overstreet's thesis and challenge. Virtually no one I have talked to has heard of this book nor its author (thanks be to Ken Markley for giving me a copy).

Something is wrong in the field of fear management. Is there such a professional field? Actually, there isn't. With fear being recognized as a very serious human problem by so many people and reputable authors, it has amazed me for some 20 years how there still is not a textbook (in English language, anyway) on Fear Management as a discipline—all due respect for current "terror management" (theory)[7]—the latter, which has appeared as an up-and-coming area of empirical research; though, it falls far short of a truly holistic-integral approach to fear management/education because it is limited by disciplinary Psychology.

If one searches a major data base on books published in the world (e.g., Worldcat) on "conflict management," there are today over 17,000 records (mostly books), and many of those are often adopted as textbooks (K-12 and post-secondary) for courses or programs in Conflict Resolution, Mediation, and Conflict Management, or Peace Studies and War Studies. In sharp contrast, on that same data base, only 11 books are found for "Fear Management" and none of them are even close to being comprehensive textbooks on the topic in the same way as the textbooks on conflict management/resolution. The most intriguing book of the 11 is *No Fear Management: Rebuilding Trust, Performance, and Commitment in the New American Workplace*.[8] From decades of research, I have found no courses, graduate programs or post-secondary degrees in "Fear Management." What most people call "fear management" is typically an in-service short course or training workshop revolving around a set of coping practices, derived from the biopsychology (and clinical aspects) of fear(s), anxiety, panic, stress, trauma, etc.

Despite this paucity, I would argue that some kind of fear management, formal or non-formal, conscious or unconscious, is going on all the time and is being taught to us through culture! In the Preface I mentioned that a major evolutionary principle or law of the universe seems to be: *when fear arises, there will be fearlessness* (i.e., fearlessness in one of its many forms, "courage" being just one of several). Yet, such a natural impulse to manage fear is not the only thing constructing our knowledge of how to manage fear. From my postmodern perspective, I believe cultural aspects (values, beliefs, worldviews) and developmental aspects (level of maturity), with their concomitant politics, are far more important in determining our relationship to fear and various culturally modified forms of 'fear.' Thus, a transdisciplinary critical holistic-integral approach needs to be cultivated today to understand the rich complexity of fear and fearlessness.

Analyzing 22 conflict management/education manuals in the twentieth century, my master's research showed that rarely is "fear" even taken into consideration.[9] Why isn't there a concept of "fear resolution" like "conflict resolution"? This unpopularity and avoidance to develop *fear management/education* (FME) as a serious field of study is an underlying core complaint of this book. Let me suggest a working conceptualization *FME* with this cultural (and educational) emphasis:

> Managing fear (and fearlessness) in formal and informal ways may involve change, coping, healing, transformation, and transmutation or liberation— depending on the functional and political knowledge-power dynamics (*a la* Foucault) and developmental capacities engaged at a particular time and situation. Managing fear, although recognizable as a set of perceptions, values, beliefs, and behaviors, is *equally* a set of teaching and learning practices (i.e., curricula and pedagogy)—as 'fear' is something created (i.e., socially constructed) as much by our knowledge about fear as anything else. Thus, *fear management/education* is an inextricable combination of knowledge and practices that need to be systematically studied and critiqued to improve humanity.

With FME as an umbrella concept for this large domain of human activity and experiences, I am attempting to add a new theoretical approach which may give feareality, fearology and FME a foundation for potential legitimation in academic, professional, activist, and broader social circles. This is an enormous task and one still in its infancy—a work in progress.

Unfortunately, unlike Bonaro Overstreet, Rollo May, and most others writing about fear or anxiety and the human condition, I have taken a route that goes beyond a reductive (depoliticized) focus on psychology of fear(s).[10] Overstreet is profoundly right-on in her challenge of humans uncritically accepting "disguises" like strength/courage, faith/hope, love/charity, as the way out and beyond fear (as so many authors teach and preach all over the world). They are often "fear-born imitations" she argues. That has been my experience also. To begin to assault that problem of fear itself disguising and "defending" itself (masking itself), I decided long ago to ask people and organizations to consider an alternative solution and replace emphasis in their teachings (theories) and practices on the virtues of strength/courage, faith/hope and love/charity to the virtue of *fearlessness* instead (or at least complementary with). Fearlessness is much more than just a virtue.

"Fearlessness," as used in this book, is a code word for "fear management" and *visa versa*.[11] "Management" turns a lot of people off these days. I use it as a verb not a noun. Try not to let the words get in the way of the spirit of what is being translated/interpreted here. You'll read of at least 15 different meanings of fearlessness within. There is no one simple definition of fear or fearlessness that is tenable in a postmodern complex world. I order the complexity of the meanings using a spectrum developmental approach that I found (generically) in the work of American integral philosopher and theorist Ken Wilber (see Chapter Two). I am excited to share this with you in the chapters ahead.

To clarify my position on the traditional premodern virtues, I support both secular and religious means of working with fearlessness as an alternative to the disguises of fear that humans are so susceptible to. There may be a more fearless form of the virtues of strength/courage, faith/hope and love/charity but I, like Overstreet, have become very skeptical of such terms and their histories of en- actments (often unjust when being justified by their perpetrators). Though, I am all for non-fear-based traditional virtues which are based on what some authors consider the "virtue of all virtues" (a meta-virtue), that is, fearlessness. I take seriously Mahatma Gandhi's (1869-1948) words: "God is fearlessness."[12] I also accept that everyone would likely not agree with Gandhi. Generally, Westerners are less familiar and/or comfortable with the term compared to Easterners (e.g., Jains, Buddhists, Hinduists, Sufists or mystics in general). I discuss this all fur- ther in the chapters ahead and point to the problems that even "fearlessness" and "fearless" or "no fear" can encounter today, as pathological constructions.

Indeed, all good virtues, ideas, people and things in human hands can be- come corrupt—corrupted by fear ('fear')—that is, unless there is excellent the- ory and concomitant critical practices that hold the best qualities (virtues) from turning rotten inside. My own work is based on a *fearless standpoint theory* (my own creation)[13] in order to study fear uncorrupted (*via* fearology)—without fal- ling into the trap (as much as possibly can be prevented) of studying fear by fear-based means. This is one theoretical device I've utilized in order to make sense of all the fear and fearlessness teachings (i.e., FME) throughout history. You will pick up roughly some of the features of the fearless standpoint theory (a transpersonal and nondual perspective) throughout the text, but it will not be elaborated further as a critical component of this book.

I do not have the luxury of enough space here to give adequate attention to my full fear ('fear') research. The next volume I wish to write and publish would be *The World's Fear Teachings* to complement *World's Fearlessness Teachings*. Suffice it to say, one cannot know fearlessness without studying fear nor *visa versa*. They are dialectically related. The other book I would like to write is *A History of Fearlessness*, because there is no such thing written or pub- lished to my knowledge. On the contrary, historians of all kinds have written fascinating scholarly books on the history of fear.[14] There appears to be a general blind-spot to seeing fearlessness flowing and crafting history equally as has fear. I am sure *The World's Fearlessness Teachings* will set that blind-spot to some light, and may it open even so slightly. Humanity and its future sustainability may hinge upon us doing so.

In roundabout fashion, the purpose of this Introduction is to give some of the historical and theoretical background to the main content in Chapters One to Five, echoing and complementing the content of the Preface. The main objective is to give an overview outline of each chapter, acknowledge limitations, and assist the reader with some thoughts in how to best utilize this book.

The latest book in humanity's FME library to come across my research desk is from American populist political author Bob Cesca. It is an eye-catcher: *One Nation Under Fear: Scaredy Cats and Fear-Mongers in the Home of the Brave (And What You Can Do About It)* (2008). The Foreword is written by another American extrovert populist with a journalistic expertise, Arianna Huffington of *The Huffington Post* and author of "Fear Watch '08: Keeping an Eye Out for GOP Fear-mongering" and "Why We Need An Epidemic of Fearlessness" and *Becoming Fearless* (see Chapter One). Cesca, like Huffington and so many others, especially in America, are fed up with the misuse of fear in politics. If you have not noticed, social critics (Al Gore, Noam Chomsky, Henry Giroux, to name only three) from diverse backgrounds have emerged with a vengeance after the "War on Terror" was declared by President G. W. Bush, Jr. and his US administration in late 2001. The critics have all condemned government and corporate agendas based on fear. It is a tip of the iceberg in terms of the larger Fear Problem humanity is being brought to face.

In the new genre of post-9/11 2001 critical analysis on the nature and role of *fear* in our world, this book supports the following restorative and emancipatory movements around the world: quality management and fearless leadership, peace/justice, strong democracy/civil society, liberation/enlightenment, ecology/environmental/sustainability, and general radical non-violence. My life experiences and career paths have intermingled in all of them. Thus, I bring three archetypal parts of myself to bear on this book's claims: *activist-self*, *educationist-self*, and *integralist-self*. The latter two take precedent in this book, as I am a professional educator with a doctorate degree in Curriculum and Instruction and I am a 27 year self-taught initiate of Ken Wilber's critical integral philosophy and theory. I present for the first time in one volume, a unique and optimistic, postmodern and post-postmodern, holistic-integral approach to FME.

At the same time as supporting the above movements, the theory of fear and fearlessness I have proposed, with its primary articulation beginning in 1989, is critical of those very movements. When post-9/11 critics have written so much about terrorism, I write about *fearism* (defined in Chapter Two). When "culture of fear" critics (like Cesca, Chomsky, Barry Glassner, Frank Furedi and others) with their rational columns of statistics and arguments, write about how people are afraid of the wrong things and ought not to be, I write about how fear within a context of fearism is not so simple to understand and alleviate. I qualify my position by asserting that a context of a 5000 year patriarchal Western

"Dominator culture"[15] (i.e., "Matrix of Domination,"[16] 'Fear' Matrix or "Fears's Empire") has installed fear-fullness and terror very deep in the human and world soul, and no simple rational "risk" statistic or argument is adequate to analyze or 'correct' what is seemingly an out-of-control spiral of trauma and irrationality (i.e., fear patterning) in the 21st century.

A philosophical and educational focus offers a unique contribution to this post-9/11 genre, largely due to my two-decade passion to plumb the depths into the patterns and motivations of why, and strategies of how people, organizations, and nations manage *fear* (and its cousins, like *terror*)—and, how they conceptualize and manage *fearlessness* (and its cousins, like *courage*). Historically, it appears the resource of fear has been well tapped, while the resource of fearlessness remains largely untapped.

A Sociology of Fear: Context for New Research on Fearuality

As mentioned earlier, my work with fear and fearlessness could most legitimately be located in the mainstream of academic research under the topic of "sociology of fear" (and risk). The whole emphasis on "risk society" (*a la* Ulrich Beck) and "safety and security" (especially, post-9/11) has brought fear out of the closet and into the eyes of researchers concerned about the sociocultural and political dimensions of how humans manage fear today. From my view, this thrust of research is a branch of curricula and strategy of FME itself.

In the last ten years, especially the last five, one can find without a lot of searching many university courses in (mainly western) Sociology departments entitled "Sociology of Fear" or sometimes "Sociology of Fear and Risk." For example a university course SOCI 421 describes the content as an examination of the "Historical role of fear in the management and control of individuals and societies. Topics include state terrorism and urban fear."[17] This was not always the case, even though "Throughout the entire twentieth century, anxiety, along with fear, was a subject of detailed research and serious scrutiny performed by psychologists [and some historians]. Sociologists for various reasons, largely neglected fear in their empirical studies."[18]

A recent major journal article by sociologist Andrew Tudor on the sociology of fear, critiques the limitations of the psychological domination of the concept and research approaches to fear:[19]

> Traditionally fear has been understood as one of the emotions (often, indeed, as a 'primary' or 'basic' emotion) and thus consigned to the tender mercies of psychology. . . . What the appropriation of the study of emotions by psychology did mean, though, was that for many years there was little attempt to develop a distinctively sociological approach to the subject. . . . [from a more holistic perspective] fearfulness is heavily mediated through the physical, psychological, cultural and social [political] environments in which it is located. . . . they are inextricably intertwined in a skein of interconnected threads. Out of this tangle emerges our emotional response. . . .

When I first started tracking the "interconnected threads" of the Fear Problem in societies, or what many have called the growing *"culture of fear"* (*a la* Chomsky, Juan Corradi et al., Furedi, Glassner, etc.), it was sociologists for the most part who were studying this (along with some political scientists, anthropologists, and urban/architectural theorists). Most of that focus on the historical, economic, cultural and political dimensions of fear in society began around 1983 when researchers across disciplines began to examine this as a major social problem. A new academic field called "sociophobics" arose at that time but soon disappeared. Chapter Two offers more details on various research movements and their attempts to understand what I label "The Fear Problem."

Much of the attention directed to the accumulating destructive *social fears* was surrounded by the emphasis of researchers (mainly criminologists) on the "fear of crime" and construction by (often unscrupulous) politicians in the late 1960s to early 1970s in the US and UK, respectively,[20] as a desperate 'social crisis' (note: with roots of moral panic and a "War on Crime" led by US government officials going back to the 1920-30s).[21] One could include the Cold War escalation (1983-85) of global fear and a concomitant planetary nuclear annihilation/terror constantly on many people's minds and deep in their hearts in those days.

One of the first (fear-based) turning points in public perception came with the introduction in 1980-83 of *The Figgie Report on Fear of Crime*[22] (geared to an American audience). It was a study commissioned by a corporate CEO (Harry Figgie) of a Fortune 500 company at the time, which opens in the Preface with the sentiments (from Harry) of what I would call a landslide discourse, a kind of Pandora's Box, opening forth the postmodern mood and climate of fear:

> From the early 1950s to the early 1960s, I traveled throughout the United States as a management consultant. My travels took me to all sizes and varieties of cities, towns, and villages. In those [good ol'] days, I had no fear of crime. I walked to restaurants, theaters, movies, and just up and down streets for exercise. I never gave a second thought to safety in those days. In the last twenty years, however, our way of life has become radically different. I can no longer travel with that former freedom. Some of my friends have been savagely attacked on city streets—even shot at and killed from moving vehicles. To some the damage has been lethal, for others permanent and debilitating. We have become fearful. We take all kinds of precautions. We all know someone who has been killed, robbed, or assaulted. We seem to be reverting to the Middle Ages, with our homes our fortressed castles and our locks and alarms our moats [i.e., "architecture of fear"]. What has happened to us? I'm not sure. But our fear of crime has become pervasive. . . . and despite widespread publicity regarding crime, and despite a vast amount of research on the causes of crime, little systematic research has been targeted at the 'impact' of crime on American lifestyles and daily living patterns. We [i.e., Harry] feel[s] responsible to bring the facts about the fear of crime to the public and its elected representatives as a public service. I feel that individuals as well as corporations have to take a leadership role. . . .

I recently came across an academic paper on educational policy in the US, where the authors lament that ever since the 1983 publication of *A Nation at*

Risk (report by National Commission on Excellence in Education), educational fear-tactics combining ever so smoothly with corporate political "terror of neo-liberalism," have ruled America's school systems from the top down, with increasing emphasis on excessive economic accountability (e.g., the "corporate university"), mistrust, erosion of strong democracy and civil rights, oppressive competition (i.e., privatization), and "abandon" of the youth generation, as Henry Giroux[23] has argued so convincingly. As context for Chapter Four, the state of education has become well-embedded in the "culture of fear."[24]

Whether listening to Harry the CEO in the early 1980s, or listening to people after September 11, 2001, one cannot deny that "everything has changed" and in fact, "We have become fearful" and it has highly altered, in a (largely) negative way, our quality of life. The popular postmodern discourse, I would argue, is just this haunting kind of "fear" (cf. Bauman's "liquid fear") overwhelming every other emotional dimension a human being or society has. Most researchers agree it has undermined social trust and the "social contract" (i.e., sociability) that goes with it. "Who can you trust anymore?," so goes the public discourse. For the past few decades, the landslide negative affect of publicity on "fear of crime" and other global and local "risks" and "dangers" has created a very different world, where "safety and security" is the number one value.[25] In many ways it is a world where people feel they are living in a "war zone" and the "enemy" cannot easily be identified. This rather pessimistic mood strongly impacts the wealthy and the poor across all differences of race, religion, gender, age and so on. This is the atmosphere or "climate of fear" that has compelled some sociologists (especially) to study the social relations, architecture, geography and ecology of fear in contemporary societies.

As much as I have drawn on this new scholarship on fear, I have typically found it lacking. The focus of the sociology of fear studies, influenced by the hegemony of *psychologism*[26] (attempting to appear "value-neutral," "objective," and "scientific"), continues to designate "fear" as a biologically-centered "emotion or feeling" just as the common dictionary or encyclopedia claims. The emphasis of the sociology of fear research tends also to focus on "fears" (i.e., "fear of x, y, z") as behaviors or self-reported experiences (easy to do statistical analysis on that kind of data). That is fine to a point, yet insufficient for developing a *critical fear theory* that addresses the power-knowledge construction (the Matrix of Domination) of the very phenomenon of 'fear' and/or fearism.

I am very concerned when "corporations" (wealthy elite CEOs, like Harry Figgie) are telling the rest of us all what the problem of fear is and what to do about it! Such elite have a lot to lose from growing crime 'on-the-streets.' Poor people don't have much left to lose. The academic and professional middle/upper class have a basic method of research framed primarily in psychological terms (including social psychology and a little sociology). The real problem is people like Harry, and he is only one example of many, who do not critique their own views of FME. They merely promote their own view and try to influence by dumping it on others uncritically. Creating fear and "moral panic"[27] is a useful tool for the elite, and always has been. Even a consummate liar, like the former US president Richard Nixon, told the (partial) truth at times and became known for his quip: "People react to fear, not love—they don't teach that in Sunday School, but it's true." Nixon promoted that and never seemed to question it ethically. Such unreflective means usually end up as "propaganda" (i.e., a "hidden curriculum") rather than good education.

So much of the "reform" (and "activist") movements in societies and in Education today, if studied critically, would likely be shown to be largely fear-based in motivation as they attempt to manage fear by creating more fear (see Chapters Four and Five). That ironic dynamic is the basic definition of the "culture of fear" that I use in this book. Virtually anyone (including myself), is susceptible to using the culture of fear (i.e., "power over") to their own ends— and under closer inspection, those ends are ethically questionable. Unfortun- ately, the Figgies and Nixon's of the world had no rich concept of fearlessness to teach as an alternative and ethical approach to FME.

Only very recently are postmodern cultural media theorists and a rare few radical critical sociologists seeing through the problems (propaganda) behind the very "label" and "meaning" of 'fear' in contemporary societies. Living in a highly techno-mediated civilization with networks of information and power, often controlled by elites, fear is rapidly being reproduced and consumed as a hot commodity (i.e., "commodification of fear" as Elizabeth Seaton called it[28]). As mentioned earlier, cultural critic Brian Massumi called it an era of an "organized fear trade." In a Baudrillardian sense, it is largely manufactured as a "false" simulacra of 'fear' from fear (I also call *culturally modified 'fear'*). This once thought to be a basic "natural emotion" is quickly becoming a non-emotion and non-feeling; rather, it is a culturally constructed perceptual *lens* or *discourse* for organizing a crisis-focused reality and at-risk society, as contemporary anthropologists (e.g., Mary Douglas) and sociologists (e.g., Zygmunt Bauman, David Altheide or Ulrich Beck) have argued (see Chapter Two).

I am more interested in "disguises" of *fear itself* (i.e., discourses of fear), which I demarcate as 'fear' with inverted commas, rather than all the *fears*. In fact, I have argued that attention on all the fears, typical of psychology's hegemonic means of studying fear, is more a distraction and inevitably prevents us from creative, holistic-integral approaches to understanding 'fear' itself as a "fear pattern" (and a 'Fear' Matrix holding together Fear's Empire). Fear research, grounded in critical theory (as opposed to functionalist theory), ought to be political, ethical and spiritual in order for real healthy change, reform, and transformation of societies today and in the future.

The point is, a sociology of fear is a good starter umbrella concept for where I am going but it has not yet as a field of inquiry developed the radical concept of fearuality, fearology, nor FME. Simply, the sociology of fear is prone to the same narrow materialist and disciplinary shackles that the psychology of fear has kneeled to—both disciplines often trying to be "hard sciences." Worse though, is how sociologists of fear are not talking about fearlessness at all! Bravery and courage are their comfortable discourse and advice. Typically, and in general, like most disciplines, they offer lots of critical analyses but little in the way of profound workable solutions. In this book I am focusing on the spirit of fearlessness and the World's Fearlessness Teachings, as the beginning stage of a recovery and antidote or counter-fear project; perhaps a revolution towards a new way of doing FME that is no longer built under Fear's Empire and the Law of Fear.

I admit I may not be the best marketer for the FME in which I write about. I don't do "flashy" "catchy" ads well, for people with a decreasing attention span. Bottomline, I'm not a very good sound-bite ('positive,' 'cheerleader,' or hope-mongering kind of) salesperson with the things I analyze systematically. So, I wrote this book as a means for a few people interested to linger with my research findings and ideas on their time. It is not a simple read for most, as it requires a new way of thinking and defining of several concepts that are familiar but are being used in a different context. I suggest reading it more than once. That said, I think it is still worth a "Reader's Digest" version, and maybe I'll write that popularized third volume someday. For now, here's my introductory (smug) "Readers Digest" quotable quote version of the book in 17 words: *"Courage is about managing fear;" whereas fearlessness is about managing fear a hell of a lot better!*

Although "courage" and its various discourses throughout human history are important, merely spouting a popular truism (i.e., "Courage is about managing fear"), as William Beaman had in a September 2006 issue of *Readers Digest* (entitled: "The Leader"), is not enough. It offers little qualitative discernment or critical inquiry as to what is a "better" managing of fear in specific contexts (e.g., in an expanding Fear's Empire). Beaman's commentary, like so many, lacks a macro-sociological analysis of humanity's situation and psycho-spiritual developmental issues. In this book, from a macro-evolutionary and developmental view, I argue that "courage" is one way of fearlessness, that is, fear management, but it is not the most complex or mature and certainly not best to use alone for all situations/contexts.

Brief Summary of Chapters

The remainder of the book includes: **Chapter One** "Do We Really Want A Fearlessness (R)evolution?," which investigates a universal theory of Defense and the relationship of natural evolutionary theory to cultural (r)evolution using examples from natural phenomena to assert operative metaphors for both a critical integral theory of consciousness and the notion of a 'quantum leap' regarding change and transformation. Five selected profiles of people and current activist movements promoting a fearlessness (r)evolution are examined to make hypothetical claims for invoking a biased view that a theory of historical fearlessness (and spirit of fearlessness) is inevitable; **Chapter Two**, "Fear Management Systems Theory: A Critical Integral Approach" lays out the methodological ground and philosophical and theoretical background for the author's unique critical holistic-integral fear management theory (following the work of the Integral Movement and Ken Wilber's writing), and thereby locates some 15 meanings of fearlessness within a universal classification system or reference system. Ten fear management systems are identified and shown in their developmental relationship (evolutionary trajectory). This provides the essential framework for others to use when developing their own critical literacy of fearlessness; **Chapter Three** "The World's Fearlessness Teachings: Managing the Human Fear Problem," by far the largest in the book, defines the global human "Fear Problem" (and Fearlessness Problem that responds to it) and tracks out the extensive and diverse literature, sacred and secular, East and West (through time), that attempts cohesively to manage fear as a system of Defense, albeit with often great confusions, contradictions and conflictual ideologies. The World's Fearlessness Teachings are ordered developmentally as seven expres-sions of the spirit of fearlessness, which include "no fear," "bravery" (and "bravado"), "courage(ous)," "fear-less," "fearlessness," and "fearless"; **Chapter Four**, "Education As Life-Long Learning: Do We Really Want to Raise Fearless Children?" invokes the reality, idea, and resistance to an education system that utilizes the concepts in my biased theory, especially the idea of historical (developmental) fearlessness. Thus, the idea of raising "fearless children" can be a goal and a great controversy, as the literature on this topic is highly contested. Several academic educators are critiqued in regard to their writing on fearlessness (and fear); thus, demonstrating how to apply Fear Management Systems theory to educational discourses. Included are a few recommendations for a new curriculum theory based on quality fear management/education for the 21st century; **Chapter Five**, "Unifying the Fearlessness Movement: Educational Implications for a New Activist Agenda" closes the book with my plea to unite the World's Fearlessness Teachings in a critical holistic-integral theory of FME, and use this theory to better understand differences and similarities of the meanings and agendas of the various groups and activist movements in the emancipatory tradition. Four important activists in America are discussed and critiqued. A new way of doing education in a new type of activist protocol is recommended, with special applications to the peace (and environmental) movement. The shift from a "Green" pluralistic worldview (Fear Management System-6) to "Yellow" integral worldview (Fear Management System-7) is predicted.

Indirectly, the book is divided in two parts, with the first three chapters containing most of the theory, and the last two chapters the application. In short, you are invited to join me on a journey of a rather long-winding developmental and cultural evolutionary theory, exposing seven different though related ways of expressing fearlessness within ten systems of fear management. Yet, aside from all the fascinating complexity we will embark upon in this book, perhaps the one most simple and worthy point to remember is that *when fear arises, so there shall fearlessness be* in order to counter fear's limitations.

So let the story begin, though not without a final caution. Like any mature socially responsible author-educator, I have to ask an ethical question about what I am presenting to the public. I am no longer interested in only "shocking" my audiences, so they'll wake up (and believe and value what I do). That's what immature rebels like to do. Rather, I want to help them 'wake up' but I know I have to be there fully to offer them support for such awakeness—and its accompanying terror (among other things). Basically, people are "asleep" to their own or the world's problems for good reasons—it is called "denial" (among other names). My specialty is "fear education" so to speak, and that has even more demanding aspects to consider. I take the spiritual educator Robert Sardello's ethical caveat very seriously: "One of the great challenges in [teaching] writing about fear is to avoid generating more fear by doing so."[29] Note, this is essentially the definition of the "culture of fear" (a type of fear management) that I spoke about earlier in this Introduction. If we are generating more fear instead of less, then our intervention to make things better (to 'wake up' people) is questionable, if not unethical. I return to this serious dilemma in Chapter Five on activism.

With the exception of Sardello, I have yet seen any author's book or article on the topic *fear* take such wise heed. Probably that is because it is easier said than done. I am still learning how to do this skillfully. The introduction material for this book is pretty terrifying at some level. Learning more about fear is not a favorite thing for people to do. I agree with bell hooks, a critical black feminist pedagogue, who wrote, "In our society we [educators] make much of love and say little about fear."[30] Why? Because we are too afraid to talk about it, too much. That's the problem. How much can one take? And everyone is different and capable of handling different amounts of fear, as they come to learn more about fear. The only 'way out' of this ethical dilemma is likely to go 'through it' and learn how to do it.

What I have attempted to do is add the notion of a 'fear' vaccine with all the fear teachings—that is, I have focused on fearlessness and enacted, what is called the "gift of fearlessness" practice in Eastern sacred traditions, a concept I return to in some detail in Chapter Three. My service intention and 'gift' is to bring you that which may free you from 'fear,' if not lessen its grip on the soul and the suffering it causes. Albeit, this focus on fearlessness does not fully take effect until you begin reading and studying the chapters. It's time to start. Feel free to contact me if you wish, and I'll support you the best that I am able to, in order for you to take-in a good amount of this research and to apply it, without having to be completely overwhelmed. Remember, this is not just information herein, it is a recollection and reinvigoration of the very "spirit of fearlessness" itself, with all my own biases of course.

Now, if you connect with the 'spirit' and attempt to use what is in this book, be prepared for a rough ride, and all the feelings of being overwhelmed. One cannot deny that the many 'great ones' who have known and walked the path of fearlessness as 'masters' have often fallen (been assassinated) under human culture's resistance to liberation. My advice: work to not let your feelings and emotions (alone) dictate the reality and what you are capable of doing along the path of fearlessness and, work to not let your so-called "rationality" always assume it is rational. Also, be prepared to die anytime. You may not until the final day. Roughly speaking, we can choose to "feel the fear and do it anyway"[31] (as Susan Jeffers teaches), or more subtlely we can choose to learn together and critically and self-reflectively work our way through—in and out of the 'Fear' Matrix.

Notes

1. I have published, through the In Search of Fearlessness Research Institute, over 30 technical papers on these topics since 1995. In particular, I recommend the following: R. Michael Fisher, "Fearology: The Biography of an Idea," Technical Paper No. 12 (Calgary, AB: In Search of Fearlessness Research Institute, 2001); R. Michael Fisher, "Disappear Fear: Action Fearology for the 21st Century," Technical Paper No. 26 (Vancouver, BC: In Search of Fearlessness Research Institute, 2007).

2. For an overview see R. Michael Fisher, "Invoking 'Fear' Studies," *Journal of Curriculum Theorizing.* 22(2006), 39-71.

3. Shoshana Felman, "Education and Crisis, or the Vicissitudes of Teaching," in *Testimony: Crises of Witnessing in Literature, Psychoanalysis, and History,* eds. S. Felman, and Dori Laub, (NY: Routledge, 1992), 1.

4. Kirby Farrell, *Post-traumatic Culture: Injury and Interpretation in the Nineties* (Baltimore, MA: John Hopkins University Press, 1998).

5. Bonaro W. Overstreet, *Understanding Fear in Ourselves and Others* (NY: Harper & Row, 1951/71), 11, 9.

6. Ibid., 90.

7. I am referring particularly to the central leaders of "terror management theory" (TMT): the co-researching and co-writing triad of Tom Pyszczynski (Professor of Psychology, University of Colorado at Colorado Springs, Sheldon Solomon (Professor of Psychology, Skidmore College) and Jeff Greenberg (Professor of Psychology, University of Arizona). Their work, although it encircles cultural context, symbolism, and sociopolitical contexts to some degree, as well as evolutionary theory (based on the late-Ernest Becker's work), TMT is still basically experimental existential psychology—a psychology of terror and the human condition. Thus, TMT with an eclectic approach still remains embedded in the discourses of general Psychology of which I am a critic. Especially I am cautious of TMT and other psychological approaches to "fear" and "fear management" which tend to avoid a wider and deeper transdisciplinary postmodern holistic-integral perspective. That said, I highly recommend the DVD on TMT entitled *Flight From Death: The Quest for Immortality*, narrated by Gabriel Byrne, produced and written by Patrick Shen and Greg Bennick, directed by Patrick Shen (copyright 2005 Transcontinental Media).

8. H. E. Chambers, and R. Craft, *No Fear Management: Rebuilding Trust, Performance and Commitment in the New American Workplace* (Boston, MA: St. Lucie Press, 1998).

9. R. Michael Fisher, "Toward a 'Conflict' Pedagogy: A Critical Discourse Analysis of 'Conflict' in Conflict Management Education," unpublished masters thesis (Vancouver, BC: The University of British Columbia, 2000). See also R. Michael Fisher, "Unveiling the Hidden Curriculum in Conflict Resolution and Peace Education: Future Directions Toward a Critical Conflict Education and 'Conflict' Pedagogy," Technical Paper No. 9 (Vancouver, BC: In Search of Fearlessness Research Institute, 2000).

10. My transdisciplinary approach (which includes disciplinary approaches but transcends them) is one more obscure and rare than interdisciplinary (which mixes disciplinary approaches but never fully transcends them), is not a study of fear and fearlessness as mere biological, psychological or psychiatric entities—that is, only focused on kinds of "fight-flight" behaviors, 'normal' or 'abnormal,' 'positive' or 'negative' cognitive thought processes, as so often is the case in mainstream, scientific/medical (and everyday) discourses on fear(s). Rather, you'll read alternatively in this treatise of at least 15 meanings of 'fearlessness'—and about 'fear' (more than a feeling or emotion) as an amorphous complex constructed relational pattern and "creative" dynamic or phenomena

that is best approached today through the diverse and combined lenses of sociology, anthropology, political science, organizational development and leadership studies, literature studies, cultural studies, urban studies, communication studies, theology, religious and consciousness studies (East and West), art, philosophy, architecture, geography, criminology, ecology, feminist studies, post-colonial and postmodern studies, etc. I also research within techno-media and popular and alternative sub-cultures (i.e., marginal or non-disciplines) for their many ways of understanding and "studying" 'fear' and how to best deal with it (and ourselves). Indeed, fear management is all about human management (i.e., self-regulation) and *visa versa*.

11. My critical theoretical orientation (with a Foucauldian discourse analysis, see Michel Foucault, 1980) lends to my work a decidedly subversive element (as least that is how the *status quo*, or Agents of the 'Fear' Matrix might 'read' me and my work). It is far too complex to enter the research behind this framework I have created to name "fearism" and its role via the 'Fear' Matrix (I trust readers may view or recall viewing *The Matrix* sci-fi film trilogy (1999-2003) by the Wachowski Bros.). You may turn to my other writing on this (e.g., footnote 2 and my dissertation cited in the Preface) and R. Michael Fisher, "What is the 'Fear' Matrix? (Part 1: Failure of Cultural)," Technical Paper No.13 (Vancouver, BC: In Search of Fearlessness Research Institute, 2002). Also, a good reference for the "sacred warrior" perspective I adopt on this is humorously translated in popular culture in the book by Jake Horsley, *Matrix Warrior: Being the One (The Unofficial Handbook)* (London, UK: Gollanz, 2003). If you are looking for a new alternative religion, apparently Matrixism has formed from the premises of the movie narrative. One can join tens of thousands of others who have signed up as members (on line). For those of a more esoteric spiritual bent there are several websites on the Internet using the term "Fear Matrix" in the context of a teaching that has come down to humans as a divine dispensation from the Ascended Masters (c.1990) and put in form as an emancipatory self-help curricula by people like Joshua Stone and others (e.g., see "Fear Matrix Removal Program"). Although I have done the 21 day self-program of this and found it useful, neither I nor the publisher (UPA) in anyway advise or promote such programs.

12. Cited in K. L. Seshagri Rao, *Mahatma Gandhi and Comparative Religion* (India: Motilal Banarsidass, 1978), 69.

13. See R. Michael Fisher, "Fearless Standpoint Theory: Origins of FMS-9 in Ken Wilber's Work," Technical Paper No. 31 (Vancouver, BC: In Search of Fearlessness Research Institute, 2008).

14. For example: From the UK, Professor of History, Joanna Bourke; from the US, Professor of Political Science, Corey Robin. See Joanna Bourke, *Fear: A Cultural History* (UK: Virago Press, 2005); Corey Robin, *Fear: The History of a Political Idea* (NY: Oxford University Press, 2004). These Western-biased books ignore, for the most part, any substantial discussion about fearlessness or fearless, and in fact, both tend to discourage such ideas or realities. Among other things, they prefer concepts like bravery and courage (and hope) as the best humans are capable of.

15. Drawing on feminist archeologists and ethnographers, like Marija Gimbutas (e.g., *The Language of the Goddess*, 1991), Riane Eisler concludes that for the past five millenia in the Western world the "Dominator" (war-based) model of culture has prevailed over the "Partnership" model (found in prehistoric, Minoan civilizations), the former geared toward masculine (male) values, and the latter more toward female values. More importantly, Eisler points out that the fossil evidence indicates a "high degree of institutionalized violence" and "authoritarian social organization" in the Dominator model, with "a basic difference between a dominator and a partnership society. . . [being] the first is held together primarily by fear and the second by trust. . . . The difference—

and it is major—is that in a dominator society, fear is systematically inculcated in us and trust (beginning with the trust between the female and male halves of humanity) is systematically undermined through dominator cultural myths and social institutions." Eisler points out that conflict existed in the Partnership model too but it was handled, characteristically with less violent outcomes. "For example, in the dominator model, conflict is emphasized, but at the same time the violent suppression of conflict is institutionalized . . .". Riane Eisler, *The Chalice and the Blade: Our History, Our Future* (San Francisco, CA: Harper & Row, 1987), 179, 182.

16. I also utilize this notion, first labeled by black feminist scholar Patricia Hill Collins in 1990, and cited by integral liberation scholar-practitioner Raúl Q. Rosado. The Matrix of Domination consists of the interlocking and interactive relations of all the forms of oppression (re: class, race, gender, age, etc.). Raúl Quiñones Rosado, *Consciousness-in-Action: Toward an Integral Psychology of Liberation and Transformation* (Caguas, Puerto Rico: ilé Publications, 2007), 67, 77-79.

17. Excerpt from The University of British Columbia (Okanagan), Canada, website in 2008.

18. Vladimir Shlapentokh and Eric Shiraev, *Fears in Post-communist Societies* (Macmillan, 2002), 5-6.

19. Andrew Tudor, "A (Macro)Sociology of Fear?," *The Sociological Review*, 51(2003), 241, 240.

20. "Fear of crime was first acknowledged in the late 1960s and early 1970s when national crime surveys were undertaken in the United States, followed by the United Kingdom and other countries." Listerborn, Carina, "Understanding the Geography of Women's Fear: Toward a Reconceptualization of Fear and Space," in *Subjectivities, Knowledges, and Feminist Geographies: The Subjects and Ethics of Social Research*, eds. L. Bondi, H. Avis, and R. Bankey (Lanham, MD: Rowman & Littlefield, 2002), 36.

21. For a good detailed analysis see Jonathan Simon, *Governing Through Crime: How the War on Crime Transformed American Democracy and Created a Culture of Fear* (NY: Oxford University Press, 2007); Ioannis Evrigenis, *Fear of Enemies and Collective Action* (NY: Cambridge University Press, 2008).

22. Research and Forecasts, Inc., with Ardy Friedberg, *America Afraid: How Fear of Crime Changes the Way We Live* (based o the widely publicized Figgie Report), (NY: New American Library, 1983), xi-xii.

23. See Henry A. Giroux, *The Abandoned Generation: Democracy Beyond the Culture of Fear* (NY: Palgrave/Macmillan, 2003); Henry A. Giroux, *Against the Terror of Neoliberalism: Politics Beyond the Age of Greed* (Boulder, CO: Paradigm, 2008).

24. Rick Ginsberg, and Leif Frederick Lyche, "The Culture of Fear and the Politics of Education," *Educational Policy*, 22(2008), 10.

25. "Safety has become the fundamental value of the 1990s. Passions that were once devoted to a struggle to change the world (or to keep it the same) are now invested in trying to ensure that we are safe. The label 'safe' gives new meaning to a wide range of human activities, endowing them with unspoken qualities that are meant to merit our automatic approval. . . . Personal safety is a growth industry. . . . Even public and private space is now assessed from a safety perspective." Frank Furedi, *Culture of Fear: Risk and the Morality of Low Expectation* (London: Cassell, 1997), 1.

26. *Psychologism* (under the aegis of scientism) is the ideology of the field of psychology, when it presents its findings and ways of doing research as the best, and *only* way, relative to other ways. It is not very easily convinced that it ought to look at its own biased ways and critique them from perspectives that go beyond the borders of the disci-

pline of psychology itself. The notion of psychologism is analogous to when a religion becomes fundamentalist and falls into the trap of religionism.

27. *"Moral panic*- an exaggerated, media-amplified, social reaction to initially relatively minor acts of social deviance. . . . Such an overreaction by media, police, courts, governments and members of the public in 'labelling' and drawing attention, far from leading to an elimination of this behavior, tends to amplify it. . . . Some theorists also suggest that moral panics [*via* racism in disguise, as one e.g.] are encouraged by governments as useful in mobilizing political support by creating a common 'threat' [or 'enemy']. Cited from David Jary, and Julia Jary, *Collins Dictionary of Sociology* (Glasgow, Scotland: HarperCollins, 1995), 427.

28. Elizabeth Seaton, "The Commodification of Fear," *Topia: Canadian Journal of Cultural Studies*, 5(2001), 1-18.

29. Robert Sardello, *Freeing the Soul from Fear* (NY: Putnam Penguin, 1999), xvi.

30. bell hooks, *All About Love* (NY: William Morrow, 2000), 93.

31. Dr. Jeffers is surely one of the most popular and "effective" teachers of FME in North America today (and I suspect a lot of the Western world). I am not a big fan of her simplistic approach of "do it anyway," etc. Nike ads in the 1990s picked up on that theme and used it for selling just about anything they produced (from their 'Third World' factory sweat shops). She is not a critical or holistic-integral theorist, rather, somewhat reductionistically (although, "spiritually") caters to a popular cultural audience of "how to" demands within the human potential movement and 'new age.' Susan Jeffers, *Feel the Fear And Do It Anyway* (NY: Fawcett Columbine, 1988).

1

DO WE REALLY WANT A FEARLESSNESS (R)EVOLUTION?

Human being – (*Homo sapiens*)- refers to all the possible traits, qualities, behaviors that this species is capable of for good or bad in association with an individual "human"

Humanity- is what human beings are endowed with *via* Creation (evolution) and thus, accomplish collectively and developmentally as a quality of consciousness for ethical actions that we would call our "best side."

I attempt to keep the above distinction in mind between the *human being* as individual, as a member of human beings (species: *Homo sapiens*), and a concept and reality of *humanity*. The latter is more abstract and philosophical. Too often they are confused in our minds and in our writing about ourselves.

In Chapter Three I articulate a natural evolutionary and cultural evolutionary framework based on Spiral Dynamics Theory, which shows there are at least nine different revolutions that human beings and their cultures have gone through collectively. Each has created memory-based intelligence systems that help us adapt to our environment—that is, survive, thrive, or even something beyond. As the theory goes: the world at any time has various percentages of these nine cultural value-memory "memes" (analogous to biological "genes").[1] This spectrum of cultural meme-intelligences are highly influential in determining much of human beings' activities and the expression of their humanity. As designated in Chapter Three, they are different "sub-species—ranging from the earliest sub-species *Homo sapiens survivalus* (c.100,000 yrs. ago) to *Homo sapiens holisticus* (c.30 yrs. ago)[2] and so on. This "rainbow" or "spectrum" view of human evolution is central (integral) to everything I write about and do.

Arguably, humanity (i.e., our best side) is inherent to our species from the beginning, but it is not necessarily dominant throughout our development, individually or collectively. The goal of the human potential movement or any agenda of human emancipation (of which this book purports to be), if it is wise, has to include a *goal of developing our humanity to its greatest maturity*, if not mastery and perfection, in and through all our sub-species—as part of a healthy, just, peaceful, and sustainable growth process. This drive, goal, motivation, or *telos* could be called God-intelligence, Life-intelligence, Creative Evolution or simply maturation. I like what Phil Nuernberger wrote about "mature thought" *via* transformational experience and transcendence, whereby adulthood attains a postconventional developmental level and "complete fearlessness" is both the means and outcome.[3] Here are the beginning strands of my Kosmology[4]—but that is getting us too far ahead too quickly.

Do *we really want more fearlessness* in the world? It depends. Some readers will want me to define what is meant by the term "fearlessness" before offering an opinion. Without going into that detail at this point, my observations indicate some people do want both evolution and revolution based on fearlessness, and some do not. The five (non-fictional) leaders profiled below (*via* a performative style fictional conference dialogue on World Fear Management) open Chapter One as radical (if not extreme) advocates on the "for" side. They, in my view, major players, really prophets, of a minor but burgeoning Fearlessness (R)evolution. Human beings' disagreements regarding the moral and practical value of fearlessness and its very possibility for humanity are nonetheless strong, if not prohibitive of such a (r)evolution, as we shall see. It is a major conflict that humanity is struggling with and in which human beings need to address. We have avoided it for far too long, perhaps until only very recently. The leaders in this chapter are raising the issue, as a case in point, and as a current call to dialogue on a new vision for humanity based on fearlessness. They see fearlessness *as in fact*, our best side or at least the *best* way to it.

I raise the issue again in Chapter Four on education (as life-long learning) and ask the question: *Do we really want to teach children to be fearless* and thus grow up into mature fearless adults, or near so? No doubt to do so would be a revolution and evolution of humanity in the way societies socialize their young and organize social order *via* religion, governance, education, culture, and economic structures overall. An underlying premise of my work and this book is that in general, our species *Homo sapiens* (meaning 'wise man'), for at least 100,000 years, has raised their offspring largely in fear and by fear-based means. The corollary is we are a relatively violent and non-peaceful species, as history has recorded domination, conflict, fear and oppression. That said, it is remarkable we live in such dense cities around the globe and most of us do not violate others at every moment, at least not physically and overtly—yet, that does not mean violation in forms of crime, fearism, adultism, sexism, racism, classism, etc. are not going on all the time. They are.

Such a thesis is nothing new, and I do not mean to indicate it is the only way we can be or ought to be. Precisely the reverse—we all are, by "law of the Kosmos" on an emancipatory journey, more or less, from *fear* to *fearlessness*. In

Chapter Three, I correlate this *historical fearlessness* movement in evolution, history, and development with Spiral Dynamics Theory and critical integral theory to build an over-arching framework (model) to assess fear management/education (FME) on this planet.

The meaning constructed and the valuing of a Fearlessness (R)evolution, in part, depends on one's perspective. It also depends on individual and collective development—that is, the evolution of consciousness or intelligence in an organization or system (what I'll later call "Fear Management Systems"). Whatever the case, what we see today in a good deal of the world is that significant numbers of people and some organizations are truly fed up with fearmongering and the destructive, toxic, violent and oppressive dynamics of what can generically be called the global "Fear Problem" (see Chapter Two).

As well as documenting some of the more recent extreme World's Fearlessness Teachings of (r)evolution, this chapter introduces ten universal perspectives (or Fear Management Systems = FMSs) as evolutionary intelligences with (r)evolutionary potentials. Each perspective or worldview is assigned a different color to validate they *all* have unique intelligences and an interrelational role to play in the whole 'rainbow' spectrum of consciousness and strategies of managing fear. A true story of a coral-colored "flower" found in Africa is introduced in this chapter as an example of the amazing intelligence of evolution on the way to revolution. It provides an articulating metaphor and expanding imaginary to embrace the concept of a *Spiral of Fearlessness*, to be used throughout this text. FME takes on a whole new look from the perspective of the Spiral.

As posited in my theory, the inherent *spirit of fearlessness* moves through a spiraling developmental sequence of intelligences (FMSs) as 'naturally' as does fear. Remember the principle: *when fear arises, then arises fearlessness*. It is an *a priori* dialectical principle of opposites, a sort of law of the Kosmos which means, in theory, that whatever Creation produces it can handle it one way or another. It will be a creative handling as Hegel and other *integral philosophers* like Aurobindo, de Chardin, Bergson, Baldwin, Whitehead, Gebser, Habermas, and Wilber have argued.[5] The fear that is produced by one of the ten perspectives, is a fear ('fear' patterning) that has an arising fearlessness ('fearlessness' patterning) to accompany it—and thus, to manage it (sometimes not so well, as we shall see). Note, the inverted (') commas are signifiers on these terms that show the concept is being used at times in an unordinary (non-common sense) way, that is, it is a term and concept under deconstruction and reconstruction (see Chapter Two). Below, this principle is articulated within a unique context of the evolution of Defense in living systems—based on another dialectical relationship that *where growth is, there is protection (i.e., defense) of that growth*—and with enough healthy growth, there can be reproduction. To reproduce is the ultimate bottomline purpose of any living system. Natural and cultural selection operate on this imperative.

I have included my own draft "Credo of Fearlessness" in the end Notes which summarizes many of the points made in this book so far.[6] Now to the fictional conference, to introduce these five selected living leaders of the Fearlessness (R)evolution today.

Some Pivotal Leaders of the Fearlessness (R)evolution

Imagine you have sat down as an international delegate in a large conference room. The occasion is a gathering of a United Nations/UNESCO joint "policy" initiative to improve humanity's fear management the world over. Organizers have called this gathering because of the current crisis of fear/terror on the planet, of which the "War on Terror" is symbolic, symptomatic and a major perpetrator. The organizers' brochure states:

> Our species has come to the brink of a major decision of how to manage fear/terror in the world. The United Nations/UNESCO policy initiative for this conference is to create a world alliance to call for and end the 'war that has no end' (i.e., "War on Terror")—because it is a fear-full and ineffective means of fear management that is creating a massive "culture of fear" in the world that is costing us more than it is benefiting us. Few, if any, are feeling more safe and secure now than before that WW-III was declared by the Bush administration in the fall of 2001 (post-9/11 period). We invite delegates to dialogue on alternatives to create a new future-positive trajectory for humanity's sake. It appears, "Modernism" has failed. We now live in a postmodern era, characterized by what some critics have labeled "Fear's Empire." Our time and empire is running down—we need to reform our ways which habitually revolve on a largely dysfunctional relationship to fear and its management. It seems we suffer from a collective "cultural pathology"[7] (in the West, especially), and we need a new cultural therapy both sacred and secular—one that starts with the word 'fearlessness.'

This is all fiction, perhaps my fantasy. Whatever the case, it is the performative and dramatic style in which I introduce five current leaders and their fearlessness teachings. Some have self-declared they are leaders of a Fearlessness Revolution and others have been interpreted as such by myself. They are pivotal voices advocating and promoting a movement of fearlessness over fear. After their introductions (given by myself as a less-than-neutral "Moderator" at this conference), and their presentations (fictional but based on their actual available teachings which are referenced in the end Notes), I'll critique and summarize these leaders and what their work means, from a critical integral theory point of view. I realize readers will not understand necessarily the critical integral theory framework at this point; you can choose to read Chapter Two now to pick-up on that, or merely wait until later after finishing Chapter Two in sequence, and return to examine my comments in Chapter One with more knowledge at that later point. I recommend the latter.

Moderator (RMF): Good evening everyone! And welcome to *Re-Visioning Fear Management for a New World.* Our first panel is made up of distinguished guests, activists, intellectuals and mountain-movers. These pivotal leaders have focused their panel presentations and discussion around the topic of fearlessness—and specifically their own version of fearlessness as a transformative, if not revolutionary force. In speaking with them prior to this session they all agreed that "fearlessness" is a controversial topic and that there is great disagreement as to its value or even its existence as possible for humans. However, their research, teaching and learning has brought them all to be convinced of its power and reality and they, like myself, agree we need fearlessness today like never before. Before the panel presentations let me quote Antonio Negri, a highly controversial, truly subversive contemporary Italian Marxist philosopher, and expert on Spinoza and our postmodern era.[8] I do this in order to set the tone for the important topic we are about to engage at this conference:

> We have in our hands the promise of a fearless society. This is what Spinoza said[9]—and what has been rediscovered by feminists, workers, students, and all those who hoped and wished that something would change in 1968 [time of the student protests in France's universities, and later in many other W. countries], four centuries after Spinoza. Something has changed: life has been reassembled in a new way.

Indeed, 1968 was over forty-years ago, and so much has changed. Yet our panel members tonight share with Negri, and indeed with Spinoza, a spirit of fearlessness that seems undeniable and ever-present—if we are ready to recognize it, follow it and nurture it in all its complexities. Hard-core empiricists and skeptics, rightfully so, will ask is a "fearless society" possible? And if so, what is the evidence? Where are the living or historical examples? Of course, it depends how strict one is in defining fearless or fearlessness. That is not my role, and the panel presenters may define these terms as they wish. With a brief search on the Internet this morning, I was able to find there are many diverse people using the term "fearless society" and it has a general connotation of being equivalent to peaceful, non-violent, just and sustainable societies. From this brief literature research one sees evidence of a long and tried tradition of the "fearless society" imaginary[10] linked to the Kung Bushman of the Kalahari before colonialism,[11] the best of native American societies,[12] the formation and ideal of socialism[13] and reconstructive Marxism,[14] the Pakistanian ideal of the democratic state,[15] resistance of the Danes to Nazis in WWII,[16] to the Shiva-Shakti folklore from the Himalayas,[17] to global education,[18] and Gandhian non-violence movements,[19] to name a few. Political and social science theorist Juan Corradi argues, however, ". . . a society in which fear is unknown has not existed and is unlikely ever to exist"[20] The following leaders are, apparently beyond such doubts. One way or another, the following selected leaders and their fearlessness movements or revolutions, quiet or noisy, small or large, are also visionaries. And as useful as that is, we also are gathered at this conference not merely to accept visionaries' proclamations, though they may be inspiring—we are here to critique each other as productively as we can, avoiding the very pitfalls of ideologisms based on fear. I ask you, and all presenters, to stay open-minded and curious—that is, I believe, one of the central characteristics of fearlessness. But you never came to hear me preach. May I now introduce our first distinguished panel presenter, **Ms. Ericka D. Jackson**. Scanning her website[21] one reads of this multiple published book author, and "breakthrough coach," launching "The Fearless Revolution," through her organizational business venture called "Convergence Center

& Ministries." Jackson, a spirited and charismatic American woman and Christian has a lot to say. She is currently "advancing in ministry . . . as a licensed Evangelist." I encourage anyone in the audience to go to her website and her interesting story of how she got to where she is today. Truly an inspiration. It's all yours, Ericka. [a 30s something vibrant black woman walks to the microphone and podium, looking everyone in the eye, with a serious smile of absolute conviction]

EDJ: Thanks Dr. Fisher. It's good to be here with so many intelligent people gathered from around the planet with the intention to re-evaluate our current situation, and by that I mean to acknowledge, without withdrawl and denial, the urgency I experience with people in my work, to better understand fear and to move beyond fear. I am totally convinced that our human potential collectively and individually is largely held back by fear. So one day, January 1, 2008, I decided to establish what I call the "Fearless Revolution" This project, open to anyone to join in, was a result of what I saw as a growing need for curriculum and programs that offer "Christian leaders and entrepreneurs with practical tools" they need to "move beyond fear" and live their dreams and true life purpose. On my website you may checkout the "Fearless Revolutionary Pack" as a primer foundation for a new kind of education on the journey to a triumphant fearlessness path. I include my book *The Fearless Living Challenge*, 12 Fearless teleclasses, and two breakthrough CD teachings on fear, entitled "Fear No More" and "Freedom from Fear," and a personal "Declaration of Fearlessness." All for $49.95. I also take international speaking engagements requests for "The Fearless Revolution Tour." We've added "Ericka's Cafe" and "The Success Store" on the website as well, so there is something for everyone. Okay, that's my business introduction, which I've learned not to be afraid of. But folks, let me say right now, the spirit of my work is not reducible to teachings and resources, and profit! The Fearless Revolution is much more than that! It represents a "stand for fearlessness" and a committed "offensive against paralyzing fear." [she flips on the computer and projector and we see on the screen a piece of text she wrote from her website, which she reads out loud]

> *The Fearless Revolution*™ - It is revolutionary in its ability to expose fear at the root. Fear is NOT [merely] 'false evidence appearing real' as some familiar teachings [like Alcoholics Anonymous] suggest.' Are you ready to take your place in the Fearless Revolution?

[the audience simultaneously whistles and calls out "Yes!" and cheers and applause ensue; the moderator intervenes with a question]

RMF: Wow! Thanks Ericka for that short and exciting introduction, I'm sure we'll all have a lot to talk about with you as this conference proceeds. Your fearlessness teaching about fear, is contradictory to what a lot of people have thought, especially in A.A., and that will be interesting to hear more about later. It is a fact that we don't all agree on these teachings. Do we? Could you define "fearlessness" for us to get us all on the same page in order to clarify your stand? [she flips a few pages on her website and the audience sees her definition in print, as she reads it out loud]

> *Fearlessness-* . . . is about clearly knowing what you have been called to do and making it happen with no hesitation, doubt, or anxiety. Fearlessness feels like waking up so excited you can barely contain yourself. You are not worried about what people think or say. Fearlessness allows you to create the life of your heart's desire and to be able to truly affect the lives you have been called to touch. It is about being 100% comfortable in your skin and with who you are. It is about expanding your channel of communication with God so He can direct your every step so you can move forward with certainty. Most of all, fearlessness is about *freedom*.

RMF: I recall King, influenced by Gandhi's fearlessness and non-violence revolution in India against British colonialism, being none to shy to spread his own American-type revolution against fear, war and hatred. Chernus wrote [he reads from a page of paper], "Why do nations act selfishly and, in so doing, perpetuate violence? Most theories of nonviolence assume that the root problem is usually some kind of fear. Nonviolence therefore must involve overcoming our fears on the way to fearlessness. Martin Luther King Jr. asked rhetorically: 'Is not fear one of the major causes of war? We say that war is a consequence of hate, but close scrutiny reveals this sequence: first fear, then hate, then war, and finally deeper hatred.'"[22] Ericka, I'd like to hear you comment on a thought I had while listening to you. I'm thinking how you are part of a few streams, legacies really, of the teachings of fearlessness. Do you recognize those streams and do they motivate you?

EDJ: I stand on great shoulders, if that's what you mean. The black leaders in the Civil Rights movement, too many to name, not merely Dr. Martin Luther King Jr., but I think of many of the less well-known women "bridge leaders" in the communities[23]—they all had an awareness of the oppression fear brings and why a non-violent fearlessness revolution, as Gandhi promoted, is essential to liberation. Then there are roots back to my Christian heritage and if you read in the Bible, you cannot help but notice God or angels, or Christ, continually telling us "Fear Not!" and "Be Not Afraid!" And most recently, I appreciate the groundwork of women, entrepreneurs for the most part like myself, who are tilling the hardened soil to get the masses growing again, up and out of the graves of fear and despair that is so palpable these days. I am thinking particularly of Dr. Susan Jeffers in the late-1980's with "feel the fear and do it anyway" and her "Fear Busters" program and then there's the amazing story and project of "fearless living" that Rhonda Britten has brought to us in the 1990s.[24] Yeah, they *all* inspire me and there's more of us, a lot more than you might think. Most of us, fearless ones, are just not so extrovert and noisy as myself, Susan, or Rhonda.

RMF: I'm sure there are more, and some of them are probably sitting on the panel with you right now.

EDJ: That's a fact! I'll let those great women speak for themselves.

RMF: Doing a quick Internet search on Google, there were 99 hits that came up with the search term "fearless revolution" and most of them are yours Ericka, but you are not alone with the idea and spirit of fearlessness in that form. Good for you. On that note, let's hear from our next presenter, known as "a prominent fearless leader"[25] and civil rights activist for over a quarter of a century. She was a leader in Bishop Desmund Tutu's "anti-fear campaign against Apartheid."[26] She was elected to the prestigious position of North American President of the World Council of Churches in 2003 and continues in that position today, though she was a member of the WCC Central Committee since 1998. The WCC, begun in 1948, is the largest ecumenical organization comprised of 340 Christian denominations and churches worldwide in 120 countries. It represents some 550 million Christians. That is a lot of potential. Her teaching is generally not concerned with the enormous energy, time and money that usually goes into physical church structures and getting memberships. She can be impatient with that aspect of white middle-class institutional Christian life. She was the spokesperson and advocate for the 2004 WCC "Decade to Overcome Violence" and remains a critic of the US foreign and domestic policies that remain intransigent to non-violent solutions to sociopolitical and economic problems. As President of the North American WCC, she met with hundreds of delegates in Porto Alegre, Brazil in February 2006, representing some four million members, where she led the initiative of prayer and repentance, backed by 34 Christian churches, and publicly apologized for those of have died and been injured in the US-led Iraq war.[27] She believes we failed to stop an unjust war, and now we need to mourn with all victims of this war. She is our next revolutionary leader of fearlessness, would you please give a warm welcome for the **Reverend Bernice Powell Jackson**. [a loud applause breaks out from the audience, and a mixed black and white heritage American woman in her 50-60s steps up to the podium like a chalice and a flaming blade]

BPJ: I'm honored to be here amongst you, and amongst the spirit of fearlessness that moves us; that moves me to challenge us to grow up! It is not an easy thing to go around and tell people in your church, or anywhere, they need to grow up. I'm always scared to do that. Let me speak about my Christian fellowship, around the world, but particularly in some parts of the United States. I recently read the book by T. Green, *Twelve Reasons Christians Don't Grow. . . Even in Good Churches*,[28] and although I don't agree necessarily with all he is saying, there is no doubt we Christians need to grow up into the postmodern world and begin to seriously account for multicultural, racial, and ethnic dimensions, and prejudice in the church. We need to internationalize not further colonize. We need to find the prophetic spirit beyond fear and redefine and declare our mission in the 21st century, not the 11th century. [a power point lights up on the screen behind her with words she reads out loud] [in 2002 B. P. Jackson gave a post-9/11 Key Note Address to her American colleagues and membership at the annual meeting of the United Church of Christ,[29] where she said:]

[Y]ou must love your enemies and pray for those who persecute you . . . do they not have meaning for us, the richest, most powerful nation in the world as well? Remember the words of a modern-day prophet, Dr. Martin Luther King, Jr., who said, "the contemporary church is often a weak, ineffectual voice with an uncertain sound. It is so often the arch-supporter of the status quo. Far from being disturbed by the presence of the church, the power structure of the average community is consoled by the church's silent and often vocal sanction of things as they are. . . . [citing Dutch theologian Henri Nouwen:]'If we want to be real peace-makers, national security cannot be our primary concern. Our primary concern should be the survival of humanity, the survival of the planet, the health of all people. Whether we are Russians, Iraqis, Ethiopians or North Americans, we belong to the same human family that God loves. And we have to start taking some risks, not just individually, but risks of a more global quality, risks to let other people develop their own independence, risks to share our wealth with others and invite refugees to our country, risks to offer sanctuary, because we are people of God.' Nouwen was saying we must take some risks for peace. King was saying the church can no longer remain a silent supporter of the power structure. Jesus was saying it doesn't mean anything if you just love those who love you or are like you or agree with you, you must love those who hate you. . . . because ultimately only love conquers fear, only love conquers hate, only love conquers injustice.

Ask me what the biggest stumbling block that 21st-century Christians need to face and overcome, as does "the global church," and I'll tell you without a moment's hesitation it is *fear*. It's "what Jesus' disciples have always had to overcome. Jesus message repeats like a chorus, "Don't be afraid of each other. Don't be afraid of the powers and principalities."[30] Call it love-work, call it anti-fear work—we need them both together, and we need them fearlessly now, as we seek to design an architecture for adult maturity in this nation, and a lot of other places. [audience applauds as she sits down]

RMF: Thanks Bernice, that gets the blood boiling. What is with you fired-up revolutionary Jacksons in the USA, there's Ericka here tonight, there's Jesse and even . . .

BPJ: Yeah, its a good soul name, isn't it?

RMF: [aware of the controversy] There's even Michael Jackson. Gotta love his emotional speech in Tom Cary's 2004 film, when Michael comes out of the California court room and tells his fans and us all "we live in a world of fear" and he too feels it but is making a choice as he looks in the mirror, and he is fighting the charges against him and not falling prey to fear in everyone around him. Then he concludes that "in the end love is more powerful than fear."[31] Wow. Good stuff. I have a question Bernice. When I look at the panel tonight, and my self, I see a lot of 'Boomer' generation folks advocating a fearless revolution, but are the younger generations interested?

BPJ: You'll have to ask them. From what I see there are many who are really pissed off at the way fear is controlling their world and future. No doubt, many of them are prey to consumerism, nihilism, and individualism. Many are deeply depressed, and seeking every means they can find, including denial, to cope with it. I believe they are terrified of the world they've inherited from the 'boomer' generation. Yet, some of them are doing great work for a fearless revolution, and a lot of them are artists and moving with the powers of popular culture. That's the way to reach young people today. For example, there's singer-songwriter *Sonia and Disappear Fear*, who is not afraid to take a political and spiritual stand as she writes on her website. [the moderator flips on computer and the website appears so everyone can read it on the front large screen]: "I pledge allegiance to the flag of Disappear Fear . . . one family under God(dess) visible with liberty and justice for all."[32] There's singer-songwriter-activist Lizzy West and her cooperative of artists, she calls "Anti-Fear Movement Agency"[33] and one could go on and on. The 1990s "No Fear!" movement . . .

RMF: Yeah, all are initiatives of what I have called the Fearlessness Movement or historical fearlessness: when fear arrives, so does fearlessness to counteract it. Humans will figure out ways to manage fear, for better or worse. And I've noticed a lot of young people, especially in the 'new age' movement have really grabbed onto the words, written by Marianne Williamson, and wrongly promoted as part of Nelson Mandela's 1994 inaugural speech when he got out of prison and was elected President of South Africa: "Our deepest fear is not that we are inadequate. Our deepest fear is that we are powerful beyond measure. . . . As we're liberated from our own fear, our presence automatically liberates others."[34] Williamson, like millions of followers, are greatly influenced by *The Course* and its premise that there are only two core emotions: Love and fear.[35] Well, time is moving and I want to turn now to our next amazing fearless panel presenter, **Arianna Huffington**. Where to start? A 58 year old [white] American non-fiction author, media entrepreneur and single career mom, with her own extremely successful on-line award-winning independent newspaper *The Huffington Post*. She has her own entry pages in Wikipedia, worth quoting [the moderator turns on the computer and the large screen shows the following from Wikipedia]:[36]

> Arianna Huffington (born Arianna Stassinopoulos on July 15, 1950 in Athens, Greece) is an author and nationally syndicated columnist in the United States. She is the founder of *The Huffington Post*, a leading liberal online news and commentary website and aggregated blog. Huffington describes herself as a 'former right-winger who has evolved into a compassionate and progressive populist.'

In a 2006 CNN television interview hosted by Costello, he wanted to discuss her new book *On Becoming Fearless in Love, Work and Life* (2006), as well he wanted to find out more about her politics and personal life. In the introduction to the interview, Costello referred to her as a "fearless political pundit" who is not afraid to go public in taking a left-leaning view in America today.[37] He also says she wasn't always so fearless. What did you tell Costello? I ask you to join me in a warm greeting for Arianna Huffington. [loud applause, as she smiles widely and steps up to the microphone and podium with total confidence]

AH: Thank you. *On Becoming Fearless* is a book that begins with the premise that fear is universal. That's not bad. The real question, one of fear management, is "do we let our fear stop us or do we go on despite our fears?" Let me tell you now, when I step forward, where I think all of us want to in order to grow, I feel fear. When I walk through the fear, and succeed or fail at the task at hand, I at least have grown a bit of what I call my "fearlessness muscle." We need to take risks to have a "fearlessness workout." Each time I risk it gets a bit easier. I'm stronger. And that's the message I want to give my teenage daughters and all women today. The book is for girls and women but it also is for men. On *The Huffington Post* I have a section called "Becoming Fearless" where I encourage everyone to write in, especially women telling their stories of fearless actions they take in the world, so as to inspire other women to take them too. I want to start a "fearlessness movement."[38] In a recent interview with AOL's Maven Bethanne Patrick, she wondered how I had the gumption in 2003 to run for governor of California, against you know who—Arnold Schwarzeneggar. She asked what started me on the "path of fearlessness"[?] My greatest role model, I told her, was my mother. I have her picture on my desk at work. What an inspiration. She was completely self-taught and "absolutely fearless about taking on challenges." During WWII, she was part of the Resistance movement against fascism and Nazism in Europe. She was hiding Jews, but when the German soldiers came into her home and asked her if she was, rifles pointing in her face, she calmly addressed them with integrity and said "No. Put your guns down." They did and they left. I was nine when she told me that story and I keep thinking how could I ever be that fearless? So I guess I keep at it, building up my fearlessness muscles. You never know when you may really need them. Even Arnold, Mr. Muscle, was a little intimidated by me, I think. A lot of people still are. The more important issue is that women are still not given adequate or equal opportunity and rewards for hard work in this country, never mind the rest of the world. Being fearless for women, in a sense, isn't an option today. It is the source for motivating real change. Oh, and I don't mean that "fearless" means without fear. I mean mastery—not letting fears get in the way and hold us back. Fear is genetic, in our DNA. To practice fearless is not dependent on being spiritual, religious, or anything else, but having the role models around us to encourage us to do the same. "As long as we keep moving and don't cling to whatever it is that we are holding on to, then we can lead a fearless life."[39] For me, it isn't a political option either. Fear has driven a lot of our politics, especially in the US, especially in a post-9/11 world. In 2006 I called for an "Epidemic of Fearlessness to Counter the Fearmonger-in-Chief" [meaning US Pres. G. W. Bush Jr.). This particular published piece plays off a notion of a "virus of fear"[40] spreading across the land. [the moderator turns on the computer and up on the wall screen the audience reads:]

WHY WE NEED AN EPIDEMIC OF FEARLESSNESS TO COUNTER THE FEARMONGER-IN-CHIEF

With the fifth anniversary of 9/11 less than a week away, and Election Day 2006 entering the post-Labor Day home stretch, we can expect the White House to play the fear card every chance it gets. As Rahm Emanuel said: "After six years, they've only got fear to sell." After all, banging the fear-gong and trying to scare the hell out of us every time they need a bump in the polls has worked like a charm for Bush and Rove. Ratcheting up the fear-mongering rhetoric is Plan A. Plan B is Repeat Plan A. The president officially kicked off the big push to the midterms with a fear-triggering speech last week in which he warned, "If we give up the fight in the streets of Baghdad, we will face terrorists in the streets of our own cities." We've seen this movie before. It's "Be Very Afraid" all over again. It has, after all, been a frighteningly effective sales pitch. Fear is a powerful, universal emotion—always there to be exploited. And that's why we need a major counteroffensive—a wide-ranging campaign to help spread fearlessness so as to inoculate the country against this shameful campaign strategy. Otherwise, we're going to once again succumb to our lizard brains and keep voting our fears—even as our logical brains . . . tell us that the fearmongers in power have made us all less safe. To this end, *HuffPost* is today launching a new feature section devoted to promoting fearlessness in all aspects of our lives. Using as its springboard the themes in my new book. . . . The life-blood of *HuffPost* will always be politics but this new section will be for those times when you want to put politics aside for awhile. And if you are one of those rare creatures that lives and breathes politics 24/7, well then, no need to click on *Becoming Fearless*. Obviously, fearlessness, though indispensable at this moment in our national life, is a great gift independent of politics. And this book is the most personal one I've ever written, dealing with my own struggle with fear and how it has shaped my life and my politics. . . . over the next two months, I intend to highlight the issues in the book that touch on the many ways the personal intersects with the political. Because the more we learn to overcome the fears that limit us and to live in fearlessness, the more we'll be able to counter the dark forces—both political and cultural—looking to keep us shrouded in a fog of fear. In the end, the more fearless we become, the more effective we will be not just as husbands, wives, parents, and co-workers but as citizens—and the more we'll be able to demand courage and authenticity from our leaders. We've had enough of spineless, fear-driven, walking-on-eggshells would-be leaders. As I've said before, the vast majority of those on the political scene are like Beltway versions of the Cowardly Lion of Oz, driven by the fear of saying the wrong thing (wouldn't want to give the other side ammo for the inevitable attack ad), of offending someone (anyone!), of going out on a limb, and, above all, of losing. As a result, we get a seemingly endless lineup of fear-driven candidates who, with each new election cycle, become a little more wrinkie-free, a little more foible-free, a good bit less interesting—and considerably more idea-free. They are so programmed to avoid the pitfalls of actually standing for something, we might as well have robots running. If this sounds like any politician you know, send them the link to our new section. As I write in the book. . . . Fearlessness is all about getting up one more time than we fall down.

RMF: [the moderator interrupts] Sorry, we don't have time to read this completely and study it now. Thank you Arianna. Are you thinking of running for President? [audience laughs].

AH: It's a little late now. I'll stick to journalism and fight the battle of the fearlessness revolution from another angle.

RMF: Well, I have seen you take an active role in the 2008 elections, with your initiating the "Fear Watch '08," to keep an eye on the GOP and fearmongering going on.[41]

AH: Yes, I really want to let all politicians and their cronies, and the public, know that we are going to be watching and unveiling all the ways that fear is misused in politics, in this election, and beyond. It simply is not intelligent, nor a way to motivate people, or run a nation, or world. We've called them on their corruption—and now they know we stand for fearlessness not fear! [the audience breaks out in cheers and applause as she sits down]

RMF: Well, ladies and gentleman, it is time to turn to our next panel presenter, who is not able to be with us in-person. However, I have a documentary summary I've written in her honor, based on research I have done on "The Lady," as her supporters call her in Burma (now Myanmar). I am speaking about the Nobel Peace Prize Laureate of 1991, the gracious and impeccable, admirable and intelligent, world leader of fearlessness, **Aung San Suu Kyi**. I wonder, and am concerned, if she is still alive. She's imprisoned again and not healthy apparently. Only those closest in the underground resistance have limited positive-contact with her as she exists in exile under house arrest by the ruling military junta of Myanmar. [a picture of Kyi, a beautiful 58 year old woman smiling softly, is projected on the wall screen; the audience is silent, then slowly the audience applauds, some people rise out of their chairs while applauding vigorously, and tears can be seen in many eyes; the moderator reads out loud from his papers:] With well over 12 books written about her life by diverse authors, Kyi has devoted to her life and work to human rights. She is an exemplar activist and political opposition leader, who practices fearlessness in everything she does. On one book's front jacket her publisher wrote the following:[42] "This Nobel Peace Prize Laureate [1991], mother of two, and devout Buddhist, is one of the most inspiring examples of spiritually-infused politics and fearless leadership that the world has ever seen." One biographer introduced her in his book as "one of the world's most renowned freedom fighters and advocates of non-violence."[43] Inspired by her father (Aung San), who was killed in her early childhood as a political and warrior-hero in Burma, her challenge with her followers, is to create a strong democracy in a country ruled by a repressive military junta, in what Alan Clements called a "totalitarian 'terror state.'"[44] In her book *Freedom from Fear* (1991/96), A. S. S. Kyi wrote, "The words used by Jawaharlal Nehru to describe Mahatma Gandhi could well be applied to Aung San: 'the essence of his teaching was fearlessness and truth.'"[45] Parker J. Palmer, the eminent spiritual adult educator wrote about "world famous agents of non-

violent change," whom he listed and reminded us of how they have "been broken open":[46]

> ... [the] Dalai Lama, Aung San Suu Kyi, Nelson Mandela, Dorothy Day, Martin
> Luther King Jr., Rosa Parks, and Thich Nhat Hahn, to name a few. Hearts like
> theirs have been broken open to a largeness that holds the possibility of a better
> future for us all.

Whitney Stewart's book entitled *Aung San Suu Kyi: Fearless Voice of Burma*
(1997), offers an example of the high regard characteristic of her admirers. Kyi
has been referred to by some as "Burma's Mandela." According to Naomi Klein,
the current military regime took power in Burma in 1988, and as representative
leader of the opposition party she was quietly jailed, but "international awareness about brutal conditions inside the Asian country skyrocketed in 1995 when
. . . [she] was released from six years of house arrest."[47] However, it wasn't long
before she had gathered opposition power, challenged the junta, and was jailed
again, which has remained the case until this day (June 5, 2008). In 1990 her
political party actually had won a country-wide democratic election but the junta
refused to give her party or her status. In an interview, she was asked once if she
was frightened by the junta, their dictator, and their brutality. She responded,[48]
"I was not frightened of them. . . . I think it was because I did not hate them, and
you cannot really be frightened of people you do not hate. Hate and fear go hand
in hand. . . . Fear is a habit. I'm not afraid." A. S. S. Kyi's original 1991 (often
reprinted) essay "Freedom From Fear" opens with the stunning and memorable
sentences, written while under house arrest, are meant for her captors and also
for the rest of humanity:[49] "It is not power that corrupts but fear. Fear of losing
power corrupts those who wield it and fear of the scourge of power corrupts
those who are subject to it." Her steadfast character under duress, warmth, and
political savvy are impressive. And as a writer, she has captured audiences everywhere. Especially interesting is her view of authentic fearlessness revolution.
She wrote in 1995, with an undercurrent of challenge to some of "Marxist" philosophy of working class revolution:[50]

> The quintessential revolution [of fearlessness] is that of spirit, born of an intel-
> lectual conviction of the need for change in those mental attitudes and values
> which shape the course of a nation's development. A revolution which aims
> merely at changing official policies and institutions with a view to an im-
> provement in material conditions has little chance of genuine success. Without
> a revolution of the spirit, the forces which produced the iniquities of the old or-
> der would continue to be operative, posing a constant threat to the process of
> reform and regeneration. It is not enough merely to call for freedom, democ-
> racy and human rights. There has to be a united determination to persevere in
> the struggle, to make sacrifices in the name of enduring truths [and Great Tradi-
> tions], to resist the corrupting influences of [personal, egoic] desire, ill will, ig-
> norance and fear.... Among the basic freedoms to which men [sic] aspire that
> their lives might be full and uncramped, freedom from fear stands out as both a
> means and an end. A people who would build a nation in which strong, democ-

ratic institutions are firmly established as a guarantee against state-induced power must first learn to liberate their own minds from apathy and fear.

While under house arrest, A. S. S. Kyi had to write on scrolls and/or on the walls of her house. One scroll was found posted on her house walls and reprinted. It was a quote she had copied down, and was obviously inspiring words by Jawaharlal Nehru during India's decolonization (i.e., Gandhian revolution of fearlessness):[51]

> Any achievement that is based on widespread fear can hardly be a desirable one, and on 'order' that has for its basis the coercive apparatus of the State. . . . it was the duty of the . . . State to preserve . . . *dharma* and *abhaya* [fearlessness]—righteousness and absence of fear. Law was something more than mere law, and order was the fearlessness of the people.

The most fascinating political and spiritual dialogue by A. S. S. Kyi and Alan Clements in *The Voice of Hope* (1997) is filled with discussion on fear and fearlessness. The "revolution of the spirit" she talks about is for all nations, and is closely linked to love, compassion, and fearlessness. Being Buddhist, for her these notions are well embedded in that spiritual tradition. Often she downplays the admiration from people world wide, and says that her colleagues and the people who are living out in the streets are much more courageous than her self. Even though she has said, in the face of her 'enemy' (captors), she is "not afraid"—preferring to love than fear them. When pushed by Clements in the interviews, she admits her fear (of herself):[52] "[Kyi:] I am afraid. I'm afraid of doing the wrong thing that might bring harm to others. But of course, this is something I've had to learn to cope with. I do worry for them though."

Clements and Kyi pursue the philosophical aspects to both peace but also revolution, as Burma (Myanmar) is clearly in need of one:[53]

> [Clements:] You have written: 'Fearlessness may be a gift but perhaps more precious is the courage acquired through endeavor, courage that comes from cultivating the habit of refusing to let fear dictate one's actions.' If truth is the basis of genuine dialogue, what is more precious than truthfulness itself?
>
> [Kyi:] People who are full of sincerity and goodwill tend not to be afraid of facing others [or the truth].

Perhaps it is fitting to leave this profile with a small excerpt from the Clement's interview with her on something very practical, which exemplifies a humble and non-dogmatic approach to her teachings of fearlessness:[54]

> [Clements:] What instigates the courage to cross the precipice of fear?
>
> [Kyi:] That, I cannot say. I think there have been people who have been inspired by the teachings of great teachers [e.g., the World's Fearlessness Teachings]. Or there are those who have been changed because somebody has shown

them what it means to live without fear. And with some people, perhaps it's not one thing, but a combination of experiences that have led them to the conclusion that they have to change. But I don't think there is one solution for everybody. Each human being is different.

So much more could be said, but let's move on. Our penultimate presenter is a resident of California, an eco-feminist, scholar, activist, poet, filmmaker, cultural critic, and author of some 20 books—**Susan Griffin**. She has had a marked impact on her readers, with books like *The Book of Courtesans: A Catalogue of Their Virtues* (2001), *Woman and Nature: The Roaring Inside Her* (1978), *Pornography and Silence* (1987) and her latest *Wrestling with the Angel of Democracy: On Being an American Citizen* (2008). She appeared in the later stages of the second wave of feminism (c.1981) with her contemporary Catherine MacKinnon (c.1990). Her writing style and artistic bent is highly appealing to many. Her depth of research and rigor that support her ideas and convictions, makes her work a welcome complement to women's scholarship. Griffin, an award winning author and a finalist nominee for a Pulitzer Prize. According to Wikipedia, she received a MacArthur grant for Peace and International Cooperation and an Emmy award for the play *Voices*.[55] At age 65 she is no waning elder, but rather leads an active life, one that is reflected in the essay she wrote entitled "Fearlessness" in *Yes! Magazine* (Summer, 2003). Please welcome, Ms. Susan Griffin. [crowd applauds loudly as she approaches the microphone and podium]

SG: What an honor to be here, and be touched, by these beautiful women.

RMF: Thanks.

SG: Oh, you too. [she blows a kiss, jokingly, to the moderator; the audience laughs]

RMF: [laughing] Thanks.

SG: You're welcome. Truly, it is breathtaking—as I have this opportunity to hear, one right after another, woman after woman, fire-up the human soul with talk of a revolution of fearlessness on this planet. None of us, usually, gets a consecutive and continuous dose of fearlessness like this! At least, I sure don't. But once before, in my long life, I did. And that is the experience I want to share with you, as I have written about in my recent article for *Yes!* magazine in 2003.[56] [she pauses, breathes deeply, centers herself and looks at everyone in the audience, glowing throughout her being]. You know, I am a long-term staunch feminist. What I am about to share isn't your status quo or stereotypical feminist position on the topic of fear and fearlessness. I am ambivalent around what many of my sisters think about this topic. I trust if I step on toes, it will be done with respect. You don't have to research long in the feminist literatures, and I recognize many feminists and feminisms, but no matter, to find they are generally not in favor of "fearless" or "fearlessness" and believe it is largely a left over of the patriarchy and its warrior-mentality; a juvenile masculinism and misogyny—all total, an intransigent inflated male-ego that believes it can conquer and transcend fear, and that that is its "goal." Our beloved sister, the late Audrey Lorde famously reminded us women activists that we don't need to wait for "the luxury of fearlessness" to take action and make things better for girls and women.[57] I agree. But I don't want to analyze the pathology of masculinity, at this point, in this brief introduction. I don't want to say all "feminists" think negatively toward fearlessness—clearly, the amazing women leaders with us today on this panel are a case in point of contradiction. There are complex arguments to be made—and may we enter them as this conference persists through the days ahead. Rather, my hypothesis is that too many girls/women/feminists have become afraid—not only of fear, but of fearlessness as well. I say that, based on my own experience, and knowing that was certainly the case for me most all of my life. Something major changed my view and attitude—my soul— in 2003, when I wrote about "Fearlessness" in the first days of the American invasion of Iraq. Strange, how we could have become so afraid of fearlessness. Or at least, most of us in the Western world. I like that Marilyn Ferguson brought this out when she was writing about the Dalai Lama. He was on tour recently and apparently teaching "Don't fear fearlessness."[58] And if the late Tibetan Buddhist, Rinpoche Chögyam Trungpa is correct, true fearlessness is more about being vulnerable than being rough, tough, and heroic. He taught that "fearlessness comes from working with the softness of the human heart."[59] But, I want to back up a bit and contextualize my experience of fearlessness and raise its value and at the same time open it to critical questioning; as I think we all ought to do at this conference. It is just too simplistic, if not dangerous ideologically, to fall into a dualistic trap that "fear" is the enemy and "fearlessness" is the solution to everything. We have to engage these concepts and realities openly, and curiously, as Dr. Fisher has called us to do on this panel. Look, I may be a new fearlessness convert, but there are good roots, reasons, and partial truths that I want to honor in how others conceptualize and feel about "fearlessness" and how they judge it—even if I may not agree. Those different views trouble me often but I think that is good for learning and critical self-reflection. Personally, I get more clear thinking from these sites of conflict and troubling, than from sites of too much harmony. For example, I recently came across a troubling blog written by a man addressing a woman he knew.[60] Paraphrasing the conversation, the man starts off telling her that he knows her well and knows she is "radiant and enlightened," He acknowledges and praises her for how many times she has "uplifted" him when he was down and struggling, though he doesn't specify how. Then he critiques her by directly challenging her apparent previous claim, that she is "fearless." He preaches his belief and value system in this regard, saying "Fearlessness is overrated. We need our fears as guideposts and motivation. I'm glad you're not fearless. And I don't think I've met anyone who is 100% fearless." Then he half-contradicts himself in the next sentence and talks about a woman he saw the other night wearing a particular kind of goofy/funky coat, and he jokingly says "I wish I was 'that' fearless." Despite the difficulties in cyberworld of knowing for sure the gender is authentic in terms of the writer "Dave," I feel this 'male-position' on women in regard to fear and fearlessness is archetypal, if not universal. Folks, look, you don't have to go very far in our culture, or any patriarchal culture for that matter, to find this attitude towards the female nature and possibilities, including the more general assumptions offered by men about the very nature of reality, that is, being human. The man is skeptical of her claim to be fearless. He thinks he knows her better than she knows herself. He thinks fear is the common ground of her make-up and being. It is meant to be that way, so we can survive. I read this with great trepidation of what it represents: I see men representing women as fearful. This is absolutely nothing new, and it is the foundation of patriarchy at its deepest level. It is pure sexism, if not subtle misogyny. He cannot love her as she claims her fearless self. He prefers her afraid. He argues "fearlessness is overrated." Then at the end he jokes about wanting to be "fearless" himself, devaluating the ascription of fearless to himself through a joke. What a put down on the woman (and all women) he is representing in his self-declared wisdom. Boy, I get mad when I read this. I wonder what that woman wrote back to him. I couldn't find her response. I would challenge this guy to come up to the panel members sitting here today, or come up to my face, and say those things to me. Of course, on cyberspace, one gets this kind of inflated bravado because you don't have to see anyone eye-to-eye. Okay. I'm cooling off. And once I'm cooled off, then I have the dilemma of sorting out what do I believe? Is he right? Is fearlessness overrated and no woman should lie to herself that she is fearless or was fearless in some circumstance? Granted, "Dave" did say no one he has met is 100% fearless, even guys. As a good first and second wave feminist I ought to acknowledge that there has been for millenium, and still is the fundamental part of us called "female fear."[61] Remember that universal—"fear of rape."? Virtually all studies by psychologists, anthropologists, sociologists, tell us the same message: women are more fearful than men, girls more fearful than boys, overall. We are the 'weaker sex' when it comes to bravery and courage. How come there is no universal "male fear"? But guys can be "fearless" and less will they be criticized. Women have this fundamental fear of being raped, and for lots of good reasons, and it has been with us so long, in patriarchal misogynous cultures of violence that fear is our 'normal' identity and ought to be so that we take the proper precautions to prevent it—that is, being raped. Isn't "Dave" telling his woman friend that she'd be better off, that is safer, if she listened to him paternalistically advising her to not be "fearless"? So, be very afraid girls and women, for that will keep you safe. And so goes the mantra and the dilemma. Don't forget the statistic that "Women are 80 percent of agoraphobes."[62] The message there: is that if women are too "fearless" they will be getting into trouble—usually sex trouble. Stay home. Be afraid! I could write volumes on that one but so many other feminists have. Fear is used to keep us in our place, in our home, under the surveillance and "protection" of the male patriarch[63] telling us who to have sex with, when to have it, and that we shouldn't even think about being fearless. The patriarchy's myths tell us we should be afraid of the penis; which feminist Germaine Greer has something to say about:[64] [she pulls out a card and reads it aloud]

Women are afraid of men. . . . They are frightened of the wrong thing. . . . There are many reasons why women do not report sexual assaults; chief among them is fear. . . . That fear has been taught to women by those who want to protect them. . . . The truth is rather that female fearfulness is a cultural construct, instituted and maintained by both men and women. . . . The myth of female victim-hood is emphasized in order to keep women under control. . . . If women are to reject the role of natural-born victim, they will have to reject the ludicrous elevation of the humble penis to the status of devastating weapon. The extent to which women have followed the phallocratic script was memorably illustrated when Loren Bobbitt cut off her husband's penis instead of his head.

[the audience breaks out into laughter] We don't get encouraged to be so fearless, as you might guess. Men have a vested interest [female audience members laugh]. All joking aside, virtually every study shows that boys and men are encouraged to be "fearless" or at least more so than girls and women. It is not that they are more fearless, it is that they report they are because girls and women have been told not to report it or to even think it—for, that would be "unsafe" and "un-lady-like," etc. In sharp contrast, I recently found another blog, this one by Evelyn Rodriguez, a woman, entitled "Time to Be Fearless." She begins her writing about types of fearlessness with a quote by a feminist artist Jia Lu. Lu points out that Venus and many goddesses are all topless. And they are so "Because they're fearless," says Lu.[65] I can just imagine what "Dave" might respond, representing the male perspective on this. Maybe, new wave feminists are going to lead the way here—and I suspect they already are in claiming the "Fun, Fearless, Female," as the recent slogan's for *Cosmopolitan* magazine, or as we see more and more pop culture images, cartoons and movies with "she-roes" who look pretty fearless, and anything but victims—behaviorally that is. I'm thinking of the very successful novels for adolescents by Francine Pascal, "Fearless™ ... a girl without the fear gene" and so on.[66] A lot of that female imagery is pretty shallow, sometimes even mechanical and ugly—women being represented as "men" basically, with a very narrow view of fearless—the masculine version. I wonder where a deeper ethical beauty, if not spiritual beauty resides in these sheroes? But that concern doesn't seem popular among the Gen X, Ys or maybe I'm just not seeing it. I'm just an old 'boomer.' Third wave, or some say "fourth wave" "urban chic" new "feminist" views of females aren't necessarily all healthy either. Okay. I must stop my rant and troubling. I've laid this out for our thoughts to come over the days of this conference. I hope I wasn't too upsetting of our comfort. Actually, I hope I was upsetting of our comfort. My own lesson, as I am now going to share with you, is that fearlessness emerges out of that discomfort but it emerges in a way I would have never predicted or thought about before this experience I had in 2003. It is an aesthetic irruption. Let me tell you how I came to see fearlessness as a "species of beauty."

RMF: If I may interrupt for a second, Susan. With time running short, and knowing you will only briefly cover your essay on "Fearlessness," I would encourage audience members to check out the Internet and read the entire, very beautiful, essay. Okay, that's all I wanted to say.

SG: Thanks. [she takes out a copy of the magazine and reads aloud]

> How can I write about fearlessness in such a time? March 8 of this year, when I willingly committed an act of civil disobedience against the war, I would not have imagined choosing this subject. The very notion of lacking fear has always distressed me. I associate this state of mind with ignorance and foolhardiness, not courage. Seasoned warriors apparently agree. Describing the psychology of combat, Glenn Grey has written that experienced soldiers learn to distrust whoever among them knows no fear. Grey sees such fearlessness and eagerness for battle as a symptom of psychosis. Those without fear are distrusted by other soldiers because their behavior is not only suicidal but dangerous to their compatriots.

[she looks up] That is one kind of fearlessness. There are other kinds. [she reads again from the article]

> Just before the start of the war, on International Women's Day, after speaking at a Code Pink rally against the war, and then marching through Washington, DC, to the police barricades formed around the public part that skirts the White House, for a few blessed hours, I encountered the other side of fearlessness. I do not think of myself as particularly brave. Ordinarily I worry about more safety and health issues than can be listed, including whether I will get enough sleep on a given night or if I will have enough to eat or money to pay my bills. I am not drawn to challenging sports such as downhill skiing. I like to swim in calm waters and enjoy a comfortable hotel. . . . A beautiful landscape, though if I am thinking more of the beauty of music now, it is because as Alice Walker and I, who had come together to Washington, DC, were brought into the capital, we saw the Washington and Lincoln monuments light up against the night sky just as we chanced to hear the voice of Mahalia Jackson on the radio. And when I think of the landscape of feelings we were just beginning to enter that night, the beauty that comes to mind reminds me of the music sung in sanctuaries of all kinds, and even of the beauty of these structures, built to serve the resonance of congregations, places whose walls echo and thereby intensify the collective sound of choirs, chants, and choruses. Together with the brilliant activists Medea Benjamin and Jodie Evans, who planned this event, those of us who had come that day to protest the war found ourselves creating a similar architecture, resonant with our very presence. Whether because of our respect for the more tender emotional realms usually assigned to women, or for the same mysterious reasons that some recipes work and others do not, miraculously this ethereal structure seemed to be holding, if even for a short time, the full dimensionality of the terrible song that had in myriad ways been keeping us all awake at night. Yet now all our nervous voices of harrying worries, our muffled sounds of doubt, the ragged shrieks of nightmare and horror that hounded us, mixed and mutated into something beautiful. That is one of the reasons why tears kept coming into my eyes. And there was another reason. This beauty made of realistic fears, hard truths, anger, resistance, uncensored speech, compassion, good will (and even the playful, erotic, irreverent use of the color pink) reached into a quiet within me as deep as any I have ever known. I was calm.

And because one thing leads to another, that in turn is probably why, despite my hunger and fatigue and the fact that I could no longer bend my 60-year-old arthritic knees, all during our arrest and the three hours it took to get us paddy wagons, according to the friends who witnessed me, I had such a fearless expression on my face. Though in truth there were other reasons too for my fearlessness. I felt joyous. The sun was out and we were all in good humor. Maxine Hong Kingston's face was radiant. Alice Walker was smiling in a famously whimsical way, as if the air itself had just whispered a delightful secret to her. Nina Utne's eyes were glistening. When Terry Tempest Williams started to leave, she lingered, had trouble tearing herself away, and then stayed. We were enjoying each other.

[she looks up] I concluded [she reads]:

In the annals of resistance, we were not especially heroic. We were not mistreated. There was of course discomfort. . . . it is true, we were fearless. What I learned that day was that the other side of fearlessness does not come from any concept, no matter how noble. Yes, we believed that we are all connected, that the world is one, that peace and compassion are better than war and hatred. But what made me fearless that day was that for a few hours I was living in a state of peace. And thus a protest I had joined to express my opinions brought me to a deeper understanding than I ever expected to have, the knowledge that fearlessness of this kind is not exclusive, belongs to neither heroes nor saints alone but to all of us. It is a mood, a cast of mind, that can be created in any assembly. It is a mood of which all the world is capable. Fearlessness is the ground of peace. A mood, a species of beauty, and perhaps also a birthright.

Thank you. [the audience is silent for a long time, then applauds]

RMF: Beautiful, Susan, well said. I think the link between Beauty and fearlessness, is a very intriguing one that deserves a lot more attention. God knows, certainly our Western world needs a serious tune-up and integral critical analysis of the deeper more fearless aspects of women's experience of Beauty[67]—that is surely, a path of liberation for women today (and I won't even talk about men's stuff around that). Anyway, a great closing that wraps up introductions, as we could all use a break. I want to say that when I planned this panel, there was no bias to picking men or women. I merely followed what my own research for years had shown—the pivotal vocal contemporary leaders of the Fearlessness (R)evolution, were women—and I'm so glad I could assemble a forum to bring them together like this. It blows me away. At the same time, there are so many other diverse souls and spirits, some alive and some passed, and so many other "movements" and organizations I would include as reflective of the spirit of fearlessness manifesting in a wave of resistance to Fear's Empire. Some other important names (in no particular order), both male and female, that stand out as leaders of fearlessness in a revolutionary sense are the late W. Edwards Deming and his "without fear" principle in organizational management and leadership (TQM), the late J. Krishnamurti in philosophy and applications to the field of education, the late Chögyam Trungpa (and students of Shambhala Warrior trainings), Chris Griscom and her 'new age' movement of healing our emotionality and soul to recover the "fearless self," Saratoga (and T.E.L.S.T.A.R) with their 'new age' movement and workshops on "The Final Elimination of Fear," Joshua Stone's unplugging from the "Fear Matrix" teachings, Osho and his spiritual teachings, the late Alice Bailey et al. and the League for Fearlessness, Marianne Williamson, Gerald Jampolsky and those teaching *A Course in Miracles*, Marilyn Ferguson, Margaret Wheatley, Rhonda Britten, Susan Jeffers, Fiona Mackie, and all the grassroots folks of the Downtown Eastside of Vancouver and their vision and projects for a "Fearless City" and so on. Thanks be to all. Let's take a break and return in 30 minutes. [loud appreciative applause]

A Very Basic Critical Integral Critique

The purpose of this short section is to critique the five chosen leaders of the Fearlessness (R)evolution. One cannot say enough good about them and their work on one level. I have written their (performative) profiles to do that. However, there is the other side too. They all fall short of providing a critical integral approach (see Chapters Two and Three) to FME, and thus, the revolution they lead in their own particular ways is limited, and in some cases distortive.

I'll begin this critique with some general comments and then proceed to specific comments. None of this is a personal attack by intention or means. It is a theoretical and philosophical critique only, however, indeed, we are all flawed as "humans" and we also need to be challenged, ideally from a compassionate and fearless place, not one based on fear, envy, hatred, and so on. You can be the judge of how well I do this. I am attempting to practice what I preach. And the first positive thing one does in a *critical integral approach* (*a la* Ken Wilber) is to "embrace" the diversity of views and give them their due validity as a particular approach to the truth about fear and fearlessness (i.e., fear management). In other words, all five of the leaders and their work on fearlessness are useful, valid, and hold some partial truth. The more 'negative' work is to critique how they are less than fully "embracing" of other views of fear management or other notions of fearlessness beyond their own. Please note, the way I wrote the above narrative dramatizations of each of these people (other than for Aung San Suu Kyi), was to make them more "integral" than they actually are in their own writing and teachings, as I have come to know them (albeit, in a limited way).

Now if you take all of those people, leaders, and organizations and movements connected to the Fearlessness (R)evolution, mentioned above, and add all the other materials written and published on fear and fearlessness in the world— what do you get? You get overwhelm. You get people agreeing and disagreeing, with contradictions. You get people taking one teaching or teacher and one method of fear management as *the* solution, and that's what they stick with (and spread often to others), whether it is particularly useful or not always. They do not generally criticize it, or even know how to. From my point of view, as a fearologist and fear educator, one arrives at a basic philosophical question: *How ought we make sense of all this information and advice?* With more questions following, like: What is the best fear management/education (FME)? How can we trust what we are taught and what we think about in judging the *best* or what is *better*? Who benefits most from a particular FME being "sold" to others? Who is privileged to create such FME knowledge-power and practices and what are their agendas (i.e., are they 'fear'-based = ignore-ance and arrogance) in doing so? How self-reflective and critical are these privileged (sometimes professional) "teachers" of their own theories and methods? Is their rationale transparent and critique invited (i.e., are they and their design of FME "fearless")? How accountable are they held by their peers, the populus, governments, or elites they serve?

These are some of the philosophical and political types of postmodern questions I cannot avoid asking, while I realize that not everyone in the world cares about them. Most people just want to "fix" others or be "fixed" with a short-term solution to plaguing fear(s), or maybe for those they care about nearest them. Taking a wider and deeper perspective, I am not interested in only symptom relief; rather, I want humanity to advance and mature its FME to undermine the causes of excess and destructive 'fear' as well. You may recall in the Preface and Introduction that only individualized, psychological, spiritual, or narcissistic means for coping with one's own fears is *not holistic* enough a foundation to build a new emancipatory postmodern theory of FME for the world, the 21st century, and post-9/11 era. My quest as a researcher is for a universal[68] integral model and theory that can help all of us with The Fear Problem (Chapter Two), in the short and long-term. It can help us understand both the diversity and contradictions in the teachings about fear and fearlessness.

With my overall purpose to provide a more global holistic-integral understanding and means of ordering the various teachings (see "spiral of fearlessness" below), one major objective is to help people develop a critical literacy of fearlessness, whereby they would, more or less, be able to critique any discourse on FME they come across and choose better which has "quality" and "rigor" and "value" and "effectiveness" for particular cases and which has not (or is less so). The aim is the development of healthier, educative, growth-full, non-violent, just, and sustainable FME practices. Arguably, without a holistic-integral critique and approach such an aim will not come about and instead we'll be left with "choices" of FME that are decidedly reductionistic and narrow-minded, if not ideological and propagandist. Unfortunately, such approaches rule FME on this planet, and have for millenia—all part of fearism itself. The latter are largely fear-based themselves in the epistemological sense. Thus, fear-based means of fear management are the 'norm.' This isn't the best approach overall and feeds Fear's Empire; though, as I'll later argue, sometimes it is developmentally appropriate when applied mindfully and with ethical care. Of course, there are a few rare exceptions and the five leaders above provide some of the better offerings on FME, and utilizing fearlessness, as you'll find anywhere. They still have problem areas that are disturbing to me. Let me explain.

Good "critical integral theory" (*a la* Ken Wilber) ought to perform a few general epistemological functions, as a necessary pursuit of making generalizations about truth claims (not to forget to mention moral and beauty claims). I want to focus, for the sake of brevity, on the *way to truth* re: fear and fearlessness and the teachings of these five pivotal revolutionary leaders. My approach is to "include and transcend" all the fearlessness teachings in my own holistic-integral theory of FME. I want to up-grade them to a postmodern world and theory, using "postmodern" as Wilber defines it—that is, contextualist, constructivist, and integralist (see Chapter Two). As well, I want to integrate the best of the premodern (magical-mythical), modern (scientific-rational) and postmodern insights available—to create an "integral" approach that "includes and transcends" them all. The five leaders teachings are less than postmodern, integral, and embracing of others views or theories, and especially divergent views are missing. None of them takes a fully dialectical view that *fear* needs to be studied in a *fearless* perspective (to the degree this is possible). They rather tend to assume fear ('fear') is the same as it always has been qualitatively, and it is only quantitatively in excess and thus requires the solution of fearlessness. They draw on "fearlessness" as a "given," in a rhetorical sense, without troubling its conceptualization rigorously and philosophically; though Kyi has drawn from the Eastern Buddhist traditions and holds a rich conceptualization of fearlessness, albeit, decidedly premodern; and Griffin (the most postmodern, scholarly, and feminist of the five) is the most creative and exploratory, trusting her experience (subjective and inter-subjective) and allowing "fearlessness" to take on a new emergent definition, quality and location (i.e., "a species of beauty"). The others (excluding Kyi) tend to use fearlessness within a psychological and human potential discourse (e.g., "Imagine your life with no fear", or "fearlessness is about *freedom*," says E. D. Jackson).

Most of them are staunch activists and link the psychological and spiritual (subjective) with the more political and cultural (objective) aspects of human life (e.g., civil rights) and in that way they are moving toward a more holistic approach to FME. However, none of them question their own FME as biased contextually or constructed and thus, relative, to a large degree—nor do they see their FME as something that may be compared to other FME approaches created in other contexts. They tend to ignore other references to research (or other conceptualizations) re: understanding fear and fearlessness (i.e., FME). They ignore, from what I have read of their work, that there are competing discourses about the value of "fearlessness" for humanity, thus, their FME comes off as naive and simplistic for the most part. They ignore equally the developmental aspects of human beings and societies, and thus they tend to suggest a "one method for all" kind of solution (Suu Kyi is a slight exception). In this sense, they are often ideological in their pedagogy, verging on righteousness and propagandist tendencies, as activists are so prone to be (see Chapter Five).

Finally, one can see that strengths and weaknesses can be found in all five leader's FME. A lack of critical theory applied to their conceptualizations of fear and fearlessness makes their work for a Fearlessness (R)evolution suspect. It needs to be filled-in, corrected and improved. Postmodern approaches to FME require us to examine biases and prejudices in our construction of concepts of fear ('fear') and fearlessness ('fearlessness'), with a nuanced relationship to multicultural (ethnocentric), racist, sexist, and classist formations of FME, and so forth—and I would add fearism and adultism. In general, they all (excluding Griffin) tend to base their FME on charismatic leadership, inspiring people through role modeling as energetic, charismatic, resilient and remarkable lives (i.e., heroic 'special people'). They tend to "coaching" people to change to a less-fear-based life of happiness and fulfillment and/or moral responsibility.

There is nothing wrong with this. It has a populist attraction common to all revolutions or activist movements, no doubt. However, I am not convinced these qualities are the best foundation for an integral educational design, fearless pedagogical architecture, and postmodern curriculum for developing a critical literacy of fearlessness. Unfortunately, the charismatic leadership model (characteristic of premodern societies, and still found in a lot modern societies as well) tends to build-in a dependency on heroic-power "leaders." They also die, sometimes suddenly, and often leave organizational vacuums and chaos, if not potential betrayal of the leader's original vision and good works, as less mature leaders often take control. My emancipatory tendency is to develop a relational (more feminine) and collaborative-based educational program that truly frees learners (eventually) from any such need to depend on one charismatic or guru-type power "teacher" and/or "leader;" thereby allowing for more diversity and types of "leaders" (and "facilitators") to emerge as needed for particular tasks and situations (i.e., a more postmodern leadership style).

However, in critical integral theory, there is also room for strong individual heroic charismatic and powerful, if not iconic, leaders. Balance is needed, for a flexible, flowing, and sustainable healthy system. And that said, I ought to point out that all the five leaders are women. For me, that is reassuring of an arising "feminine" force (difficult as that is to define) and form that the spirit of fearlessness is taking today—at a time when the masculine (really hyper-masculine) has dominated in our world (particularly the West) for far too long. I look forward to women's input in FME for the 21st century and I trust they will examine seriously the value of critical integral theory and a postmodern theory of fearlessness, as found in this book. If I could leave one recommendation with all the five beautiful souls profiled here, it would be to not let "fearlessness" become a marketing device (e.g., "Fearlessness, Inc.")[69], keep it growing in conceptualization and do not copyright or trademark the "Fearlessness R(e)volution"—it's for everyone!

Turning to the Evolution in (R)evolution

The prophetic educator-activist-scholar in India, the late Vinoba Bhave (1895-1982), an honored student of Mahatma Gandhi, spoke of the message I wish to communicate to all:[70] "The goal of education must be freedom from fear. . . . Until education [learning] is really based on fearlessness there is no hope of any [transformational] change in society."

This book focuses particularly on fear management/education (FME) as a key domain of reality, theory and practices, whereby an ideal education, which Bhave spoke about (one that is based on "freedom from fear"), could develop and our humanity could deeply transform and evolve toward something more healthy, sustainable, and mature, than what we see dominant today. The overall evolution of humanity, from this perspective, is one from *fear* to *fearlessness*, to state the theory I proposed in rough terms early on. The challenge is to determine *what is fearlessness*? Throughout this book I argue it is vastly more complex than we normally think, and that the traditions generally teach. The conceptualization requires a postmodern upgrade. In this next section I present an evolutionary and developmental view of the "spiral of fearlessness." This is new and unique to all the World's Fearlessness Teachings. It is a concept and holistic-integral theory outlining and ordering ten fear management systems and seven basic forms of fearlessness that have evolved in human evolution so far.

It is a developmental and educational premise of this book that we are as a species at a junction of evolution, a transition, where we are moving from what transformative integral educator Edmund O'Sullivan calls an era of "terminal cenozoic" (and "terminal stage of modern history") to an "emergent ecozoic" era.[71] Later, I classify this within Fear Management System (FMS) theory—marking out a shift from a dominating FMS-5 (Modern = Orange) to FMS-6 (early Postmodern = Green) with potentials of FMS-7 (late Postmodern Integral = Yellow), and more rarified FMSs-8 and 9 (post-Postmodern Holistic = Turquoise and Coral).

O'Sullivan explains this era transition, our challenge to "survive," and the need to adjust our present and future education for a "period of historical decline":[72]

> We humans all over this planet, who have the privilege of witnessing a new century, are descendants of a magnificent history. For good or for ill, in our own times, we are the recipients of the legacy of 'modernity.' In our own times, the peoples of the earth are being nudged or pushed into something that is being called 'post-modernity.' There is a transformation taking place that is both exciting and fearful.... We are in need of an evolutionary transformation that transcends the forces of modernism [and its shadow-side] and includes them [their positive side] at the same time. . . . The coming transformation will transcend and include these [best] features of modernity, incorporating their essentials and limiting their powers (Wilber 1996:70). . . . the fundamental educational task of our times is to make the choice for a sustainable planetary habitat of interdependent life forms over and against the dysfunctional calling of the global competitive marketplace. . . . The emergent [ecozoic] vision of life deeply challenges the economic globalization [cenozoic]. . . . In Anthony Giddens' (1990) terms, the juggernaut [of economic globalization = cenozoic] crushes those who resist it. . . . This choice for what I would label an ecozoic [Green] vision can also be called a *transformative* perspective because it posits a radical restructuring of all current educational directions. To move towards a planetary education it will be necessary to have a functional cosmology that is in line with the [ecozoic] vision. . . .

These are macro-scale generalizations within an evolutionary discourse. Thomas Berry, to whom O'Sullivan draws upon, called it "the geo-biological story of the planet."[73] Beyond egocentric and ethnocentric worldviews, it takes a consciousness of not only a *global worldview* to see this, it takes an even more embracing and mature and compassionate *cosmological worldview* and evolutionary perspective of Life itself—to *see* on such a grand scale or narrative as

O'Sullivan and many others have asked humanity to do in the past four or five decades. Unfortunately, most of humanity (80% or more) are simply not capable of that macro-scale worldview for multiplex reasons. They don't have the information and/or haven't put it together and/or they are excessively exploited and suffer in poverty and from diseases, and/or they are more concerned about local "survival" of their body, ego, and the few loved ones around them. Most humans on earth are not into "saving the planet" but more "saving" their job, food and water stocks, housing, capital, family, community, religious and cultural symbols, and maybe a nation—that is, they tend to want to preserve those who are relatively of like-mind and like-values.

Technically, as Wilber and other integralists have said, the vast majority of people and organizations on the planet are still at egocentric and ethnocentric levels (or worldviews) and, as such are a long ways away to developing a worldcentric, or even further expansive cosmocentric worldview (see Chapters Two and Three). To care about the development of our "species" *Homo sapiens* or a conceptualization of "humanity" on a millions of years time scale is way too big of an idea to interest them. O'Sullivan, somewhat naively (magically = FMS-2 Purple) wrote: "A full-planetary consciousness opens us up into the awesome vision of a world that energizes our imagination well beyond a marketplace vision. Our planet is a shared dream experience."[74] For the very vast majority this is an abstract (even fluffy and dreamy) philosophy or worldview maybe, but it does not operate practically, ethically, cognitively, or emotionally on a daily basis for the vast majority. That's why the Eco-Movement (Green FMS-6) has had a very difficult time getting people around the world to transform significantly their everyday life styles (i.e., current hegemonic cenozoic values and worldviews), which tend to put Life and "humanity" at-risk (for e.g., to stop or reduce driving their air polluting automobiles or consuming so many products and services, based on non-renewable oil and gas, that are not essential to voluntary simplicity and a small "eco-footprint").

Reality-check. Let's not include in our statistical ramble, for the moment, the non-'First World' countries (with 80% of the population). In North America maybe 20% of the population on a good day will think to live a life style consistent with the transition from a "terminal cenozoic" to an "emergent ecozoic" era. Most (over half) of those 20% (call them the "Eco-Green elite") are likely still struggling to survive the financial, social, and emotional stresses of the day, so in their fear (deficit and narcissistic thinking) tend to make choices less than ecozoically ideal for their bodies and minds, their families, communities, or all humanity (never mind all species on the planet).

If "fearlessness" is put in front of their faces as another way to live beyond fear-based reality, the vast majority of this Eco-Green elite (less than 20% of the North American population), based on this author's 20 years experience teaching, reject or deny (ignore) they have anything new to learn about fear or fearlessness. Ignore-ance *(Thanatos)* and arrogance *(Phobos)* reign as components of the 'Fear' Matrix (fearism) over the vast majority, even those highly aware, caring, and loving Eco-elites who want to "save the planet"—even in the post-Al Gore ("global warming") ethos this has not changed substantially. There is

no concrete data to prove this. It is based on my observations and intuition. It is
so subtle and common we don't see it.

I am suggesting (hypothetically) that *is* the general *reality* we have to accept
today. To fight against reality willfully and disrespectfully is not going to do
anything but cause more distress, fear, and damage. Once we accept that (reasonable) hypothesis, then we can move on in our rehabilitation, and accept that
it is only what is now. We can then reject that reality is fixed or completely determined; we can accept we are agents in bringing about the changes we want.
Some freedom exists and that is an amazing resource. True freedom, as that beyond fear, is more powerful than we can imagine. Accepting the 'statistics' I set
forth above means realizing (without denial) *it is* what the vast majority are *only*
capable of, based on limiting conditions of the moment and the era. Critics may
claim I am delivering a pessimistic view, which is "too negative," and itself is
based on fear and deficit (limiting) thinking. I trust the critics will read further
on through this text, to see that the critical holistic-integral theory presented and
philosophy behind it, is exuberantly positive toward humanity's future evolution
and also realistic of the risk of de-evolution or extinction.

O'Sullivan et al. have it dead right when they say we are (especially in the
West) going through the crisis of a major epochal transition (cenozoic to ecozoic), or whatever you want to call it. That truth is worth studying and applying.
However, it lacks a larger evolutionary vision and a critical integral (developmental) vision to see the ecozoic for what it is—it is not the only 'alternative'
better way to move for evolution of consciousness. Actually, ecozoic won't do
the trick to move us from a world based on fear ('fear') to a world based on fearlessness. That's the point of the critique here of O'Sullivan. I pick-up again this
critique of what Wilber calls "Eco-Camp," and bring in a more "integral" eco-
view of David Korten's in Chapter Five. Simply, activists need to look at FMSs
theory to improve their way to a transformational (R)evolution.

The Spiral of Fearlessness, Cultural and Spiritual Selection

We die to fear of Spirit to be reborn into the Spirit of fearlessness.
                                                                - Iyania Vanzant

Vanzant's dictum[75] is another way of saying (r)evolution of consciousness
is a movement of Spirit in the Kosmos from *fear* to *fearlessness*. The principle:
when fear arises, so then arises fearlessness to manage it. What critical integral
theory offers is a way to 'map' out the movement of Spirit onto a spiral pattern
of growth and development. If this is sounding too metaphysical or religious and
spiritual, I suggest bypassing the words and language and see what is being said
as a secular development of the "spirit" of Life itself.

First, I want to share a couple short autobiographic true stories on the inherent spirit of fearlessness. Story One: over a decade ago, I was working as director at the In Search of Fearlessness Centre and Research Institute, Calgary, Alberta, Canada. *The Centre*, as our conscious community called it, was a small

office space of 300 sq. ft., housed in a suburban working class mini-mall—a hair dressor's business on one side of us, and a co-op housing agency office on the other side, with a camera shop, a non-chain small corner grocery store and small ethnic restaurant to complete the business sector we shared our 'home' with. *ISOF*, as we called it, was a unique (if not weird) drop-in space for the public to experience and study the way to create a *'fear' vaccine* (and a lot of other things). It was a location for my library, research and writing, counseling and teaching adults *via* liberation seminars, workshops and courses. I co-founded and created a School of Sacred Warriorship (1993-96) for the more hearty souls to really dig in to challenging the *'fear' virus* that was dominating our world.

One hot summer day, I smelled the toxic scent of tar coming in under the door of the ISOF office. It was coming from the back alley. Overnight, the owner of the mini-mall had ordered a paving crew to lay down a smooth layer of black asphalt over the once bumpy gravel and weed-infested back parking lot. Sometimes I would eat my lunch sitting there on an old pail watching the grasshoppers, ants, and cabbage white butterflies feeding on the plants. From now on, there was no such enjoyment to be had. The pavement buried all that life. I watched the steam coming off the still warm pavement, cursing under my breath the death-making mentality that "needs" (is addicted to) homogeneity and comfort. I couldn't believe anyone really cared to have a paved parking lot behind the mall, as the pavement in front of the mall was more than enough to service all the vehicles that came to shop. The industrial logic of this occasion was beyond me and actually sickened me. About a week later, I went for a walk out back behind the ISOF Centre and couldn't believe what had grown through the black top. Hundreds of bright yellow dandelion flowers on long thin stems (no leaves in sight) had pushed their way up through probably two inches of packed down fresh pavement. The drive way was stark in contrasting colors and shapes, as the black background highlighted the sunny bright yellow flower heads and light green stems. The pavement was virtually ruined as the thrusting destroyed the smooth surface. I couldn't help but smile. A metaphor came to mind instantly. This was the "Essential Rebel." You cannot keep the rebel down or buried. It is a spirit in Life itself that refuses to be defeated and dominated, without a fight.

It was a parking lot—conflict site, I thought at the time. Here was the conflict being played out. The paving crew tries to wipe out all of the Natural by imposing the Cultural. The imposition and domination, frankly, just rude, gross, and violent, is unwilling to attend to that which is being dominated. Hey, no one asked the dandelions, the ants, the butterflies what they thought. Hey, no one asked the tenants, who rent offices in the mini-mall what they wanted, or the neighbors in the community what they wanted.

Yet the 'Yellow Lions' had their own way to respond, as an "essential" resistance and rebellion to the Cultural perfectionist (mono-cultural) mentality of the industrial worldview and its values. The Natural has its own rules and ways and it also has the power to destroy as well. Looking at the scene brought tears to my eyes. I had been attempting to teach people for years at the Centre that there is a spirit inside them always—that, no matter how much oppression one has faced, that rebel spirit, essential to life, would resist oppression. It was the way I explained fearlessness as always being where fear is. Most people got it but here was the exemplar narrative to tell in order to demonstrate the reality of what I was saying—a simple story of basic "Life." The principle, is that Life wants to reproduce, and to do that, it must defend itself (it's life) so that it can grow and mature to reproduce. Tapping into that power of defense that can break through two inches of pavement—a first step to tapping into the process of liberation itself. There is a spirit of fearlessness, not created by humans, but by evolution (Creation) that is billions of years old—an intelligence that knows what and how to do it—that is, how to live and defend itself. Defense (like an immune system) is first Natural, however, it becomes Cultural (often pathological) as in forms of the "Twisted" and "Normal" Rebel archetypes I used to teach about (e.g., could be a "Hell's Angel gang member", or "corporate leader," respectively). The archetype of an Essential Rebel might take the form of a Jesus Christ or Gandhi = "Fearless One," etc.

A week later or so, I went out behind the Centre and found another three inches of fresh pavement had been laid on top of the Yellow Lions again. I also smelled the unmistakable pungency of "weed killer" all around the edges of the pavement. I surmised that this time, the attack of the owner and crew was first a good shot of poison and then three inches of casket. It worked. Telling this story, many times now, taps into the Spiritual dimension of the event. I have given the Natural and Cultural relationship a particular meaning, from a particular perspective. Most people seeing the happenings behind the mini-mall wouldn't have likely thought too much about it. The Spiritual is the way to bring the integrative lessons of Life and Death, of Domination and Subordination (conflict and violence) to "light" and "awareness" or "consciousness" as some would say. I cannot say what 'good' that Spiritual does, as I didn't save the Yellow Lions or other creatures at all. I never felt that was my role. However, this occasion has inspired my teaching that fearlessness exists as deeply as the very impulse to survive. It is in all living systems, perhaps even in non-living systems. I thank this occasion, Natural-Cultural-Spiritual, for this teaching.

Story Two: fascinated by how evolution by natural selection occurs in the individual, as well as how that translates to the social organization by cultural selection, the following true story came to me while reading Robert Ardrey's *African Genesis* (1961).[76] It was the early 1970s and as a young 20s something studying ecology, ethology and evolutionary stuff like sociobiology, Ardrey's popular science books on primate behavior and early hominid's and their evolution toward us *Homo sapiens* was a millions of years journey I found compelling, as I searched for ancient clues to why humans behave the way they do. I never doubted that we were still animals, despite our obvious differences from even our closest evolutionary cousins the chimpanzees (the latter having around 1% difference in their genetic code from ours).

Growing in the shadows underneath the idyllic optimism of hippie counter-culture, I also wondered what humans were capable of—the not so good and their potential best. I was well aware of the environmental crisis of the 1970s, Earth Day, and the collective fear humanity may not make it to the 21st century.

The true story Ardrey told was from one of his trips to Kenya at Olduvai Gorge, where at that time the oldest human fossils were being dug up and studied. The famous late Dr. Louis S. B. Leakey had been working there for years, leading the archeological investigations. Leakey went for a walk with Ardrey and pointed out a beautiful shrub with many coral-colored blossom clusters somewhat like the shape of a lilac flower. They stopped to admire it. Then Leakey grabbed the branch and shook it. The blossoms dissolved into fragments and began flying up into the sky and around them. This is a species of "flattid bug," said Dr. Leakey. Within less than a minute the bugs drifted back to land on the same branch which they had left. Watching in speechless amazement, Ardrey wrote,[77]

> They alighted in no particular order and for an instant, the twig was alive with the little creatures climbing over each other's shoulders in what seemed to be random movement. But the movement was not random. Shortly, the twig was still and one beheld again the flower.

Looking more closely now at the coral-colored "flower," Ardrey described how the architecture of this flattid bug society was made:

> At the tip of the insect flower was a single green bud. Behind it were half a dozen partially matured blossoms showing only strains of coral. Behind these on the twig crouched . . . [all others] with wings of purest coral to complete the colony's creation and deceive the eyes of the hungriest birds. There are moments when one's only response to evolutionary achievement can be a prickling sensation in the scalp.

As the two discussed this amazing feat of flattid bug mimicry as a defense system against predation, Leakey explained that the "coral flower" did not imitate any existing species of flower known. It was uniquely a creation of the flattid bug society itself. In listening to this story again, it is as if "art" and the Cultural are at work even in the insects. Upon close examination, Ardrey reported that there were individual bugs with all green wings (that formed the bud tip) and some with half green and coral that formed leaf like shapes, and then a mixture of pure coral-colored wings ranging in shades of light to rich dark coral. These latter bugs arranged themselves with precision to form gradients that gave a three-dimensional quality to the coral shape, with darkest on the outside and lighter toward the middle. Upon doing research on the Internet, I found some reports of flattid bugs also having a yellow winged variety with the green and coral, and thus a central yellow structure (like stamens, and pistils of a flower) were mimicked as well. Leakey explained that each batch of eggs laid by a female flattid bug has all the variations of colors needed. Somehow, unknown to science, these bugs meet and form colonies of beautiful "flowers" when they are resting.

Ardrey and Leakey, as well as others (like authors Colin Wilson in 1971 and Marilyn Ferguson in 1980), have puzzled over how Darwinian natural selection could have ever produced such a complex socio-cultural *life strategy* in an insect. I published one of my first articles on this anti-predator adaptation in 1976.[78] The flattid bug's "collective instinct" (or "intelligent design") with its ability to mimic a flower was apparently even mentioned in the 1964 Alfred Hitchcock film "Marnie." Colin Wilson in his book *The Occult* was first to offer a meta-physical explanation that transcended strict Darwinian genetic explanations which do not suffice. Wilson wrote,[79]

> Life increased in the warm seas, and developed its own kind of purpose—instinctive purpose [*telos*]—and its own kind of senses. And as the tiny organisms developed into fishes, birds, mammals and insects, they also developed their most important instinct: the community sense. And it is arguable that this community instinct [for cooperation and defense], like the homing instinct and the premonition of danger, was telepathic. [he cites Ardrey's story]

Stretching Darwinian (or neo-Darwinian) evolutionary principles, Marilyn Ferguson had read Wilson's interpretation and suggested a "communal consciousness" does likely exist, even among insects, and the telepathic means of communication evolved because it works, but it is not necessarily selected or determined by genes alone. Ferguson, with her own agenda for human collective consciousness transformation, wrote,[80] "The flattid-bug community is, in a sense, a single individual, a single [unifying] mind, whose genes were influenced by its *collective* need [for unity]. Is it possible that we too are expressing a collective need, preparing for an evolutionary leap?"

Complex ideas are flowing in these interpretations, and are far beyond the scope of this book to address adequately. Suffice it to say, all of us re-reading Ardrey's story of the flattid bug are puzzled by a wonderful mystery of communication, order, and life strategy of defense that is not merely individual and not merely genetic-controlled. There is good evidence that consciousness (intention) can control gene expression and thus behavioral outcomes (see genetic biologist Bruce Lipton's work[81]). No reductionistic (scientific empirical) explanation is sufficient, it seems. The challenges to gradual, or mutational change, in evolutionary theory are now common, and Wilson and Ferguson are writers who are part of that challenge. Quantum physics, dissipative structures theory, chaos and complexity theory and so forth, are all interesting and may free our minds from believing that change and transformation (or revolutions) happen only by chance and very slowly. At the sociocultural level of organization, the principles of evolutionary change are somewhat different, somewhat more fluid and potentially radical. Most contemporary evolutionists and developmentalists agree about that. We are now in the realm beyond the Natural, where the Cultural selection processes (even Spiritual) require focused attention.

For our purposes, the above two stories are indicators of an inherent Defense life strategy and Intelligence (or strategies and intelligences) that have evolved in the domains of the Natural, Cultural and possibly even in the Spiritual. The argument of this book is that *Defense* (as the spirit of fearlessness) is crucial in order to understand conflict and violence, and ways to peace and sustainability. Any good FME has to look at genetic and evolved life strategies at the sociocultural and spiritual levels as well. At this point, with judicious artistic and heuristic license, it is illustrative to use Ardrey's story of the flattid bug to a "new level" or meta-explanatory level in order to represent briefly my own integral FMSs theory and the hypothesis of a *spiral of fearlessness* as a core construct in any notion of (r)evolution.

First let's define an evolutionary "strategy" from Dr. Valerius Geist's amazing integrative cross-disciplinary work in ungulate mammalogy, keeping in mind that the ten fear management systems (i.e., FMSs with their colors) are based on organizing principles ("laws" and "rules") and evolutionary developmental theories of *life strategies* (Val Geist), *value-memes* (Don Beck) and *Kosmic habits* (Ken Wilber). For any Foucauldian's you could call these "*discourses*" or "*epistemes*."[82] Roughly, these theorists approach these life patterns or growth intelligence systems from the perspective of Natural (Geist's definition), Cultural (Beck's definition), and Spiritual (Wilber's definition); they are intimately interrelated, analogous, if not somewhat homologous in evolution and development:[83]

> *Life Strategy* = "If the driving force of evolution is indeed reproductive fitness ["minimize expenditures on maintenance in order to maximize reproductive fitness"], then genes are subject to conditions that can best be summarized as grand strategy, strategy and tactics of survival [according to life rules]. . . .

Geist's synthesis of volumes of empirical research on the bioenergetics of organisms, applies universal generalizations to notions of "fitness," and "quality of life." Whether an individual chooses to reproduce their biological genes in offspring during a life time or not, Geist's "organism theory" suggests the same "policy of the gene" will apply, more or less, to answer questions of who we are, how we are shaped, what we do, and what we become. The evolutionary policy rules are "logical derivatives of the theory of evolution" based on natural selection of the highest quality of "fitness" to pass on the biological genetic code that an individual organism was given from its ancestors.[84] The overall grand strategy of living organisms is to 'pass on what you were given' and if possible, depending on conditions, do it more efficiently and even make quality improvements on what is passed on. The Natural gene code, acting through individuals and conditions for expression, delivers the ultimate motivation of life—that is, more life. In other words, it is all about *survival strategies* to enhance *survival rates*. Yet, eventually, all organisms, at least as individuals, die. Natural universal laws seem to operate for all organisms.

Exactly how an *organismic system* (individuals + environments) optimizes its *passing on* Life-imperative before passing on (as in death-imperative), is very complex, beyond the scope of this book to discuss. From the seven general Natural rules[85] for all organisms that Geist has arrived at, there could be dozens of life strategies developed (and hierarchically ordered) through behavioral adaptations (and possibly later through physiological adaptations, and possibly later still through physical adaptations).[86] He noted diverse strategies of "resource exploitation," "predator avoidance," "parental investment," and so on, are highly interrelated "for a small change in one dominant adaptation may have rather great repercussions on other adaptations [life strategies]."[87] In the largest sense, the greatest life strategy of evolution and development is to Defend (*via* the seven rules) optimal *passing on*, be that passing on a genetic code, a set of life strategies, a set of ideas, symbols, values, beliefs, or even spiritual practices and truths. The latter two types of passing on are evolutionary and developmental imperatives based on Cultural selection and Spiritual selection. As I see it, the greatest life strategy of Defense (survival-plus) is *fearlessness*. That said, remember, at least 15 different meanings for fearlessness are covered in this book, so my intention above is to give readers a sense of the essential 'root' spirit of fearlessness in evolution, not to give a strict and only definition or meaning to the term.

The most innovative theory of Cultural selection utilized in this book on FMSs, is Spiral Dynamics theory, based on the concept (and reality) of the value-meme (v-meme):[88]

> *Value-Meme* = "A Meme is an information/energy core that radiates commands, instructions, cultural programs and social norms into the minds of people. Think of them as pieces of hot uranium that impact everything within their reach. They are forms of 'psychological DNA' that contain the coded messages [discourses] which create different life forms [and strategies] based on a predetermined script and set of instructions. As such, they simply replicate the core message [values] over and over again throughout any system. In Chaos Theory they are called fractals. In biology the parallel structure is genes. Some examples of memes would be the Puritan Work Ethic, the Marxist or Free Market Impulses, the animistic beliefs common in some 'tribal' groups, etc. You will note that they spread their influence across every aspect of society—religion, the workplace, families, public safety, education, politics, etc.

Following Beck's research and theory of v-memes, moving in a spiral dynamic configuration throughout human evolution, it is imperative to keep in mind that v-memes are that which "shape human choices, establish priorities, and set the tone of families and teams [and organizations, as well as individuals]. These [nine core v-memes] are the basic themes in life's symphony. Sometimes they are harmonious; sometimes in discord."[89] V-memes, like life strategies, significantly determine the architecture of our worldviews and the way we privilege (value) seeing and acting in the world. Each is united to the overall goal of "passing on" the accumulated wisdom and intelligence of life itself but each has their own agenda of how best to do that—that, then is where conflict, fear, and even violence begins. The "passing on" can also have a destructive aspect, as in a mutation (e.g., gene for a deadly disease), or a pathological psychological or cultural trait (e.g., a vicious ideology).

In the integral (and transpersonal) philosophy of Ken Wilber, another deep "structure" has been hypothesized to capture the general principle or law that the Kosmos does not waste anything gained, and thus tends to find ways to maintain and reproduce what worked in the past for the present and future. Wilber defines one of his ideas of what that "structure" may be:[90]

> *Kosmic Habit* = "What follows are twenty basic tenets (or conclusions) that represent what we might call 'patterns of existence' or 'tendencies of evolution' or 'laws of form' or 'propensities of manifestation.' These are the com-

mon patterns or tendencies... in all three domains of evolution—the physio-
sphere [matter], the biosphere [life], and the noosphere—[mind]—and tendencies that therefore make this universe a genuine *uni-versum* ("one turn"), or an
emergent pluralism undergirded by common patterns [deep structures]—the
'patterns that connect' [as the late G. Bateson said] . . . I don't want to get involved in intricate arguments over whether these are 'eternal laws' or simply
'relatively stable habits' of the universe, and so I will be satisfied with the latter. . . . [However,] Reality is not composed of things or processes; it is not
composed of atoms or quarks; it is not composed of wholes nor does it have
any parts. Rather, it is composed of whole/parts, or holons.

Wilber's theory of holons is taken up in greater detail in Chapter Two. Just
as genes are the structures of focus for Geist (Natural selection), and memes are
the structures of focus for Beck (Cultural selection), holons are the structures
(Kosmic habits) of Wilber (Spiritual selection). Wilber's integral model is the
most complex and integrates (generally) the other two. All the holons of the
universe have a commonality when they interact, says Wilber, and the twenty
tenets are the "habits,"[91] analogous to Geist's seven rules, with many life strategies carrying out those habits/rules in different environments and contexts.
There is no point making this more complex at this time. My aim is to show
there is some significant scientific and evolutionary basis for FMSs as life
strategies of Defense (i.e., of fearlessness).

Recall that the detailed description of this integral FMSs theory is found in
Chapter Two and Three. At this point, the basic introduction to the theory comes
in an image and a narrative "fictional" imaginary. Think of walking in the African grasslands in the area where Leakey and Ardrey were talking. You see a
bush that is glowing with rainbow-like brilliance in the sunshine. Upon closer
inspection, one sees each branch on the bush has a translucent aura of colored
light spiraling around it in a whorl beginning at the base of the branch with a
Beige coloring that eventually blends into a Purple light on the other side of the
branch, which blends into a Red light on the other side of the branch, and on up
the branch to the tip are the following colors in the same spiraling structure:
Blue to Orange to Green, to Yellow to Turquoise and to Coral at the end of the
branch but it grades off into invisibility as it transcends the length of the branch
as if it goes on into infinity. Which it does, at least theoretically. You have just
been introduced to the basic holistic-integral model of the evolution of worldviews, or what in Spiral Dynamics theory (Beck et al.) are called *value-memes*,
sort of like Natural "genes" but rather they are "memes" because they are (non-
structural) deep structures—human-made, and rather invisible patterns of the
Cultural and Spiritual. In short, Cultural and Spiritual evolution of consciousness has produced these v-memes ("habits").

I have used the v-memes found in Cultural and Spiritual evolution to peg on
the concept of a FMS; roughly, for each v-meme there is a different FMS (num-
bered) as follows because they start with the most simple systems and evolve to
the most complex (following the laws or rules of development and evolution of
living systems theory as Geist, Beck, Wilber have articulated): FMS-0 (no
color), FMS-1 Beige, FMS-2 Purple, FMS-3 Red, FMS-4 Blue, FMS-5 Orange,

FMS-6 Green, FMS-7 Yellow, FMS-8 Turquoise, FMS-9 Coral. There are ten FMSs known to have evolved in human history (phylogeny) and within an individual human's life time (ontogeny), one could potentially develop and evolve through (and utilize) all ten, or not. Mostly, development is limited by various factors and people and their organizations or cultures and often development gets "arrested" somewhere on the spectrum—usually, below FMS-6. However, research has shown there are at least these ten available at the current time. In future human development there are likely to be more than ten.

If you imagine yourself back at the branch in Africa glowing with these colors of light, look at how they are assigned colors that have a general pattern. On one side of the branch the colors are warm colors, Beige, Red, Orange, Yellow, Coral, while on the other side of the branch the colors are cool colors, Purple, Blue, Green, Turquoise. This is done intentionally as a reminder that the warm colors evolve as FMSs with the focus of innovation on the "individual" or "singular" unit (holon) of development. Curiously, evolution seems to like to 'balance' itself, meaning its life strategies, intelligences (or consciousness levels) develop from one side to the other side of the branch and the cool colors evolve as FMSs with the focus of innovation on the "communal" or "plural" unit of development. In general then, evolution of FMSs occurs along a grand pattern/principle of movement from I to We, all the way up the spiral and onward. Later, you will learn that by the time one reaches FMSs 8 and 9 there is hardly any differentiation between I or We focus, as there is a complete merging of the two focuses in FMS-9 Coral (sometimes called "nondual consciousness").

The FMSs colors are coded in memetic pattern with a link to genetic coding. They are hypothesized to have evolved like Kosmic habits or life strategies of defense. Defense used very loosely here, is the spirit of fearlessness moving along the spiral of growth and development, or the spectrum of consciousness. The next thing to imagine is looking closer at the colored lights spiraling up the branch. They are joined as one, even though they have their particular differentiated location or specialized set of life strategies. The spiral of fearlessness is one Spiral, or one Spirit, which has evolved in the Natural world and modified itself into the more invisible (intangible) realms of the Cultural world and Spiritual world. They evolve one from the other, unfolding, and growing, meeting different conditions at different occasions in the evolution of the planet. They are like 'One Mind' (Consciousness), with differentiated "minds" or intelligence systems designed for managing fear (also conflict and violence).

If you look at the imaginary spectrum around the branch closely between FMS-6 and FMS-7 there is an "abyss" or dark "gap," where it is hard to see where they blend from Green to Yellow, although, theoretically they do, as far as the model is concerned. The reason for this gap is very significant. The researchers have labeled the spiral as consisting of three different tiers: the 1st-tier (FMSs 0-6), the 2nd-tier (FMSs 7-8) and, the 3rd-tier (FMS-9). If you look closely at the colored lights on the branch there is another smaller gap between Turquoise and Coral. The 1st-tier FMSs (other than FMS-0) are more or less fear-based in their design and consciousness. They make decisions based more on fear ('fear') than Love. That's the not so good news, even though each FMSs is a brilliant intelligence system with elegant life strategies of defense for managing fear ('fear') as well. There are however "pathologies" that are unconscious to the operation of these FMSs as well. The 2nd-tier FMSs begin the reversal of this 'fear'-based phenomenon. That's the good news. If development can get over the gap from Green to Yellow, and it is not easy, as all research shows so far, then Turquoise is acquired rather quickly and easily. Further development on to Coral, is a rather difficult affair once again—over another gap. The FMSs of the 2nd and 3rd tiers more or less utilize decisions and organizational life strategies that are less and less fear-based and more and more mature and Love-based all the way up.

The integral spiral model of FMSs allows us a 'map of the territory' of intelligence systems of defense (i.e., life strategies of fearlessness) that have evolved in the maturing of the planet's consciousness. The map is a generalization (theory) based on real data collected. Yet, it is still an imaginary map, much like the map of a DNA structure, as seen in illustrated form in a book or a 3-D model of it in a lab. They are models or maps, crudely representing some reality below the obvious surface of appearances. The spiral of fearlessness is a movement from fear-based to Love-based. It is a movement not arbitrary, as so many postmodern poststructuralist thinkers might argue, rather, here, it is a movement choreographed by life strategies (Kosmic habits or tenets) and ruled by the Natural, Cultural, and Spiritual "laws" of evolution outlined by Geist, Beck, Wilber. Because this proposed movement is theoretical (not meaning it has no evidence), and posited by "integral" thinkers/philosophers, one ought to conclude it is an "integral movement" that is at hand—is reality—at least, reality at the deepest levels/patterns of 'invisible' operations.

The journey of operational dynamics is the *spirit of fearlessness* in action roughly aligning with seven terms that this author has identified as best to represent "fearlessness" as the Spirit (and its defense), each interpreted at each FMSs or color on the whole "rainbow" spectrum. Noteworthy, is that all colors of the rainbow are valuable, and so is the case with FMSs and the seven phenomenon of fear management. Recall the seven ways of fearlessness—that is, cousins of fearlessness mentioned earlier in this book. For example, *Bravery* is the best term for the phenomenon of the spirit of fearlessness interpreted at the earliest (most immature or junior) stages of development or evolution of consciousness (i.e., primarily at FMSs 1-4). *Courage* is the best term for FMSs 5-6a, and *Fearless* is the best for FMS 6b. Crossing the first abyss or gap on the spiral of fearlessness, comes FMS 7-8 where the more precise use of the term *Fearlessness* best fits, and following that, development is the most mature of all with *Fearless* as the best term for FMS 9. There is a subtle distinction in this theory for FMS 0 (no color), which is taken up in a later chapter but the best term for that is *No Fear*. Later, the term and phenomenon of *Bravado* will be discussed as arising in the 1st-tier FMSs as a "twist" of interpretation and a "pathology" that travels through the spiral of fearlessness (i.e., as the 'shadow' of fearlessness). These critical definitions and discourses of the seven ways of fearlessness for managing fear ('fear') will allow readers to build a critical holistic-integral theory of FME and a means to critically analyze what anyone is teaching about fear and fearlessness. That's the best outcome of such a theory as this. Testing and experience will tell how well it actually works.

Maybe the example of the flattid bug colony evolution is extreme. It does however point us toward the issue of "sociocultural" evolution *via* Beauty (i.e., capital 'B' Beauty as in the ancient triad of "Truth, Beauty, and Goodness" as the determinant and referential positions for determining "quality"). The question arises, how 'beautiful' did the coral colored 'flower' (anti-predator strategy) have to be to work really well—that is, to act as a significant life strategy which brought about survival fitness for the flattid bug as a species (or at least as "subgroups" or "sub-cultures" or "colonies")? Is Beauty a factor in Cultural selection, or even Spiritual selection processes of evolution? Susan Griffin's story earlier in this chapter makes this author wonder how powerful of an influence Art/Beauty/Aesthetics have in our development and evolution? These are big questions that won't be answered in this text, but this chapter has offered them up, among others, to re-appraise perhaps some of our thinking about evolution, and seeing life strategies as not merely about "genes" or even "memes" but involving the triad of archetypal values of wisdom and compassion. Steve McIntosh (*Integral Consciousness*, 2007) in his new integral philosophy has made the claim that Truth, Beauty and Goodness are universal "Kosmic habits" of sorts, and they are the best way to understand evolution across the domains of Natural, Cultural and Spiritual. Time will tell if this is the best way to organize an integral philosophy and theories.

Maybe the notion of a Fearlessness (R)evolution as presented here is an extreme idea. Whether there is such a (r)evolution going on or not is debatable. Theoretically, any movement across a gap in the three tiers of the Spiral is (r)evolutionary. Yet, arguably, a conception like Fearlessness (R)evolution does accomplish at least one important claim, as does the spiral of fearlessness concept: *there is irrevocable data pointing toward a universal resistance against accepting the normalization of fear ('fear') on this planet—and this appears to have been so for an extremely long time*. It is from this finding of my own research that I suggest you be cautious in accepting the very common discourses of our societies that claim "fear is natural, fear is normal" so don't worry about that. "Fear makes us human and creative" etc. These claims, I trust I have shown so far, are highly dubious and likely to merely feed into the building of Fear's Empire. They are largely uncritical statements, as far as I see, that stereotypically and rhetorically come out of fearism itself. We need to challenge them, and their subtle (or not so subtle) aim to terrorize us, while looking like they are calming our worries with such discourses.

In the rest of this book such an argument will be made and pushed as far as it can be—radically—to claim that any normalization of fear ('fear'), and concomitant normalization of bravado-based (really, 'fear'-based) distortions in the FMSs is equivalent to 'evil.' "Evil" used here as "Live" spelled backwards. Prepare yourself. The journey is about to get a lot more interesting. In the next chapters the World's Fearlessness Teachings offer superb insights to both the upside and downside of "fearlessness" and its seven cousins.

So, do we really want a Fearlessness (R)evolution? It depends on who you ask. It depends on whether they are operating out of the first-tier or not. If they are, as 98% of the world's population is, then they don't want such a revolution and frankly, they likely don't even think about it seriously. If one is operating out of an integral perspective (FMS-7 Yellow) or above, the answer to the question is positive. Readers of this book, you will have to ask what you really want, and why. Then ask what does the Spiral want? or what does the Spirit want? After an answer—well, then action—and a lot of messy and complicated fear management details. I leave you with the question: *On what basis can we develop the best architecture, curriculum and pedagogy for FME in the 21st century?* Perhaps, you have better questions to throw into the 'pot.' I welcome them; we need all the creative intelligences working on The Fear Problem.

Notes

1. Spiral Dynamics Theory, as I use it here generically, was created by Don Beck and Christopher Cowan in the mid-1990s, two students of the American psychologist, the late Dr. Clare Graves (1914-1986). See Chapter Two. I have been trained in Spiral Dynamics Technology (Levels I and II), by Dr. Beck and Dr. Marilyn Hamilton.

2. These sub-species names and figures are taken from a poster produced by the National Values Centre, Inc. publication (written by Don Beck), distributed in their courses.

3. The higher levels of postconventional development for humans includes a development of spiritual knowledge: "A transformational experience, it alters the identity of the individual and eventually leads to wisdom, complete fearlessness, and objective awareness of mind and its resources. . . . [as the Tantric master] Exploration of the mind as well as the rest of the persona occurs only through relentless objectivity and fearlessness." Phil Nuernberger, "The Structure of Mind and its Resources," in *Transcendence and Mature Thought in Adulthood*, eds. M. E. Miller, and S. R. Cook-Greuter (Lanham, MD: Rowman and Littlefield, 1994), 109, 104.

4. I'm using "Kosmology," with a postmodern epistemological (if not mystical) sensibility, as the philosopher Ken Wilber uses it, with a 'k' (*a la* ancient Greek Pythagorean sense), to indicate more than a cosmos. The cosmos more in common use today tends to emphasize the empirical (obviously recordable)'outer' exteriors of the universe and reality, whereas the former indicates *both* those exteriors but also the 'inner' less visible and recordable interiors of the universe as consciousness. See for example, Ken Wilber, *Sex, Ecology, and Spirituality (Vol. 1): The Spirit of Evolution* (Boston, MA: Shambhala, 1995).

5. Steve McIntosh, *Integral Consciousness and the Future of Evolution: How the Integral Worldview is Transforming Politics, Culture and Spirituality* (St. Paul, MN: Paragon House, 2007), 159-160.

6. This "Credo of Fearlessness," unique to my approach, is a work in progress and set of "orienting generalizations" (as Ken Wilber offers in his own philosophical work): "*Credo of Fearlessness:* (a) Love and fear are great powerful sources, energies and motivators, (b) Love is not enough: as the general conditions of fearism (*cum* terrorism) today, and development of the self/society and its insecurities, on average 99% of human beings and their organizations choose fear over Love, and thus undermine Love (i.e., undermining trust, justice, freedom, morality, beauty, high intelligence), (c) fearlessness is the answer: which can undermine and prevent this fear-based choice (patterning) that is

so dominant everywhere and which is the root source of all forms of violence, oppression, and evil, (d) fearlessness is not a mere choice, it is what we are in essence and have to grow and develop into so as to manifest its most powerful advanced levels; it demands we know intimately how this fear, Love, and fearlessness dynamic works, and in order to know it so intimately (inside and out, holistically and integrally) involves good critical theory and disciplined emancipatory practices informed by the very best transdisciplinary (and cross-disciplinary) research on fear and fearlessness, (e) humans are not totally bad and all to blame for this current situation, yet, they are responsible to improve it by furthering their own development and maturation, as no other being is comparably capable of doing so, (f) the major block to awareness and effective development and utilization of the above points in the Credo are ignore-ance ('fear' in the form of *Thanatos*) and arrogance ('fear' in the form of *Phobos*, often called "hubris" in wisdom traditions of the West)—immature human beings as a whole believe they already understand Love, fear, and fearlessness good enough (their pragmatic default) and believe there is little new to learn, and they can hardly imagine there is a new and improved perspective in which to learn more and, (g) the next block to the effectiveness of the above is the problem of hope and hopelessness, neither of which are particularly helpful (i.e., transformative) to the mess humanity is in, opening the 21st century. Fearlessness is hereby, the better alternative and replacement for hope ("hope" that has become too saturated with fear to be helpful)." "Radical hopelessness" is also valuable (see later in the book). So ends the Credo, and one could think this document would be a basic foundation for a new "philosophy of fearlessness" or "School of Fearlessness," even maybe a "Church of Fearlessness"—time will tell.

7. A point made by transformational educator Edmund O'Sullivan recently. Edmund O'Sullivan, *Transformative Learning: Educational Vision for the 21st Century* (Toronto, ON: Ontario Institute of Studies in Education/University of Toronto Press, 1999), 3.

8. Antonio Negri (with A. DuFourmantelle), *Negri on Negri: In Conversation with Anne DuFourmantelle*, trans. M. B. DeBevoise (NY: Routledge, 2004), 29.

9. See also, Hanna Sharp, "Why Spinoza Today?, or, 'a Strategy of Anti-Fear,' *Rethinking Marxism,17*(2005), 591-608.

10. For a summary see R. M. Fisher, "The Movement Toward a Fearless Society: A Powerful Contradiction to Violence," Technical Paper No. 10 (Vancouver, BC: In Search of Fearlessness Research Institute, 2000).

11. W. S. Barnard, *Onsnuwe Wereld 10* (Miller, n.d.), 214.

12. B. M. Pritzker, *A Native American Encyclopedia: History, Culture, and Peoples* (NY: Oxford University Press, 2000), 235.

13. M. Desai, *The Story of My Life* (Pergamon Press, 1979), 65.

14. Sharp, 591-608.

15. I. Azam, *Sons of the Soil: Some Poems, Short Plays, Stories and Articles About War* (London Book Co., 1974), 347.

16. Following Arendt's fascinating account of this story, I suggested a "fearless culture" was involved to disable the Nazi's work in Denmark. Hannah Arendt, *Eichmann in Jerusalem: A Report on the Banality of Evil* (NY: Penguin, 1994), 174-175. R. Michael Fisher, "Capitalizing on Fear: A Baseline Study on the Culture of Fear for Leaders," unpublished document (Minneapolis, MN: Intellectual Architects, Ltd., 2004), 15-17.

17. V. Verma, *The Emergence of Himachal Pradesh: A Survey of Constitutional Developments* (Indus Publishing, 1995), 24.

18. On the NGO website for Global Education Associates, Samdhong Rinpoche (endorsing the organization) said that GEA, using E. and W. approaches, and materialist and spiritualist too, is offering a balance of "outer and inner life so that a peaceful and

fearless society can emerge in the 21st century." Retrieved October 10, 2008 from http://ww.g-e-a.org/endorsements.html.

19. B. K. C. A. Chandiwala, *At the Feet of Bapu* (Navajivan Publishing House, 1954), 270.

20. Juan E. Corradi, "Toward Societies Without Fear," in J. E. Corradi, P. W. Fagen, M. A. Garretón, eds. *Fear at the Edge: State Terror and Resistance in Latin America* (Berkeley, CA: University of California Press, 1992), 267.

21. The following material is taken, in part, from Ms. Jackson's website http://www.erickajackson.com.

22. I. Chernus, "World War II and the Origins of the Cold War: Toward a Nonviolence History," in *Nonviolence for the Third Millenium: Its Legacy and Future*, ed. G. S. Harak (Mercer University Press, 2000), 83.

23. For example, "bridge leadership," not as showy, prophetic and preachy, is based on connecting family legacies and communities in the background. It is crucial work in social movements and women are often leaders. During the Civil Rights Movement, Helen Bass Williams (mixed black and white) was an exemplar (according to sociologist Mary O'Hara), among others. Mary Lee O'Hara, "'Let it Fly': The Legacy of Helen Bass Williams," unpublished dissertation (Carbondale, IL: Southern University of Illinois Carbondale, 2004), 6.

24. Rhonda Britten, *Fearless Living: Live Without Excuses and Love Without Regret* (NY: Dutton/Penguin Group, 2001). Also see her website "The Fearless Living Institute."

25. Excerpt from Rev. J. B. Guess, "Don't Ever Say What You're Never Going To Do," *United Church News* (Aug.-Sept. 2005). Retrieved April 2006 from http://www. ucc.org/ucnews/sept05/leader.htm.

26. ibid., 1.

27. Excerpts from X. Diego, "US Christian Leaders Apologize for Iraq War," February 25, 2006 (Inter Press Service). Retrieved March 2006 from http://www. commondreams.org/headlines06/0225-03.htm.

28. T. A. D. Green, *Twelve Reasons Christians Don't Grow. . . Even in Good Churches!* (Xulon Press, 2007).

29. Excerpts taken from Key Note Address Oct. 18, 2000, Connecticut Conference. Retrieved June 1, 2008 from http://www.ctucc.org/news/AnnlMtg02/bpjkeynote1.html.

30. Guess, 1.

31. Excerpts from *The Michael Jackson Story: Man in the Mirror*, directed by Tom Cary and produced by IMAVision/Oasis International ©2004.

32. Excerpt retrieved May 1, 2007 from http://www.soniadf.com/.

33. See www.lizziewestlife.com.

34. Marianne Williamson, *A Return to Love: Reflections on the Principles of a Course in Miracles* (NY: Harper Collins, 1992), 190-191. For the story (myth) of this quote being attributed to Nelson Mandela's presidential speech, see http://skdesigns. com/internet/articles/quotes/williamson/our_deepest_fear/.

35. According to Harman and Rheingold, In the mid-1960s a sudden altered state of consciousness and higher creativity infiltrated an otherwise "conservative" academic educator and psychologist by the name of Dr. Helen Schucman (Columbia University). Schucman found herself to be a "channel" for a spiritual entity and wrote down, with help from a friend, the entire set of teachings that are world famous now. It's a long story well worth reading about, as a spirit of fearlessness that came into our postmodern times with the 'bible' for much of the 'new age' movement, entitled *A Course in Miracles*. See Willis Harman, and Howard Rheingold, *Higher Creativity: Liberating the Unconscious for Breakthrough Insights* (Los Angeles, CA: Jeremy P. Tarcher, 1984), 115-118. See

Foundation for Inner Peace, *A Course in Miracle* (Tiburon, CA: Foundation for Inner Peace, 1975).

36. Retrieved June 2, 2008 from http://en.wikipedia.org/wiki/Arianna_Huffington.

37. Retrieved May 18, 2008 from http://transcripts.cnn.com/TRANSCRIPTS/0609/15/ltm.o4.html.

38. Ibid.

39. A. Huffington (in conversation with B. Patrick), "Becoming Fearless," 2006. Retrieved December 2, 2006 from http://coaches.aol.com/business-and-career/feature/_a/interview-with-arianna-huffington/20060908145309990001.

40. The phrase "virus of fear" has been used in fiction and non-fiction writing since at least the early 1920s, and later into the 1980s-90s, with growing popularity since. It refers to the contagious quality of "fear" when it spreads from individual psychology to others—that is, when it becomes a social and symbolically constructed experience and power. It is likely Ms. A. Huffington borrowed the idea from Shmuel Boteach's popular self-help book published a year before her own book. Boteach wrote, "We must immunize ourselves against the virus of fear, or it will infect us all." S. Boteach, *Face Your Fear: Living With Courage in an Age of Caution* (NY: St. Martin's Griffin, 2005), 16. Independent of the above authors, I have used the phrase "fear virus" (or 'fear' pattern virus = FPV+ as an analogous notion to HIV+) since the early 1990s.

41. See Arianna Huffington, "Fear Watch '08: Keeping an Eye Out for GOP Fearmongering," *The Huffington Post*, June 25, 2008, http://www. huffingtonpost.com/arianna-huffington/fearwatch-08-keeping-an-e_b_109262.html.

42. A. S. S. Kyi and A. Clements, *The Voice of Hope* (NY: Seven Stories Press, 1997).

43. J. Wintle, *The Perfect Hostage* (Hutchinson, 2007).

44. Kyi and Clements, 10.

45. A. S. S. Kyi, *Freedom from Fear and Other Writings*, ed. M. Aris (UK: Penguin, 1995), 183. [original essay "Freedom from Fear," 1991]

46. Parker. J. Palmer, *A Hidden Wholeness: The Journey Toward an Undivided Life* (San Francisco, CA: Jossey-Bass, 2004), 179.

47. Naomi Klein, *No Logo: No Space, No Choice, No Jobs* (NY: Picador, 2002), 330.

48. Alan Clements, "We are Still Prisoners in Our Own Country: An Interview with Aung San Suu Kyi," *The Humanist*, 57(1997), 19, 21.

49. A. S. S. Kyi, "Freedom from Fear," in *Violence and its Alternatives: An Interdisciplinary Reader*, eds. M. B. Steger and N. S. Lind (NY: St. Martin's Press, 1999), 313.

50. Kyi, 183.

51. Kyi and Clements, 18.

52. Ibid., 30.

53. Ibid., 56.

54. Ibid., 179.

55. Retrieved June 5, 2008 from http://en.wikipedia.org/wiki/Susan_Griffin.

56. Susan Griffin, "Fearlessness," *Yes! Magazine*, (Summer, 2003). Retrieved April 18, 2005 from http://www.futurenet.org/article.asp?id=604.

57. Audrey Lorde insisted: "we cannot wait for 'the luxury of fearlessness.'" Cited in Susan Bickford, *The Dissonance of Democracy: Listening, Conflict, and Citizenship* (Ithaca, NY: Cornell University Press, 1996), 137.

58. Marilyn Ferguson, *Aquarius Now: Radical Common Sense and Reclaiming Our Personal Sovereignty*. Boston, MA: Weiser Books, 2005), 154.

59. Chögyam Trungpa, *Shambhala: The Sacred Path of the Warrior* (Boston, MA: Shambhala, 1984/2007), 36.

60. Posted by "Dick the Boomer" (May 08, 2006). Retrieved April 2, 2007 from http://happy.blogs.com/jayne_says/2006/05/fill_in_the_bla.html

61. Margaret T. Gordon, and Stephanie Riger, *The Female Fear* (NY: The Free Press, 1989).

62. Germaine Greer, *The Whole Woman* (NY: Alfred A. Knopf, 1999), 286.

63. Ibid., 286. "Feminists have argued that the emphasis upon women as targets for attack functions as an instrument of social control. The object is not protection but the engenderment and maintenance of fearfulness."

64. Ibid., 280.

65. Quote excerpt from Evelyn Rodriguez, "Time to Be Fearless." Retrieved October 11, 2007 from http://evelynrodriguez.typepad.com/crossroads_dispatches/2006/12/the_time_has_co.html.

66. See for example, Francine Pascal, *Bad* (NY: Simon Pulse, 2002).

67. I highly recommend the research and writing of my daughter on this topic. See for example, Vanessa D. Fisher, "Beauty and the Experience of Women's Identity," *AQAL: Journal of Integral Theory and Practice, 3*(2008), 68-86.

68. Lest readers misunderstand this, critical integral theory also keeps itself wide open to the various surface and local cultural practices that are not so universal or deep-structured. It is the combination and integration of the best of local and universal that is the ideal quest here. That said, the framing in this book is decidedly focused on universal aspects, and that is because it is a largely deductive theory being developed for the first time (although, it has lots of inductive aspects to it as well, for e.g., in Spiral Dynamics Theory based on empirical studies, and on years of my own teaching and practices). Later works, can apply it to specific and local cases to test the theory and correct it. One cannot do all that in one introductory text, with the wide scope that I have taken on.

69. Starla Sireno of San Francisco, for example, has recently called her executive coaching and consulting practice "Fearlessness, Inc." with no definition of *fearlessness* offered on her website, nor an appreciation of fearlessness as a concept in the Eastern wisdom literature. This I believe cheapens the concept of fearlessness.

70. Vinoba Bhave, "The Intimate and the Ultimate," Excerpt from M. Hern, *Deschooling Our Lives* (Stoney Creek, CT: New Society Publishers, 1996). Retrieved June 2, 2006 from http://www.learningnet-india.org/Ini/data/publications/revive/vol1/v1-6b8.php.

71. Edmund O'Sullivan, *Transformative Learning: Educational Vision for the 21st Century* (NY: Zed Books, 1999).

72. Ibid., 1-2.

73. Thomas Berry, "Foreword," in *Transformative Learning: Educational Vision for the 21st Century*, Edmund O'Sullivan (NY: Zed Books, 1999), xi.

74. O'Sullivan, 3.

75. Iyania Vanzant, *Until Today!* (NY: Simon and Schuster, 2000), 19.

76. Robert Ardrey, *African Genesis: A Personal Investigation into the Animal Origins and Nature of Man* (NY: MacMillan, 1961), 65.

77. Cited in Ferguson. Marilyn Ferguson, *The Aquarian Conspiracy: Personal and Social Transformation in the 1980s* (Los Angeles, CA: J. P. Tarcher, 1980), 162.

78. R. M. Fisher, "Coral-colored 'Flower'—An Anti-predator Adaptation," *Calgary Field-Naturalist, 88* (1976), 148.

79. Colin Wilson, *The Occult* (Watkins, 2006), 159. [original published in 1971]

80. Ferguson, 162.

81. The DVD *Biology of Belief ("Lite")*, recorded in 2005 at "What the Bleep Do We Know! Conference, Berkeley, CA (Mephis, TN: Spirit 2000, Inc., ©2005) is a good entry to Dr. Lipton's research (see the Internet for other resources on this topic).

82. See for example, Michel Foucault, *Power and Knowledge: Selected Interviews and Other Writings, 1972-1977* (NY: Pantheon Books, 1980).

83. Valerius Geist, *Life Strategies, Human Evolution, Environmental Design: Toward a Biological Theory of Health* (NY: Springer-Verlag, 1978), 2.

84. Ibid., 1.

85. Ibid., 2. According to Geist, "What must an individual do to maximize its reproductive fitness? It ought to do the following: (1) Minimize expenditures on maintenance so as to save a maximum of resources for reproduction, (2) Maintain physiological homeostasis. That is, keep healthy and unharmed, (3) Create and maintain access to scarce resources essential for reproduction, (4) Reduce directly the reproductive fitness of others, (5) Support individuals with similar gene compositions in relation to their relatedness, (6) Grasp every opportunity to expand into unutilized resources, (7) Mate with individuals equal or superior to itself in maximizing reproductive fitness. These rules apply to all individuals regardless of what species, provided they are reproducing sexually. They apply simultaneously, so that a compromise must be struck by an individual to the extent that it follows the dictates of one rule rather than another. Therefore, these rules cannot be deterministic (philosophers, please note!). Furthermore, individuals can and do opt out of reproduction and then act contrary to at least some of these rules until the opportunity arises for them to enter into reproduction. These rules imply the existence of very basic mechanisms of monitoring and evaluating alternatives and adjudication between them."

86. Ibid., 14.

87. Ibid., 11.

88. Don Beck, excerpt from "V-Memes: A Self-Discovery Process" worksheet (Denton, TX: The National Values Center, Inc., 1994), back cover.

89. Ibid., inside cover.

90. Ken Wilber, *Sex, Ecology, and Spirituality: The Spirit of Evolution (Vol. 1)* (Boston, MA: Shambhala, 1995), 32-33.

91. Ibid., 34.

FEAR MANAGEMENT SYSTEMS THEORY:
A Critical Integral Approach

Including myself, no one likes to be put in a box or fixed under a label or have a stereotype applied by others. However, some general boxes are useful to help others understand where we come from, especially as writers and educators. I have been asked if I am a communist, socialist, evolutionist, capitalist, Marxist, Trotskyist, humanist, liberalist, environmentalist, holist, existentialist, postmodernist, poststructuralist, spiritualist, nondualist, artist? To which I reply, "yes," in part, with qualification. And yet, if push comes to shove, I really am an *integralist*, and I hold it is the *best* box of them all. Why? Because it sincerely respects and critiques all the other boxes, while offering a truly 'new' visionary, unitive and pragmatic developmental perspective that neither of the other boxes holds about reality and human beings. However, I am not an advocate of *integralism* (or any ideologism)[1] where the 'ism' reflects a rigid self-reifying "methodolatry" (as the late artist-educator Ken Beittel (1922-2003) would call it)[2] that dismisses or denies the validity of other methods and perspectives.

Two generic (English) dictionary meanings of *integral* appeal to my sense of the term: "essential to completeness" and "lacking nothing essential" which are foundations of the term *integrate*, meaning "to form or blend into a whole: unite" and "incorporate into a larger unit [whole]."[3] The term *holistic*, in part, would apply here. If human beings are to make good decisions, it is best that they make them upon means and knowledge that are as complete in the essentials and embracing of as much reality as possible in 'capturing' a good representation of Reality or the Whole (not that any absolute fixed Real or Whole exists or is likely entirely knowable to a human mind). On the politically controversial side, I would be the first to acknowledge that any philosophy (ideology) or action which values and moves toward "integration" by majority domination or violence and appropriation of a subordinate minority (e.g., 'black' people into 'White' society), is not necessarily an ideal. An integralist (sacred or secular), as I use that term, would abhor and condemn such abuse. Many people have used the term "integral" for all sorts of purposes with differing definitions, too many to overview here. I also know that those who call themselves "integralists" today do not agree on everything either. My view of a *critical* integralist stance and *critical* integral philosophy is my own version, albeit, created from what others have articulated as well. Later, I articulate the importance of keeping the word "critical" in integral philosophy and theory. However, for brevity sake, I won't always include it throughout the book.

The integralist task is to challenge the scientists, existentialists, humanists, eco-holists, spiritualists, and others to 'get off their high moral horse' as the holders of the best (or final) reality perspective to take on the planet (or universe). I have come through those camps and still utilize their better findings. I love what they offer, yet, the integralist camp has shone above them all; proving to me a more highly evolved and mature view of reality, while admitting there are ever higher levels or perspectives yet to reach beyond an integral worldview. No one, and no ideological group likes to admit the limitations of their own value-based worldview in relation to reality and the human being. Many scientists, religionists, spiritualists, existentialists, humanists, and eco-holists, in my experience are characteristically incapable of good self-reflective criticism and are mostly intransigent to admitting that the evolution of consciousness (or spirit) goes beyond their favorite views, values, and moral commitments, as well as the views and values they critique and have placed themselves morally above.

Roots of an Ethical Philosophy and Commitment to Maturity

> We are not bad, we are frightened. – Jeanne Segal

Whatever theories, approaches, concepts, advice or practices you encounter in this book, the aim toward which they are utilized here is an ethical one. My ethical (i.e., integral) philosophy and commitment, complex as it is, could be boiled down to the profound and mature claim that transformational therapist Jeanne Segal made in her book *Living Beyond Fear* (1984)[4]. Her realist-optimistic philosophy about human beings and humanity has deeply stuck with me since I read it 25 years ago, as the first serious transformational book on fear management I put into practice.

The *critical integral approach* takes a similar philosophic stance as you'll read in more detail in Chapter Two. Suffice it to say at this point that its basic idea is that human behavior and thinking is not "all bad," not "all false," nor "all wrong" no matter how bad, false, and wrong it may be, or may appear and be judged by others. All such judgments have their biased and relative perspective and thus cannot judge in any absolute sense; which does not mean there are no universal agreements that can be reached on ethical matters. Postmodern, this unique compassionate perspective of *integral philosophy* is most appealing to me because it is rigorously sensitive to the real empirical dynamics of human development and evolution. It is not merely a 'story' based on pre-modern myths, metaphysics, or modernist beliefs alone. Yet, integral philosophy recognizes "humankind is an essentially tragic figure with a beautifully optimistic future," says Ken Wilber,[5] and it recognizes the reality of the crucial role that fear ('fear') plays in our predominantly immature stages or levels on the journey from 'beasts to the gods,' as Plotinus once remarked. And finally, it recognizes the first condition of spiritual integrity is the "spirit of fearlessness" and thus the pursuit of an ideal for humanity. The *Bhagavad Gita*, one of the oldest recorded books of wisdom, puts *abhaya* (fearlessness) as *the first* virtue of any sustainable and just commonwealth.[6] Ethical fear management is thus essential to human evolution, leading us beyond the hegemonic fear-based stages or levels of development toward maturation that is absolutely *fearless* (see Chapter Three).

How different the world would be if we saw and remembered that "bad" behavior (i.e., thinking and behavior that is immature, violent, and/or pathological) is not who we are but who we've become through our developmental processes up to the present time. As we have become more and more frightened by our biological vulnerability and because of accumulated life's hurts and fears, we usually do less and less humane and loving things, especially if our fear management has not been the best. For most of us "maturing" (i.e., getting older) leaves us more bitter, resentful, mistrusting, isolating, if not mean. We stop caring about others (the whole) and neglect and abuse the environment and body that sustains us. Luckily, there are some wonderful exceptions.

Our lack of caring (wholeness) is equivalent to our level of chronic inner fearing (i.e., fear of being hurt again, fear of Other, fear of ourself, fear of Life/Death, fear of fearless, fear of Spirit, etc.). Care-less is an identity-formation that's frozen in an egocentric worldview or what David Korten, author of *The Great Turning*, calls "Imperial consciousness," as the fear-based foundation of oppressive "Empire" mentality and behaviors. He wrote of the deep challenge to transform our societies:[7]

> [a "mature society" would] . . . support every individual in negotiating the pathway to a fully mature consciousness. [Wilber calls this pathway a "spectrum" or "spiral"]. . . . Creating a mature society, however, requires leadership by people of a mature consciousness ["mature worldview"]. . . . Cultures and institutions afflicted with the addictions of Empire [i.e., Fear's Empire] throw up active ['fear'] barriers to the acquisition of a mature consciousness and favor leaders who act from an Imperial Consciousness [e.g., U.S. President G. W. Bush Jr., especially after 9/11]. The Imperial consciousness is a normal and essential stage in the developmental process of children. In adults, however, it is sociopathic.

In fear ('fear'), we become self-centered and more or less dissociated and wayward from the ethical path of maturation and ethical development (i.e., fearlessness, wisdom and compassion). As I posited earlier, the pathway of growth, development, and evolution itself can be seen as one from *fear to fearlessness* individually and from a *culture of fear* to a *culture of fearlessness* on a macroscale. History, somewhat of a 'nightmare' (said James Joyce) is a record of the wobbliness of that movement and direction. It is certainly not always straight-forward, and during 'crisis' times seems to be heading backward. Historians, like Zeldin, have often constructed and taught a far less emancipatory perspective of history than I. He wrote,[8]

> The history of fear over the centuries shows that liberation from fear has from time to time been achieved, by two methods. The first has been with the help of fear itself, by escaping from one fear to another, which contains more hope. The second has been through curiosity about something quite different, which has temporarily blotted out the awareness of danger.

Whatever the historical conditions and reality of humanity's struggle, I agree that with new growth comes new fear(s) and challenges that humans need to learn about and overcome. That is fear management as a process moving dialectically between fear and fearlessness all driven by an inherently ethical *historical fearlessness* unfolding developmentally (a modified version of Hegelian theory).

Figure 2.1 is an overview phenomenological 'map' I created to remind me of this path of fearlessness on the way to maturation. It is available to us all to negotiate as best we can. It marks out very general, archetypal, and universal stages of progress of the soul's journey.

Figure 2.1 Path of Fearlessness: Stages of the Soul's Journey

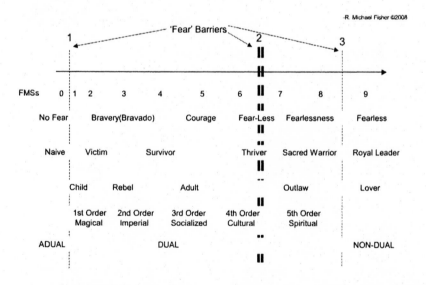

Notice first and foremost the three ontological and epistemological *'Fear' Barriers* that correlate somewhat with Korten's quote above as he conceptualizes "barriers to the acquisition of mature consciousness." One could do an extensive description of the phenomenology of the *'fear' barrier* but that is not appropriate and too complex for this book. I have written about the 'Fear' Matrix as one metaphor to capture the notion of moving in and out and across these barriers. Korten, like many others before him, writes about a "cultural trance" as the means by which the 'normal' often operates, and by which we humans are kept behind the 'fear' barriers and unable to progress in maturation, and so on. I suggest readers look at any of my earlier writings and also the brilliant sociological critical phenomenology of Fiona Mackie on discovering the 'fear' barrier(s) in our everyday conditioning of perception.[9]

Where exactly "mature" begins and ends is not the point, for maturation is a continuum along this spiral pattern (which is shown in a flat table here for graphic simplicity). Figure 2.1 simply shows what several depth-developmental theorists have roughly agreed upon, although I have arranged these theorists' continuum (or spectrum) evolutionary models on one map, with my own version of 'Fear' Barriers. "Stage" is a loosely used term here. I actually would prefer to use postmodern language and call them "discourses"[10] but that's a fine technical matter. For Korten, it is not until the 4th Order (Cultural consciousness) stage has been reached that the label "mature society" is appropriate, and after that is an even more mature stage at 5th Order (Spiritual consciousness). Let's look at the various theorists in Figure 2.1 from top to bottom. My particular original model includes the top three continuums: FMSs 0-9, No Fear to Fearless, and Naive to Royal Leader. "Mature" in my model begins with FMS-6, Fear-Less, and Thriver (as an archetypal pattern) with at least two later more mature stages available. You may recognize that other authors you have read may have some similar names and/or I have borrowed some of those names to mark out stages of growth and development (for e.g., "Sacred Warrior" and "Royal Leader" are borrowed from Chögyam Trungpa). The next continuum down is from existential-spiritual psychologist Sam Keen.[11] "Mature" for Keen begins with "Outlaw," with a more mature stage as the "Lover." It is important to note that his theory claims that "Adult(hood)," as 'normally' constructed in most societies is about half-way along the path of development. Keen has offered us what I would call a "post-adult" post-conventional critical model that challenges pervasive "adultism."[12] This is painful important and neglected. The next continuum down is from the political-ecological critic David Korten, of which I have already discussed. He utilizes several developmental theorists—primarily Harvard educational psychologist Robert Kegan's work on "Orders" of hierarchical development.[13] The next continuum down is from Ken Wilber's work and a good number of other philosophers and spiritual teachers, who have experienced and talked or written about the full-spectrum nature of reality and consciousness. "Mature," for these theorists, would begin and end in "Nondual."

Various arguments could be put forth to suggest Figure 2.1 shows development from an Idealist perspective in that there is some final ideal stage that all humans can and are meant to reach. Frankly, I would not make such a rigid or fatalistic idealist claim that way, nor would any of the theorists whom I have cited. They all, as do I, acknowledge that having an ideal has to be real (i.e., empirical in some measure). Meaning, there are people (sometimes groups, less likely societies) that have attained reliably a stage of development to the far right in Figure 2.1 (i.e., FMS-9, Fearless, Royal Leader, Lover, Non-Dual). As well, such theorists would say, as would I, not all people are born with the same capacities, constitutions, nor do they live in adequate (or ideal) conditions throughout life to actually achieve the far right—most mature stages or levels. However, all of the developmental and evolutionary theorists I draw on here, would claim that all human beings are drawn along this continuum by a Natural, Cultural, and Spiritual *telos*—that is, a drive of historical fearlessness (call it "compassion" if you like). Figure 2.1 is a map that reminds us, at least, "we are not bad, we are frightened," at least more so to the left and less so to the right of the diagram. This book is conceptualized and written from a mature perspective, at least, on the right side of 'Fear' Barrier 2. Others may judge if this is true. All of the theorists I am drawing on here would also say this long path of fearless-ness, or journey of the soul, is difficult and more difficult than most can imag-ine. It is largely inconceivable to those who have not attempted to cross the thresholds/barriers marked on Figure 2.1. The 'fear' barriers are not merely psy-chological or spiritual (all in the "mind"), but physical, sociopolitical, cultural and historical as well.

Some spiritual (nondual, absolute) teachers tend to disregard this kind of developmental map, and would say it is all too complex and "enlightenment" is much more simple and available to all human beings right now—the "power of now"—and all one has to do is stop "thinking" (using "mind") and achieve full Self-Realization (i.e., the far right mature side of Figure 2.1) because that is the Ground of Being of only that which is Real (i.e., beyond the illusion of all rela-tive reality = stages). These teachers are correct at some level of interpretation if one accepts radical Absolute Nonduality (i.e., nondual consciousness which is not a stage and nor are there stages from that perspective) as the only Reality as that which is before and after all other consciousness. As useful as those nondual teachings may be, I would argue they are only "partial" and yet powerful for transformative growth. Too often the nondual teachings (and/or how they are interpreted), tend to fall into the *"pre/trans fallacy"* trap which Wilber articu-lates, as we shall see. In simple terms, the far right of Figure 2.1 is confused with the far left, even though there are many characteristics of the extreme right and extreme left that do seem to "overlap." That is enough technical philoso-phizing for our purposes. I wish lastly, as a premise for this work, to point out that this map is foundational to a universal fear management model/theory. To grow along the path of fearlessness requires awareness, healing and ontological growth to the higher levels of consciousness and intelligence available to us. Humanity has already developed the "grooves" (templates) for these, yet every-one starting from birth has to go through the stages one by one (and no skip-ping). Anyway, I am convinced of the "truth" in this map (not the *only* one and not *all* the truth) as highly valuable for marking out a skeletal curriculum of FME in the 21st century.

Relying on critical integral theory (*a la* Wilber), this chapter and the next will sketch out the philosophical and theoretical basis for the above premise. What will not be so evident in the pages ahead is my own 30 years or so learn-ing of this truth from a great many teachers and guides. One guide, in written form, has been Jeanne Segal. In this context, I would add to Segal's dictum: *We are not bad, we are developing (i.e., maturing).* Ken Wilber's classic book *Up From Eden* (1981), a personal favorite, is a transpersonal view of human evolution with that exact same message on a macro-scale.

We are struggling to develop maturity from fear to fearlessness as not mere surface behavioral change, but a deep structural transformation of the very way we "see," "sense our self" and "act" in the world ethically. I can safely say that I wouldn't know transformation was possible for human beings unless I had repeatedly experienced it and witnessed it in many others as well. Although far too many "teachers" and "therapists" to acknowledge here, I ought to mention those who have influenced my maturation journey most. The first (in no particular order) were those leaders I witnessed personally and received various transmissions of awareness from, beyond what I could have imagined was possible for human beings and/or myself. They are as follows: Jean Robertson, Brugh Joy, Matthew Fox, Jon Amundson, Charlie Kriener and Saratoga/Mikhail. Next, in no particular order are the many who's writings lept out and resonated with my soul, taking me into new frameworks of analysis and knowing of the world and myself: E. F. Schumacher, Alan Watts, Ivan Illich, Henry David Thoreau, Jiddu Krishnamurti, Gregory Bateson, George Leonard, George Land, René Dubos, Loren Eiseley, Harvey Jackins, John Heron, Henry Giroux, M. Scott Peck, Arnold Mindell, R. D. Lang, Paulo Freire, Chögyam Trungpa, Ernest Becker, Sam Keen, Valerius Geist, Carl Jung, Rollo May, Myles Horton, Michel Foucault, Charles M. Johnston, Robert A. Masters, Joseph Campbell, James Hillman, R. Buckminster Fuller, Jeanne Segal, Shaun McNiff, Marilyn Ferguson, Rudolf Steiner, Ken Beittel, and most importantly, by far the most consistently influential is Ken Wilber.

It is hard to admit they are almost all men, as I am a particularly feminine and feminist-oriented man. Yet, I have met far greater "men" than "women" not because they are men but because they are mature, often masterful, human beings working and writing out in the wide world as leaders with great impact (at least on me). There are also far more men published to read about. I am committed to encourage more women to lead the way in new ways in the future. Like other writers, I am quite convinced, at some level, women are "spiritually" more advanced (mature) than men overall. I agree, in general, and unlike men (biologically), that "women embody enlightenment" as spiritual teacher Eckhart Tolle has suggested.[14] Clearly, in terms of contemporary fearlessness they already are "fearless leaders" as Chapter One indicates. Several great mature women are brought forward in Chapter Three from the ranks of the World's Fearlessness Teachings. On average, our socialization and educational systems do not well promote ongoing maturation of girls and women to move beyond 'normal,' from fear to fearlessness. The context of living in mostly a pathological patriarchy ensures females are constructed as 'weak and afraid,' dependent on, and in service of masculine male-centered dominating power (see Chapter Three). It has been wonderful over the years to see women scholars and others writing about the fear-based structure of pathological patriarchy and challenging it, though on the whole my research shows women's thinking, imaginary and theories about fear and its management is not one bit more advanced than men's—and that is not very advanced (i.e., not very holistic-integral).

The Integral Movement

This chapter outlines the basic theory of Fear Management Systems (FMS-0 to 9), which is my original work based heavily on the critical integral approach (Wilber, et al.). To introduce the FMSs and the principles of the theory, one ought to contextualize this within what has been called the "Integral Movement" and is sometimes referred to as the "Integral Revolution" for a potential future "Integral Age." Some biographical information on Ken Wilber in this regard is offered below. The underlying subtext is to link the Fearlessness (R)evolution (Chapter One) with the Integral Revolution and postulate how each may help each other to bring about a non-violent transformation of individuals and societies, if not the global village itself. That said, the critical integral approach does not in any way see such a transformation as a "harmonious," "unified" or simplistic change and turn. It is envisioned and theorized rather as developmental and multiply-stratified, filled with conflict (reversals and progressions).

That said, there is a need to critique these and all movements or revolutions. The premise of this book is that *fearism*[15] is largely controlling the various expressions of both the Integral Movement and the Fearlessness Revolution. Unfortunately, as well, fearism is more or less informing the World's Fearlessness Teachings and their interpretations. The correction ultimately for this hegemonic discourse of fearism can come from a critical integral theory of fearlessness based on FMS theory. Likewise, "*Flatland,*" in Ken Wilber's fearless analysis, is a crucial conceptualization, among others like "*Atman Project*" (and "*Phobos-Thanatos*"), which are illuminated in this chapter, as the deep level destructive formative (organizational) forces that most profoundly get in the way of and pathologically twist the development of humanity and consciousness. Maturity is inhibited systematically. Wilber's darker conceptualizations above are a new way of seeing and managing, if not transforming, "evil." In this light, the discussion below casts Wilber's offering to integral philosophy and the Integral Movement as qualitatively distinct and essential to the overall emancipatory projects on this planet. His work is required for any FME in the 21st century.

To understand the widest view of the roots of the Integral Movement one has to trace back through what Steve McIntosh has recently called the history of "*integral philosophy*" and/or more generally what Wilber and others have called "Integral Studies." The overview here is brief and insufficient to a good understanding of the history and philosophers McIntosh introduces as core leaders, past and present, of an integral philosophy. Those seeking more nuance and depth ought to read McIntosh's *Integral Consciousness and the Future of Evolution* (2007), a welcomed contribution to this field. Like myself, McIntosh got into integral philosophy through a basic intuitive inquiry as to the nature and role of *cultural evolution*, the latter being a concept highly critiqued today by many (not all) postmodernists (i.e., post-colonialists, poststructuralists). Wilber is a unique postmodernist, as will be shown below. In Chapter One a distinction was made between Natural, Cultural, and Spiritual domains, and the life strategies and evolutionary development patterns within each of those domains. The argument has been that the Cultural interprets the Natural, and the Spiritual corrects (ideally) the Cultural mis-interpretations, and the latter does so to avoid deep "cultural pathologies." This does not exclude however, that Natural and Spiritual domains may also have pathologies. However, it is arguable that the 'Fear' Matrix has largely grown upon the fermentation of mis-interpretations (and dissociations) within the Cultural (see Chapter Three).

McIntosh introduces this project of integral philosophy and its embedded interest in spirituality (i.e., spiritual evolution) as an outgrowth of cultural evolution:[16]

> . . . this search for the causes of cultural evolution led me to the discovery of a new way of seeing things best described as *integral philosophy*. Integral philosophy is a new understanding of how the influences of evolution affect the development of consciousness and culture. Although aspects of it have been around for a long time, it's only since the late 1990s that the essential elements of integral philosophy have been coming together into a coherent whole. The power of this new philosophy becomes self-evident to those who use it because it actually raises their consciousness. It's a philosophy of evolution that literally causes evolution.

I find McIntosh's book a 'new agey' overzealous positive "sales-pitch" for integral philosophy and McIntosh's own unique integral theory approach. He is not the most scholarly of the integral thinkers today. His lack of systematic attention to *critical theory*[17] and problematics of integral theory and philosophy (i.e., his de-politicization of it) leaves much to be desired. His pragmatism (results-centered approach), as a practitioner-of-mind for the most part, comes through as he wrote, "This book, however, is not so much about a philosophy as it is about the results of this philosophy—the newly emerging worldview known as *integral consciousness*."[18] However, his basic definitions of integral philosophy and his historical overview chapter on it with particular core philosophers is well worth reading. His synthesis of each "level of consciousness" on the Spiral (or spectrum) is very helpful and is used by myself, in part, to articulate a summary of the FMSs later in this chapter.

Although McIntosh has a substantial disagreement with Wilber's integral philosophy/spirituality,[19] McIntosh agrees with Wilber's general project which is to bring attention and research to the premise and reality that "no philosophy can be truly 'integral' unless it acknowledges the significance of humanity's experience of spirit and attempts to account for and integrate this ultimate human concern."[20] Any Cultural Studies cannot ignore religion and spirituality nor merely reduce religion and spirituality to secular terms of understanding. One can hear in this integral agenda a clear acknowledgement that the Spiritual is not reducible to Cultural, and in fact the former has the capacity to re-interpret the Cultural, integrating the Cultural perspectives but also transcending them (especially, the "distortions" of the Cultural mis-interpretations). What becomes a very exciting area in the Integral Movement is the interest in *"integral culture"*[21] as a mature advance in the evolution of culture(s). This topic is taken up later in regard to FMSs. Readers interested in a rich survey of the literature on integral philosophy and theory will have to turn to more sources than what is provided here (the Internet is a good start).

With a somewhat Western bias, who are the integral philosophers, consisting of a continuum of thinkers and their ideas, according to McIntosh? They are: Hegel "The First Integral Philosopher" (1770-1831), Bergson "The First Post-Darwinian Integral Philosopher" (1859-1941), Whitehead "Spiritual Philosopher for the Ages" (1861-1947), Teilhard de Chardin "Master of the Internal Universe" (1881-1955), Gebser "Prophet of Integral Consciousness" (1905-1973); and with more developmental psychology slant to their philosophies he includes: James Mark Baldwin (1861-1934), Clare W. Graves (1914-1986), Jürgen Habermas (1929-), Wilber "Framer of Integral Philosophy's Twenty-First Century Synthesis" (1949-). Quite the legacy of ideas. Arguably, Wilber is the most postmodern-integral synthesizer of them all. Progressive spirituality leader, Rabbi Michael Lerner,[22] referred to Wilber as, "[O]ne of the most creative intellectual synthesizers of our time. His integration of spiritual wisdom with the most significant work in science, psychology, social theory, and social science is a masterpiece of creativity and insight."

McIntosh wrote in Chapter Seven on "The Founders of Integral Philosophy,"[23]

> In this chapter we'll become familiar with the origins and development of what can now be recognized as the *integral canon*. Knowledge of these origins is important because seeing where integral philosophy has come from helps us recognize where integral philosophy is going, and how it is part of a developing stream of thought that has included some of humanity's most gifted thinkers. . . . Just as modernist consciousness arose during the Enlightenment through the power of a New Philosophy [of Reason], the rise of integral consciousness is likewise being brought about by a popular philosophical revival wherein the power of philosophy is being reclaimed by ordinary people who are using it to see things more clearly and to make life better in tangible ways. . . . Integral consciousness represents the future of cultural evolution, and this worldview of the future is becoming available now to those who would use integral philosophy to illuminate their minds and hearts with the light of integral values.

Yes, there is a new philosophy, theory and ideology called "integralism" to watch for, participate in, and critique. It isn't for everyone. Not all will be "integral" (or integral-interested) so to speak, nor do all people need to be. However, if you are a "leader" or "teacher" of some kind in this world—an integral perspective or being integral, is fairly important. For those who have not centered their own development or organization yet "at integral" (i.e., approximately FMS-7 and just across to the right of 'Fear' Barrier 2 on Figure 2.1), they may develop toward it and find and/or create adequate conditions to support it. Similarly, as one cannot just be "fearless," likewise, "integral" is something we grow and develop into, or not. To be stabilized developmentally 'at integral' is not the same as merely having cognitive state experiences or thinking about or even understanding "integral." I won't even enter the problematics and complexity of being 'at integral' on the various developmental lines (re: Wilber's AQAL theory). This general point will come back time and again throughout this book.

Many will also resist anything "integral," as is the case for "fearlessness" or "fearless." That may be subtle resistance or outright oppressive violent resistance. I have experienced this on many occasions. And Wilber, a critical theorist of sorts, is not naive about this and writes about it lots. We'll return to this developmental principle/theme in a moment. As McIntosh emphasized in his quote earlier, integral philosophy tends to advance the consciousness of the learner and practitioner. Thereby, it is not meant to be merely abstract or intellectual. The integral approach is a new paradigm and philosophy which is slowly being incorporated into the methodologies of the social sciences and even the hard sciences, says McIntosh.[24] For readers interested specifically in my application of "an integral attitude toward 'fear'" see my earlier writing.[25] I prefer to call it *integralist* thought and theory—or, *critical integral theory* and practice. The "ism" ought to be used on the term "integral" when it actually becomes, more or less, pathological and ideological (political) to the (paradoxical) point of denying or dismissing other forms of knowing, knowledge, etc. Wilber, long ago, applied this linguistic distinction to "science" when it becomes "scientism" and that is a good distinction. Unfortunately, followers of integralist thought and philosophy don't usually make this distinction and thus, use "integralism" in a positive, perhaps naive, sense.

McIntosh noted that several thinkers were the first to coin the term "integral" independently in the last century or so.[26] What is *integral*, integral consciousness, integral methodology, or integral reality frame, integral vision, etc.? These are huge questions that cannot fully be answered here, due to shortage of space. There will be indicators of what they are, but remember that different theorists and philosophers and followers will sometimes define these things differently, though a core of ideas are usually universal. FMS-7 (Yellow, Integral = Fearlessness) is the focus of this chapter, along with the other FMSs. Wilber's version of integral is the one primarily used by myself.

Ken Wilber

I have been reading, studying and applying Wilber's work since 1982. Around 1995 there were like "5 hits" on "Ken Wilber" on the Internet. Today, there are 800,000 "hits" and so many books and articles it would take half a life time to read them all and summarize *who and what Ken Wilber is about*. Wikipedia (on the Internet) has a very good introduction. McIntosh gives his version of Wilber and his work in an introduction to what he calls the "Framer of Integral Philosophy's Twenty-First Century Synthesis." He wrote,[27]

> Wilber's work has carried forward and expanded the canon of integral philosophy in a number of important areas. . . . Wilber has effectively updated evolutionary philosophy by skillfully incorporating many of the significant advances in science and philosophy that emerged during the last quarter of the twentieth century. Moreover, not only has Wilber expanded the content and contemporary relevance of integral philosophy, he has also enlarged the frame of integral

philosophy's reference. That is, Wilber has developed a model of evolving reality that reveals the internal universe in new and important ways. . . . Wilber's four-quadrant [AQAL] model reveals aspects of reality that heretofore have not been fully recognized or understood, and so in certain respects this new frame of reality does for the *internal universe* what Descartes' philosophy did for the *external universe* during the Enlightenment.

McIntosh goes on to describe how Wilber synthesized large bodies of knowledge, East and West, across disciplines, and gave due recognition "of the universal whole-part [holonic] structure of all evolutionary development [which] reveals how systems manage to maintain their integrity in the face of increasing complexity [and challenging environmental conditions]."[28] Such is the basis for FMSs theory as well. Structures (soft as well as hard) exist and evolve as systems—they can become, more or less universal, and reproducible. Wilber often calls them "deep structures" or "Kosmic habits" (i.e., more invisible) as compared to the more visible "surface structures" of Life systems. Most important, for our purposes, is that Defense, as fear management = spirit of fearlessness, is foundational to the integrity of living systems. Defense systems (FMSs) to a large degree consist of Natural "life strategies" and Cultural "v-memes" (Chapter One).

Wilber then offers another piece of theory significant to understanding an integral approach and perspective. McIntosh continues,[29]

> In his formulation of integral philosophy's twenty-first century synthesis, Wilber also skillfully illuminated the connection between developmental psychology and evolutionary philosophy. Although Hegel, Gebser, and Habermas had each in their own way recognized how consciousness and culture develops through distinct stages, Wilber demonstrated more clearly how these stages [or levels or waves or deep structures] have shaped the historical evolution of human culture and how they are now defining the problems and opportunities of contemporary society. . . . Wilber . . . was able to go beyond Habermas's insights about postmodernism by following Graves ["spiral dynamics theory"] in showing how the postmodern way of seeing actually arises from a distinct worldview that occupies a position in between modernism and integralism. As a result of his enlarged understanding of postmodernism as a historically significant stage of consciousness, Wilber has been able to transcend postmodernism more thoroughly than Habermas by clearly recognizing postmodernism's enduring contributions [*via* deconstructionist methodology and other methods or paradigms of knowing and critique] as well as its debilitating falsehoods [i.e., partial truths].

Two important conceptions appear in this quote: (1) stages or levels of development in integral philosophy (and theory) and, (2) Wilber is a postmodern integral philosopher, by far beyond others in McIntosh's list. On the second point, Wilber, a staunch critic of extreme (deconstructive, flat) poststructuralist postmodernism, has a unique and compelling reading of postmodernist thought and consciousness. His reading, and my reading, would approximately locate the following (see Figures 2.1, 3.1): "Modernism" (FMS-5), "Postmodernism" (FMS-6), and "Integralism" (FMS-7), respectively as hierarchically (holarchically) related in developmental terms. Again note, ideally a better way to write this would be to take the "ism" off these terms, to make a distinction between their healthy and pathological sides. Wilber clarified that,[30]

> Postmodern philosophy is a complex cluster of notions that are defined almost entirely by what its proponents *reject*. They reject foundationalism, essentialism, and transcendentalism. They reject rationality, truth as correspondence, and representational knowledge. They reject grand narratives, metanarratives, and big pictures of any variety. They reject realism, final vocabularies, and canonical description. [This is what Wilber would call "deconstructive postmodern"] [Referring to the "constructive" side of the postmodern, Wilber concluded:] Incoherent as the postmodern theories often sound (and often are), most of the 'rejections' stem from three core assumptions: (1). Reality is not in all ways pregiven, but in some significant ways is a construction, and interpretation (this view is often called 'constructivism') . . . (2) Meaning is context-dependent, and contexts are boundless (this is often called 'contextualism'). (3) Cognition must therefore privilege no single perspective (this is called 'integral-aperspectival').

Integral philosophy and theory is thus postmodern (*a la* Wilber), or rather, more accurately, it is *late-postmodern* or *re-constructive postmodern* or *post-postmodern*. Integral (sometimes called "integral consciousness," "vision-logic," or "aperspectivism") critiques the limitations and pathologies in postmodern thought (i.e., limitations and pathologies of pluralistic perspectivism) and offers alternatives to solving problems; this is no different than postmodernists rejecting the pathologies of modernists and modernists doing the same to premodernists. As well, on point (1) above, integral includes systems (holistic) theory and developmental and evolutionary theories. If one does not buy into or accept any validity of these domains of theories, then they will not accept anything substantial about integral theory either. These are often theories based within a philosophy of holism (holistic philosophy). The notion of holistic therefore is essential to the foundations of integral philosophy and Wilber's work, albeit, he is also a staunch critic of holism and overly simplistic (and "flat") *holistic* thinking[31] as it has developed so far. The quick working definition Wilber offers is as follows:[32]

> *Integral:* the word means to integrate, to bring together, to join, to link, to embrace. Not in the sense of uniformity, and not in the sense of ironing out all the wonderful differences, colors, zigs and zags of a rainbow-hued humanity, but in the sense of unity-in-diversity, shared commonalities along with out wonderful differences. And not just in humanity, but in the Kosmos at large: finding a more comprehensive view . . . that makes legitimate room for art, morals, science, and religion, and doesn't merely attempt to reduce them all to one's favorite slice of the Kosmic pie [same applies to the Natural, Cultural, Spiritual realms]. And, of course, if we succeed in developing a truly holistic or integral view of reality, then we will also develop a new type of critical theory—that is, a theory that is critical of the present state of affairs in light of a more encompassing and desirable state, both in the individual and the culture at large. The integral paradigm will inherently be critical of those approaches that are, by

comparison, partial, narrow, shallow, less encompassing, less integrative [yet, also acknowledging that the less integrative approaches are also useful for their own appropriate conditions and development].

"Integral" is thus holistic, yet rather more accurately is *holistic-plus*. It has integrated the best of postmodern and modern holistic thought and has transcended it as well. In the last chapter, I suggested that a "Green" eco-holistic movement (based in FMS-6) ought to be replaced by a "Yellow" integral movement (based in FMS-7)—or more accurately, from an integral perspective, we ought to have *both* as leading corrections to our current cultural and environmental malaise and other world problems. The technicalities of the integral paradigm and holistic systems theory (arguments for and against) are too complex to enter into here. The notion of "stages" in development is a taboo for most postmodernists. The notion of "no stages" or "no depth" in development is a kind of taboo for integralists. Yet, what is at the base of the use of stages (sometimes called "levels," "altitudes" or "waves" by Wilber) is to make distinctions in quality and depth. Yet, remember that no one stage *per se* is better than any other in all circumstances. Wilber's arguments and writing on "hierarchy" vs. "heterarchy" etc. are long and worth checking out but beyond the scope of this chapter.

From our perspective here, each stage (and/or FMS) of cultural development is unique and intelligent for a particular set of conditions and life strategies. They unfold and evolve one from the other as needed by circumstances and the essential creativity of evolution itself. However, the earlier systems (and 1st-tier in general) tend to be more fear-based (immature, dualistic) than the latter ones (2nd-tier and 3rd-tier, nondualistic). That is very significant when looking at planning curriculum, pedagogy, and policies for how best to manage fear ('fear') (see Chapter Four). Following the foundational premise of critical integral theory, most fear management theories and approaches are often "dangerously" incomplete, partial, distorted, un-holistic, and un-integral. Rarely have fear management discourses (especially of the 'mainstream') incorporated postmodernist and/or integralist perspectives. Such discourses cannot see their own implicit fear-based discourse. Thus, the need for an integral FMSs theory, with a FMS-7 view of FME, and fearless standpoint, and concomitant integral FME agenda for the 21st century. FME, generally speaking, is behind the 'eight ball' as they say. Especially with 9/11, we're all pretty much on catch up duty—as the generic fear (terror) problems increase in complexity and offer more severe challenges than our current accessible fear management approaches can handle well.

To further introduce Wilber and his work, several authors writing about Wilber together make up a collage or portrait of sorts, that gives the reader a further sense of "Wilberland" (or what I call "Integraland") as opposed to "Flatland." Critical futurist and theorist Richard Slaughter wrote,[33]

Until recently the dominant futures project was essentially an expression of a late-modern outlook founded on notions of prediction, forecasting and control. While other 'layers' of futures work, other traditions and ways of knowing were always available, the framing of Futures Studies (FS) occurred out of a broadly reductionistic framework—what Wilber calls 'flatland.'. . . the future was essentially 'more of the same.' For some time FS has needed a wider, richer view. [he proposes "Future Studies an Integral Agenda" using Wilber's work for theoretical support]

Lew Howard, in his popularized watered-down book on the basics of Wilber's work wrote in the Preface:[34]

> My desire to write this book has developed over a period of years. When I was introduced to the works of Ken Wilber about seven years ago, I found his ideas to be interesting and inspiring. I read more of his books, and when his [eight volume] *Collected Works* were published, I bought and read them all—which took me a couple years. This evolved into a serious study of all of Wilber's works.

Howard's is a common experience for me too, like many others around the world who have found Wilber to be a good writer, public intellectual, and teacher of philosophical-spiritual dimensions of reality. Wilber chose to drop out of his formal higher education pursuits and write professionally as an independent scholar. Rather humorously, another common experience for us who read and study Wilber comes in the next part of Howard's Preface:

> Ken Wilber opened an integral worldview that was new to me. It changed my approach to spiritual practice. I began to see relationships and principles behind what I read in the newspaper or saw in tv. I began to see the deeper [structural] basis of disagreements between individual people—and between collective groups. I was, and am, deeply moved by the glimpses of Wilber's personal life as revealed in his books, *Grace and Grit* and *One Taste*. . . . Wilber expresses his rich feelings and he is an authentic person, who shares his real-life experiences. In my enthusiasm for Wilber's ideas, I talked to my friends. I led a 10-week discussion group on his book, *A Brief History of Everything*. I found many people just did not understand it, or see how it applied to them. Others could not see how to fit Wilber's ideas into their current belief system.

Indeed some, like Brad Reynolds,[35] have argued Wilber's conceptualization of an *integral vision* is foundational to an *Integral Revolution*. These two precise words together have a powerful emancipatory Modernist resonance and political history associated with the French Revolution,[36] communism, Marxism,[37] European socialism,[38] the Gandhian non-violent movement,[39] Artaud's "real revolution,"[40] surrealism and the avante-garde,[41] revolutionary psychology,[42] some Buddhist activism,[43] and so on. These pre-Wilberian notions of Integral Revolution basically involve revolutions that are economic, social, political, moral (spiritual), cultural and psychological. They are intended as total "integral" revolutions or theories thereof, not partial—that is, not merely revolutions where one corrupt, oppressive, or unaware group takes over from another corrupt or unaware group and nothing substantially transforms, in an integral (holistic) sense. No real transformation. There has to be some "higher" ethical consciousness shift (transformation), to some extent, for an integral revolution.

Wilber, speaking from his American perspective, however, has a very unique 2nd-tier view of an integral revolution:[44]

> When we talk about an integral revolution, let's be very clear what we mean by this. The truly necessary revolutions facing today's world involve, not a glorious collective move into Green [FMS-6] or even into second tier, but the simple, fundamental changes that can be brought to the Purple, Red, and Blue waves [levels or stages] of existence at home and in the world at large. . . . No [one] society will ever simply be *at* an integral level [FMS-7, Yellow]. . . . Thus the major problem remains: not, how we can get everybody to the integral wave. . . .

No, that won't happen. Evidence and experience, from an integral perspective, suggest that at best we can facilitate the movement and growth of the 1st-tier FMSs up a level or two and we do that from a Yellow (Integral) FMS-7 perspective of management and leadership—that is, a leadership (emancipatory management), more or less, not ruled by Fear's Empire (or the 'Fear' Matrix). This would be an ideal integral organization/culture but it is not a "utopia" in the modernist sense, as Wilber's caution suggests in the quotation.

Readers may be uncomfortable with how management is a common or central term in this book and theory. At integral we are no longer avoiding the term, as Green (FMS-6) often does. Many streams of postmodern and post-colonial discourse (especially, feminism) have painted "management" as a euphemism for dominator-paternalistic economic (i.e., FMS-5) control and order (FMS-4). However, FMS-7 positions management otherwise, while accepting the partial truth of the FMS-6 criticism and caution (re: "managerialism," as Foucault analyzed). There is a healthy and ill-healthy management, and no need to throw out management all together. It won't happen anyways. There will not be a total utopian anarchist or democratic collective that operates on full justice, peace, and the common good—without needing *management* (as a verb).

This book and critical integral theory (and FMSs theory) are primarily macroscopic approaches to understanding and managing systems and cultural change (evolution of consciousness), etc. They may also examine micro-levels and meso-levels as well, but ultimately, integral demands a viewpoint well 'up and out of the fray of the everyday "trees"—rather, focusing on the "forest." We need all perspectives however, in order to work and facilitate a healthy change and developmentally-sensitive transformation in living systems. Integral tends to be a 'natural' coordinating approach—and less a hyper-extremist adrenalin-pumping approach to social activism. Wilber reminds readers that Boomers and their 1960s (onward) revolutionary spirit was great and admirable in gains for humanity. However, it had (still has) a tendency toward emotional narcissism and grandiosity (i.e., fantasy utopias or chaos and disruption for chaos and disruption sake = win-lose scenarios of a victim mentality). Wilber calls this tendency "Boomeritis."[45]

In a general naiveté overall, radical Boomers did not predict well how mass societies change and transform—that is, how effectively they resist to do so. Wilber warns future transformers and revolutionaries, "Unless we can get over the Me generation. . . . get over ourselves. . . . [there will be no] *integral revolution*"[46] (see Chapter Five). A Yellow Revolution, and what Wilber calls an emerging "Integral Age,"[47] is the potential correction to the FMS-6 Green Revolution or "Great Turning" as Korten calls it, or so the critical integral theory suggests[48] —and, in regard to FME for the 21st century and an emancipatory non-violent agenda. This contrast and contestation will remain the premise for this book.

Roger Walsh, Professor of Psychiatry and Human Behavior in the School of Medicine and Professor of Philosophy and Anthropology in the School of Humanities at the University of California Irvine, has no hesitation of putting his own reputation on the line by supporting Ken Wilber and his work. He wrote, "Ken Wilber is one of the greatest philosophers of this century and arguably the greatest theoretical psychologist of all time."[49] "Widely regarded as the leading theorist in the growing field of transpersonal psychology . . . his work has not yet figured much in the controversies of radical ecology,"[50] wrote Michael E. Zimmerman, former Prof. of Philosophy, Tulane University. That said, there are a plethora of critics of his work from lay and scholarly sources. When Wilber steps out to write about religion, sociology, politics and other fields, beyond psychology, he is on rather shaky ground— however, that is not to say he ought not attempt to do so.

For the most part, scholars in philosophy have completely ignored Wilber's work as have most academics. Wilber is not a professional institutional scholar or academic, rather he is best located as a professional intellectual writer, independent scholar, and public intellectual (as I have argued at great length elsewhere[51]). Wilber has inspired a formidable network of integral thinkers and practitioners around the world, most of which have come together under his initiative to start the Integral Institute in 2000 and later a virtual Integral University. The point is not the success or lack thereof regarding these ventures, rather it is to point out Wilber's unique role in the future evolution of consciousness and education. His work continues to feed the growing theory of critical integral fear management. For a more in depth review of the author's connection of Wilber and fear management theory see my earlier writing.[52]

Critical Integral Fear Management Systems Theory

In a recent interview with Don Beck, a leading exponent of Clare Graves theory of cultural stages and evolution, Beck said, in regard to the shift to 2nd-tier[53] (i.e., to the right of 'Fear' Barrier 2 in Figure 2.1):

> There was [in Graves's research] the *dropping away of fear*, which is perhaps the most significant marker. Fear seemed to have vanished. Now caution didn't, but fear did. [to which the interviewer remarked:] The dropping away of fear would certainly signify an enormous shift in human consciousness and in the motivations that shape our existence. [italics added for emphasis]

Indeed, this is the significant aspect of Spiral Dynamics (integral) theory[54] and cultural evolution that concerns us here, of which Graves's research pointed to, and one can find in Abraham Maslow's psychological developmental theory[55] as well. There is a significant shift (rightfully called a *transformation*), all conditions being right, across the abyss, across 'Fear' Barrier 2 from 1st-tier to 2nd-tier.

The spirit of fearlessness in evolution manifests in at least ten generic recognizable and universal forms in which to manage fear at the cultural and organizational level, which have analogous and interrelated aspects at the individual psychological level as well. I have called them FMSs-0 to 9. Beck et al. gave these "colors" which are appropriately used here for FMSs. The advantage of knowing all FMSs is that one has an increased vocabulary and set of critical distinctions as to use in regard to these FMSs and as to how to best learn about them. Most people use one or two of the FMSs almost unconsciously. Often they use one FMS (or discourse of fear and fearlessness) to solve the "fear problems" at levels which it is not capable of solving. This leads to frustration and often violence. One may have heard the story that northern Inuit (used to be Eskimo) tribes have 23 names or so for "snow." That is because they have made very fine distinctions in types of snow, which is really important when managing (and adapting) one's way in a world covered mostly by snow throughout the year. The analogy is that one needs to learn a critical discernment of many types of FMSs (intelligences of Defense) to manage one's way well in a world filled with fear ('fear')—that is in the context of a "culture of fear."

The remainder of this chapter is a quick summary of the FMSs that I have identified so far. The base qualities of the FMSs are derived from the good summary of consciousness (or v-memes or worldviews) provided by Steve McIntosh, as mentioned earlier in this text. In a nutshell, *"fear management"*[56] is the essential life-process of securing Defenses—and, thus the integrity of the organism/system against threat (real or perceived) by one or more means that have evolved naturally and/or culturally (sometimes spiritually). From reading the writing of thousands of authors on fear and fearlessness (i.e., the World's Fearlessness Teachings), in general, seven ways of fearlessness can be aligned along the continuum of FMSs, as is pointed out in Chapter Three. However, to learn a more critical fearlessness literacy it is good to also have at least a skeleton awareness of the cultural worldviews that McIntosh has outlined on the Spiral. Before we begin that overview, it is useful to take McIntosh's warning about misusing hierarchic (really, holarchic) classification systems in integral practice. He wrote of the "stages" which analogously applies to "FMSs":[57]

> The systematic structures that populate the internal universe are subtle and complex. They are better compared to ocean currents than to architecture. The very idea of a 'stage of consciousness' is something that must be held on to lightly and understood, not as a material object, but as a pattern of relationships that exhibit systematic properties. Understanding the stages of consciousness starts with the kind of discussion we are about to have, but using this understanding to help further cultural evolution involves a practice of seeing that

avoids oversimplifying, pigeonholing, or stereotyping. As you will come to see for yourself, the stages of consciousness are real; however, what follows is a description of their reality rendered at a level of generality that [is limited but that] facilitates its usefulness.

In describing the "Spiral of Development," a basic conceptualization of integral theory, McIntosh summarizes what each "stage" means overall:[58]

> According to integral philosophy, each stage of consciousness is a *natural epistemology*, an organic way of making meaning with its own distinct view of the world that arises from a specific set of problematic life conditions and their corresponding solutions. These stages function as living dynamic systems that organize both entire human societies as well as the minds of the individuals who participate in those societies. . . . The spiral's structure is dialectical because its growth exhibits the familiar pattern of *thesis, antithesis,* and *synthesis* [in a Hegelian sense]. . . . the stages . . . on the right side of the spiral tend to be more individualistic, emphasizing the *expression of the self*; whereas the stages on the left tend to be more communitarian, emphasizing the *sacrifice of the self* for the sake of the group. This spiral structure is not a deterministic blueprint that cultural evolution is bound to follow, but it does trace a real pattern of development, the recognition of which is backed by decades of research.

Unfortunately, McIntosh, following in the tradition of Spiral Dynamics and a lot of Wilber's interpretations of v-memes, leaves nothing much said about FMS-0 or 1, that is, *No Fear*. In McIntosh's model FMS-0 or 1 is "archaic consciousness." McIntosh justifies this omission with some partial truth, saying "Our description of the stages of the spiral . . . starts with the tribal stage of consciousness, because this is where human culture, and therefore human consciousness, nourished and molded by culture, arguably begins."[59] Although there is not the space here to take up this omission in integral theory of the "Natural" before the "Cultural," it ought to be said that McIntosh's notion of "natural epistemology" (or "natural theology" in his other writing) is highly problematic when the cultural evolution of consciousness is his main interest and he arguably, actually, leaves out the Natural life strategies (Chapter One) that accompany millions of years of evolution, if not billions of years, prior to the evolution of what could be called human "culture."

There is another problem with relying on the Cultural (as McIntosh and Beck do), and that has been pointed out in the work of Ernest Becker and TMT in the previous Chapter and throughout this text. The 1st-tier FMSs (or "stages" of consciousness) are Cultural phenomenon that have a fear-based structure and design (more or less, within the 'Fear' Matrix). That is, they are attempting to manage fear by largely a fear-based motivation; the result: there is not a lot of healthy non-fear-based FME or analysis going on. Yet, they are the "stages" and FMSs that are best available for certain conditions, at least, theoretically they were best at one time. Things change. New systems are required for the changes. This makes this all a very dynamic and complex process when looking at fear and its management, individually and collectively. The point is, from a critical integral perspective (i.e., fearlessness FMS-7, 2nd-tier) one has to be critical of

FMSs in all the 1st-tier because of their motivational design based in fear ('fear'). Thus, we want to learn about them, release them from their worst pathologies, and recover their intelligence to manage fear. And at the same time recognize their embedded reality in the Cultural, not so much the Natural—and this is particularly the case with FMS-2 (Purple, Magical) or what McIntosh calls "tribal consciousness."

With all those cautions and partial truths, I shall proceed to unveil the skeleton of FMSs along the Spiral of Development. Keep in mind that McIntosh is the better source for full details of each stage of consciousness, of which 18 parameters are identified for each stage.[60] In regard to this introductory text, only a few parameters may be directly engaged to identify the basic architecture of each FMS.

Fear Management System- 0 (no color, adual)

- located prior to (to the left of) 'Fear' Barrier 1, adual consciousness (no "self" sense, pre-egoic, naive, innocence, a relatively "harmonious" psychology of being), an organizational design based on motivation instinctively (Natural) directed to adapting to life and death forces but still without a conscious sense of the "need to survive" (i.e., without a fear of not surviving)—with little if any capacity to symbolize fear (i.e., 'fear') and thus manages fear as totally in the animal-based alert (instinctual) systems of protection; e.g., baby in the earliest stages of development within the womb and peri-natal, and found in some very early hunter-gatherer groups; see *No Fear* in Chapter Three).

Fear Management System- 1 (Beige, Survival)

- located in transition across 'Fear' Barrier 1,[61] earliest dual consciousness (similar qualities to FMS-0) but a slight emergent "self-sense" as distinct from the environment and a beginning awakening to a vulnerability of the organism to the environment; motivation is highly instinctual (Natural) directed to adapting to life and death forces with an awareness of the "need to survive" in order to have continuity of individuals and the collective small hunting and gathering group; very basic marking of time in symbolic representations begin as "language" develops—these may be involved in managing early anxiety around time/mortality and suffering; beginnings of storing early traumatic experiences and marking them into the existence of everyday life; e.g., Mbuti Pygmies who still have a Natural fear management system without a taboo (moralism) values system based in the form of "Good vs. Evil"; yet arguably, there is an inherent life principle/ethic that unconsciously says: *I have a right to survive* (early form of ecological wisdom ensures that to be so, as much as possible); in modern discourses this FMSs gets recognized as animal-like, instinctive fear reaction (fight-flight-freeze) based in biology (neurophysiology) and perceived by many as a "gift of fear" for survival.

Fear Management System- 2 (Purple, Magical, Tribal Consciousness)

- "perceived life conditions: a mysterious, threatening, and spirit-controlled world where spirits must be placated and fear drives many decisions; worldview and values: sacrifice self for kin and tribe [clan], respect and obey chiefs, clan, customs, and taboos, follow sacred rituals, preserve sacred places and objects, honor the spirits and the ancestors. . . . Pathology: superstitious; violent; slavery to the group; docile; naive . . . [examples] some indigenous peoples, and children . . . Exemplary leaders: Chief Seattle; Chief Joseph" with 5% of world's population and less than 1% of the world's wealth and power.[62] Main fear revolves around "Good spirits vs. Bad spirits" and bravery (sometimes bravado) becomes a major part of ritual and initiatory rites (see *bravery* in Chapter Three), which more or less appease the "spirits" (gods, goddesses). Specifically "fear of losing favor of Good spirits" controls the organization of culture. Ethically: "Good Blood, Good Spirits are Right." Fear projection (defenses) begin to develop and get codified in communalist-dominated rituals, rites and taboos. To break a taboo is terrifying, yet ultimately fearlessness must advance to do so, for the next FMS-3 to evolve. Pre-democratic clan-centered hierarchies compete with each other for political (and genetic) power without a sophisticated weaponry. Basically, what Korten identifies as "1st Order Magical."

Fear Management System- 3 (Red, Rebel, Warrior Consciousness)

- "The warrior stage of consciousness and culture arises as a result of the inevitable transition from the long and stable stage of tribal culture to a more complex form of human social organization. In human history, as tribes become successful, as they develop wealth and new technologies, their expanding populations bring them into conflict with their neighbors. And as life conditions become increasingly warlike [competitive], a new worldview emerges. This worldview can be aggressive and egocentric, but it can also be splendid and noble."[63] With this the warrior specializes in its role with *bravery* (often *bravado*) and concomitant "warrior codes"[64] of conduct, and with individualizing as a unique personality or individual thus tends to become more conflicted with the generic and communal "tribal" codes of ethical conduct (and taboos); but breaking taboos of FMS-2 is necessary when the conditions are (chaotic) threatening and tribes attempt to overtake or wipeout other tribes in warfare thus warrior archetype "craves honor; fears shame;" a major fear is lacking sufficient bravery and thus, being a prey rather than a predator. Pathology can easily set in here with "violent; ruthless; moral bankruptcy of egocentric ethics ["express self, the hell with others"]; always at war"—tendency of 'gang mentality' driven by Might is Right! Highly rebellious individualism (fixated "terrible twos" or "rebellious early adolescent" stage) can also attribute to much destruction. Exemplary leaders Attila the Hun; Genghis Khan; . . . Tupac Shakur; Johnny Rotten"—estimated percent of world population 20% with about 5% of the world's wealth and power.[65] Modern clinical psychology often sees only the pathological side of this FMS that can be extreme "no fear" types or affective or "behavioral fearlessness" as discussed earlier in this text. The most important aspect of fear-lessness is "action" (behavioral focus)—with heroic displays (often violent to-ward others) to keep others (especially enemies) "terrorized." Most political terrorists, with an anti-democratic interest, fit in and utilize this FMS against FMS-4 but also against all other FMSs above FMS-4 where democratic political processes are most valued. The big secret fear of FMS-3 is to find out that "ter-rorizers" are "terrorized." That means, the violent terrorist looks so brave but is terribly afraid, but this system has amazing dissociative and denial capacities and defense mechanisms psychologically to block that "truth" (i.e., a critical self-awareness of personal fault—because the shame (a cousin of fear) would be seen as just too painfully great and devastating to the egocentric self). What Korten defines as the most destructive fear-based systems as "2nd Order Impe-rial"; by which he also includes the pathological side of FMS-4.

Fear Management System- 4 (Blue, Mythic, Traditional Consciousness)

- this social FMS has to control the rather "barbaric" ruler-ship of the earlier FMSs, especially Red egocentric—we move now to developing traditional eth-nocentric values and motivations often with their paternalistic formulation of a "promise" or "bargain" or "covenant" with Greater Other: for example one might say: "I am fearless. Without Fear. I leave fear to Him," as a Muslim col-league once wrote to me.[66] Such a formulation is classic premodern FMS-4, which attempts to manage fear (even to become fearless" to some degree) by giving over fear(s) to a superior (often paternal) archetype/symbol or projection of a great Father (or Mother) figure like a God or Goddess or even the State. FMS-4 is "Traditional consciousness, also known as 'conformist consciou-ness,' which arises in response to the brutal and chaotic life conditions created by the warrior level [or stage] that came before it. This is why traditional con-sciousness tends to perceive the world as 'evil,' requiring salvation and law and order [i.e., more structure and systematic management!]. While this stage of consciousness can now be identified with the many forms of religious funda-mentalism found throughout the world, not all those whose consciousness is centered in this stage are fundamentalists. [Group sports organizations and] [m]ilitary organizations, government bureaucracies, and conservative political groups provide contexts in which this stage of consciousness flourishes."[67] Here a pre-given "social role" identity is utmost, and members will sacrifice self for the good of the whole society, religion, nation/state. Fear is controlled by "safety in numbers—of sameness." Fear is controlled by order, hierarchies of power over with clear boundaries, status, and structures of dishing out punishment— the greatest fear is guilt brought on to those who disobey the order(s)—such individuals are charged with treason, with abandoning duty, with being uncivil, traitors, and so on. There is an immense fear of social rejection built into virtu-ally all the discourses of "appropriate" behavior, individually and communally. Institutions are created to handle this management of emotional life and it is essential as cities are now growing with vast numbers of dense populations of difference. Black n' White (written upon mythic narratives) ethics works well (for some; usually those in power). Pathology "rigid intolerance; dogmatic fanaticism; prejudice; fundamentalism; chauvinism"[68]—see *courage* and courageousness (Chapter Three) as a beginning form of fearlessness in the discourses but still basically *bravery* (*bravado*) are the strong underpinning behavioral orientations (highly masculinized)—especially, pathological forms. The ethic is "My Country/Belief is Right!" which means "Yours isn't!"—and that is perceived by fear-based processes and enemy-making. Institutional terrorization is the operations of this FMS far too often as "Fear of God" and/or "Fear of State" (Monarchy, etc.) is maintained for fear management. The people remain in fear of authority as the "social contract" for the protection (safety and security) offered by that God, State, Monarch, etc. Thomas Hobbes's W. philosophy of precursor early modern FMS-4 logic of social organizational design, is based on manipulating the fear of the people (see FMS-5 analysis and endnotes on this). It is hard to find a really healthy FMS-4 today at the operational level (they need to be built, but from a 2nd-tier perspective). The 'Fear' Matrix is believed to have grown most severely and effectively when this FMS emerged and dominated so much of the world's operations. Issues of secular and sacred elements of FMS-4 are crucial to look at in a more nuanced investigation into this worldview. They may serve to control "terrorists" (pathological FMS-3) but often end up being a sanctioned state "terrorism" or in the case of Christian history (for e.g.) the Inquisition and the Crusades were carried out in righteousness (bravery) of FMS-4 to supposedly "calm the fears" of the people and any threats to order and stability. Police brutality, unjust military operations, and militarization of public spaces follow along this line, as has been seen in much of the post-9/11 era. Exemplary leaders "Winston Churchill; Pope John Paul; Billy Graham. . . . estimated percent of world population: 55% [and] Estimated percent of wealth and political power: 25%."[69] The healthy side of FMS-4 (and FMS-5) is what Korten would likely call "3rd Order Socialized," while the pathological side is closer to his "2nd Order Imperial."

Fear Management System- 5 (Orange, Success, Modernist Consciousness)

- it is important to recognize on the Spiral of Development that by the time we reach FMS-5 (which our "modern" "scientific" mind can most easily understand of all the FMSs), 80% of the world's population is prior to Modern—that is, the vast majority of the world's population at this time in history has a "center of gravity" in basic values and worldview that is traditional Pre-Modern (for e.g., meaning, they have not yet found full or strong democracy and made a "separation" between Religion and the State). When one takes this reality in, it is enormously humbling, especially to those of us lucky enough to live in conditions of modernity (relatively stable "democracies") and realize we are only about 20% or less of the world's population in believing in (and/or achieving success at) the Modern worldview and thus, operating on its advanced fear management system. The "Culture Wars" between Pre-modern worldviews and Modern worldviews is enormous, and it has risen to a head in the last 50 years or so of Postmodern times (in the West, that is), where even newer worldviews (and FMSs) are being added into awareness of modern people's and seen as a threat (for the most part) to both Modern and Pre-modern peoples. "Traditional consciousness [FMS-4] has been present in various forms for at least the last five thousand years. . . . The first significant emergence of modernist culture appeared in the fifth century B.C. during the Golden Age of ancient Greece. The triumph of reason over myth was evident."[70] Reason (rationality) is the 'great' philosophical fear management system—it is the basis of science (another form of fear management system)—these methodologies manage the superstitious fears (and irrationality, at times) of the earlier "stages." This is the predominant discourse of fear management in most texts and teachings of the World's Fearlessness Teachings (especially, in the 'mainstream'). Individual autonomy is highly valued in FMS-5 and that gives individuals a Right to Reason (and logic and achievement) beyond what merely has been taught by the tradition and its view of the 'best way' to be or 'best way' to manage fear, or be courageous, moral, and so on. Indeed, *courageousness* (see Chapter Three) is highly valued at FMS-5 but it is highly individual (compare to FMS-6 which is more communal). This is the beginning FMSs of existential philosophy, that is, the primarily secular philosophy (e.g., Kierkegaard, Nietzsche, Schelling, Fichte) that has most focused, historically speaking, on understanding the human condition of fear, terror, and how to best adapt to it and not be controlled by it or controlled by those who use it against us. Elsewhere, I have written a brief genealogy of FMS-5 (Modern-Existential discourse).[71] Right to Reason is a Right to Freedom from Fear (as another major dictum of FMS-5). Pathology: "materialism [individualism]; nihilism [secularism]; exploitive [technicism, scientism]; unscrupulous; selfish [narcissism]; greedy."[72] As well, a kind of "left-brain" dominance—where analytic logical (masculine) thinking (instrumental reason), etc. becomes overly dominant over feelings, ethics and social concerns—often this gets hooked into economic capitalism which plays upon the value of individuals being able to overcome oppressive and limiting aspects of one's location in life—thus, "success" is highly prized, but the great fear that accompanies it is "fear of failure" (i.e., of "being a loser"). Exemplary leaders: "John F. Kennedy; Bill Gates; Margaret Sanger; Carl Sagan; Issac Newton. . . . Estimated percent of world population 15%. . . . Estimated percent of wealth and political power: 60%."[73] It ought to be recognized that between FMS-4 and 5 the estimated wealth and political power in the world amounts to 85%. This is very significant to understand which FME theory and practices are going to be dominant on the planet in a globalizing way. Remember, with this much wealth and power, FMS-4 and FMS-5 are always afraid of losing it—and that dictates a good deal of their management activity and thus, their efforts and strategies to maintain this privileged position will be well developed with an increasing "global worldview" perspective as we move from FMS-4 into FMS-5. Globalization, its worst sides, as economic and value-based colonialism (see Korten's "Imperial" consciousness), is based on these two FMSs and particularly the latter. FMS-6, as we shall soon see is abhorred by this globalizing combination and thus attempts to correct it.

Fear Management System- 6 (Green, Sensitive, Postmodern Consciousness)

- if the emergence of a significant percentage (maybe 20% of the Western populations) of FMS-6 is equated with postmodernist thought as some authors have suggested, then it has given rise to what could be called the 1960s "Love Revolution"—ideal-seeking (often romantic) youth led this movement for the most part (e.g., 1968 university student riots in France and then spread around the world). "In academia the rise of postmodern values [particularly since the early 1980s with deconstructionist philosophers like Jacques Derrida] produced a new 'critical paradigm' that sought to deconstruct the [oppressive] canon of Western [colonial] knowledge by showing the subjectivity [and relativity] of what had been previously understood as 'objective.'"[74] Science was now questioned as mere social construction and with a politics of objectivism that destroyed or severely hurt people of all kinds, if not the Natural itself. Postmodern consciousness is a highly sensitive consciousness to perceiving oppression (virtually everywhere, in every kind of form of 'ism')—it detects and unveils where possible the "presence of exploitation [victimization]; corrupt hierarchy; environmental degradation; shallow materialism; suffering of others [of difference and marginal existence]."[75] This worldview tends to promote a non-violent resistance, use of arts for resistance, a 're-enchantment' of the Natural and "whole person" (body/mind), and a fundamental egalitarian principle of inclusion behind social organization and democracies. It has a "worldcentric morality" by which it recognizes the worth of all beings in the world, and asks for the first time systematically, "what is the best thing to do for the planet?" "Exemplary leaders: John Lennon; John Muir, Martin Luther King, Jr.; Margaret Mead; Joan Baez; Allen Ginsberg."[76] It also has a pathological side (which it typically neglects to acknowledge and is vicious to defend against any criticism): "value relativism; narcissism; denial of hierarchy; contempt for modernism and traditionalism."[77] A strong political correctness (communalism) pervades FMS-6 ideology and it can turn into a "Green Inquistion" (*a la* Wilber) of its own right, where paradoxically, it disallows individuals to have a different view than "Green." Its Ethical Stance is the Right to Be Sensitive (a Subject) and have subjective experience that is valid and true and worthy. Self-esteem is of particular critical importance in this FMS, and it has been a strong advocate of healing and transformation of trauma (hurts, violence, fears, and terrors) from our past. It is this massive soft technology of self-reflective awareness of healing and therapy (holistic health movement, and human potential movement, 'new age') that has arisen to manage the fear and terror. However, FMS-6 is often driven by a "fear of being hurt again"—meaning, it tends to operate out of an over-determining victim-identity and hyper-sensitivity to being hurt (note: some critics of the "culture of fear," like Furedi, have critiqued the pathology of FMS-6 as being a "therapy culture" and a non-progressive society which has come to "fear progress" avoid "risk": see Beck's "risk society" concept[78]) and thus, in some ways, limits human creativity—in its worst form, Furedi believes that it has turned to a kind of "culture of emotionalism" and "politics of emotion," and dangerous growing "misanthropy" (i.e., hatred of humans[79]); Sunstein has critiqued this social movement as well, based on what he calls the "laws of fear" (i.e., overly privileging laws made for victim-survivors) that are more and more ruling our postmodern world in the form of the "precautionary principle"[80]—all basically attempting to manage fear. However, FMS-6 has a strong tendency to reproduce fear—and ends up with a strange admixture of patterns that 'fear fear itself' like no other time in history has done so (see Corey Robin[81]). As wonderful as FMS-6 has been it has truly *not* been able to create a culture of fearlessness from the embedded human condition of a culture of fear. In fact, because FMS-6 admires (sensitive) *courageousness* as its ultimate value it tends to disregard and denigrate *fearlessness* (i.e., FMS-7 and 8, 9)—that is, fear of fearlessness. FMS-6 has clearly neglected doing its homework and recognizing the vast traditions (especially in the East) of *fearlessness*. Thus, we see a FMS-6 ideal of inclusivity turns rather to be exclusivity, believing it has the *best* (only) fear management approaches of all, as it rejects for the most part, any discourse of fear management of the 2nd or 3rd tiers. This is a huge problem for FME on this planet. FMS-6 is the 'top' of the 1st-tier FMSs and rightfully has evolved to be in that position to "correct" the fear problems created by the earlier FMSs; but then it cannot see anything higher than itself (a typical characteristic of the 1st-tier competition for dominating discourses). My research has shown there is a small but growing "correction" to these problematics within FMS-6 which requires distinction and thus a FMS-6a and FMS-6b (and likely FMS-6c) have been created. FMS-6b is led by theorists and practitioners like Gavin de Becker and Forrest Church (see discussion of *fear-less* in Chapter Three), who have led the way toward re-examining how "over-sensitive" (over-fearful, and irrational, exaggerated, or "unwarranted") ways of managing worries, fear, threat, and violence are, in the end, likely to produce worse outcomes, and more fear and violence than they intended. Korten calls this FMS-6, "4th Order Cultural." To break out of the cycle of the culture of fear, Fear's Empire, or 'Fear' Matrix of the 1st-tier, one needs to seek more mature forms of the evolution of consciousness and FMSs found in the 2nd and 3rd tiers.

Fear Management System- 7 (Yellow, Integral, Integral Consciousness)

- McIntosh wrote,[82] "the postmodern worldview [FMS-6] needs to be transcended and included by a new evolutionary development in consciousness. Further cultural evolution will be required in order for our society to find realistic solutions to the growing problems of the world. And this further cultural evolution can now be recognized in the form of the newly emerging integral stage of consciousness." The proper location of "fearlessness" as we saw in Figure 2.1 the "quantum leap" to the 2nd-tier from the 1st-tier, is marked by a significant reduction in the production and consumption of 'fear'-based toxicity due to fear-based motivations (including, the mostly unconscious production of culturally-modified 'fear'). At the 2nd-tier the entire spectrum of consciousness and FMSs can be seen—those prior to FMS-7 are well known, those above FMS-7 are intuited or known in part, even though they may have not been attained yet as an operative center of gravity for the individual or organization at FMS-7. Theo-

retically, FMS-7 is the best place of "managing" the entire spectrum (Spiral) —
and the entire human Fear Problem (Chapter Three) due to the emergence of
"*vision logic*."[83] This Yellow fear management system is able to "think" and
"operate" beyond the full constraining limitations (i.e., cultural trance-blindness)
of the 'Fear' Matrix. It intuits the spirit of fearlessness running through all of
evolution (i.e., Spiral of Fearlessness) and draws upon the World's Fearlessness
Teachings to access a critical discerning wisdom and compassion needed for
contemporary problems. This is critical to a truly emancipatory project, curriculum and pedagogy for FME in the 21st century (see Chapter Four and Five).
This entire book is written from this location. Only at FMS-7 does one become
interested to study and know the architecture of the 'Fear' Matrix itself — and the
main reason is because it can actually be detected (somewhat obviously) for the
first time in the developmental continuum. You cannot 'fix' what you don't see
'broken.' The issue of greatest concern is the rising levels of toxicity produced
within the unsustainable "ecology of fear" (as Mike Davis, calls it[84]) that is the
'Fear' Matrix mega-system. Unlike FMS-6, Yellow Integral consciousness is
less concerned with internal "fears" and merely seeing fear as biopsychological
or emotional problems to be "solved" or overcome by *bravery* (*bravado*), *courage*, or *fear-less* strategies. A deep ethical sensibility[85] grows up and matures at
FMS-7 and "revival of philosophy; seeing spirituality in evolution; envisions
overcoming the Culture Wars; renewed insistence on achieving results," as
McIntosh suggests — with an interest in new organizational structure such as a
"world Federalism" and "global systems economy"; "Exemplary leaders: Albert
Einstein; Teilhard de Chardin; Alfred North Whitehead; David Ray Griffin; Ken
Wilber."[86] A renewed sense of "progress" is experienced globally. However, it is
not a monological or purely fanciful notion of progress with the arrogance of
Modernism. McIntosh elaborates further,[87]

> Locating integral consciousness within its place along the spiral of develop-
> ment. . . . reveals the many similarities between the modernist worldview and
> the integral worldview. However, we can distinguish modernist values from in-
> tegral values in the way that integral consciousness embraces and includes all
> the healthy values of postmodernist consciousness (and the other stages) in its
> evolutionary transcendence. And this transcendent act of inclusion makes the
> integral worldview significantly different than modernism. But despite the ma-
> jor differences, we can still see many parallels between the emergence of early
> modernist consciousness during the Enlightenment and the emergence of inte-
> gral consciousness in our time. Consider the following similarities: modernist
> consciousness values progress, integral consciousness values evolution; mod-
> ernist consciousness sees the good life in an abundance of status and material
> possessions, integral consciousness sees the good life in an abundance of con-
> sciousness — the abundance   that comes from the continuous development of
> the inner life. Modernists are fascinated by external technologies such as ma-
> chines and electronics, and similarly, integralists are attracted to internal tech-
> nologies such as psychospiritual practices. When modernism first appeared, it
> had a new approach — reason and the scientific method. Now integral con-
> sciousness likewise brings a new approach — dialectical evaluation and the
> compassionate use of the spiral as a method of relating to the good in each level

and seeing the bad in appropriate perspective. [Modernist = "discovery of the big picture of the *external* universe" and Integralist = "discovery of the big picture of the *internal* universe"].

Re: Yellow Integral FMS-7: estimated percent of world population and power and wealth politically is less than one percent. It's pathology tends toward being "elitist; insensitive; aloof; lack of patience [arrogance]"[88]—many of these symptoms have been part of the criticisms thrown at Ken Wilber (and sometimes the whole Integral Movement) over the decades, and not surprisingly, as he has claimed he writes much of his work from an integral vision-logic perspective. As well, I have experienced the integral fear of complexity and massive amounts of knowledge that one needs to assimilate and work with to resolve problems (e.g., the Fear Problem). Harvard integral psychologist, Robert Kegan, has thoughtfully brought this problem forward as the demands of today's world are increasing and our mental capacities are lagging behind.[89] He says we are generally "in over our heads" and that is even more prevalent when one enters the second-tier for the first while. There can be an ongoing sense of "overwhelm" and sometimes "paranoia" (i.e., the 'Fear' Matrix is out to bring you down); and of being so alone, unsupported, incapable to find sufficient paid work and sustainability on projects on this journey of integral (FMS-7). No one yet has studied the negative effects of fully crossing the abyss into FMS-7. This integral worldspace promises better conflict management in all realms, but the doubt is immense in terms of "real capacity" and effectiveness to do so. Conflicts often seem to grow when integralist thought is brought in, rather than diminish (at least, that is the first reaction). Research is lacking and often integralists seem to brag about results of conflict management with little real solid back-up that would convince one (or others) that integral is offering the powerful 'technology' it says it is. Critics of integral are everywhere and some of the internal criticism (and "attacks") within the Integral Movement itself, are despairing to some degree, as integralists should know better—but don't act any different than what we have seen historically in most all other movements that undermine themselves from the "inside." The demands of the actual "integral methodology" seem far beyond what even self-proclaimed "integralists" are capable of doing. Talk is 'cheap' but real operational integral practice is a rarity. There is a tendency for a hyper-masculine identification (power play) with Yellow Integral as well—and a much stronger feminine (feminist) presence is required to grow a healthy and sustainable FMS-7. There is an ongoing sense of "being rejected" (not surprising as research shows that they are less than one percent) with one's "integral analysis" because it is either not understood at all or is perceived as being "too out in left field" or "too abstract" or "unrealistic." Most of these critiques, partially true, tend to arise from a desperation and fear projecting from the 1st-tier of not getting results quick enough, as the world collapse is envisioned as deeply threatening and coming a lot sooner than later. Integral approaches seem "long term" and "someone has to put out the fires now!" Integralists are too philosophical to be of much help to pragmatists—so it appears to the critics. Integralists may accuse the critics of breeding more "fear" (and a culture of fear) in their desperate short-term solutions; and thus, integralists see that there is little accumulative intelligence produced in those short-term interventions. On the positive side,[90] there is the invincible Sacred Warrior awakening of a true regard and application of *fearlessness* (e.g., "gift of fearlessness"; see Chapter Three) as the basis for an "Integral Culture" (and Revolution)—and such an awakening (for the most part) sustains the soul and will beyond victimization or survivalist patterns (so common in FMS-6)—making this FMS unique from all previous. Courage and courageousness are seen as "personal" precursors to the development of "transpersonal" fearlessness, and onward to *fearless*. Unfortunately, "integralists" have not yet embraced the importance, conceptualizing, and emancipatory practices of FMS-7 as outlined in this book. McIntosh, characteristic of most "integralists" tends to see "moral courage" (p. 92) as integral, whereas I would see "moral fearlessness" as appropriate to 2nd-tier (see Chapter Three *fearlessness*). Even Ken Wilber or Don Beck write (or talk) rarely about "fear" and less so about "fearlessness."[91] The ideal ethical right of FMS-7 is "No One Is All Right Or All Wrong" and the responsibility with that is: *not to make anyone fear for their safety or security, or have their power, status and privileges diminished because they have different views of what is right or wrong.* At the same time, this ideal principle is not actually attainable when there are 1st-tier v-memes and worldviews dominating (often with weaponry that can threaten the whole). Thus, arguably, under some circumstances "fear" is the only language certain individuals or organizations (especially Red FMS-3) understand. However, this conscious use of "fear" is seen by FMS-7 as merely temporary to minimize damages potentially caused by 1st-tier pathologies.

Fear Management System 8 (Turquoise, Postintegral Consciousness)

- there is good evidence, says McIntosh that currently America (like many other highly industrialized Western nations) is rife with three major conflicting distinct subcultures (i.e., Culture Wars): *Traditional*, *Modern*, and *Countercultural* [Postmodern].[92] From an integral FMSs perspective Culture Wars is a historical and political battle for who gets 'top' control of the FME on the planet(?): FMS-4 (Blue), FMS-5 (Orange), and FMS-6 (Green), respectively. In earlier discussions in this book: *fear is power (and the knowledge/discourse of fear is even greater power)* (due credit to Foucault). With more pressures from the need to advance in cultural evolution and to respond well to the current crisis of Culture Wars (paradigm wars, etc.), FMS-7 (Yellow) and FMS-8 (Turquoise) are beginning to arise (simultaneously) at some significant level but one ought not to be overly optimistic because the percent of the population and power and wealth of these 2nd-tier FMSs is extremely small (less than one percent). However, as McIntosh points out, true as that may be, there are postintegral levels of consciousness, and some esoteric individuals or small groups have arisen throughout history that manifest these elite qualities. However, McIntosh says little about them in his summary because, for him, "as soon as we go beyond what can be observed culturally, as soon as the only subjects we can research are essentially spiritual teachers, we have gone beyond the confines of public philosophy and entered the realm of spirituality."[93] His view is not necessarily the only view for a delimiting conceptualization of "public philosophy" (or "public intellectual" work). That issue aside, he makes an important note that with Turquoise (FMS-8) one is called to bring in a stronger discourse of "Spiritual" (no matter how one wants to define it). The Cultural discourses of FMSs 1-7 shift, for McIntosh, and he prefers to now speak of Spiritual discourses (FMSs 8-9). For me, technically speaking, FMS-7 ought to also be in the Spiritual discourses, (i.e., Korten's "5th Order Spiritual") but that is a minor point of contention among some spiritualists. Like McIntosh, there is a sense of the *Spiritual* coming to 'correct' the *Cultural* (meaning, the Cultural's accumulating misinterpretations of the Natural throughout evolution). McIntosh is quite right to argue "... the contours of what can be termed 'postintegral culture' cannot yet be described in detail."[94] There's no general agreement across the disciplines of knowledge that evidence is substantial and valid to describe such a postintegral culture anywhere in human history. Some 'new agey' or esoteric spiritualists might want to argue that early human history had produced such "postintegral" cultures such as mythic or real "Atlantis" or "Shangrhila." I would agree with Wilber, such ascription would likely be more a "pre/trans fallacy"[95] than reality (from an evolutionist's or integralist's perspective, that is). Those issues aside, FMS-8 and FMS-9 do not have to be completely identified with a "postintegral culture" and/or with "spiritual teachers" (as McIntosh's focus revolves around). Rather, one can surmise the *discourse* of these senior mature and emancipatory levels of consciousness and correlate them with issues of fear and fearlessness (i.e., FMSs available). Another way to do this is to acknowledge that the *existential discourse*, throughout Western human history has been perhaps the most vigilant in pursuit of knowledge about fear (and its cousins, anxiety, angst, dread, terror) and courage (i.e., fearlessness); in Figure 2.2, I have summarized some of the major theorists of FMS-6b through to FMS-9, locating them from the view of an existential fearanalysis. Although much could be said about this diagram, it is a rough first-guide to some distinctions that may be helpful in an integral fearanalysis. Notably, the FMS-6b has a strong tendency to evolve *via* a downloading from FMS-8 and/or 9—what I call a *"spiritual by-pass"*; often seen in spiritualism movements (esoteric Gnostic cults), some nondual mystics, 'new age' folks and those who don't like integrative 'shadow' work all the way down and all the way up—i.e., the Ascenders. The spiritual by-pass often takes the form of "spiritual" FME teachings (from FMS-8, 9), but interpreted primarily through the FMS-6b Humanistic-Existential discourses. A good example of this is McIntosh's *Integral Consciousness* book that has been useful for general mapping of the FMSs underlying structure in this chapter. The main critique is that FMS-7 *fearlessness* (i.e., Integral-Existential) is underdeveloped through the habit to enact the spiritual by-pass. The result is a FMS-8 that is "more spiritual" than "existential" or "integral."

Figure 2.2 Spiritual By-pass in the Higher FMSs

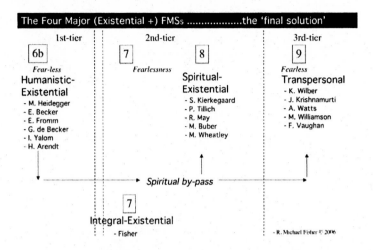

What that means, from my study of the discourses, is that FMS-8 tends to be ungrounded in good critical integral fearanalysis, and that is not a useful bias when clearly the world's Fear Problem is growing at an unprecedented rate in a post-9/11 era (World War III = "War on Terror" or "War on Fear" by any other name). FMS-8 can become driven by Spiritualism, just as any of the three major domains can become pathological to some degree, as in Naturalism or Cultural-ism. McIntosh's strong link with critical integral theory helps his perspective from going too far off but this is not the case with so many other "integralists" or 'Green' and/or 'new age' (spiritualist) authors who preach Turquoise without a good integrative teaching of Yellow first (e.g., Eckhart Tolle, Thich Nhat Hanh, and others). Indirectly, McIntosh recognizes some of the problem here in his discussion of "current limitations of polite spiritual pluralism."[96] One of the wonderful unique qualities of Turquoise (FMS-8) is that one's self-identity be-comes entrained deeply (transpersonally) with the identity of the Kosmos (i.e., Kosmocentric worldview). The notion of "self" vs. "Other" virtually disappears, and thus fear('fear')-based motivations equally disappear. The detection of "sub-tle" energy flows, connections, relationships, and feminine ways is another ma-jor feature of intelligence so needed that FMS-8 provides. See *fearlessness* (Chapter Three) for more subtle masculine and feminine distinctions between FMS-7 fearlessness and FMS-8 fearlessness. The Ethical imperative or right at FMS-8 is "The Spiral is Right." This roughly translates as *what is best for the Spiral* (of development, consciousness) *is best and ought to be done*. The notion of "human rights" or "animal rights," etc. have been included but transcended (i.e., no one creature is given that much priority of value, relative to the whole of Creation-in-the-making and a reality that "Life" will take care of itself and the extinction of this or that species, that no longer serves "Life," well, isn't a big deal to the Kosmos).

Fear Management System 9 (Coral, Nondual Consciousness)

- in Spiral Dynamics Theory, we have now entered the realm of the 3rd-tier, which I have identified in Figure 2.1 as a (rarified) crossing of 'Fear' Barrier 3 in human development of consciousness. In many of Wilber's earlier writings he emphasized that this "level" is not even a real "level" to be attained as a "stage" of development. He used to call it the essence of the Ground of Being prior to all distinctions—yet, later he refined his thinking to agree with developmental evolutionary theory and the reality that nondual consciousness is not adual consciousness as pre-given ontological condition before consciousness. The technical precision of labeling Spiral Dynamics Theory's "Coral" worldview with nondual is less than to be desired. There is little space here to develop the arguments and trace through various anatomies of these higher mystical stages of consciousness. Wilber has usually divided the transpersonal levels into Psychic, Subtle, Causal, Nondual and variations thereof.[97] My FMSs classification of manifestations of the spirit of fearlessness is relatively less precise than Wilber's but to suggest it is generally useful to work with generalizations that the Psychic and Subtle is similar to Yellow (FMS-7), Causal to Turquoise (FMS-8) and Nondual to Coral (FMS-9). Nondual consciousness is grown into as all the 'Fear' Barriers (Wilber calls "repression barriers") are surpassed. Again, no culture we know of has attained such a center of gravity and a few rare individuals may have, and most often they are "spiritual teachers" (gurus) or monastic-type activists. The names of the transpersonal thinkers and practitioners in Figure 2.2 are merely there as exemplars pointing to and valuing FMS-9 (Fearless), but not necessarily fully embodying of FMS-9. The image of what a fully fearless person is seems beyond most of our imaginations. How is fear ('fear') managed in this place where there is "no self" and thus, no self that has no fear = *fearless*? Really, not much can be said here (see Chapter Three on *fearless* and concrete examples), at least, not by myself. Words and concepts fail miserably to touch the most evolved reality of existence depicted on the 'map' of the journey of fearlessness. Discourses on the nondual (Absolute) and fearless do however exist across most all spiritual and philosophical traditions. One has to practice the practices and go through the legitimate procedures of validation that involve a fearanalysis and "testing" by the adequate (i.e., achieved nondual *fearless* ones). The ethical imperative or right is non-detectable, not of interest to this stage or level. If anything, most basically, FMS-9 holds the 'bar high enough' to aspire to *living and loving beyond fear and coping*. The empirical evidence of interest of diverse discourses across diverse populations that positively use terms like "fearless" or "no fear" and "without fear," "freedom from fear," etc. need to be taken quite seriously (as well as critiqued, as has been done earlier in this book). This author would hypothesize that such discourses are symptomatic of a great Spiritual longing within most human beings (if not all), which seeks to "finally" be free from fear ('fear'). If anything, FMS-9 recognizes this Spirit as *fearless*— as effortless—as one recognizes their own breath and heart pulsating from a Source not of their own making but not apart from their own making. The paradoxical logic of FMS-9 nondual is to be expected, and as it is, embraced. *Fearless* emerges spontaneously by grace or by thunder-bolts of lightening—it is not merely an altered meta-physical truth, or mystical "state" (i.e., psychospiritual phenomena). FMS-9 *fearless* is a "system" (in and out of the 'Fear' Matrix)-- and that is, all quadrants, levels, lines, types, etc. It is very complex. There is no formula for *fearless* and there is no need to seek safety and security because the latter do not exist; not from this nondual perspective. I have experienced the nondual as "the zero of consciousness," as Robert Pirsig[98] once called it, as that place of awareness of being both free of all mind-stuckness, yet knowing the next stuckness is just around the corner as ideas, theories, and intentions pour in to take on the next problem of existence as one steps back into dual reality of the suffering body/mind system in the Cultural. I have called this a dynamic movement "in and out of the 'Fear' Matrix," perhaps, equivalent to the Buddhist notion of the bodhisattva who returns to the world after enlightenment to serve to free all others before one can declare one is free—but if nothing else, FMS-9 acts as an analytical (yet ethical) location for a provocative conceptualization of a *fearless standpoint theory* (see *fearless* in Chapter Three)—and from that theory one sees the seven ways of fearlessness as all one and the 15 or so different meanings of fearlessness as means and ways of liberation.

A Few Closing Remarks

As readers you have taken a whirlwind surfing tour of most things integral. From critical integral theory (in a sociological sense) to integral consciousness (in a psychological and philosophical sense), to integral vision (in a spiritual sense) and to the Integral Movement and Revolution (in a political sense). Integral is an approach endless in its unfolding of possibilities for re-evaluating our sense of self, thinking, and inheritance from Premodern, Modern, and Postmodern eras, while stretching us simultaneously forward into the rise of Post-postmodern (Integral) or what some are now calling Transmodern.[99] These major worldviews and their values are what concern us in developing a futures-oriented and effective FME.

There is no fixed blueprint for any of this. The FMSs themselves are at best "orienting generalizations" (hypotheses) for how the Natural, Cultural, and Spiritual domains integrate their functions for the evolution of consciousness. With time they may be empirically "proven" to be "real" in ways that satisfy more people than they do at this present time. Lest it be said that *integral*, as used here, is a means for transformative and emancipatory ends, depending on how well it is constructed and utilized. My interest is in developing consciously an integralist sensibility and more ideal, an integralist culture, as the late integral sociologist Pitrim Sorokin (1889-1968) called for as critical to the world:[100] "In the current sociopolitical crisis, he [Sorokin] sees the only hope in a new integralist philosophy which can and must become the basis for a new integralist culture." The tricky part, even if we agree there is a distinct quality worth supporting in an "integral culture," is that we have only a vague sense of what that is to look like. It is too new on the planet. Also, there will be all due resistance to "integralist culture" formations (groups) because they have in the past history been not all that wonderful and often associated in political terms with a fascist, religionist, communalist, nationalist, and/or extreme unification conservative elements,[101] — not exactly what Gebser, Wilber, Sorokin, McIntosh nor myself are thinking of in a contemporary conceptualization of integral consciousness, values or culture. However, more research and writing on the politics and history behind the "integralist" movements needs to be done so a political transparency is unveiled behind these discourses that infect all things integral. That aside, like anything else, *integral*, in its contemporary framing in this book, can also be abused or mis-used. That is why a *critical* integral theory and practice is recommended, which critiques itself continuously for hidden ideologies and curriculum.

McIntosh has given a wonderful summary of integral consciousness and integral philosophy and its uses for the future. He has shown that an integral spirituality is an outcome (if not a motivation) for the more analytical work of an integral methodology. He, like myself, is convinced that (to some degree) an integral philosophy,[102]

> . . . can provide an orienting generalization that can be used in the empirical evaluation of the different spiritual teachings [including the World's Fearlessness Teachings]. . . . This method of evaluation is found by looking at the 'fruits' of those teachings: Do they *vanquish fear* and promote compassion? Do they increase morality and loving-kindness? Do they result in evolution? [italics added for emphasis]

May we take those evaluative questions, and others, forward to look at the field of Education (Chapter Four) and Social Action (Chapter Five). However, in the next chapter we must enter into a more thorough and integrally-sensitive analysis of the seven basic forms of which the spirit of fearlessness takes place *via* interpretive perspectives on a spectrum—and as they have been spoken, written, and enacted for millenium as FME or The World's Fearlessness Teachings.

Notes

1. Ken Wilber, in my studies, was first to point out this distinction in his early writing between "science" and "scientism." Ken Wilber, *Eye to Eye: The Quest for the New Paradigm* (Garden City, NY: Anchor Press/Doubleday, 1983), 20-25, 28-31, 46.

2. Kenneth R. Beittel, *Alternatives for Art Education Research: Inquiry into the Making of Art* (Dubuque, IO: Wm. C. Brown, 1973), 1.

3. Webster's New Collegiate Dictionary, *New Collegiate Dictionary* (Toronto, ON: Thomas Allen and Sons, Ltd., 1981), 595.

4. Jeanne Segal, *Living Beyond Fear: A Tool for Transformation* (Hollywood, CA: Newcastle, 1984), 88.

5. Ken Wilber, *Up From Eden: A Transpersonal View of Human Evolution* (Garden City, NY: Anchor Press/Doubleday, 1981), ix.

6. The ethical and spiritual Hindu (Sanskrit) view of "fearlessness" is as one of the cardinal virtues: "Fearlessness is the fruit of perfect Self Realization—that is, the recovery of nonduality" (according to *Brihadaranyaka Upanishad 1.4.2*). Retrieved November 11, 2007 from http://www.experiencefestival.com/a/Abhaya/id/57934.

7. David C. Korten, *The Great Turning: From Empire to Earth Community*. San Francisco, CA: Barrett-Koehler and Bloomfield, CN: Kumarian Press, 2005), 48-49.

8. T. Zeldin, *An Intimate History of Humanity* (NY: HarperCollins, 1994), 169.

9. Fiona Mackie, *The Status of Everyday Life: A Sociological Excavation of the Prevailing Framework of Perception* (London: Routledge, 1985), 164-181.

10. *Discourse* has many different meanings depending on the discipline and context in which it is being defined and used. Throughout this book I prefer the following Foucauldian conceptualizations: "*Discourse* then, consists of recurrent statements and wordings across texts (Foucault, 1972)," as Luke has defined it. And "discourses are not simple groupings of utterances or statements, but consist of utterances which have meaning, force [power], and effect within a social context," as Mills described. A. Luke, "Text and Discourse in Education: An Introduction to Critical Discourse Analysis," ed. M. W. Apple, in *Review of Research in Education, 21*(1995-96), 15. S. Mills, *Discourse* (NY: Routledge, 1997), 13.

11. Sam Keen, *The Passionate Life: Stages of Loving* (NY: Harper and Row, 1983).

12. Although much could and should be said about *adultism* there is little space here to pursue this. It is usually a label for the 'normalized' oppression of young people (and children) by dominant adults in a society. It is invisible to most of us and only recognized usually in extreme "child abuse" cases. It is co-relational with fearism. My use at this point in the text is in regard to how the very model (assumptions) that we adults have about "adulthood" (or equivalently "human") as the end of the line of development is oppressive. It is oppressive to further development and evolution of our species; and thus, Keen's *post-adult* (or equivalently post-human) perspective is heartily embraced from a critical integral perspective.

13. One could read any of Robert Kegan's books, but a more general and convincing work to support the hierarchical model of development (with higher stages of maturation), I refer readers to Wilber's comment: "For example, in the widely regarded text *Higher Stages of Human Development* (edited by Charles Alexander and Ellen Langer), the works of thirteen top developmental psychologists—including Piaget, Kohlberg, Carol Gilligan, Kurt Fischer, Howard Gardner, Karl Pribram, and Robert Kegan—are presented, and of those thirteen, all of them except one or two present models that are hierarchical in part, including [the feminist] Gilligan for female development. These conclusions are based on massive amounts of experimental data, not merely on theoretical speculations. That is not to say that all of these developmental lines are *only* hierarchical; many of their features are not. . . . But crucial aspects of all of them appear to be hierarchical in important ways. Furthermore, there is a general consensus that no matter how different the developmental lines might be, not only do most of them unfold holarchically, *they do so through the same set of general waves* [stages], which include: a physical/sensorimotor/preconventional stage, a concrete actions/conventional rules stage, and a more abstract, formal, postconventional stage." Ken Wilber, *Integral Psychology: Consciousness, Spirit, Psychology, Therapy* (Boston, MA: Shambhala, 2000), 29.

14. Eckhart Tolle, "Women Embody Enlightenment" (excerpt from *The Power of Now*), *Common Ground*, March 2008. Tolle wrote, "The number of women who are now approaching the fully conscious state already exceeds that of men and will be growing even faster in the years to come." Although that may be true, and I suspect it is, that achievement of a "fully conscious state" does not necessarily mean they have (or will

have) the best critical integral theory and practices to bring to a global fear manage-ment/education agenda as I propose in this book. The same would apply to men reaching such a state. Wilber, in much of his later writing, offers good critique on the difference between achievement of "state of consciousness" and "stage of development" in which "states" are actualized individually and in cultures collectively.

15. *Fearism* is the systematic (often unconscious) production and perpetration of fear ('fear') on others for the purpose of obtaining power for abusive control, punish-ment, and manipulation of people, other species, and the environment. Fearism, as a process and discourse hegemony, creates an experience of fear that is normalized and naturalized, whereby the term "fear" is skewed to mean whatever those in elite power positions, who control much of the originary fear production (and its "management"), want it to mean, and whatever they want to teach others it means. Fearism is dedicated to keeping the cultural matrix of 'fear' operative and relatively invisible, while preventing any systematic critique and exposure of the real dynamics of fear ('fear') and fearism. With fearism, you don't even feel or see the fear anymore—that is, if you don't look deep enough (fearlessly enough). You won't read that in your average textbook on fear and its management. You won't read that in the therapists office or hear that from the psychia-trist at the clinic or priest at the pulpit. Fearism is attempting right now as you and I communicate, to erase (or skew, diss) any memory of this book's contents, and mostly to erase (or skew, diss) the author's name and who wrote this about fearism. Why? Because a serious critique of our current FME (i.e., knowledge about fear and fearlessness) and fearism itself is at the foreground of the communication here. If you have seen *The Ma-trix* sci-fi film (1999-2003) by the Wachowski Bros. you'll get what I mean about how the Agents are everywhere in society (i.e., in The Matrix or what I call 'Fear' Matrix) trying to "delete" any hackers who attempt to "awaken" others from the enslavement to The Program (i.e., Fear's Empire). Universal 'paranoia' intended, but only for dramatic effect. I'm not trying to make a 'mountain out of a mole hill' either. If you can under-stand the concepts of classism, racism, or sexism (as examples of oppression), then you need only apply that understanding analogously to fearism (*cum* terrorism).

16. S. McIntosh, *Integral Consciousness and the Future of Evolution: How the Inte-gral Worldview is Transforming Politics, Culture and Spirituality* (St. Paul, MN: Paragon House, 2007), 2.

17. There are many different definitions of "critical theory," some more radical than others. However, this does not necessarily mean "critical thinking" or necessarily even "critical philosophy" as they are popularly used terms. Rather, I am using a philosophical but highly political (and particularly sociological) definition of critical theory (somewhat more "Continental" and European etc. than American traditional), of which Wilber's work is embedded (see the Frankfurt School of critical theory and its latest evolution in the writings of Jürgen Habermas). Most basically such a theory emphasizes "power rela-tions" and challenges the very structure of an oppressive society (dominators and subor-dinates). Again, I remind readers of my take: Wilber's earlier pre-1997 writing is more richly and accurately "critical theory" than after that period. The unfortunate tendency of contemporary "integralists" is to attempt to be advocates of a 'value-neutral' methodol-ogy for integration and wholeness, as if the integral approach is so—it is definitely not. My caution points to the political hidden agenda (ideologies) (see Endnote 83) that lurk in all integral theory and philosophy. Readers interested in critiques and new suggestions for a critical integral theory and integral critical theory ought to consult excellent papers by: Daniel Gustav Anderson, "Of Synthesis and Surprises: Toward a Critical Integral Theory," *Integral Review*, 3 (2006). Retrieved November, 1, 2008 from http://integral-

review.org/current_issue/documents/; and Martin Beck Matustík, "Towards an Integral Critical Theory of the Present Age," *Integral Review*, 5 (2007): 227-239.

18. Ibid., 2.

19. In terms of spiritual faith commitments, basically McIntosh is more (Western) "Christian" and Wilber is more "Zen Buddhist-Hinduist" (Eastern). Thus, McIntosh believes Wilber mixes his religion with his philosophy in "bad faith," and McIntosh attempts to pull those apart and keep philosophy where it ought to be ("pure") and what it does best and leave religion/spirituality to religious faith commitments of individuals and groups and/or to theology. Of course, neither Wilber nor McIntosh (or any integral philosopher) would deny the intimate relationality between philosophy and spirituality. It seems to come down to an issue of debate about how one defines "spiritual" (Spirit) and "philosophy" (*Philosophia*)—and that's where I have difficulties with McIntosh's clean distinction (and likely Wilber would not agree with McIntosh on that point as well).

20. Ibid., 227.

21. A conceptualization of *"integral culture"* appeared in Charles Johnston's marvelous (and too often ignored) integral philosophy and theory book (1986). He also had a community of people living and studying his work (i.e., an integral sub-culture). It is the earliest mentioning I'm aware of among contemporary integral thinkers. It is obvious that McIntosh ignores it and prefers to suggest that integral philosophy and theory never really got going until the "late 1990s." McIntosh is not correct on that point, unless he means got "popularized" in certain 'circles' in the late 1990s. See C. Johnston, *The Creative Imperative: A Four-dimensional Theory of Human Growth and Planetary Evolution* (Berkeley, CA: Celestial Arts, 1986), 92 [originally copyrighted in 1984].

22. Michael Lerner, *Spirit Matters* (Hampton Roads Publications, 2000), xii.

23. McIntosh, 151-152.

24. Ibid., 159.

25. R. M. Fisher, "Fear is . . .", Technical Paper No. 16 (Vancouver, BC: In Search of Fearlessness Research Institute, 2003), 8-15.

26. McIntosh, 180. Although McIntosh doesn't give them big headliners in his book, he acknowledges that Sri Aurobindo, a guru of Hindu spirituality, and sociologist Pitrim Sorokin, (and Jean Gebser) arrived at the term "integral" "independently without knowledge of its use by others. While these three writers were not all referring to exactly the same thing, we can see how they all had a similar vision of what was to come."

27. Ibid., 191.

28. Ibid., 192.

29. Ibid., 192-193.

30. K. Wilber, *The Marriage of Sense and Soul: Integrating Science and Religion* (NY: Random House, 1998), 120-121.

31. The evolutionary concept of holism (after Jan Smuts) and *holon* (after Arthur Koestler) and *holarchy* (after Wilber) have differences but enough similarity to attract Wilber's attention (and synthesis of their work) in his earlier writing, where he wrote that they agree upon a basic generalization as theories: "'we may conclude that the psyche—like the cosmos at large—is many-layered ('pluri-dimensional'), composed of successively higher-order [hierarchical] wholes and unities and integrations'; in other words, 'the same force that produced humans from amoebas produces adults from infants [ontogeny recapitulates phylogeny].' This observation is also confirmed by modern developmental psychology, which subscribes, in whole or part, 'to the concept of stratified stages of increasing complexity.' upon which Wilber bases 'a fairly well-balanced and comprehensive model of the Spectrum of Consciousness' [similarly, I bases the model of FMSs theory]". Wilber cited in B. Reynolds, *Embracing Reality: The Integral Vision of*

Ken Wilber: A Historical Survey and Chapter-by-Chapter Guide to Wilber's Major Works (NY: Jeremy P. Tarcher/Penguin, 2004), 181. Most postmodernists throw out "hierarchies" and "deep structures" and "developmentalist models" as "Modern" or "Pre-Modern" conceptions that we must simply outgrow because of their problematics. Wilber, like myself, would agree with some of the postmodern critiques but not all. Indeed sexism (gender), classism, racism, and colonialism etc. are not often brought forward enough in Modernist and Pre-Modern theories of development. He attempts to rescue and re-integrate into a late-postmodern (or integral) approach the best findings (he calls "orienting generalizations" of truth) of Modernity (and Pre-Modernity) and their hierarchical and structuralist theories. Our use of "holistic" here is highly problematic as well, as technical complexities in definitions are a bit of a nightmare, depending on which theorist one is talking about. The other problem is that "Holistic" is sometimes used in Wilber's writing with Turquoise v-meme (FMS-8). And that complicates the critique of Wilber's view of "holistic systems" thinking (FMS-5 and 6). For the most part, readers will have to navigate this as best they can, and trust that the context of use in the main text of this book will give a relatively clear sense of use and meaning intended.

32. K. Wilber, *A Theory of Everything: An Integral Vision for Business, Politics, Science, and Spirituality* (Boston, MA: Shambhala, 2000), 2.

33. R. Slaughter, *Futures Beyond Dystopia: Creating Social Foresight* (London, UK: Routledge Farmer, 2004), 115, 113.

34. L. Howard, *Introducing Ken Wilber: Concepts for an Evolving World* (AuthorHouse, 2005), xiii.

35. B. Reynolds, *Where's Wilber At?: Ken Wilber's Integral Vision in the New Millenium* (St. Paul, MN: Paragon House, 2006), 46, 341, 350-354.

36. F. A. Ridley, *The Revolutionary Tradition in England* (National Labour Press, 1947), 190.

37. "[T]he ideas of Marx, the champion of integral revolution." L. Von Mises, *Planning for Freedom: And Other Essays and Addresses* (Libertarian Press, 1962), 94.

38. P. H. Box, *Three Master Builders and Another: Studies in Modern Revolutionary and Liberal Statesmanship* (Freeport, NY: Books for Libraries Press, 1925), 112.

39. I. B. Tikekar, *Integral Revolution: An Analytical Study of Gandhian Thought* (Sarva Seva Sangh Prakashan, 1970). War Resisters International Triennial Conference, *Liberation and Revolution: Gandhi's Challenge* (War Resisters International, 1969), 64.

40. "[Antonin] Artaud speaks in the name of what he calls an 'integral revolution,' which would not just change the social structure but would aim at 'unbalancing the actual foundations of things and the perspective on reality.' For him it would not be enough if power passed from the hands of the middle class to the working class." Artaud paraphrased and cited in D. Francois, *The Self-Destruction of the West: Critical Cultural Anthropology* (Editions Publibook, 2007), 232.

41. Breton, leading Surrealism as an art (social) movement, created a "platform of integral revolution, with an interest in psychoanalysis, investigations carried out by spiritualists and mystics, primitive rituals and myths." J. Guimón, *Art and Madness* (The Davies Group, 2006), 165.

42. S. A. Weor, *Revolution of the Dialectic: A Practical Guide to Gnostic Psychology and Meditation* (Thelema Press, 2007), 48.

43. J. Filliozat, *Religion, Philosophy, Yoga: A Selection of Articles*, trans. M. Shukla (Motilal Banarsidass, 1991), 144.

44. Wilber, using one of his fiction character's voices (from *Boomeritis*), cited in Howard, 383.

45. See K. Wilber, *Boomeritis: A Novel That Will Set You Free* (Boston, MA: Shambhala, 2002). Elsewhere, Wilber wrote, "Thus, it seems that my generation is an extraordinary mixture of greatness and narcissism, and that strange amalgam has infected almost everything we do. We don't seem content to simply have a fine new idea, we must have the new paradigm that will herald one of the greatest transformations in the history of the world. We don't really want to just recycle bottles and paper; we need to see ourselves dramatically saving the planet and saving Gaia and resurrecting the Goddess that previous generations had brutally repressed but we will finally liberate. We aren't able to tend our garden; we must be transfiguring the face of the planet in the most astonishing global awakening history has ever seen. We seem to need to see ourselves as the vanguard of something unprecedented in all of history: the extraordinary wonder of being us. . . . [an awful lot of] 'heroic self-inflation'. . . . the Culture of Narcissism is antithetical to an integral culture (because narcissistic, isolated selves strenuously resist communion)." K. Wilber, *A Theory of Everything*, 3-4. Wilber, in Endnote 1 (Chapter 10 in *Boomeritis*, Retrieved July 1, 2005 from Shambhala's website, http://wilber.shambhala.com/html/books/boomeritis/endnotes/ch10.cfm/) wrote, "So, when we say 'Boomers were the first green generation [operating FMS-6 predominantly], a significantly larger percentage of Boomers—perhaps up to 30% or 40% of them—reached the green wave as their general center of gravity. 'Center of gravity' for an individual means that the proximal self-sense is basically identified with that level (although many other developmental lines might be at other levels). Thus, for example, the stereotypical Boomer that we are discussing . . . has a cognitive line of development that is at yellow [FMS-7 maybe]; a self-sense whose center of gravity is green; numerous subpersonalities at red [FMS-3] and purple [FMS-2]; and an internal recoil against, or repression of [*via* dissociation], one's own blue [FMS-4] and orange [FMS-5] (which means that the subpersonalities at blue and orange are internally alienated and therefore *projected* onto others where they are aggressively attacked)."

46. Ibid., 397. Wilber here is using one of his fiction character's voices.

47. According to Wilber, the integrative sophistication of "integral" "did not really start to come to light until the closing decades of the 20th century and the dawn of the Integral Age." K. Wilber, *Integral Spirituality: A Startling New Role for Religion in the Modern and Postmodern World* (Boston, MA: Integral Books/Shambhala, 2006), 282.

48. *Boomeritis*, (Endnotes: Chapter 10; Endnote 1) http://wilber.shambhala.com/html/books/boomeritis/endnotes/ch10.cfm/. Wilber wrote here that "no generation is simply 'at' a level [stage] of development, just as no society is simply 'at' a level. When we say 'Boomers were the first green generation' or 'Millenials might be the first yellow generation,' these are extremely simplistic generalizations. In order to grasp the demographics more accurately, you need a 'phase-4' model of quadrants, levels, lines, states, and types. You can then analyze much more carefully the distribution of consciousness in each individual, culture, generation, society, species, and so on. . . . [the Boomeritis] psychograph is quite typical[ly]—a green alliance with red/purple in hatred of blue/orange, and all the interior grandiosity and outward rebellion that would ensue—. . . . (This does not rule out subsequent psychological dynamics: e.g., once boomeritis has alienated its own healthy blue, it often compensates by reactivating a morbidly rigid blue system—we saw this with the Green Inquisitors. But all of that is subsequent to the basic psychograph of the GREEN/red pathology [i.e., boomeritis dis-ease and what he also calls "Mean Green Meme"]." Wilber, like Don Beck (Spiral Dynamics) has said often that "Green" (in its pathological forms) has been one of the most destructive forces on the planet in the last forty years or so. It does everything possible to attack any worldview or perspective that is in the 2nd-tier or 3rd-tier. In political terms, Wilber has examined this

as the "Green liberals" problem, where classically the "liberal of the Enlightenment was free Left (free, in that individual freedoms were championed in the face of the herd mentality and ethnocentric religion; Left, in that the cause of human suffering is corrupt and repressive social institutions; all human are born equal, but society treats them unfairly. This free-Left orientation was thus often a revolutionary politics—if society is unjust, get rid of it, which France and America did). Civil libertarians carry on this free-Left orientation, arguing the free rights of individuals over almost any challenge. Green liberals, are almost always order Left [not free-Left]: they want their values—whether multicultural, feminist, or otherwise—imposed on society as a whole, through both education and governmental action. This is why order Right and order Left have often aligned forces to make the strangest bedfellows. For example, some conservatives and some radical feminists have both called for bans on pornography: what they have in common is their willingness to impose their values on others; which overrides their liberal and conservative differences. It has been generally noted that liberalism started out free Left—arguing that government should stay out of the lives of individuals—and slowly tended to become order Left—arguing that big government must interfere with individuals on a daily basis, for moral reasons. . . . However, just as clearly, order Left—in addition to its healthy and important contributions—is also the major home of boomeritis (post-conventional green pluralism infected with preconventional narcissism), and boomeritis wants to interfere with peoples' lives just for the power of it all. Order Left has thus become the home of boomeritis feminism, boomeritis multiculturalism, boomeritis ecology (aka ecofascism), and so on [pc politics]." K. Wilber, *A Theory of Everything*, 164. We see here in these quotes Wilber at work with his cultural *therapia*, of which he most clearly "attacks" (especially in his pre-1997 work) and calls for integral thinkers to work at cleaning-up their own internalized Boomeritis (emotional narcissism). This is a huge topic beyond what can be covered here adequately in a few endnotes. The relevance of most of this comes with the FMS-6 (Green, Sensitive) and its tendency to try to dominate all other FMSs and assume it has the only psychological and moral corrective to fear. This author takes the position that until FMS-6 is willing to correct its own "Boomeritis" biases and adopt a FMS-7 to some degree, there is little reason to expect any significant change on this planet in terms of improving FME.

49. Retrieved April 17, 2007 from the *Integral Naked* website http://www. integral-naked.com.

50. Excerpt from Michael Zimmerman, *Contesting Earth's Future: Radical Ecology and Postmodernity* (Berkeley, CA: University of California Press, 1997), 198.

51. R. M. Fisher, "Postmodern Developmental Philosopher *Par Excellence*: Ken Wilber's Role in Education, Part I (Introducing Ken Wilber)," paper submitted, 2007, to *Interchange: A Quarterly Journal of Education*.

52. R. M. Fisher, "Wilber and Fear Management Theory," Technical Paper No. 17 (Vancouver, BC: In Search of Fearlessness Research Institute, 2004).

53. D. Beck, (interviewed by Jessica Roemischer) "The Never-ending Upward Quest," *What is Enlightenment?* Fall/Winter (2002), 124.

54. Spiral Dynamics Integral (or SDi) has been a major part of the Wilber-Beck integration and integral paradigm and teaching; albeit, they have disagreed on several aspects and more or less parted ways in recent years. Spiral Dynamics theory has an integral consciousness structure/perspective/approach especially when it comes to analyzing cultural worldviews (and v-memes).

55. See Maslow in regard to the distinction between people who operate primarily from need-values of ego [1st-tier] and Being-values [2nd-tier] that transcend the ego. Abraham Maslow, *Toward a Psychology of Being* (NY: Van Nostrand Reinhold, 1968).

See Maslow's distinction on a more collective (paradigmatic) level in his critique of knowledge and science: where he identifies "deficit-motivated" and "safety-need motivated" and "ego-centered" research [1st-tier] and "growth-motivated" and "problem-centered" research [2nd-tier]. Abraham Maslow, *The Psychology of Science: A Reconnaissance* (NY: Harper and Row, 1966), 20-32. According to Brussat and Brussat, "In his book *Creativity in Self-actualizing People,* Maslow writes: 'It seemed to me that much boiled down to the relative absence of fear. They ["actualizers"] seemed to be less afraid of what other people would say or demand or laugh at. . . . Perhaps more important, was their lack of fear of their insides, of their impulses, emotions, thoughts.'" Frederic Brussat, and Mary Ann Brussat (n.d.). Retrieved March 22, 2007 from http://www.spirituality andpractice.com/films/films.php?id=5249.

56. The more complex nuance here is that fear management is not just defensive or retractive (i.e., creating "walls" or "barriers" or coping mechanisms to prevent the overwhelming of the biopsychosocial systems of living things, as Freud in part identified "defense mechanisms" as essential to some stability for the living system—albeit, they can go overboard to excess and cause neurosis and psychosis). TMT (terror management theory) from social psychology is based on Ernest Becker's theoretical work in the 1950s-70s which focuses on the existential predicament of the human organism and the notion that all culture is a defense mechanism against that assault on "self-esteem" from a place of vulnerability of the organism before the consequences of a sometimes hostile environment and ultimate mortality. TMT explores the "immortality projects" that are created through cultural devices, such as worldviews, values, belief, symbols etc. The connection of TMT with understanding "evil" is worth examining as FME develops in the next decades ahead. Two excellent resources on TMT or the DVD *Flight from Death: The Quest for Immortality* mentioned in the previous chapter and T. Pyszczynski, S. Solomon, and J. Greenberg, *In the Wake of 9/11: The Psychology of Terror* (Washington, DC: American Psychological Association, 2002). For a more in depth reading of TMT from an "integral" perspective see R. M. Fisher, "Toward an Integral Terror Management Theory: Use of the Wilber-Combs Lattice," Technical Paper No. 24 (Vancouver, BC: In Search of Fearlessness Research Institute, 2007).

57. McIntosh, 33.

58. Ibid., 34-35.

59. Ibid., 37.

60. The 18 parameters McIntosh uses are: (1) Perceived life conditions, (2) Worldview and values, (3) Contribution to the spiral, (4) Pathology, (5) Contemporary examples, (6) Organizational structures, (7) Exemplary leaders, (8) Estimated percent of world population, (9) Estimated percent of wealth and political power, (10) Techno-economic mode of production, (11) Key technologies, (12) Type of medicine, (13) The true, (14) The beautiful, (15) The good, (16) Average neurological activation, (17) Transitional triggers, (18) Other names for this stage.

61. Probably, more accurately, the 'Fear' Barrier 1 is open and porous, and consciousness at FMS-1 flows easily back n' forth; at later stages of FMS-2 this "return" to adual is largely repressed, denied, "walled off," except in cases of psychotic breaks or psychotropic drug-induced states of consciousness (i.e., regressions).

62. Ibid., 36.

63. Ibid., 39.

64. See Rick Fields, *The Code of the Warrior: In History, Myth, and Everyday Life* (NY: HarperCollins, 1991).

65. Ibid., 40.

66. 'Him' in this passage refers to Allah. My colleague, a woman educator born and raised in Pakistan, also added to this claim saying "I do worry though. I am only human." With a thorough analysis of this secular and spiritual discourse of FMS-4, it would show links to an interpretation or FME that is highly dependent on conformity to a superior power/being/authority (often paternalistic); see Hobbes and Middle-eastern religions where this FMS is very prevalent in their discourse. My colleague here was Pakistanian, albeit, raised under the British schooling system. Her desire for "fearless" (which is a facsimile but not FMS-9 as used in her quote) is part of a long traditional pedagogy and socialization in a lot of East Indian cultures, as one anonymous speaker suggested: "India and its culture have always adored the spirit of fearlessness and heroism, and infused the same in people." Retrieved September 19, 2004 from http://www.ganehaspeaks.com /blog_Dussehra_Its-time-to-worship-heroism-and-fearlessness_519.jsp.

67. Ibid., 42-43.

68. Ibid., 44.

69. Ibid., 44.

70. Ibid., 48.

71. "A *fear management system* is a basic 'habit' that has evolved in humanity for the purpose of handling a particular kind of worldspace, worldview, consciousness perspective, and so forth. FMS-5 is half-way along this developmental or evolutionary spectrum. A much larger document would be required to do justice to this FMS and the theory behind it. . . . Like all FMSs, the FMS-5 is valuable, powerful, and inherently limited; having gained its strength from all the FMSs (0-4) before it. FMS-5 has evolved from FMSs 0-4.... FMS-4 (Blue v-meme) is organized around a strict hierarchy often associated with Religion (or religious values and morals)—that is, "right vs. wrong" and anything that threatens the religious/moral structure of the institution (or governing body) is an assault to its sovereign and unchallengeable authority. FMS-4 is typical of organizational power, in order to manage fear, that creates a lot of fear within it. The primary premodern fear in the Judeo-Christian and Islamic traditions is "Fear of God" as a basic orienting philosophy and organizational (emotional) ethos. This means fear authority. Fear those in power over you who are of the status of the "Divine" (or "Godly" or "Good"). Such a structure can be utilized in secular State organizing as well, or you can find it in a family system where the traditional (most often man/father) authority is passed on through the FMS-4 design. The Tradition, Authority, Religion, State, will tell you what is right and what is wrong, and never shall there be any gray areas between.... That's the basic quick picture. FMS-4 gives most people who want it (and/or are forced to live in it), the *security* (perceived or real) they need to *not* feel so afraid of the world, and afraid of themselves, and afraid of rebellion or revolution to authority, etc. But the rule is "Fear God" or "Fear the State," or "Fear Other," first and foremost—as the condition of the 'social contract'—then, the God or State will protect you from others (and all threats to your well being)—at least, that's the 'logic' of FMS-4. The reality is that FMS-4 presupposes and reinforces that the Traditional Authority gets most all the police, soldiers, weapons, and economic power to incarcerate and/or destroy those who are a threat to its (Security) SYSTEM." FMS-5 is driven, in part, by a powerful arising spirit of fearlessness (in existential terms), whereby there is a refusal to be controlled by fear of others, and fear and terror within the self and its vulnerabilities before a cosmos that seems unmeaningful and uncaring toward any particular individual organism. The transition to FMS-5 is long and involves many powerful existential (and some spiritual) thinkers: in the 17th century Pascal, Spinoza, Hobbes, and in 19th century Kierkegaard, Nietzsche (influenced by Schelling and Hegel, respectively), Fichte—and into the 20th century with Schleiermacher and Heidegger, Sartre, Camus, Freud, Kafka (the latter, forming the basis

of FMS-6b). One example of the powerful potential (symbolically) in the FMS-5 declaration comes in statements from Voltaire and "no more myths" or Nietzsche and "God is dead" (the latter meaning "Fear of God is dead." See R. Michael Fisher, "Conceptualizing a Fearlessness Philosophy: Existential Philosophy and a Genealogy of Fear Management System-5," Technical Paper No. 23 (Vancouver, BC: In Search of Fearlessness Institute, 2007), 9-11.

72. McIntosh, 50.

73. Ibid., 50.

74. Ibid., 56.

75. Ibid., 56.

76. Ibid., 56.

77. Ibid., 56.

78. For example, U. Beck, *Risk Society: Towards a New Modernity*, trans. Mark Ritter (London, UK: Sage, 1992). U. Beck, *World Risk Society* (Cambridge, UK: Polity Press, 1999).

79. F. Furedi, *Therapy Culture: Cultivating Vulnerability in an Uncertain Age* (London: Routledge, 2004).

80. C. Sunstein, *Laws of Fear: Beyond the Precautionary Principle* (Cambridge, UK: Cambridge University Press, 2005).

81. C. Robin, *Fear: The History of a Political Idea* (NY: Oxford University Press, 2004).

82. McIntosh, 60.

83. Ibid., 82-83 "Wilber refers to this emergent capacity as 'vision-logic,' which he describes as follows: 'Where the formal-mind [modernist consciousness] establishes higher and creative relationships, vision-logic [post-formal-mind] establishes networks of those relationships. The point is to place each proposition alongside numerous others, so as to be able to see, or 'to vision,' how the truth or falsity of any one proposition would affect the truth or falsity of all the others. Such panoramic or vision-logic apprehends a mass network or ideas, how they influence each other, what their relationships are. It is thus the beginning of a truly higher-order synthesizing capacity, of making connections, relating truths, coordinating ideas, integrating concepts.' According to Wilber, vision-logic represents an integration of intellectual capacity with intuition in a way that brings together the body and the mind so as to produce this new ability to recognize relationships and approach problems with enhanced creativity. In my experience, this new epistemological capacity of integral consciousness can be best described as 'dialectical evaluation,' because unlike reason or logic, this new ability is centered in *volition* rather than *cognition*. That is, the new insights provided by 'vision-logic' come about through the use of our *will*—it's a process of evaluation informed by head and heart—as opposed to the exercise of reason and logic, which is more analytical and strictly cognitive. The process of integrally informed dialectical evaluation recognizes how conflicting values and worldviews actually work together within a larger evolutionary system, mutually supporting each other in opposition, in a manner that can be compared to the function of a tension strut in an architectural structure. Through dialectical evaluation we can see how the elements [e.g., FMSs] of any evolutionary system work together in their mutually supporting roles of thesis-antithesis-synthesis. However, it is only by appropriately *valuing* each element of the system that we can actually correctly perceive its crucial function within the system as a whole. This involves more than simply 'weighing the alternatives' and assigning different values to various components; it is a way of understanding and appreciating that requires an intuitive sympathy achieved only by entering into the alternative perspectives that generate the opposing values. When we look at evo-

lutionary processes without this ability, all we can see is conflict; but when we come to recognize the unfolding of larger internal structures through time, we can begin to better appreciate how they fit together within a larger purpose, and this allows us to engage these structures more creatively. Recognizing this, Robert Kegan [developmental psychologist] actually defines integral consciousness as 'the capacity to see conflict as a signal of our over-identification with a single system.'" McIntosh also points out that this integral ability "relies on the expanded vertical perspective provided by integral consciousness. This enhanced epistemological capacity is very real and very powerful." This extra long quote is worthy of study, and one ought to read Gebser, Wilber, and McIntosh directly on these topics. The point McIntosh is making is a good one and highlights "integral consciousness" (FMS-7) is a major location (epistemology) for doing healthy and sustainable *conflict management/education* (or as I mentioned earlier in this text, the Domination-Conflict-Fear-Violence dynamic is the essential form in which to analyze, if we are ever to figure out "non-violence" and move toward building societies based on it). The other point of the long quote is to show how *structure-functionalist* in sociopolitical orientation McIntosh is; or, more precisely, how his articulation of vision-logic is ideologically functionalist (in contrast to critical or conflict theory). My critiques throughout the text attempt to offer a bare basics toward a more *integral conflict theory* view and more radical politics. McIntosh, typical of so many "integral" (spiritual) thinkers today, brings in FMS-8 (if not 9) to justify and explain the nature of conflict on the planet (and among differing worldviews, etc.). This can be rather glib, bloodless, 'new agey' (e.g., sounding like "appreciative inquiry" *a la* David Cooperrider et al.) and somewhat disconnected or dissociated from real 'ground battles' going on (in all four quadrants and across the discourses and v-memes of reality)—and thus, downplaying the view of the Sacred Warrior archetype (or Outlaw) appropriate to FMS-7 (Yellow, Integral Consciousness). The structural-functionalist cannot let go of seeing that the 'System' is basically all working fine—just a few tweaks needed here and there and that all the tensions (conflicts) are really part of the dialectical 'play' of the cosmos (System). Structural-functionalists generally are white bourgeois folks or upper class and relatively 'very comfortable' (extraordinarily privileged) in their every day living conditions compared to how most of the world lives and thinks. The structural-functionalist will avoid notions of a 'Fear' Matrix or any other theoretical and deeply ethical framework that postulates something that is 'near' conspiratorial (i.e., oppressive systemically, like the Matrix of Domination or Wilber's "Atman Project" which I have called 'Fear' Project in evolutionary development of consciousness). I acknowledge that such a conflict theory (critical) view is in the minority amongst most integral (spiritual) thinkers and theorists. Even Wilber is overly structural functionalist at times in his post-1996 writing and lectures. A better (or balancing reading of the *critical integral method* (epistemology of vision-logic), in part, is found through my transfiguration of the meaning of v-memes, Kosmic habits, etc. *via* FMSs theory but also can be found in a lesser radical version in Jack Crittenden's, "Foreword: What is the Meaning of 'Integral,'" in K. Wilber, *The Eye of Spirit: An Integral Vision for a World Gone Slightly Mad* (Boston, MA: Shambhala, 1997), vii-xii. On a technical point: those who believe I am overly dichotomizing "structural-functionalism" vs. "conflict theory," may I offer the research knowledge I have collected that many sociological theorists and others have tried to "blend" these two oppositional positionings (*via* synthesis). Those attempts in literature reviews pale in doing justice to the "conflict theory" (perspective). Randall Collin's offers the best argumentation on this—that is, concluding the two views are incompatible—meaning, they are *not* blendable (i.e., to be mushed into a heap or mix of distortive eclecticism). The 'include and transcend' rhetoric and practice of most "integral" theorists (and standard vision-logic definitions) has to be taken very critically in this regard, as usually there is not near enough vigilance applied. Unfortunately, this is all too complex to go further with, even though it is very important politically (and epistemologically). "Integralists" will continue to be challenged (if not rejected outright by many critical theorists) as being "too conservative" politically for a very long time, unless they (i.e., most "integralists") acknowledge this issue (and bias), which "integralists" tend to skirt around. Some of this political problematic is discussed again in Chapter Five, where the "critical theory" tradition (and Conflict Tradition) need to be better integrated in the latest forms of critical integral theory (cf. "spiritual-by-pass" phenomena). FMSs theory is one way to do this. Building an Integralist Coalition, especially one that embraces (realistically and in a healthy way) critical (conflict) theory and radical revolutionary (and evolutionary) politics is one sub-textual aim of this book. Of course, no "integral" theory is going to please all people of all political stripes. I support diversity of views too—but not if we don't talk to each other about our differences. Randall Collins, *Four Sociological Traditions* (NY: Oxford University Press, 1994).

84. Mike Davis, *The Ecology of Fear: Los Angeles and the Imagination of Disaster* (NY: Vintage, 1999). Technically this is not a 2nd-tier perspective or FMS-7 analysis, but more a FMS-6b which is barely starting to awaken to the absurdity of FMS-6a (and thus, offers itself a nascent "victim" critique).

85. McIntosh, 84. In particular, with the three primary value spheres (according to McIntosh): "*The true*: harmonization of science and spirituality; the evolutionary significance of values. *The beautiful*: nature; the arts of each level in their emergent phase; the unification of extreme contrasts. *The good*: evolution; the prime directive." The last notion of "the good" is very important, but too involved of a theory to discuss here in any depth. Wilber has called this the "Basic Moral Imperative" (in *Sex, Ecology and Spirituality*) and Don Beck, Wilber, etc. have called it "The Prime Directive" of which ultimately there is a transpersonal recognition of the *telos* of Spirit itself in the evolution of consciousness (what I would call "spirit of fearlessness") toward the becoming of a greater moral planetary intelligence (see also FMS-8 Turquoise).

86. Ibid., 84.

87. Ibid., 85-86.

88. Ibid., 84.

89. Robert Kegan, *In Over Our Heads: The Mental Demands of Modern Life* (Cambridge, MA: Harvard University Press, 1998).

90. Ibid., 92-93. McIntosh also discusses, with a welcomed sensitivity and experience, the foibles of integral and its pleasures. He tends, in contrast to myself, to play-up the positives—for example, "So you may ask: What does it really feel like to have integral consciousness? Well, there is a feeling of amused anticipation, like knowing a big secret that's about to be revealed; there's a feeling of pleasure associated with a sense of wonder—a feeling that must have been felt by the early modernists when they realized just how powerful human reason, the scientific method, and constitutional democracy could be. And with integral consciousness there is a feeling of conviction, a sense of confidence in 'the way forward' that arises from the new truths of the integral worldview. This new feeling of confidence is accompanied by a sense of optimism about the inevitability of evolution, and as this feeling of confidence matures, it can be recognized as a form of moral courage. But perhaps the most significant feeling associated with integral consciousness is the way it makes you feel about other people. The practice of integral consciousness definitely results in an increased sense of compassion, sympathy, and respect for those about whom you previously felt consternated. However, accompanying this enlarged feeling of compassion is also a new sense of realism about the inherent

limitations of those who dwell in these older worldviews. I have a direct personal experience of integral consciousness, and thus I know that it is a historically significant new level because I can see how extremely useful it is. Yet integral consciousness is more than just a tool for problem solving; it's an identity-providing platform for cultural allegiance, a worldview that invites our passion and our loyalty. As integral practitioners we have to see ourselves as ambassadors of the future." Two concepts of focus for McIntosh (characteristic of contemporary American "integralists") in the above quote are "moral courage" and "ambassadors"—these are typically (and arguably) more "Green" (FMS-6b discourses) than "Yellow," as readers will see our differences throughout the text in interpreting Integral and self-proclaimed "integralists" (FMS-7).

91. Apparently, Wilber talks about "How fearlessness grows as your sense of self expands" as one topic on his massive lectures from his 10-DVD set (*Kosmic Consciousness*, Sounds True, Inc., ©2003). At $99.95 retail, I have not yet been able to afford purchasing this.

92. McIntosh, 93.

93. Ibid., 95.

94. Ibid., 94.

95. According to Brad Reynolds "The culmination of years of research, the pre/trans fallacy is perhaps one of Wilber's most novel theories clarified through the lens of transpersonal psychology." Basically, a pre/trans fallacy, in Wilberian terms, is a fallacy of interpretation that conflates the "lower" with the "higher"—based on an interpretation from the "middle" when it examines the "higher" and sees it as the "lower." It confuses developmental distinctions because the "middle" position tends to believe it is highest (e.g., of FMS-6 seeing all FMSs above it as really below it). See B. Reynolds, *Embracing Reality*, 27-28 and several other pages).

96. McIntosh, 130.

97. See Wilber, *Sex, Ecology and Spirituality (Vol. 1)*; Chapter 8 "The Depths of the Divine," pp. 279-316.

98. Robert M. Pirsig, *Zen and the Art of Motorcycle Maintenance* (NY: Bantam Books, 1976), 279.

99. See for example Paul H. Ray, "The Rise of Integral Culture," *Noetic Science Review*, #37 (1996). Retrieved August 11, 2007 from http://www.noetic.org/publications/ /review/issue37/r37_Ray.html.

100. Excerpt from Barry V. Johnston, *Pitrim A. Sorokin: An Intellectual Biography* (Lawrence, KS: University Press of Kansas, 1995), 241.

101. For example in the 1930s and the formation of the "Integralist Party" in Brazil, not unlike the same ideological forms of fascism growing in Europe at the time. See Todd L. Edwards, *Brazil: A Global Studies Handbook* (ABC-CLIO, 2007), 56.

102. Ibid., 130.

3

WORLD'S FEARLESSNESS TEACHINGS:
Managing The Human Fear Problem

World's Fearlessness Teachings- any teaching, East or West, North or South, sacred or secular, oral or written, published or unpublished, immature or mature, which attempts to manage fear better, is a valid expression of the spirit of fearlessness and its role in the emancipation of human consciousness and society.

Human Fear Problem- the generic term and phenomena which involves many of human being's worst problems that are traceable to a source in fear ('fear') —that is, how well we do fear management/education.

Culture of Fear- is the attempt to manage fear and ends up creating more fear not less because the "cultural" system(s) which shape the fear management/education are themselves fear-based and usually do not recognize it or they deny it.

Introduction: The Fear Problem

To be clear: whatever humans agree or disagree upon in regard to the nature and role of fear and its problematics, the human Fear Problem is a fear management/education (FME) problem. Complex as a conceptualization of these matters are, the above generic (and insufficient) definitions are at least a place to start. They make critical distinctions in our 'normal' language and theorizing for a 21st century global FME. On a different day the above definitions would likely change (evolve), often extending into labyrinthal conceptualizations or even new angles and new terms included. That dynamic quality is because of two main reasons: (1) the nature of fear ('fear') is constantly changing (evolving) and can be seen from multiple-developmental perspectives and, (2) my mind is relatively full and whirling with all the research I've collected, so I can spin-off as many versions as needed, depending on the intention for that day or the problem-at-hand to be solved. The dynamic relativity of the definitional constructions is highly contextual, not fixed from a monocular single-perspective. Obviously, there is a highly subjective element of interpretation involved. Thus, if you are looking for only objective fixed "scientific" definitions here (or a nice clean Glossary), you are going to be disappointed. I am more interested in the meaning (power discourse) of things than mere objective and/or abstract (politically-neutered) definitions, especially when it comes to the study of fear ('fear') and fearlessness. At the same time, the basic definitions above would remain much the same over time, and thus, a workable generalization (or hypothesis) with subjective-objective aspects and individual-collective aspects, which can be used for some interesting results.

The rather awkward introduction to this chapter is underwritten by the epistemological theory of Wilber's AQAL[1] (four quadrant) basic model of integral knowledge and knowing. However, my framing of fear ('fear') goes much further than Wilber's or anyone else's that I have found in the past 20 years of research. Yet, ultimately, I craft these rather loose definitions (meanings) from the perspective of a postmodern transdisciplinary fearologist and integralist, attempting to achieve a perspective on fear ('fear') from a "fearless standpoint" or FMS-9 (i.e., including but transcending the perspective of fear ('fear'), fearism, the culture of fear, Fear's Empire, and what I call the 'Fear' Matrix and the 'Fear' Project(ion)).

With all due limitations and imperfections, this new theory of fear management is built from 2nd-tier Fear Management System-7 (Yellow, Integral, Fearlessness), described in the previous chapter. It seems one of the greatest problems of human knowledge about FME is that it has *not* demanded we research and understand fear from the point of view of fearlessness (i.e., including but transcending perspectives from bravery or courage in 1st-tier FMSs prior to FMS-7)—rather, than constructing most of our knowledge of fear from the point of view of fear ('fear') itself. I am thus positing (ever so briefly and grossly) that: 99.99% of people argue that the greatest Fear Problem we have is merely "excess fear" or "fear of death" etc. The integral fearologist rather, argues that our greatest suffering due to the Fear Problem arises because of partial, inadequate, pathological, and often distortive knowledge about fear and fearlessness (i.e., FME). Of course such distortive knowledge is related to attitudes, beliefs, values and worldviews (see Chapter Two). Such is my postmodern educator's slant with its Foucauldian edge, toward a critical analysis of *power-knowledge-fear* dynamics. The late Michel Foucault's (1926-1984) philosophical-political "power-knowledge" idea[2] is a very powerful analytic tool, and even more so as I have added "fear" to it by necessity and for completeness. I see the best "unit" (or discourse) formation for fearology to study is knowledge-power-fear, rather than only studying fear(s) alone. However, that is all a topic for my next book.

The Preface, Introduction, Chapters One and Two ought to provide readers with several premises, principles, and perspectives upon which I work from in the study of fear ('fear') and fearlessness ('fearlessness'). They are not 'normal' and can be difficult to understand. Those platforms won't be repeated here, yet it must be said again that there is no way I can do justice in one first book to these topics. I have already mentioned this current book does not focus on all the research I and others have done on "fear" (and/or what I prefer to call 'fear'). My next book is *The World's Fear Teachings* which would cover a vast range of the complex postmodern philosophical, educational, and political problems of analyzing *how best to know fear ('fear') in a post-9/11 era?*

The human fear problem (with or without capitals) is enormous and overwhelming at times to even contemplate—and that alone is part of the problem of the human Fear Problem. Arguably, it is too big and too scary to investigate fully (i.e., holistically-integrally). Most people don't have the 'stomach' for it. In this book, my initial attempt to deal with this is to create more "order" for examining Fear Management Systems (FMSs), as one example. Because of that "fear of fear" problem if you will, and/or just being "apathetic," human societies have not achieved the best FME they are capable of yet. That's becoming a huge problem with the post-9/11 "War on Fear" (i.e., "War on Terror" as "the war without end") forcing humanity to travel down a slippery slope to designing virtually *everything* we do based on priority principles of a "security culture," "victim culture" (i.e., culture of fear) or an "architecture of fear."

Fortunately, at least humanity has recognized the universal nature of the fear problem as a basic issue in the UN's Universal Declaration of Human Rights (1948).[3] Complaining as a critic of human beings and their lack of enthusiasm to tackle the fear problem more rigorously is, however, not very useful either. The words "cowardice," "lazy," "apathetic," or "stupid" come to mind. Not all that productive. Chapter Two began with a quote that guides me to see humans as not 'bad' but 'afraid.' Our humanity is lost in direct proportion to accumulative 'fear.' Of course, we are at times amazingly "brave" and "courageous," and seem to utilize fearful events to be humane. Yet, what really turned me around from thinking the vast majority of humans were *apathetic* about the fear problem came from an interdisciplinary study of modern terrorist regimes from the southern cone of Latin America. Juan Corradi *et al.*[4] found that the middle class majority in LA countries (1970s-80s), with dictators ruling the countries by fear/terror, were suffering from what critics called "apathy." They would not go out and vote or rebel or support the people who were rebelling against the dictatorships. Hordes of "the People" "disappeared." General civil society had broken down as well as democracy under these barbaric conditions. What the researchers discovered, and reframed, from years of research after-the-fact (when the regimes had gone for the most part) was that the non-active privileged and somewhat powerful people in those societies were apathetic as citizens *because of fear*—and not mere individual psychological fear, though that was certainly part of it. Rather, the researchers found a *network of fear* that was more subtle and insidious. It was a dynamic that needed to be called something else. They called it the "*culture of fear.*" Such an oppressive culture had been constructed both by the dictator regimes *and* by the middle *and* elite classes (and the more obvious victims as well). In postmodern perspective, the *cultural dimension* (as well as political) became the focus of new research to attempt to understand how cultures of fear establish themselves, create themselves, and eventually destroy themselves. The greatest power runs in the cultural sphere, according to these researchers. And I agree. That study published in 1992 is a classic reading, if not one of the most comprehensive empirical studies ever on the psychological, historical, sociocultural and political dynamics of fear and fearlessness in modernity.

A critical phrase I read somewhere, more or less, speaks to my experience living in the last few decades: *Be afraid, the fear industry tells us: be very afraid.* It will likely sound familiar to many readers. That is our major fear problem today. Some voices beyond my own, are raising the issue and what needs to be done about it. For example, The eminent American historian of emotions Peter N. Stearns has recently called us to examine "the fear problem" collectively as civil societies and as a world:[5] "Addressing what can fairly be called the fear problem involves responsibilities from leadership and the general public alike."

Artist-philosopher-activist Eduardo Gáleano rather humorously captures the essence of our contemporary (and insidious) global fear:[6]

> *Global Fear:* Those who work are afraid they'll lose the jobs. Those who don't are afraid they'll never find one. Whoever doesn't fear hunger is afraid of eating. Drivers are afraid of walking and pedestrians are afraid of getting run over. Democracy is afraid of remembering and language is afraid of speaking. Civilians fear the military, the military fears a shortage of weapons, weapons fear a shortage of wars. It is a time of fear. Women's fear of violent men and men's fear of fearless women. Fear of theives, fear of the police. Fear of doors without locks, of time without watches, of children without television; fear of night without sleeping pills and day without pills to wake up. Fear of crowds, fear of solitude, fear of what was and what could be, fear of dying, fear of living.

In 1997 a colleague-visionary[7] and myself worked diligently to plan and design a first international conference on The Nature and Role of 'Fear' that would happen in the autumn of 1999 just before the turn of the millenium. We were interested in principle-centered systems and leadership. "Fear" was the theme chosen for our first conference of a series of ten over the next decade. We wanted to address, *via* a holistic-integral systems approach, the most important issues facing global ethical management and leadership in the future, in the largest sense of those terms. Our public relations document in 1997 began as follows:

> **Theme #1: The Nature and Role of 'Fear'**—This is the first international conference on 'fear' with such a systematic approach to understanding this phenomena. Historically, "we are at a peak fear point. . ." says author Gavin de Becker (1997) in his best seller The Gift of Fear. Although most people would agree that 'fear' is one of the most powerful and universal human experiences, there is a multitude of different views from lay persons, professionals and

scholars about the best ways to deal with it. Some see 'fear' as the enemy and cause of all war, violence and evil, while others see it as a friend and gift for survival. A new awareness of the importance of 'fear' in areas such as education, politics and business management is likely in the next few years. The definition of 'fear' is multi-dimensional and complex, while often contradictory from discipline to discipline. Some say that there are only two kinds of 'fear' and others say that 'fear' hides behind a thousand disguises. The language for the hundreds of different kinds of 'fear's fills encyclopedias. The focus of this conference is not on 'fears' or phobias ("fear of x, y, z) so much as on 'fear' itself. Despite the contradictions on how best to deal with 'fear,' the public generally knows that 'fear' is increasing rapidly in the late 20th century and it is likely to be an issue critical psychological educational, social and political concern in the 21st century. The first conference of the "Learning Under Fire" [series] is dedicated to what seems to be the crucial component that often inhibits trust, cooperation, learning, and creativity in principle-centered systems. Some of the key questions to be explored include: a) What is 'fear'?, (b) How do we best know 'fear'?, (c) How accurate is our information on 'fear'?, (d) How can we apply what we know best? and, (e) What further research is required to provide us with the most integrative knowledge about the nature and role of 'fear' in principle-centered systems?

Little did we know while planning this what would have emerged at the beginning of the 21st century with the "War on Terror" (post-9/11). *Fear* ('*fear*') had rapidly become one of the most talked about and troubling topics of social-political and economic debate in many of the world's most powerful nations. Many critics accused the US and UK, among other countries, as creating their own 'invisible' form of dictatorships ruled on a "politics of fear." And the Wachowski Brother's screen play *V for Vendetta* (2006)[8] is the best artistic portrayal of the future of fear and civil society in the Western world. A must see film.

Our 1999 conference never got off the drafting board design phase; although many people internationally were contacted, who ought to have been curious and supportive of this venture. In the end, they were rather uncommitted and no funding could be found. Many told us that the holistic-integral design of the conference was groundbreaking as we had attempted to cross disciplines. But more than that, we had a model of knowledge construction built-in to the design of the conference that was mind-boggling, including three major models of important theorists: Banathy's Nine "Evolutionary Dimensions," Wilber's "Four Quadrants" and Dilt's Six "Logical Levels." The idea was to have debates and various forums, games and so on that would bring out knowledge from different experts on the topic of fear ('fear'), no matter what their discipline or orientation. Then we would filter the knowledge they brought collaboratively— creating through an "integral" transforming system of the three major models of organization we had brought together for the conference series. The results to come from such a synthesis would then go back to the participants and stimulate creation of a vast international network of learning organizations that would put the new knowledge into practices to 'make the world a better place to live.' It sounded good at the time. We were a bit naive.

In 2000 I tried reaching out again by initiating a rigorous invitation to "fear" experts around the globe to come together in a common dialogical forum to address the topic. Not much happened. Over the years experience shows various kinds of "fear" (management) experts, leaders, and teachers from the biological to the spiritual are not that interested to bring their wisdom together to address the global Fear Problem as an integrated collective force (see Chapter Five).[9] They showed no interest for meta-theories or holistic-integral frameworks to organize our knowledges on fear or fearlessness—and how best to manage them in the challenging 21st century ahead. From another direction, equally exasperating, has been the ignore-ance of a critical integral theory of fear and fearlessness by the Integral Movement. They just don't seem to take it in that the *biggest difference* between "integral" (2nd-tier consciousness) and non-integral (1st-tier) is the issue of "fear" and moving beyond it as the main motivation. I can only say, in general, the 'Fearlessness (R)evolution' (the 'experts' on fear and how to go beyond it) and the 'Integral Revolution' (so-called) are unfortunately still trapped in the coding discourses of 'normal' ways of talking about and understanding the nature and role of fear ('fear'). Their 'revolution' is mere 'reform,' not radical or transformative enough. They are still predominantly enslaved by 'fear' (fearism and adultism) itself. I trust this book and new theory of fear management will slowly convince some of them to change their rather recalcitrant attitudes.

The painful disappointment from this reality of our times has remained deep in my psyche and heart. The reasons for the apathy are complex, some rational and some irrational (i.e., 'fear'-based). No one is to blame—its a systems problem. It seems virtually everyone is caught up in hyper-speed with their own pursuits, fame, and marketing (i.e., obsessive careerism). Of course, they would all likely retort: "we're just too busy." And so, then what? Now, as a species on planet earth we've been caught 'behind the eight ball' playing catch-up, and not doing so well. A tragic future narrative for humanity seems reasonable within the next decade to two—with no intention on my part to add to the fearmongering.

Today, we have a post-9/11 era and tidal shockwaves of uncontrollable 'fear' flowing over this planet—everyday, everywhere, "liquid fear," according to postmodern sociologist Zygmunt Bauman.[10] Sociologist and culture of fear critic Frank Furedi insightfully remarked that,[11]

> It is not hope but fear that excites and shapes the cultural imagination of the early twenty-first century. And indeed, fear is fast becoming a caricature of itself. It is no longer simply an emotion, or a response to the perception of threat. It has become a cultural idiom through which we signal a sense of growing unease about our place in the world. Popular culture continually encourages an expansive alarmist imagination through providing the public with a steady diet of fearful programmes about impending calamities—man-made and natural. . . . Today we are simply encouraged to regard fear as our default response to life itself. . . . Misanthropy [hatred of humanity and its quest for progress] has gained unprecedented influence in Western societies. It is the fear of ourselves as human beings that underpins the normalization of fear in contemporary soci-

ety.... That is why it is so important to *rebel against our culture of fear*. [and "conservativism of fear"] [italics added for emphasis]

Despite the apparent short-term success of US President Obama's *Audacity of Hope*[12] campaign (and charismatic leadership) this past year, I for one am not convinced "hope" (or "the American Dream") is the best sustainable alternative to "fear." I suggest "fearlessness." Thus, I go down a very different road, that is, a radical (integral) postmodern analysis of FME than does Furedi and most others studying fear. Also, I think we need to develop a healthy construct (idea) of a "culture of fearlessness" rather than merely "rebel against our culture of fear" as Furedi suggests. Where is the systematic integral vision of a viable alternative? How may we construct it—individually and collectively, in the dynamic shifting context(s) of today and the future emerging?

The upside of our times of 'great fear' is the 'great fearlessness' emerging simultaneously, of which this chapter elaborates through what can be called the World's Fearlessness Teachings. As in Chapter Two, these teachings are underlain with an existent, though mostly invisible, spirit of rebellion against the 'Law of Fear' and its limitations, its toxifying potential, and its power to corrupt the Beautiful, the Good, the True, especially in a post-9/11 era.

My last introductory point regarding the Fear Problem involves the dangers of "the normalization of fear" as Furedi pointed out, keeping in mind the controversial nature of talking about fear, as if it is only "negative." Truly Dozier, is partially right that "Fear brings out the best and worst in human beings."[13] It depends on how you define "fear" (or 'fear') and how you locate it within a particular narrative and larger context beyond individual biopsychological interpretations of fear. I take a highly precautionary view of any positive-discourse regarding fear ('fear'). But that's jumping ahead too fast. I'll return shortly to my rationale for that methodological strategy, that is, a "hermeneutics of doubt," as Ricoeur might have called it if he were alive today.

The 'Fear' Matrix

Some might argue (and have) that I am creating an unnecessary, rather 'negative,' tragic sounding scenario regarding fear. Indeed, I have created 'fear' within a particular biased imaginary, yet it is based on the research I have collected and my best interpretations along with a lot of other interpretations of history, development and evolution. Data and experience, not mere belief or fantasy or delusion, have led to the biased 'maps' and theories I work with. Figure 2.1 (Stages of the Soul's Journey) is a map of the path of fearlessness that distinguishes a continuum of growth, transformation, possibilities and ways of managing fear (i.e., FMSs). Figure 3.1 below offers a variation of the same map with the demarcation and illustration conceptually of the Fear Problem and 'Fear' Matrix. Figuratively and theoretically, following the curving line across the graph, one sees the relative amount of toxicity in the global Life system as a whole. The toxicity is speculative and theoretical. The slow evolution of accumulating fear ('fear') is noteworthy and somewhat predictable through time. The peaking of fear ('fear') is relevant to the state of danger our species and living systems face today. The dynamic underlying Figure 3.1 is also evident in that as fear rises so does fearlessness, that is, *if* the more advanced FMSs (7-9) can actually be increasingly engaged effectively for the demand of the times. However, the diagram shows that it is possible the toxicity peaking curve may not be pulled down or "corrected" in time and thus, causing irreparable damage with a realistic threat of extinction for ours and others species. This depicts visually a hypothesis of the Fear Problem and potential correction *via* a gradual decline of accumulating toxic 'fear,' based on the trends mapped out and the developmental logic behind Figure 3.1. The fine details cannot be engaged in this book but rather my future book on fear. Suffice it to say, the idea of the 'Fear' Matrix

Figure 3.1 Evolution of Fear Management: An Integral View

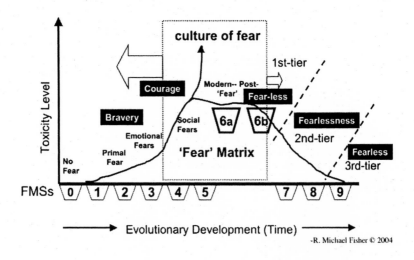

(and "culture of fear") has a lot do with the Fear Problem. The 'Fear' Matrix is growing as indicated by the arrows. It is a virtual (no less powerful) reality of the Cultural in its most pathological aspects, in which fear-based means of fear management (1st-tier), operating in a twisted "bravado" life strategy, are not working all that well to clear away excess 'fear' accumulations. A 'fear' and violence cycle is created. Later in this chapter a few specific examples of this kind of bravado are described in the form of a false or shallow "fearless" strategy and discourse. These have become very common in the Western world, especially in the last ten years. A helpful analogy for understanding the accumulation problem in the structure of the 'Fear' Matrix, is that *stress* may be natural but *distress* is toxic and culturally produced *via* coping strategies that lead to chronic distress. When stress rises due to many factors, and there is no returning to approximate 'equilibrium' in an organism or living system, then chronic distress patterns (i.e., toxic 'fear' patterns) are formed. Any doctor will tell you that chronic stress is on the rise. It is difficult to recognize often because people with it feel it is the 'normal' state and most everyone else also seems to have it. Some have called this a corruption of the natural recovery cycle, whereby a living system is chronically overly "stressed" or "challenged." Overwhelm, sets into the system as manufacture of the chronic 'fear' pattern occurs (e.g., fearmongering). It cannot recover, especially as the repeated traumas set in and build the distress levels up to "hyper" and excessive proportions. One could say the fear-immune system (i.e., spirit of fearlessness) is somewhat compromised under such conditions.

The hegemonic *culture of fear* phenomenon operates thus, in a largely unsustainable and ultimately oppressive way. The lack of a *healing culture* is a big part of this problem, and 'fear' accumulates likewise and is directly related to a *coping culture* (1st-tier FMSs as predominant). We are more and more as a species coping with fear ('fear') rather than healing and transforming it, to use popular jargon. The pollution is accumulating faster than we are cleaning it up. It's a self-regulation problem of the System.

The 'Fear' Matrix is a self-reinforcing *fear pattern* and architecture of fear, where 'fear' has become the 'norm' organizing motivation and framework for social life. The 'Fear' Matrix is thought to have arisen particularly with FMS-4, although its source goes back into the pathologies of the earlier FMSs. However, at FMS-4 (Blue, Mythic, Imperialistic), there is a very strong organizing structural dualism of "Good" vs. "Bad" and "Right vs. Wrong" in terms of "the best way to go" (see Chapter Two). FMS-4 represents the major civilizations and their religions, governing bodies and armies; often they are very powerful "Empires" which have (and many still do) operated in a largely pre-democratic paradigm. Note, that even an advanced pluralistic democracy (FMS-6) like the United States may fall back and regress when under intense distress (fear, terror) such as with 9/11. And Islamic intelligence can return to 9th-10th century dogma moral codes to attempt to run countries in the 21st century (call it "fundamentalism" by any other name). Under certain conditions the discourse of FMS-4 (its healthy and pathological sides) may rule again, as FMS-4 has always been the highly organized fear management strategy (a type of fearlessness) that often violently reins in Red Warrior (FMS-3) systems (i.e., less organized, uncivil, unruly, rebellious, "terrorist," gang-like, or "barbaric" aspects of civilizations in early development).

Theoretically, the 'Fear' Matrix is unsustainable as its toxic oppressive and violent impacts grow daily. Identifying and naming this 'Fear' Matrix complex is a first step toward better "managing," if not eliminating it; but such interventions or "corrections" will have to come from designs at FMSs-7, 8, 9. The most likely and easily accessible FMSs is 7 (Yellow, Integral). From a 2nd-tier perspective there is no "one person" or "one system" to blame for the mess we are in. Only 1st-tier systems typically scapegoat "one source" in simple dualistic cause-effect linear thinking. FMS-6b starts to see through this faulty thinking but it is not until FMS-7 to 9, when engaged, that a more holistic-integral analysis can be done and "many sources" are seen as part of the Fear Problem or 'Fear' Matrix. Fearism, as I argued earlier, is pivotal and revealed at FMS-7.

The 1st-tier is working hard right now to promote "bravery," "courage," and "fear-less" to counter the overwhelming aspects of the cancerous growth of the 'Fear' Matrix and "culture of fear." This is especially the case with the FMS-6 (Green, Sensitive) as this FMS has been the Postmodern emergence to "correct" the pathology of Modernism and Pre-Modernism. Nonetheless, Zygmunt Bauman is critical as to just how effective postmodernity as a philosophy and way of organizing reality and society will be. He perceptively wrote that,[14]

> Postmodernity has not allayed the fears which modernity [and its pursuit of lib-eralist freedom] injected into humanity once it left it to its own resources; postmodernity only *privatized* these fears. . . . With fears privatized [psycholo-gized] the temptation to run for cover remains as potent as ever. But there is no hope left that human reason, and its earthly agents, will make the race a guided tour, certain to end up in a secure and agreeable shelter.

However, Green FMS-6 (immature postmodernity) is particularly trouble-some because it fights hardest against hearing that there is any FMS (or FMSs) that might be more advanced or mature than it is. Such 'grand' evolutionary or developmental narratives are usually rejected outright by FMS-6. My point is, the FME discourses or FMSs are highly competitive, that is, when your vision is restricted to the 1st-tier systems (including immature postmodernity). Readers may see why the heavy "against" and "victim" qualities of Green arise when it meets Yellow, as FMS-6 is the "top" ("improved") FMS of the spectrum shown in Figure 3.1. The problem is, as pointed out earlier, all 1st-tier FMSs are pri-marily fear-based in motivation as researchers like Graves, Beck and Cowan, and others have shown. Each of the 1st-tier FMSs are incredibly intelligent, par-tial truths, and legitimate means of FME. Equally important, is to recognize their weaknesses and biases, as well as their pathologies—pathologies, they seem inherently to deny.

Fear-Positivists' Position

Elsewhere, I have written about several "movements" in the world that one could call the *enemies of fearlessness*.[15] For now, I'll focus on one specific 'en-emy.' In the West (especially, North America) where I live, most people lately have a knee-jerk reaction when I talk about fear ('fear') the way I do. They de-fend (what I call) the Western canon on fear and courage. It is largely a domi-nant white male middle-upper class discourse on fear management. They defend vociferously that there is a *positive-side* to fear, albeit, they may acknowledge it has a negative-side too; the latter, when fear is in excess relative to the reality-threat of the situation. Rather than listening well to a potentially new view of fear ('fear') that I propose, they typically interrupt and trot out the Western canon of teaching (i.e., hegemonic discourse) that says *the best* way to manage fear is to use it and go through and beyond it—that is the *true* definition of cour-age, rather than denying fear or dismissing it or making it only a negative aspect of human life. I label this *"fear-positivism."* Arguably, it is an (unconscious) ideology (discourse) found in virtually every book I have read on fear and courage in the Western world. Westerners believe it is true and defend it. They've made it *the* canon (meaning, *the* truth). It is based in premodern and modernist Western philosophy, religion, and psychology (for the most part). It is a severe discourse barrier to a more postmodern holistic-integral approach to the topic. I won't trace out its history, but some of these issues come forth in the following section of this chapter.

Elsewhere, I have written in some detail of the failing project of "fear-positivists" and the danger in their 'logic' (and beliefs) regarding fear.[16] If their goal is to make "fear" less negative and fearful and create that kind of positive energy around it so we will learn more about it, then I am all for that. However, that aim does not justify the means. Fear-positivists typically are reductionistic not holistic. They are not integralists. They adopt a 'good-enough' definition of fear based in the Natural biological-psychological (individual) domain of reality and use that as the foundation for their entire argument: that is, "fear is a natural survival mechanism." They also argue such a *natural fear* then spurs on and creates the necessary dialectical tension for human (if not cosmic) creativity and progress. Based on these premises, fear is then constructed as the very motivator creativity and Life—of goodness, truth, and even beauty. That's where I am very cautious of the slippery slope to travel, where fear is being reinforced, defended and justified (uncontested) as "essential" and "natural" etc. What fearmonger ('fear' pattern/discourse) in the world wouldn't want to capitalize on that? The 'Fear' Matrix is constructed on this very idea.

They argue the very source of *courage* is actually due to fear, for as they say (or write) often "without fear there would be no courage." Analogously, that is like saying "without suffering" there would be no "acts to try to prevent suf-fering." This is a faulty, weak, and potentially harmful 'logic.' And when ap-plied to fear, by a Western civilization that has been known to be fear-based for 5000 years of pathological patriarchy and domination (*a la* Eisler), one really wants to be extra cautious of making fear so positive. Of course, it depends how you define fear. The fear-positivists[17] (using FMSs 5, 6) are not character-istically interested in my complex postmodern integral (FMS-7) definitions or conceptualization of 'fear' and its management. They may acknowledge modern technomedia have constructed fear in slightly new (or more) ways and thus, made fear increasingly easily misused. However, that is as far as their analysis tends to go. They stick with their 'good-enough' (reductionistic)[18] definitions and they shy away from any suggestion of a link between "culture of fear" and the 'Fear' Matrix notion, or an idea of fearism that keeps us not knowing well what fear ('fear') actually is and how it operates so 'normally' (but oppress-ively). Indeed, I have been derided and laughed at by fear-positivists when I suggest we go beyond the habitual Western canon and its notions of fear and courage. The resentment in their tone and facial expressions is vivid and—rather painful to me.

Regardless, I persist and suggest critically that "natural" and "essential" in regard to fear ought be challenged today. That's part of a critical literacy of fear-lessness for the 21st century. Fear-positivists are predominantly thinking in premodern and modern conceptualizations of fear. In a postmodern (post-9/11)

era there are too many good criticisms to ignore for us to settle on past easy
definitions of "natural fear" or "essential fear" (and confusing that with "normal
fear")—and thus, make them positive fears because of such reductionistic essen-
tializing (i.e., committing a "naturalistic fallacy" in philosophical terms). They
always haul out the W. canon discourse: "If you were being attacked by a saber-
tooth tiger you would be glad fear is there." I listen and think who is that talking? What discourse or FMSs is coming through this person? What power does
it have? Who's power is it and what does it serve? On and on I ask critical questions that the speakers typically do not ask of their own utterances and claims to
truth.

    When I suggest to fear-positivists "*What if our very definition and concep-
tualization of fear and how to best manage it is impartial, incomplete knowledge, distortive or even pathological knowledge?*," they shrug such foolish
thinking off, and more or less mock at the absurdity of it. They assert their confident ignore-ance and reclaim the Western canon, as if there is nothing new to
learn about FME in our times. They promote a confident rational attitude (FMS-
5) or what singer/songwriter Issa critiqued as "happy, happy," when we might
be better off with "happiness" as "an absence of being afraid of fear."[19] The fear-
positivists *appear* to defend not being afraid of fear. When I ask them, they typically demonstrate a virtual complete ignorance about the Eastern canon of fear
and fearlessness. All they know is that the word "fearlessness" itself is distasteful, if not repulsive to them (or some embrace it naively without knowing what
it means). The fear-positivists interpret fearlessness means the end of fear (being
only human) or worse, denial of fear, which all seems an infectious lack of courage to them. End of discussion. There's not much more they want to talk about.
This is a huge barrier on the quest to 'light-up' the FMSs-7 to 9.

    My hypothesis is: *the greatest fear is that we may not know as much as we
think we know about fear*. Such doubt, not happy happiness, would put our entire FME into question. Based on decades of research, that's the big secret
"greatest fear" and it has not yet even been labeled—until now! Next up, you are
about to read what the World's Fearlessness Teachings (East and West) have to
say about FME, so you can make your own discernments on these issues.

Reviewing The World's Fearlessness Teachings (WFTs)

    This section is of major importance in the overall purpose of this text, as the
mindful (sometimes critical) documenting of the WFTs, and a constructing of a
Fearlessness Tradition (and critical integral theory) from them, is pivotal in the
battle with Fear's Empire. This author did not create this project and review
because of only rational aspects of thought. Indeed, rational was what followed
the arational intuitional vision and inspiration for this collecting and documenting process. It all started with a shamanic journey I had taken on November 4,
2007, after having worked with a shamanic holistic practitioner named Angela
Prider[20] in Vancouver for a few months. The fifth dreamtime inner journey was
recorded and the following is an excerpt taken from notes immediately after the
journey:

I lit a candle, after awaking from a dream that was a positive experience of me as a teacher/guide/therapist in a setting of rehabilitation of youth and families and a new job-career track upon which I had just been hired on the first day of work. It felt enlivening and got me up. . . . [deciding to do a self-guided shamanic journey] I turned on the tape of the 15 min. of drumming I had recorded last week, and soon I was lying on my back in bed and in my imagination going to my power hole in the ground; setting my intentions . . . I slipped below the earth's surface into limbo space again. I was going to be patient and not try to push things; and so slight images or ideas or senses happened and I felt a sense of coming up out of a hole in the earth in the middle of a desert. I also knew I may have to go where Penny Camel [my power animal] lives, . . . any way, I had this sense of coming up underneath its body and legs and thus was shadowed over by it as my power animal. And in retrospect that's a good place to be as I am starting to get the image of the power of this creature. . . . I had a sense of greeting Penny Camel and quickly I felt it knew what to do and took me to see the tents on the sand. The wind was blowing them, or so I imagined it was windy in the desert. I then was guided to the door opening of a large tent, of which I was expectant there would be master teachers, as that was one of my intentions of asking for. I could not see anyone particular as an image or recognizable feature in the tent but sensed there was candle light and a warm presence. I was welcomed there in some way. But I literally don't recall being there in a physical presence nor were they physical beings. It was not formal or ritual-like but just a sense of reception. I eventually thought they would offer guidance and I was ready and it was like a "melting of hot wax into and onto me"—as the message form that came from them as a collective of higher wisdom teachers.

The journey went on but the main 'transmission' had occurred. The master teacher-leaders (souls) in the tent were the Ancient Ones and the Contemporary Ones, all of whom were teachers of fearlessness from around the world. They wanted yours truly to collect their teachings in one volume and publish it in an encyclopedia. No one had brought their 'voices' altogether before. Of course, the 'terrifying' task was accepted. It was an honor to do so. As enormous as the task was, and felt in the infusion *via* the hot wax that went into this one mortal human soul, there was relief that I was no longer the sole author. This was to be a collective authorship. Only R. Michael Fisher would be the scribe, of sorts. Soon after this journey the energy shifted within and without and the task was underway. A book outline was constructed with a prospectus for publishers. Estimated length of *World's Fearlessness Teachings: An Encyclopedia of Sacred and Secular Wisdom for a Non-Violent World* was 1200 pages (three volumes). From the prospectus:

Purpose: To best meet the urgent need for fearlessness on this planet, a diverse body of wisdom literature is required which is accessible in encyclopedia-form so as to be relatively non-biased, non-dogmatic and readable; whereby, diverse individuals, groups, and nations, can sort through the human legacy of fear management and make better critical assessments of their own and others' attempts to cope with, manage, and potentially transform fear and our relationship to it. This volume puts most all of that diverse knowledge together in one

volume [three smaller volumes], never done before, and organizes it alphabeti-
cally so readers can access what is most interesting in a short-time, thereby not
having to read tonnes to get to the 'gems.' This book's fearlessness teachings,
sacred and secular, inherently will inspire and connect readers to the roots of a
universal life 'spirit' that rebels and resists the imposition of excess oppressive
fear on our lives and other beings in earth's ecosystems.

It seemed many publishers never responded because this was a huge project
and I was relatively unknown and unproven in the book publishing world. The
one offer that came in from University of America Press was heartening but they
wanted a different book, yet, still wanting the essence of the book as a review of
the WFTs through my 'eyes.' The book would be a technical monograph first
and foremost, and that meant it would have to have a critical context and theoretical underpinning for what I have to say that is new about fearlessness (and
fear).

By the time the publisher got the new book prospectus, there were three
very full very large binders sitting on my desk all ready to go as notes and
quotes for the encyclopedia. Within months, the letters A, B, C, were completed
in first draft form, ready to be sent to a publisher, if one were to be interested.
What better way to begin to review some of the WFTs than to give some excerpts from the ms for the encyclopedia, starting with the seven ways of fearlessness: *no fear*, *bravery* (and twisted *bravado*), *courage*, *fear-less*, *fearlessness*, *fearless*. At the time of writing this current book, only a few of the ways
have been reviewed in the encyclopedia ms under A, B, C.

My first task was to define "World's Fearlessness Teachings." When first
conceived it referred to identifiable traditions in philosophy, religion, or disciplines of scholarly repute. Soon that seemed too restrictive. If the spirit of fearlessness was everywhere that fear was, as a first principle for the new book, then
everything written down or said and recorded in some way was potentially a site
to find fearlessness teaching us something. This meant that popular culture also
had to be included. It meant that "teachings" involving some suggestion as to
how to "best" manage fear were worth including. WFTs is therefore used very
loosely here with advantages and disadvantages. Sometimes the teachings are
unconscious and sometimes very conscious. Sometimes they are of poor quality
and sometimes of high quality. This qualitative distinction ought to become
fairly evident as examples are given side by side below. As well, contradictions
and conflicts in these teachings do surface. Let's begin with *no fear* (FMS-0)
and work along the spectrum of consciousness through to *fearless* (FMS-9).

No Fear

I wake up, and I have no fear. I go to bed without fear. Fear, fear, fear, fear.
Yes, tear is a word that is not in my vocabulary. . . .   -Steve Martin[21]

... if you had no fear you would have been dead long ago.   - D. Viscott[22]

Everyone is not as 'gifted' (or successful) with "no fear" as Martin quips. Although, one could fantasize being "born without the fear gene" as protagonist Gaia is in the very successful contemporary juvenile fiction series *Fearless*, penned by Francine Pascal. Yet, for many like Viscott such a condition would be deadly. Our attitudes and beliefs about fear and fearlessness vary and sometimes conflict. *No Fear* (FMS-0) as one of the seven ways of fearlessness I have ordered in this chapter, is foundational and a beginning point to understanding FME. What I offer, however, is still only a skeletal first overview.

Clinically, going back some 50 years to experimental psychology research on antisocial personalities, D. T. Lykken showed that some individuals when hooked up to a galvanic skin response machine (i.e., lie detector) and exposed to frightening stimuli, did not register a significant physiological reaction of fear, or at least did so to such a minor degree they were truly well outside the 'norm' and were labeled "fearless." Researchers believed a substantial degree of such a trait was genetically inherited, rather than psychosocially learned or due to structural brain damage. Other research by Lykken et al. tended to link this 'no fear' trait to antisocial behaviors as these individuals were not inhibited in regard to forbidden things nor very afraid of authorities (i.e., parents and teachers or older siblings, etc.), who threatened them with punishment for misbehaving.[23]

With Lykken publishing an article entitled "Fearlessness: It's Carefree Charms and Deadly Risks" in the pop psychology magazine *Psychology Today* (1982), a definite legacy of negative attitude (even fear) colored the public's perception of "no fear" or "fearless" as extremes and thus, illegitimate ways and discourses for fearlessness (i.e., fear management). On the contrary, Jerome Kagan's psychological research identifying a naturally occurring "fearless temperament" in your average children 24 months or less, has attempted to 'normalize' (i.e., de-pathologize and de-stigmatize) these qualities to some minor extent.[24] The internationally recognized psychologist on fear and courage, S. J. Rachman reported that,[25]

> For most of us fear is a familiar emotion, and it is difficult to imagine life in which it plays no part. However, there is a small number of people who are relatively impervious to fear [e.g., the late Henry Cooper, a former heavyweight champion boxer, according to Rachman].

Despite this strong negative connotation to "no fear" or "without fear" (applied to individuals), a movement of popularizing the term and discourse has poured into Western culture beginning in 1989 and flourished with youth through the 1990s *via* the "NO FEAR!" (x-treme sports) logo and slogandia on t-shits, decals for automobiles, and just about any other kind of product one can think of (check the Internet). This is a discourse of fear management best located in FMS-3 (Red, Warrior) with *bravery* (*bravado*), see below and in later chapters. As well, there is a considerable amount of political discourses on "without fear" and "freedom from fear" that show up in modernist FMS-5 and 6, all of which are discussed much later below with *courage* and *fear-less*.

Other uses of the discourse of *no fear* show up in self-help literature occasionally. Gerald Jampolsky, a famous spiritual-psychiatrist of the 'new age' wrote, "When someone is occupied with helping another person, [s]he experiences no fear."[26] Another international 'new age' author-teacher, James Redfield, wrote of an altered state of consciousness (mystical experience) where he was "totally without fear. . . . I had a feeling of perfect well-being."[27] The late venerable Chöygam Trungpa Rinpoche (1939-1987), a Shambhala Tibetan Buddhist teacher, wrote,[28]

> Fear comes from uncertainty. If you know exactly how you are going to handle this frightful situation, then you have no fear. . . . There is no fear if you really have a compassionate relationship with yourself, because then you know what you are doing.

Seemingly contradictory, Trungpa 12 years later wrote emphatically,[29]

> True fearlessness is not the reduction of fear, but going beyond fear. In order to experience fearlessness, it is necessary to experience fear. The essence of cowardice is not acknowledging the reality of fear.

Martin Luther, the great 16th century Christian Reformationist, wrote,[30] "For there are two classes of people on earth. Some are wicked and unruly; they pay God's Word no heed and live as they see fit—smug, unabashed, and without fear." For Luther, good Christians were opposite that, and "easily frightened" by "reason of tender hearts and consciences." Somewhat contradictory, is the internationally-renowned humanist leader and Christian Jean Vanier, who writes a book entitled *Be Not Afraid*,[31] and the late Pope John Paul III stated at the front of his book "from the outset: 'Be not afraid.'"[32] Of course, somewhat paradoxical, most Christian teachers and leaders following the Bible closely, teach that "fear of God" is essential to good Christian ethical practice.

The late Jiddu Krishnamurti, spiritual teacher and philosopher, wrote, "One has to find out for oneself what it means to die; then there is no fear, therefore every day is a new day. . . . in that there is love." Contemporary and popular Zen Buddhist teacher Thich Nhat Hahn, encourages a similar reflection on death and its transcendence in his book *No Death, No Fear* (2003).[33] New Age teacher Gregg Braden teaches that 90% of our fear is not ours, but comes to us through history and society's fears. He reminds his followers to "Remember the No 'Fear' Option."[34] Huber, a Buddhist author noted critically: "'Without fear, wouldn't you just walk out into traffic?' The belief is that being afraid keeps you from doing something dangerous or just dumb. But that's one of the processes fear uses to protect itself."[35] Sounds like my argument for the case of fearism.

With all these discourses regarding *no fear* (or "without fear"), the meanings vary depending on the author and the tradition they come from. From an academic perspective, typically, "no fear" is used rather sloppily and is ill-defined (mostly, ignoring a definition at all) What is confusing often is that the rhetoric, especially from spiritual teachers (especially from the East), tends to blur with "fearless" (FMS-9) as meant in a critical integral theory of fearlessness, where in the former *no fear* is designated as that state (or level) before "fear" (FMS-0) (see Figure 2.1). At times we have to examine the reality from within the level or FMS and at other times, we also have to step back and survey the reality from a standpoint that sees the whole spectrum. The latter is accomplished at 2nd tier, from where the 'maps' I offer derive their imaginary. Writing about these perspectives at the same time is not easy. Hopefully the context in which the analysis is exploring at any point in this text will reveal the perspective. The reality is that things are not so clean cut. We have to accept the flipping back n' forth of perspectives as we attempt to communicate about them.

A lengthy explanation is due. For summary purposes, the quotes above are often referring more to "fearless" or "fearlessness," respectfully, to FMS-9 or FMSs 7, 8. This *pre/trans fallacy* (*a la* Wilber) is confusing FMS-0 (*no fear, adual reality*) with FMS-9 (*fearless, nondual reality*), all which is discussed later. Remember, this holistic-integral classification is not characteristically applied in your average discourses on fear management or fear education (i.e., FME). This is a first, rather rough and humble, attempt to sort out the differences in how fear is managed differentially, by applying consistent nomenclature to those differences. It will likely take most readers a bit of extra re-reading of these chapters to get more familiar with the language and 'mapping' schema, to then be able to apply it to any analysis of discourses of 'fearlessness.'

In the 'story' of the unfolding of the evolution of consciousness (Figures 2.1 and 3.1) there is a developmental period, individually and collectively for humans where the condition is *adual*—that state and that sense of being where no individual self (organismic sense) has yet emerged to distinguish itself consciously from the environment (and/or womb or mother). Wilber, early in his career, described this within an evolutionary context and Perennial Philosophy framework,[36] which recognizes a "unity consciousness or supreme identity" as that which we already are and which is the very Ground of Being upon which all sentient beings participate. He continued:[37]

> . . . but that we progressively limit our world [as Spirit or Self] and turn [*via* involution] from our true nature [essence] in order to [enter creation *via* evolution as manifest in materiality] embrace boundaries [differentiation]. Our originally pure and unitive consciousness [adual] then functions on varied levels [e.g., FMSs], with different identities and different boundaries. These different levels are basically the many ways we can and do answer the question, "Who am I?" [and 'What is real?'].

"Our originally pure and unitive consciousness," as Wilber suggests—this is the location of *no fear* (FMS-0, no color), before the *dual* emerges and greatly shapes most of the rest of our lives. Of many possible other stories, Bill Moyers interviewing the late Joseph Campbell (1904-1987), the great postmodern mythologist and critic, gives us a good representation of this universal original stage, consciousness, or level of existence, where there is *no fear* but the quick transition to primal fear (see Figure 3.1) is evident:[38]

BM: Do you think there was such a place as the Garden of Eden?

JC: Of course not. The Garden of Eden is a metaphor for that innocence ["paradise"] that is innocent of time, innocent of opposites, and that is the prime center out of which consciousness then becomes aware of the changes.

BM: . . . what happens to it? Isn't it shaken, dominated, and corrupted by fear?

JC: That's it. There is a wonderful story of the deity, of the Self that said, "I am." As soon as it said "I am," it was afraid.

BM: Why?

JC: It was an entity now, in time. Then it thought, "What should I be afraid of, I'm the only thing that is." And as soon as it said that, it felt lonesome, and wished that there were another, and so it felt desire. It swelled, split in two, became male and female [dual], and begot the world. *Fear* is the first experience of the fetus in the womb. There's a Czechoslovakian psychiatrist, Stanislov Grof, now living in California, who for years treated people with LSD. And he found that some of them re-experienced birth and, in the re-experiencing of birth, the first stage is that of the fetus in the womb, without any sense of "I" or of being. Then shortly before birth the rhythm of the uterus begins, and there's terror! Fear is the first thing, the thing that says "I." Then comes the horrific stage of getting born, the difficult passage through the birth canal, and then— my God, light! Can you imagine! Isn't it amazing that this repeats just what the myth says—that Self said, "I am," and immediately felt fear?

Campbell and Moyers continue the conversation of these universal mythemes in human history and development, and speak about the archetypal "Rebel" spirit that disobeys God or some other parental-authoritative deity-figure. Campbell concludes from his life-long research that "Life really began with that act of disobedience."[39] To keep the developmental logic of the sequence in tact of which they are speaking to: (1) *no fear* in the adual "Self"(or deity), (2) *fear* in the awakening to a dual "self" in time, body, language, concepts, and "self-consciousness" and, (3) *no fear!* as the first expression or FME discourse of a dualistic life of the individual (man or woman, or child), who is driven to "rebel against," as Campbell says, any prohibition and/or taboo by any authority figure (e.g., God in the Garden of Eden, e.g., mom or dad or doctor in the birthing room), and/or any pre-given limitation by a common social group norm; and/or the emerging 'I' simply rebels against limitations imposed on it due to physicality, artifice, pain, hurt, violence, fear (oppression-repression dynamics) from without and/or within.

Thereby, *No Fear* has two meanings in this creation-centered ontology and narrative of development: the first, is for all intense of purposes completely unconscious *no fear* as simply and literally meaning there is not enough "self" structure or conscious awareness to register an experience one could call "fear." It is a *pre-fear* existence of being not against anything nor threatened by anything, at least not yet; the second, is slightly conscious of a "self" and thereby "otherness" (or "stranger") all around it and even within it, and it knows enough to know that it is all of a sudden experiencing some sense of ongoing subtle or overt risk and threat from "otherness" (which is usually experienced as something very 'big' or 'great' (like the Cosmos, an immortal God, like Mom, like a cultural symbol, etc.), relative to the very small vulnerable organic mortal self-sense. And it may even be hurt by that "otherness" because the "otherness" is operating on a different agenda (apparently) than the early "self."

Campbell reflected on God saying to Adam and Eve, for example, in the discourse of "Thou shalt not!" a taboo[40] (i.e., a fear-based invocation to obey authority and norms, and to be afraid of breaking them, that is, be afraid of some punishment to come by maintaining an "existential" ongoing "fear of God."[41] — and in the Bible story that rebellion was "sin" and the price to be paid for willful sin against the tradition, authority, taboo, and so on). It looks as if the pre-modern Judeo-Christian 'story' (and/or Islamic 'story' but it is also a much larger story across varied traditions of thought, both sacred and secular) is one of "Do not try to be without fear, and especially fear of God." Later in FMS-4 (*courage*), we'll encounter contradictions around this narrative and fear management strategy (worldview). According to Campbell, this universal dialectical pattern of authority-rebel (conflictual) drama is embedded in the emergence of *human fear*, which will, more or less, stay with the organism (humans) from that point onward because of dualism and its "opposites" (i.e., self vs. Other, and Life vs. Death, and so on goes the struggle of existence). Of course, there is the option presented in all these stories for redemption from the consequences of fear and sin (or dualism = Fall[42]). That is the possibility of the "transcendent," as Campbell says; there is always the "means to 'transcend,' to go past duality"[43] and thus past fear and its limitations. Which, in critical integral theory means to grow and develop (include and transcend). Simply, we do or we do not "grow" into duality and then nonduality. As evolution's law seems to suggest: We all start growth from aduality (FMS-0, No Fear).

The spirit of fearlessness, thus, can also be found in these stories/ myths/traditions of cultures *via* the concept of redemption *via* transcendent possibility. Fearlessness is also in the individual but we also have to grow into fearlessness (along the spectrum, up to FMS-7, for instance). At the organismic level, for example, the inherent *fearlessness* arises, more or less, the moment *fear* appears. Returning to the myth: the impulse to "transcend" and/or to "rebel" against imposition and limitation, which is an attempt to make the organism fearful of something big, great, divine, hurtful — is a responsible and intelligent impulse I call the *spirit of fearlessness*. Recall, the basic Life principle and assumption in the philosophy and theory behind this book: *when fear arises, then arises fearlessness*. In its very first appearance developmentally, this inherent fear management principle shows up in the form of FMS-0 (no color) represented by the discourse pattern of *no fear* (in two sub-forms): (1) mere existence without knowing fear and, (2) a rebellion to fear. Another way to put this, is that fearlessness is the way of Defense for all Life systems so they can maintain and grow and reproduce eventually. In the first instance, it is difficult to apply a concept of fear management in the pre-fear formation but theoretically it is operating *via* the earliest forms of fearlessness as Defense (i.e., as an attempt to keep the intra-uterine organism (baby) in biopsychological homeostasis). *No fear* is a useful strategy to maintain (albeit, unconsciously) a relatively "unitive harmony" around the uterine 'paradisical' (innocent) experience. Arguably, it is a useful strategy to prevent overwhelming the organism biopsychologically in this very vulnerable condition at pre-birth or just after birth.[44] Another way to put it, is that fearlessness *via* "no fear" is operating to act as an early 'immunization' against fear—at least, against excessive accumulating fear and its toxicity. In other words, the baby is being protected to stay relatively "un-awakened" for the critical early stages of becoming and manifesting into the corporeal dimension on earth. Evolution, at one level, seems somewhat "sensitive" to organisms' vulnerability. One can think of the descriptions of prey about to be eaten, whereby the prey species may enter a genetically pre-scripted life strategy to go "unconscious" (freeze, play dead) because their living organic system is not capable of handling the full-awakened traumatizing experience (i.e., terror) of being eaten alive/awake/conscious. One could call this a proto-type of ethical "gift of fearlessness," of which some have misconstrued to be a "gift of fear" (e.g., de Becker[45]). Recent pre-natal psychological research shows that a lot of intelligence is forming with the early nervous system and brain of the baby *in utero*. Early emotional experiences are happening. My argument here is that the earliest experiences are not of a "self" (an "I am")—not yet.

At this early level of development the Natural selective forces to defend and grow (i.e., FMS-0) are already being impacted, as the myth suggests, by the Cultural selective forces (i.e., FMS-2), in order to obey that which comes before you in terms of socialization and enculturation processes. Even the modern medicalized childbirthing model and practices (i.e., Cultural) are known to be highly traumatic to the Natural, and thus, many postmodern families, dulas, midwives and some feminist doctors are now educating others as activists for a "childbirth without fear."[46] Such education around liberal (if not liberating) childbirth practices is itself a type of FME. It is the spirit of fearlessness manifesting at what later will be identified (primarily, but not entirely) as FMS-6a (Green).

Of course, this evolutionary (historical) and developmental story is more complex than what can be written about in a very short space; but more to the point, the descriptions and explanations are as much metaphor as reality *per se*. Keep the idea in mind that the discussions here are 'mappings' based on experience and traditional wisdom teachings but they are still only 'maps' and not the 'territory.' They are partial truths. One could critique them at great length. They ought to be studied and critiqued, as all the traditions and WFTs ought to be. However, they are teachings to be regarded with great respect too. It is balancing criticism and respect that is a difficult thing to do; one rarely ever finds it in contemporary discourses, especially in the early postmodern period. Critical integral philosophy attempts to "correct" the excesses of deconstruction (critique) in most postmodern philosophy, and embraces the best of the Pre-Modern and Modern wisdom that is available. Analogously, integral philosophy attempts to integrate Natural, Cultural and Spiritual likewise. Albeit, the integration is now in a Postmodern era context (or lens)—in this case, this author is slowly building a postmodern theory of 'fearlessness' (and 'fear').

'Fearlessness' is not to be taken lightly, or with only one familiar idea or discourse from some tradition, discipline, or habit of thought. That is why, 'fearlessness' is represented here in multiple ways and forms, as any good postmodern theory ought to, because reality is multiply-complex beyond simple answers, beyond black n' white, as they say. 'Fearlessness' is presented here moving from interpretations (contexts of meaning = FMSs 0-9) that are *adual*, to *dual*, to *non-dual*. Psychiatrist-artist and integral creativity theorist Charles M. Johnston, relates these to *first space, second space,* and *third space* as holonic patterns in the "creativity cycle" of all living organisms and systems.[47] Creative growth here means transcendent (*telos*-directed) movement along this path (transcendence = translate and include earlier levels into higher senior levels and transform, so that new more complex-intelligent-adaptive structures and accompanying new life strategies, emerge). Thus, I present a path of 'fearlessness,' of creativity itself, of healing and maturation, and a path of liberation from fear,[48] and perhaps, even from 'fear' is possible—is real. But we have to start somewhere and this view above overall tends to take an evolutionary stance (not rejecting an involutionary perspective) for illustrative (simplifying) heuristic purposes of the model.

No fear FMS-0 is the preferred Natural way of managing fear in a precognitive, pre-fear, pre-self, pre-boundary, pre-individual, pre-traumatized, pre-violent, pre-civilized, pre-human, pre-personal manner—using these latter terms with great caution and due respect of their potential abuse as conceptions. Even these labels are problematic. However, for our purposes here, the problems can be minimized if claims are qualified with 'good' theory, meaning, and good integral theory.

Campbell in the myth quoted above stated that this *adual* condition "is the prime center out of which [dualistic] consciousness then becomes aware of the changes [opposites and conflicts of existence]." He acknowledged its universal reality in a historical reflective context, as a pre-historical context and way of living and managing life's challenges. Generalizing, and accepting there are multiple meanings for this time and state of being (with evolutionists, involutionists, and creationists, all contending for a different focus and perspective on the human 'story'), one could speculate this is and was a time of animal-instinctual practices of our primate and hominid cousins, in an evolutionary sense. One could speculate this is how most animals exist, largely with a genetic deterministic aspect to basic survival behaviors. One could speculate this is the pre-natal experience (consciousness) of the human baby *in utero*. This is the time (i.e., innocence) before the "Fall" (i.e., post-innocence) in more metaphorical, existential and religious terms.

There is a distinct Natural domination that *no fear* is embedded in a time of pre-Cultural, and even perhaps pre-Spiritual influence. According to Willoughby, Margaret Mead's ethnological studies of early (pre-highly technological) cultures indicated some do exist "which are characterized by almost no anxiety."[49] That may not be the same as *no fear*, but "almost" is the key word. Yi-Fu Tuan, the eminent human geographer, has discussed the problem of scholarly trends and ethnographers relativistic value-biasing of their interpretations of cultures and ways of life in the (paradisical) past, especially in pre-industrialized societies. He wrote,[50]

> In recent years still another trend is discernible: the tendency now to denigrate village life for its superstition and envy, manifested in bitter factionalism and witch hunts, and to elevate the life of simple hunters and gatherers to a state approximating that of Eden. However, few people living in the manner of Paleolithic times remain on the scene for modern ethnographers to study. The recent literature is therefore focused on a few small and scattered groups, and it is not surprising that most of these are to be found in a nurturing tropical environment. Of carefree and harmonious societies, perhaps the best documented is that of the Mbuti Pygmies in the northeastern corner of the Congo rain forest. . . . An outstanding fact concerning the Mbuti Pygmies is that they have no concept of evil. Without such a concept there can still be alarm, but the special components of human fear—dread, suspicion, anxiety—are much diminished.

Key words: fear is "much diminished," fear is not completely absent. However, interestingly, Tuan (paraphrasing Colin Turnbull's work with the Mbuti), says they still have "alarm." The "alarm response" sometimes called "fear response" in modern psychology and philosophy is Natural (biological). It operates as a Defense against predation and other natural threats but apparently does not involve Cultural constructed threats which derive from conceptions of "evil." Note: I would prefer "alarm response" to "fear" as the term most appropriate to the Natural domain (FMS-0 discourse = "gift of fear"). So far, critics of this change of language are reluctant to change their wording and conceptual framework. This is an important point when we come to FMS-2 (Purple, Magical), which is a FMS characterized by a Cultural worldview embedded in a fear-based dualism of "Good vs. Evil" (see Chapter Two). Later, you'll see that Tuan's description of the Mbuti Pygmies is closer to FMS-1 (Beige, Survival) than to FMS-0.

All these controversial expressions or stories of FMS-0 are understandable as they are difficult to grasp conceptually as an adult reading this text and looking back to the evidence of one's own life or searching for evidence from ethology, anthropology, archeology, biology and psychology (i.e., child development), or theology. Perhaps the best methodology of accessing this "innocent" location is ultimately a radical phenomenology or a poetics. These technical points aside, the *no fear pattern* (FMS-0) is an undeniable discourse and imaginary that is compelling nonetheless. We have to start the 'story' somewhere, while acknowledging "there is no beginning and there is no end" as the song goes. I am relatively convinced that FMS-0 is the foundation or template for the rebellious *and* emancipatory spirit driving the women leaders of the Fearlessness (R)evolution in Chapter One. As I have said all along, sometimes this 'spirit' is more or less healthy and sometimes pathological. We require informed-cautiousness to inquire into the FMSs and "rebels" and "revolutionaries." Yet, whatever we find, the instinctual originary intuitive Defense is well-intended, from a Kosmological and evolutionary perspective, which I'm constructing.

This is a very early time developmentally, a time and experiential field that we generally don't well remember, though we may intuitively sense at some point in our early life phases (some would say perhaps in other life incarnations) we had "no fear." From a Zen Buddhist perspective, for example, Huber wrote, "Children don't know there is anything to be afraid of. . . . Children are naturally fearless; they are open to the world and to exploring and learning from it."[51] The topic of "fearless children" and parenting and educating is taken up in some detail in Chapter Four. What is relevant to consider in this discussion of *no fear* and "child consciousness" (to use that latter term loosely) is what Chris Griscom, a new age spiritual teacher, put before us:[52]

> The child [originally, or metaphorically] is not afraid of the unknown. . . . The child consciousness that resides within us still possesses a holographic way of perceiving things and has both the joy and the ability of being able to enter into new experiences, other dimensions, and to fearlessly seek and enjoy adventures. [she calls this the "fearless self"]

Artist Robert Genn, wrote "According to Maslow the traits needed for eminence [in one's creativity and art] are 'child-like spontaneity, fearlessness in the face of the unknown.'"[53] The tendency to romanticize (and overly-romanticize) "childhood" from an adult (and relative) perspective, is something we ought to stay away from in a critical holistic-integral theory, as Wilber has warned us.[54] However, the discourses circling around this "innocent time" and *no self* ("paradisical time" of pre-self) are worthy of study and critique. They are meaningful in shaping the way we start our human 'story' and how we construct our "human nature" (and from that, our "human condition" and "human potential").[55] They have, no doubt, a significant impact on our worldviews, beliefs, cultures, values, and actions—and thus, our fear management strategies and FME in general.

Bravery (and Bravado)

Fearlessness ways such as *no fear* and *bravery* are discourses of Pre-Modernity. Of course, they have been used in Modernity and Postmodernity, and still are. The postmodern critical integral theory of 'fearlessness' classifies them more stringently based on evolutionary and developmental logic, across the domains of the Natural (adual), Cultural (dual), and Spiritual (nondual). The research and theories that support this classification system are virtually all dominated by (Western white) men. This is not necessarily a problem in itself, but it is more problematic when the actual terms of the seven ways of fearlessness are primarily (not exclusively) attached to and signify socialized 'male behavior'—usually, with positive connotations (but not always). *Bravery* and its twisted version *bravado* are characteristically used with males and are typically encouraged by masculinist cultures (Western especially). We'll turn to that 'story' in a moment. In other words, 'men' (problematic as such a category is to define) are likely to slant their understanding of male bravery (and bravado) to the point where they cannot even see their own theoretical or philosophical assumptions and premises behind their assigning concepts and meaning to this label. Some alternative is required, or at least, some complementary tension is required in this construction of this major form of the seven ways of fearlessness.

In order to construct a balanced originary narrative for *bravery* (and its corresponding FMS-1, Beige-Survival; and FMS-2, Purple-Magical, and FMS-3, Red-Rebel—see Chapter Two), I utilize Judy Grahn's research and controversial evolutionary theorizing (see *Blood, Bread, and Roses: How Menstruation Created the World*, 1993) about the origins of dualistic consciousness and culture (i.e., the "creation of the world" from a historical-cultural perspective). Her work is based on the complex "metaformic" principles and processes of women's "menstruation." Defining of all these terms will come as this discussion unfolds. Thus, we start the analysis of the discourse of *bravery* from a feminine-feminist-womanist lens.[56] As far as this author knows, this is a first, in terms of systematically studying fearlessness. After laying that groundwork in the feminine, we'll turn to the actual World's Fearlessness Teachings on *bravery* (*bravado*) to integrate what takes shape under Grahn's influential ideas.

Instead of the Joseph Campbell "hero" mytheme (meaning, usually "male hero" *via* Sun-archetype and/or blade-image of the Hunter-Warrior) as the major player in understanding human development and bravery historically, Grahn would have us rather turn to the "menstruant" (meaning, "female menstruant" *via* Moon-archetype, chalice-image of Caregiver-Nurturer) as the major player in understanding bravery herstorically. Studying the living traditions in Kerala, South India, Grahn's doctoral research found corroborative evidence of matrifocal lineage and practices in goddess art and "goddess religion" which confirm the findings of archeomythologist Marija Gimbutas (re: "Old Europe" 40,000 – 1500 BCE and a unified worship of goddesses by neolithic farming people). Goddess figures recovered from archeological sites in Gimbutas's work and from contemporary temples in Karala by Grahn, confirm the specific important attention that was given to vulva, breasts, eyes and the color red in the spirituality of these times and places—a focus which has typically been downplayed or omitted by male (and/or non-feminist) researchers work on ancient and contemporary cultures and religion. According to Grahn (following Gimbutas's claims) there is significant evidence "of a single goddess tradition involving multiple forms and functions, which are different yet united in the Sacred Feminine—a river that may run under all humanity, as the oldest known identified religion/cosmogony."[57]

Grahn points out that various understandings, values, beliefs, and emotions around "blood" are highly controversial and conflictual across cultures and in some cases lead to oppressive caste systems and other forms of social hierarchical differentiation. "In Christian culture [and patriarchal cultures, generally], only male blood is sacred; naturally flowing female blood, especially menstruation, is hidden [and feared]."[58] Goddess worship, being somewhat revived today,[59] has its concomitant primary deities characteristically celebrate the menstruation of women. It reveres the crossover or transition to womanhood (menarche). Even more significant perhaps, is the honoring of the process and rituals around the menstruant (the one having menstrual flow), and their symbolic cultural and creative power that shapes culture and psychological development. Her research fervently challenges patriarchal hegemony in regard to the role of gender in connection with divinity and cultural evolution. She wrote of the goddess practices and their role as in[60]

> . . . contradistinction to the mainstream US and European Darwinian origin story resting on sexual selection and supposed male development of culture from hunting and 'superior intelligence'—that non sequitur. Metaformic theory, following this study, now posits more confidently that menstrual practices are the wellspring of human culture, bubbling from Jayakar's river of female wisdom. Male practices, including agricultural, horticultural and craft processes, have been deeply entrained to women's rites. Menstrual rites and the sacred feminine have also been the conduit for powerful radiant emanations that, shaped and named within women's rites, appear to have become living metaforms of both beneficial deity and destructive forces. . . . The paradoxical character of the goddess is also the paradoxical character of humans and of life. Relationships between women and nature have always been cultural. Human generative processes and cycles are at the center of culture and cognition; ritual,
> stemming from menstrual cultural processses, is embodied literacy, taking many forms. [she posits a notion of "Liberatory Evolution" in contradistinction to current oppressive evolutionary theory as constructed mainly by men and their ignore-ance of the goddess and role of the menstruant in cultural evolution]

Grahn's important contribution to this finding is the application of metaformic theory and concepts like "cosmetikos," as "ways we are taught to order the cosmos through our bodies" whether we know this embodied teaching and knowing consciously or unconsciously (e.g., in religious rituals or mere social custom/habit). Grahn's metaformic theory "postulates that human culture evolved from the connection between the lunar cycle and the menstrual cycle."[61] For Grahn and her students, people and traditions are, more or less, "constructed metaformically, that is to say, ritually"[62] and the base formative ritual is that associated with menstruation (i.e., body-based, and symbolized into ritual-based). The spectacular and critical journey of the *menstruant* can give a memory-tracing back many tens of thousands of years in human evolution. Grahn's most difficult but exciting challenge to us all in re-configuring the evolution of our cultural ancestors (and applying that to today) is "learning to think with metaformic theory," with a variety of benefits, not the least being to acknowledge and better assimilate differences and conflicts in customs, rituals, beliefs and religious practices around the world.[63]

Drawing on Grahn's book (*Blood, Bread, and Roses*) on metaformic theory and menstruation, this I summarize briefly (and inadequately) an interpretation of the 'story' she posits, with a particular focus on rites and ritual as Defense systems to the fear and terror of existence, as seen through the evolution of an adualistic mind or consciousness to a dualistic mind, or as referred to earlier under the *No Fear* discussion. What defense, *via* a notion of bravery, emerged in this evolutionary significant change? For Grahn, the major concept and distinctive behavior has to do with what she calls sacred "separation" (where *sacred* means "set apart" as in Sabbats[64]) in the development of rites, ritual, magic, culture and dualistic consciousness. This plausible explanation she offers begins generally with the powerful co-relation (and entrainment) of menstrual cycling with moon phase cycling (approx. 28 day monthly cycle)—all of which is related to sexual reproduction as a basic Darwinian imperative in Natural selection. One ought to keep in mind that females in earlier primate cousins did not cycle every 28 days but more like once or twice a year, or even less in some chimpanzee populations. According to the late Robert Ardrey (1908-1980), author and ethologist, the female hominid 'invention' of (female) "year-round-sexual responsiveness" (including monthly estrus) was "perhaps the most astonishing innovation that had ever come about since the biological introduction of sex itself, a half-billion years ago."[65] However, Cultural selection is a 'quantum leap' of sorts beyond (but including) mere Natural selection and genetic imperatives of biological materialist sexual reproduction.

The Grahnian metaformic story of menstruation begins some four and half million years ago. She suggests,[66]

> How terrifying the first ventures into separation [dualism] must have been, for at the very beginning of the changes from primate to human, archeologically dated at around four and a half million years ago, there were *no words* to describe the vision. Wordlessly, a more conscious female pulled her sisters into seclusion with her. . . . With the act of sitting together [as entraining menstruants] in the dark, the early woman entered a new world of consciousness [potentially one could call this the first woman's movement, vision, thought, act of advancing culture] Their minds that had as yet and perhaps for millenia to come no other expression than menstrual separation, the creation of [dualistic] consciousness by distinguishing menstruation from other [normal] activities. . . . she stepped out of Chaos, and across a terrifying abyss of mind. What makes the Abyss so ominous is that to enter human mind we step out of the security of instinct, the [safety] net of animal mind [in the Eden myth of the Bible this was the terrifying "sin" of the taking of the "tree of knowledge" and responsibility for the awakening distinction of "good and evil"] and enter the frail social construct of a rite, which is only held in place externally and accessed through cultural memory and repetition. The farther we get from inner knowledge, the more dependent on the external [cultural] mind we become. The Abyss yawned before those who did not keep the separation, for in their newfound understanding they established a principle correspondence: without menstrual separation, there *was* no light. Menstrual seclusion rites continually created light and separated it from dark. Without menstrual separation and the emphasis taboo placed on the seeing of light, the idea of light having a source would have flickered and gone out.

With all speculation as to what our female ancestors were actually doing millions of years ago in this evolution of the Natural animal mind to Cultural human mind, the "menstrual logic" behind this emergence is compelling. It is never clear what caused what in linear logical time but the more complex interaction of physiology, environmental conditions, life strategies and brain development and mind development, with rites and rituals, is undeniable. The power of entrainment of women's menstruation with each other, and then being noticed to align with the dark and light of the moon cycle in corresponding rhythm, placed a symbolic 'specialness' on the menstruant who, according to Grahn's research, was isolated from the normal routines of daily life of the early group/tribe. This was universal and so were the taboos that accompanied the menstruant who was *not* allowed to: (a) have her feet touch the ground when they were in the isolation of darkness in a cave, (b) not to have light fall upon them from the sun or moon, (c) not to look at people or things for fear of the "Evil Eye" she could possess and cause destruction. These broad general universals also had many variants that developed from them over the course of her-story.

Grahn's important point is that the awareness of the entrainment power with other women with the cosmic forces beyond the earth (i.e., with the moon and sun's light reflecting off it), created an externalization of "self" awareness beyond the "no self" (no fear) awareness of the animal mind living in the normal routines of everyday rhythms and Darwinian survival logics, strategies, and time. The menstrual logic and time was shamanic, visionary, women-centered, based in darkness—emerging into the light of day when she had finished bleeding. Grahn tells of how girls at the end of menarche would be taken by other older women and shown earth, water, and other species as though the menstruant had never seen them before and "In this way, seclusion reenacts the original awakening of human consciousness."[67] "Menstrual seclusion rites reenacted [dramatized] their own discoveries, returning women back along a path of unraveling time, to the chaotic mind before light was seen."[68] The taboo of fear (and awe) surrounding the menstruant by others in the group/tribe is palpable in Grahn's description:[69]

> Nor could she gaze at bodies of water, for fear of causing a flood; if she were to look at trees and plants, they would wither [so it was believed]. She had to protect the sources of water. . . . She had, in her blood rites taken as a whole, complete power over all that humans depend on for their lives, all we had deciphered about the universe—for, as I have argued, it was menstrual consciousness that first created all these elements [as distinctions]. And so many of the rites involve silence, as though they were laid down during the long eras before speech, when action alone did the creating. . . . Hers was the power of raveling and of unraveling, since what consciousness (spirit, mystery, and mind) gives us, it can also take back. And the power of creation and destruction, as at one time evidently all humanity believed, was in the woman's blood.

For purposes of this book, it is important to imagine and theorize of the power of the menstruant and the menstruant's journey in relation to the survival Defense systems of the group/tribe. Just before that, however, let us summarize the interpretations. Women, following the metaformic pattern of Grahn's explanation, are the embodiment of Creation and Destruction, that is, "power of raveling and of unraveling" and "power of creation and destruction." Menstruant's were constructed within their groups/tribes in the metaformic of a Goddess of Birth and Death symbolically. They were the embodiment of the relationship of the human-Divine principles both struggling and enjoying their co-existence and their seeming paradoxical qualities in and above the everyday circumstances and laws of Nature and survival itself. The women's unique and powerful physiology of bleeding led them to this symbolic power as their minds led them to "new consciousness," which we call today "dualistic"—that is, a construction of a distinct subject and object, seer and the seen. It separated them from mere naive primordial "unity" in Nature and from the role of men in culture. Simultaneously, a separation-menstruation-logic placed the role of women at the heart of the culture of the group/tribe. It placed them in the cosmogonic originary and formative imagination of all "The World." It was awesome and it was (perhaps) terrifying. In this way the experience is consistent with our previous discussion by Joseph Campbell, retelling the more abstract mytheme of "I am"—that is, dualistic consciousness and concomitant birth of human fear.

Gimbutas noted that the Goddesses of these earliest times of the birth of human culture and religion are "Life-givers [but] are also death-wielders. . . . The concept of regeneration and renewal is perhaps the most outstanding and dramatic theme that we perceive in this symbolism" and thus the Goddess is an immanent (not transcendent) metaform of Nature itself (and *visa versa*), according to Gimbutas.[70] The menstruant's bleeding brought forth, through embodied correspondence and associative 'magical' thinking, the great fear (trauma) of flooding and death that early humans on the savannahs of Africa must have experienced repetitively, as they often lived close to river valleys because of their richness of food and water. Grahn wrote,[71] "The Flood can be described as loss of consciousness, overwhelming mental as well as physical chaos, the quality of being 'lost.' The Flood myth, in all its permutations, is surely the most universal of the ancient stories."

I cannot help think of the postmodern ascription of "liquid fear" and flooding used by Bauman (or "fluidification" by Massumi), mentioned throughout the first chapters of this book—what ancient feminine vs. masculine terror is being manifested in postmodern discourses? Following Wilber's extensive synthetic study of the evolution of consciousness in human individuals and as that is correlated to human cultural development in history, it can be said that a major universal principle of growth and development is "each new step [in consciousness] also creates new fears, new diseases, new pathologies," says Wilber in his early 1980s writing.[72] And in this book, I suggest that when new fear arises there is new fearlessness arising with it. This is the nature of the Kosmos itself. It has to do with 'correction' of potential fear ('fear') patterns. It leads to a healthy *differentiation* (i.e., expansion and complexity building) in growth processes, and away from *dissociation* (i.e., unhealthy contraction and regression and simplistic reductionism). Wilber further adds an important insight to this time:[73]

> Man [sic] had finally 'come up from the apes' as a self-reflexive being, and was therefore open to anxiety and guilt (the Scientific Fall); and [s]he *also* became aware of the fact that [s]he was *already*, originally, and priorly divorced from Spirit (the Theological Fall).

Common to Grahn, Gimbutas, Campbell and Wilber above is the "Fall" story of this amazing awakening in evolution of consciousness to the duality of existence, but at the same time the existential terror (fears) that go with it. There is a long explanation of that in their writing and many others who have studied consciousness development—which, revolves, more or less, around the evolution of fear/terror. That, however, is not the focus of this book. What is of most interest is how fearlessness, in its unique diverse forms, is emerging along with this transition from adual (FMS-0) to dual (FMS-1, and further into FMS-2, 3). Theoretically, the first fearlessness strategy, I call *bravery*, is the impulse and manifestation that goes with the menstruant's journey each month into a "separation" from the group/tribe. This is a vulnerable situation for a young female in her first menarche and/or a group of such females, or even for more experienced women. There are increased threats for sure to such adventurers, menstruants, going off without the full protection of the group/tribe, especially from the larger males/warriors who apparently stayed clear away. Predators and other invading males from other groups/tribes would be a major factor in increased threat. So, under these circumstances the evolution of bravery is likely to have occurred, but of course it was sanctioned by the group/tribe, although there is nothing in the women's feminist writing on menstruation that I have read that makes a big deal out of the menstruant's bravery upon bleeding. This is in contrast, as we shall see later below, where the "hero's" bravery is fore-fronted as he goes off on his rites of passage and journey of "separation" from the group/tribe/civilization (e.g., in a vision quest). The menstruant isn't reported to have carried weaponry at all with them or had it available at the bleeding sites in the dark caves. This either was not the case in fact, or it has not been reported.

Hypothetically, it can be assumed that the power and ferocity of the menstruant comes from another source than big muscles, skills of fighting and killing, or use of weapons. Rather, we are dealing with the likelihood of a "power" of two major sources: (1) within, that the menstruant carries as a symbolic referent of the Goddess and, (2) without, the power assigned to the menstruant by the magical believing group/tribe that she belongs to.

There are no "brave acts" reported in the feminine, woman's, or feminist versions of the menstruant's journey, as I read Grahn's work. Yet, clearly, this was a frightening time for them as it was for many in the group/tribe. The awakening of dualistic consciousness is quite (or apparently) terrifying. The *feminine bravery* for these menstruants exists in menstrual time and consciousness as a necessary (and relatively limited) *following* of the body: that is, a slowing down, the flow of red waters (the flood), the unconscious reverie, and the stillness of darkness. It consists of walking away and walking back; that is, of separating and returning. It involves a great risk and trust that what is happening to them is meant to happen, yet, it is beyond their total control as an individual (egoic mind). And for the group/tribe likewise, menstruation is beyond their total control, rules and regulations. It is an occasion of 'special' cosmic enactments, or the energies of a 'greater Other-ness.' The great forces of Nature and the Goddess are at play. And in these earliest hominids no scientific explanations are advanced to explain away one's fear/terror. Rather, magical rites, stories, and ritual, are created to locate, contain, and thus, manage (and story) the somewhat overwhelming fear. Equally, "Like magic, ritual is the act of transforming consciousness," as Elinor Gadon says.[74]

The Defense system of bravery for the menstruant is in ritual form (i.e., magical thinking of the earliest forms of dualistic consciousness). All the accompanying "regulating" taboos imposed on the menstruant and process of women's bleeding time (moon time) are arguably, the very structures of management of fear—fear of death and destruction—fear of the vulnerability of an organism living in a world that is harsh at times and takes it's toll. The birth survival rate was not all that 'good' compared to standards of survival for offspring for most humans today (at least, in the First World and Second World nations). The menstruant, if they got pregnant, carried the potential for new life but also for immanent death. No wonder females, women, feminists, are so feared, especially by men who have passed on their genetic code to the woman but then have little obvious connection with the success or failure rate at birth and in the immediate perinatal caring environment. Mother's survival rate also was not all that great back then, relatively speaking. All the male could do was protect the vulnerable pregnant female and mother and child from predators and other aggressive acts. But evidence (*a la* Goodall) studying chimpanzees living in the wild shows that many deaths come to vulnerable females and mothers and their children from sources that the alpha male has no way to prevent.

The defense to survive involves a growing consciousness to the effects and affects of death (i.e., mortality as distinct from immortality). New emotions arrived in early hominids like shame. "Shame," says Grahn, "is consciousness of ability to do evil, and it is a fundamental human quality"[75] with dualistic consciousness and culture. Arguably, animal adualistic consciousness has *no fear* and thus no shame. Shame[76] is a cousin of fear, like guilt. Dualistic consciousness brings a rampant increase in this new species of fear—whereas in the adualistic consciousness, death is not thought about reflectively in a future sense. The adualistic mind is in present time only, life and death are more or less witnessed but with little connection to causality of them as natural principles. Once the menstruant evolved as the "symbolic" metaformic principle of the Goddess and Life (Natural) principles, then came the "new" problem and accompanying 'new' fear, shame, and responsibility for doing evil; that is, to bring about destruction because of will, of acts that an emerging "self" does now that it is separated from Nature or the Divine. These are the characteristics of FMS-2 (Purple, Magical) that are outlined in Chapter Two. Grahn explains the paradoxical feelings and reality of managing the "power of blood" (i.e., the power of fear) in this feminine (discourse) perspective of cultural evolution:[77]

> The problem with everything that accrued to the power of blood is that it all had to be knit together and held in place with increasingly elaborate ritual [and taboos]. For as memory and predictive skills increased [with dualistic consciousness], so did the law of cause and effect that told people their own actions ['good' or 'evil'] were what raised and lowered the light, kept the sky in place, held back the floods, and made the yams proliferate. The more the external [dual] mind knew about the world, the more effort was needed to maintain

it. As technologies of household arts and food purification, of hunting and earliest gardening developed, people took on more complex and demanding work in every sphere. It must have seemed at times that the taboos knitting sacred human life together, with the growing multitude of deities and spirits, would collapse society under their weight. . . . The solution to the gathering burden of knowledge [i.e., conscious awareness of one's choices for 'good' and 'evil'] was the establishment of separate select groups of people who would enact [with 'professional' precision] taboos in behalf of everyone else. . . . boys as well as girls would have been selected for a special life, a life of rigorous training and intense seclusion, to maintain the most extreme taboos [fears] for the people, to specialize in keeping certain rules of 'the path' for the sake of the village as a whole.

No longer able to solely depend on mere animal instincts (i.e., adual consciousness) to survive in a world of the Natural, the emergent separation processes of menstruation brought forward operationally the nature of will, decision, and actions that an individual or tribe may bring about that cause (or were corresponding to) Life and Death. The Cultural responsibility and burden of that was "shame"—because we made mistakes or thought we did and thought we were to blame (or someone was to blame) for the not so good things (i.e., traumas, or environmental accidents, etc.) that happen as part of living. This was new to human beings in these earliest groups/tribes. The use of magic, ritual, rites, taboos, and later specialized "professional" shamans, sorcerers, medicine man (including women who took on those roles) added a new Spiritual dimension into everyday life. Grahn would argue the very first of these spiritual (healing and corrective moral) roles were dominated by women, menstruants, and those women that attended to the ritual around menstruation.

The loss of dependency on animal instincts, as Grahn argues, created a new vulnerability of relying on cultural rules and taboos, all of which were symbolic fear-based compensations and self-regulating means to reconnect the human with the Divine and with the Natural (Nature's instinctual ways) and maintain that intimate harmonious connection as much as possible—believing that to lose it would bring destructive and 'evil' things to their land and people. That was also a reality not mere belief. With excess fear, of course, that belief could become distorted by symbolic dualism (dissociation) and create superstitions that eventually became more terrifying than the reality of what was actually a threat (i.e., a "culture of fear" syndrome, as discussed previously). This is a theme we shall return to over and over in this book, as fear and fearlessness 'battle' for domination and privilege to assess risks—to assess what is "real." As well, these cultural rules and taboos, and specialized magical "professionals" were dealing with the inner psychic demand on these early humans and their new dualistic consciousness. One demand was how they experienced shame and responsibility for all Life and Death—a responsibility that was no more intense than in the menstruant's journey and experiences of getting pregnant and facing the risks of death of the infant prenatally or perinatally. To lose an offspring carried huge implications physiologically and psychologically (including culturally). A second demand, to sometimes have to kill an offspring (as in infanticide) also carried huge implications. The future of the group/tribe depended primarily on these willed actions of the female. The demands of early women's work and world, are so apparent. The fear of life and death collapsed upon each other in this first stage of emerging dualistic consciousness, and its existence regarding managing fear—a fear that was more and more symbolic (socially constructed) in the Cultural domain, further and further removed from the Natural domain.

The Goddess metaformic, based upon the female body and moon-menstruant's condition was given the "power of blood" that corresponded to Life and Death. To manage (if not control) that real and symbolic psycho-cultural burden well (at least most of the time) was accomplished with the assignment of *immortality status* to the deity (i.e., Goddess = menstruant). As Gimbutas wrote of the Goddess, "Life-givers are also death-wielders. Immortality is secured through the innate forces of [sexual reproduction] regeneration within Nature itself."[78] The search for safety and security, as part of Defense systems, is inherent, as has been argued throughout this text. However, in the early stages of the Cultural, one of the most powerful symbolic substitutions (or fear projections) occurs in order to psychically handle the burden of a world of cause and effect, world of time, world of responsibility (apparently) for Life and Death and continuity of Creation in the face of Destruction (i.e., the force of Good and Evil, respectively). The human had to take on the "power of blood" as the power of Immortality, of which the menstruant-Goddess co-relation was created. This is the mortal-immortal co-relational bond. It ensured, as Gimbutas suggests, that mortals could help (possibly ensure) that "Immortality is secured" (correspondingly, that mortality is secured)—and they did that *via* life strategies that were biological, cultural, and spiritual. This refers to the integral theme began earlier in this book that the Natural, Cultural and Spiritual domains are critical conceptualizations to understanding FME in our human past, in the present, and in the future. Wilber and Ernest Becker, and other male theorists of the evolution of consciousness have seen this phenomena of Defense as well and have called it, for simplicity here, the "Immortality Project." Which I have previously called the 'Fear' Project.[79] It ends up being a project that is both a necessity and imperative of fearlessness and a great vulnerability to fear-based dissociative symbolic distortions, whereby fear overall is actually increased instead of lessened (i.e., the anatomy of the "culture of fear" syndrome, as I have defined earlier).

The result of the imperfection of this fear management strategy has led to great horror and violence on the planet. However, that is a fearstory to leave for another book (see also Wilber's book, *Up From Eden*). That said, as this discussion of *bravery* unfolds, the fault in the Defense system of the premodern discourse is going to expose the emergence of a twisted pathological version of *feminine bravery* and *masculine bravery*—toward what is *bravado* overall as a Defense strategy to manage fear/terror. No one gender is total cause or blame for this down-side or 'shadow-side' of human evolution. Both (all) are responsible.

For the moment, it is best to draw on actual discourses that one can find in the WFTs on *bravery* and *bravado* (and its cousins). From there I pursue more theorizing as to how they are characteristically discourses written mostly by men and apply to the "hero" archetype and journey. Joseph Campbell's rendering of the hero, psycho-mythically, is a foundation for understanding but it unfortunately is mostly meant for males (but not totally). I am aware there are many other "gender" (queer) formations one could deal with in this discussion, but there simply isn't space to give all attention here. It is worth noting that Campbell near the end of his life said that he would have revised his "hero" conceptualization and narrative, because he constructed it without knowing Marija Gimbutas's (feminist) archeo-mythological work[80] (upon which Grahn and I have largely drawn upon to understand the menstruant narrative).

Growing up in Western highly developed nations, we generally learned that a "brave" was an indigenous male who was a warrior. That's my limited white male urban learning, at least. They were extraordinarily brave in facing the enemy and in hunting dangerous game. White English dictionaries typically construct the meaning of bravery as "a quality or state of having courage, being dauntless" and so on. Then one has to define what "courage" means. In this holistic-integral theory, *courage* (FMS-5, Orange, Scientific and FMS-6, Green, Sensitive) is located in a modernist discourse of ways of fearlessness to manage fear ('fear'). Indeed, in common discourse and teachings by others, bravery and courage are often used interchangeably.

Another distinction important to this text is mentioned elsewhere, when I wrote,[81]

In most cultures and in common language, bravery is held in higher esteem than the qualities of bravado or braggadacio, the latter two being often more a superficial immature attitude to 'show off' based on an inflated egoic-style of one's individual strength, and less on their moral and ethical commitment to the Good and True and Beautiful for all of society. The authorities of the State often mark bravery as equivalent to the 'soldier in battle' sacrificing for their nation as the highest good a citizen can partake in (as with Aristotle's view). Sadly, feminist psychotherapist Dorothy Rowe (1987) pointed out that some evidence shows 'It is the bravest men and women from the [military] Services [during and after war]' that suffer most from mental breakdown.

Common and moral sense traditions from the WFTs may even mock bravery, such as the Aesop's fable: "It is easy to be brave, from a safe distance." Often the discourse refers to an extraordinary act of will that is engaged in the face of danger and/or fear—for example: "But bravery is never the absence of fear, as much as a presence in spite of it."[82] In a discussion on the sport of boxing a correspondent wrote, "A brave man is one who recognizes a danger, he feels the fear, but he controls the fear and faces the danger."[83] In a poem written by Joanna Baillie (a Christian perspective), she declares the brave man as one who is not free from feeling fear, as that would be stupid and irrational, if danger were near, but rather the brave has a noble soul that dares danger above and beyond what Nature would shrink from and tell him to run away.[84]

All of the above quotes (discourses) have a theme of not extinguishing the Natural realm in which fear is located but positing the implicit moral imperative to include but transcend Natural fear in a 'higher' ("noble soul") from which the Cultural (if not Spiritual) realm is invoked as a strategy of fear management.

Humans, unlike animals, are expected not to be victims of fear nor of Nature, as that is our very definition of being *human*—that is, to be brave. Thus, we ought not flee fear because of superstition, irrationality, and cowardice. Dualistic consciousness in other words, requires we willfully act, take charge, and assess and reflect on reality and risk (danger and fear). However, says an African Ewe proverb: "There is a time to show bravery and time to show 'fear,' i.e., cautious retreat."[85]

On the shadow-side of bravery, with her critique of Western culture, Rowe wrote, "By denying painful facts and emotions we become brave."[86] As a fear management strategy and defense mechanism, *denial is power* and will play a key role in the distinction later of twisted (if not pathological) *bravado* from healthy bravery. Confusing denial with bravery is what Rowe is pointing to, and what many women and feminists, and security experts like de Becker, have pointed to in the WFTs.

Next, we see religious and spiritual traditions using the term bravery: "One of the grandest, bravest characters in the history of the race is the law-giver and moral reformer, Moses. . . . this 'Man of Law' stands as a sturdy bulwark of the highest good [sometimes called "moral courage"]."[87] This Christian discourse on Moses as the archetypal brave 'Man of Law' is something that emerges fully in the FMS-4 (Blue, Mythic) discourse of premodernity. Yet, it is still very powerful and active today, whereby "law" and "bravery" are configured together as a moral fear management strategy of control—both control outwardly and inwardly. In contrast somewhat (though with a similar theme) to the above Christian Western discourse, Eastern spirituality teachings from Swami Vivekananda speaking to youth wrote, for example, "Be moral. Be brave. Be a heart-whole man. Strictly moral, brave unto desperation. Don't bother your head with religious theories [FMS-4]. Cowards only sin, brave men never, no, not even in mind."[88] Vivekananda is more interested in the disciplined mind approach to bravery and morality, rather than a social (institutional) "law-based" (and mostly fear-based) approach. Vivekananda, like many others, teaches fearlessness more akin to a nondual (3rd-tier) and/or 2nd-tier strategy. It is seductive to pursue the connection here of "sin" with "fear." I shall refrain.

Pragmatic and functionalist perspectives on bravery are common. In secular Western philosophical literature René Descartes in the 17th century wrote "bravery is an excess of courage which is always good, provided that the end proposed is good."[89] In ancient Greek Athenian culture (*Philonides*) wrote, "Even the bravest should fear shame, the law, the displeasure of their superiors or their community, or the commission of an offense against the gods."[90] Again, bravery is honored but *not* if it is without fear—especially, without fear of shame. Shame being critical in the development of dualistic consciousness, and shame seemingly associated inherently with woman's culture and FMS-2 (Purple, Magic), as discussed earlier around menstruation logic and consciousness in the earliest hominids becoming human. I am acknowledging this past evolutionary step and the role of shame (or guilt: the cousins of fear), but I am *not* claiming that shame, guilt or fear are *essential* "controls" for social order in all situations (as Hobbes, Nathanson[91] or others may argue), or even in postmodern times. That is all open for debate and indeed we need to look at the role of feelings and emotions in any good FME. I simply cannot go into these areas fully in this book. Although, it is worth quoting Beck and Cowan on the relationship of Cultural v-memes and some emotional aspects of FMS on the evolutionary continuum. They summarized that,[92]

> While there is no sure correlation between v-MEMEs and temperament, the cool colors are generally more authoritarian; the warm colors more flexible. Rigidity is high in BLUE [FMS-4] and GREEN [FMS-6]. Dogmatism passes from a High in BLUE to its Low in YELLOW [FMS-7]. Guilt surfaces in BLUE; disappears in ORANGE [FMS-5]; resurfaces in GREEN; drops away again in YELLOW. 'Don't fence me in!' demands for freedom are the highest in RED [FMS-3]; somewhat mollified into a quest for autonomy at ORANGE; and become unemotional individualism without isolation in YELLOW. BEIGE [FMS-1] experiences distress and delight based on biological satisfaction; PURPLE [FMS-2] lives with fear [shame] and superstition; RED is caught up with anger and avoiding shame; BLUE deals with an almost perpetual guilt burden; ORANGE is manic in its competitive urges to win in this life; and GREEN carries great responsibility for others and the burden of caring so much. What emotionality there is in YELLOW is based in feelings about one's own performance and failures of systems to function as needed [for the whole-health of the Spiral]. TURQUOISE [FMS-8] seems to reactivate outer-focused spirituality and Zen-like emotions [Coral, FMS-9] based in liberation of consciousness without ceremony or groupiness. Keep these points in mind and you can avoid many of the personality-based pitfalls change [in individuals and organizations] presents.

In non-Western traditions and highly communal cultures, with teachings of fearlessness, there can be a taboo of strong regulation against interpersonal conflict (i.e., prideful bravery) as in the Ifaluk tribe:[93]

> What is notable about the value placed on bravery is that it is not associated with interpersonal confrontation. The man who conquers fear in the face of the threat of another's aggression is *not* brave, but either foolish, or more likely, simply 'bad.'

In a more aggressive northern peoples, the warrior tradition of the Vikings sees "truth is only for the brave; that joy is only for him who does not fear to be alone; that life is only for the one who is not afraid to die."[94] And bravery, in its healthy side, encourages diversity as adult educator Lindeman wrote,[95] "We should, if we were bravely intelligent, beg individuals to give us their difference, not their sameness. Nothing exciting can happen in a world of uniformities and homogeneities."

A common discourse of the human potential movement (and 'new age'): "Our wounds speak not of our weakness, but of our bravery. Life is not given to us because it will be easy. It is given to us because we are capable of it."[96] The above quotes are definitely biased toward men (but not always), and definitely diverse in meanings, sometimes contradictory. And this brings us to the archetype of the "hero," and a faith (a reality) that in the hero is the spirit of fearlessness—capable of handling fear and the life challenges that comes to us. At least, in most cases. Not everyone or every group or organization, for many reasons, is able to be brave enough—and many succumb to victimization and never recover from a fate ruled by fear ('fear'). "Brave enough" for what?, that is the question. And a very complicated question, which this text can only begin to address adequately. Keep in mind the orientation here is *brave enough* to "act" against fear ('fear') and violence (i.e., hurting and suffering, oppression and repression), and for love and non-violence (healing and joy, liberation and freedom).

In many ways, this decision is like the decision to be on the side of Life or the side of Death-making, in symbolic and real terms, or the side of Creation or Destruction-making, or Good and Evil, in symbolic terms; however, one wants to define them. I am not suggesting these dichotomies are absolutely real but they are symbolic of qualitative oppositions (forces and demands) that the dualistic mind and consciousness experiences as Cultural evolution unfolds (i.e., between FMS-1 to 6); which remain critical distinctions in more subtle yet powerful forms in FMS-7 and 8 as well). For example, an organism is either "hurting" or "healing" not both, or an organism is either "dead" or "alive" not both. In other words, to make a *decision* to be on the side of Love or fear, on the path of fear (1st-tier) or path of fearlessness (2nd-tier to 3rd-tier), is real and "bicentric" (as I call it).

Indeed, there are many different ways and traditions that speak to and about this notion of *bravery* as a way of fearlessness involving conscious decision (but not always). The WFTs are rife with these bi-centric (absolutist) oppositionalities as part of moral and ethical principles to guide behavior, be it individual or collective. Postmodernity (especially extreme poststructuralism and its valuing of "individualism" as an ideology) has attempted to erase all communal absolutes like dualities, dichotomies and binaries. That is likely having very destructive ethical and moral consequences overall. Of course, a relatively small percentage of the world's population is operating *via* postmodernism. As Zygmunt Bauman was quoted earlier, "Postmodernity has not allayed the fears which modernity injected into humanity." And arguably, postmodernity is adding its own set of new fears to the pot. Fearlessness ('fearlessness') is that which brings us out and beyond fear ('fear') and the limitations of fear (and 'fear'). And the argument all along has been that we have to grow with and into fearlessness at its highest stages or levels, we cannot just decide willfully and be there, at least not for more than a very short time (in a "state" vs. a "stage"). The 'fear'-based patterns are powerful to undermine the evolutionary trajectory of consciousness (as declared in the Credo of Fearlessness in Chapter One). Such is the developmental logic of the "dialectic of progress"[97] followed here; as well, change and transformation logic is followed here—for example, a good principle to keep in mind with evolutionary change (especially Cultural) is: "leaps forward are often preceded by desperate regressive steps backward," as Beck and Cowan[98] have found in living systems. Freud knew "regress" in a therapeutic or integrative sense, comes usually before we can "progress." A generalization seems useful: dialectically, from a systems perspective, sometimes we're timid and regress, sometimes we're brave and progress—it depends on developmental and environmental conditions and contexts. This is the realistic-optimistic view I adopt here.

Simply, the discourse on bravery above, diverse as the WFTs are, seems to direct us at the deepest formative foundation to take on the qualities of bravery for the growth of the evolution of consciousness, from adual to dual to nondual, whether we act bravely by conscious choice or not. Overall, we are 'called' through evolution to embody and enact the systematic telic drive or 'spirit' to advance, not to regress overall. Overall progress is the creative imperative 'choice' of Intelligence in the Kosmos. What most of us still have to learn is that it comes with "no guarantees." Life is a (no-guarantees) struggle, relatively speaking.

Having looked at the feminine role of menstruant bravery in the evolution of cultural consciousness, let's now look at the complementary masculine role of heroic bravery, and arrive at a complementary, critical, and holistic-integral definition (conceptualization) for *bravery* (and *bravado*) in our future.

The late Ernest Becker (1924-1974), eminent existentialist researcher and philosopher of the late 20th century, and Pulitzer Prize winner for his book *The Denial of Death* (1973), wrote an entire thesis around the role of *"the heroic."* For him and others, it was the foundation for understanding human nature and cultural evolution, which in many ways is a particular interpretation of the spirit of fearlessness itself. Although, Becker never (apparently) used the word "fearlessness" (as most pure existentialist wouldn't). Becker argued that,[99]

> In times such as ours there is a great pressure to come up with concepts that help men [sic] understand their dilemma; there is an urge toward vital ideas, toward a simplification of needless intellectual complexity. . . . One such vital truth that has long been known is the idea of *heroism;* but in "normal" scholarly times we never thought of making much of it, of parading it, or of using it as a central concept. Yet the popular mind always knew about how important it was . . . William James—who covered just about everything—remarked at the turn of the century: 'mankind's common instinct for reality . . . has always held the world to be essentially a theatre for heroism.'

Philosophers (all males), especially Emerson and Nietzsche, knew our central calling and primary task is "the heroic," says Becker. From this Beckerian lens we can see the overall development of the social sciences (with Marx onward) and psychology (with Freud onward) representing a detailed account of the "problem of human heroism."[100] Becker, a transdisciplinary thinker, also brought forth the idea of narcissism as central to understanding the inherent urge toward heroism. He wrote,[101]

> As Erich Fromm has so well reminded us, this idea is one of Freud's great and lasting contributions. Freud discovered that each of us repeats the tragedy of the mythical Greek Narcissus: we are hopelessly absorbed with ourselves. If we care about anyone it is usually ourselves first of all. As Aristotle somewhere put it: luck is when the guy next to you gets hit with the arrow. Twenty-five hundred years of history have not changed man's basic narcissism. . . . It is one of the meaner aspects of narcissism that we feel that practically everyone is ex-

pendable except ourselves. . . . Our organism is ready to fill the world all alone, even if our mind shrinks at the thought. This narcissism is what keeps men marching into point-blank fire in wars: at heart one doesn't feel that *he* will die. . . . [i.e., he feels immortal]

Freud explained that the unconscious dimension of humans knows neither death nor linear time. In the human organism's physiochemical and genetic recesses there is a feeling of immortality. For Becker, humans are not able to escape this animal nature and selfishness of narcissism (i.e., a most intimate primal defense).

As Defense, by evolutionary design, the organism protects itself and its own identity and integrity. Survival and preservation are literally protoplasmic. Becker argued that invasions by 'other' are minimized and result from a self-nurturing aspect so basic to life and humans. The organism attempts to keep pleasure as its main experience. Awareness of the suffering with death and mortality is one of the aspects the organism tends to act against—thus, the narcissistic and heroic (rebel) impulse. The narcissistic self-empowerment is essential to the organism in its environments. Call it self-esteem, as Becker did—a foundational built-in "self-worth" (and need for it). The great psychodynamic psychologist, Alfred Adler, promoted such a view that what we need most as humans is a feeling of security in self-esteem. This is a primal motivation. For Becker, this self-asserting "natural" narcissistic complex of heroism feeds on symbolic powers attributed to it also by the culture within which it exists. Humans necessarily want to feel they are valued both in the universe and in their groups and societies. It seems we don't like to be second-best, at anything.[102]

I find Becker's work compelling, albeit, at times without a postmodern developmental sensibility. He articulates the deeply structured Natural Defense system (fearlessness) of the human being. Although, Becker's analysis is not so focused on physical needs, one cannot deny his *heroic logic* of the interior self-needs—both socially, and yet individually, as in psychological needs of the human being based in organismic survival and its inherent natural narcissism (i.e., self-love). He asserts that this is a "physiochemical" and "protoplasmic" need but it is also desire—an inherent *organismic bravery* (heroism). The rest of his book goes into this in great detail.

For Becker, the striving to assert oneself is the (masculine-agentic) heroic in human nature (albeit, Becker is not a feminist nor does he make due recognition of the differences in gender in his theory of heroism). Yet, his is a plausible universal heroic: which is to assert oneself, more or less, against the communal social structures, traditions, and taboos and against disease, death, decay and threats of danger. Sounds like universal Defense. The archetypal Hero (like the Rebel) is the risk-taking, standing up, assertive, and individuating aspect of human nature. Albeit, each individual in each unique circumstance does not necessarily manifest this form of healthy narcissism in the same way. Some are more overt and some more passive in their "self-love" and heroic expressions. And when humans move out of the adual organismic bravery he speaks of, the dual consciousness creates an even stronger "cherished narcissism" that constitutes itself in cultural symbols, images, abstractions of immortality.[103] The heroes that the self mimics, emulates, and attaches to, are universal and a constant practice like biological and cultural imperatives to seek significance and greatness—all built-in to an inherent narcissistic foundation.

This is the heroic bravery of FMSs-1 to 3, most particularly, though aspects of this can be found all the way along the continuum of the evolution of consciousness and FMSs. Emulation and enactment of great, strong, wise (if not immortal) human beings in a group/tribe is a selection process that is rewarded in the Natural (e.g., increased "fitness" for the future genetic line, ancestors, or species *via* differential passing on one's genetic code over others doing so) *and* Cultural realms (e.g., differential passing on one's cultural code of ideas and values, beliefs, over others doing so). It is a means of gaining power and privilege and sometimes becomes out-and-out dominance *via* certain heroic characteristics, of which bravery would have to be pivotal. In part, this is useful to survival: meaning, first useful to maintenance functions, then to reproduction functions. Simply, the "heroic" qualities are important to Life in its struggle against the forces of the Natural and Cultural worlds where chaos and crisis are part of existence. Evolution thus, is boosted against devolution by the basic organic and psycho-cultural narcissism of which Becker describes so well.

FME in the future ought not ignore Becker and his theory of "hero systems" (also see TMT, as I've mentioned in earlier chapters). There's little space here to elaborate on Becker's *heroic logic* (i.e., a masculine metaformic theory on the evolution of culture). Suffice it to say, he is well aware of the diversity of "hero systems," as he calls them. Around the planet they are magical, mythic — religious and secular—some even scientific and so-called "civilized." He acknowledges most of us moderns shun away from hero systems especially, more pathological forms (e.g., Caesar, Charles Manson, Hitler, and/or any dictator-types). However, Becker's important point is that we need to be careful how we judge the great "heroes" of history, and from what perspective we assess them— not to 'throw the baby out with the bath.' He argues it is not their individual fault alone for a corruption of the heroic drive but rather the way in which the society (context) designs and manages its hero system and funnels its roles.[104]

To deny the heroic its naturalness and potential good because of some bad examples of its abuse, is not what Becker recommends. The hero system as archetypal Defense is also a creative system for innovation in development. The educative and psychological problem is to become more conscious of one's path to manifesting the "feeling of heroism," as Becker called it.[105] Such is a necessary self-analytical and critical process, because the evidence shows that a heroic impulse can be twisted, distorted, and turned pathological as well as pathologized, by the overall hero system (or FMSs) one lives within.

According to Becker, the postmodern climate of the 1960s-70s was indicative of a crisis of bravery and the heroic. Youth felt there was no longer a meaningfully constructed heroic for them in their culture. They were being ascribed a role (like today) of a consumer. It was not what they wanted to be, or at least for many that rebelled against the system in heroic fashion.[106] They dropped out and some turned to anti-hero worship, many left traditional religion as no longer providing a valid hero system for the world and the future they had to live in.

The acted out and were largely scorned, sometimes coerced, beaten, incarcerated, and some were killed. The mainstream society saw them not as heroes at all. One could make a case for many "terrorists" today, who are caught in pathological hero systems.

One cannot leave Becker without seeing the relationship between this primal instinct of narcissism-bravery as a fear management life strategy and the "terror of death" from which it proposedly emerges. The emerging of dualistic consciousness in the evolution of culture creates an awareness of one's death and the responsibility for death of self and others (as we saw similarly the great burden of responsibility with the menstruant logic). The way to manage that great burden of awareness (fear and shame) with mortality, is through constructing a defense mechanism called the Immortality Project, as discussed earlier in this chapter. The Beckerian heroic impulse or rebel impulse is a deeply structured project of the organism and culture to create itself into the immortal (often, Divine), so that it can ultimately overcome fear of death (if not Death itself, symbolically). Becker suggests that heroism is basically motivated in a kind of reflex in confrontation with the terror of death awareness. Societies may call this bravery or courage—to face death. We adore this as it moves us deeply, and perhaps contemplate in their actions, we are not yet (or may never be) so brave. Yet, we are often motivated by them and their brave actions. Becker believed "the hero has been the center of human honor. . . . Man has elevated animal courage into a cult."[107]

Joseph Campbell, as early as 1949 in *The Hero with a Thousand Faces* recognized the "imagery of schizophrenic fantasy [studied by psychiatrist John Weir Perry] perfectly matches that of the mythological hero journey," of which the basic universal pattern is:[108]

> . . . first, of a break away or departure from the local social order and context; next, a long, deep retreat inward and backward, as it were, in time, and inward, deep into the psyche; a chaotic series of encounters there, darkly terrifying experiences, and presently (if the victim is fortunate) encounters of a centering kind, fulfilling, harmonizing, giving new courage; and then finally, in such fortunate cases, a return journey of rebirth to life. . . . in my own published work [on the mythical hero journey] . . . 1) separation, 2) initiation, and 3) return: 'A hero ventures forth from the world of common day into a region of supernatural wonder: fabulous forces are there encountered and a decisive victory is won: the hero comes back from this mysterious adventure with the power to bestow boons on his fellow men. [sic]

Again, without space for an in depth analysis and comparison of the sacred "separation" of Grahn's menstruant and Campbell's hero, it is reasonable to claim they are virtually identical in foundational pattern. This is because of the way dualistic consciousness emerges in cultural evolution at its earliest levels in structured FMSs (especially FMS-1 to 3). What is important to note is that the men and their heroic logic are much more reliant on a discourse of bravery and courage (often used interchangeably) than is the discourse of women and menstruant logic. Yet, we can assume or conclude that both logics are critical in the evolution of humanity and the development of Immortality Projects of Defense (i.e., fear/terror management). At a deep level there seem more important similarities in the herstory of the menstruant and history of the hero than differences. Despite that, one cannot ignore the blatant denial of men writing about the hero as if the menstruant did not exist in cultural evolution and consciousness development. And one can somewhat empathize with the strong dismissal (if not dissociation) of feminist authors like Elinor Gadon who, in my view overplays the wonderful (if not romantic) qualities of the female-Goddess archetype (implicitly embodied in the menstruant journey) over and above the hero (implicitly the embodiment of the God(s)). She wrote,[109]

> The truth of the Goddess is the mystery of our being. She is the dynamic life force within. Her form is embedded in our collective psyche, part of what it is to be human. She is Gaia, the dance of life, and her song is eros, the energy of creation. . . . Wholeness is not the hero's journey of individuation and separation, which has been glorified since Homer. . . . [re: her chapter:] Why Men Need the Goddess: The Hero's Journey is Not the Way to the Goddess [and in contrast Joseph Campbell's hero journey is a] . . . journey away from the Mother [and]. . . . escape from the body, transcendence, [and] is precisely the problem.

From a critical integral perspective, the value and interpretive problem arises when a theorist attempts to privilege either the hero logic or menstrual logic without an attempt to integrate their different and mutually informing perspectives (e.g., masculine and feminine). If some form of *wholeness* is truly sought, then an integral way is the best way. One has to wonder about the usefulness of popular books by women, like Carol Pearson *The Hero Within* (1986), where the feminine (menstrual logic) is ignored; yet, other popularized books on *The Heroine Journey* (e.g., by Maureen Murdock, 1990) are attempting to correct the over-emphasis on the hero and replace it with heroine (or for some authors, "shero"), especially for women. This is not to deny, arguably, there is a huge conflict between these two archetypal paths or journeys that have attempted to get into our knowledge systems and FMSs in cultural evolution. This is not to deny, arguably, most of Western history has dominated herstory and the two archetypal paths are not on the same political playing field.

Ken Wilber, implicitly addresses this conflict and has called this, more abstractly, the "arch battle" of 2500 years in the Western world—between "Ego" (heroic) and "Eco" Camps of the "best way to go" to attain salvation or enlightenment.[110] We need both, and without both 'fear' (*Phobos* and *Thanatos*) will rule development, if given free reign—and the Immortality Project will twist, distort, and turn both the masculine bravery and feminine bravery of these archetypal forces into an unnecessarily destructive *bravado*. That said, however, because the menstrual form of feminine bravery has been so marginalized (virtually made invisible) throughout Western civilization's progress, there must be the extra responsibility placed on male authors (especially) of the heroic, to come to terms with their more than half of the distortion and pathology of inherent heroism-narcissism of which Becker acknowledged.

For our purposes, we come to bravery and heroism-narcissism as healthy Defense (fear management) impulses, devised by millions (if not billions) of years of evolution. That's the good news of the spirit of fearlessness manifesting in various forms or life strategies. The bad news is that within cultural evolutionary processes various kinds of traumatization (individually and collectively), may develop disabling pathological strategies of coping rather than healing. Overall this tends to lead to a coping system that operates primarily on fear ('fear') and utilizes FMSs in ways that end up creating more fear ('fear') rather than less. Thus, interpretive "errors" (mis-education) in FME is characteristic of the 1st-tier FMSs as the Cultural interprets the Natural. This is a critical differentiation dynamic, not merely of the past, but still with us continually today as we learn and develop our humanity. This is identified in Figure 3.1 as a culture of fear syndrome or metaphorically a 'Fear' Matrix—lodged right in the beginning-middle of the evolution of consciousness spectrum. It cannot be avoided, nor explained away. It is extremely complex to explain and fully understand. The beginning (if there is such a thing) of the strong-shadow side of bravery begins in FMS-4 (Blue, Mythic), although I have argued its roots come from the earliest levels of human development in primeval times (FMS-1, 2, 3), where culture was just forming due to the emergence of dualistic consciousness from adual consciousness. This shadow is called *bravado* (and its cousins, for e.g., *macho, braggadacio*). The start of the 'Fear' Matrix at FMS-4 is institutionalized bravado.

We can identify critically these distinct discourses of the pathology of bravery through some examples given below from the literature. However, first let's utilize the herstory and history, including an overall fearstory, from the above, to construct a working definition of *bravery* (from an integral lens):

> The best use of *bravery* is to see it as a discourse of the primal inherent impulse to rebel to oppression and limitation—to assert its inherent narcissism and accept its special role in life (masculine or feminine): that is, bravery is the impulse to behave to advance evolution of consciousness against the forces of devolution (regression)—thereby, bravery is best kept in use as a description of an action/act of bravery, not deeply reflected on as we see in a notion of "courage" but more as an animal instinct with some cultural cloaking. Often, bravery is an act that is done without a lot of thought or will. It happens and is over. The bravery diminishing as quickly as the occasion for its emergence. After the fact, the so-called brave one often creeps away feeling very afraid or simply in denial of what had happened as anything much to do with them being brave in character or personality. It just happened. There is little interest to take on the social or existential responsibility of the spirit of bravery (fearlessness), because it is not thought about in an ethical way. It is performed and that's its greatest expression and (limited) 'gift.'

The "gift of fear" or fear-positivist discourses today (*a la* de Becker and his followers) very much fit this discourse of bravery. These fear-positivists rely on the genetic or evolutionary potential in "fear" (defined biopsychologically) as the resource for brave acts in horrific circumstances, that seem in some cases even "inhuman"—for example, adrenalin . . . often performing amazing feats of bravery, with urban myths like the mother lifting up the car with one hand and pulling out her child with the other, etc. Again, this is not the book to go into the depths of arguments about "what is fear?" However, be very cautious about the habitual 'mantra' of the fear-positivists which always assumes, as if by logical deduction they must be right, that "without fear then there would be no bravery, courage, etc."[111] Later, below, this logic is turned on its head.

Now, let's turn to the pathological (i.e., Cultural) side of bravery (and "fear" and "fearlessness"). Elsewhere, I've critiqued much of the so-called fearless rhetoric in popular culture:[112]

> . . . from a non-dual consciousness standpoint (i.e., fearless) [FMS-9]. Suffice it to say, that 99.99% of what is touted as "fearless" or "No Fear!" (especially in the West) is a lot of dualistic fearful hyperbolic egoism (usually, hyper-masculine machoism), exploited by unscrupulous entrepreneurs and politicians. I am not ignoring the plethora of accounts from developmental psychologists that believe "fearless" or "fearlessness" is a pathological condition. . . .

Bravado is a "fearless" kind of attitude, temperament, personality and life-style, typically associated with strength, bravery, courage, braggadacio or extreme high-risk taking behaviors that appear to be enacted "without fear." Some people and sub-cultures praise bravado, especially male teenagers and early 20s somethings. Typically, it is intimately associated with sports teams, gangs, police forces, military, and nationhood defense systems and organizations. There is an inherent premise in these systems that one has to 'out shine' and/or out compete others in order to 'stay on top' and gain power over another in order to 'win' some goods, affections, self-esteem, awards, protection, and ultimately more power (e.g., in capitalism and colonialism). Bullying, gang-mentality, ego-centrism, ethnocentrism and chauvinism (FMSs 2-3) function along these lines revealing symptomatically bravado in sometimes highly sophisticated hierarchical organizations of all kinds; including the civilization process itself as it gets distorted by fear ('fear'). Fear ('fear') is typically masked and denied.

In an earlier chapter Bonaro Overstreet provided one of the best critiques on how "disguised fear" is too often the basis of depictions and enactments of "strength" in our world. Strength turning to power-over, she says, and often entire cultures will reinforce striving for this disguise (denial) that can be dissociative and destructive (violent).[113] One could argue much of arrogance and pride can turn into or is being reinforced unhealthily by bravado—that is, a twisted and distorted way of fearlessness in the earliest FMSs (generally between FMS-2 to FMS-4 but a good deal of the 1st-tier).

Some cultures and individuals do not approve of bravado because it is usually a pretense, defense, or mask over one's real nature, feelings and thoughts. It is hard to trust someone who acts out bravado-like behavior all the time, attempting to show absolutely no human vulnerability. The meaning and value of bravado is therefore relative and ambivalent overall. In much of psychology, criminology, or feminist literature, and philosophies going back to Aristotle in the Western world, one finds a negative connotation with bravado. For example,[114]

Too much fear [worry, anxiety] is globally inhibiting, while too little promotes recklessness. . . . Most people have a moderate amount of inbred worry, although our popular culture is fond of idealizing individuals [hero's] whose worry is nonexistent. . . . When we identify with their bravado we treat ourselves to the vicarious thrill of a temperament most can never experience.

Some authors, like in the above quote, link bravado or worry-less-ness in children to a higher risk of becoming criminals. However, from an integral perspective, bravado, good or bad to some—is more likely, a little bit of both—depending. It is important to assess bravado in its full contextual-environmental aspects and include gender, class, race, age factors and other conditioning such as biopsychological temperament, family history, culture, and so on—that is, in how one is also taught to be fearful, less fearful or fearless, or guiltful, less guilty, shameful or shameless. We also need to be critically aware that the biased view of those in elite-power, who can say they represent the establishment *status quo* and the "civilized" (as opposed to "barbaric"), may be quick to attack or suppress any recklessness or bravado because the standard (middleclass) definition of modern "citizenship" is "marked by rationality and a quiet passion for order, security, and peace."[115] Such an uncontested view of citizenship or being civil is clearly based on humility and/or guilt and shame under the aegis of the powerful authorities. Potentially a pathological passivism and conformism can result. *Bravado* surely is not this at all. It is an attitude of challenge to that pre-given dominating order and authority, with its default to conformism and passivism. There may be good reasons that such a *status quo* order of "citizenship" be challenged, especially if that citizenship definition and the way it is enforced (socialized) are not fair to all citizens, as history has so often shown to be the case. In some secular institutions (for e.g., the US Constitution), there is support for bravado built-in (i.e., valid and right-use of weapons and revolt by the people against corrupt government).

Religious and sacred traditions often teach their followers not to be totally obedient to the secular powers of the earth, but to give only their full obedience (and fears) to a God above and beyond the earth (e.g., residing in Heaven). Thus, more or less, bravado can be seen as an extreme of bravery, and at times, in limited ways, useful to challenge and resist social oppression. It is part of the 'spirited' movement of fearlessness. Sometimes it is more healthy than others. Sometimes bravado can undermine emancipation efforts by its overly biased attitudes favoring sexism (i.e., the masculinization of hero and hero-worship). The intention is not to overly pathologize *bravado* as is done in psychological (biomedical) discourses, under terms like "affective fearlessness" or "biological fearlessness."[116] We also need to include drug-induced bravado. Regardless, a more sensitive philosophical, spiritual, sociopolitical and cultural reading is also required to understand bravado.

Our fearstory of fearlessness, unfolding through rules and life strategies, shows that *bravery* emerged appropriately and adaptively with the development of the Cultural and dualistic consciousness (FMS-1, Beige, Survival) and was put into ritual and taboo forms of social organization with magic rites (FMS-2,

Purple, Magical). The very interesting change that *bravado* indicates in this evolution is a rancorous and extreme arrogance of development in some cases
where FMS-3 (Red, Warrior) reinforces an extreme agentic rebellion against
FMS-2 as social order and FMS-4 (Blue, Mythical) as social order. There is no
way to say exactly how the twisted *bravado* traits got culturally selected, but
what is likely is that they were selected by the drive of narcissistic Eros in consciousness evolution toward a greater individualist orientation (as a further
elaboration on the Beckerian "hero")—and as an emergent "self" became an
emergent and exuberant "ego-self." This is found where an individual, egocentric morality, and a hero system (culture) function along these values and cognitive structures. And as Freud maintained, "The ego is first and foremost a body-
ego" during the early stages of development.[117] The body-ego tends to be driven
and shaped to a large degree by "instinctual, impulsiveness, the pleasure principle, involuntary urges and discharges [usually highly reactive in a reptilian complex and emotional in a mammalian complex as far as the brain system's in operation predominantly]."[118] People and sub-cultures that identify with their "bodies" (as symbols of danger, of pride, of violence, etc.) are giving off a message
"I am my body," in a somewhat similar consciousness structure of materialist
values. Such material-identity, at a more sophisticated level (FMS-5 Orange,
Success), shows up as "I am my car or house or bank account." It is not surprising that bravado and its cousins braggadacio and macho are heavily influenced
by "body-image"—pursued as signs of *strength-muscularity* in males especially.
One could argue signs of *beauty-sexuality* in females serves similar ends.

In the postmodern world, the traits of bravado are becoming more and more
appropriated into the construction of the "female" or "urban chic." Sex (and
'porno') videos and websites express un-ashamed aggressive female erotic (if
not 'immoral' or 'degrading') bravado. Some performances are, arguably 'beautiful art.' Cyber-glitzy sexy "sheroes" on TV and in movies are often tough and
muscular (if not machine-like) just like the macho guys. Body-building and martial arts, even women's wrestling, are a significant part of Western(ized) postmodern bravado-extreme-culture today. How much of it is driven by fear and
fearlessness in the form of bravery turning to bravado? *Cosmopolitan* magazine
in the 1990s began the "*Fun, Fearless, Female*" slogan which has proven to be
very attractive to many women. And more studies are showing that young
women are increasingly attracted to gangs and overt physical violence in our
schools and beyond (as defense mechanisms).[119] Many of these trends leave a
difficult situation for feminist theorists to explain, as it appears being "feminist"
is being masculinist—that is, being oppressed means it is "best" to mimic one's
oppressor. But what then is women's liberation today?

One could say, as evolution of consciousness grew with more differentiation and complexity, at one point an "exuberant ego" (as Wilber has called it)
emerged that was a kind of hero-in-excess; full of self-confidence, arrogance
and pride. Some religious traditions like Christianity, for example, labeled
"pride" a sin in an attempt to control it. They recommend maintaining "fear of
God" and humility as the primary moral corrective strategy. Yet, Ernest
Becker's main point is not to attack bravery (or its cousins) and its excesses or

even its pathologies *per se* but to rather look at the context in which bravery was emerging and forming. Unfortunately, this takes us into a larger discussion beyond our purpose here. Simply, bravery and its cousins (even its twisted varieties) are a result of a co-relation between individuals and systems of organization—i.e., "hero systems." If there is a pathology, one ought to look to the system, as least, as much as one ought to look to the individual labeled a "troublemaker." One could surmise that more intelligent, that is holistic-integral designs and policies regarding today's "hero systems" and future ones too, is a great way to deal more effectively with "terrorists" and all the various forms of excessively violent bravado we see today all over the world (see Chapter Five).

A final point is to realize that in both feminine and masculine ways of bravery, that is, respectively, in the menstruant and hero paths throughout evolution, the life strategies could be identified and organized around four basic major strategies (all arising as a response to fear and danger): (1) *flight*, (2) *fight*, (3) *freeze*, and the more recent addition to the literature is (4) *"tend and befriend"*[120] (a feminine and/or feminist version). Arguably, the menstruant metaformic brought us the latter two strategies and the hero the first two. Clearly, the first two have been the classic and common discourse when it comes to defining "fear" and its responses. Fear and the fear response are actually fearlessness—that is, fear management strategies (or FMSs). Flight, fight, freeze, tend and befriend, are all fear management strategies. They are ways to reduce (bring to equilibrium) the distress, toxicity, threat and danger of both external elements of life existence and also the internalized elements of life existence that go with them.

It is the 'blind spot' of our culture of fear, of fearism, and the biased lens of fear-positivists that has led so many people (lay and professionals) to confuse *fearlessness* with *fear* itself; thereby, missing the inherent spirit of fearlessness that arises when fear arises. This reality can only be seen from a critical integral perspective or fearless standpoint theory. This book attempts to upgrade these four basic strategies of fearlessness and create seven ways of fearlessness, and then place those into ten FMSs based on a hierarchical (really holarchic) developmental logic, as shown in Chapter Two.

Courage(ous)

The fearlessness ways of *no fear* and *bravery* outlined so far represent discourses of fear management in the earliest realms of human consciousness and evolution. *Courage* and *courageousness*, from the research of many, is a discourse one might best locate at the pivotal location of transformation from small groups/tribes to the first villages and cities of thousands (and tens and hundreds of thousands) of diverse peoples living closely on a shared linguistic and universally coded system of economic regulations and moral-social rules. Let's call it "society." The societal rules and regulations, more complex than those of a unified small tribe/group, may have been both formal (written down) or informal (part of everyday cultural knowledge). This period has been called a "farming mode" or "farming consciousness" by some, but Wilber prefers to call it a "mythic-membership consciousness" (FMS-4, Blue, Mythic) that arose some 12,000 years ago with farming practices and new social organizations that humanity had not previously encountered or needed. Wilber wrote,[121]

> [Hu][m]ankind was starting to wake up, and wake up very quickly, from its prehistoric slumber in subconscious Eden. . . . when man [sic] became a farmer, he sustained the most prodigious mutation in consciousness that had yet appeared. . . . The ability and necessity to delay and control impulsive animal gratifications, emotional-sexual impulses, and typhonic magic, in favor of temporal and mental goals, was also heightened . . . by simple virtue of the large number of people living in close proximity. . . . [it was] a basic and profound expansion of consciousness [and brain development which] *allowed* man to picture the future more clearly, and thus plan and farm for it. . . . what *allowed* it was the full-fledged emergence of language; what *compelled* it was a new and heightened [terror of and experience of] death seizure [i.e., mortality awareness].

As I've suggested earlier, the spirited fearlessness of earlier times was rebellious, heroic, and somewhat individualizing, as differentiation in growth is inevitable and characteristic of evolution. However, the discourse of fearlessness also needed to 'balance' the hyper-individualism of bravery (e.g., *bravado*) with a hyper-communalism (e.g., *courageousness* as virtue). In simple terms, the project of personal freedom (with potential for anarchy), even in its infancy, has to be controlled as Becker had suggested.[122]

Volumes could be written about this transition and its demands, and its pressures for quick cultural evolution toward conformity. Wilber argues that there was a great need at this time for "some sort of internal, psychological control of social organization."[123] I would posit that although many different, often conflictual, uses of "courage" and "courageous," "fortitude," etc. are used in the WFTs (East and West), the shift from courageous behavior to a *virtue of courage* (*a la* Aristotle, and Western chivalry traditions of the Middle Ages) is a substantial shift in practices of fearlessness in human evolution. Miller wrote,[124]

> [Courage] [c]onstrued narrowly as the capacity to face death [early on in human history] in feud or war, courage was frankly granted to be necessary to defending self, family, and one's own against external threat, and thus absolutely crucial to securing the space in which other virtues could develop.

Historically, Miller noted that distractors and staunch critics of the notion of courage eventually began to fear its abuses, in "that courageous people may seek to foster the very conditions that make courage necessary."[125] For example, create more wars to create more courage. Recall here, a similar problematic in the underlying logic of fear-positivists: fearful people may seek to foster fearful conditions that make courage necessary—that is, 'without fear there is no courage.' Isn't that fearmongering in order to produce "courage," so-called?

The virtue aspect is the inner psychological control aspect of social organization, required with the strong pull to be an integral *social self* in a social body, of which is held together by strong mythic stories (and accompanying social fears and taboos, especially the use of "guilt;" see FMS-4). Joseph Campbell and others believe this had the power to hold great classical civilizations together in city-states, theocracies and dynasties or empires (e.g., Egyptian, Sumerian, Aztecian, Roman, Ottoman, American). Of course, this membership consciousness is the core of nationalism that we see in modern and postmodern times. Great bureaucracies and their economic and military-industrial organizations grow from this membership consciousness, all the way to globalism that we see today. Such great social enterprises need to have people feel both courageous and guilty (fearful) in order to be able to serve as good citizen-workers, and good military-warriors to defend the great social structures that have been built. But that is jumping ahead too quickly.

More than all the other seven ways of fearlessness, *courage* has been studied and written about the most by far (in sacred or secular texts). From the earliest Western ancient philosophers like Aristotle and Aquinas, many have written extensively on this topic, of which I won't repeat or try to summarize here. This section will be brief. In general, what we know for sure, is that "courage," however it is particularly defined, is extremely important to the survival and flourishing of humanity. Masculinists psychologists, Moore and Gillette wrote, "Only a massive rebirth of courage in both men and women will rescue the world"— and that courage, at least for males has to be coming from a mature man not merely a man with an immature (wounded) ego-centric hero stance.[126] The latter is more bravado than the former, which fits for courage.

Suffice it now to give a few examples of discourses that exist and to note how courage and fearlessness are often confounded, as are bravery and courage. Mostly the conceptions are used interchangeably by most every writer, with few significant exceptions. The aim of this volume is to put all the fear management conceptions of fearlessness ways into order with a developmental logic in order to critique ways that "courage" is constructed and used. There is a lot of power in defining "courage" in certain ways, and we ought to look to see who is doing the defining as much as what the definition is and how that defining shapes the expression of courage-power (or courageousness), throughout history.

One ought to expect an often paradoxical and confusing history of fear and courage, as Rush W. Dozier Jr. articulated:[127]

> Clearly consciousness and the rational [civil] fear system can, with patience and persistence, be trained to overcome the primitive [animal] system's aversion to risk. Yet we ignore at our peril the evolutionary wisdom embodied in the brain's primitive system. We can use the rational fear system to instill an attitude of courage and self-sacrifice sufficiently strong to overcome the innate fear of death. . . . Suppressing our natural fear of death can lead not only to courageous soldiers, but fanatical terrorists and suicide bombers.

Dozier is writing about Defense and development within Natural and Cultural domains. He shows how interpretations and uses of courage (the spirit of fearlessness) may vary. In the context of a post-9/11 era especially, the notion of bravery and courage or fearlessness and fearless are at times ambiguous as to their social worth. Often the attribution of 'positive' or 'negative' value to them is dependent on to what end the act of courage is aimed. For example, Richard Dawkins wrote of the "insane courage" of Islamic fundamentalist-terrorists in the world today.[128] This notion of extremism *via* insane courage has also been used in fiction writing and in describing soldiers and general egotistical behavior of the precociously gifted and insane.[129] The assigning of courage, in the positive sense, to such acts of honorable self-sacrifice and success against fear, threat, and difficult odds, brings us to notions more aligned with existential thought and critical theory (FMS-5, Orange, Success and FMS-6, Green, Sensitive). The latter, more to do with an inner psychological state of affairs, whereby one learns both self-discipline and self-analysis (i.e., as Wilber argued: an inner 'social regulation' psychologically-induced). Authors often want to distinguish (in Aristotelian fashion) a "moral courage,"[130] "genuine courage,"[131] "true courage,"[132] "enlightened courage,"[133] or "fearless courage" (*a la* Brady),[134] in contradistinction to a reckless, if not pathological, "courage."[135] It seems, in general, even without finer distinctions and definitions, humans generally want to give *courage* a positive and noble spin, and a connotation that supports our view of the world and of social order and goodness. "Studies have shown that virtually all cultures admire courage," says Dozier.[136] "[I]t is the most frequent theme of all world literature . . . courage makes for better stories than its corresponding vice [cowardice]."[137] Maya Angelou wrote, "History, despite its wrenching pain, cannot be unlived, but if faced with *courage*, need not be lived again."[138] Courage, one way or another is a major factor pushing and/or pulling humanity progressively forward in development (i.e., at least, in the latter part of the 1st-tier).

Sociologist Juan E. Corradi, historically speaking, suggested that for the "proud aristocrat and the virtuous [Western] citizen, courage is intrinsic to status."[139] In other words, according to Corradi, one is generally expected to be courageous as an aristocrat, whereas lower classes (and barbarians) are not necessarily given the same socially-ascribed virtuous character of courageousness, among other positive virtues of the elite *status quo*. These premodern and modern discourses of courage are changing with postmodern times. According to adult educator and feminist, Elisebeth VanderWeil:[140]

'For subjugated groups that are only newly articulating their knowledge, the movement from inchoate, deeply private, silenced knowledge to public performance is an act of great courage' [Hayes and Flannery, 2000, p. 150]. The courage shown by marginalized people—women, racial minorities, elderly, queer, physically disabled, all of the above, etc.—to make their voices heard and their experiences known within educational, and other, settings brings to clear focus the sentiment expressed by Rogers (in Hayes & Flannery, 2000): 'Courage is integral to the self expression of self, and tracing what it has meant through history to be courageous, finds a definition that illustrates the connection of voice, mind, and emotion in a compelling manner: 'to speak one's mind by telling all one's heart.' (p. 96) Courage in the face of fearsome transformation can propel education. . . . Courageous responsibility for one's actions, for acting in the world in a more authentic way is a characteristic shared by this study's leading educators [Palmer, Starhawk, Noddings, Boler, Parks Daloz].

In this latter formation of discourse on *courage* and *courageous* we see the emergence of "self expression of self" and "authentic way" showing up as very interior psychological and existential ideas. To explore those further one would have to turn to the legacy of discourse on fear and courage in the writings of the existentialists from Kierkegaard, Nietzsche, Heidegger, Jaspers, Tillich, Rollo May, Sartre, Camus, and so on. They were the (largely early postmodern) inner explorers *par excellence* of the 'courage to be' in the face of the fear of death, personal meaningless and loss of faith, be it sacred or secular approaches. A highly influential thinker in the Western world, Rollo May linked courage directly to "the virtue of maturity" when he wrote, "In any age courage is the simple virtue needed for a human being to traverse the rocky road from infancy to maturity. . . . it is in confronting [fears, anxieties] rather than fleeing these that courage is essential."[141]

The Western world has also been highly influenced by Aristotle's teachings on courage and temperance as base virtues to regulate the basic appetites of fear and pleasure, though, as Hauerwas and Pinches explain, the management of fear is not repression:[142]

> [re: courage and temperance] Their purpose is not to repress these appetites [fear and pleasure] but to form them to function rightly. Hence courage does not eliminate fear—that would be wrecklessness. Rather courage forms us to have fear in the right amount, at the right time, about the right things. Granted, a reckless person may appear to do just what a courageous person does but he [sic] is not acting courageously as he does, for he is not being properly affected by fear. It follows that courage is not only difficult to practice, it is difficult to recognize.

Perhaps, call it "right fear" or "right courage"—nonetheless, it is difficult too recognize and practice.

Western existential writing is vast and beyond the scope of this book. Yet, one can see its deepest roots in Stoic philosophy (i.e., pre-Aristotelian tradition) in ancient Greece. Writing on Stoicism, K. Campbell, proclaims in classic Western fashion:[143] "Fear is natural and in some cases justified, and to get rid of all fear is not a sensible plan. Fearlessness may well make us foolhardy, or heedless, and so destructive of ourselves and others. . . . Fear calls for courage. . .".

Courage-positive authors and discourses, sounding like Campbell's quote, are very common, especially in the Western world (i.e., the Western ethical canon). They also tend to be fear-positivists; they define fear in positive and natural terms, and then define courage as the essential dialectical pair to fear, equally natural, equally positive, and ontologically co-dependent. Writer, Cynthia Lamb, clearly articulates this discourse: ". . . without fear there can be no courage, and no satisfaction. For if we ride easily to victory, what have we won?"[144] There is always an ethical and social component to assigning courage, more so than bravery. Yet the courage discourse is never very interested in the complexity of the power construction of fear-knowledge or fear itself (as we see in *fear-less* in FMS-6b and *fearlessness* especially in FMS-7 Yellow, Integral). The courage discourse has little curiosity in qualitative differences in fear and 'fear'. Rather, it focuses on when fear is "too much" (abnormal) in a quantitative scaling. A little fear is a good thing, they claim. The focus is on "fears" (fear of x, y, z), and documenting the fears and phobias *ad nauseum*, filling book after book with such classifications and "how to" diagnose them and overcome them.

Courage-positive authors' interest in fear is generally shallow as is most often their advice. They create manuals in the religious traditions full of statements like "Fear Not!" (e.g., the Bible). And they create manuals in psychiatry and psychology with marketing titles like "Nothing to Fear!"[145] as well. There is a systemic (patriarchal) paternalism always lurking behind this (parental) advice of how to manage fear and courage: "Don't be afraid," or "Be courageous and brave." And in postmodern secular society "No Fear!" is another version of this with an extremist (individualism) bravado component (FMS-3). I have argued, implicitly, that there is authoritarianism always lurking in FMS-4, where *courage* originates as a discourse, and is carried on through (more subtlely) in different advanced streams in FMS-5 (existential) and FMS-6 (social activism).

All of these *courageous* discourses, more or less, promote a kind of heroism of "human character" and "civilization" (i.e., social control). But critics like Ernest Becker would say be very cautious as "Human Character" is "a Vital Lie." He wrote, ". . . if the basic quality of heroism is genuine courage, why are so few people truly courageous?"[146] Mind you, it is a lie, he says, most of us never admit. We are mostly accepting prisoners in denial—'slaves' to social systems that have told us what is "courage" and what is "fear" and they have told us to conform to the ideology of control—that is, the 'norm' fear ('fear') management system that large groups, cities, nation-states and empires must keep in place to *manage* (i.e., suppress) chaos and rebellion, and change, transformation, if not revolution and liberation.

Earlier in this book, I and others have begun to see through this discourse and have called it what it really is: Fear's Empire (the 'Fear' Matrix). The oppressive systemic message is deep in the secular writing of Thomas Hobbes (17th century) as the modern political theorist (of fear), who best articulated the dilemma of this way of organizing civil societies *via* managing fear and fearlessness. The message boils down to: *Be Afraid, Be Very Afraid.* Today, this phrase is showing up everywhere in books, articles and speeches by those in avid resistance (literally, "anti-fear campaigns"[147]) to the post-9/11 "culture of fear." And then, paradoxically, *Be Not Afraid!* (meaning, We, the Church, the Government, the Military, etc.—we will ensure your safety and security ultimately, so, *be not afraid*, just do as we say, think as we think and we'll call it "courage" to do just that; and then (while you fear us) we'll tell you it is honorable, noble, civil, and so on. The general idea is obvious—an insidious discourse of paternalism behind it, which Foucault called "pastoral power" and "governmentalism." According to political historian, Corey Robin, ". . . Hobbes believes that a state built upon fear can support a world of humanistic endeavor; in fact, he argues, it is a necessary condition for such endeavors. . . . [it is ultimately] a counter-revolution of fear."[148] Hobbes and most Modernists are not really very radical—at least not when analyzed from a 2nd-tier perspective. The Hobbesian view, thus, is far off from supporting a Fearlessness (R)evolution. With that kind of history of functionalism and its courage-positive and fear-positive discourses of power, one ought to be very cautious of this discourse. One ought to look for more FMSs beyond FMS-5 and 6, such as we shall see in the next few sections below.

If one is forced into a gross generalization: *Courage* is perhaps overall better than *bravery*, indeed, but *fearlessness* is even better, and *fearless* even better. The question is, "better for what, when, who?" The reality is, one has to grow into them all; they develop and evolve with consciousness, each with a valuable role for certain conditions and development. This is a fearlessness FMS-7 perspective itself and conflicts highly with the activist sentiments of Frances Moore Lappé and Jeffrey Perkins (like multitudes), who insist *You Have the Power: Choosing Courage in a Culture of Fear*[149] is the best way to go. They (i.e., FMS-5 especially and some FMS-6) assume 'courage is always a choice,' as if we all have the same choice (essential agency) under some abstract universal set of conditions of 'freedom' to choose. I think not.

In Chapters Four and Five this issue will be addressed further. For now, the fearlessness perspective is based on an idea of developmental differential "choice-making" (agentic) capacities. One cannot force any of the seven ways of fearlessness on anyone (including oneself), especially if one wants them to manifest in their best and healthiest forms—that is, forms or ways of the spirit of fearlessness. Remember, they all, more or less, can show up as pathologies with the twist of *bravado* (in males or females) excessively determining their expressions; though, in general, the trend of development, following the principle of historical fearlessness, is that there will be less and less pathologies (ignore-ance and arrogance) along the evolutionary spectrum from *no fear* to *fearless*. The point is, we need critical discernment of them all from a holistic-integral lens— that is, a critical literacy of fearlessness. Let's conclude a view of courageous here by Osho, a spiritual teacher (2nd-tier or even 3rd-tier perspective), who wrote:[150] "Fearlessness happens if you go on being courageous and more courageous. That is the ultimate experience of courage—fearlessness: That is the fragrance when the courage has become absolute."

Fear-Less

According to "The Gospel of Fearlessness" (from a Gandhian philosophy website), there is an interpretation of the critical importance of fearlessness that Gandhi always emphasized throughout his life:[151]

Fearlessness is the first requisite of spirituality. Cowards can never be moral! Every reader of the [*Bhagavad*] *Gita* is aware that fearlessness heads the list of the Divine Attributes enumerated in the 16th Chapter. . . . Fearlessness is a *sine qua non* for the growth of the other noble qualities. How can one seek truth or cherish Love without fearlessness? . . . . the brave are those armed with fearlessness. . . . Fearlessness connotes freedom. . . . Perfect fearlessness can be attained only by him [sic] who has realized the Supreme. . . . Let us fear God and we shall cease to fear man.

The *Gita* is one of the most ancient "bibles" (holy books) of humanity. It has been at the basis of much of the development of Eastern philosophy, spirituality and religions (e.g., Hinduism, Buddhism). Mahatma Gandhi used many sacred texts (including the *Gita*) to develop his own philosophy of fearlessness as a basis for a spiritual, ethical, and political (just) life. The message is that there is no way toward non-violent revolution (in the Gandhian sense) without fearlessness. Theoretically, fearlessness as a meta-virtue is the basis of ending all violence. These are complex issues that this entire book *World's Fearlessness Teachings* (WFTs) pivots upon.

The above language and quotes from "The Gospel of Fearlessness," as problematic (and perhaps distasteful to North American or European ears) as they are, with seeming contradictions within this piece of text, is at least making the WFTs significant. That is, spirituality must first and foremost be based on *fearlessness*. First the virtue of fearlessness; then, all other virtues will follow in a healthy fashion. That's the message of the Eastern wisdom texts (like the *Gita*). Analogously, that's a similar but different message offered by the 1st-tier view of courage, as Miller suggested: ". . . with courage secured the other virtues will take care of themselves."[152] For FMS-5 and 6 there is no need seen or envisioned of anything beyond "courage" as the 'be all end all' of FME. In fact, these top of the 1st-tier discourses, with a tone of smugness and superiority, implicitly believe (and would argue) that any attempt toward something called "fear-less," or fearlessness or fearless or without fear, etc. is merely a fear of fear (a running from fear and trying to eliminate it). They see such words as indicating cowardice or denial, or simply foolishness or inhumanity. They generally have no patience (or curiosity) for the 2nd-tier and 3rd-tier discourses of FME. They're easily enraged about the suggestion of emancipation, liberation or enlightenment, which calls for the 'elimination' of fear. This will likely make more sense as you read through the rest of this chapter.

Drawing opening attention to the fearlessness quotes and a particular Gandhian fearlessness discourse at this point is crucial. It directs attention to the explicit emergence of the Spiritual domain in our discussion of the ways of fearlessness as "correction" of the Cultural (1st-tier) and its mis-interpretations of the Cultural (and of the Spiritual). We come to a great abyss, threshold, and (potential) transformation with our next way of fearlessness, called *fear-less* for lack of a better name. This is FMS-6b as mapped out earlier in Figures 2.1 and 3.1, as it lies just before the crossing of 'Fear' Barrier 2 into the 2nd-tier. We are at the edge of leaving, in a developmental and evolutionary perspective, the cultural consciousness of the 1st-tier FMSs. We are leaving the "Survivor" archetype and moving into the "Thriver" stage.

Here, spiritual consciousness is being filtered through the highly pragmatist (functionalist) *fear-less* discourse, whether that is in secular or sacred language forms or not. Fear-less is a discourse that has arisen from the Natural, through the Cultural, and is just barely emerging existentially toward the Spiritual, although the actual discourses of fear-less may or may not be overtly sacred and may sound quite profane/secular. This matters not from a critical integral theory perspective. Below, one gets a sense of how bravery or courage are significantly different discursive and linguistic conceptions than fear-less (and its other forms as in fearlessness and fearless).

The deeper structure of fear-less (FMS-6b, Green, Sensitive) is what is of formative interest here. In one way, it could be said that fear-less is the precursor for the future evolution of ethical discernment in FME. Although, clearly the ethical discourse has also been found in the writings and teachings on bravery and courage in previous discussions. However, fear-less is the linguistic template so to speak, which uses the words *fear* and *less* united by a hyphen, yet still uncertain, ambivalent and hesitant, as to its own unfolding destiny and full possibility as an unhyphenated condition and reality—on the way to a most mature form of FME, which is called *fearless* (FMS-9, Coral, Non-Dual).

For many readers the odd or unusual appearance of *fear-less* as a term itself is understandable. I created it (specific to FMS-6b) but it was inspired directly from one author who has greatly influenced the identification and formation of the fear-less FMS-6b. Gavin de Becker, a successful American security consultant, author, activist and humanitarian, published his third book *Fear Less: Real Truth About Risk, Safety, and Security in a Time of Terrorism* (2002)[153] just after the September 11, 2001 terrorist bombings in America (the worst ever in its history). This high profile attack on American soil from within, has created a whole new genre of writing about fear management and education on the planet, especially in America and the Western world. The following discussion focuses on this secular cultural discourse that de Becker leads and promotes, although one can find it in other literature on contemporary (post-9/11) "safety and security" discourses (e.g., Schneier[154]), and in what Frank Furedi and other social critics have called a "fear culture," "victim culture," "precautionary culture," "security culture," etc. (i.e., a culture of fear).

More or less, the intention of all the WFTs and this entire book are dedicated to "less fear" rather than more. The prevailing more contentious issue is should we "eliminate fear"? Let's hold off on that for the moment. Individually and collectively FME overall is concerned with this task of fear-less. The next issue of contestation is: how best can we go about doing this? However, since 9/11 'the world has changed' and so have the discourses around FME, and these questions are thus dynamic and ever-evolving, if not quite unanswerable.

Fear-less exemplifies this post-9/11 turnaround or awakening to "terrorism" but also to the "culture of fear" as the context for our every day lives. Both of these contexts have been around (to some extent) in human societies for a very long time, even though they may not have been called by these names. Regardless, this current climate of fear and concern about terrorism and the culture of fear is the basis of all of de Becker's very practical crisis and primary intervention work. He has his own unique and provocative approach. Like myself, he likes to take an interdisciplinary approach to the topics of fear, risk, safety and security, anti-violence, and justice. Similarly, he is a fan of Ernest Becker's existential philosophy of fear and the hero. However, distinctly, he is no "theorist." His focus is practice and activist-education. De Becker's work, popular as it is today, also needs to be critiqued. I do so here, using mostly Forrest Church's framework, rather than an in depth critique of de Becker's writing *per se*.

Church takes the fear-less discourse (FMS-6b) further along in a holistic sense than de Becker.

Gavin de Becker, owner and president of a large corporation, works as a professional security consultant, often for high profile government officials and movie stars. His firm protects them from harm and violence. His passion has also moved into the realm of public life in general, and teaching people how to use their own inner intuitive (Natural) resources to predict and avoid (as much as possible) violence. His first book *Gift of Fear* (1997) was an American best seller and he ended up on Oprah, with her recommending it to millions of watchers of her program.

Forest Church, a top minister in the Unitarian Universalist's organization in America (and another author of the *fear-less* discourse), recently wrote a book on fear and listed Gavin de Becker's work as first of "Seven Fear Experts" we ought to all pay attention to. Church wrote,[155] "*The Gift of Fear*, a collection of [true] stories and lessons by one of the nation's leading experts on crime and violent behavior, is the best single discussion of what I call fright."

Like de Becker, and so many writers on FME, they seek some basic typology to organize the various forms (types) of fear. After discussing the problems of such typologies, Church admits they are mostly all imperfect, and he chooses an experience-based model of "five underlying types of fear" (not focusing on "fears" *per se*). Like de Becker, Church provides a quite advanced (somewhat integral) approach, that one finds generally in the writers using a *fear-less* discourse (e.g., Cayce, 1980[156]). Fully articulating a developmental or evolutionary perspective to his five types of fear (which dialectically are five types of fear management), Church locates "fright" as the foundational form of fear and way of fearlessness, which he equates with de Becker's "true [or natural] fear." Church identifies "fright" (stage or level one, equivalent to FMS-0 to 1) within an appropriately justified Natural discourse:[157]

> FRIGHT (FEAR CENTERED IN THE BODY) Fright triggers the body's re-
> sponse to physical danger. Innate and reflexive, it is the one fear for which we
> should all be thankful. It may even save our lives. . . . [he cites science's dis-
> covery of the flight-fight responses of stress and the amygdala in the emotional
> brain]. . . . Fright is a vestige from our distant ancestry, when fear was our con-
> stant companion. Today it makes us jump more often than we need to. In fact,
> we can mark human progress by how many more false alarms we experience
> than our forebears did. One feature differentiates fright from the other forms of
> fear. It takes place completely in the present rather than visiting from the fu-
> ture, where imagined dangers lurk. Other forms of fear may linger after a
> physical scare, thereby appearing to be extensions of fright, but direct, instinc-
> tive, physical fear passes with the danger, whether that danger is perceived or
> real.

Church's second category is "WORRY (FEAR CENTERED IN THE INTELLECT)." The remaining types are "GUILT," "INSECURITY," and "DREAD." He wrote,

If fright is triggered by danger, worry by imagination, and guilt by conscience, insecurity almost always comes packaged with inadequacy [re: "a form of narcissism," he suggests]. . . . [and] Dread and anxiety distinguish themselves from all other fears by having no fixed object.

He calls "Dread" the "most philosophical of fears" and anxiety can often be fear of fear itself. These are important insights by Church and helpful to FME but his theory is loose and could use grounding in developmental and evolutionary theories. Yet, it is clear he aligns his spectrum from the most concrete "physical fear" (he also calls "fright") to the most "centered in the soul" "philosophical fear" he calls "dread."[158] The progression from matter to soul (or spirit) is part of his attempt (in my words) at a holistic-integral perspective. It is nearly a 2nd-tier perspective, but not quite. Arguably, the *fear-less* discourse (FMS-6b) never can fully see itself or its model from a meta-level perspective (or integral view or 2nd-tier). Such a consciousness and meta-overview perspective is only available with the substantial emergence of FMS-7 (Yellow, Integral). It is however, a precursor form to a spectrum or holistic-integral model.

Church's *fear-less* (like de Becker's) lacks a strong political (radical) critique. Fortunately, it does move beyond reductionistic psychologism or religionism and begins to bring in a modest critical political (cultural) critique of how fear ('fear') is used and abused in a social context (i.e., a culture of fear). We'll see this exemplified in de Becker's work in a moment. To push an integral analysis here momentarily, is to see that Church (and de Becker) are making a crucial distinction in their models of FME by positing, implicitly for the most part, that we have to understand fear (and the fearlessness spirit) as *Natural vs. Cultural*—a conflict view.[159] For Church, a man of the cloth (minister), he is more spiritually-oriented in his teachings than de Becker. Thus, Spiritual is overt in the FME of Church compared to de Becker.

For Church, his concept of fright is a Natural reality and discourse that is "a gift" (de Becker would agree). De Becker wrote, "Intuition [like fright] connects us to the natural world and to our nature."[160] This is the accurate basis of the fear-positivist attitude and discourse, mentioned earlier in this book. Myself, like Robert Augustus Masters, prefers "fright" as an entirely different, albeit, interrelated category of phenomenon compared to fear (or 'fear').[161] In radical distinction: fear is not what our animal, instinctual, Natural world of experience is about. Yes, there is fright because danger can and does often exists in real terms in the real world, depending on where one lives—even in a totally "natural world." This is basic survival instinct and concomitant "fright" process—whereby a concept or term, like alarm or "alert response"[162] fits well.

Simply, it is not *fear* that keeps us from running out on the street in front of an oncoming bus (although, it could be), it is *natural intelligence* (instinct, or as de Becker says, "intuition" of danger) that stops us from doing so, and it does that through the mechanism of fright or alert response (stress) systems (i.e., FMS-0 and early FMS-1), which are literally millions of years old in design and life strategy of adaptation for organisms. From my perspective, *evolution* (i.e., accumulated survival and Defense intelligence) is the "gift," not fear. As I've hinted at earlier, it is the *spirit of fearlessness* (as "gift") that protects the person who might potentially run out on the street in front of an oncoming bus. Thus, fearlessness is not the problem nor is danger the problem nor is fright or alertness. Fear is a problem (meaning, fear cannot be extracted "purely" from 'fear'). But the larger complex significant problem comes with how we recognize, interpret, and enact FMS-0 (the Natural systems of fear management and ways of fearlessness).

And how we manage FMS-0 (i.e., *no fear*) takes on intriguing twists and turns in human evolution and history due to Cultural (mis-)interpretations and uses of FMS-0. This begins in FMS-1 (to the least extent) and continues as Cultural evolution through the remaining cultural FMSs 2-6. The heavy influence of the Cultural begins with FMS-2 (Purple, Magical) as discussed earlier in the menstruant and hero archetypal patterns of growth and development, both individually and collectively. In Church his "fright" is Natural, and the four remaining types of fear (rightly called "fear") are Cultural, with the last one, verging on the Spiritual. Yet, like de Becker, Church is an American pragmatist and argues for practical means: "One key to fighting fear is to divide and conquer, breaking it up into manageable pieces."[163] The *fear-less* discourse tends to be a "protectionist" (survivalist) discourse with a tendency to reductionistic, logical-rationalistic, and underlying (usually unconscious) ideological functionalist-managerialism (i.e., masculinism,[164] paternalism, if not Hobbesianism) tone and structure. De Becker, as a business person, cannot be too politically critical (in public, at least), of the clients and *status quo* establishment that he serves, and who pay his business bills and mortgage payments. We'll see less (sometimes much less) of this kind of functionalism discourse and approach to FME in the (critical, radical) Spiritual domain of FMSs 7-9 (i.e., *fearlessness* and *fearless*).

Let's turn to de Becker now, to see the gifts and limits of his *fear-less* theory and American male-based (masculinist) "protection" discourse (i.e., his FME approach). De Becker's a regular kind of upper middle-class white heterosexual American business man, at one level, yet, he has a rather traumatic autobiography that impacts his humanistic default program to "protect" others (as well as teach others how to protect themselves). Survivor-Thriver archetype is central (see Figure 2.1). There's no indication he reads or studies the practices of fearlessness and fearless from the Eastern traditions nor critical theory or sociological conflict theory traditions.[165] Rather, he is focused on Western psychological and criminological analysis and experiences. We see this similar rationalist-male Western bias in Church's teachings (i.e., his Aristotelian ethical discourse).

Church continues in his introduction to de Becker and the basic teachings behind *The Gift of Fear: Survival Signals That Protect Us From Violence*:[166]

For more than twenty years, Gavin de Becker has worked with and learned from leaders in the criminal justice field. His clients include many public figures [maybe even Oprah, whom de Becker has called a "friend" in one of his books] whose prominence places them in danger. De Becker's expertise grew from more than merely a professional interest. He first learned about the ravages of violence, intimidation, and fear at home. By the age of ten, he had witnessed his mother shoot his abusive father. By thirteen, he had seen his sister assaulted and had endured serious beatings himself. Under these circumstances, he learned to assess dangerous situations. And as he grew older, he learned how to protect himself and those around him from violence. The techniques he developed do not demand unique talents or skills, he says. He simply began with his childhood experiences and let his ghosts become his teachers. . . . Violence is not random. In fact, it is quite easily predictable. We need only listen to our [true] fear to develop our predictive [protective] capacities. Fear speaks to us in the form of intuition, a detective aide available to everyone if only we heed it [and not "unwarranted fear," as de Becker calls it]. Intuition born of fear is an organic bodily [unconscious] function similar to breathing or blinking. . . . Intuition seems magical only because we are so used to logical processes that lead us step-by-step toward solutions for our problems. . . . Our mind, trained originally by the need to survive, is constantly on the lookout for danger. . . . it remains hardwired to protect us from physical harm. . . . Not all fear is helpful. When fear lingers, it serves no practical purpose. "Remaining in a state of fear [distress] is destructive" [says de Becker]. Only as we learn to work with fear can we begin to use it selectively and strategically. . . . We must discern whether what we fear has the ability truly to harm us.

For de Becker (like Church), the problem is "Worry" and all the other human-created derivative Cultural formations or types of "fear." *Worry* (i.e., distorting the true risk by unwarranted fear), and *denial* (i.e., ignoring natural survival instincts or intuition from the unconscious) are two bug-a-boos for de Becker and his FME teachings. Keep in mind that he was responsible to protect not only his younger sister in an often chaotic household, but he even had to protect his mom from some of her consorts that used violence against her. He 'learned every trick in the trade,' as they say; because he had to and because he learned that denying there was danger or worrying about a future danger that wasn't yet present was not good strategy for any of his family members that he loved. Action (i.e., safe action) counted high on the young de Becker's value-scale and it had to be based on intelligent data collection and prediction. His books are full of aphorisms, for example: "Whether it is learned the easy way or the hard way, the truth remains that your safety is yours. It is not the responsibility of the police, the government, industry, the apartment building manager, or the security company,"[167] and "Justice is swell, but safety is survival."[168] Arguably, he couldn't use his physical power or rely much on others with physical power in moments of crisis, when dealing with threatening or irresponsible (drugged-up) adults much bigger and stronger (at least in principle). I'm sure as a young boy he learned life strategies by trial-and-error, fear, and fearlessness. He was also probably somewhat 'lucky' he saved more than he lost. I highly recommended checking out his original work to learn more.

However, the focus of this analysis of *fear-less* discourse is more on the quality of its sociocultural and political critique, especially in a post-9/11 context of risk (or "risk society" as sociologist Ulrich Beck called it[169]). There is a severe social "crisis" that de Becker and so many others are teaching us about. This is where de Becker's fear-less discourse offers significantly important insights that perhaps deserve as much or even more emphasis than his popularizing psychological (often individualist) insights in his work. He noted in *Gift of*

Fear that "Among individual crimes, assassination has the greatest impact on the American psyche. Bullets have demonstrably influenced most presidential elections in the past forty years."[170] This is chilling enough to be said in 1997, but with the current U.S. Elections 2008 in full swing, when this writing is being laid down, there is a real potential resonance with this truth as Democrat (and 'black man') Barack Obama is leading in the Presidential race.

In tracking the arising methods of "fame" in the U.S. in the last forty years or so, de Becker noted that many "Elements in society were pioneering the skills of manipulating emotion and behavior in ways that had never been possible before: electronic ways. The media were institutionalizing idolatry."[171] Cultural critic-scholar, Sarah Ahmed, called this new era as one dominated by "affective politics." And fear in its culturally constructed (mediated) forms, she argues, is a major player in that game of emotional manipulation and power.[172] Having studied several high profile assassins and other mass murders, de Becker notes the dangerous combination of "daredevil" (bravado) fantasies and pathological narcissism in murders, with the construction of fame in American media and politics. The reality for assassins is that they "do not fear they are going to jail — *they fear they are going to fail. . .*".[173] And that distinction, says de Becker is one we better understand and use in our work to undermine the positive-feedback cycle of violence and fame (celebrity status) that tends to accompany these people and their heinous crimes. They fear they are going to fail being recognized in their lives. Famous assassins, he noted "Each inspired to make it in Hollywood but gave that up for a faster, easier route to identity. . . . with a single act of fraudulent heroism, with one single shot, they could be forever linked to their famous targets."[174]

Violence, for young people (and for gangs), is the fastest way to celebrity — meaning, the way to get a power-identity. Their violence looks "fearless." They want a 'fearless-identity,' one could say. That drive, that spirit of rebellion and heroism is very powerful—virtually unstoppable. We all have a little of it in us. Truly, with severe abuse in childhood accompanying many of these people (mostly men), there are twists in this narcissistic pursuit to matter—that is, to be seen and kept in the immortal records of historical memory (trauma). It's sickly twisted.

Where de Becker really shines in his analysis is where he details the way media cover these events and the way police or federal agents get caught in the rhetoric of the public media formats for entertainment and celebrity-making (see Chapter 13 in *Gift of Fear*). Ernest Becker called these "hero systems" which determine the healthy or pathological expression of the "hero." Of course, news media want to use emotionalism to get more people watching, and thus sell more advertising, as sociologist David Altheide has studied this culture of fear for years—making the public more and more afraid, while selling them stories and experts, products and services, that are supposedly going to make them feel more safe and secure.[175]

In his declaration about fear (and its cousins), de Becker wrote *"Worry is the fear we manufacture*—it is not authentic. . . . Most often, we worry because it provides some secondary reward."[176] The construction of worry today is an "economy of fear" as many have argued. I'd call it the social construction of 'fear.' "Real fear is objective," says de Becker, "but it's clear that we are not."[177] The distortion of the probability of risk to dangers is a massive panic-industry. De Becker has popularized, along with others like filmmaker Michael Moore, this bizarre and destructive state of affairs that constructs the "culture of fear" and 'Fear' Matrix (see Figure 3.1).

De Becker closes his 2002 book (post-9/11) on *Fear Less* with his passionate philosophy of fear management and advice for Americans:[178]

> We've all been through a lot, and many things are different now. Let's keep them different, and not go back to the same divisive [Culture Wars], attention-seeking, counterproductive attacks on one another that we'd all gotten so used to. We've got plenty of enemies around the world to think about, and if we take a break from chewing on one another, I think we'll find cooperation to be the most effective route to safety. . . . Just as we can find compassion for those who hate us and for those who serve in government, so, too, can we find compassion for ourselves. It is just fine that we felt fear, just fine that we canceled some plans, just fine that we didn't know what to do or how to react to a terrible trauma that still seems unreal. Our nation has been terrorized. What we lost at the start of this war was our peace of mind, and it is time to take back that beachhead. Before we do, there may be some benefit in consciously feeling our fear [rather than denying it] for just one more moment, because fear can carry us closer to the truth of who we are. When we are frightened, our options multiply enormously. . . . In that willingness to do things differently resides the opportunity—the privilege—to change our lives in ways we might not have in the absence of fear.

De Becker's "Thriver" archetype is clear—the opportunistic (pragmatic) fear-positivist attitude can be seen in the quote, as fear invokes itself as a valuable resource for positive changes. This is the 1st-tier (fear-based) discourse self-reification pattern in open display. No need for fearlessness, here, in the FMS-6b narrative. In true existentialist fashion (FMS-5, Orange, and 6b, Green), de Becker concludes that "At core, unwarranted fear is the fear of death" and to live is to risk living and dying—both, not one or the other; and "September 11 is our reminder to live—to live as fully as possible, and to live with less fear of one another than we used to."[179] The secular humanist always nudges the Spiritual realm whenever compassion is evoked. De Becker's politics is a *politics of compassion* or as many feminists have said, the overcoming of a *politics of fear* must come from "love for one another" and it won't be easy—and, as the late black lesbian activist-poet Audrey Lorde claimed "we cannot wait for the 'luxury of fearlessness'"[180] but rather we must pursue with moral courage the love and compassion to free all peoples now.

The "gifts" of the *fear-less* discourse are released and its limits revealed. The post-9/11 direction for a world based on compassion and love is recommended in some discourse that both includes and transcends everything covered in this chapter so far. However, as we shall see in the next way of fearlessness (FMS-7, Yellow, Integral), that without a true *fearlessness* discourse the compassion de Becker et al. suggests will only be a wish not a reality in a cultural-based world so deeply in the grips of the 'Fear' Matrix. As we saw, the *fear-less* discourse (FMS-6b) cannot yet let go of the 1st-tier 'fear'-based structure and its very cultural definition of what it is to be 'human,' to be part of humanity (i.e., its identity-addiction to fear). That all (theoretically) can be healed and transformed as we grow and mature to receive the WFTs. They recommend another (more holistic-integral and Spiritual) FME solution and challenge— *fearlessness* itself.

Fearlessness

> *Fearlessness* (perspective): is not easy to describe; it is something that needs to be experienced to be understood well. First, there is a decided decline of interest to study "fear" and "fears" (fear of x, y, z). The research on these is seen as more distracting of truth, than revealing. The emphasis of study (almost totally) becomes the "discourse" construction of culturally-inscripted (manufactured) 'fear.' An ethical imperative is characteristic of this fearlessness perspective (FMS-7), and that is the awareness that there is no "right fear" (valid as it is on the level of reality in the 1st-tier); rather, one sees through and dissolves "rationalist" disguises in the 2nd-tier of fearlessness and concludes what was justified as "right fear" is quite "wrong fear." The end of the 'fear'-game is nigh.

Welcome to FMS-7 (Yellow, Integral) and its somewhat ambiguous and provocative views on the discourses along the continuum of FMSs—and of FME itself. This is mostly rather radical stuff, which you won't find in contemporary texts on fear management, nor talked about on popular tv talk shows. Be prepared for a smorgasbord of sampling, a kind of pastiche (or collage) of material for *fearlessness*. It is not all linear-logical and organized to satisfy a 1st-tier sensibility for order and clarity. To do fearlessness due justice as a form (FMS-7) would require a book-length articulation, with lots of art, illustrations, models, parables, and poetry.

Thus far some 15 meanings of fearlessness, including the quote above, have arisen in the text. I have not always pointed them out directly, preferring to let them be absorbed within the context of the writing. At times however, they have appeared in overt forms, including but not limited to:

(a) God is fearlessness,
(b) being truly human is fearlessness,
(c) fearlessness is the epistemic lens (FMS-7) through which this entire book is conceived and written,
(d) fearlessness is a Spiritual *cura* and *therapia* for the ailing problems of a Cultural world ruled by 'fear,' (Fear's Empire, 'Fear' Matrix, etc.)
(e) fearlessness is the base of the 2nd-tier FMSs and thus the base of an ethical response to the world that is no longer 'fear'-based,
(f) fearlessness is the path between the two arche-motions Love and fear,
(g) fearlessness is the way of the Great Reversal (or Korten's "Great Turning") required in development, transformation, and healing,

(h) the "gift of fearlessness" is an ancient tradition in Eastern spiritual teachings,

(i) fearlessness invokes a vital imaginary for contemplation of and curricular direction toward an enlightened society.

To make things more complex, the spirit of fearlessness and historical fearlessness have been concepts that run throughout the text, suggesting that when fear arises there is a *telos* of fearlessness—arising to meet the demands and limitations of and around fear ('fear'). I've claimed the spirit of fearlessness is manifest in at least seven different forms (i.e., from *no fear, bravery. . . to fearless*) depending on the perspective taken, and the level of development (evolution) of the individual, organization, culture, society, etc. Some of these meanings have barely been mentioned, some have been given more detailed descriptions, but most have been dealt with thus far very inadequately. Despite space limitations, I have to bring forward a few more new meanings of fearlessness, like "fearlessness paradigm," and "Fearlessness Movement" and "Fearlessness Tradition" in this section. All 15 or so meanings create a multi-layered composite of *what fearlessness is* (or *means*). In postmodern fashion, there is no *one* definition of fearlessness that exists nor that likely ever will. The conflicts, contradictions, and agreements over fearlessness have yet to be catalogued, and a history of fearlessness has yet been attempted across the wide diversity of views across time.

There are some objective aspects one could argue make up fearlessness, as experimental and clinical behavioral psychologists prefer, but mostly there are subjective interpretations in the WFTs. They are based on experience and insights tested (sometimes) and passed on through generations, and in some cases for millenia. Each WFT is valid. Yet, not all of them are equally true, beautiful, good, or useful. One ought to bring a critical lens to them all. Amongst them, there are gems that will likely be very helpful to FME for humanity in the 21st century. The holistic-integral collage here is simply a rendering, an image, a portrait or profile of the concept and reality. Readers are encouraged to check out the additional references as original sources, and refer to condensed overviews in other publications.[181]

With many tensions running through the varied interpretations of fearlessness are conflicts, if not wars, around the nature of being human and existence itself. One of the more outstanding tensions is between seeing Life as "Defense," and in a very different tenor, seeing Life as "Caring." The former is the foundational lens that I have brought forward into the discussion of fear and fearlessness (i.e., FMSs and FME). In many ways my approach is a typical "male" view of reality and being human. Arguably, it is a "warrior's" way (see below), as the appropriate articulating archetype for 2nd-tier. In contradistinction, the notion of *caring* has captured the attention of women and a "female" (and/or feminist) view of reality and being human. The tension revolves around developing ethics and questioning—that is, on what basis might a good quality ethics be derived? The following quote from feminist philosopher-educator Nel Noddings's book *Women and Evil* (1989) demonstrates this well:[182]

[discussing the dominating philosophical orientation of a Western masculine hero-tragedy narrative, she wrote:] It includes the notion Ricoeur endorsed: 'Man enters into the ethical world through fear and not through love.' We cannot deny that fear inspires some ethical thinking, but so does love.

Noddings's earlier more popular book, not surprisingly, was entitled *Caring: A Feminine Approach to Ethics and Moral Education* (1986). Of all of her many books, Noddings never uses the word "fearlessness" or "fearless." This is common among many feminists, especially of the second wave and older (prior) generations. These women prefer "courage" and "caring" in combination. The point here is to ask these women, and others who focus more on caring, to at least bring a new fearlessness perspective to "Defense" and see that underneath caring is *defense of love*, and thus, defense of the being(s) we love. They are not necessarily incompatible constructs or realities, especially not if 'fear' is managed well (*via* 2nd-tier perspectives), or not absent at all as in FMS-9 (*fearless*). To defend one's offspring from dangers, for example, is an act of caring fundamentally. If this isn't done well, there will be fewer options for "reproduction" (biologically, or culturally) and for further caring and love in the future.

Moving across the 1st-tier perspectives to a 2nd-tier perspective (i.e., integral consciousness or view/theory) is what happens when we come to *fearlessness* (FMS-7). In Figure 3.1, with fearlessness, there is a stepping out of the 'Fear' Matrix completely (at least for a moment, perhaps longer). From a view outside of the 'Fear' Matrix, one sees its construction (at least in part). This is the moment of freedom from *fearism* and its means of "hiding" the fact that fearism is controlling so much of our lives, of which terrorism is only an extreme form thereof. Fearlessness in this 2nd-tier context gives us a "heightened perspective" way up on the Spiral, and we see the whole Spiral with all the FMSs. This is the location of deconstruction and reconstruction (in postmodern fashion) of everything we think we know about fear and fearlessness, and about the very nature of being a "human" (and adult, maturity).

Ken Wilber, in his earlier books (cited previously in this text) argues for a spectrum of worldviews or levels of consciousness in holarchical order. We encountered the existential level or worldview at FMSs-5 and 6b, and now we enter the *transpersonal* level worldview, of which there are three subsets in Wilber's work. My point: the *human being* in this fearlessness deconstruction and reconstruction is not quite what we thought it was in the 1st-tier (i.e., within a view inside the 'Fear' Matrix). The human being in the 1st-tier is generally narcissistic and egoistic (especially in the FMSs-3 to 6). The fear-perspective is "personal" in FMSs-3 to 6, and that makes up a good deal of our experience as human beings as a whole. If one judges human beings or a notion of humanity by a personal perspective, that is a "projection" of one's own state or reality onto the whole of our species; it can be distorted. Thus, we commonly see when a person feels fear so chronically (even without knowing it) as to identify with it and thus, makes it 'normal' or 'natural,' then they will want the rest of their peers (and humanity) to accept that *fear* is normal or natural for them too. If one cannot see the 'Fear' Matrix or does not know how to get beyond it, then they will deny such a place, state or level even exists in consciousness; and they deny it not only for themselves but then project that onto all of humanity. Such 'fear' projections are distortive (ignore-ant), at best, and pathological (arrogant), at worst. The "authorities" of the 'Fear' Matrix, who most benefit from mis-uses of 'fear,' like to keep this 'normal' and 'natural' fearstory going. This is accomplished primarily through fearism as a virtually an invisible ideology like any 'ism.'

Such is the everyday reality most everyone lives, more or less aware of fearism's destructive impacts. Critical theorist, the late Henri Lefebvre (1901-1991), in his critique of Modernity, called it "Terrorism and Everyday Life,"[183] and critical theorist Stanley Aronowitz called it "terror of the everyday world."[184] These critics were talking about a world long before 9/11. I would call the low-grade chronic "terror of the everyday" a symptom of fearism, and sometimes it builds and then "explodes" in all out terrorism in many forms as in despotic regimes, or random acts of political terrorism to name a few extremes. War, by any other name, is also an explosion of fearism, as is any abusive violence toward another being. Although Lefebvre or Aronowitz, like most critical theorists, are not integral thinkers (2nd-tier), they are pointing to one of the 2nd-tier's revelations: *there is something terribly wrong with the world; and that is a 'fear-'game that has become seductively 'natural and normal'*—conflating the two.

At FMS-7 there is very little (if any) 'fear' projection onto humanity and its evolution (and possibilities). The fearlessness perspective is "transpersonal" or sometimes called "trans-egoic," and "trans-ethnocentric." One's expanding sense of self-identity (and perception) is shifting to a global-centric and/or cosmocentric worldview (*a la* Wilber), that transcends one's historical and cultural roots. One can find evidence for this "shift" across the abyss, which earlier I called *'Fear' Barrier(s)* in the developmental literature of Jean Gebser, Clare Graves, Abraham Maslow, Robert Kegan, Suzanne Cook-Greuter, Sam Keen, Don Beck, Ken Wilber,[185] and others (see Figures 2.1, 2.2, 3.1).

FMS-7 *fearlessness* demands we challenge our preconceived 'norm' definitions and meanings of terms and concepts, including our image of ourselves, or our organizations—and in this case, concepts like fear, fearlessness, violence, and human being—are up for grabs. In essence, FMS-7 (8 and 9) are not attached to a conceptualization that 'to be human is to be fearful (or to suffer)'— that is, *fear* and *human* must (ought to) go together as some eternal "moral" existential principle and reality—that is, *this is the way it is and has always been and will always be*. These relative claims and positions are all a socially constructed (even arbitrary). They are 1st-tier cultural 'myths' or worldviews and experiences, limited by the blind spot of a 1st-tier perspective. It is not the experience or truth as seen from outside of the 'Fear' Matrix and thus outside of the violent ways of fearism. Many of the WFTs point to this in texts and practices.

That said, the risks and difficulties (and terror) of achieving and maintaining 2nd-tier or 3rd-tier perspectives, among the general populations on this planet, are enormous (see discussion in Chapter Two). Often FMS-7 (or 8, 9) are kept nourished in monasteries, small cliques, mystical clans, esoteric (cult-spiritual) groups, and so on (some significant examples are profiled below). Psychiatrist and spiritual teacher M. Scott Peck once said in a lecture I attended (paraphrasing), that if you or your organization are one step beyond the 'norm' of society you are likely to be heroic, but if you are two steps beyond or more, you will be perceived as an enemy. And in a discussion by Al Gore and others, there was a comment made that if you want to be elected as a political leader you ought not be more than half-a-step beyond the 'norm' of the people. Accordingly, there are (apparently) no elected world political leaders at this time centered in their consciousness at *fearlessness;* there have been some historically (e.g., Mahatma Gandhi, Martin Luther King, Jr.), and they often were assassinated. This political reality is quite disheartening, if not damned discouraging for anyone to want to pursue the path of fearlessness all the way—that is, across all the 'Fear' Barriers. It hardly seems worth it, from one perspective, anyway. Such is the price of growth, integrity, and reality. Two principles come forth: (1) in most cases, when there is not a physical/mental disability involved, individuals change and develop (potentially) much faster than cultures, creating problems and, (2) junior FMSs have a tendency to destroy violently those FMSs emerging beyond their grasp (see Chapter Two).

Fearlessness (FMS-7, Yellow, Integral) is difficult to get a simple handle on as to what it is and what it does. In fact, fearlessness is easier to "see" or "imagine" as a conscious movement from one set of dominant qualities, more or less, towards a new referent of qualities of which, it is assumed in this theory, are better in some way (i.e., less violent and more liberational). At least, this is the perception. Therefore, "unplugging" from the 'Fear' Matrix and culture of fear *is* a movement toward a *culture of fearlessness.*[186] The tracks of that movement indicate fearlessness exists. But to find fearlessness itself, is impossible. We record experience on the journey and describe the culture it produces. What I do know, is that there is a strong pull to remain in the inertia of the dominating 'Fear' Matrix (Fear's Empire) overall. That means, movement is difficult across the abyss from 1st-tier to 2nd-tier. The WFTs tell us this over and over, especially when examining the discourses of the FMSs-7 to 9. And as I have said all along, not everyone is capable of attaining a center of gravity of existence or consciousness (as operational) at FMS-7 fearlessness. People and organizations have to *develop into fearlessness* just like any of the other expressions or ways of fearlessness previously discussed in this chapter. Life conditions and many complex factors based on disciplined practices and so on are going to determine growth and evolution of consciousness. Ken Wilber argues that the "vast majority of humanity . . . has not yet stably reached the rational-egoic level [FMS-4, 5]."[187] An attainable goal humanity could set, or at least some people could set, is to have a few leaders and groups of thinkers on the planet grounded in and effectively utilizing FMS-7 fearlessness to manage the most challenging problems facing humankind today and in the future. This political, leadership and educational theme is further developed in the next chapters.

From FMS-7 the view of the path of the soul is one of both living the virtues but also of rigorous critical inquiry. The late venerable teacher Jiddu Krishnamurti (1895-1986), the most articulate epistemologist on the problem of fear in the 20th century, described the discipline required:[188]

> If you want to understand something, if you want to understand fear, you must obviously give your whole attention to it. . . . The disciplining of the mind to wipe away habit merely creates another habit. But in observing fear without verbalization, without condemnation or justification, [without assigning 'positive' or 'negative'] there is a spontaneous discipline from moment to moment—which means that the mind is free from the habit of discipline.

The "habit of discipline" is another 'fear' pattern (i.e., addiction pattern of 'fear'). Krishnamurti saw through that limited awareness of the 1st-tier. One cannot use a 'fear'-based approach, like habitual discipline, to remove a habit that is 'fear'-based itself. The fearlessness teaching here is that *'fear' will not dissolve 'fear'* but *'fearlessness' can.* A whole book could be devoted to the depths and practices of 'fearlessness.' For our purposes here, suffice it to say that a holistic-integral FMS-7 is not "for" or "against" fear; rather, it is interested in a full inquiry into fear (and 'fear') from a *fearlessness paradigm*, and particularly a notion of *fearanalysis* (like psychoanalysis). This book is a performative demonstration, in part, of both this paradigm and way of critical analysis.

One could speculate on a fearlessness paradigm that is both feminine (with the menstruant metaformic design) as inquiry practice, and masculine (with the hero-warrior metaformic design) as inquiry practice. At this point, I have not integrated these two. The focus has been on the more familiar, along the masculine approaches. However, by the time one has developed into the 2nd-tier there is a considerable amount of integration of masculine-feminine. Whatever the case, it takes great "spontaneous discipline"[189] to be a researcher of 'fear' and 'fearlessness' from a holistic-integral perspective. It takes the commitment of a *fearologist* to make it foundational to all FME. Far too many people on the liberational quest, be it secular or sacred, continually miss this FMS-7 disciplinary holistic-integral and critical work. This entire text is devoted to attempting to raise awareness of how much the FMS-7 (with fearanalysis) is needed and neglected. I have constructed FMS-7 (in a Wilberian manner) as a postmodern analysis. This latter perspective is typically dismissed (or ignored) by FMSs-8 and 9—which, are often constructed as more "spiritual," "groovy," "sexy" and "light." These latter two FMSs are not the primary location of the Sacred Warrior (or postmodern). They tend to be more premodern. Without the healthy integrative Sacred Warrior (FMS-7) in place as foundation, the higher FMSs and stages of development (e.g., Lover or Royal Leader) will tend to falter, twist, and distort as pathologies. They become anachronistic with the world context we live in today. Typically the leaders and their advocates and practitioners will not be able to discern their own 'fear'-based distortions and pathologies very well.

Power so easily corrupts our gurus and leaders, who may have the highest ethical intentions. As Burma's political opposition leader, Aung San Suu Kyi has said, *fear corrupts power*. She, like Bonaro Overstreet, said, "The most insidious form of fear is that which masquerades as common sense or even wisdom. . .".[190] They are with 'heads in the clouds' or in their passions of convictions of the "higher." These are what Wilber aptly called "the Ascenders." As a teacher of the soul path of 'fearlessness,' I have seen this "spiritual bypass" (Figure 2.2) in hundreds of people while working in the In Search of Fearlessness Project since 1989. I have conducted three years of doctoral graduate research on the concept of *fearless leadership* to attempt to address these problems theoretically.[191]

Rinpoche Chöygam Trungpa, the late great Tibetan Buddhist (American) teacher of the Shambhala Tradition, was an inspiration early on for the In Search of Fearlessness Project (ISOF). His book *Shambhala: Sacred Path of the Warrior* (1985) is a classic text (teaching) for understanding *fearlessness* and some of the FMS-7 and FMSs above that. However, Trungpa's work is decidedly premodern (magical) in many ways, and fails often to integrate the best of modern and postmodern (and post-postmodern integral) findings of many authors and disciplines. For this reason Trungpa's definition of "fearlessness" "fearless" and "warrior" are useful but somewhat distortive from a 2nd-tier point of view, as are his own conceptualizations of "fear." His famous, often repeated dictum is: "True fearlessness is not the reduction of fear, but going beyond fear."[192] Trungpa, like so many, taught that we have to experience fear to know fearlessness and practice fearlessness. Partially true as that is, most every definition of "courage" (and most of "bravery") in secular and sacred traditions have this same dialectic formula for a definition. Fear is conceived rather naively—not as a postmodern complex conception of 'fear' (within a culture of fear). The definition of fearlessness is mostly 1st-tier ('fear'-based) in its discourse formation.

Trungpa often used the four terms (bravery, courage, fearlessness and fearless) interchangeably. His developmental "curriculum" lacking clear distinctions, can get stuck in 1st-tier perspectives and their FMSs. 'Fear' and fearlessness thus, can become pathological in some individuals,[193] with various twists, as was parts of his own life in America a testimony. He was apparently a practicing alcoholic and died prematurely due to his toxic addiction, which most of his students denied while it was in progressive stages.

The wonderful liberation work of the larger Shambhala Tradition (and followers of Trungpa and other Tibetan teachers and their students) and current training centers in the world, ought to be carefully examined by anyone pursuing the path of fearlessness and sacred warriorship. I was recently sent an inspiring excerpt by Trungpa (and/or paraphrasing him), from a colleague, entitled "Ocean of Dharma of Fearlessness":[194]

> Over the centuries, there have been many who sought the ultimate good and have tried to share it with their fellow human beings. To realize it requires immaculate discipline and unflinching conviction. Those who have been fearless in their search and fearless in their proclamation belong to the lineage of master warriors, whatever their religion, philosophy, or creed. What distinguishes such leaders of humanity and guardians of human wisdom is their fearless expression of gentleness and genuineness—on behalf of all sentient beings. We should venerate their example and acknowledge the path that they have laid for

us. They are the fathers and mothers of Shambhala, who make it possible, in the midst of this degraded age, to contemplate enlightened society.

This is a beautiful Tradition and resource of the World's Fearlessness Teachings. As FME and good fearwork, it needs to be studied with all due caution and critique—especially from the position of a critical integral theory of fearlessness. Jeremy Hayward's interpretations of Trungpa and Shambhala is inherently a good contemporary improvement.[195] What has been most inspiring in Trungpa's emancipatory leadership is his declaration and optimism toward what he called "Creating an Enlightened Society," I'd call a generic *culture of fearlessness*. Trungpa wrote,[196]

> The Shambhala teachings are founded on the premise that there is basic human wisdom that can help to solve the world's problems. This wisdom does not belong to any one culture or religion, nor does it come only from the West or the East. Rather, it is a tradition of human warriorship that has existed in many cultures at many times throughout history.

In ancient Tibetan folklore there is a strong ethical distinction of two worlds or "kingdoms" that exist: Setting Sun Vision (Kingdom) or Great Eastern Sun Vision (Kingdom of Shambhala). The former is usually always dominant, the latter is the possible alternative idea or utopia. The former is 'fear'-based (Fear's Kingdom or Empire), the latter is love-based. The task of the warrior on the sacred path, as Trungpa explained, must choose one (i.e., Great Eastern Sun Vision) and reject the other. The sacred warrior is radically different than our usual negative association of warrior as an aggressive violent militaristic 'agent' of a group or State, who's only interest is in their own welfare. He defines this further:[197]

> Warriorship here does not refer to making war on others. Aggression is the source of our problems, not the solution. Here the word 'warrior' is taken from the Tibetan *pawo*, which literally means 'one who is brave.' Warriorship in this context is the tradition of human bravery, or the tradition of fearlessness. The North American Indians had such a tradition, and it also existed in South American Indian societies. The Japanese ideal of the samurai also represented a warrior tradition of wisdom, and there have been principles of enlightened warriorship in Western Christian societies as well. King Arthur is a legendary example. . . . The key to warriorship and the first principle of Shambhala vision is not being afraid of who you are. . . . When we are afraid of ourselves and afraid of the seeming threat the world presents, then we become extremely selfish. We want to build our own little nests, our own cocoons, so that we can live by ourselves in a secure way. . . . We must try to think beyond our homes, beyond the fire burning in the fireplace, beyond sending our children to school or getting to work in the morning. We must try to think how we can help the world. . . . you can start with yourself. The important point is to realize [as warrior] that you are never off duty. You can never just relax, because the whole world needs help. While everyone has a responsibility to help the world, we can create additional chaos if we try to impose our ideas or our help upon others. . . . The

Shambhala teachings are not based on converting the world to another theory [or vision].

Trungpa's fearlessness teachings here are excellent and reflect an open-mindedness to not impose or try to convert others (based on 'fear'). The issue is to support development in the right direction—that is, away from the Setting Sun Vision (of 'fear') toward the Great Eastern Sun Vision (of Love). The path is the way of the warrior—the way of fearlessness. This, Trungpa is very clear on. It is basically the same open-minded approach that ISOF has taken since its inception in 1989. I co-founded the School of Sacred Warriorship as another project in 1993 to assist this task. There were a lot of writings on the sacred way of the "warrior" appearing in many domains of the Green movement and social activism as well as 'new age.' What they all lack generally, is a systematic study of 'fear' and 'fearlessness'—and they rarely incorporate the full study of the Shambhala Tradition (Trungpa's work).

The twists and turns of activist-rebels becoming warriors and Outlaws was (and still is) as much disastrous as helpful, one could argue (see Chapter Five). The point here, however, is to note that in Figure 2.1 there is a double thick line illustrating 'Fear' Barrier 2 as the abyss. Moving from 1st-tier ('fear'-based organizing within the Setting Sun Vision) to 2nd-tier (fearlessness-based organizing within the Great Eastern Sun vision) must occur at 'Fear' Barrier 2. Arguably, it is the most difficult passage for the uninitiated, untrained, uneducated, and undeveloped. Trungpa did not speak/write a lot about this, that I know of. ISOF theory has offered a lot of teaching about this through a set of six 'fear' vaccines[198] to assist individuals or groups on this journey to and beyond the 2nd-tier (or 'Fear' Barrier 2). Because fearlessness is not usually properly understood, most questors end up in the "Thriver" (or super-Survivor) stage, more or less, with sometimes very complex ethical and nondual (contemplative) philosophies and spiritual costuming as rationale for their "way."

In other words, they tap into the wisdom of the higher FMSs-8, 9 and download them into an operative functional FMS-5 or 6 (via the "spiritual by-pass"), where they actually live and act, and interpret the higher FMSs from. Thus, inevitably, they distort the higher wisdom of the Outlaw and Lover (to use Keen's terms) or Sacred Warrior and Royal Leader (to use Trungpa's terms). Trungpa, like this author, and others, have long known that the Sacred Warriorship of fearlessness (FMS-7) has to be vigilant to guard against any distortions of the WFT's and traditions. Yet at the same time, FMS-7 offers a critical integral critique of all such teachings and traditions. This is not an easy task and one not yet mastered by myself. The holistic-integral perspective, however, is one of the better theories that is capable of making distinctions of the ways of fearlessness ('fearlessness') and when they get twisted in 'fear'-based forms of bravado (ego, narcissism).

Figures 2.1 and 3.1 map out the life and reality of the worldviews (FMSs) of the 1st-tier which are challenged and "reversed" ("resisted") as one moves into 2nd-tier and the duty of the Sacred Warrior (Outlaw) in FMS-7. At the same time evolutionary "progress" is made by going forward not backward (i.e., into a "retro-regress," as Wilber calls it). Fearlessness at FMS-7 has to be a progressive discipline of well-informed "Defense" that discerns the strong tendencies of individuals and organizations to come across the 'Fear' Barrier 2 but turn then back (due to cowardliness or unconsciousness due to prior traumatic and repressive 'fear' patterning). Such retro-regress is a returning back toward the 'norm' where they have built their entire (often comfortable) identities and received the rewards (i.e., economic and cultural capital = power) for conforming to the cultures of their history and current lives. Don't forget: *The 'Fear' Matrix wants you* but *only as you conform. When you no longer conform, then it simply deletes you.* See Chapter Five and discussion of the sci-fi movie meta-narrative entitled *The Matrix.*

There is, as Trungpa says, no rest for those who practice the tradition of fearlessness and fearless leadership, in this sense. The Setting Sun Vision wants you as the 'Fear' Matrix does. Arguably, this Sacred Warrior vigilance is the same for those who practice holistic-integral traditions of critical theory (e.g., Wilberian). And before that, many critical theory traditions, especially since the 1960s have argued this kind of "reversal" vigilance is required "against" the pull of the 'norm' (i.e., everyday terror). To abandon ship, so to speak, is to be a 'traitor' of the liberation movement on the one-hand and on the other-hand to leave the 'Fear' Matrix is to be seen as a 'traitor.' When one crosses permanently 'Fear' Barrier 2 there is immense *terror* to experience and overcome both internally and externally. The entire culture(s) from which you have arisen in the 1st-tier will 'attack' every fabric of your way of being—as they make you an 'enemy of your family,' 'enemy of the state,' 'alien' and a 'threat' to *status quo* "Security" (i.e., captial 'S').

Simply, 'Be Prepared' for major conflict, if one sincerely follows 'fearlessness' forward in the evolution of consciousness as the *telos* of historical fearlessness implies and directs us. In FMS-7 this quality of going forward and backward, of rebelling and then giving-in (or giving-up as 'betrayal' to your group) is all part of the journey of the soul, or of any organization that is striving to cross the 'Fear' Barrier 2. Expect it. There is no need to blame or condemn those who cannot "hold" the 2nd or 3rd-tier perspectives (FMSs). That *is* the reality of where their development *is* at, and the conditions around them (more on that in the latter chapters). We are a long way from seeing sustainable cultures of fearlessness anywhere, and for good reasons. However, discernment of *cowardice* is something FMS-7 keeps intact (see below).

Fearlessness (FMS-7), as a discourse, is relatively, both wise and compassionate. It is not something we usually see in political movements of liberation. The 20th century Gandhian non-violent movement in India, against the British Empire, was likely one of the most successful in modern times at doing both well. Yet, it was not without its errors, failures, and critics—but that's another study. More importantly, Gandhi's revolutionary activism, a movement still active around the world today informing other social movements, revolved around the practice of *satyagraha* (non-violence) and concept *ahimsa* (fearlessness). For many ethical thinkers, this is still a highly respected WFT of principles and a model for action, politically and spiritually. According to Joan Bondurant,[199] Gandhi's interpretation of the ancient Eastern practice of *satyagraha* boils down to "non-violence" as lived in one's everyday life and applied rigorously in the field of social and political conflict (i.e., battles for justice). Democracy, according to Gandhi, cannot properly function without these practices based on fearlessness. Acharya Mahaprajna, a contemporary Sikh spiritual teacher, wrote,[200]

> . . . Lord Mahavir emphasized much more the importance of fearlessness than of non-violence [but] this spirit of non-violence is implicit in fearlessness; without fearlessness this spirit cannot manifest itself in life. A coward can never be truly non-violent.

Gandhi's life of fearlessness was a renunciation of the will to kill or to damage; yet, he was not rigid or absolutistic in his interpretation of the principle of non-violence. Perhaps his genius, and obvious transformative impact on India's emancipation from the British Empire (of 'Fear'), was his contextual flexibility to utilize *satyagraha* and *ahimsa* (as premodern ethical precepts of Hinduism, Jainism, Buddhism). Gandhi's view of *satyagraha* as "passive resistance" to unjust authoritarianism and abuse of power or fear over others included resistance that may involve taking up arms and killing. "Gandhi guarded against attracting to his satyagraha movement [a FMS-7 movement] those who feared to take up arms . . .", according to Bondurant.[201] However, for Gandhi, any taking up of arms for such resistance (and ultimate Defense) had to be accompanied with a disciplined practice of *ahimsa*—that is, love, goodwill, self-suffering as all part of courage and fearlessness. One had to overcome fear and had to be aware of how fear motivates violence, which is not acceptable ethically to the practice of the *satyagrahi* (Sacred Warrior or Outlaw). Gandhi wrote,[202] "The votary of non-violence has to cultivate the capacity for sacrifice [without revenge] of the highest type in order to be free from fear. . . . He who has not overcome all fear cannot practice *ahimsa* to perfection."

In this Tradition, the *satyagrahi* (having "overcome all fear") vows to obey the laws of society as sacred first; and then and only then may they practice discernment, find flaws in those laws that are unjust, and rebel against them to change them for improvement. There is no room for rebelling just to rebel against authority and thus spread more fear ('fear') with ensuing chaos.

FMS-7 defense, like Gandhi's interpretation of *satyagraha* and *ahimsa* requires we move beyond the 1st-tier motivational paradigm of 'fear'-based actions of defense. The Defense of "life" (or Truth, Beauty, and Goodness) at the integral level of consciousness in 2nd-tier or 3rd-tier (nondual) is profoundly different than immature egoistic 'fear'-based actions. Overcoming the "fear of death" or harm for Gandhian revolutionaries is essential but it is done with ethical intention, never to prove how one can be brave or courageous as part of *bravado*, narcissistic heroism with egoic inflation.

This is *ethical fearlessness* being engaged as I discuss Gandhian ideals of revolutionary practices. There is a threshold ('Fear' Barrier 2) that must be crossed to attain the practice of "*ahimsa* to perfection" or to attain the "perfect love that casts out fear" as the Biblical dictum suggests. The word "perfect" in these teachings is there for good reason. Perfect Love, like perfect non-violence (i.e., non-revenge, non-hate, non-ego) is a highly demanding ethic and consciousness to attain. What the ancient Eastern traditions of philosophy, religion and spirituality teach is that a "Reversal" must take place in one's life and convictions as well as their awareness. On the other side of 'Fear' Barrier 2 the initiate of non-violence awakens to the Sacred Warrior and leaves (unplugs) from the "setting-sun vision [which] is based on trying to ward off the concept of death, trying to save ourselves from dying. The setting-sun point of view is based on fear," proclaimed Trungpa.[203]

The ancient Warrior Tradition, which I call the ancient *Fearlessness Tradition*, can be drawn on as wisdom and guidance on the 'other side' of 'Fear' Barrier 2. Cowardice is now no longer tolerated as an "excuse" for one's choices and actions that are based on fear ('fear') and what Trungpa called the habit or role of "cocoon[ing]." He wrote,[204]

> The way of cowardice is to embed ourselves in a cocoon, in which we perpetuate our habitual patterns [individually and collectively]. When we are constantly recreating our basic ['fear'] patterns of behavior and thought, we never have to leap into fresh air or onto fresh ground.

In his discussion of how to be a "warrior" in the Shambhala (FMS-7) tradition, Trungpa discusses the metaphoric role "darkness" plays in the cocooning process of cowardice. He wrote,[205]

> In the last chapter we talked about the dawn of the Great Eastern Sun. However, in general, we are much more accustomed to the [seduction toward] darkness of the setting sun world [of 'fear'] than we are to the light of the Great Eastern Sun [of Love]. By darkness, we mean enclosing ourselves in a familiar world in which we can hide or go to sleep. It is as though we would like to re-enter our mother's womb and hide there forever, so that we could avoid being born. When we are afraid of waking up and afraid of experiencing our own fear, we create a cocoon [of defense mechanisms] to shield ourselves from the vision of the Great Eastern Sun. He prefers to hide in personal jungles and caves. When we hide from the world in this way, we feel secure. We may think that we have quieted our fear, but we are actually making ourselves numb with fear. We surround ourselves with our own familiar thoughts, so that nothing sharp or painful can touch us. We are so afraid of our own fear that we deaden our hearts.

Perhaps one of Trungpa's most important passages, the above quote refers to our tendency for our evolving consciousness to retro-regress when "waking up." It seems just too painful, hard, and terrifying. "Darkness" thus, especially for the male hero/warrior, becomes pathological, unlike the healthy darkness (retreat from the everyday world) that I discussed in the menstruant's journey earlier. The integration of a healthy version of "darkness," brought about by hero and menstruant metaformics, again, is a future task. For now, what we see is a fear of awakening, nicely performed in the dramatics of the sci-fi movie *The Matrix*. In the 1999 first film, the female protagonist named Trinity (who is relatively freed from the Matrix of 'Fear') 'calls' on a computer screen for Neo (who is not yet freed from the Matrix of 'Fear'). She types: "Wake up!" The movie plot begins. All spiritual and secular traditions of emancipation, one way or another, call for this. The call to wake up is a call to enter and keep going along the path of fearlessness and not use 'cocoon' excuses to avoid it—that is, to avoid the fear of death, but also the fear of life—that is, to avoid the transpersonal responsibility for Death and for Life. I have written elsewhere about this problematic of "waking up."[206] These are great existential themes in the history of Western philosophy and spirituality but they extend further into the transpersonal themes of enlightenment as well.

Gandhi's point is difficult to accept within the FMS-6 discourse—seen in *The Matrix* narrative. That is, fearlessness (FMS-7) requires both the responsibility to bring about 'death' as well as to bring about 'life' (i.e., dying and birthing). That is why sometimes one has to be assertive and stop violence with violence. The former violence being based on 'fear' and the latter being based on 'fearlessness.' That is the point of Gandhi's interpretation, and which I see as valid and quite characteristically FMS-7 logic. At this perspective of the 2nd-tier (Yellow, Integral) there is no mere wishing for "equality" and "non-violence" without looking straight into the terror of oneself, and seeing that most of our "need for peace" is actually based on a deep "fear of being violent"—that is, fear of killing, fear of taking another's life. When such fear is operating, say these 2nd-tier WFTs, there will be no authentic "non-violence" or "peace." It is a projection, facade, a denial, a distraction. Ultimately, such "good" ethical claims and activist attempts are, deeply and insidiously, 'fear'-based (i.e., shadow projections). They are often based on self-fearing, self-loathing and/or hatred of humanity itself (what Frank Furedi called "misanthropy"). Feeding the culture of fear, they tend to deny their own hidden shadowy violent motivations. I have experienced this personally being a peace activist for years, and witnessing it in various situations, including in my counseling office with peace activists as clients in therapy.

A. Mahaprajan, speaking without a politically correct (Green, Sensitive) 'filter' (i.e., speaking from fearlessness), recently said in order to be totally free from fear we must not fear violence by pretending to be peaceful:[207]

A coward can never be truly non-violent. The man [sic] who is too much attached to life, who is afraid of dying, cannot be non-violent. A friend said the other day that the Jains in India almost outnumbered the Sikhs and yet the Sikhs managed to get their way while nobody paid any heed to the Jains. I said, 'I don't want to enter into a lengthy discussion, but one thing is clear. The Sikhs are not afraid of dying [some anyway]; the Jains are [some anyway].'

The Jains are known for their 'extreme' practices to be non-violent to everything. That may be quite appropriate to certain conditions but quite inappropriate to other conditions. This is a complex topic beyond the scope of this book but it is implicitly relevant as we come to the critical integral perspective (FMS-7) of this book. Fearlessness here is *not* politically-neutral nor trying to be above enacting appropriate justice and/or law as required. If that means, for an extreme example, killing a person (or group) who is killing many other persons out of a 'fear'-based motivation, so be it. Gandhi, and Martin Luther King Jr. (as a few examples), knew this. To *not* act rightfully, from fearlessness, is violent—or in the Jain's case it is fear. That is cowardice. In my own language, be it cocooning, or peace-making, the "coward" archetypal pattern or discourse is one of being an Agent of the 'Fear' Matrix— and simultaneously, its "victim." To be such is to "choose" (consciously or unconsciously) to *refuse to let go of the power of fear*—be that in oneself (i.e., 'fear is a great motivator') or in others that one may support to use the power of fear (i.e., 'fear brings effective social order'). Cowardice is usually an alignment with some affinity group (or sub-group, or team), which desperately needs to "win"—at any cost, for any cause— the egoic goal is to not "fail" or be a "loser," nor to "be left out." This performance or 'game' is characteristic of the 1st-tier FMSs and incongruent with FMSs of the 2nd-tier or 3rd-tier.

Regarding Sikhs vs. Jains and who is the most fearless(?), that is not a generic discernment I can make, as exposure to actual practitioners of Jainism has not been part of the research in this book. However, the quote above does raise the point being made about critically inquiring into our motivations (our cowardice), even when on the surface the rhetoric or behaviors (rituals) may seem so benign—that is, loving, peaceful (idyllic).

Another example of the denial of FMS-6a is in the peace movement. There is a wonderful DVD documentary entitled *Think Peace*, produced during the 2006 World Peace Forum in Vancouver, BC, Canada.[208] At one point one of the peace activists, and co-founder of Green Peace, laments emotionally with anger "Why would somebody be opposed to a peace movement?" Is he kidding? The FMS-6a has no clue, nor capability to empathize with another worldview (or worldviews), like FMSs-1-5 which make up most of where the world actually operates. The FMS-6a is a 1st-tier perspective and thinks everyone should "think peace" just like it does. It literally can't understand "why" someone in FMSs 1-5 would be against FMS-6a, and it literally cannot critique itself to see that it is against all the other FMSs on the spectrum that don't think like FMS-6a. We'll see this explained in more detail in Chapter Five. This same co-founder of Green Peace, typically of the 1st-tier ('fear'-based motivational paradigm) then says in the interview on the DVD, "I'm on the side of peace." Yeah, no doubt he is, and by placing himself there, he seems blind to seeing *that* as an act of 'war,' relative to the other FMSs on the spectrum? Of course, nowhere in the film is "peace" actually defined by these peace activists; they don't need to define it because 'they get it' and they're waiting (impatiently) for 'others to get it.' One of the purposes of this book, like the DVD *Think Peace* is to open dialogue and re-think the limitations of FMS-6 Peace (Green, Sensitive)—that is "Green Peace" as the only construction available to the liberation of humanity. The alternative, I suggest, is "Yellow Peace" (i.e., FMS-7 perspective). From a (fearlessness) Defense perspective: *peace is fundamentally a response to fear and a means of managing fear* (i.e., "war" and toxic conflict, and domination, etc.).

This is why the Fearlessness Tradition tells us (at FMS-7), as Sacred Warriors, that we are required to study fear ('fear') and fearlessness ('fearlessness') in *all* of its dimensions intimately, across the spectrum. We are to see through (or attempt to embrace) the many forms, ways, and disguises of 'fear' and fearless-ness. That is a life-time study. Of course, fearlessness here does not mean to "study only" and avoid taking just, right, and sufficient corrective action in the world. This level of fearlessness is all about integrity, integration, or what is more sophisticatedly referred to as *critical integral praxis* (see Chapter Four and Five). FMS-6a (especially) really doesn't like any of this discussion on violence, non-violence and peace, because FMS-7 sees things very differently. FMS-7 is a relatively mature perspective and consciousness that understands FMS-6 well and has integrated its better aspects but has also evolved beyond it. Having cri-tiqued FMS-6, FMS-7 is attempting to solve the problems that FMS-6 could not solve, as well as some problems that FMS-6 actually created and still creates (adding to the Fear Problem).

FMS-7 is clear, there is no workable (foreseeable) solution like egalitarian-ism in all things, as FMS-6 (Green, Sensitive) would like to see (fantasize). The ideal of egalitarianism is wonderful, but it has not proven a solution to the more complex problems of a postmodern world, and that is FMS-7's assessment at this time (of course, from my biased view and fearanalysis). And FMSs-7 also needs to be critiqued and 'balanced' as FMS-8 is designed to do—that is, to ex-pand the spirit of fearlessness intelligence even further along the spectrum.

It is very important in distinguishing the discourses of a 2nd-tier fearanaly-sis from a 1st-tier fearanalysis (especially FMS-6), because there is a significant shift of focus from looking at "personal fears" (fear of x, y, z) to looking at the 'fear' patterning in a formalistic (or developmental "structural") manner. The deep pattern is of special interest. That is why the very use of FMSs period is utilized in a 2nd-tier integral analysis. FMSs are not "personal" *per se* but rather are discourses that flow throughout human history and participate in and enact cultural evolution and even biological evolution to some degree. FMS-6 tends to take the remarks of FMS-7 (in particular) as if they were personal, for example, in discussion of cowardice by Trungpa and Mahaprajna. FMS-6 hears FMS-7 as "superior" and "arrogant." FMS-6 tends to feel criticized and sensing that it is being blamed for producing all the "cowards" *per se*. They (the discourse of FMS-6) feels FMS-7 is elitist and judgmental, putting people down in an insen-sitive (pathological) hierarchical (egoistic) manner. FMS-6 characteristically interprets FMS-7's ethical discernment through its own lens of critique of FMS-5 (and FMSs junior to that). It mistakes "discernment" for "judgment." Underly-ing the Green (FMS-6) discourse is the question: *Who is really more courageous or fearless?* Green believes it is. Yellow believes it is. The difference is, Green takes it personally (egoically), Yellow is primarily only interested in the dis-course formation and its consequences.

Point being, we ought to be looking for deeper formalistic patterns when operating in the 2nd-tier. This research has found a deep pattern of a spirit of fearlessness (i.e., historical and ethical fearlessness)—a *Fearlessness Movement*, which manifests in 15 or so meanings of fearlessness, and what is worth calling a Great Tradition or *Fearlessness Tradition*. The WFTs reveal this, if one looks for it. At this point in our discussion of *fearlessness* at 2nd-tier, the emphasis is on Defense, Warriorship, Fearanalysis, and dichotomous distinction of what is on the side of the 1st-tier from the 2nd-tier—as one crosses problematically back and forth over 'Fear' Barrier 2. However, one is reminded not merely to interpret *fearlessness* from FMS-7, but also from FMS-8 (Turquoise, Global) (see Figures 2.1, 2.2, and 3.1). The latter, is a more communal view and 'softer' asesthetic of a "unitive," "universal," and "global" perspective. A healthy ideal: "Turquoise thinking is fully integral and uses the entire Spiral; sees multiple levels of interaction; detects harmonics, the mystical forces, and the pervasive flow-states that permeate any organization," according to Wilber.[209] It is an understanding of fearlessness as less about Defense and more about Caring, but with a very subtle energetic and intelligence in how caring operates as compassion (beyond 'fear'-based operations). This is where the metaformics (feminine, feminist) theories of menstruation (birthing journey), uncovered by Judy Grahn et al., are likely to be a major part of FMS-8.

What interests me most at this point is FMS-7, the transitional FME approach at the highest tension (conflict) at 'Fear' Barrier 2. In Search of Fearlessness Project (ISOF) is one of the only such projects to have been developing the FMS-7 perspective systematically. Not only have 15 meanings of fearlessness been revealed but, in the following pages 15 paradigms (of the Fearlessness Tradition) make up deep structures that manifest in the WFTs and construct an ethical bi-centric distinction, much like we saw with Trungpa's "Great Eastern Sun" vs. "Setting Sun." The former being the *way to go* for quality life and evolution of consciousness and society, the later being the *way to leave behind* or deny the great potential before us.

In secular philosophy (and some spiritual paths within it), this bi-centric (dichotomous) distinction between "Living" vs. "Dead" qualities and thought was prevalent in German philosophy between 1880 and 1930.[210] It went out of fashion after that, and any such simple ethical categories were usually discarded overall. One can recognize a resonance with early dichotomies of "Good" vs. "Evil" in FMS-2 (Purple, Magical)—it is a theme that won't go away in evolution and history, but it goes underground now and then and changes forms with the times. FMS-7 is not afraid to 'tackle it' and deal with 'Evil' once again, but this time from a 'fearlessness' perspective, not from a 'fear'-based perspective as we are familiar with in 1st-tier discourses of most forms of religion, ethical philosophy and popular moral standards.

In FMS-7 a more complex dichotomous fearanalysis marks out a 'map' (e.g., Figures 2.1 and 3.1) for the journey of recovery (a "Reversal"). Growth forward *via* recovery, healing, transformation and transmutation of 'fear' is virtually universal in the individual and collective aspects of development. If growth and healing exceeds beyond the "Dead" ("Evil") side of the dichotomy there is a freeing and liberating from forces that act in the world to prevent 'fearlessness' and the 2nd-tier and 3rd-tier FMSs from operating. In a previous publication I summarized 15 paradigms (that I know of) which compose a Great Fearlessness Tradition (of which ISOF works with).[211] For our purposes they will be mentioned in short form only as a resource for Reversal work, from a 2nd-tier perspective. They are listed here not in any particular order:

15 Bi-centric Paradigms of the Fearlessness Tradition (Movement)

(1) *Living Process vs. Addictive Process* (Schaef)
Dr. Anne Wilson Schaef, of Wilson-Schaef Associates, Inc. (Boulder, CO), is the addiction and healing expert with many books. She is a feminist and a leader of the "Living Process System" model and "Deep Process Work" which reaches into the deeper traumatic roots of the healing needed to "cure" addiction; as most addiction therapists know, there is "Stage-I recovery" which is the basics of learning to stop addicting to the point of it ruining your life and others' lives with it—and there is the more rare "Stage-II recovery" which focuses on the deeper wounds around intimacy,[212] which act to motivate the addictive "substitutions" for love, based on 'fear.' A pivotal text of Schaef's bi-centric model is *Beyond Therapy, Beyond Science: A New Model for Healing the Whole Person* (1992); her model and experience shows that one cannot be in an "addictive process" and "living process" at the same time, they are interrelated but contradictory processes.

(2) *Love vs. Fear* (many wisdom traditions)
This classic dichotomy has the largest universal "truth" or historical tracings of a foundational theory and set of practices of healing and liberating oneself from 'fear.' Eastern and Western mystical traditions, and the mainstream religions of the world (and some philosophies) have this dichotomy well established into their basic design and beliefs. The most popularized, in the human potential and 'New Age' movement in the past 30 years or so has been *The Course in Miracle* (1975). It is published by the Foundation for Inner Peace (Tiburon, CA), and has many teachers worldwide, influencing millions of people's lives for the better. Dr. Gerald Jampolsky's book *Love is Letting Go of Fear* (1979) is a classic example of this tradition. The argument is that one cannot be in Love, if they are in Fear, and visa versa. Suffice it to say that "Fear" (capitalized) in this paradigm is more metaphysical in construction than a common sense notion of psychological (personal) "fear"; however, they are intimately related.

(3) *Good vs. Evil* (many wisdom traditions)
This dichotomy of how to divide the world up is as ancient as history itself. The exact meaning of what is 'Good' and what is 'Evil' (be it secular or sacred in its dimensions, is variable based on cultures and different time periods). The most systematic theorizing and philosophy of these polar opposites is found in the tradition of theology and the particular sub-discipline called "theodicy" which is an attempt to understand how these two polarities emerge and operate and how we can move from Evil to Good. Typically, one cannot be in 'Good' and in 'Evil' at the same time.

(4) *Sunrise Vision vs. Sunset Vision* (Trungpa)
Has already been discussed in this text somewhat.

(5) *Benign Reality Pattern vs. Distress Pattern* (Jackins)

In the late 1940s a union leader, Harvey Jackins, began to discover what happens when people breakdown emotionally and how to facilitate their healing (of distress and trauma). A grassroots movement called Re-evaluation Co-counseling developed and continues to this day to foster amazing liberational work worldwide. For Jackins, "Benign Reality" is our inherent human nature and the nature of the universe (it is 'Good'), and when we are hurt and not encouraged to heal our hurts we form "distress patterns" which cloud the experience, memory and actualization of "Benign Reality"—thus, causing human suffering. Characteristic of the dichotomous paradigms, distress is 'fear'-based and one cannot be in Benign Reality while in a 'fear'-based pattern. The classic textbook by Jackins is *The Human Side of Human Beings: The Theory of Re-evaluation Counseling* (first ed. 965).

(6) *Red Pill vs. Blue Pill* (Wachowski Bros.)

The metaphor and (meta-)narrative of the healing transformation and liberational journey in contemporary pop cultural sci-fi filmmaking, comes to us today in the Wachowski Brothers' hit trilogy *The Matrix* (1999-2003). You have to watch the first film to see the Red Pill vs. Blue Pill choice of the initiate (Neo). Blue Pill puts you back to sleep in the illusions of the everyday world, Red Pill wakes you up to how you are a "slave" of the everyday world, etc. You take one pill or the other, not both. An excellent, radical book on this movie and some of its more profound implications can be found in Jake Horsley's book *Matrix Warrior: Being the One* (2003).

(7) *Heaven vs. Hell* (Cohen)

Christians, for example, will readily recognize this bi-centric conceptualization, with roots going back a few thousand years in Western thought. However, one of the most original and detailed mappings of the paradigm of liberation is that of "Hell" ('fear'-based worldview) and "Heaven" (Love-based worldview) that has been created by the guru of evolutionary spirituality, Andrew Cohen, based out of his ashram in Massachusetts. His primary work has been to find the contemporary way to "Enlightenment." He has many books and runs the community and organization that published the more popular *What is Enlightenment?* magazine. His view (and model) marvelously and aesthetically depict these two worldviews, and again, one cannot be in Hell if they want to be in Heaven. The latter, Cohen calls the way of the "Authentic Self" vs. "personal self."

(8) *Healing vs. Coping* (Fisher)

This author, co-founder of the In Search of Fearlessness Project (1989), has taught that we live primarily in a coping culture in the Western world, and have done so for probably thousands of years. The opposite of coping with a wound (trauma) is to heal it. Without healing our wounds and reclaiming our natural healing capacities to do so, we end up in a "culture of fear" because coping is motivated by 'fear' patterns and healing is motivated by 'Love' patterns. The path in between these two is the path of fearlessness, according to Fisher. The current book you are reading is the classic text to understand the fearlessness path. Characteristically, one cannot be healing if they are coping and coping often prevents healing.

(9) *Benign Circle vs. Vicious Circle* (Robertson)

Drawing some from Re-evaluation Co-counseling, Jean Robertson, an activist-community leader in Canada, has created an elaborate (well-tested) model of the "Vicious Circle" (dynamics of fear, mistrust, hurtful cycle) and "Benign Circle" (dynamics of love, trust, cooperation cycle) of communications. She is co-founder of Common Ground Learning Community (1980-1989) in Olds, AB, and is now promoting her model as the "Living Room Context." Typically, one cannot be communicating in trust and mistrust at the same time.

(10) *Moksha vs. Maya* (Eastern wisdom traditions)

Basically, *maya* is the 'fear'-based illusory world of form and temporality (duality, self, ego). The nondual *moksha* is beyond and incompatible with the suffering cycle of existence of *maya* (or karma). Generally, a movement out of *maya* is the way of enlightenment or *nirvana* as Buddhists use the notion of *moksha*. See the Internet for distinctions.

(11) *Eros-Agape vs. Phobos-Thanatos* (Wilber)

Integral philosopher Ken Wilber, a contemporary leader of the "Integral Movement" world-wide, has been writing and publishing a radical new philosophy for the past 30+ years. His earlier work (prior to 1997) is amazing in universal scope by its synthesis of wisdom and research East-West, throughout time and across cultures. He has posited that living systems function universally upon the same deep structural (habitual) patterning and dynamic forces of "Eros-Agape" (Love pattern) vs. "Phobos-Thanatos" ('fear' pattern). The analysis is more metaphysical than psychological, but they are related of course. These two great meta-patterns or forces are discussed at length in his classic work *Sex, Ecology, and Spirituality* (1995); since that time he has left emphasizing this model in his latest post-metaphysical teaching and writing.

(12) *Creation-Centered Cosmology vs. Fall/Redemption Cosmology* (Fox)

In the early to mid-1980's Fr. Matthew Fox, a Dominican priest in California, was challenging the Catholic teachings of a 'fear'-based "Fall/Redemption Cosmology" that underlay the exoteric ('normal') form of the Church and its teachings. Having studied Christian mystics, and from his own experience, Fox saw a love-based esoteric (universal) stream deep in the religious traditions that was more "Creation-centered" without a starting point of "original sin." His classic work appeared in his book *Original Blessing* (1986); not surprising he was excommunicated by the Catholic Church and labeled a heretic. One of his latest ventures is the creation and development of Wisdom University, California.

(13) *Wholistic vs. Mechanistic* (Hatala's)
Rick and Lillas Hatala are spiritual-based corporate leadership consultants and entrepreneurs in Western Canada. Having studied the esoteric traditions around the world, they have created a synthetic integrative model based on the distinction between a largely 'fear'-based "Mechanistic Paradigm" vs. a Love-based "Wholistic Paradigm" (and "Organic Paradigm"), which develops sequentially with conscious choice and practice. Their book is entitled *Integrative Leadership: Build a Foundation for Personal, Interpersonal and Organizational Success* (2004). They claim their model is "integrally-informed" (in the Wilberian sense) but it is very original and a breakthrough in the business consulting literature. They are planning an Integrative Energy University in the next few years. Another wonderful book arising from a business management consultant is Jack Gibb's *Trust; A New View of Personal and Organizational Development* (1978, new edition in 1991), where he helps us understand organizational dynamics based on a paradigm of "Trust" vs. "Fear." When one is dominant the other is sub-dominant. They are incompatible realities.

(14) *Paradigm of Hope vs. Paradigm of Fear* (Lerner)
"For the past several thousand years, much of human society has been torn by a struggle between two worldviews or ways of understanding what it is to be human. . . . [i.e.,] paradigm of fear and paradigm of hope." Recently, this claim comes from the American Rabbi Michael Lerner, Editor of the revered *Tikkun* magazine and author of many books and articles. See especially his article www.tikkun.org/magazine/tik0603/lerner-fear. A similar dichotomy is found in Riane Eisler's feminist philosophy-archeology (based around Marija Gimbutas's findings) that "Dominant Hierarchies" based on fear and mistrust have long ruled the Western world; these are incompatible with a more feminine (feminist) "Partnership" model based on trust and cooperation. See Eisler's classic book *The Chalice and the Blade* (1987).

(15) *Second-tier vs. First-tier* (Beck)
The extensive values psychological research of Americans like Clare Graves (1950s-70s) and his students, such as Don Beck (later Chris Cowan), have produced a theory of v-memes ("like cultural-genes") to explain human behavior and development individually and collectively. Their classic version or the model has appeared in Beck and Cowan's book *Spiral Dynamics* (1996). They have argued that there are about nine empirically identifiable v-memes that have evolved as intelligent systems (this author has modified them and labeled them "Fear Management Systems") over time in human history, which are, in various combinations operating today. The first six v-memes (1st-tier) are more or less fear-based, and then there comes a "quantum leap" in development (that is possible) in which the next v-memes (2nd-tier) which are no longer mainly motivated by fear. One can find correlates of this theory of development in Abraham Maslow's work, especially in *Toward a Psychology of Being* (1968).

One ought to remember that many of these bi-centric ethical paradigms arose independently by the various theorists, philosophers, spiritual teachers and their students. No doubt many of them have influenced each other along the way. These paradigms of a Fearlessness Tradition present a universal message that cannot be denied. Yet, despite the simple dichotomy in concepts, these are only 'maps.' The reality of living the dynamic between (in and out) of the bi-centric aspects of the paradigms is "messy." Life is not divided up into such neat binary packages and sides. Most critics of these bi-centric models suggest there is a continuum between the extremes and such polarities are to be downplayed. However, the concept of "center of gravity" (in Spiral Dynamics Theory) was referred to in the previous chapter and remains salient to this discussion—that is, when a person's (or organization's) development and conditions have brought them into one side of the paradigm (or FMS) as distinct from another—meaning, their "center of gravity" revolves around a consciousness and set of actions that truly are motivated by one side of the paradigm *not* the other. A real difference and incompatibility arises between the paradigms. Of course, it is a probability that this is so, and there are always exceptions or "leaks" from the paradigm and a falling back into the other (less ethical) paradigm of these universal pairs.

Reality is (I'm guessing), the majority of people today on the planet have no idea of the variety of these bi-centric paradigms, or they do not care about them, and/or they interpret them in a 1st-tier perspective only. The research question remains: How valuable are they actually in people's lives, and how valuable might they be, and how real and true are they to the nature of "reality" (i.e., human nature, human condition and human potential)? I am quite convinced they all are useful, more or less, as ethical guide posts along the journey of the soul, consciousness, and society. Without the bi-centric distinctions there is a danger-ous collapse of knowing "which way to go," in order to lead an ethical life. I believe we are seeing this confusion in our current postmodern era. Without these types of distinctions (and paradigms of practices), without accessing the WFTs at their profound ethical depth, where are we to derive criteria to critique and assess the quality of FME along the continuums of life?

Fearlessness (FMS-7) has had some 20 pages devoted to it so far in this section, indicating its significance in my work. However, the time has come to move on and slowly wrap-up Chapter Three with a final appraisal of *fearless*. Beyond doubt, I am suggesting that a Fearlessness Tradition exists, and a 'fear-lessness' critique/theory as well. To date, no one has systematically put these together. Eventually, that will happen. The analogy could be with the sociologi-cal work of Randall Collins, who put the "Conflict Tradition" together as a cri-tique, theory (conflict theory), and movement, throughout Western history.[213] I envision a day when that analogy becomes a reality and the mainline disciplines of sociology, anthropology, psychology, political sciences, criminology, law, business management and organizational development, theology, etc. take a serious look at the power and potential of a new critical theory (East-West, North-South) for analysis and planning. This would be a *critical fearlessness theory*, based on holistic-integral theory, fearology, and the WFT as documented however briefly in this book. The critical importance of enabling and uniting the Fearlessness Tradition and Movement cannot be underestimated—thus, Chapter Five makes its entry with that plea.

After ISOF's rise (1989) and fall (1998) as an organization, I had been researching and writing to figure out what went wrong; why did it collapse, at
least, in its first community manifestation in Calgary, Alberta, Canada? This is
not the first time in history (herstory) that various visionary leaders have witnessed the painful collapse of a radical movement. Usually they follow that with
a reflective incubation and exile. They attempt to think through and write about
their theories of revolution once again, before they pass away. ISOF Project is
still going strong—in spirit—in the spirit of fearlessness. I expect new forms
will emerge in the future; its inevitable, no matter how much one sees Fear's
Empire growing and dominating (e.g., post-9/11 era). That said, it gives one
great moral strength to carry on a Tradition (still unrecognized), when one finds
that other's have acknowledged the importance of fearlessness in our future and
attempted to lead movements to make that known. The following historical note
is one such event that won't be forgotten by this author-fearologist.

While researching on the Internet a few years ago, I found a reference to a
1931 brochure entitled *The League of Fearlessness*, sitting in the archives of
The New York Academy of Medicine library. After a long and rather expensive
process, the rare brochure arrived. The text was a revelation. The validation
sunk in. There are no other references to be found listing this document and
"movement," from a massive search I did in newspapers, books and articles
from around that time period of 1931 (focused in the U.S.A.). The opening lines
of the brochure read as follows: "The League *for* Fearlessness, An International
Movement To Free The World From Fear, Organized in New York October 17,
1931."

There it was—an international movement directly dedicated to "Fearlessness" as the means "To Free The World From Fear." Why had this never appeared in all previous research since 1989? Why had no one (apparently) told
me about this movement? Who were these people who envisioned and organized
this global movement—The League *for* Fearlessness in 1931? From the best I
can gather from the brochure, the group of some 50 people gathered somewhere
in downtown New York City in 1931. The contact name and address for the
group reads: "Address all communications to Foster Bailey, Sec., 11 West 42nd
Street, 32nd Flr., New York City." Although no information is given as to the
spiritual background of The League, one can follow some of its origins through
researching Foster Bailey, a 33rd degree Freemason, and husband of the famous
occultist, the late Alice Bailey (1880-1949). Indeed, this is the kind of project
Alice would have initiated or supported fully. Anything further about the people
involved is speculation, just as it is impossible to say why there seems to have
been no successful follow-up of activity beyond the brochure—at least, nothing
in recorded history.

What I do know is that this international movement was not superficial but
based in esoteric wisdom teachings in and around the Freemasons[214] and other
sources. The brochure tells us more:

THE INITIAL PROGRAM OF THE LEAGUE
I. To reach the public with appropriate literature dealing with the present world
problem and presenting the need for mobilizing the power of right thought to

free the world from fear. To send out literature in English, French, German and other languages, proclaiming the doctrine of fearlessness and confidence and to inspire writers and speakers everywhere to rally to the cause of pushing open the door of a new era of peace and prosperity by action based on clear thinking and courageous living.

II. To cooperate with all groups and organizations throughout the world whose programs include activities in harmony with the purposes of the League, by supplying them with literature and with speakers, and by seeking to increase and strengthen their work in all ways acceptable to them.

III. To inaugurate a world-wide practice of noontime recollection at which moment every member will daily consciously link him[her]self, by the power of thought, with the constructive forces of fearlessness and truth and with the power of good which controls the destiny of [hu]mankind.

IV. To establish a department of research and study of the causes and cure of fear, with relation to the life of the individual and the welfare of the community, the nation and the problems of modern civilization....

The League was (is?) a movement meant (at least) to contradict, enlighten, and liberate a post-WWI population that was in the midst of a climate of fear — that is, the crisis of progress in the Western world was steeped in the challenges of the "Dirty Thirties" ("Great Depression"). The last few sentences (aims of the organization) read:

d. To expose fear as an aspect of the great illusion and to meet it with the constructive power of the mind.

e. To offset the present negative world condition by a counter-current of belief that [hu]man [her]himself is master, that [s]he has all the powers of a divine nature and can control [her]his own destiny, and that the human family has a glorious heritage toward which it inevitably moves.

Fearlessness is referred to now and then but it is not actually defined in the brochure. Clearly, there is an emphasis on the "power of the mind" and changing it, as the best way to change our destiny. In other writings Alice Bailey (channeling Djwhal Khul) has spoken of the "utter fearlessness" that is essential to solving the world problems,[215] but again fearlessness is not actually defined. In the end there is a lot of mystery about this international movement and one wonders if it went underground because it was 'too risky' to be so out front and center with fearlessness at that time in (American) history. The total brochure is reprinted in another of my publications.[216] It is worth absorbing, in terms of the scope and commitments made by its members and applications to today and future FME.

One idea behind The League for Fearlessness, the ISOF Project, and other forms of the Fearlessness (R)evolution (e.g., in Chapter One), is the archetypal *"gift of fearlessness"* tradition. Here is another of the ancient (Eastern) meanings of fearlessness that still exists today in some cultures and religions. Maria Hibbets, a religious scholar, wrote an extensive paper that,[217]

> . . . explores medieval South Asian gift discourses from Jain, Theravāda [Buddhist], and Hindu Dharmasāstra sources, which list and discuss a variety of prescribed [ethical] gifts. Such lists generally include a category of gift known as the 'gift of fearlessness' (*abhayadāna*), wherein refraining from harming others is considered a species of gift giving. This type of gift and the discussions concerning it unite generosity and nonviolence in a way that is suggestive for understanding how some medieval South Asian theorists conceived of the gift, human nature, and altruism.

With variations on the theme across the various philosophical and religious traditions of South Asian cultures, the basic notion is to practice a disciplined lifestyle of complete nonviolence, and to do so is to give the ethical "gift of fearlessness."[218] Such a choice of lifestyle or orientation is one of great kindness and has exceptional power to free others from fear. One Sikh website on guru philosophy reads: "Fear not, frighten not."[219] According to the ethical precepts the Buddha taught: "He is the Master who, having himself reached the castle of fearlessness, invites and leads them [all others] to the same."[220] In these Eastern traditions the mudra of *abhaya* (hand gesture of right hand raised with palm facing outward and fingers upward) means *fearlessness* (and for some it means "fearless").[221] It is a gesture to offer protection and is characteristically offered by the *bodhisattva* but not exclusive to the highly developed *bodhisattva*. According to Stanley Kopp, a Buddhist psychotherapist, the *abhaya* mudra of fearlessness is a gesture that announces that one will face their fears in this life, and not pass them on to others unnecessarily (e.g., the Buddha).[222]

Carlos G. Valles, a Jesuit priest living in India, wrote about the gift of fearlessness as an essential practice (virtue) of the spiritual person, but it may also be used in common everyday life of the 'ordinary' people of India. He described a father doing this regarding his son, who had done something very wrong and was caught by his father doing it. Instead of approaching the boy with discouragement and threat or fear of punishment, he surprised the boy saying "You have nothing to fear. Nothing from me in this case. I grant you the gift of fearlessness in your dealings with me. Tell me whatever you have to tell me. . . . You have nothing to fear."[223] The implications of such a practice in our basic socialization, relationships and education could be profound. It is a gift indeed that an adult, or anyone, would take such responsibility for their power-position and not "pass on" their fears to others because they believe it will do them good. Reality is, at FMS-7 there is a totally different way to live, and to manage fear ('fear') itself. One must not misuse 'fear.' Valles noted that Gandhi's revolution was based largely on this 'gift' as well. A great lesson is available in the WFTs that speak about this gift of fearlessness. Unfortunately, Westerners generally seem quite ignore-ant of this tradition.

Before leaving *fearlessness* (FMS-7, Yellow, Integral) behind and introducing *fearless* (FMS-9, Coral, Nondual), it ought to be said that my survey so far has been a smorgasbord with more surfaces than depth. One has to make such a compromise in a review book as this is. However, to add a few items of dessert to the menu before leaving the meal, there are three more aspects of 'fearlessness' offered below in brief form: (1) "four-fold fearlessness," (2) listing the past and/or present organizations of the global Fearlessness Movement, (3) examining 'fearlessness' as epistemology (i.e., inquiry). These are all, 2nd-tier foundations for building, in part, a healthy, more mature, integrative 3rd-tier or nondual way of FME on this planet.

Buddhist philosophy (e.g., Trungpa's Tibetan-Shambhala Warrior Tradition) has offered many insights that could likely benefit people of all traditions and non-traditions, sacred and secular. The Buddhist concept of "four-fold fearlessness" is one of the most advanced ancient ideas one finds in the literature on fearlessness in general. It would require more study and practice to fully understand, than what can be presented here. In fact, it is so advanced that one cannot find hardly anything written about it in English translations. I believe, Westerners are at a great disadvantage to explore this topic without an Eastern teacher or guru. The Internet has a few rare mentions of four-fold fearlessness and most all the Buddhist literature on the market (in English) has no mention of it. In R. A Gard's book on *Buddhism* (1962), an overall reference book to Buddhist literature, one cannot even find the words "fear" or "fearlessness" in the text. However, when it comes to identification of the attributes of the Buddha, Gard wrote, "primarily a fully 'enlightened' being"; the Buddha is said to have acquired the ten powers and "the four *vaicāradyas* ["grounds of self-confidence"]" and so on. Gard inserted "grounds of self-confidence,"[224] which is very different than the interpretation given by Chinese Buddhist scholar-Master Yin-Shun, who spoke of the attributes of buddhahood as "four-fold fearlessness."[225] What is apparent is that most Buddhist interpretations are not nearly as focused on fear and fearlessness as I might like. There is no depth of discussion in these two texts on what exactly four-fold fearlessness is, conceptually or otherwise. This remains a delightful notion yet to be unfolded as we find more and more meanings for fearlessness in our search. Admittedly, my presentation is from a Westerner's rather awkward perspective on these spiritual matters outside my own expertise, experience, culture, and history.

As mentioned earlier in this book, I have undertaken a major project to document the WFTs in an encyclopedia. As part of that project an emerging list of Fearlessness Movements (as new social movements or old social movements) has emerged — not because it is complete or systematic, only because it seemed obvious to begin to make. The names or people involved from this list may or may not be representing a 2nd-tier perspective of 'fearlessness,' but many are to some degree, although only ISOF is basically integral (*a la* Wilberian) by design; most are indicative of the significant emergence of the spirit of fearlessness or at least the concept of "fearlessness" in their writings and teachings (at some point in time). In no particular order:

Fearless Resistance Alliance, Global Renaissance, The New Thought Movement, United Nations Human Rights, Schools Without Fear, Earth Community Movement, Death of the School Movement, Unitarian Univeralists, Shambhala Institute, Omega Institute, A Course in Miracles, The League for Fearlessness,

In Search of Fearlessness Project, Lucis Trust, Fear Matrix Removal Program, T.E.L.S.T.A.R., Alcoholics Anonymous Free School Movement, Freedom from Fear Foundation, Eupsychian Network, Aquarian Conspiracy, The Light Institute, Human Potential Movement, New Age Movement, Self-Realization Movement, Attitudinal Health Movement, Peace Movement, Existentialist and Spiritual Movement, Culture of Fear critics, Spiral Dynamics, Integral Movement, Anti- or Non-Violence Movement (Gandhian *satayagraha* Movement), Religion, Religious Freedom Movement, Socialism, The Fearless Revolution Movement, Anti-Fear Movement, Anxiety Disorders Association, Re-evaluation Co-Counseling and Co-Counseling International, Transpersonal Psychology Movement, etc.

On top of those movements and along with them are the "teachings" (symbolic or otherwise systematic) of a multitude of individuals, past, with some still living (as we know it), listed in no particular order:

Aung San Suu Kyi, Amma, Jiddu Krishnamurti, Gavin de Becker, Erich Fromm, Abraham Maslow, John Heron and Barbara Langton, Chris Griscom, Pema Chödrön, Charles D. Bass, Osho, Paulus Tillich, Noam Chomsky, Chöygam Trungpa Rinpoche, Sai Baba, Rhonda Britten, Forrest Church, Benjamin Barber, Margaret Wheatley, Aristotle, Harvey Jackins, Matthew Fox, Socrates, Saint Thomas Aquinas, Alice and Foster Bailey, Dalai Lama, Ken Wilber, Swami Akshara, Maitreya, Marianne Williamson, Arianna Huffington, Nelson Mandela, Bernice Powell Jackson, Ericka D. Jackson, Martin Luther King Jr., David Korten, Rosa Parks, Susan Jeffers, Tielhard de Chardin, Vinobā Bhave, Mahatma Gandhi, Joshua Stone, Michael Lerner, Thich Nhat Hanh, Robert A. Masters, Saratoga, Deepak Chopra, and many others mentioned in this book.

There is some arational quality and purpose behind listing together these branches of the Fearlessness Movement and its peoples. I like the intimacy suggested, as they are juxtaposed in the same place and space within a unifying context—separated only by a comma or thin space between lines. It intimates a breaking down of barriers between them. It makes a difference but that difference is not yet understood. Perhaps, Chapter Five will illuminate such subtleties, as I attempt to address "unifying" the Fearlessness Movement and (R)evolution for the future.

And finally, to 'fearlessness' as epistemology (i.e., critical inquiry) and perception itself. This is a huge topic, which I have addressed directly in previous publications[226] which will not be reviewed fully here. This book is an application of a *'fearlessness' epistemology* in part—in that, it searches in open-inquiry of 'all' the possible sources of understanding of and meaning of 'fearlessness.' It is an attitude, coherent with critical integral theory, to be curious and have 'eyes-wide-open-24-7' when it comes to the topic of fear and fearlessness. That's a beginning. As well, much literature and teaching has been devoted to discovering "fear" by going into it so as to really know it and know yourself. The WFTs are full of this kind of directive (paradigm) or inquiry method, and often it is called "fearlessness." For example, Jeremy Hayward, and important contemporary Buddhist educator, speaks about fear of death as a barrier to enlightenment and as a source of suffering. He wrote, "Recognizing it is fearlessness. . . . When you realize it, when you stay with it, which means that you let yourself quake."[227]

Practicing fearlessness (for some) involves (often) a lot of quaking (not surprising The Quakers have long known this process). That said, and valid as such an inquiry is, sometimes it seems odd that 'fearlessness' is so often constructed and defined (and understood) in the prevailing literature based on an inquiry into fear ('fear'). It is as if looking into the 'mirror of fear' then fearlessness is revealed. Do we ever doubt this premise and method? Ought we? Now, what would happen if we straightforwardly posited that 'fearlessness' is best known when it inquires into fearlessness? When we look into the 'mirror of fearlessness' then fearlessness is revealed. The latter approach seems not of interest, or has not been written about in the Fearlessness Movements, so far.

Basically, 'fearlessness' as inquiry involves "radical perception: being present and imaginally open"[228] from the start, according to transpersonal psychologist, author, artist, facilitator, John Heron, writing in his book *Cooperative Inquiry* (1996). He suggested that,[229]

> Radical perception [and radical phenomenology as method] means paying heed in an extraordinary way to the process of perceiving. . . . It is the ability to open up fully to our participation in reality through our empathic communion with it, and unrestricted perceptual patterning of it. It means owning our creative transaction with what is given. We find this behind the screen [mirror] of language in the immediacy of felt attunement and unrestricted perception (Wahl, 1953). This immediacy [primary cognitive processing] takes us into the lived world of primary meaning: the deep tacit experiential pre-understanding that is beneath language, and of which the conceptual meaning of language is a continuous, partial and limited transformation. This kind of holistic awareness of how our world is being and how it is patterned through our creative minding of it, is a central inquiry skill. It involves the two complementary components of radical perception: being present and imaginal openness.

I call this "radical trust" as part and parcel of 'fearlessness'—that is, not letting cultural conditioning ('fear'-based motivations) over-interpret or over-determine what we see and how we see it, and what we do with it. What Heron is addressing is a powerful 'fearlessness' method of inquiry (epistemology) into a formation of perception, reality, and experience; we may want to call "Natural" (FMS-0) before "Cultural" (meaning, before 1st-tier FMSs 1-6)—though, that is a complicated argument and not necessarily what Heron would want us to consider. He wrote,[230]

> This world of primary meaning is unrestricted perception, consciousness-world union, which is anterior to every distinction [i.e., adual] including that of consciousness and nature (Merleau-Ponty, 1962). It is apprehended by a fearlessness which [citing Trungpa] "means being able to respond accurately to the phenomenal world altogether. It simply means being accurate and absolutely direct in relating with the phenomenal world by means of your sense perceptions, your mind and your sense of vision. Attunement with the other, empathy, harmonic resonance, is the way of communion, of participating in the interior

world of the other. It grounds and complements and is inseparable from everything I have to say about imaginal openness.

Heron's work, in complement to Wilber's work, exploring integral and
transpersonal bases for human understanding and development, is communal
and relational,[231] whereas Wilber's is more cognitive and individual in focus.
Most writing on philosophy and spirituality involving fearlessness is like
Wilber's approach, though the gift of fearlessness tradition is obviously not and
Heron's work is not. This last quote is important as Heron does not use "fearless" or "fearlessness" hardly ever. When he uses it, he means it. He uses it
forthright and appropriately as a very special way of inquiry, a way that is at
base the only way to "attune" to reality beyond what is in "one's head" (or in
conceptual thinking). One could argue many meditation and yoga traditions
likewise help foster this 'fearlessness' of inquiry, beyond fear, and beyond
'normal' ways of knowing. 'Fearlessness' as a form of perception then, is the
way to "accurate" knowledge and knowing, which is critically in short supply
today on so many levels, as we experience distortions and lies in most every
domain of everyday life. It is hard to trust anything. 'Fearlessness' is a way of
radical trust (as critical ongoing inquiry and development of intelligence), not
mere hope nor mere faith.

Trungpa's view, like most Buddhist philosophy, tells us to leave hope and
pursue fearlessness[232]—and I heartily agree, because 'fearlessness' involves
radical phenomenological inquiry and not merely hoping (or acting upon hope)
for anything. One could say, that's a lie, for surely fearlessness is hoping to get
beyond fear—the very notion of "in search of fearlessness" mentioned in this
text is a "searching" and that is a "hoping." On the surface, using a linguistic
and conceptual analysis, that may be a worthy logical argument to put toward
myself or anyone advocating the pursuit of 'fearlessness.' However, when we
turn to Heron's dictum and a postmodern (integral) notion of 'fearlessness' as
inquiry (beyond fearlessness)—there is search for "accuracy" not "hope."

One doesn't hope for accuracy either, when practicing 'fearlessness' as it is
meant here. One merely works to become aware and clear enough from fear
('fear') as the *modus operandi* of perceptions (of reality). Fearlessness is not
about hope. Perhaps those who wish to still argue may write critiques. That
would be good. Perhaps also they would study and practice some of what the
WFTs offer. That would be good. There is no need to hope that this will be the
case, at least not from a FMS-7 perspective. Maybe Arianna Huffington (see
Chapter One) is correct that "Fearlessness is contagious"[233] with or without
hope. No argument, I would make, would attempt to undermine people's need
for hope or discourage hope; the point, rather, is that *fearlessness does not arise
from hope* (nor *visa versa*); though, in many ways they have an analogous positioning in human affairs and contain inspiration when times are dark and the
going very tough. A critique of hope/fear[234] is beyond the scope of this book and
will find its place in the next volume.

Fearless

Phil Nuemberger wrote,[235] "The skilled Tantric is fearless, unafraid of other's opinions, and not driven by the need for acceptance and approval. [commitment to truth is first and foremost]. To pick one quote and discourse that uses *fearless* is difficult as there are so many, including some definitions and meanings very diverse and controversial. The above quote is a discourse from the Eastern yogic traditions and sounds very individual and psychological. One could say such a "fearless" Tantric practitioner is highly self-actualized and above and beyond being frightened into being or thinking or acting in 'fear'-based ways because some authority or majority wants them to. For some this is a positive trait, in this sense. Yet, for others they would be in shock of this claim, even in disbelief of it as possible and/or many would see it as negative, if not pathological, in social terms. We saw this dominating doubt and criticism with discussions of *no fear* and *fearlessness* earlier.

In the West, those who study courage, from a psychological or sociological view, would agree with the above quote only in part but would take the term *fearless* more literally. W. I. Miller, in his Aristotelian discourse-bias, argued that men in the military have their own "hierarchy of fear-management techniques,"[236]

> . . . some nobler than others, and what they desire is a technique that drives fear, whether fear for their lives of fear of shame, out of their consciousness. They subscribe to a view, it seems, that courage demands, if not quite fearlessness, that fear stay modestly in the background. They are not conceding courage solely to the few psychotics who lack normal fear response. . . . What though of those people claimed to be utterly fearless? For one thing, they are very rare. It is striking how many of those uses of the word 'fearless' do not pretend to describe the inner state of the actor. They are meant rather to register the awe of the observer. 'He did not know what fear was' or 'he acted fearlessly' means only that 'he acted *as if* he did not know what fear was' or 'he acted *as if* he were fearless.' Some dispute whether there are any naturally fearless people except in fiction and fantasy. True, some people are born without functioning pain receptors. They do not fear pain. . . .

Miller's quote reveals the *bravado* (bravery) qualities discussed earlier in this chapter and how they can be a part of the path of fearlessness but are not the most matured (or ethical) forms of fear management. And in some cases are quite immature and led by the motivation to "impress" others. The human mind has an incredible capacity to dissociate, to deny, and to even re-wire the pain-fear-danger *alert system*. The dissociative process of 'mind control over body,' or over pain, is well documented in other sources and will not be discussed here. Even meditators in spiritual traditions have been held in awe as being "fearless" because they can withstand physical pain without wincing and without withdrawl from the source—that is, when most 'normal' humans would be screaming and withdrawing from the pain.

Whole traditions of thought, e.g., "science of mind," etc. are devoted to a cognitive mind-over-matter philosophy and technology, that works to a large degree to 're-interpret' what pain is and what one's relationship to it can or ought to be. Through reframing techniques of interpretation, "fear" isn't what it was thought to be—and thus, can be overcome, more or less. This is an extensive discussion beyond my interest here. The emphasis of the ascription of "fearless" to these people is given by those who focus on the obvious physicality and behavior of such "fearless" ones; and in doing so, judge their behavior relative to their own (and the 'norm'). Thus, such fearless ones are indeed 'abnormal'; rather than, as an attainment by practices of maturation (i.e., evolution).

The motivation of some (so-called) "fearless" meditators, can range across a wide variety of situations and individuals. Some Buddhist monks are famously known to have used meditation as a fearless social political resistance to oppressors and their abuse. These examples of FMS-9 (in some cases) are discussed further below. And keep in mind that sometimes fearless is held as the ultimate of non-violence, as in "To see beyond fear and suffering is the path of the fearless one, and the compassionate one."[237] And other times, like in the famous quote by the black psychiatrist-activist Frantz Fanon in the decolonization processes: "At the level of individuals, violence is a cleansing force. It frees the native from his inferiority complex and from his despair and inaction; it makes him fearless and restores his self-respect"[238] (gender bias noted here).

In this book, indeed, the seven ways of fearlessness and 'fearlessness' are a kind of hierarchy of fear management techniques as well. They are more than techniques or behaviors. They include physical techniques but are also powerful discourses of ways of knowing, teaching, learning, and being. Again, like with fearlessness (FMS-7 and 8) with an ethical intention. The critique of Miller is welcomed as we come to examine critically *fearless* as it is a word that removes the "ness" from fearlessness. No longer are we talking about a quality of relative fearlessness, rather we are referring to fearless in an extreme, as Miller calls it "utterly fearless." And rightly so, Miller attacks the real or imagined *bravado* egoic (dualistic) quality in much of the discourses around "fearless" (or "no fear").

In reading Eastern spiritual traditions one finds a more favorable attitude toward fearlessness and fearless compared to the Western sacred and secular traditions, which tend to prefer *bravery* and *courage* as terms to describe the highly mature and noble states of human beings. Later, I argue this is very unreliable in typically Western (masculinist-capitalist) contemporary popularizing discourses, where "fearless" is attached as a quality or sign to almost any behavior or product. Both fear and fearless can be superficially and grossly commodified. Nonetheless, if we look in the Eastern philosophical and spiritual traditions there is the distinction of an extreme accomplishment, of ultimate aim in growth and development. It is marked by both fearlessness and fearless, sometimes these words used interchangeably. However, often we see accompanying adjectives like "utterly" or "ultimate" or "totally" added to *fearless*, which gives a sense of the extreme form or qualities involved. The contemporary (and very popular) Hindu spiritual teacher Sai Baba Gita teaches,

> Of all the great virtues, fearlessness occupies the place of primary importance. It is the ideal virtue. Unless you have fearlessness, you will never be able to live comfortably. Be it in the secular field, in the battle of life in the world, or

be it in your struggles in the realm of the spirit, you must never leave room for fear to creep in. It should find no place in your life. . . . When you are filled with fear you cannot shine in the world. Therefore, The *Gita* taught that you must become totally fearless. . . . Only a fearless person can achieve victory in great undertakings. A person who is truly fearless will have detachment from all the objects of the world and be saturated with the love of God. On the other hand, one who is egoistic about his body and his worldly accomplishments will be charged with fear. Attachments to the worldly objects and egoism will never be entertained by a person who is free from fear.

Here we get a sense of a rarified state and/or stage of being. And one must read these accounts in that context. Though, we also ought to recognize they are descriptions, partial and inadequate to what they describe, as dualistic language and abstractions are inadequate, in regard to the nondual domain we are entering. However, they do communicate about something real—that is, real from a 3rd-tier (nondual) perspective. *Fearless* is a discourse and FMS-9 that crosses over 'Fear' Barrier 3 (Figures 1.1 and 3.1). Each crossing of 'Fear' Barriers is a dangerous and enlightening leap across an abyss—each more rarified than the next, as we encountered in the crossing to 2nd-tier (e.g., *fearlessness*, FMSs-7 and 8). That said, one ought to be very cautious indeed in describing or judging what *fearless* is or isn't. A lot of our judging is dependent on our perspective (worldview) and development. A critical holistic-integral perspective starts by validating these discourses as reflecting, to some degree, a real developmental phenomena (albeit, it is both objective and subjective).

Fearless has many meanings just like fearlessness, depending where one is coming from in interpreting it. Yet, we are pushed with the arrival of FMS-9 to acknowledge fearless (so far) as the 'top' or most mature (most intelligent) position of the continuum of FMSs. At least, it is hypothetically useful to 'map' it as such, and suggest as the previous chapter indicated, that consciousness evolution has reached FMS-9, and we are potentially all touched by it in some way, even if only for a moment, or even as an ideal fantasy or imaginary. However, FMS-9 for some is much more. They are touched by it, embedded in it and enact its intelligence. These are "great ones" for sure, in our fearstory. They are the nondual mystics, sages, and bodhisattvas of differing kinds,[239] whether they are from a religious tradition or not. They are highly "spontaneous" and "disciplined." The FMS-9 however is not reducible to individuals, rather, it is a discourse (or intelligence system) and can become a "culture" or "environment" or "system" as well—the latter much more slow and difficult to attain.

Speaking at the individual level, one could pick names and try to locate *fearless*, but that can be restrictive and force us to think of (famous or infamous) personalities too much. In a metaphoric, if not empirical sense, a nondual *fearless* discourse does not care about personalities; there is no person, no self, no ego, and no fear ('fear'), in this advanced FMS—that is, from a Wilberian perspective. Maybe a better tact is to conceive of fearless (and FMSs in general) as metaphoric "landscapes." I suggest, as integral educator Clifford Mayes has proposed, that his "Unitive-Spiritual Landscape" is the highest mature domain of development along a spectrum of seven (or eight) landscapes.[240]

For most of us, fearless is an incredulous claim, and too foreign to take seriously. Perhaps so. There is no need to try to convince anyone of its truth or value, at least not from nondualistic (transpersonal) consciousness. If one is truly interested there are many sources to read on the nondual traditions and practices (e.g., Wilber's early admiration for nondual "Madhyamika (Buddhism)"[241] or Zen). That said, it seems worthy to keep Heron's transpersonal model and "states of personhood" as another (complementary) formulation that avoids overly-Eastern philosophies of "no self" but rather constructs an evolutionary and developmental model of personhood that moves from adual (Heron's "primal person," and "spontaneous person") to dual (Heron's "compulsive person," "conventional person" etc.) on up to nondual (Heron's "charismatic person").[242] Heron doesn't use the term "fearless" specifically in his version of the charismatic person. Whereas, Wilber is willing to assign fearless, sparingly and discerningly; and this is the holistic-integral critique perhaps most important for understanding Coral FMS-9 *fearless*.

To begin this critique let's look at where Wilber assigns the enigmatic concept *fearless*. In Wilber's latest new introduction to a 2nd edition (2000) of his book *Grace and Grit* (a story of his life with his wife Treya and her death from cancer), he wrote,[243]

> Treya simply had no split between her public and private selves. I think that was exactly part of her enormous integrity, and I think that was directly related to what can only be called her fearlessness. There was a strength in Treya that was absolutely fearless, and I do not say that lightly. Treya had little fear because she had little to hide, from you or me or God or anybody. She was transparent to reality, to the Divine, to the world, and thus had nothing to fear from it. I saw her in much pain; I saw her in much agony; I saw her in much anger. I never saw her in fear. Her presence changed you. . . . It drew you into being present to the Present, it reminded you to wake up." [cf. Trinity in *The Matrix* film]

Treya's own transcript in that book *Grace and Grit* shows she had self-admitted fear(s). Ken's own paragraph, moving as it is, is not fully consistent as he says she "had little fear" and says she "was absolutely fearless," and then says "I never saw her in fear." Was she beyond fear, or in fear, or had some fear? Was she still touched by and controlled somewhat by 'fear' itself in the context of a culture of fear? Who's to know? Unfortunately, she's not around to answer for herself. One letter Ken published in this 2nd edition from a surviving cancer patient, who knew Treya reads: "How she was fearless, not because she lacked fear, but because she immediately embraced it, even when it became obvious that she would soon die." Everyone interprets their own version. Yet, the assigning of "absolutely fearless" (by Wilber) is a reminder of the discourse found in much of the enlightenment literature of the East (and some from the West).

On one popular culture website Ken Wilber is even labeled "the Fearless Leader of the Integral Age."[244] I suspect Wilber would never label himself that, nor would I. FMS-9 is a great attainment off in the future perhaps, and yet is still a worthy and demanding concept, practice, if not an ideal. What is important is not to think that one "should" attain it as a stage of development (more than just a temporary state). Wilber himself acknowledges that Treya was more developed than he in this area of life, and she was more fearless than he. He also acknowledges an important (intriguing) point in all this "hierarchical" distinction: "And I really do believe that any one of us can meet Treya [or others of "absolute fearless" attainment] again, any time we wish to do so, by acting with honesty, integrity, and fearlessness—for there lies the heart and soul of Treya."[245]

In simple non-elitist discourse, Wilber casts Treya in archetypal (Goddess) garb. She, is not merely a person but more a set of qualities, we could sincerely call "fearless." Reflecting on his first enlightening meeting with her, he wrote:[246]

> She was beautiful. But what exactly was it? There was an energy that seemed literally to radiate from her in all directions; a very quiet and soothing energy, but enormously strong and powerful; an energy that was very intelligent and suffused with exceptional beauty, but mostly an energy that was *alive*. This woman said LIFE more than anybody I had ever known. . . . Her eyes looked at, and through, everything. It wasn't that she had a penetrating glance—that's much too aggressive—it was simply that she seemed to see through things, and then perfectly accept what she saw, a kind of gentle and compassionate x-ray vision. Eyes committed to truth. . . . You trusted her immediately; an enormous integrity. . . . She appeared the most self-confident person I had ever met, yet not proud or boastful in the least. I wondered if she ever got flustered; it was hard to imagine. Yet behind the almost intimidating solidness of her character, there were the dancing eyes, seeing everything, not ponderously, but wanting rather to play. I thought this woman is game for anything; I don't think anything scares her. . . . she could shed density and float all the way to the stars, if she wanted.

One senses Wilber is describing 'buddhahood' (or a yogini) in this female contemporary and relatively ordinary form—a pattern—a set of qualities of personhood at the highest level of Being. Words simply fail to do Her (or Him) justice. The use of the words "energy," "beauty" and "alive" by Wilber remind me of Susan Griffin's essay on fearlessness as a species of Beauty (Chapter One). I suspect fearless is likewise another species of Beauty, Truth, and Goodness.

Fearless, fully alive and radiant in Beauty, seems to be the grace upon which consciousness evolution endows all sentient beings. We don't have to attain a level of cultural greatness in our own lives (if that is not meant to be nor is attainable directly and personally). Treya's life was hardly famous or great, compared to others in history and herstory. Her premature death with cancer perhaps prevented earthly accomplishment and fame. We have access through grace to practice and prepare our vehicle for that reception and touching of those who have attained fearless. Is it the same quality or not as Treya's—or some other 'Great One' of FMS-9? That is irrelevant from a nondual FMS-9 perspective. It is not about personal striving to get the attainment. Fearless is a receiving and integrating of FMS-9 intelligence. It exists. It can be learned and received because it exists (as a legitimate discourse, at any rate). No need to despair not getting it. Fearless is not a need for human beings. To need it is to reject it. Such is the paradox of nondual reality, as perceived and longed for (by many not all) from a dual perspective.

Wilber, again very sparingly, uses the fearless term in one more place in his 30 years of writing and researching. He uses *"fearless shallowness"* in a critique—arguably, from his many, this is his *most important* critique for our times. This argument unfolds slowly as it is rather technical. In the preceding chapter some of these critiques of Wilber, Beck, McIntosh et al. and integral philosophy overall, came to the foreground as a basis for a critical literacy of fearlessness. However, now is appropriate timing to include Wilber's attack on "fearless shallowness" or "Flatland" (again, see Chapter Two for more basic theory and details).

One could claim Wilber's entire scholarly life is dedicated to understanding, teaching about, and undermining a "flatland ontology" (*ontology-* is about the "nature of being and/or reality"). He is critiquing equivalently (though not exactly his words) a *false fearless ontology* (based on an extreme postmodern *bravado* twist) that has formed in the great fearstory of human evolution and development, especially, since Modernity (some 300 years ago). If anyone misses this, unfortunately, they miss the best of Wilberian ethical thought and critical theory combined. Sadly, most miss it, at least for awhile. Okay, here it is in a few fragments, according to one of Wilber's most dedicated students and interpreters, Brad Reynolds:[247]

> Wilber uses the four quadrants to critique any type of flatland reduction or reductionism, whether gross (atomistic) or subtle (holistic). A 'modern flatland ontology,' whether filled with 'flatland atomists' or 'flatland holists,' must be avoided, according to Wilber, including 'systems theorists and the structural functionalists,' and therefore "virtually all of the 'new paradigm' and 'ecological/holistic' theories." He includes a strong critique of modernity's 'fundamental [largely secular] Enlightenment paradigm,' which Wilber heavily censures, especially its unwarranted demotion of 'all degrees of interior depth to mere functions of exterior span.' Indeed, as Wilber explains, 'The holistic paradigm of the Enlightenment collapsed a Kosmos that was [in Pre-Modernity] both vertically and horizontally holarchic . . . into a flatland cosmos . . . a flatland web [of shallowness] that replaced vertical depth with the great universal system of [horizontal] interlocking span.' Nevertheless, [in integral style] Wilber insists it's not so much that 'systems theory and eco-holism is wrong' but rather they're just incomplete.

Wilber's technical integral jargon aside for the moment, the outcome of his ontological critique and ethical positioning is looking like it must be either Premodern or Postmodern, as he attacks Modern Enlightenment for its version of a reductionistic "Flatland" (aka "Shallowness"). He attacks Flatland as the proposed hegemonic guide, coaxing us to conform with it as the *only* reality, as the *only* possibility—as a "flatland cosmos" and vision (or "oops philosophy"[248]). He attacks how it "fearlessly" boasts as the *only* way to make sense of life and death and everything in between them. He attacks how this has been the legacy of much of "Science" (really, "scientism" as Wilber argues) in our era.

Wilber is not about to align merely with Pre-Modern (sacred or secular) discourses either, nor merely with Postmodern (sacred or secular) discourses completely; albeit, his work is *postmodern-plus* (i.e., integral) and his work is *modern-plus* (i.e., he likes integral versions of holistic and systems theories). He is not typically conservativist nor progressivist *per se*, in simple terms. Basically, he's rather hard to pin down politically and philosophically in easy dichotomies such as conservative or liberal. That said, he is highly dichotomous on ethical/ontological/epistemological grounds (some may call, ideological, of which I call bi-centric). *Wilber is against "Flatland."* At least, he was, overtly in his earlier pre-1997 writing (which includes what he technically refers to as his Wilber-1, Wilber-2, Wilber-3, Wilber-4 phases). Reynolds notion, in the above quote, that Wilber is involved in a critical (conflict theory) "censure" of Flatland (eco-holism, structure functionalists, etc.)[249] is a de-politicized euphemism, and even more so when Reynolds says that Wilber thinks these philosophies are "just incomplete." That is true, but to say "just incomplete" is hardly where Wilber (again, early-Wilber pre-1997) is coming from in his attack. You have to listen to his Wilber-phase 4 discourse in his last pages of his book *A Brief History of Everything* (1996) to 'get it'—that Wilber is not merely a little upset about the "incomplete" quality of Flatland (i.e., *flatland* ontology, epistemology and ideology):[250]

Good-bye to Flatland [what follows is him asking & answering]

Q: So in all of these cases—the problems with the culture gap, with vertical integration, with environmental ethics—they all hinge on a rejection of flatland[?].

KW: Definitely. We are talking about the possibility of a coming transformation [reversal and revolution], which in many ways is already in motion. [cf. Marilyn Ferguson's "Aquarian Conspiracy" in the 1980s]. But I don't believe this new transformation can harmoniously proceed without integrating the Big Three [It, I, We = four quadrant view or integral ontology, epistemology, ideology]. The dissociation of the Big Three [also the True, the Beautiful, the Good or Science, Art, Religion] was the gaping wound left in our awareness by the failures of modernity, and the new postmodern transformation will have to integrate those fragments or it will not meet the demand of the twenty tenets [Wilber's earlier principles of holons]—it will not transcend and include; it will not differentiate and integrate; it will not be able to evolve further; it will be a false start; evolution will erase it. We cannot build tomorrow on the bruises [pathologies] of yesterday. Among numerous other things, this means a new form of society will have to evolve that integrates consciousness [Spiritual], culture [Cultural], and nature [Natural], and thus finds room for art, morals, and science—for personal values, for collective wisdom, and for technical know how. And there is no way to do this without breaking the stranglehold of flatland. Only by rejecting flatland can the Good and the True and the Beautiful be integrated. Only by rejecting flatland can we attune ourselves with Spirit's radiant expression [spirit of fearlessness] in all its verdant domains. Only by rejecting flatland can we. . . .

"The gaping wound" and "culture gap"—ominous terms, which require more integration in the future, as critical integral theory develops. Suffice it to say, these are pivotal notions and challenges for any *cura* or *therapia* ahead, both theoretically and practically, philosophically and politically or spiritually. An integral and future FME cannot ignore them. Similarly, an integral philosophy (or FME) cannot ignore the ferocious 'calling' in Wilber's lament above: "Only by rejecting flatland" is ushered in—ten times in 28 lines of text (pp. 336-337). It is slam poetry, if nothing else, and Wilber's not holding back (he concludes):

> In flatland you can only be an Ascender or a Descender. You either deny any existence to flatland altogether (the Ascenders), or you try to make it into God (the Descenders).
>
> Q: So we really have come full circle here, right back to the archetypal battle at the heart of the Western tradition—the Ascenders versus the Descenders.
>
> KW: Yes. The purely Descended approaches [Eco Camp] absolutely despise the Ascending paths [Ego Camp] [to liberation], and blame them for virtually all of humanity's Gaia problems. But not to worry, the loathing is mutual: the Ascenders maintain the Descenders are simply caught in self-dispersal and outward-bound ignorance, which is the real source of all humanity's turmoils. The Ascenders and the Descenders, *after two thousand years*, still at each other's throat—each still claiming to be the Whole, each still accusing the other of Evil, each still perpetuating the same fractured insanity it despises in the other. The Ascenders and the Descenders—still crazy after all these years.
>
> Q: The point is to integrate and balance the Ascending and Descending currents in the human being.

In this kind of dialogical Socratic format, I think Wilber is at his best, writing with spontaneous discipline and animation (just as in his first novel *Boomeritis*). It 'hits' more artistically than analytically, but always both. There is such a sense of Spirit writing through Wilber in these more artistic texts, whether you like the concepts or ideas so much. A spirit of fearlessness is very present, even if temporarily in a state experience, as *fearless* (FMS-9). It is not always that way with Wilber's writing and teaching.

The electricity in his last few pages of *Brief History of Everything* is a virtual blood-letting ritual. It is hard to describe in words, but the narrator calls for a sustainable spirituality for the world and future, one that is not "split" (schizoidal) into *Ego Camp* ('other-worldly' involutionist schools of thought) vs. *Eco Camp* ('this-worldly' evolutionist schools of thought). One hears the echoes of Plato, Whitehead, and other great integral thinkers that have known the Western traditions 'blessings and curse,' and known the urgent need for a new philosophy and spirituality that no longer keeps up this "culture gap" and no longer pours salt on or pisses in the "gaping wound." No one wins in the archetypal battle—not this way—of one Camp against another. Wilber attempts to synthesize the best of Western and Eastern, secular and sacred, in a new version of humanity's fearstory.

I am not suggesting that Wilber has the answers to all this wounding. However, his work is the *best* this author has read on the subject of "Evil" and "Flatland." Yes, that is what Wilber brings up together in his opus *big book* entitled *Sex, Ecology and Spirituality* (1995) and the follow-up (much shorter) passionate dialogue to it in his last great book *A Brief History of Everything* (1996). After that, these real pivotal issues: the "archetypal battle" "after two thousand years" fade away under more of Wilber's evolving creative thoughts and new (more functionalist) theories. Yet, always lurking below, one has to come back to Flatland and Evil, and Wilber's integral analysis and solutions—which no other contemporary "integral theorist" can stand alongside with head-to-head-heart-to-heart. No, they cannot match the soulful prophetic text and eloquent passionate intellect because no other contemporary "integral theorist" operates in *fearless* (FMS-9) as much as Wilber—and, we know where he "got" the *fearless* stik from—his beloved, *philosophia* Treya. Other contemporary "integral theorists" groom the FMS-7 and 8 but rarely dip into the FMS-9 so deeply—and none of them have Wilber's critique down as tight and metaphorically open simultaneously, as Wilber with his notion of "fearless shallowness" (see below). Wilber does more than others when his writing starts to 'runs with the wolves.' That's all part of a larger hypothesis worth further investigation. Yet, what is most important here transcends comparisons, and rather puts the responsibility on the reader of critical integral philosophy and theory right where it *ought* to be—on Flatland and Evil—meaning the battle between "Good and Evil" and "*Integraland* and Flatland." Too bad Wilber doesn't use the term Integraland. It is quite precisely what his early work was flying the flag for—a way in and a way out of the way we battle Flatland and Evil. A new route (maybe a "third way") is inevitable. Wilber is *onto it* big time. He was onto it some 15 years ago when he was penning those two critical texts above.

In his most recent and remarkable text *Integral Spirituality: A Startling New Role of Religion in the Modern and Postmodern World* (2006), Wilber talks a good deal about *shadow* but only one very brief mention of the concept "flatland" on one page.[251] That's it. It is a different, somewhat muted, Wilber-text-integral world, than prior to 1997. Some now call it Wilber-5. It appears, in part, more like Wilber-re-tired. Not that I am looking for more of old-Wilber, actually, the preference is for less Wilber and more Spirit—and less Ken and, perhaps, more Treya-Ken. Whatever!

And what's all this got to do with *fear* and *fearless*? Lots, more than can be covered adequately in this book. Yet, start one must and it comes down to understanding early-Wilber's fearanalysis. It is remarkably good, and unlike any other contemporary "integral thinker." Simply, Wilber identifies the "Ego" (Ascender's camp) and "Eco" (Descender's camp) in archetypal battle for "the way" to liberation. Neither can offer the 'goods,' so says Wilber. Not alone. And when they go off on their own, as they do predominantly, they spin off and from a new base called *"Phobos and Thanatos"*—respectively, the pathological sides of "Eco and Ego." Wilber wrote,[252] "And thus, to return to my point at the be-

ginning . . . stuck with these two variants of flatland ideology [Eco and Ego],
any intuitions of deeper and higher occasions become immediately misinter-
preted in terms of one or the other of the monological paradigms."

His point: *two variants of Flatland exist and even though they appear to be
in great battle against each other (and are at some level), they are both of the
same Evil source—that is, the 'Fear' (Project)*. The 'fear' is, as Wilber rightly
identifies it, none other than the oppositional (and pathological) forms of *Phobos*
and *Thanatos* relative to the benign Love forms that run the Kosmos, that is,
Eros and *Agape* (respectively).[253] This is not mere subjective opinion or my own
particularist-obscurant reading of Wilber's Kosmology—and of Wilber's theodicy. Rather, it is very evident in his 1995-96 writing. Flatland is 'fear' manifest
in pattern, and any way to get into it, under it, and transform it, as Wilber calls
us to do, must be based on what I would call a *fearless standpoint theory*.[254] And
Wilber (in part) just that standpoint in these texts (he's always had it from his
earliest writing, more or less). It is a nondual perspective, a 3rd-tier view, and a
FMS-9, more or less.

His *fearless* standpoint theory is evident, if only partial, in his prophetically
critical declaration against Flatland and what he called "fearless shallowness."[255]
He wrote,[256]

> It is often said that in today's modern and postmodern world, the forces of
> darkness are upon us. But I think not; in the Dark and the Deep there are truths
> that can always heal. It is not the forces of darkness but of shallowness that
> everywhere threaten the true, and the good, and the beautiful, and that ironi-
> cally announce themselves as deep and profound. It is an exuberant and fearless
> shallowness that everywhere is the modern danger, the modern threat [the mod-
> ern evil], and that everywhere nonetheless calls to us as savior. . . . lost . . . in a
> world dedicated to surfaces and shadows, exteriors and shells, whose prophets
> lovingly exhort us to dive into the shallow end of the pool head first.

If critical integral theory (*a la* Wilber) is anything of a 'savior' it is so in
saving us from "prophets lovingly" guiding us into Flatland—both versions—
both ideologies—Ego and Eco—with a noose around our necks. Welcome to the
'force' (seduction) of Fear's Empire. And that noose, Wilber knows is 'fear.'
The worst part, as Wilber knows, is that "fearless shallowness," or what I have
called false fearless ontologies (and discourses), is the latest mutant 'Agent
Smith' of Fear's Empire or 'Fear' Matrix. We have to be vigilantly critical of
discourses of "fearless" today, in the plethora of forms it manifests. That's the
whole point of this discussion and introduction to FMS-9 *fearless*. FME cannot
ignore this without great peril, if one wants to be so dramatic. No one else has
used this phrase "fearless shallowness." Wilber is ahead of this 'game.' His understanding of the 'Fear' Matrix is crucial to its undermining and any liberation
from it. Indeed, a rarified post-postmodern critical integral theorizing and phi-
losophizing at 3rd-tier.

Fearless standpoint theory (FST), inspired (analogously) by "feminist
standpoint theory" acknowledges a privileged 'real' and epistemological posi-

tioning for analysis and solutions with an emancipatory purpose. Wikipedia's (relatively 'neutral') basic definition is that,[257]

> *Standpoint feminism* argues that feminist social science should be practiced from the standpoint of women or particular groups of women as some[who?] claim that they are better equipped to understand certain aspects of the world. A feminist or women's standpoint epistemology proposes to make women's experiences, instead of men's, the point of departure. As theorized by Nancy Hartsock in 1983, standpoint feminism is founded in Marxist ideology. Hartsock argued that a feminist standpoint could be built out of Marx's understanding of experience and used to criticize patriarchal theories. Hence, a feminist standpoint is essential to examining the systemic oppressions in a society that standpoint feminists claim devalues women's knowledge. Standpoint feminism makes the case that because women's lives and roles in almost all societies are significantly different from men's; women hold a different type of knowledge. Their location as a subordinated group allows women to see and understand the world in ways that are different from and challenging to the existing male-biased conventional wisdom. Standpoint feminism unites several feminist epistemologies. Standpoint feminist theorists attempt to criticize dominant conventional epistemologies in the social and natural sciences, as well as defend the coherence of feminist knowledge.

Any remnant or accumulated "marxophobia"[258] aside, one ought to see the point of reference to feminist theory. A *fearless epistemology* at FMS-9 (Coral, Nondual) and 3rd-tier is conceived theoretically just as Hartsock et al. have for feminist epistemology in terms of choosing (and further articulating critically) a counter-standpoint (view and worldview) that is subordinate to a predominant oppressive standpoint. For FME, the predominant view is 'fear'-based (call it "pathological patriarchy" as Wilber does or whatever; cf. Riane Eisler). The emancipatory 'savior' is an alternative view, philosophy and theory—with an epistemological critique that (ideally) does not fall into the same traps and motivations of the 1st-tier oppressor-epistemologies (and ontologies). Arguably, feminist standpoint theories have not faired so well in transcending the 1st-tier.

All along, FMS-9 has been the FST for the interpretations of all the FMSs and ways of fearlessness. How else could one do this "accurately" with ethical discernment if they did not draw upon to the "best" view (FST). For women, attempting liberation, they also did this in their own way and established the "best" view in feminist standpoint theory—and most interestingly, standpoint feminism is articulating a philosophical methodological positioning that tries to "unite" all the other feminisms, more or less. This is also an aim of this author, using FMSs and FME and FST as uniting methodological positionings that can act as umbrella concepts and means for all the disperate (if not desperate) attempts to manage fear in the world.[259] The WFTs need that kind of uniting FST 'best framework' or 'best practice.' Albeit, "best" is qualified as largely unexplored, incomplete, and groping at this time in fearstory. We've a long way to go, just as the feminists do.

And one of the reasons there is still such a long way to go, so to speak, is the problem of finding the 'right direction.' Flatland offers "all directions" as valid, but lacks vertical developmental distinctions. Beyond that problem is that *fearless* only appears fully when there is *terror*. Remember, that a premise of the Credo of Fearlessness is that *when fear appears, also then will fearlessness appear*. That's true up to FMS-8, but after that, any movement across 'Fear' Barrier-3 requires something more—the abyss is enormous (and not). This time the Credo of Fearless emerges as the next morph for FMS-9 and for FST. It arises with a new premise and principle: *when terror appears, also then will fearless*. We are now in the realm of extremes. Yes, there is no doubt about that. It is rarified territory for most humans (say 0.00001%). Without going into this in more detail, the reality of *fearless* is deeply entrained with the profound (often sublime) reality of *terror*. This entrainment does not mean they are ontologically-dependent in the sense of claiming 'without terror there is no FMS-9 fearless.' It is too simplistic to cast that dialectic, especially in the subtle dimensions of the 3rd-tier.

Regarding "terror," in this context, the vast majority of fearworkers, conflictworkers, culturalworkers or feministworkers, etc. just don't go there, at least, not long enough nor not deep enough. They come up with rather mute forms (false forms) of "fearless ideology"—sounding like and looking like, more and more, *bravado* (in feminine and masculine forms). You may recall the "Fun, Fearless, Female" dictum of *Cosmos* magazine I mentioned earlier. It is "fearless shallowness" (Flatland) as Wilber says, by any other name—it is "evil" (Evil, with a capital)—it is Phobos-Thanatos, etc. Without consistent and deep integral work in/with *terror*, says FST, not much will really transform significantly, either individually or collectively. And all this raises us to the 'call' of our current awareness and the events of what postmodern philosopher Jean Baudrillard called "The Spirit of Terrorism."[260] If "terrorism" (including a WWIII named after it, that is, the "War on Terror") is calling us to awaken—it is calling us to *fearless* (FMS-9) right now! Will we answer the call for a leap to new FME in the 21st century? Not everyone can, will, or ought to make the leap—it is developmental.

Two remaining fragments remain to close this chapter and discussion on *fearless*, which arise from writing the encyclopedic version of *World's Fearlessness Teachings* prior to this book. There is a very strong resistance to "fearless" anything by a long historical Western discourse coming mostly from Aristotle, the ancient Greek philosopher (384-322 BC), a student of Plato and teacher of Alexander the Great. His influence is powerful in so much of what we think in the West, and especially around fear and fearlessness (i.e., FME). I ended up suggesting the "fear-positivists" (who love "courage" as opposed to anything like "fearlessness") were followers of a classic Aristotelian position (interpretation). It is largely pre-modern—but Aristotle was a modern thinker too, in many ways. Without going into the full classic argumentation of Aristotelian thought on fear and courage and fearlessness, suffice it to say that the encyclopedic entry for "Aristotle" was shaken-up by a very interesting paper written and published by a contemporary philosopher-scholar, Michelle Brady (2005).[261]

Brady's re-interpretation of the classic version interpreters (typically Hannah Arendt's work) of Aristotle on fear and courage offers a radical notion of "*fearless courage*," as one of Aristotle's definitions of "courage." Her complex arguments are worthy of study (beyond the scope of this discussion). Basically she shows that Aristotle believed in "fearless" as *good* (i.e., ethical virtue) in circumstances of facing a "noble death" (i.e., terror) and "courage" is better applied for lesser demanding situations of fear. Brady's reading of Aristotelian ethics (from *Nicomachean Ethics*, Book III), suggests that Aristotle saw through the 1st-tier, perhaps even the 2nd-tier to 3rd-tier, at least conceptually and philosophically, if not experientially. He posits for us the hierarchic differentiation of fear management so needed in the West between a discourse on "courage" and discourse on "fearless." Maybe in time Westerners will catch on and catch up on Aristotle's support for FMS-7, 8, 9, which fear-positivists refuse to legitimate (and tend to use classic Aristotelian logical arguments to do so—apparently, they haven't read Brady yet). And if Westerners are to continue to distrust the fearless discourse, they may want to read another critical theory paper by scholar Hasana Sharp (2005) on Why Spinoza's[262] (Western) philosophy is "A Strategy of Anti-Fear" made for a post-9/11 world.

And lastly, after so much philosophical and analytical conceptualizing of *fearless*, there is an image of it that remains in memory, at least for me, and maybe others who saw it. The story goes back to 1963 or so when Buddhist monks in some Asian countries protested the American-led Vietnam War. They prepared themselves for self-emolation by fire. The picture that hit the front pages of major American daily newspapers at the height of the war, was of one particular small monk in a lotus meditation position completely wrapped in flames, melting flesh, charred skin and garments. Other monks stood around him in a circle. An empty gas can appears at the edge of the photo. The scene is dead center on one of the major downtown intersections of some city. People are in crowds watching in the distance with horror. Cars stopped. The monks are all panic-free.

The eyes of the one burning monk are closed and calm. Reports were made by journalists notified of the event, that not a wince of the body was made during the complete burning to death. This is FMS-9, by any other name. The U.S. President at the time saw the photos and heard of these stories. The people everywhere were outraged at the destructive war, and too many people "burning" in villages in Vietnam. It was a stylistic form of "theatre of the absurd"[263]—a publicity stunt, in gross terms, which seemed to work. Ultimately, it was a spiritual trans(per)formance of the highest ethical order—*when terror arises fully, there will be fearless*—if we look and trust radically and deeply enough!

Notes

1. Ken Wilber's "AQAL" involves an ontological and epistemology (as well as ethical = non-violent) model (theory) of the Kosmos and how the Kosmos knows itself (i.e., how it develops and evolves as consciousness and creates means (methodologies of inquiry) for knowing itself). AQAL is short-hand for quadrants, levels, lines, types. I recommend you read more on the Internet or in any of Wilber's books (1995 onward), or read others who have written about his work.

2. To explain Foucault's postmodern theory of power-knowledge in a nutshell is difficult (it is also controversial, for e.g., some would argue he is not postmodernist, etc.).

Without entering the technicalities and problems involved in interpreting Foucault or assessing his strengths and weaknesses, I would locate his work as a re-visionist theory of social domination (i.e., theories about social conflict, violence, injustice, oppression and justice and liberation). What Foucault did was to challenge older "modernist" ideas about class and power, as Marxism tended to dominate that thinking. This short quote by Foucauldian interpreters summarizes Foucault's important 20th century re-vision (i.e., a needed complication of understanding "power" dynamics, individually and collectively): "the necessary centrality of a particular class (classically, the proletariat) to the struggle against 'domination' had to be critically rethought. A class could no longer be seen to act as a 'subject in history' — and yet neither could it be a purely determined economic effect. To this extent the stress on class analysis itself had to be dropped or at least restricted or supplemented. It needed to be replaced by a theory of constraint (or 'structure') and enablement (or 'agency'), locked into a broader conception of society than economistic [*a la* Marxian] models had allowed. Such a theory would need to think of the 'wielders' of power as being just as inextricably caught in its webs [Matrix] as the supposedly powerless. It would have to see power in terms of *relations* built consistently into the flows and practices of everyday life, rather than as some *thing* imposed from the top down. In short, the predicament of Marxism showed the limitations of mechanistic determinism [and verly simplistic binary categories of 'powerful' and 'powerless'], and the need for a more subtly historical and detailed [discourse] analysis of the local and specific effects of power [*via* cultural aspects]. This, among other things, is what Foucault was to provide." Alec McHoul, and Wendy Grace, *A Foucault Primer: Discourse, Power and the Subject* (Washington Square, NY: New York University Press, 1998), 7. Foucault linked power with knowledge flows in the everyday world, just as I have linked FME with such flows, and thus, one needs to ask who gets privilege and power (status) and control in constructing discourses of FME (i.e., power-knowledge-fear)? How can such power-knowledge-fear (i.e., FME) be critiqued, especially, when as Foucault says, we are all embedded in the "web" of the relations by which such power-knowledge-fear is produced and consumed? See also my quotes from Massumi in the Introduction on the serious postmodern problem of distinguishing our "selves" from "fear."

    3. "Freedom from fear and want" is foundational to the former U.S. President F. D. Roosevelt's 1940s "Four Freedoms," essential to developing any universal human rights. F.D.R. delivered this formulation of worldwide social and political objectives in his State of the Union Message to Congress on January 6, 1941. In 1946, after establishing the United Nations, Eleanor Roosevelt, the Unites States ambassador to the UN, was selected to head the newly formed Commission on Human Rights to determine the constituents of humankind's inalienable freedoms. According to Clements, "She and other members of the commission were determined to write a document that would live and last, a document that would protect and empower men and women [and children], irrespective of color, creed or culture. Their goal was to establish a universal framework for all beings to realize their highest potential and live in freedom and dignity. Thus on December 10, 1948 the Universal Declaration of Human Rights was adopted by the UN General Assembly stating that 'freedom from fear' was [hu]mankind's highest aspiration." Alan Clements, "Editorial," *Spirit in Action: WorldDharma Monthly Newsletter, Vol. 1* (1999). Note the ethical philosopher and feminist, Martha Nussbaum, has published 10 "Central Human Capabilities" as a universal document which adds nuance and sensitivity to the current UN document on human rights. She has given fear its due recognition in #5 which states: "*Emotions*- Being able to have attachments to things and people outside ourselves; to love those who love and care for us, to grieve at their absence; in general, to love, to grieve, to experience longing, gratitude, and justified anger. Not having one's emotional

development blighted by fear and anxiety." Cited in Robert E. Goodin and David Parker, "Introduction: Symposium on Martha Nussbaum's Political Philosophy," *Ethics, 111*(2000), 6-7.

4. Juan E. Corradi, Patricia Weiss Fagen, and Manuel Antonio Garretón, eds., *Fear at the Edge: State Terror and Resistance in Latin America* (Berkeley, CA: University of California Press, 1992), 3.

5. Quote taken from Peter N. Stearns, *American Fear: The Causes and Consequences of High Anxiety* (NY: Routledge, 2006), 219.

6. Eduardo Gáleano, *Upside Down: A Primer for the Looking-glass World*, trans. Mark Fried (NY: Henry Holt, 2000), 78.

7. Ian Dakers, creator of the *Inflow Matrix* system.

8. *V for Vendetta*, directed by James McTeigue, produced by Joel Silver, Grant Hill and Andy and Larry Wachowski (© 2006 Warner Bros.). Note this is the same production-artistic team who produced *The Matrix* (1999-2003).

9. That said, there have been other smaller initiatives by other people to bring "experts" from various disciplines together to share about their research on fear in public and scholarly forums, for example, "Fear: Its Political Uses and Abuses" organized in 2004 by the New School of Social Research in New York; also scholarly journal issues totally focusing on "fear" have shown up in *Urban Studies, 38*(5-6), 2001; *Hedgehog Review: Critical Reflections on Contemporary Culture, 5*(3), 2003; *Capital and Class, 80,* 2003; *Social Research, 71*(4), 2004.

10. Z. Bauman, *Liquid Fear* (Cambridge, UK: Polity Press, 2006). See also Z. Bauman, *Liquid Times: Living in an Age of Uncertainty* (Cambridge, UK: Polity Press, 2006).

11. F. Furedi, *Culture of Fear Revisited: Risk-taking and the Morality of Low Expectation* (London, UK: Continuum, 2006), vii, ix, xi, xxi. As much as Furedi critiques both the Right and Left, he is very critical of the current "radical" Left (activists), who he sees feed upon and reproduce a "conservativism of fear" because they have a "fear of the future." All of which stifles human creativity in society and accompanies that with misanthropy (hatred of humanity and its notion of progress).F. Furedi, *Politics of Fear* (London, UK: Continuum, 2005), 10-11.

12. Barack Obama, *The Audacity of Hope: Thoughts on Reclaiming the American Dream* (Crown, 2006).

13. R. W. Dozier Jr., *Fear Itself: The Origin and Nature of the Powerful Emotion that Shapes Our Lives and World* (NY: St. Martin's Press, 1998), 13.

14. Z. Bauman, *Intimations of Postmodernity* (NY: Routledge, 1992), xviii.

15. R. M. Fisher, "Defining the 'Enemy' of Fearlessness," Technical Paper No. 6 (Calgary, AB: In Search of Fearlessness Research Institute, 1997).

16. R. M. Fisher, "Disappear Fear: Action Fearology for the 21st Century," Technical Paper No. 26 (Vancouver, BC: In Search of Fearlessness Research Institute, 2007), 8-14.

17. There are far too many fear-positivists to name, though a few good contemporary examples are the following: Rush W. Dozier Jr., *Fear Itself* (1998); Michael Clarkson, *Intelligent Fear: How to Make Fear Work for You* (Toronto, ON: Key Porter Books, 2002); Samuel N. Gillian, *The Beauty of Fear: How to Positively Enjoy Being Afraid* (Bronx, NY: Phemore Press, 2002); Gavin de Becker, *The Gift of Fear: Survival Signals that Protect us from Violence* (NY: Bantam Doubleday Dell, 1997); Harriet Lerner, *The Dance of Fear: Rising Above Anxiety, Fear, and Shame to be your Best and Bravest Self* (NY: HarperCollins, 2005); Elisebeth VanderWeil, "Accepting a Ring of Fire: Stories of

Engagement with Fear in Transformational Adult Learning," unpublished dissertation (Spokane, WA: Gonzaga University, 2007).

18. Usually, fear-positivists boast (and defend) their foundational "natural" or "normal" definition of fear extracted from contextual historical, cultural, and political nuance—that is, omitting multiple perspectives for defining and conceptualizing fear. They like using the English dictionary meanings for fear, as if the dictionary is 'neutral.' There attempts are simply partial and naive (perhaps, even lazy). I sense they are terrified to go 'deeper' into their own fear of not knowing what fear ('fear') is. They don't like to be questioned on that either. Yes, it is scary but a critical and truly radical 'fearlessness' perspective (2nd-tier) requires we go all the way and not be limited in our epistemologies by 'fear' itself. The human Fear Problem will not be resolved (or transformed) by partial and timid means.

19. Issa, "Dragon Dreams" CD, from the song "When We Are Queen," (© 2008, IssaLight.com).

20. Angela Prider's shamanic and therapeutic work is accessible from her website: www.westcoast-shamanic.com.

21. S. Martin, *Born Standing Up: A Comic's Life* (NY: Scribner, 2007), 169.

22. D. Viscott, *Emotional Resilience; Simple Truths for Dealing with Unfinished Business of Your Past* (NY: Random House, 1996), 72.

23. R. D. Hare, D. J. Cooke, and S. D. Hart, "Psychopathy and Sadistic Personality Disorder," in *Oxford Textbook of Psychopathology*, eds. R. D. Davis, T. Millon, and P. H. Blaney. (NY: Oxford University Press, 1999), 570.

24. Jerome Kagan, *Galen's Prophecy: Temperament in Human Nature* (Boulder, CO: Westview Press, 1997), 49.

25. Stanley J. Rachman, *Fear and Courage* (NY: W. H. Freeman, 1990), 297.

26. Gerald Jampolsky, *Teach Only Love; The Seven Principles of Attitudinal Healing*, (NY: Bantam, 1983), 2.

27. James Redfield, *The Celestine Prophecy; An Adventure*, (NY: Warner Books, 1994), 101.

28. Chögyam Trungpa, *Cutting Through Spiritual Materialism*, (Boulder, CO: Shambhala, 1973), 108.

29. Chögyam Trungpa, *Shambhala: The Sacred Path of the Warrior* (Boston, MA: Shambhala, 2007), 33. [original published in 1985]

30. Martin Luther, "Sermons on the Gospel of St. John, Chpts. 14-16, in *Luther's Works, Vol.24*, ed. J. Pelikan (St. Louis, Missouri: Concordia Publishing House, 1961), 14.

31. Jean Vanier, *Be Not Afraid* (Toronto, ON: Griffin House, 1975).

32. Pope John Paul III, *Crossing the Threshold of Hope*, (Toronto, ON: A. A. Knopf, 1994), 4.

33. Thich Nhat Hahn, *No Death, No Fear: Comforting Wisdom for Life* (Riverhead Books, 2003).

34. Gregg Braden, *Awakening to Zero Point*, video, 1996, (see www.lauralee.com).

35. Cheryl Huber, *The Fear Book: Facing Fear Once and For All*, (Zen Meditation Center, 1997), 23.

36. Serious readers may note that Wilber has more or less left his reliance on the Perennial Philosophy in his later phases of integral writing (post-metaphysical philosophy), but it still has partial truth; and importantly "There is much evidence that this type of existence or knowledge [i.e., the Perennial Philosophy] is central to every major religion—Hinduism, Buddhism, Taoism, Christianity, Islam, and Judaism—so that we can justifiably speak of the "transcendent unity of religions" and the unanimity of primordial

truth." Ken Wilber, *No Boundary: Eastern and Western Approaches to Personal Growth* (Boulder, CO: New Science Library, 1981), 3. [original published in 1979]

37. Ibid., 4.

38. Joseph Campbell (with Bill Moyers), *The Power of Myth*, ed. Sue Flowers (NY: Doubleday, 1988), 50-51.

39. Ibid., 51.

40. According to Grahn, spiritual feminist author, poet-teacher, "Besides sacred, taboo also means forbidden, valuable, wonderful, magic, terrible, frightening, and immutable law. Taboo is the emphatic use of imperatives, yes or no, you must or you must not. Taboo draws attention, strong attention, and is in and of itself a language for ideas and customs." Judy Grahn, *Blood, Bread, and Roses: How Menstruation Created the World* (Boston, MA: Beacon Press, 1993), 5.

41. Many authors, too many to mention, have given a more in depth (mystical) reading of this phrase and Biblical imperative, where the meaning in Hebrew original translation is "awe of God" (as Fr. Matthew Fox once told me). Second-tier FMSs would claim likewise.

42. From an involutionary perspective, and/or merely a psychological model of development, the mythical "Fall" (or "Great Reversal") narrative, common around the world, "was primarily the awakening of self-conscious knowledge that correctly disclosed, among many other things, that men and women were *already* and *priorly* alienated from true Spirit. . . . That was not an *actual* Fall from spiritual Heaven [say the esoteric involutionists and Gnostics, and a lot of Western theology], but a move up from Earth. . . . [say evolutionists and developmentalists] To this true awakening . . . were added natural guilt . . . neurotic guilt . . . and guilty pride . . . all cascading over each other in a nightmare of terror. The texts from just that period [in Cultural development], the second and first millenia B.C., show just that horrifying moral atmosphere [Fear's Empire]—in both East and West alike." See Wilber for much detailed description of two different kinds of "Fall" experiences in human evolution. Ken Wilber, *Up From Eden: A Transpersonal View of Human Evolution* (Garden City, NY: Anchor Press/Doubleday, 1981), 293.

43. Ibid., 50.

44. With mother-child linked intimately during pregnancy, one could argue that *no fear* (FMS-0) is operating in both mother and child to keep the "fear" managed so as to keep the birth system in as least amount of biopsychological turmoil (distress, trauma) as possible. Why? Intuitively speaking, it produces "better" quality offspring and nurturing peri-natal environments to increase the chances of health and survival during relatively high risk times (i.e., pre-natal, peri-natal). Arguably, with less fear (distress, trauma) going on in the mother and child, the more likely a 'good' quality bonding is made after the child is born and suckling (of course, this is in ideal conditions, with no biopsychological complications with the mother or child). Dr. Nané Ariadne Jordan, a homebirth expert and dula, has informed me of the work of Dr. Michel Odent (see Internet) and others, who have specialized in birthing and the interrelationship of fear during that process. FME in the future ought to utilized this research on mothers and birthing as foundational to curriculum and pedagogy.

45. As *The New York Times* endorsement reads on Gavin de Becker's inside best-selling popular book cover: "The ability to predict and protect oneself from violent behavior [i.e., terror and traumatization], largely through one's own intuition ["true fear," says de Becker], is the central premise of de Becker's book—thus fear is a gift [of survival]. The book taps anxieties of an era." Gavin de Becker, *The Gift of Fear: Survival Signals that Protect Us from Violence* (NY: Dell, 1997).

46. Grantly Dick-Read's classic book in 1969 *Childbirth Without Fear*. Republished many times; this book represents the intention of a non-violent birthing process. M. Oden and G. Dick-Read, *Childbirth Without Fear: The Principles and Practice of Natural Childbirth* (Pinter and Martin, 2005).

47. "In the small rhythm of childhood, first space is the period during which the maternal bond is far stronger than the will to self assertion; the time before standing, exploring, and no-saying [Rebellion]. . . . In cultural evolution, it is the stage in which the individual identifies primarily with the circle [0] of the [group] tribe or village, and separate ["I am"] identity has yet to become a significant reality. In a creative event, it holds the last part of the mystery of incubation, and the first glimmerings of inspiration. It is that period when the intangible magic of germination predominates over solidity of form." Charles M. Johnston, *The Creative Imperative: A Four-dimensional Theory of Human Growth and Planetary Evolution* (Berkeley, CA: Celestial Arts, 1986), 81.

48. As Wilber wrote, "one can transcend fear and angst by transcending self and other [dualism]. . . . seeing that self and other are one, the individual is released from the fear of living; seeing that being and non-being are one, the individual is released from the fear of death [so one is released from suffering]." Ken Wilber, "Odyssey: A Personal Inquiry into Humanistic and Transpersonal Psychology," *Journal of Humanistic Psychology, 22* (1982), 63.

49. R. R. Willoughby, "Magic and Cognate Phenomena: An Hypothesis," in *A Handbook of Social Psychology, Vol. 1*, ed. C. Murchison (NY: Russell and Russell, 1935), 502.

50. Yi-Fu Tuan, *Landscapes of Fear* (Minneapolis, MN: University of Minnesota Press, 1979), 36.

51. C. Huber, *The Fear Book: Facing Fear Once And For All* (Zen Meditation Center, 1997), 61.

52. Chris Griscom, *The Healing of Emotion: Awakening the Fearless Self* (NY: Simon and Schuster, 1990), 61, 129.

53. R. Genn, Retrieved May 1, 2004 from http://www.cgroup.com/capa/rgenn2.htm.

54. Wilber has warned of the problems of Romanticism ('child innocence,' or 're-enchantment of the world' scenarios and) argumentation in many of his works, of which a good basis for his points can be found in Ken Wilber, *The Marriage of Sense and Soul: Integrating Science and Religion* (NY: Random House, 1998).

55. Elsewhere, this author has written on these three distinctions in some detail and of their relevance for integral theory and philosophy, especially in regard to critique. R. M. Fisher, "A Guide to Wilberland: Some Common Misunderstandings of the Critics of Ken Wilber and His Work on Transpersonal Theory Prior to 1995," *Journal of Humanistic Psychology, 37*(1997), 47-54.

56. A good deal could be cited as to these terms, and too complex it would be to sort out for our purposes. The postmodern view is that there are many feminisms, many gender formations (not just male and female) not all compatible philosophically or politically. Womanist views (often associated with women-of-color) have emerged often to suggest a woman's perspective that may or may not be (white) "feminist." Feminine refers to a more broad category of qualities that many traditions have differentiated, and in some cultures like the ancient East *yin* and *yang* may be used to differentiate them. This author combines the three terms as a diversity in unity, only in that they have enough general overlap of interest in a particular lens of analysis and view on the world-reality overall.

57. Judy R. Grahn, "Are Goddesses Metaformic Constructs?: An Application of Metaformic Theory to Menarche Celebrations and Goddess Rituals of Kerala and Con-

tiguous States in South India," unpublished dissertation (San Francisco, CA: California Institute of Integral Studies, 1999), 309, 311.

58. Ibid., 314.

59. Ibid., 314. "A crossover seems to be happening in the US, Canada, Australia and Europe, with a renewed interest in goddess worship. There is much discussion about the work of Marija Gimbutas and her philosophic followers, such as Riane Eisler, author of the *Chalice and the Blade*. Grassroots movements have established goddess worship, and women travel to sites considered both sacred and ancient. Not coincidentally, there is also a renewed interest in the honoring of menstruation and the celebration of menarche."

60. Ibid., 314-315.

61. Ibid., viii.

62. Ibid., 313. Grahn posits a notion of "cultural obversity" (as intervention into psychosocial intolerance and fears) as perhaps more meaningful, nuanced and useful than "cultural diversity."

63. Ibid., 313.

64. Grahn, *Blood, Bread, and Roses*, 15.

65. Robert Ardrey, *The Hunting Hypothesis: A Personal Conclusion Concerning the Evolutionary Nature of Man* (NY: Atheneum, 1976), 92-93.

66. Grahn, *Blood, Bread, and Roses*, 15-16.

67. Ibid., 16.

68. Ibid., 17.

69. Ibid., 18.

70. Marija Gimbutas, *The Language of the Goddess* (NY: Harper San Francisco, 1991), 316.

71. Grahn, 30.

72. Wilber, "Odyssey," 66. "Wherever there is other, there is fear; wherever there is self, there is anxiety—that is a Buddhistic and Upanishadic absolute." Wilber, *Up From Eden*, 333.

73. Wilber, *Up From Eden*, 312.

74. Elinor W. Gadon, *The Once and Future Goddess: A Symbol for Our Time* (NY: Harper and Row, 1989), 273.

75. Grahn, *Blood, Bread, and Roses*, 172.

76. A good deal of intense study on *shame* exists in the literature across disciplines but is beyond the scope of this book. However, the most basic distinction, most would agree on, is that guilt is feeling "bad" for a behavior done (see FMS-4 Blue-Mythic) and shame is feeling "bad" about the core of the self that did the behavior (see FMS-2 Purple, Magic).

77. Ibid., 173.

78. Gimbutas, 316.

79. The "Immortality Project" (or "Dualism-Repression-Projection") or "Atman Project" can be read about in great detail in Wilber's earliest writing in *Spectrum of Consciousness* (1977), *The Atman Project* (1980), *Up From Eden* (1981). For a similar reading, but from an existentialist perspective, not a transpersonal perspective as in Wilber's work, see E. Becker, *The Denial of Death* (NY: Simon and Schuster, 1997). [original published in 1973] Becker's work has been taken up by social psychologists and studies of "terror management theory" (TMT, e.g., Pyszczynski et al.), which offer powerful evidence for the way that the Immortality Project works across cultures and through time, as a defense to the terror of existence (meaning, of living with dualistic consciousness). But as a defense, the Immortality Project has also flaws, fatal sometimes.

80. Thanks to Dr. Nané A. Jordan for this information (pers. comm. January, 27, 2009).

81. Fisher, *Encyclopedia of the World's Fearlessness Teaching* (in progress), 93.

82. From an anonymous father, poet, of an anonymous woman who shared e-mails with this author; personal correspondence, 1998.

83. Taken from a website (no address given) in 1997.

84. Cited in C. L. Allen, "How We Can Handle Our Fears," *Sign of the Times* (1985) June, 3-5.

85. Cited in D. Bondevac, W. Boon, and S. Phillips, *Beyond the Western Tradition; Readings in Moral and Political Philosophy* (London: Mayfield, 1992), 56.

86. Dorothy Rowe, *Beyond Fear* (London: Fontana Paperbacks, 1987), 67.

87. C. Norton, "Victory over fear," no date. Retrieved March 12, 2007 from http://www.anglefire.com.realm/csu/victory.htm

88. Cited in S. P. Ruhela, *Quotations from India* (M. D. Publications PVT, Ltd., 1997), 9.

89. René Descartes, "The Passions of the Soul," in *The Philosophical Works of Descartes*, trans. E. S. Haldane & G. R. T. Ross, (London: Cambridge University Press, 1975), 412. [original published c. 1650]

90. K. J. Dover, *Greek Popular Morality: In the Time of Plato and Aristotle* (Oxford, UK: Basil Blackwell, 1974).

91. Books by Donald L. Nathanson, a psychotherapist and scholar are a valuable source of information and contention, for example *The Many Faces of Shame* (NY: The Guilford Press, 1987), and *Shame and Pride: Affect, Sex, and the Birth of the Self* (NY: W. W. Norton, 1994).

92. Don Beck, and Christopher Cowan, *Spiral Dynamics: Mastering Values, Leadership and Change* (Cambridge, MA: Blackwell, 1996), 75.

93. Catherine A. Lutz, *Unnatural Emotions; Everyday Sentiments on a Micronesian Atoll and their challenges to Western theory.* Chicago, IL: University of Chicago Press, 1988), 198.

94. R. Blum, *The Book of Runes* (NY: St. Martin's Press, 1982).

95. C. E. Lindeman, *The Meaning of Adult Education* (Montreal, QB: Harvest House, 1961), 36. [original published in 1926]

96. From John Robbins and singer-songwriter Anne Mortifee (unknown source).

97. Reynolds summarized "five important hints or a set of tenets" within Wilber's theorizing that are useful to explain the advance and regression, good and bad news of development and evolution (re: humans). Rehabilitation of Cultural Evolution, to be effective and nuanced enough, requires at least an understanding of the five tenets, of which "The Dialectic of Progress" is but one (he cites Wilber): "each stage solves or defuses certain problems of the previous stage, but then adds new and recalcitrant—and sometimes more complex and more difficult—problems of its own"—and this comes out to an awareness and acceptance (citing Wilber again): "The more stages of evolution there are—the greater the depth of the Kosmos—the more things that *can* go wrong." The other four tenets are: "The distinction between Differentiation and Dissociation," "The difference between Transcendence and Repression," "The difference between Natural Hierarchy and Pathological Hierarchy," and "Higher Structures [levels, stages] can be Hijacked by Lower Impules [structures, levels, stages]." Brad Reynolds, *Embracing Reality: The Integral Vision of Ken Wilber (A Historical Survey and Chapter-by-Chapter Guide to Wilber's Major Works)* (NY: Jeremy P. Tarcher/Penguin, 2004), 352.

98. Beck and Cowan, 75.

99. Ernest Becker, *The Denial of Death*, 1.

100. Ibid., 1.

101. Ibid., 2.

102. Ibid., 3.

103. Ibid., 3.

104. Ibid., 4.

105. Ibid., 6.

106. Ibid., 7.

107. Ibid., 12.

108. Joseph Campbell, *Myths to Live By* (NY: Bantam Book, 1978), 207-208.

109. Gadon, 369-370, 372-373.

110. Ken Wilber, *Sex, Ecology, and Spirituality (Vol. 1): The Spirit in Evolution* (Boston, MA: Shambhala). See also B. Reynolds, *Embracing Reality*, 261.

111. If one looks up the words "without fear there is no courage" (for e.g.,) on the Internet (Google search), 2800 'hits' appear (June, 21, 2008).

112. Fisher, "Invoking 'Fear' Studies," 59-60.

113. Bonaro W. Overstreet, *Understanding Fear in Ourselves and Others* (NY: Harper and Row, 1971), 92-95. [original published in 1951]

114. T. Lewis, F. Amini, and R. Lannon, *A General Theory of Love* (NY: Random House, 2000), 48.

115. D. R. Margolis, *The Fabric of Self: A Theory of Ethics and Emotions* (New Haven, CN: Yale University Press, 1998), 151.

116. The problematics of the "ascendence into adolescent 'fearlessness' has been reearched sensitively and holistically by J. Goodey, BOYS DON'T CRY: Masculinities, Fear of Crime and Fearlessness, *The British Journal of Criminology, 37* (1997), 401-418. "Affective fearlessness" as a clinical concept has been discussed earlier in this book. "Behavioral fearlessness" as one personal coach is promoting is sophisticated but truly disturbing (see FMS-5, Orange, Success) as to where unabashed bravado can go. From an ad on the Internet: "What can unleash your new power and ability to fearlessly attract, approach, seduce and succeed with women even more than any other 'inner game' work? Ironically, it's NOT 'inner game'!. . . . With exclusive training, tips, and access (purchase links) to the ORIGINAL and exact resources (that you can acquire yourself) over the past 5 years that have allowed me (and now other students) to be grounded so strongly in Feminine Alpha Cognition and masculine strength resulting in behavioral fearlessness, powerful sexual communication and nonverbal body language around any and all women." Retrieved April 1, 2007 http://www.masterinnergame.com.

117. Freud cited in Wilber. Ken Wilber, *The Atman Project: A Transpersonal View of Human Development* (Wheaton, IL: The Theosophical Publishing House, 1982), 20.

118. Ibid. 21.

119. See for example, Jody Miller, *One of the Guys: Girls, Gangs, and Gender* (NY: Oxford University Press, 2001).

120. S. E. Taylor, L. C. Klein, B. P. Lewis, T. L. Gruenewald and et al., "Biobehavioral Responses to Stress in Females: Tend-and-Befriend, Not Fight-or-Flight," *Psychological Review, 107*(2000), 411-429.

121. Wilber, *Up From Eden*, 87-89.

122. Becker, 46.

123. Wilber, 102.

124. William Ian Miller, *The Mystery of Courage* (Cambridge, MA: Harvard University Press, 2000), 5.

125. Ibid., 5.

126. Robert Moore, and Douglas Gillette, *King, Warrior, Magician, Lover: Rediscovering the Archetypes of the Mature Masculine* (NY: HarperCollins, 1991), 41.

127. Dozier, 229.

128. Richard Dawkins, "Design for a Faith-based Missile," *Free Inquiry, 22* (2001-02), 8.

129. J. Sumpton, *The Hundred Years' War* (University of Pennsylvania Press, 2001), 117. H. Carrington, *Psychic World* (Kessinger Publishing, 2003), 52.

130. R. M. Kidder, *Moral Courage* (NY: William Morrow, 2005).

131. Susan Bickford, *The Dissonance of Democracy; Listening, Conflict, and Citizenship* (NY: Cornell University Press, 1996), 151.

132. Miller, 6.

133. D. Khyentse, *Enlightened Courage* (Ithaca, NY: Snow Lion, 1993).

134. Michelle E. Brady, "The Fearlessness of Courage," *Southern Journal of Philosophy, 43*(2005), 190.

135. Dozier, 19. "the daredevils, the risk takers, the heroes—not only cope with fear, but become to relish being in extremely dangerous situations." E. Becker has called this often a type of "false courage." E. Becker, *The Structure of Evil: An Essay on the Unification of the Science of Man* (NY: The Free Press, 1976), 186. [originally published in 1968]

136. Dozier, 19.

137. Miller, 8.

138. Maya Angelou, *Life Doesn't Frighten Me* (NY: Stewart, Tabori and Chang, 1993).

139. Juan E. Corradi, "Toward Societies Without Fear, in *Fear at the Edge: State Terror and Resistance in Latin America,* eds. J. E. Corradi et al. (Berkeley, CA: University of California Press, 1992), 273.

140. Elisebeth VanderWeil, 45-46.

141. Rollo May, *Man's Search for Himself* (Toronto, ON: New American Library of Canada, 1967), 191.

142. Stanley Hauerwas, and Charles Pinches, *Christians Among the Virtues: Theological Conversations with Ancient and Modern Ethics* (Notre Dame, IN: University of Notre Dame Press, 1997), 152.

143. K. Campbell, *A Stoic Philosophy of Life* (NY: University Press of America, 1986), 23.

144. Cynthia Lamb, *Bridgid's Charge* (Corte Madera, CA: Bay Island Books, 1997), 16.

145. F. Kent, *Nothing to Fear: Coping with Phobias* (NY: Harper and Row, 1979).

146. Becker, 47.

147. Artist, Lizzie West and *Anti-Fear Movement Agency* is one good example. See http://www.lizziewestlife.com/.

148. Robin, 47.

149. Francis M. Lappé and Jeffrey Perkins, *You Have the Power: Choosing Courage in a Culture of Fear* (NY: Jeremy P. Tarcher/Penguin, 2005).

150. Retrieved October, 19, 2007 from http://osho.com.

151. Retrieved July 1, 2002 http://www.mkgandhi.org/philosophy/fearlessness.html.

152. Miller, 8.

153. Gavin de Becker, *Fear Less: Real Truth About Risk, Safety, and Security in a Time of Terrorism* (Boston, MA: Little, Brown & Co., 2002).

154. Bruce Schneier, *Beyond Fear: Thinking Sensibly About Security in an Uncertain World* (NY: Copernicus Books, 2003).

155. Forrest Church, *Freedom from Fear: Finding the Courage to Act, Love, and Be* (NY: St. Martin's Press, 2004), 177.

156. Hugh Lynn Cayce, son of the late great psychic/author Edgar Cayce, has written a wonderful book (based on a lot of his father's teachings) that covers in the first chapter a good deal of the basic spectrum of "fear patterns of the body and mind" (soul and spirit) and the various types of philosophies and psychologies throughout Western history that have attempted to make sense of fear and how to best manage (or transform) it. Such holistic and integrative scope is rare to find in any one book on the topic. H. L. Cayce, *Faces of Fear* (Cambridge, MA: Harper and Row, San Francisco, 1980), 5. Church's book is also open to this spectrum analysis but from a more superficial, though not insignificant, way. He lists seven "fear experts" (and entrepreneurs and potential 'competitors' to his own book and ideas) in his final chapter and thus guides readers to a greater scope of FME beyond his own biases. This is pedagogically impressive and very rare graciousness among the world's fearlessness teachers, especially in a postmodern world.

157. Church, 10-11.

158. Ibid., 14-15.

159. Although I have said the *fear-less* (FMS-6b) discourse is not politically radical in its critique, it is so at a very subtle level in that it makes a commitment to a sociopolitical "conflict theory" (perspective and analysis)—and this is the first time in the evolution of FME (FMSs) that we see this necessary shift. Earlier FMSs, generally, tend toward a more functionalist FME discourse.

160. de Becker, 13.

161. See Robert Augustus Masters's teachings. He is a psychospiritual trailblazer and shamanic visionary, as well as a master psychotherapist. R. A. Masters, *Truth Cannot be Rehearsed: Talks, Sessions, and Essays About the Art of Being Fully Human* (Vancouver, BC: Xanthyros Foundation, 1990), 138-139.

162. "When ethologists and psychologists say that animals such as geese and rats experience fear and other emotions, they are not suggesting that these states are the products of the kind of cognitive process that in humans typically precedes fear. So how do we define fear? If we define it as cognitive in order to accommodate what seems to be an essential feature of human fear, we exclude fear in geese and rats." M. Matthen, "Biological Universals and the Nature of Fear," *The Journal of Philosophy*, XCV (1998), 105. Exactly, my point! No harm is done to animals or humans in this distinction. Human cognition, as we might define "human" or "humanity" as a self-conscious being, then is also a "Cultural being" as this text has used throughout—as a shift from FMS-0 to FMS-1 and up to FMS-6. What the distinction reclaims is the "right" for humans to criticize "fear" in all its forms, without criticizing "fright" or "alert response." The criticism is Cultural (and/or Spiritual) attacking not the Natural, but the Cultural (and in some cases "spiritual") pathologies in the discourses around fear, fearlessness, and FME in general. For a good critique of the complex concept of "fear" in the field of psychology, see Jerome Kagan, *Three Seductive Ideas* (Cambridge, MA: Harvard University Press, 1998).

163. Church, 103.

164. That said, de Becker is very sensitive to women and their experience (especially as victims and survivors, whom he interviews often). He is also critical of masculinist (i.e., sexist) attitudes in our Western culture toward "intuition" and in particular he wrote: "Husbands chide their wives about 'feminine intuition' and don't take it seriously. If intuition is used by a woman to explain some choice she made or a concern she can't let go of, men roll their eyes and write it off. We [men] much prefer logic, the grounded, explainable, unemotional thought process that ends in a supportable conclusion. In fact,

Americans worship logic, even when it's wrong, and deny intuition, even when it's right." Becker, 12.

165. That said, it must be acknowledged he was a 'student' of sorts of cultural critic and philosopher Ernest Becker, and the radical feminist psychiatrist Alice Miller (see References in *Gift of Fear*). He also wrote of the need to reclaim, in each of us, a "critical inquiry to people," who may be a threat to us and not let merely so-called "experts" on violence (i.e., authorities) do that critical work (see *Gift of Fear*, 11).

166. Ibid., 177-179.

167. de Becker, 11-12.

168. Ibid., 12.

169. Ulrich Beck, *Risk Society: Towards a New Modernity*, trans. Mark Ritter (London, UK: Sage, 1992). U. Beck, *World Risk Society* (Cambridge, UK: Polity Press). U. Beck, "An Interview [by J. Yates] with Ulrich Beck on Fear and Risk Society," *The Hedgehog Review: Critical Reflections on Contemporary Culture*, 5(2003), 96-107.

170. de Becker, 280.

171. Ibid., 283.

172. Sarah Ahmed, "The Politics of Fear in the Making of Worlds," *Qualitative Studies in Education*, 16(2003), 377-398. S. Ahmed, *The Cultural Politics of Emotion* (NY: Routledge, 2004). S. Ahmed, "Be Very Afraid!," *New Internationalist, 376* (2005), retrieved October 19, 2005 from http://www.newint.org/issue376/be-very-afraid.htm.

173. de Becker, 295.

174. Ibid., 297.

175. David L. Altheide, *Creating Fear: News and the Construction of Crisis* (NY: Aldine de Gruyter, 2002). D. L. Altheide, "Notes Towards a Politics of Fear," *Journal for Crime, Conflict and the Media, 1*(2003), 37-54. D. L. Altheide, "Mass Media, Crime, and the Discourse of Fear," *The Hedgehog Review: Critical Reflections on Contemporary Culture*, 5(2003), 9-25.

176. de Becker, 347.

177. Ibid., 353.

178. de Becker, *Fear Less*, 194-195.

179. Ibid., 196-197.

180. Lorde cited in Susan Bickford. S. Bickford, *The Dissonance of Democracy;Listening, Conflict, and Citizenship* (Ithaca, NY: Cornell University Press, 1996), 137-138.

181. R. M. Fisher, "A Movement Toward a Fearless Society: A Powerful Contradiction to Violence," Technical Paper No. 10 (Vancouver, BC: In Search of Fearlessness Research Institute, 2000). R. M. Fisher, "An Integral Fearlessness Paradigm," Technical Paper No. 20 (Vancouver, BC: In Search of Fearlessness Research Institute, 2006). R. M. Fisher, "History of the Fearlessness Movement: An Introduction," Technical Paper No. 22 (Vancouver, BC: In Search of Fearlessness Research Institute, 2007).

182. Nel Noddings, *Women and Evil* (Berkeley, CA: University of California Press, 1989), 244.

183. Henri Lefebvre, *Everyday Life in the Modern World* (Transaction, 1984), Chapter Four.

184. Stanley Aronowitz, *False Promises: The Shaping of American Working Class Consciousness* (NY: McGraw-Hill, 1973), 42.

185. See a good summary by Ken Wilber, *"Integral Psychology: Consciousness, Spirit, Psychology, Therapy* (Boston, MA: Shambhala, 2000).

186. "Culture of fearlessness" has been used by a few different authors from different FMSs, for example Jones and Gosling speak historically of Lord Nelson's great skills

of commanding the men in his military forces, in extremely difficult times, as he had an "ability to inspire his officers and men and maximize their performance creating a culture of fearlessness and superiority [against the enemy]" [FMS-4]; whereas Crush speaks historically of the resistance fighters and Black Consciousness in Africa during its recent colonial battles and cites Wilson who wrote, "The Biko Generation inspired the culture of fearlessness" among blacks in order to persist successfully in revolt to the oppression [FMS-6]; and Jon's discussing Tibetan Buddhist ancient tradition, suggested the enlightened society, with a mythic source imaginary in the notion of Shangri-La, is a real phenomenon—he wrote, "The society of Shambhala is believed to have been a culture of fearlessness, dignity, and compassion. Its sense of responsibility and its compassion are believed to be rooted in the practice of meditation. . . . [it] represents an ideal for secular society. . . . From the Shambhala perspective, each one of us is a fearless warrior" [FMS-8]. S. Jones, and J. Gosling, *Nelson's Way: Leadership Lessons from the Great Commander* (Nicolas Brealey Publishing, 2005), 175; J. Crush, *Power of Development* (NY: Routledge, 1995), 245; T. Jon, *Mindful Knitting: Inviting Contemplative Practice to the Craft* (Tuttle Publications, 2004), 40. Note: assigning one FMS per discourse above is very gross, as often more realistically a combination of FMSs are involved, though there is one dominant usually, and the dominant FMS is what I have ascribed above.

187. Wilber, *Up From Eden*, 323, wrote: "This majority is still caught in uroboric, typhonic, magical, and mythical desires, bodily self-protective states, and a general refusal to even recognize or respect *other* personal selves. And one does not and cannot reach the trans-personal without first firmly establishing the personal. . . . National governments—which have a disproportionate hand in present and future history—are today, with few exceptions, organizations of thinly rationalized typhonicisim, animalistically self-protective, and therefore perfectly willing to dash to hell the entire world in an atomic holocaust, simply to prove their own cosmocentric ability to do so... In America (and Europe), where the New Age is most loudly announced, a significant majority of individuals are suffering from the stresses of these civilizations' failures to support truly rational and egoic structures, and thus these individuals are actually *regressing* to pre-personal, cultic, narcissistic pursuits, as Christopher Lasch has made very clear. Often, however, the cults of Narcissus claim that this regression is actually a pursuit of trans-personal realities, or at least 'humanistic' freedom. The 'New Age' movement is thus, in my opinion, the strangest mixture of a handful of truly trans-personal souls and masses of pre-personal addicts."

188. Jiddu Krishnamurti, *The Collected Works of J. Krishnamurti* (Krishnamurti Foundation of America, 1991), 175. [excerpt from a lecture given in 1959]

189. Although Krishnamurti uses this concept "spontaneous discipline" it first came to my awareness through my experience as an artist, then reading artist-educator Ken Beittel's writings (cited earlier).

190. Alan Clements, *Instinct for Freedom: Finding Liberation Through Living* (Novato, CA: New World Library, 2002), 225.

191. R. M. Fisher, "Fearless Leadership In and Out of the 'Fear' Matrix," unpublished dissertation (Vancouver, BC: The University of British Columbia, 2003). Available as a free pdf online http//: m1.cust.educ.ubc.ca/Artography/phd.php

192. Trungpa, 33.

193. This author's repeated experience with Buddhists (Western white North Americans who take up Buddhism), especially Shambhala trained ones, is that they espouse "fearlessness" and try to live by it using (habitual) discipline instead of spontaneous discipline (*a la* Krishnamurti), but they are quite first-tier (competitive) in orientation toward it because they show little curiosity at all to learn other perspectives, like those

ISOF and others have developed. The pre-modern conditioning architecture of Shambhala tradition, as learned by contemporary westerners, shows through—they seem afraid to "pollute" their "clean" ("purist") tradition (teachings) with 'other.' This is hardly appropriate (or fearlessness) for a postmodern world. Ken Wilber, an integrally-informed Zen Buddhist by tradition, is also critical of a similar pattern, what he calls "boomeritis buddhism" that has taken over much of contemporary movements in the Western world (particularly America). See Wilber's 2002 book *Boomeritis: A Novel That Will Set You Free.*

194. Thanks to Bob Camp for sending this from his copy of *Shambhala: The Sacred Path of the Warrior Book and Card Set* (based on Trungpa's thought and writings), edited by Carolyn Rose Gimian and copyrighted by Diana J. Mukpo (Boston, MA: Shambhala, 2004).

195. J. Hayward, *Sacred World; A Guide to Shambhala Warriorship in Daily Life* (NY: Bantam, 1995).

196. Trungpa, 5.

197. Ibid., 9-11.

198. ISOF's six 'fear' vaccines: (1) fear and fearlessness information, (2) liberation peer counseling/healing (3) spontaneous creation-making, (4) community-building, (5) School of Sacred Warriorship training, (6) vision quest. Later (2006) *fearanalysis* was added as a 'fear' vaccine itself, though it is part of (1).

199. Joan V. Bondurant, *Conquest of Violence: The Gandhian Philosophy of Conflict* (Berkeley, CA: University of California Press, 1965), 23-24, 28-29.

200. A. Mahaprajna, "Freedom From Fear: And the Freedom Must Be Total," Retrieved June 29, 2008 from http://www.greaterkasmir.com/full_story.asp?Date=27_6_2008&ItemID=7&cat=11

201. Bondurant, 28.

202. Cited in Bondurant, 29.

203. Trungpa, 45.

204. Ibid., 51.

205. Ibid., 51-52.

206. R. M. Fisher, "'Unplugging' as Real and Metaphoric: Emancipatory Dimensions to *The Matrix* Film Trilogy." Technical Paper No. 33 (Carbondale, IL: In Search of Fearlessness Research Institute, 2009).

207. Mahaprajna, 1.

208. Produced by David Maidman and Directed by Corey Ogilvie (©2007 DreamHouse Creative, Inc. and Production, Inc.) See http://www.thinkpeace.com.

209. Wilber, *Boomeritis*, 30.

210. A. Newman, "Aestheticism, Feminism, and the Dynamics of Reversal," *Hypatia*, 5 (1990), 195. Readers might note that philosophical critique of "reversal" in secular literature tends, as in Newman's formulation, to see it as negative and unhelpful to progress. A major reason for this difference is that Newman's work is decidedly a 1st-tier perspective. Reversal, from a 2nd-tier perspective, is a very different phenomenon and critical to ethical transformation (or *metanoia* in theology = "change of heart").

211. Fisher, "History of the Fearlessness Movement," 6-12.

212. Thanks to Dr. Gary Nixon, an integrally-informed therapist, from the addictions program at the University of Lethbridge, AB, for clarifying this two-tier conception in personal communications and in his publications.

213. Randall Collins, an internationally respected American sociologist-historian-theorist, has written many books and articles in his long career. His most valuable one to this author is *Four Sociological Traditions* (1985, later edition 1994). There Collins

documents "The Conflict Tradition" as an emancipatory movement throughout Western cultures, in forms of philosophy and theory—not merely within "sociology" *per se*. Collins is an integrative thinker of vast scope and intelligence, and this chapter on the "Conflict Tradition" is overwhelming in that it shows how important a particular view, he called the "conflict vision" is to understanding many thinkers and their theories and philosophies through time. He really maps out the conflict discourse, by any other name. Of course it is not totally complete, or detailed, but it brings together the great thinkers who have, in a variety of forms, talked about a basic argument within a line of thinking. He wrote, "A line of thought going back many centuries emphasizes social conflict. This sounds like it studies only certain dramatic events, but the perspective is much broader and includes all of what goes on in a society. Its main argument is not simply that society consists of conflict, but the larger claim that what occurs when conflict is not openly taking place is a process of domination. Its vision of social order consists of groups and individuals trying to advance their own interests over others whether or not overt outbreaks take place in this struggle for advantage. Calling this approach the *conflict* perspective [as opposed to the *consensus* perspective in sociological literature] is a bit of a metaphor. The word focuses on the tip of an iceberg, the spectacular events of revolution, war, or social movements; but the viewpoint concerns equally the normal structure of dominant and subordinate interest groups that make up the larger part of the iceberg submerged below. This conflict vision of society is rarely popular. Conflict sociologists have usually been an intellectual underground. Prevailing views of one's own society have usually stressed a much more benign picture." His historical map of the Conflict Tradition includes diverse great thinkers and activists like Hegel, Marx and Engels, Nietzsche, Weber, Simmel, Mannheim, Gramsci, Frankfurt School (critical theorists), and many others, including himself. R. Collins, *Four Sociological Traditions* (NY: Oxford University Press, 1994), 47. If readers could replace the word "conflict" in the above quote and ideas with "fearlessness" then they would see what this author's future work is going to look like in bringing the WFTs in under one roof and making it applicable to mainstream academic discourses as well as esoteric uses. Bottomline, Collins recognizes that one cannot have both a conflict perspective and a consensus perspective, they are incompatible, as are the other dichotomous paradigms of fearlessness listed in this chapter. Despite this, many sociologists and others have tried to "white-wash" the dichotomous distinctions of Collins (and this author), arguing they can be "blended" or "integrated." That's a whole other story for another book. Suffice it to say: be very cautious of "the third way" method and ideology being promoted by so many people in our times. The intention is a good one to 'get around the bipolarity' and oppositional but one always has to look at the motivation for doing so, and the reductionism and loss of distinctions that may be very important to keep in dichotomies (e.g., the 15 paradigms): one might see that this author's notion of "path of fearlessness" is actually a postmodern attempt to provide the "third factor" in the bi-centric concepts that are used, e.g., Love vs. fear. The connecting thread and way is fearlessness. See the Credo of Fearlessness in Chapter One.

214. On a Christian website, for example, concern exists about the "New World Order" that esoteric spiritualists, like the Freemason's, are attempting to build as part of the "New Age." They claim: "Alice Bailey, Director of the House of Theosophy in the early part of this century, writes about the role of Freemasonry in the coming New Age and in the realization of the appearance of the Great One [which the Christians interpret as Antichrist] and the reason for all this tremendous secrecy. Actually, Bailey is writing as a conduit for her demonic 'Guiding Spirit,' Master DK." Retrieved November 10, 2006 from http://www.cuttingedge.org/news/n1081.cfm. All part of the Masonic Movement, apparently. It is beyond the scope of this book to examine these details other than to say

The Baileys have a very interesting history in occultism in the 20th century and beyond. Foster Bailey has written articles on the Lucis Trust website, with all the occult symbolism of a New Age. Alice died in 1949 and her husband Foster in 1977. It is well-known, in certain circles that the Freemasons were central in the forming of the American Constitution and have impacted American culture and institutions in 'high places' at times.

215. Retrieved October 11, 2007 from http://energyenhancement.org/AliceBailey/BK/MAGIC/magi1146.html.

216. Fisher, "History of the Fearlessness Movement," 13-16.

217. Maria Hibbets, "Saving Them From Yourself: An Inquiry into the South Asian Gift of Fearlessness," *Journal of Religious Ethics*, 27(1999), 437.

218. Ibid., 456.

219. Retrieved May 22, 2004 from http://www.sikhe.com/gsdno/articles/bookreview/thesikhsinhistory.htm.

220. Cited in J. Hastings, ed., *Encyclopedia of Religion and Ethics* (Part 23) (Kessinger Publications, 2003), 202.

221. C. Humphreys, *A Popular Dictionary of Buddhism* (London: Curzon Press, 1976), 25.

222. Stanley Kopp, *Raise Your Right Hand Against Fear; Extend the Other in Comassion* (Minneapolis, MN: Compcare, 1988), 149.

223. C. G. Valles, *Let Go of Fear* (NY: Triumph, 1991), 205.

224. R. A. Gard, ed., *Buddhism* (NY: George Braziller, 1962), 61.

225. Yin-Shun (Venerable), trans. W. H. Yeung, *The Way of Buddhahood: Instructions from a Chinese Master* (Wisdom Publication, 1998).

226. R. M. Fisher, "An Introduction to: An Epistemology of 'Fear': A Fearlessness Paradigm," Technical Paper No. 2, (Calgary, AB: In Search of Fearlessness Research Institute, 1995). R. M. Fisher, unpublished. ms., *Spectrum of 'Fear.'*

227. Ken Wilber, *Grace and Grit: Spirituality and Healing in the Life and Death of Treya Killam Wilber* (Boston, MA: Shambhala, 1993), 382.

228. John Heron, *Co-operative Inquiry: Research into the Human Condition* (London, UK: Sage, 1996), 119.

229. Ibid., 119.

230. Ibid., 120.

231. Another very good complementary approach to transpersonal (and integral) theory is Jorge N. Ferrer, *Revisioning Transpersonal Theory: A Participatory Vision of Human Spirituality* (Albany, NY: State University of New York Press, 2002).

232. See for example, R. Shikpo, Fremantle, F., and Hutchens, D., *Never Turn Away: The Buddhist Path Beyond Hope and Fear* (Wisdom Publications, 2007).

233. A. Huffington (interviewed by Linda Frum), "No More Fears: Arianna Huffington Was Once Terrified," *National Post*, September 30, 2006. Retrieved December 18, 2006 from http://www.canada.com/nationalpost/news/story.html....

234. The interrelational enmeshment ("dis-ease") of fear/hope as a pattern is a topic this author has written about in many other places, noting that "powers" (elites) of all kinds have used this combination to keep us in "fear" (and "hope") but always in the 'Fear' Matrix. The way they operate is by creating *fear*, then selling *hope*. It is the oldest way to manipulate people, and is opposite the "gift of fearlessness" tradition talked about in this chapter. As Osho, the spiritual guru wrote, "The ego is always coming out of fear. A really fearless person has no ego." Reality is, as far as this author's analysis goes, hope is an ego-control-game" (and ego defense)—not bad, just not very mature. It can also be pathological—people get addicted to "hope" (/fear). Hope is an early form of expression of fearlessness that runs throughout human evolution, and it gets its due regard in the 1st-

tier, but not the 2nd and 3rd-tier, where it is integrated but transcended for *fearlessness* as the better expression (FMS). Jiddu Krishnamurti's work also is a good example of fear-analysis beyond fear/hope (thus 2nd-tier and above). See Osho's wonderful nondual fearanalysis at http://www.paulcopps.com/Books%20-%20Osho%20Courage.htm.

235. Phil Nuemberger, *Strong and Fearless: The Quest for Personal Power* (Yes International, 2003), 9.

236. Miller, 85, 129.

237. Gabriel Roth, (with J. Loudon) *Maps to Ecstasy; Teachings of an Urban Shaman* (San Rafael, CA: New World Library, 1989), 27.

238. Jean-Paul Sartre in the Preface to Fanon's *The Wretched of the Earth* wrote, "For the only true culture is that of the revolution; that is to say, it is constantly in the making. Fanon speaks out loud; we Europeans can hear him, as the fact that you hold this book in your hand proves; is he not then afraid that the colonial powers may take advantage of his sincerity? No; he fears nothing. . . . Have the courage to read this book, for in the first place it will make you ashamed, and shame, as Marx said, is a revolutionary sentiment." Frantz Fanon, *The Wretched of the Earth*, trans. Constance Farrington (NY: Grove Press,1965), 12, 14, 133.

239. Wilber in *Sex, Ecology, and Spirituality* identifies three major types: nature-nation mystics, deity mystics and nondual mystics (see Chapter Eight).

240. Clifford Mayes, *Seven Curricular Landscapes: An Approach to the Holistic Curriculum* (Lanham, MD: University Press of America, 2003), 125.

241. Ken Wilber, *Spectrum of Consciousness* (Wheaton, IL: The Theosophical Publishing House, 1977/82), 57, 65-71, 86, 94.

242. John Heron, *Feeling and Personhood: Psychology in Another Key* (London, UK: Sage, 1992), 53. In likewise complementary fashion (with its own problematics), Clifford Mayes offers a bifurcation (at FMS-9) of "monistic" (Eastern) and "dualistic spirituality" (Western) as legitimate options for the highest unitive-spiritual landscape or level on the spectrum of development. Clifford Mayes, "A Holarchic Approach to the Classification of Curricula," paper under review, 2007, 30-37.

243. Wilber, *Grace and Grit*, (2000 ed.), front matter.

244. Excerpt from "Kosmic Links" Retrieved June 1, 2007 from http://www.kosmictom/com/category/andrew_cohen/.

245. Wilber, *Grace and Grit* (2000 ed.), front matter.

246. Wilber, *Grace and Grit* (1993 ed.), 7-8.

247. Reynolds, 237-238.

248. Wilber, *Sex, Ecology, and Spirituality*, vii.

249. See this in my earlier discussion in this chapter on "conflict theory" vs. "consensus theory" (also the latter is called "structure-functionalism" in sociological discourse). Truly, here we see Wilber's embedded emancipatory and revolutionary battle— that is, his conflictwork (early-Wilber pre-1997) as a follow through from Habermas and the critical theory (i.e., conflict theory, Conflict Tradition) school of analysis. It is well-known in integral circles that Wilber has written of Habermas as the world's greatest living (sociological) philosopher. Virtually everyone seems to miss this reading of Wilber as a "conflict theorist"—at least, in his early foundations. Troubling as it is for me, the mid-career Wilber seems more "functionalist" (less "radical" as a conflict theorist-philosopher). His students (e.g., Reynolds) seem to really become more so straight-functionalist than Wilber himself. This needs scholarly correction in the future—that is, the future of the Integral Movement itself. Historically, Wilber's vision for a more "public" profile in his own teaching and his vision of an Integral Institute (and spin off "institutions") began in 1997, when he gathered with 100s of "experts" and financial backers

to "go public" in a big way—that is, to be commercially viable. This, dramatically, and synchronistically, is the same year his writing and publishing shifted to being "less radical." And one can only imagine that his need for others, especially financially, led to compromising a big part of his manifestation of the spirit of fearlessness. Again, that's a fearstory . . . Wilber may have let fear (from all involved in the ventures) run ahead and take control too much. Then when 9/11 'hit' in 2001, many of the primary money-lenders dropped out of the projects and Wilber 'has struggled financially ever since, and his work is less politically radical, one could argue, in proportion for his need for support and financial back-up—that is, to go "public" with "profit."

250. Ken Wilber, *A Brief History of Everything* (Boston, MA: Shambhala, 1996), 336.

251. Ken Wilber, *Integral Spirituality: A Startling New Role for Religion in the Modern and Postmodern World* (Boston, MA: Integral Books/Shambhala, 2006), 285. I have not yet poured through every line of this book to look for "flatland" but it is obviously and typically somewhat absent or rendered rather vacantly, just as in his later works (post-1996).

252. Wilber, *Sex, Ecology, and Spirituality*, 515.

253. I wrote elsewhere, "*Eros* and *Agape*, the two 'patterns of Love," in Wilber's (1995, p. 338) Kosmology have met the enemy and it is *Phobos* and *Thanatos*, the two patterns of 'fear.'" R. M. Fisher, "*Thanatos* and *Phobos*: 'Fear' and its Role in Ken Wilber's Transpersonal Theory," unpublished paper, 1997, 2. And Wilber in *SES* (1995) calls them two "patterns of Love" (capital 'L'). Unfortunately, he never got around to naming the (dissociated) shadow-side of the two as "patterns of 'fear,'" or what is appropriately a 'Fear' Project(ion) dynamic.

254. *Fearless standpoint theory* (FST) goes back a long way in this author's prior thinking and writing (inspired by "feminist standpoint theory"). Elsewhere I wrote, "I have returned to systematically and critically read 'Wilber's most controversial book to date' (according to his student Reynolds, 2004, p. 33)—that is, *Up From Eden* (1981), as part of Wilber's Phase II theorizing about cultural evolution of consciousness. This was my first and my favorite book of Ken Wilber's. . . . It is the most neglected of his work by his followers and other readers, in my opinion. It is probably one of the most important contributions of his work to getting at the shadow-side (repressed) of human development. It is the most comprehensive book on the cultural history and evolution of fear ['fear' patterning and organization]." R. M. Fisher, "Fearless Standpoint Theory: Origins of FMS-9 in Ken Wilber's Work," Technical Paper No. 31 (Vancouver, BC: In Search of Fearlessness Research Institute, 2008), 1. This quote is really acknowledging Wilber as a fellow integral fearologist (not a title this author would give to any other contemporary integral thinker). Readers ought to read this technical paper for more details on FST but still so much more needs to be articulated on it that has not been written yet.

255. In his tongue-in-cheek critique of Kramer's "The Guru Papers" and of Goldsmith's "The Way: An Ecological World-view," Wilber in *SES* wrote, "Although [their approach] utterly lack[s] any depth, they make up for that in a type of fearless shallowness . . . that confers great confidence on their reductive pronouncements [i.e., "authoritarian dominance of Descent"] and makes happy the hand of Thanatos that they so freely wave. . . . Hence the Divine egoism coming to us as our glorious saviors, themselves already saved." Wilber, *Sex, Ecology, and Spirituality*, 741. Often his critique is aimed at extreme poststructuralist postmodernism (especially, as egoically, and narcissistically glorified in domain of research and writing called Cultural Studies).

256. Ibid., xi.

257. Retrieved July 5, 2008 from Wikipedia at http://en.wikipedia.org/wiki /Standpoint_feminism.

258. "One of the difficulties with remembering Marx [as a major player of the contemporary Conflict Tradition] is the 'knee-jerk 'marxophobia'' (McLaren, 1997, p. 171) faced by those who draw, however critically or circumspectly, on his work. Marxophobia holds that even to mention Marx is to engage in un-American behavior and by implication to support the genocide and repression exhibited by totalitarian communist regimes throughout history. . . . Indeed, Marcuse, West, Davis, and others draw attention to the democratic impulse in Marx, while Fromm sees Marx as concerned chiefly with spiritual liberation." Cited in S. D. Brookfield, *The Power of Critical Theory: Liberating Adult Learning and Teaching* (San Francisco, CA: Jossey-Bass, 2005), 19. Reader's ought to note that Wilber himself once wrote (early-phase, about the same time he was writing his most prophetic works that were published in 1995-96): "My own feeling is that a theory of world transformation will in effect be a 'mystical Marxism'—that is, it will cover the intricate relations between the 'material-technological-economic' base [*a la* Marx and other materialist thinkers] of any society and its worldviews [*a la* spiritualist aspects and thinkers]." K. Wilber, "Paths Beyond Ego in the Coming Decades," ed. Roger Walsh and Frances Vaughan, *Paths Beyond Ego: The Transpersonal Vision* (Lost Angeles, CA: Tarcher/Perigree, 1993), 263. This latter comment by Wilber, simply an appropriate comment from a critical integral theory (i.e., integrating a balance of materialist-spiritualist values and interests), is never mentioned by his followers, students, or Wilber himself anymore. It is Wilber's "radical" political side that appeared, and unfortunately, later disappeared as Wilber wanted to appear less controversial in America—as the American political scene was turning more and more conservative (Republican) into the mid-late 1990s onward.

259. And tangentially, this critical integral FMSs theory is cursory, and naive attempt to "unite" the disperate (if not desperate) integralisms that are out there today calling themselves "integral theory" of one kind or another, each with their fav "integral thinkers" or "integral theorists" (leaders and institutions and journals) and "integral theories." The conflict is immense (and usually just ignored by the conflicting players who off doing their own thing), and for the most part, not very productive to an overall synthesis or cohesive force that could make significant impacts in the world. That's a speculative opinion, of course.

260. Jean Baudrillard, *The Spirit of Terrorism and Requiem for the Twin Towers*, trans. by Chris Turner, (London, UK: Verso, 2002).

261. Brady, 189-191.

262. Baruch de Spinoza (1632-1677), a Dutch philosopher, was thought to by postmodern philosophers (Deleuze, Guattari, and Sharp) to have outstanding integrity. According to Wikipedia "Spinoza's moral character and philosophical accomplishments prompted 20th century philosopher Gilles Deleuze to name him "the absolute philosopher." And Sharp seems to indicate Spinoza was operating within (somewhat) a *fearless* (FMS-9), albeit, that is not her language to describe his work. Deleuze and Guattari 1994 wrote, "Spinoza is the Christ of philosophers" (cited in Sharp, p. 591). Hasana Sharp, "Why Spinoza Today? or, 'A Strategy of Anti-Fear,'" *Rethinking Marxism, 17* (2005), 591-608. Wikipedia excerpt Retrieved July 5, 2008 from http://en.wikipedia.org/ wiki/Baruch_Spinoza.

263. "'The Theatre of the Absurd'. . . a phrase used in reference to particular plays written by a number of primarily European playwrights in the late 1940s, 1950s, and 1960s . . . the style of theatre which has evolved from their work. The term was coined by

the critic Martin Esslin, who made it the title of a 1962 book on the subject." Retrieved from http://www.123exp-art.com/t/04224091988/.

4

EDUCATION AS LIFE-LONG LEARNING:
Do We Really Want to Raise Fearless Children?

One generation . . . could transform the world by bringing into it a generation
of fearless children. . . . Education is the key to the new world.
                                                                    - Bertrand Russell

This quote has always taken my breath away, not because it is some simplistic, idealistic or spiritual romantic view, but because it was delivered by a
very staunch rationalist, secularist, and critical eminent international Western
male philosopher, the late Bertrand Russell[1] (1872-1970). I wish I could believe
it was true that Education is the key to a new world. With all doubts in mind, I
pursue in this chapter my specific recommendation (ideal) for fear manage-
ment/education (FME) as a source of renewal that can begin to transform the
way we conceptualize Education in the 21st century.

The previous three chapters have offered theory for the last two chapters.
Chapter Four examines further our contemporary educational context, particularly in the highly technological and developed nations of the Western world.
I briefly examine the embedded relations of "educators" (parents, caregivers,
leaders, etc.) in the culture of fear (including fearism and adultism)—that is
Fear's Empire. I conclude that most of our schooling (i.e., fear education) regarding fear and fearlessness is well behind the times.

Demands of the future, coming in many ways, serves to worsen the situation through largely outdated psychologies and pedagogies of fear. I extend a
modernist definition of education into a postmodern critical view of life-long
learning, so that we can better understand the role of fear management *as* education—and thus, open up the so-called 'expert' *discourses on fear*[2] and how best

to manage it to a critical pedagogical analysis. Of course, managing fear ('fear') is inevitably about managing humans but it is not limited to that. We have to include systems and structures (architectures and landscapes), which also need to be managed (redesigned)—based on a new paradigm or imaginary of 'fearlessness.'

Lastly, I cover the work of three important contemporary and diverse educators on fear (Henry Giroux, Parker Palmer, Rick Ginsberg) and critique their work as a practical application of the Fear Management Systems (FMSs) theory presented in earlier chapters. It would take a book to give due justice to the themes brought forward here and for the issue of education and possibility of raising fearless children. Space is limited, so I merely stir questions, make outrageous claims, and for those interested I point out ways to pursue issues further.

Introduction: 21st Century Educational Context

"Knowledge is the best cure of fear caused by ignorance." This quote from a website on snakes,[3] is very common in the history of ideas and Western philosophy. Similarly, scholar Ruth N. Anshen in the mid-60s described the shifting emphasis to which knowledge ought to be used, as crises in the 20th century were clearly going to continue into the future:[4] "Knowledge . . . no longer consists in a manipulation of man [sic] and nature as opposite forces, nor in the reduction of data to statistical order, but is a means of liberating [hu]mankind from the destructive power of fear."

Knowledge, education, modern living—all a 'promise' of redemption from fear and superstition that has plagued premodern humanity. Myth or reality? Whatever the case, there is enough partial truth in this *knowledge* vs. *fear* claim for it to continue to stick and remain very popular in common discourses. However, the "fear" I have addressed in this book is not just individual or collective psychological (or cognitive-based) fear(s) but 'fear' patterning. I mean 'fear' as a construction embedded in fearism (and adultism[5]). I mean 'fear' as an addiction (i.e., addictive pattern/process = cycle of hurting/violence).

Where coming to know the unknown may help solve some fear(s), the situation today is more complex and well beyond what a basic psychology of fear can deal with—a point I have made all along as a transdisciplinary fearologist. Educators are being challenged to no longer rely on only simple common discourses, habits, 'value-neutral' psychologies and pedagogies of fear. My dream is for the field of Education to divorce (or at least separate) from the hegemonic domination of the field of Psychology—at least, until we educators can think for ourselves about topics like the emotions and learning, fear ('fear'), and fearlessness ('fearlessness'), risk and safety/security in a postmodern historical, cultural (and artistic), philosophical, spiritual, and political context.

Unfortunately, Psychology and the modernist biomedical (scientific) model it heavily relies upon, have largely been controlled by the State (elite and *status quo*), just as so much of Education has been. Joanna Bourke, in *A Cultural History of Fear* makes this point repeatedly in regard to how political (war-based) agendas take control of both psychological and educational domains of a society under the rhetoric of "safety and security" (i.e., 'emergency') measures.[6] This pattern she noted goes back more than a hundred years before 9/11 and the Bush administration's reactions and return to conservativism in educational policy. Readers may note, overall, that I take a "critical psychology"[7] stance as opposed to the dominant approach of a so-called "value-neutral" stance of Psychology-wedded-with-Education today.

I opened this book (Preface) with the general question: What foundation can we build upon to enact 'great cause' toward what sociologist Elise Boulding calls a "culture of peace" and what I would call a "culture of fearlessness"; rather than what we have now with a dominant societal agenda which reproduces a predominant "culture of fear" and "war culture"? Arguably, the latter produce fear-full children, who become fear-full adults, even though the expression and kinds of fear(s) may look different on the surface at different ages. As Thomas Merton reminded us in the opening of this book, as well, a fear-full person following the 'Law of Fear,' rather than the 'Law of Love,' is going to be a violent person, more or less, in some way or another. Is it really that simple?

In this chapter I begin to address the complexity of raising and educating children in a culture of fear as the predominant context of the 20th-21st century. I have not found a better, more poetic and poignant, introduction to the problematic *postmodern educational context* of the times than the four lines penned by French author-philosopher Albert Camus in 1946, just after the end of WWII (and the end of the "promise" of Modernity):[8]

The 17th century was the century of mathematics;
the 18th century that of physics;
the 19th century of biology; and
the 20th century is the century of fear.

To add a (post-9/11) fifth line: [and] *the 21st century is the century of terror*. That says it all in a nutshell, as to what 'reality' has turned out to be for us humans living in the so-called "First World." Albeit, I am not claiming "terror" is all there is in our new century. I am merely saying we cannot ignore its vast impact and dominance which has created an undeniable "climate of fear." The postmodern mood of doubt of progress is vivid in Camus's existential complaint. The unthinkable modern atrocities (natural disasters left out for the moment), still act as 'ghosts' witnessing our unfolding human and technological growth: the Holocaust, nuclear attack on Hiroshima-Nagasaki, various ethnic cleansings and wars, various nuclear plant and chemical spills, global warming, 9/11 and post-9/11, 'melt down' of the global economic system.

It is logical to me that any emancipatory or non-violent foundation for our future, is ultimately educational. We are going to make the "Great Turning" (*a la* Korten) as societies and individuals from fear to fearlessness, from immaturity to maturity, not by force but because we are openly learning, creating, and using intelligence to do so. Living in a century of fear/terror does make this task a good deal more complex and challenging. However, the energy is 'a stir' for some significant transformations for many. To enact fearlessness (FMS-7), at least in part, by a few, as core to that foundation, we are going to require a new framing of the kind that Jeanne Segal offered us earlier in this book: *we are not bad, we are frightened* (or as Brian Massumi suggested *we may have become fear*). I have no doubt such an ethical transformation in our way of seeing ourselves and each other, as simple as that gesture offered by Segal, could make such a great difference in our socialization and education in the future.

Then add the historical fearlessness principle to that foundation: *when fear arises, so then does fearlessness* (whether we recognize it or not). The FME agenda is one of developing knowledge for making recognition possible: that is, developing a critical literacy of fearlessness, and perhaps as Chris Griscom suggested, developing the "fearless self" that is our divine essence. In more secular, and simple terms of possibility thinking, "we know deeply that the other side of every fear is a freedom."[9] These ideas have immense potential to negate, or at least counter-balance, the heavy desperation and despair that accompanies living in chronic fear without vision of anything beyond fear and more fear to follow— and thus, more suffering. Albeit, living in Fear's Empire, unfortunately, most people are not aware of this. 'Ignorance is bliss.' But I am not talking of an ignorance in a common sense way of merely being naive (i.e., un-learned, un-awake, un-aware, un-mindful) about something; I speak rather of *ignore-ance* as an active (perhaps, unconscious) form of *resisting* learning something more, something new, something that will force one to change the way they value, think, form subjectivities, and hold certain beliefs as invincibly sacred. Ignore-ance in this sense can be both healthy and unhealthy for growth and development, depending on what learning is being resisted, by what means, and to what ends.[10] It makes me think how and why this book's messages are so often resisted.

Add one more aspect to the emancipatory foundation: the *gift of fearlessness*, as mentioned in the last chapter. To live so as to not create fear in others unnecessarily or pass on your fear to them, is indeed a great gift—especially, as we look at the current dynamics of the culture of fear which capitalizes on passing on the fear ('fear' pattern) virus and fearism itself. What new forms of education are needed for these new and challenging times?—is a vast question with many smaller questions and lots of details, all beyond the scope of this book. The Credo of Fearlessness I provided in Chapter One is the beginning of a statement one may refer to now and then, as we build a new "School of Fearlessness" on the planet (i.e., many schools and other sites of emancipatory teaching and learning), like nothing we've seen and like nothing, perhaps we have dared imagined.

I wish to imagine and offer you a quick summary of what my FME agenda is all about. As a fearologist, if I were to meet an "expert" on fear, be they a secular psychologist or maybe a spiritual guru, I would ask them what they thought of the idea of a Fearlessness (R)evolution and if they thought the Educational System ought to be dedicated to nurturing fearless children and adolescents in the next generation? And I would tell them, that as I listen to their answers, I would be classifying the discourse and FMSs that they utilize. If they asked why I do that?, I would tell them that is one of the important things a researcher-educator of FME does. Such a practice involves my concern for the development of a healthy and sustainable humanity *via* a set of social practices. It's about time that human beings put all knowledge (and discourses) about fear ('fear') and fearlessness ('fearlessness') on the same platform, without excluding any of them. These experts' (or non-experts') responses would be recorded among many others' views. This equalizes their validity to exist and recognizes they have some partial truth to tell—but not *the* only truth. This approach I promote is good pluralist thinking. It values diversity, with criticality, as the basis of any democracy. Everyone has a right to their view and to be heard (in principle, anyway). This is a great pluralistic idea of late-modernity, which attempts (ideally) to level the playing field of differential power relations—that is, of the dominant and subordinate 'voices' in societies.

I'd tell these 'teachers' (experts) that as a postmodern fearologist and critical pedagogue, I must however, go one step further beyond merely validating their diverse views. Not only do I classify and then place all FME discourses on the same platform, I discern and critique them from a 2nd or 3rd-tier perspective of fearlessness, and locate the discourses these experts use along a developmental and evolutionary continuum or spectrum of consciousness worldviews, which I have labeled FMSs 0-9 (Chapter Three). Wilber's critical integral theory, a post-postmodern approach, guides me to do so. Pluralist arrangements are good but not enough for critical literacy and discernment of fearlessness ways.

I'd tell these experts that my first goal of this FME work is to put everything about fear and fearlessness 'up-for-grabs'—that is, I put it up to be seen, to be critiqued, and to let people see what the discourses (and advice) is, relative to the other discourses available among humanity's accumulative intelligence. Yes, we ought to be able to compare, pick, and choose—what FME approaches, knowledge, and advice, we think most appropriate for our own uses in various cases. I do this to create an "Option Curriculum" for *fear education* in the 21st century; with a clear distinction made between emancipatory fear education and an oppressive *pedagogy of fear*[11] (cf. Miller's "poisonous pedagogy"[12] concept).

Regarding an ideal Option Curriculum, I want to ensure there is no power-over "hidden curriculum" (ideology) lurking in the expert's FME discourses that listeners or readers may be manipulated by, without knowing. The criteria for what is "propaganda" and what is good elicitive educative practice are brought out and a dialogical approach to knowing is encouraged. The vulnerability of the learner ought to be taken into account by the teacher and/or expert. And a humbleness is required by experts—meaning, that just because they may be a content-expert on fear and fearlessness (FME) does *not* equate necessarily that they are good critical pedagogues (i.e., good teachers, educators) on this topic or in general.

That is an image of the ideal fear education I would like to see, eventually. The Fear Problem, fearism, the 'Fear' Matrix, or Fear's Empire, are all too powerful of contexts to ignore or dismiss lightly. Experts, *via* increasing professionalism, have taken over so much of the "advice-giving" of highly industrialized civilizations in the last century or so. We require empowered learners from the grassroots to discern, and find their own "expertise" both inside themselves and by utilizing good holistic-integral knowledge. We ought not ever forget how 'fear' itself shapes power-knowledge-fear dynamics that have an agenda, at some level, to not reveal the truth about how fear ('fear') predominantly rules us. The fearologist and critical pedagogue in me enters the conversation with experts through a "hermeneutics of suspicion" like that the philosopher Paul Ricoeur wrote about—not closed-mindedness, but curious suspicion of the role that fearism is playing in all our discourses of FME—especially experts in powerful and influential positions. That same healthy suspicion (but not 'fear'-based), includes critique of my own discourses of FME. Learners and teachers (and experts), if they aren't already, are invited to begin practicing this holistic-integral approach to FME.

I am not claiming there are no authorities regarding FME, nor am I saying there should not be such, I am merely saying a good starting point for FME ought to be a curious doubt, in postmodern fashion, of any authoritative 'voice' on the topic. And equivalently, an attitude of deconstructing the discourses spoken or written or performed is required—followed by an attitude of reconstruction, where everyone builds their own curriculum and pedagogy, more or less, as to what they want to take from the FME and what they don't. They ought to also know why they so choose. It ought not be based on mere habit or intuitive hunch alone; and it ought not be based on desperation ('fear') which grabs the first answer to 'fix' pain and fears. I have provided a structure and model for such discernment on reasonable integral grounds. Unfortunately, it does ask us to do our homework and it demands a good deal of attention and energy. I realize, this is a hard sell these days.

This is my future vision. It will not happen overnight. And for so-called realists, pragmatists, survivalists, and ideological zealots, that is simply not good enough. They all know, as their experience has proven, that people are afraid of change, even when it is the best thing for them. Conclusion: you have to make them change, they claim. And the sooner the better, because there is an "emergency" (the safety and security discourse card is played)—and so they make their authoritative "fearless" plans for reform or possibly revolution—and make them without public or democratic processes. There simply isn't time for that.[13] Now, these change-makers return to 'fear' (and its cousins, shame, guilt) as a most efficient motivator of change. I challenge such ideas (and conventional wisdom) though, as I recall reading somewhere a cute quip: *people are not afraid of change, they are afraid of someone trying to change them*. Big difference! Regardless, as the Machiavelli's and Nixon's of the world know, fear is a better motivator than love—that is, if you are a propagandist and not an educator.

Do we have time left for that change in our attitudes towards FME or will we go extinct because we did not manage our fear and crises well? If we do or do not, is not the concern here. The crises (real or imagined) we face today and tomorrow will merely push the universal transformative dilemma—that is, to "grow or die" as George Land[14] would say, sooner rather than later. Focusing on that question of extinction is likely 'fear'-based itself and thus it diminishes our overall intelligence to come up with better solutions. In the moment, more important things are afoot than trying to predict an unpredictable future. In the end such a question ends up merely *scaring ourselves to death* over it.

I suggest an alternative radical direction for thought beyond the fear of mass extinction—yet, not suppressing nor denying the real feelings that go with an impending sense of danger, real post-traumatic affects, and potential further massive loss and trauma. My neighbor in the co-op housing units where I lived had a big sign on his door: "I'm not sick of Global Warming, I'm sick of Global Warning!" Aren't we all getting 'sick' (literally) from one scare after another—one face of fearmongering after another—on the news, or next door? My neighbor's sentiment is one I relate to and one I have critiqued based on how environmentalists, like Al Gore, (mis-)use the current culture of fear for their own convenience to sell their 'emergency' messages. Of course, just about every business or political party enterprise is capitalizing on this too. Indeed, I have pain and grief every day with the loss of quality I experience in the world of the early 21st century. I process it appropriately *via* healing and turn the energy of grief to a futuristic vision and what I can learn from it to help and improve things.

Key word: *learning*. In describing our "pedogenic illness" (*a la* Ferguson) we inherited in the industrial-military complex of the modern Western world, Marilyn Ferguson's view fits my own: [15]

> If we are not learning and teaching we are not awake and alive. Learning is not only like health, it *is* health. . . . [but unfortunately] schools have been the instruments of our greatest denial, unconsciousness, conformity, and broken connections.

Most of pre-modern and modern school learning has characteristically been "shock learning," which is fear-conditioned learning by any other name. Scare-after-scare is not the best way to learn. And it is still going on today in a culture of fear far too frequently, along with "maintenance learning," both of which futurist-type educators like myself and progressive leadership gurus like Warren Bennis have critiqued. Bennis wrote (citing the futures research report of Botkin et al. *No Limits to Learning*, 1979),[16]

> ['maintenance learning' - most common, transmits the known about a known world that is expected to be recurring; compared to 'shock learning' when we are overwhelmed by rapid change] 'humanity waits for events and crises that . . . catalyze or impose this primitive learning by shock [fear]. . . . Shock learning can be seen as a product of elitism, technocracy and authoritarianism. Learning by shock often follows a period of overconfidence in solutions created solely with expert knowledge or technical competence and perpetuated beyond the conditions for which they were appropriate.'. . . both maintenance learning and shock learning are less learning than they are accepting conventional wisdom. Society or one's family or school says this is the way things are . . . and you accept what you're told as gospel. You forget that there is a self that must be listened to.

I cannot think of a better articulation of the way human beings have traditionally learned about "fear" itself (meaning: the sorry state of FME at the present time). The maintenance ("equilibrium perspective")[17] and shock learning approaches are not good enough for the complexity of our times and the future coming. How can a shock learning based on fear teach us how to learn about fear? It depends what the goal is? And the goal of shock learning is (like "future shock" *a la* Toffler or "shock doctrine" *a la* Klein) only more fear, not less. The culture of fear dynamic feeds on, and is definable, by this exact learning pattern, which is more accurately called "conditioning" not "learning." Critical adult educator Roger Boshier noted (following Botkin et al.) that as the future becomes more complex with more crises, there is a distinct style of politics and ideology that flow along with "learning by shock." He says it is fundamentalism [both secular and religious] and it is "by definition . . . the opposite of learning. It is a reaction to undigested complexity and, in some parts of the world, gnawing at the social fabric."[18] Indeed we need a new psychology of learning beyond the hegemonic "fear of freedom" (*a la* Fromm) that seems to rule most all school learning and socialization in the industrial-military complex of Fear's Empire. Far too many critics to mention have also lamented this about this fact.

I think one of *the* wisest postmodern challenges to maintenance and shock learning is provided by literary critic and teacher Shoshana Felman, who named our era the "post-traumatic century." She has worked with Lacan's post-Freudian ideas of psychoanalysis and its role in education. She asked, regarding,

> *Trauma and Pedagogy-* Is there a relation between crisis and the very enterprise of education? To put the question even more audaciously and sharply: Is there a relation between trauma and pedagogy? In a post-traumatic century, a century that has survived unthinkable historical catastrophes, is there anything that we have learned or that we should learn about education, that we did not know before? Can trauma *instruct* pedagogy? Can the task of teaching be instructed by the clinical experience, and can the clinical experience be instructed, on the other hand, by the task of teaching?

Felman turns disciplinary chauvinism on its head—both educational and clinical worlds and authorities/experts, she claims, need to ask how the other can mutually *instruct* the other. And to do so within a context of a post-traumatic century (a century of fear) from which our learners and clients come from, are coping with, and are attempting to move beyond.

Similarly, other critical theorists have asked how we ought to make political meaning of social practices and 'Education After Ground Zero?,' that is, after dropping the H-bomb in Japan or "Education After Auschwitz"—as they bring us to awareness of the dark shadow-side of human knowledge/progress /education and the intimate exchange with "crisis" and "pedagogy."[19] I interpret Felman's questions as a needed critique of "educators" (meaning, trained teachers and administrators K-12 and in post-secondary levels) who are fearful, if not terrified, of entering the deep domains of the existential and spiritual psychological/spiritual and ethical and political concerns of humanity. Notice, Felman does not oppressively criticize their being fearful, she merely asks us to ask more about the contemporary role of fear (trauma, crisis). Typically, teachers want to leave such issues of "psychology" to psychologists and biomedical psychiatrists, therapists and social workers. They also want to leave the "irrational" and "arational" domains to others, because Education (meaning: knowledge) is of the domain of the Rational[20] (as Western Greek philosophy have largely constructed it).

In general, institutional professional teachers dare not trespass and act outside of their professionalized rigid "teacher" role—a role largely constructed for them by the State and elites who pay their salaries—a role legitimated by State powers to keep the *status quo* in place, unquestioned. I have experienced this deep fear in teachers and whole public educational systems for decades—which is really 'crazy' because fear (i.e., fearuality) is such a foundational aspect of human experience and learning. Elsewhere, I have written a report on the status of what I call "fear education," noting the lack of a holistic-integral approach.[21] The critique I offer is not so much what to do with fear ('fear'), it is what to do with our dominant FME and "reform" discourses, which are simultaneously teachings and political discourses of power/knowledge, as Foucauldian educational theorist Thomas Popkewitz[22] has, among others, argued.

Teachers believe, oddly enough, they are experts at learning, not mental health. Is that line really so easy to draw? When does learning become therapeutic and therapeutic become learning? It is socially constructed (even arbitrary). It can be changed. Felman, like myself, knows that the divide is fuzzy—much as is the line between these disciplines arbitrary and unsustainable; especially, as fear *via* trauma and trauma *via* fear is unavoidable as the contingent everyday way we are living our lives, at least in most countries on the planet (post-9/11). Of course, Felman rightfully is asking the clinical experts likewise to overcome their fear and specialization to ask how they can better become critical pedagogues in our times, and not retreat safely to their discipline that needs not be informed by any source beyond the clinical world of knowledge.

I would add to Felman's questions and ask the educational and clinical world to come out from hiding, and further expand and embrace how sociology, anthropology and other disciplines and experts (and lay persons) can also inform pedagogy for our times and future—and *visa versa*, how a *pedagogy of fearlessness* is distinct from a pedagogy of fear, and how such pedagogies *instruct* all of these disciplines of knowledge. This is why we need a holistic-integral approach to FME? But I am jumping ahead and down a road that is beyond the scope of this book.

And learning comes from teaching and *visa versa*—cradle to grave (lifelong), not merely in traditional schools. However, let's start with a useful critical distinction between *schooling* and *education*, as defined by progressive educational theorists Aronowitz and Giroux:[23]

> Schooling . . . takes place within institutions that are directly or indirectly linked to the State through public funding or state certification requirements. Institutions that operate within the sphere of schooling embody the legitimating ideologies of the dominant society. Such   institutions generally define their

relationship to the dominant society in functional and instrumental terms, though, of course, room is also provided for forms of critical pedagogy.

Aronowitz and Giroux, as reconstructionists of schooling rather than anti-schooling radicals,[24] note that "critical pedagogy" (grounded in "critical theory")[25] is often gutted by "constraining ideological and material conditions" of the power elites of the State-run schooling. Often, in my experience, the "critical" ends up in the curricula of (public) schooling under the rhetoric of a liberalistic politically-neutered "critical thinking." They continue, showing the contrast whereby *education* is ultimately the term best used for authentic emancipatory aims:

> Education is much more broadly defined, and used in this context takes place outside of established institutions and spheres. In a radical sense, education represents a collectively produced set of experiences organized around issues and concerns that allow for a critical understanding of everyday oppression as well as the dynamics involved in constructing alternative political cultures [futures]. As the embodiment of an ideal, it refers to forms of learning and action based on a commitment to the elimination of class, racial and gender oppression [I would add adultism and fearism]. As a mode of intellectual development and growth, its focus is political in the broadest sense in that it functions to create organic intellectuals, and to develop a notion of active citizenry based on the self-dedication of a group to forms of education that promote models of learning and social interaction that have a fundamental connection to the idea of human emancipation.

Aronowitz and Giroux's postmodern distinction is both radical and integrative — that is, it combines traditional with the new and relevant of the times. It is both modern and postmodern — beginning a 'bridge' to what I would call *critical integral education* (*a la* Wilber). Unfortunately, there is not the space in this book to deal with comparing those forms. Aronowitz and Giroux, like Wilber, have embraced the better aspects of premodern, modern and some postmodern educational ideas and have transcended them with integrative and (somewhat) integral-like perspectives. Thus, their philosophies are both conservative and liberal in the widest political sense. Readers will judge my own work on FME likewise — both conservative and liberal and something beyond.

My point is to show that FME belongs in both schooling and education domains but particularly in the emancipatory education domain, which Giroux later has identified as "public pedagogy." Postmodern education (e.g., Aronowitz and Giroux) has rightfully attacked the State ownership and Corporate privatization (and fearmongering[26]) that has accompanied so much of Western schooling and public education under the economic (managerialism) and excessive-capitalist ideology of neoliberalism and neoconservativism for the past several decades.[27] Educators as "transformative intellectuals"[28] and public pedagogues are, for Aronowitz and Giroux, to embrace the entire living curriculum of life/learning outside of formal schooling walls and economic-capital formats for learning. Thereby, the Cultural domain has been a large part of the postmodern education they promote. Not surprising then, as I agree with this notion of public pedagogy, FME is most concerned with the concept of "culture of fear" and "World's Fearlessness Teachings" as foundational to a good postmodern education about 'fear' and 'fearlessness' for the 21st century.

"Teachings" and "learning" are everywhere, and even more radical post-structuralist notions of "life-long learning" (e.g., see Richard Edward's conceptualization of a postmodern "learning society"[29] and Zygmunt Bauman's notion of education for a "liquid-modern era"[30]) include but transcend traditional ideas of "educational systems" owning and appropriating *the* only legitimate power of knowledge. FME is everywhere, and everyone has a right to make out of it what they think is *best*—albeit, well-informed, ethically responsible, and non-fear-based in their learning and discernments. Good education (and FME) most values the process of 'learning to learn,' as the cliché goes. It less values getting a product.

The critical literacy of fearlessness promoted in this book is to be attained by a unique learning process and embrace of the knowledge from traditional and radical, sacred and secular, high culture and low culture, and so on. Such a task requires a commitment from learners—an *epistemological fearlessness*[31] itself, which can be found theoretically within FMS-7. No educational theory or model to date, that I have seen, takes a FMS-7 approach to fear education (FME). Elsewhere, I have researched on the potential of Wilber's critical integral theory for advancing educational theory into a 2nd-tier post-postmodern or integral perspective,[32] but we are a long way from that yet.

Education and Fearlessness

Vinobā Bhave (1895-1982), a prophetic educator-activist-scholar in India and honored student of Mahatma Gandhi, suggested that,[33]

> . . . our whole education should be based on fearlessness, and so should the whole social and political structure. . . . The goal of education must be freedom from fear. . . . Until education is really based on fearlessness there is no hope of any [significant or transformative] change in society.

In characteristic contrast to the Eastern view (e.g., Bhave), Western philosophers are less confident in fearlessness as the base of good education. Plato (428 BCE-348 BCE), an important W. Greek educational philosopher argued,[34] "Let us not forget that there are two qualities which should be cultivated in the soul—first, the greatest fearlessness; and, secondly, the greatest fear." Plato was concerned with the problem of "bravado" (excessive unethical boldness) in youth especially without the discipline of respect and reverence for elders which fear is supposed to ensure. This difference is a large topic that educators have yet to fully engage in debate, and I will not attempt it here.

More pragmatic, the challenge before us can be formulated in regard to seriously asking: *how do we want to design and implement FME in the 21st century?*—for individuals, groups, organizations and even nations. The self-reflexive aspect to the question is: *who is competent to design and implement*

FME based on a fearlessness approach (or fearless standpoint theory)? And
*how might we best include the World's Fearlessness Teachings into our curricu-
lum and socialization?* I can barely touch on these broad important questions
here. Reality is—no one, no organization, at least not in the mainstream, is likely
even thinking about such systemic questions. I have not seen or heard of such a
venture.

There was one FME project in which I was involved. In the mid-1990s,
with a family therapist in Colombia, an interdisciplinary group of helping professionals worked with Bogota's civic officials to create a 'fear' vaccine for
25,000 children on Day of the Dead (Halloween)—which crossed borders into
Canada.[35] Education and therapy borders also were crossed during this unique
and successful public pedagogical project of FME on a grand scale. No doubt
other examples of such projects have occurred, and more are expected in the
coming decade. Despite these unique efforts, beyond the 'school walls,' fear
education is still immature. This book is a first to responsibly awaken leaders
who might intuit the great need for such a systematic approach to FME now and
in the future. From a 2nd-tier perspective, a critical integral theory's overall purpose is to improve FME for the Spiral (see Chapter Two) but on a practical level
it has to be an education that aims to, and is more or less effective in, undermining the culture of fear and Fear's Empire ('Fear' Matrix). In order to limit the
conversation for this short chapter, let's look first at what the situation is in
terms of fearlessness in academic and professional educational writing (K-12,
adult, and higher education). The focus is to apply FMSs theory to a few examples of discourses used by 'major' players.

The Eastern gift of fearlessness, which I have mentioned in FMS-7, ideal as
it is, has implications for education/socialization. It has roots in premodern
Hindu educational philosophy as one spiritual guru pronounced might be: "The
first great virtue derived from education is fearlessness. Knowledge destroys
fear."[36] Both caring (compassion) and knowledge (wisdom) are at the base of all
ethical development. Arguably, great quality emancipatory education must be
based on fearlessness to produce it. In the Western schooling discourses there is
something quite different. Particularly in the 1990s, with a FMS-5 (Orange,
Modern) discourse in educational circles, one could witness an emergent FME
movement among diverse advocacy groups and professionals—for example, we
saw calls for: "schools without fear,"[37] "peaceful school communities," "safe
schools,"[38] teaching math "without fear,"[39] teaching peace "without fear,"[40]
"fear-free education zones"[41] and a plethora of calls for ensured "safety" and
"security" in general. Mostly, it was (still is) "victim culture" (*a la* Furedi) calling for mostly State-power (authorities and agents thereof) to take charge and
make people feel "safe" (a virtually impossible task, and a dangerous road to go
down). Based on my research of these movements (and texts), the concept of
"fearlessness" or "fearless" was not mentioned nor is "fear" defined or conceptualized with any systematic rigor or postmodern sensibility. Typically, they are
1st-tier FME discourses without a full holistic-integral or emancipatory trajectory; though the spirit of fearlessness is there, because the fear is there in the
people.

Arguably, and ironically, the "without fear" discourses may feed Fear's Empire, as much as try to manage 'fear' better. At the same time, FMS-5 is clearly the operative modernist discourse behind the design of the Universal Declaration of Human Rights (and the UN)—regarding the right to a freedom "without fear," as mentioned earlier in this book. One could also, if there was space, make an argument that the "culture of trust"[42] discourse, common in organizational development and business management literature, and now in educational policy and schooling literature, has similar FMS-5 foundations with a bit more FMS-6 (Green).

The "without fear" discourse is similar to another trend in North America. You may recall from earlier chapters that the NO FEAR! slogandia of popular (youth) culture (and business) in the West took off in the 1990s as well. A growth industry, it was (still is) cool to 'diss' fear—totally! It was (still is) all pretty much depoliticized (i.e., psychologized, individualized) egocentric rhetoric (i.e., 1st-tier discourse of fearlessness = spirit of fearlessness in immature stages). Earlier in this book *no fear* was shown to belong to FMS-0, although one wouldn't want to claim that the NO FEAR! slogan is only retro-regressive, but that is a hypothesis, because there was an enormous emergence of the "culture of fear" dynamic in the 1990s. As well, the early 1990s represented the end of the Cold War, the fall of the Berlin Wall, and just maybe a renewed thrust of freedom for all (or its opposite)—thus "fearless" and "without fear" kinds of rhetoric are likely FMS-9 (Coral, Nondual) being downloaded into a more egocentric FMS-3 ("Fuck You!" kind of NO FEAR! rebel *bravado* energy). It is complicated but worth further future analysis because the quasi-fearless or false *fearless* discourse is pervasive at this time in the Western world, and arguably, is spreading like a 'virus.' It is likely quite *retro* and pathological, involving a Wilberian pre/trans fallacy (Chapter Two).

Plato's ancient caution in the quote above is thus reasonable to some extent, but it also needs to be critiqued with nuance from FMSs theory. Troubling confusion, and or outright objections, may thus easily arise when we feel and/or think about a vision of raising "fearless children" or "children without fear" (see later below). This latter topic is a good one to get people of all kinds talking, or at least get their heart beating and body temperature rising, about the nature of public (civic) life today and the role of education/socialization. To apply FMSs theory, let's turn to three important contemporary 'players' regarding fear and fearlessness and emancipatory education, as examples to critique. I picked these three among others,[43] especially because of their overt labeling of the "culture of fear" as the major contemporary context of educational theorizing and critique.

Henry A. Giroux

An icon of critical theory and pedagogy (*a la* Paulo Freire) in the field of education and communications, Giroux, a secular humanist, is the most important educator writing on the culture of fear today. Apparently, he began using the term "culture of fear" in a 2001 paper, written prior to 9/11,[44] with many to follow. He has long criticized politics and educational policy (mainly in the

USA), for its increasing domestic militarization in public spaces, deep distrust and fear of youth by adults and school leaders, and oppression due to class, gender, and race. Though not the first to write explicitly about the "culture of fear" in the field of Education, he is the first (and so far only) educator to use those terms in a published book title (2003) in the field of Education.[45]

Always a fighter for the marginalized (under-represented), for oppressed teachers, the democratic sphere, civil society and the role of "school culture" to provide nurturance for them, he (along with Aronowitz) in the early-1980s onward condemned the trend of school policy and conditions in much of the USA (and elsewhere). In 1985 he criticized eloquently a fear-based reformist schooling agenda based on "near hysterical description of education as providing human capital to commerce or socialization models that speak to the limited task of transmitting dominant culture"—and, he was determined to recreate emancipatory conditions and theory for a curriculum which would replace the current ones but "refrain from finding techniques to displace it by fear."[46]

What kind of FMS(s) does Giroux employ in his texts? I'll sample only his early works here. He is all for going beyond fear and anxiety as primary motivators, but he never fully defines "fear" in the context of his work nor attempts to make it all 'bad.' He doesn't gloat on about it in the way some fear-positivists do. Rather, his main fear management concepts are *civic courage* and *hope* as counter-methods and pedagogies to excessive fear in education. He never mentions the words or concepts "fearlessness" or "fearless" or "without fear." He appears cautious to not build up some idealistic liberation vision of freedom from all fear. He's no revolutionary of fearlessness. Rather, he is a pragmatist educator/leader/intellectual, in common American fashion, in that way. Let's listen to the discourse of FMS-5 (predominant) in Giroux's 1983 text:[47]

> [drawing from Agnes Heller's 1976 notion] Civic courage is a central concept here and it represents a form of behavior in which one thinks and acts as if one lived in a real democracy. It is a form of bravery aimed at exploding reifications, myths, and prejudices. At the same time, civic courage is the organizing principle that informs and defines a notion of literacy grounded in the grammar of self-determination and transforming praxis.

When we place this FMS-5 courage (rationalistic) discourse within his emphasis on behavior (social action), we get a FMS-4 discourse that not surprisingly uses the term bravery. He continues:[48]

> . . . [re: citizenship education] students should be educated to display civic courage. . . . its goal is a genuine democratic society, one that is responsive to the needs of all and not just of a privileged few. . . . [citing Heller] 'The fundamental bravery of this way of life is not military heroism but civic courage. Whoever says no to the dominant prejudices and the oppressing power.'

Giroux's and Heller's discourse is beyond pure FMS-4 "military heroism" or FMS-3 rebel (bravado) heroism. The intellectual maturity of civic courage, rather, shows the FMS-6 discourse (courage as well) with a postmodern sensitivity to the marginalized (victims).

Readers may review the criteria for the FMSs again from Chapter Three. For Giroux "the development of civic courage is the bedrock of an emancipatory mode of citizenship education." His pedagogical solutions are implicitly to move *away from fear and towards courage* in students (and teachers and parents). His solutions are based on critical thinking (rationalist discourse), clarifying values (cognitive emphasis) and building political structures of resistance.[49] Typically, he doesn't talk about emotions or feelings, other than to criticize the current literature in the field of citizenship education as bordering on "despair" (meaning, too negative and "frozen"). He asserts we need vision "to dream, imagine, or think about a better world."[50] He is a bit of a hope-monger[51] (i.e., "hope" is constant and explicit in his pedagogical discourse. I'll not cite those uses of hope, but it has a FMS-4 root in it. The latter hopeful and courageous discourses are typical of FMS-6 (with aspects of FMS-2 re: dream, fantasy, magical, imaginary techniques). He says he doesn't see his kind of civic courage (citizenry) as only involving debate that is intellectual and based on insight, but also on action (behaviors). However, like most critical pedagogues, his view of *fear* and *courage* are 'thinly' theorized and he does not overtly draw on the WFTs, for the most part, in order to articulate what wisdom of FME is available philosophically and spiritually. He's more a typical political culture activist when it comes to FME.

He also doesn't raise criticism of his own views as good critical theory and pedagogy ought to—because of that lack, his FME discourse tends toward repetitive bombastic propagandist (ideologism), even though he critiques those things in other's. I have heard him give talks and as compelling and passionate as he is, he is a bit of a 'bull in a china shop.' One can't get a word in edge-wise and he "tells" you how to best manage fear, his way, and does not offer other views to consider as having partial truths as well. His delivery style in "lecture" seems to use intimidation (fear), even if he doesn't know it or intend to do so (it is this aspect that strikes me as FMS-3 strategy with a bravado-masculinism base). All of his discourse is pretty much 1st-tier (still 'fear'-based in a subtle way). His FME is not holistic-integral (FMS-7). His writing on the "culture of fear" is disappointing, as he never cites anyone else writing about it, and thus, his work lacks collaborative richness (FMS-8); and, he never well defines the conception either. It seems to be used by him (and/or his publishers) for 'sexy' affect in marketing (FMS-5) his previous repetitive mantras.

Parker J. Palmer

Three years before Giroux, Palmer, a Quaker, spiritual teacher and educational guru for some, used "Culture of Fear" (a first) as the title of a chapter in his very popular book *Courage To Teach* (1998).[52] A year before that he published what I see as one of the most insightful, transformative, and postmodern (2nd-tier) FME dictums in the field of education of any contemporary writer in the field. He wrote,[53] "Education's nemesis is not ignorance but fear. Fear gives ignorance its power." One can hear echoes of Aung San Suu Kyi's dictum here, from a few years earlier. Recall, she said it is not power that corrupts but fear (Chapter One). Palmer in this dictum challenges the idea that mere "rational" (reason) discourses on knowledge/education are the answer to the fear problem. He actually attacks the objectivism (and scientism) beneath arguments that dominate Western educational philosophy, curriculum and pedagogical rationale.

Courage to Teach contributed to his swelling impact within some progressive circles of education, as he challenged directly and vociferously the "culture of fear" in the field of Education (especially, in university academic culture). Palmer, promoting a conception of "Integral Life: Integral Teacher"[54] (not to be conflated with or mistaken for *integral* as used in this book or by Wilber), however, is no fan of "fearlessness" or "fearless," or "without fear" and rather promotes *courage* and *trust* to defuse the negative impact of excessive fear (cf. VanderWeil as another one of the educational fear positivists and Palmer fans).

His FMS-6a and 6b discourse (with some 2nd-tier FMS-8 spiritual underpinning), comes through in an autobiographical reflection about his youthful desire:[55]

> As a young man, I yearned for the day when, rooted in the experience that comes only with age, I could do my work fearlessly. But today, in my mid-sixties, I realize that I will feel fear from time to time for the rest of my life. I may never get rid of my fear.

Despite Palmer's well-tested wisdom and compassion, on many practical levels working effectively with people as a teacher and human being, his discourse, arguably, is not matured or evolved (yet)—that is, as a center of gravity in 2nd-tier and across the threshold of 'Fear' Barrier 2. His discourse (in the quote above) lapses back into an egoic-personality-based self-identity to make his 'weak' (implicit) argument against fearlessness (FMS-7, 8) or fearless (FMS-9). "I may never get rid of my fear," he wrote. That may or may not be true, it depends. But that's not my critique. FMS-7, 8, 9 do not "think" in this 'I'-centered (and 'my'-centered) way when it comes to going beyond fear and/or emancipation from fear ('fear') (see Chapter Two and Three). Most disappointing to me is to witness a unique and important leader/educator/model (in his 60s) make a solid prediction about the rest of his life (and development), without (apparently) consulting the WFTs or other post-adult possibilities developmentally (i.e., 2nd-tier and 3rd-tier, as in Figure 2.1).[56]

Although Palmer is not a hope-monger in the way Giroux is, his "belief" (at FMS-6) is apparently fixed and pre-determines much of what will be in his own development. One has to ask, is Palmer afraid of developing too far, too fearlessly, beyond his spouse, family, peers, spiritual community, and culture? Why? He obviously intuited a maturational "fearless" (FMS-9) possibility in the quote above. Yet, his dominating attitude in the discourse is hardly one of emancipatory transformative learning, and that is a critique he (and others) may wish to examine more closely, as Palmer teaches a transformative learning context to others.

I sense his impact on thousands of educators (especially in the US) is enormous and thus, his FME teachings are one of the biggest obstacles to an integral FMS-7 emergence in the field of education. He is still, with both feet, embedded in the 'Fear' Matrix and glimpses beyond it (FMS-6b), while drawing somewhat on his Quaker background of the spiritual (FMS-8). One cannot dismiss his true courage and insight to see that the power of fear and culture of fear has to be named and claimed as a matrix of sorts that reproduces fearism/terrorism (albeit, Palmer does not use "fearism" in his conceptualizing). This courageous acknowledgment is the truly wonderful breakthrough that Palmer has brought forward. However, his discourses on fear and how to manage it, that I have read, are decidedly (although not completely) traditional, modernist, and unnuanced.[57] He does not investigate with a critical epistemology, or seem to question the nature of fear ('fear') itself and that it may not be understood by us humans as well as we think (i.e., no FMS-7 in his thinking). Of equal neglect, is the omission to engage the culture of fear critics (e.g., Furedi, Giroux, Glassner, etc.), and thus, this makes his conclusions about the culture of fear in his own critique, limited and "personalized." His promotion of things holistic, integral, trustful, and whole, etc. are also suspect because he doesn't acknowledge the developmental and evolutionary full spectrum of consciousness with an East-West sensibility (i.e., integral wholeness and a healthy form of *fearlessness* and *fearless*), as this book does.

Rick Ginsberg

The last example of applying FMSs theory to education comes in a recent (2008) unsuspected mainstream journal publication (*Educational Policy, 22*(1)). It is devoted to the role of fear in education, albeit, focused on contemporary America. This genre of a total journal issue being devoted to contemporary problematics of fear ("new scholarship on fear," as Brissett called it)[58] is welcomed indeed, and is part of a trend seen in other academic journals in the last few years (post-9/11), for example: *Hedgehog Review: Critical Reflections on Contemporary Culture, 5*(3), 2003; *Capital & Class, 80*, 2003; *Social Research, 71*(4), 2004. Note that the *Educational Policy* issue is four years or more behind the other disciplines in this regard of featuring "fear" as an academic topic of concern. This is characteristic, as the field of Education (primarily schooling) is conservative by definition (although, it need not be). It is usually not the forerunner of radical debate on critical cultural and political issues. And I suspect it may be one of the last disciplines to acknowledge that it produces more fear than it eliminates through knowledge (i.e., FME). That said, one cannot find the terms or discourses of *fearlessness* or *fearless* (FMS-7 discourses) included in any of these recent academic works, suggesting they are all 1st-tier in their FME discourses. Education as a field is not unique. The discussion of fearlessness, apparently, is even further behind than serious discussions about fear, as we saw in the writing of Giroux and Palmer previously.

The *Educational Policy* (2008) issue is remarkable, nonetheless, as this is the leadership and administration/management domain of Education. Although there are 11 articles in this issue with "fear" in their titles, the two lead articles are co-written by Rick Ginsberg, School of Education, University of Kansas, and that caught my attention to feature his work here. He is lead author of both articles "Introduction: What's Fear Got to Do With It?," and "The Culture of Fear and the Politics of Education."[59] Ginsberg is not well known as an icon like Giroux or Palmer, but he has been long interested in the softer human and emotional side of leadership. In the co-written book (Ginsberg as lead author), he concluded that fear is underneath all the really negative and nasty behaviors in most organizations, including the field of Education. He sees fear as an "emotion" (within psychological discourse) and "flight-fight" behavior pattern. Nothing very radical there: "Fear can spur you on to achieving great heights or cloud your thinking and lead you astray," he remarks.[60] Implicitly then, the real FME issue for Ginsberg, common to most other educators, such as Lehr and Martin, is to ask: "Does fear have a positive side? If so, how do we determine when fear is working for us and when fear is working against us?"[61] However, unlike most educators, Ginsberg systematically brings in the context for making that discrimination through his citing of the sociological and political culture of fear critics like Barry Glassner especially, and Corey Robin. However, Ginsberg does not articulate in any depth these critics' views nor create a theory of the culture of fear and how it might actually morph our everyday psychological conception and definition of fear and how best to manage it. Thus, Ginsberg's discourse remains within scientific modernist discourses of FMS-5 and within FMS-6, the latter which is sensitive to the emotional (affective) and "human side" of educational and leadership enterprises.

Although Ginsberg in his "culture of fear" article is highly critical of American education, he is not radical in wanting to completely overhaul it. He is not likely to be accused of being anti-American (rather, he more so falls into bravado and questionable Americanism[62])—yet he points out the corrupt propagandist (some times hysterical) fear-based elements in policy development by the State, who are overly influenced by media. He cites fearmongers Richard Nixon and Adolph Hitler back-to-back to open the article.[63] But then, there is in his discourse no FMS-7 questioning of our need to better understand fear (and the culturally modified versions of 'fear'), beyond psychologism which has dominated the definition of fear as a "feeling or emotion." He doesn't question how the predominant 20th-21st century political and sociological contexts (i.e., propaganda and affective politics), that he nods to in citations, may alter our very subjectivities (as Massumi suggested), nor does he point out they may alter the very FME that is hegemonic already—of which critical educators may have to challenge, deconstruct and reconstruct. He is not, for the most part, a very creative postmodern thinker on FME. In good FMS-5 (masculinist) fashion, his primary values and interests regarding fear and its management, are calmly rational analysis and planning *via* information and knowledge, in order to overcome the negative (disruptive) side effects of too much fear as our motivation for actions.

Ginsberg, unlike Giroux and Palmer, engages (in a minor way) the culture of fear critics as he develops his FME philosophy and teaching. One thing they all have in common is they have largely ignored any of the research and theorizing I have done, and that I have sent their way for feedback. They seem content with their own views and choose not to engage in dialogue with me or each other, that I know of. They don't cite each others' work either. I find that narrow-minded, if not epistemologically unethical, and unprofessional practice. That said, I applaud sincerely their work on FME, we can use all we can get. It is all there to learn from, all with its own validity and partial truths as we continue to build our collective intelligence of which the spirit of fearlessness remains the 'thread' of all such initiatives (such a position is FMS-7 and some FMS-8). That position is a high-calling, I realize—and calls forth different archetypes for an image of the "teacher" or "educator" beyond State controlled images/roles. Perhaps, Clifford Mayes calling for "The Teacher as Shaman"[64] is a good example of a FMS-7 "Outlaw" or "Sacred Warrior" (post-adult), or "Fourth Order" discourse (see Figure 2.1). Even though that is only one, not the only valid one, of many archetypes for teachers at all levels on the spectrum of consciousness and development in evolution.

Fearless Children?

Although this book documents a powerful and provocative, if not mostly underground, Fearlessness Movement (i.e., historical ethical fearlessness) in history and evolution—such a movement or direction is highly contestable. The 1st-tier discourses of FME want nothing to do with it—that is, they see anything "fearless" as a dis-ease or threat to order and control. From a 2nd-tier (FMS-7) position, I have argued elsewhere there is substantial evidence of a universal developmental movement towards a "fearless society" and have included educators (and other social critics, spiritual leaders and philosophers) who support that and promote a notion of "fearless children."[65] There are simply too many important quotes and arguments to make a positive (albeit, cautious) case for raising "fearless children," as space is limited here. Recently, I have found books, websites and programs/lectures offered in the public educational domain (mostly for adults), which use promotional terms like "a fearless approach to learning,"[66] "fearless learning"[67] or "fearless parenting."[68]

Despite these initiatives and titles, one would find it hard to imagine "fearless children" as the goal of public education anywhere, except in maybe some of the radical free schools or alternative education. From what I have read of the supporting texts for "fearless children" by educators, or others, there is a lack of a systematic definition of "fearless" (or "fear"). The term becomes self-evident but not convincing to critics, like myself. If "fearless" is not mere marketing hype (e.g., like "No Fear" discussed in Chapter Three), or pathology (e.g., like "fearless shallowness" as Wilber calls it, discussed in Chapter Two), then it must be grounded in FMS-9 discourse to be worthy of the name. Rarely is that the case from what I have read. Yet, FMS-4, 5, 6 discourses, will challenge FMS-7 discourse, asking: "Surely, Michael, have you lost your sense of priority and proportion of what children in the world need today? You must know the atrocious statistics of child poverty in the world, even in the so-called First

World—it is simply tragic that so many children live without clean running water, sanitation, shelter, food, and die prematurely due to disease and wars. And you say our priority ought to be 'fearless children?' Get real! The children will be a hell of a lot less afraid when they have the basics in Maslow's hierarchy of needs met, and be free from violence." That is a very compelling point of argument (the "safety and security" discourse) against a FMS-9 emancipatory perspective re: children or youth, or adults. I don't disagree with that general critique.

Theoretically, "fearless" (FMS-9) is developmental—you have to grow into it. FMS-9 is not natural or essential, or of our essence, at least not from a critical integral theory perspective (*a la* Wilber, and myself). The conditions and environment plus the developmental stages and lines of individuals are factors in how "mature" one reaches in a life time. The romantic idea of human nature as "fearless" and only oppressive societies make children fearful, is a nice radical FMS-6 liberalist (modern) idea with FMS-2 ("magical child") fantasizing and even with 'new age' FMS-8, with some FMS-9 partial truths. It doesn't, however, hold up well as 'fact,' if one really gets critical-integral and looks developmentally at what children are empirically capable of (let's not pull a pre/trans fallacy). Yet, FMS-6a critics are right in that you also have to get base level needs/priorities clear when we are talking about child-raising and education. FMS-6b (existentialist) critics are *all for* "fear-less" as foundational as an outcome of good safety and security practices (e.g., de Becker). However, we cannot forget that it takes "fear-less" parents and caregivers etc. to create non-violent (peaceful) world spaces to nurture healthy, creative and ethical children to enact "fear-less"—never mind any FMSs beyond that in the 2nd-tier or 3rd.

The real contentious problematic in this discussion however, comes when one moves into a larger historical, social, cultural, political, philosophical, and spiritual analysis of the "culture of fear" as context for children's development, and for socialization and education. Then things get way more complex, and a 2nd-tier FMS-7 perspective really angers the FMS-6 folks. That's my experience anyways. FMS-7 argues that we all have to be better *'fear' critics*.[69] FMS-6 responds: "Michael, so you are hopeful that being a 'fear' critic is going to help the world—the children?" And I respond: "Not really. I choose not to hope for anything. I am interested in systematic critical analysis of 'fear' that is not 'fear'-based itself—and that is what I believe will help matters (e.g., our FME)." Such critical literacy of 'fearlessness' is much better than hope, and it is ultimately much better than trying to obsessively 'put out fires' and forget to 'see what is causing them.' You got it. FMS-7 perspective, pursues critical analysis of 'the causes' and embraces and includes the passion and wisdom of the FMS-6 critique (and all the 1st-tier FMSs) but transcends its limited 'fear'-based modes of analysis of fear ('fear' and 'fearlessness') and how best to manage it.

I recommend a spectrum of understandings and approaches to learning and teaching, based on Spiral Dynamics theory,[70] critical integral theory, and my own FMSs theory. FME has to be more holistic-integral than it is now. Even "peace educators" (like Jan Arnow, for e.g., with FMS-6 discourse)[71] are not supportive of a notion of fearless children but again, definitions are weakly (not holistically) constructed by her to make such claims. Peace educators/activists have to seriously look at Gandhi's ethical "fearlessness" construct in the peace movement and Aung San Suu Kyi's as well, to name a few examples of FMS-8, and FMS-9 (see Chapter One, Three). The peace and non-violence issue relevant to FME, will be taken up, somewhat, in Chapter Five.

I am all for what radical pedagogues Fischman, McLaren and Sunker have challenged of teachers (especially) in a post-9/11 world:[72] "How could we become victims a little less, not innocent but at least conscious consumers? How could we be fearless teachers and critical educators? How could we teach others [children and youth] to be like that?" Teachers, and parents, are far too 'scared' today to be politically incorrect. They are far too frightened to "risk" pedagogically, for fear they will be criticized as putting children (or other teachers, or education itself) at risk, etc. And scared they are by many discourses of 'fear' from diverse sources, which in the vast majority of cases systematically undermines their sense of empowerment (agency).

As long as we are thinking being an "adult" is all there is—is the end of evolution—is the end of our capacities and identities—then, Fear's Empire has won. It has kept us in "adult-slavery" (another twisted form of adultism, I'd guess). My 'maps' of the soul's journey and the basic FMSs theory presented, show that being an "adult" is half-way in our developmental spectrum of possibility. It is half way to becoming fearless. I take that serious, and especially as an educator. The *authentic transformative educator* is one who has, more or less, penetrated beyond 'Fear' Barrier 2. Only with that vision and new identity, perhaps, as a "warrior pedagogue"[73] or "fearless warrior" the likes of some qualities of Che, Malcom X, King, Chávez, or McLaren,[74] and with the integrative sensibilities of the women leaders of the Fearlessness (R)evolution in this book, will any serious reform and transformation occur in the field and discipline of Education.

Ultimately, I recommend focusing on what we "adults" can do differently to get our thinking and social practices beyond the blinders of fearism (Fear's Empire)—and from there, the children will do just fine, progressing as evolution pushes and pulls them—toward *fearless* (our "highest" potential intelligence of "Defense"). FMSs are D.I. (Defense Intelligence) systems. Children will do that because us "adults" are not getting in their way. All my research of decades listening to children, collecting their art and watching them, shows me *they* have their priorities straight: they do *not* want anything, *not* even their basic needs, if it comes with the price tag of "fear." In other words, if it was their 'first choice.' Just ask them. Ask them if they want to be fearless, and ask them what they would do to help the world if they were really fearless? And ask them what they think we (adults) should do to not suppress their 'first choice'? Ask them how they would have us adults manage our fear better?

No child is going to operate fully in FMS-9, at least not theoretically, based on a critical integral perspective. All definitions aside about "fearless," there is a quality and spirit of freedom and fearlessness that exists in humans, regardless of their limitations. We adults (and post-adults) need to listen to it and see what it wants us to do; though listen with informed discernment and maturity, a fearless standpoint, a FMS-7 perspective. The idea of children or especially youth being 'free and fearless' itself raises resistance in most of us, if not loathing and a desire to suppress and discipline *via* punishment and oppressive control management (recall, the psychological research literature that continually describes "fearlessness" as a state of pathology in children; see Chapter Three).

There are, however, good reasons for this vein of 'hatred' of so-called "fearless" youth —for one, because Hitler (mis-)used this idea to promote his pedagogy of the Third Reich. In chilling seductive discourse (sounding like emancipation), Hitler spoke implicitly of his FME:[75]

> My pedagogy is harsh. Weakness must be chipped away. The youth that will grow up in my fortress will frighten the world. I want a brutal, authoritarian, fearless, cruel youth. Youth must be all of this. The light of the free marvelous beast of prey must once again shine from their eyes. I want my youth to be strong and beautiful.

With due caution as to this English interpretation of the German text, this twisted and pathological FMS-3 (and FMS-4) discourse is amazing in mixing "fearless" with "brutal" and "cruel"—and anything else that is seductive to the outraged and hormone-pumped youth of difficult times. It is the discourse of 'war' and 'battle' free from its own self-critique. It is too bad Hitler's 'prey' was not 'fear' itself—or Fear's Empire. Rather, he only fed into it by an immature and toxic FME that wanted to "frighten the world" more than it already was. This is ultimately (pragmatically) a form of fearism *cum* terrorism. The "fearless" of FMS-9 is the exact opposite of Hitler's agenda—or opposite of any fearmonger, or fear-colluder.

In conclusion: rather than asking *Do We Want Fearless Children?*, I'd ask *Do We Want a Fearless Context* to raise and educate amazingly intelligent and ethical children, with great *existential capacity*[76] (FMS-6b onward)? And how would we know when we have a fearless context? We would know because we experience "fearless speech" in children, adults, teachers, etc.; which has been practiced by critical postmodern pedagogues like Peter McLaren and his "pedagogy of revolution" against (Fear's) Empire.[77] A question we who so love an "open society" (so-called) have to ask: But what does it take to create such—and is that the same as a "fearless society"—and what is the role of non-violence and/or violence in its attainment? Big questions, beyond what this book can fully address. Suffice it to say, following the revolutionary pedagogy of one "fearless" educator, Peter McLaren, I have to agree that "The tension between violence and non-violence has remained undiminished throughout modern history and this book does not attempt to exercise a reconciliation."[78]

After the philosophy of the late J. P. Sartre's (1905-1980) existential vision, I close with Hazel E. Barnes's ethical-democratic Sartrean challenge to us all (i.e., FMS-6b):[79] "A society not afraid to envision transcending itself must be made up of persons who are free and *without fear*, but individuals cannot live freely, creatively and safely except in a free and open society" (italics added for emphasis).

And, with all due caution, and developmental and evolutionary sensibility, of which critical integral theory an FMSs theory demands, *not everyone should, nor can be* what revolutionaries may shout about and demand. As much as I admire the educational activists, warriors, and revolutionaries, I find their FME typically lacking a holistic-integral perspective. They do not usually draw on the WFTs enough, nor make their definitions and conceptualizations of the forms of fear and fearlessness (Gandhi a wonderful exception), clear enough.

In contemporary times, in North America, Peter McLaren (with Kris Gutierrez) in 1995 led the educator's 'pack,' so to speak, when they discussed the evolving and threatening postmodern form of fear ('fear'): "we are witnessing the hyperreal formation of an entirely new species of fear."[80] Indeed, and what a great lead that was for the rest of us to follow further in our *fear education*. I recommend the WFTs to assist us in doing so. This book offers up-dated holistic-integral perspectives for life-long learning that have previously not been available in one volume and with one address: that is, the address of *fear management/education*. Critical, radical and revolutionary pedagogues, like any pedagogues, can no longer in good faith, deny, ignore or diminish the essential role of fear ('fear') and fearlessness ('fearlessness') in all their educational initiatives. May Education recover the spirit of fearlessness within and bring it back to its proper emancipatory role.

Notes

1. Excerpt retrieved March 11, 2004 from http://geocities.com/arguivog1/Glauco/HomePage/FightThePower/FTPengl.htm.

2. Although I have used the term "discourse" in a generic, yet political sense, throughout this text, I now come to be more specific that one of the best ways to study fear ('fear') and the culture of fear today is to study the unit that sociologist David Altheide has identified as "discourse of fear." See, for example, D. L. Altheide, "Mass media, crime, and the discourse of fear," *The Hedgehog Review: Critical Reflections on Contemporary Culture*, 5(2003), 9-25. A similar case for a unit-specificity for study, and political strategic study of emotions, has been made by Megan Boler, a feminist educator, in her identification of the "discourse of emotion." See M. Boler, *Feeling Power: Emotions and Education* (NY: Routledge, 1999). In my own work in the paper "Invoking 'Fear' Studies" (2006), I make an important distinction between "discourse *of* fear" (which feeds Fear's Empire) and a "discourse *on* fear" (which attempts to understand and undermine Fear's Empire).

3. Retrieved October 29, 2008 from http://www.uga.edu/srelherp/ecoview/Eco1.htm

4. Ruth N. Anshen, "Epilogue: What World Perspectives Means," in *The Meaning of The Twentieth Century: The Great Transition*, Kenneth E. Boulding (NY: Harper Colophon, 1965), 203.

5. In my dissertation I did not hold back my critique and divorce from the discipline of Education. I claimed that until the field of Education is willing to look at its State-borne, fear-borne collusion in fearism/adultism, "education" is nothing but a furthering of the oppression of human potential and a lot worse things that are leading to unsustainable practices on this planet. I also claimed that fearism is the base 'ism' of all other 'ism' (dis-eases) known in human cultures. The next significant base 'ism' intimately connected to fearism is adultism. "Every human has experienced the targeted

status of youth and oppression of adultism," wrote diversity educators Love and Philips. Barbara J. Love, and K. J. Philips, "Ageism and Adultism Curriculum Design," In *Teaching for Diversity and Social Justice*, eds. M. Adams, L. E. Bell, and P. Griffin (CRC Press, 2007), 370. Indeed, adults are the first Agents of the 'Fear' Matrix we all encounter as human beings, and without healing that adultism and learning about it, it reproduces fearism as 'the power to use fear over others' to gain privileged power, status, control, etc. It is all an addiction to 'power over' (i.e., 'fear' over)—and children, youth, get 'hit' the most. Of course, as we grow up to become adults, we then can reproduce the fearism/adultism dynamic on other children and youth and on and on goes the cycle of violence/oppression/hurting. My research in my dissertation acknowledged that it is almost impossible to find significant text or dialogues happening on adultism in Education circles anywhere. This breeds, in my view (theorizing), the need for a "Rebel" archetype (or Rebel Standpoint Theory) to resist that adultism, and in the more mature stages (i.e., 2nd-tier) this becomes (for e.g.). the "Outlaw" or "Sacred Warrior" archetype (see Figure 2.1). When adultism is recognized in rare cases by thoughtful critics like Love and Philips then it is typically FMS-6 discourse, but I also have outlined a FMS-7 perspective on adultism, whereby it is a type of thinking and discourse that maintains there is no stage of development for humans beyond "adult." In thus denying the realities of "post-adult" development (Figure 2.1), then adultism is even more oppressive and also maintains itself as a 1st-tier outlook on humanity and thus, will be fear-based in many ways—primarily, it engages and reproduces pedagogies of fear (as mentioned throughout this text).

6. Her survey is of the last 150 years in the UK and USA. Joanna Bourke, *Fear: A Cultural History* (Emeryville, CA: Shoemaker and Hoard/Avalon, 2006).

7. I am speaking in terms of "critical psychology theory" like "critical race theory" and "critical disability theory," and so on. These all, unlike the 'norm' theories, do not claim political value-neutrality (which is impossible anyway). See the welcomed edited volume by Dennis Fox and Isaac Prilleltensky, *Critical Psychology: An Introduction* (London: Sage, 1997). I would refer to my own work with the distinction (counter-hegemonic discourse) of "critical fear theory" and not mere "fear theory."

8. Albert Camus (1913-1960) won the Nobel prize in 1957 for literature. He wrote these lines on "the century of fear" first in his underground newspaper *Combat* (as part of the underground French Resistance to the Nazis), and less than a year after the US military dropped the atomic bomb on Hiroshima-Nagasaki, Japan in 1945. Often associated with existentialism, he was devoted to challenging the (postmodern) philosophy of nihilism. Not an author/teacher/artist who directly commented on the fearlessness movement, or used the terms "fearless" or "fearlessness" *per se*, Camus, a leader and defender of the "artistic imagination," was a rebel and Outsider, never easily settling to conform to the mainstream. Anderson compares Camus and French feminist Luce Irigaray, finding them fundamentally alike: "Both write from a position of creative revolt, challenging the terror [fear] exercised by the dominant cultural ideologies. Both accord significant attention to the threat posed by culturally contaminated [fear-based, propagandized] language." The original words of the four lines were in French and have been translated to English by colleagues. They were first found by this author cited in J. E. Corradi, "Toward Societies Without Fear," in *Fear at the Edge: State Terror and Resistance in Latin America*, eds. J. E. Corradi, P. W. Fagen, and M. A. Garretón (Berkeley, CA: University of California Press, 1992), 267. K. H. R. Anderson, "*La première Femme*: The Mother's Resurrection in the Work of Camus and Irigaray," *French Studies*, 55(2002), 30.

9. Marilyn Ferguson, *The Aquarian Conspiracy: Personal and Social Transformation in the 1980s* (Los Angeles, CA: J. P. Tarcher, 1980), 294.

10. Aronowitz and Giroux discussing "blocks" to development, draw from Shoshana

Felman's writing on "ignorance" as active negation (e.g., unconscious process), and "refusal of information"—suggesting that "ignorance is a form of knowing that resists certain forms of knowledge. Ignorance is, in a sense, a form of knowledge defined by the way it actively resists certain knowledge. The pedagogical question that emerges from this type of analysis is what accounts for the elements of repression and forgetting at the core of the dynamic of ignorance [what Felman pursues in later works as part of crisis/trauma processes of resistance to learning, of which researchers Smith and Jones call "neophobia" as a fear of learning anything new, and Ferguson called "gnosisphobia"]; put another way, what account for conditions that posit for individuals or social groups a refusal to know or to learn." *Fearism* is systematic ignore-ance of the truth about fear and fearlessness. Any new FME will have to deal with this curricular and pedagogical dilemma of ignore-ance (which I have called, relying on Wilber's work, a great 'fear' pattern as *Thanatos*). Stanley Aronowitz, and Henry Giroux, *Education Under Siege: The Conservative, Liberal, and Radical Debate Over Schooling* (South Hadley, Massachusetts: Bergin and Garvey, 1985), 159. S. Felman, "Psychoanalysis and education: Teaching Terminable and Interminable," *Yale French Studies, 29*(1982), 29-30. Martin R. Smith, and Ellen T. Jones, "Neophobia, Ontological Insecurity, and the Existential Choice Following Trauma," *Journal of Humanistic Psychology, 33*(1993), 89-109.

11. I use *FME* (fear management/education) throughout in a generic sense, which can be good quality or not so good. Similarly, with *fear education* I use it as a short-hand term for FME. The *pedagogy of fear* is a different beast, of which I am highly critical and against. Brent Malin describes it well, as he critiques it simultaneously: "Pedagogy of Fear- Fear is a very real social construction with profound consequences in our everyday lives. As such, it is an important component of the cultural processes with which we concern ourselves on a daily basis, and one too often overlooked by cultural critics. If we take fear seriously as a specifically social phenomenon, rather than only as a personal experience, then we open our eyes to the intricate workings of a variety of cultural practices. Our education into the discipline of fear begins early. . . . Although no formal curriculum exists, the pedagogical tactics are well in place. What are 'dunce caps' and 'sitting in the corner' but tools for teaching the unembarrassed child to keep his or her unruly actions in check?. . . . We were to learn these lessons well because those who didn't—those who didn't fear authority, feel remorse, or worry about humiliation—would surely wind up as delinquents, mobsters, and serial killers. After all, aren't psychopaths people who don't feel an obligation to the social order, who don't fear the consequences of a breakdown of social rules. . . . fear and its friends are not our own, but held in some communal stock of public pathos." Brent Malin, "Be Afraid, Be Very Afraid: The Pedagogy of Fear," *Bad Subjects*, May-June, 2000. Retrieved October 17, 2002 from http://bad.eserver.org/issues/2000/50/malin.html. See also on the "pedagogy of fear" the following: M. Tatar, *Off With Their Heads!: Fairy Tales and the Culture of Childhood* (Princeton, NJ: Princeton University Press, 1993); Michael Welton, "Cunning Pedagogics: The Encounter between the Jesuits and the Amerindians of 17th Century New France. Canadian Association for the Study of Adult Education Proceedings. Retrieved March 12, 2004 from http://www.oise.utotoronto.ca/CASAE/cnf2003/2003 _papers/mweltonCAS03a.pdf.

12. Alice Miller, *Thou Shalt Not Be Aware: Society's Betrayal of the Child*, trans. by Hildegarde and Hunter Hannum (NY: Farrar, Straus, Giroux, 1985).

13. Critical postmodern pedagogue and cultural critic, Giroux, makes a good argument for how "emergency time" is constructed by elites and other change-makers to create extreme conditions for policy changes and draconian actions (i.e., breaking normal laws), and thus, create the perception that safety and security is at-risk, and everything is

at risk (e.g., we are at war). This emergency time thus, based on fear (and false "truths"), usurps normal time, "public time," and democratic time. President G. W. Bush's way of handling 9/11, and the War on Iraq, etc. is a classic recent case of this nightmare distortion of fearmongering for political and economic, not moral nor democratic, ends. Totalitarianism and dictatorship regimes operate in just this created "chaos" and "emergency" constructions. See Henry A. Giroux, *The Abandoned Generation: Democracy Beyond the Culture of Fear* (NY: Palgrave/Macmillan, 2003), 7-15.

14. George Land, *Grow or Die: The Unifying Principle of Transformation* (Leadership 2000, Inc.). [original published in 1973]

15. Ferguson, 282.

16. Warren G. Bennis, *On Becoming a Leader: The Leadership Classic* (Da Capo Press, 2003), 67-68.

17. Roland Paulston, Roger Boshier, and many other adult educators have charged that the dominant hegemony of maintenance learning is operational within the "equilibrium perspective" (or lens), which is that of the *status quo* (i.e., structure functionalism). The alternative or critical lens is a "conflict perspective" with transformative learning as its method, all of which is shunned by the equilibrium perspective. This is a topic I have mentioned in this book earlier but is beyond the scope of what can be covered here.

18. Roger Boshier, *Introduction to Adult Education* (Adult Education 412) (Vancouver, BC: The University of British Columbia, Continuing Studies and Technology, 1996), 43.

19. See for example, F. Pöggler, "'Education After Auschwitz' as a Perspective of Adult Education," in *Adult Education in Crisis Situations: Proceedings of the Third International Conference on the History of Adult Education*, eds. F. Pöggler, and K. Yaron (Jerusalem: The Magnes Press, 1991), 223-230. The late critical theorist, Theodor W. Adorno (1903-1969) first coined this phrase (question) in essays after WWII, and a new sense of a new future/context was required after the tragedy of so many traumatic decades of modern history. In 1966 Adorno wrote a now famous passage in his essay "Raising Children After Auschwitz": "The very first claim for education is that there will be never a second Auschwitz." Excerpt from an article by Ido Abram, 1998, translated from a Dutch local newspaper. Retrieved May, 2, 2006 from http://www.humanbing.demon.n/ humanbeingsweb/Library/abram.htm. One can feel the "negative" approach, and postmodern skeptical (precautionary principle of fear) working in these discourses. Some neo-Marxian postmodern critical pedagogues have recently picked up on this theme, for example, Henry A. Giroux, "What Might Education Mean After Abu Ghraib: Revisiting Adorno's Politics of Education," *Comparative Studies of South Asia, Africa and the Middle East*, 24(2004), 3-22.

20. See the argument made by artist-researcher-teacher, Barbara Bickel, "Embracing the Arational Through Art, Ritual and the Body," Paper presented at the 3rd International Conference on Imagination and Education, July 13-16, 2005 (Burnaby, BC: Simon Fraser University). B. Bickel, "From Artist to A/r/tographer: An Autoethnographic Ritual Inquiry into Writing on the Body," *Journal of Curriculum and Pedagogy*, 2(2005), 8-17.

21. I wrote, "This report offers the first known summary on the status of *fear education* [analogous to *sex education*] in Western society, and probably the world. The results of studying fear education for the past 13 years casually, and the last four years intensely, have shown that fear education [like FME] is not yet an entity (or field) self-reflective, never mind critical of itself. Fear education is now as inadequate as sex education was 100 years ago. With such an important topic as fear (and fearless), it is concluded that the lack of systematic study of fear education itself, may be equally as much of a problem to healthy human/global functioning, as fear is." R. Michael Fisher, "Report on the Status of

Fear Education," Technical Paper No. 15 (Vancouver, BC: In Search of Fearlessness Research Institute, 2003), 1.

22. Thomas Popkewitz, *A Political Sociology of Educational Reform: Power/ Knowledge in Teaching, Teacher Education, and Research* (NY: Teachers College Press, 1991); T. Popkewitz, *Struggling for the Soul: The Politics of Schooling and the Construction of the Teacher* (NY: Teachers College Press, 1998).

23. Aronowitz, and Giroux, 131-132.

24. Ibid., 132. "For radical teachers, it is imperative that strategies be developed that take as their starting point an understanding of how knowledge and patterns of social relations steeped in domination come into being in schools, how they are maintained, how students, teachers, and others relate to them, and how they can be exposed, modified, and overcome, if possible. We suggest that such a strategy can be organized around a [transformative] pedagogy that argues for a notion of critical literacy and cultural power, while simultaneously presenting a strong defense for schooling as a public service."

25. For these terms, generally, I am using the equitable and scholarly treatment of them by Stephen D. Brookfield, *The Power of Critical Theory: Liberating Adult Learning and Teaching* (San Francisco, CA: Jossey-Bass, 2005).

26. Aronowitz and Giroux, 64. The 1980s-90s American moral panic of "educational excellence" that came along with the organizational business reform movement from *In Search of Excellence* by Tom Peters et al., was a "standards" movement by any other name (e.g., "quality" management, "corporate culture" agenda, etc.). The crisis in schools and problem of "illiteracy" etc., came as a counter-revolt to much of the 1960s-70s revolt and emergent progressivist (often Leftist) movements. Aronowitz and Giroux noted: "There is, of course, a serious problem with the literacy of the American people. Some aspects of this question reside in elementary skills. But, for the most part, this is a misplaced emphasis, a slogan that is oriented to promoting fear and anxiety so that a new wave of school policy [reforms] may be accepted." I for one, was interested in the slogan and how it caught on, but I quickly realized in 1989 that a new version (more mature) was required and that is why I coined "In Search of Fearlessness." The opening introduction to *In Search of Excellence* tells it all, as the authors wrote: "Wherever we have been in the world . . . we can't help but be impressed by the high standards of cleanliness and consistency of service we find in every McDonald's hamburger outlet. . . . it really *is* extra-ordinary to find the kind of quality insurance McDonald's has achieved worldwide in a service business." Thomas J. Peters, and Robert H. Waterman Jr., *In Search of Excellence: Lessons from America's Best-Run Companies* (NY: Harper and Row, 1982), xix.

27. See Stanley Aronowitz, and Henry A. Giroux, *Postmodern Education: Politics, Culture, and Social Criticism* (Minneapolis, MN: University of Minnesota Press, 1991).

28. Aronowitz and Giroux, *Education Under Siege*, 23-45.

29. Richard Edwards, *Changing Places?: Flexibility, Lifelong Learning and a Learning Society* (London, UK: Routledge, 1997).

30. "Having compared the pedagogical ideas and educational settings of 13 different civilizations, Edward D. Myers noted (in a book published in 1960): 'the increasing tendency to view education as a product rather than a process. When it is regarded as a product it is conceived as something that can be 'got,' complete and finished [solid].'. . . . Myers did not like what he found; he would rather have education treated as a continuous, whole-life endeavor. . . . In its 'solid' stage, now bygone, modernity—itself a reaction to the frailty of the pre-modern *ancien régime* fast losing its holding power—was obsessed with durability [terrified of non-durability]. . . . The ultimate horizon of the modern [educational] overhaul of the human condition was a society in the 'state of per-

fection'. . . . The radical transformation was to result in a rationally conceived, scientifically designed and forcefully built order that would make all further transformation redundant and uncalled for. . . . It seems, though, that the present [postmodern or late-modern] crisis is unlike the crises of the past. The present-day challenges deliver heavy blows to the very essence of the idea of [modern] education." Bauman then talks about how the "liquid-modern" world less 'solid' seeks a freedom of movement and the new, embraces the unknown, etc. but it too is frightened in a different way—by the "duration of life." Clearly, both of these educational frameworks are still fear-based, and an integral FME ought to include and transcend them on the way to fearlessness. Zygmunt Bauman, "Educational Challenges of the Liquid-Modern Era," *Diogenes, 50*(2003), 18-19.

31. I have adopted this ethical, educative, transformative, and methodological notion from Kierkegaard's existential (spiritual) writings. See R. Johnson, "Neither Aristotle nor Nietzsche," in *Kierkegaard After MacIntyre: Essays on Freedom, Narrative, and Virtue*, eds. J. J. Davenport, and A. Rudd (Open Court, 2001), 155; H. J. Cloeren, *Language and Thought: German Approaches to Analytic Philosophy in the 18th and 19th Centuries* (Walter de Gryter, 1988), 131; Roland Paulston, "From Paradigm Wars to Disputatious Community," *Comparative Education Review*, August (1990), 395-400.

32. R. Michael Fisher, "Postmodern Developmental Philosopher *Par Excellence*: Ken Wilber's Role in Education, Part 1 (Introducing Ken Wilber)." Paper under review, *Interchange: A Quarterly Review of Education*. As well, I have discussed this in R. M. Fisher, "Ken Wilber and the Education Literature: Abridged Annotated Bibliography." Invited and hosted by holistic educator, Dr. Ron Miller, at http://ww.pathsoflearning. net/resources_writings_Ken_Wilber.pdf

33. Shriman Narayan, Vinobā, *Vinobā: His Life and Work* (Popular Prakashan, 1970), 125. V. Bhave, "The Intimate and the Ultimate," Excerpt from M. Hern, *Deschooling Our Lives* (Stoney Creek, CT: New Society Publishers, 1996). Retrieved June 2, 2006 from http://www.learningnet-india.org/Ini/data/ publications/revive/vol1/v1-6b8.php.

34. Plato, *The Dialogues of Plato*, trans. Benjamin Jowett (NY: Scribner, Armstrong, 1874), 28. [original may have been published nearly 2000 years ago]

35. This Colombian-Canadian 'Fear' Vaccine Project was created in collaboration with Maria Solorzano in Bogota, Colombia. She organized musicians, therapists, teachers, artists, holistic health practitioners and many others. The Canadian event was much less dramatic and involved far less resources and numbers of participants. The joint-results were to be documented and published but communication with Ms. Solorzano ended without any explanation a few weeks after the event. She did however inform me of the great success (reduced violence on the streets on that day of traditional social chaos in Bogota) in her view. I have no access to the data they collected. With Bogota's very unstable and violent political history (terrorism) I have grave concerns of her safety. It is a long, interesting, and somewhat tragic story to be told some day.

36. Ranganathananda, *Eternal Values for a Changing Society* (Bharatiya Vidya Bhavan, 1984), 408.

37. J. B. Lehr and C. Martin, *Schools Without Fear: Group Activities for Building Community* (Minneapolis, MN: Educational Media Corporation, 1994); A. H. Francis, ed., *Schools Without Fear. Proceedings of the 14th Annual International Alliance for Invitational Education Conference* (Greensboro, CA: International Alliance for Invitational Education, 1996); N. Wetton, *Schools Without Fear* (Forbes Publications, 1998).

38. S. Miller, J. Brodine and T. Miller, eds., *Safe by Design: Planning for Peaceful School Communities* (Seattle, WA: Committee for Children, 1996); J. L. Arnette and M. C. Walsleben, *Combating Fear and Restoring Safety in Schools* (NCJ 167888) (Washing-

ton, DC: Department of Justice, Office of Justice Programs, Office of Juvenile Justice and Delinquency Prevention, 1998); R. R. Verdugo and J. M. Schneider, "Quality Schools, Safe Schools: A Theoretical and Empirical Discussion, *Education and Urban Society, 31*(1999), 286-307.

39. P. Bernstein, *Math Without Fear: A Concrete Approach to Mathematics* (Philadelphia, PA: Lutheran Settlement House, 1992).

40. Jan Arnow, *Teaching Peace: How to Raise Children to Live in Harmony—Without Fear, Without Prejudice, Without Violence* (NY: A Perigree Book, 1995).

41. D. Conway and R. R. Verdugo, "Fear-free Education Zones," *Education and Urban Society, 31*(1999), 357-367.

42. For example, Mark Olssen, John A. Codd, and Ann-Marie O'Neill, *Education Policy: Globalization, Citizenship and democracy* (Thousand Oaks, CA: Sage, 2004), 196. These researchers show that all the neo-liberal "accountability" rhetoric and tactics are actually undermining the "culture of trust" in educational organizations, when they are intended to improve it. Another example, of the ironic and paradoxical "culture of fear" dynamic I have talked about throughout this text.

43. Other than my own work on this topic, with more space, I would have included bell hooks, Claudia Eppert, Kathyrn Ecclestone, Pauline Lipman, Catherine Scott and Elisebeth VanderWeil, etc. For an in depth annotated bibliography on these authors and others (with full references), see R. Michael Fisher, "Culture of Fear and Education: An Annotated Bibliography," Technical Paper No. 28 (Vancouver, BC: In Search of Fearlessness Research Institute, 2007).

44. Henry A. Giroux, "Mis/education and Zero Tolerance: Disposable Youth and the Politics of Domestic Militarization," *Boundary: An International Journal of Literature and Culture, 28* (2001), 1-92.

45. Henry A. Giroux, *The Abandoned Generation: Democracy Beyond the Culture of Fear* (NY: Palgrave Macmillan, 2003).

46. Aronowitz and Giroux, *Education Under Siege*, 20.

47. Henry A. Giroux, *Theory and Resistance in Education: A Pedagogy for the Opposition* (South Hadley, Massachusetts: Bergin and Garvey, 1983), 116.

48. Ibid., 201-202.

49. In general terms (not FME terms) re: his strategies of resistance to hegemony, his approach is somewhat integral (but not developmental in terms of a Wilberian notion of development sensibility). However, impressively, he sees thinking, values, behavior—and individual and collective aspects (subjective and objective) as important to utilize as domains of knowledge and reality—this is, quite AQAL (to use Wilber's terms; see Chapter Two). This is why Giroux is a postmodernist.

50. Ibid., 203-204.

51. Some of Giroux's discourse can be traced to Freire's "pedagogy of hope." Paulo Freire, *Pedagogy of Hope; Reliving Pedagogy of the Oppressed*, trans. R. R. Barr (NY: Continuum, 1994). I highly recommend Peter Taubman's postmodern critique of hope-mongering in education (especially, in the Western world, and America). He wrote: "What I am going to argue is that at this particular [conservative] historical moment, teaching, and writing about teaching and education, may mean giving up hope, renouncing the desire to cure, reform, or rescue. . . . [i.e., if they are based on hidden or repressed fear ('fear')] It may be that hope for a better world, the desire to cure, and the belief in agency are not only defenses [fears] against the terror of the abyss but in fact work against what we hope for, what we desire, and what we believe in. In fact they may keep us from exploring at a deeper level. . . . They may keep us from exploring what is of most importance to us." P. Taubman, "Teaching Without Hope: What is Really at Stake in the

Standards Movement, High Stakes Testing, and the Drive for 'Practical Reforms,' *Journal of Curriculum Theorizing, 16*(2000), 25. Recall, as I argued earlier in this book, *fearlessness* is the recommended replacement for *hope* in FME in the 21st century, based on holistic-integral theory of FMSs—even though, likely Taubman would disagree with this, as much as Giroux. For them "fearlessness" would sound too utopian (idealism) —which it really isn't, as I argue based on a lot of research—it is merely developmental and evolutionary. For another supportive reference of the value of radical hopelessness in learning and therapy, with counseling attention, see also Gary Nixon, "The Transformational Opportunity of Absolute Hopelessness and Non-Attainment," *Voices: The Journal of the American Academy of Psychotherapists,* Summer (2001), 55-66. In African-American studies, Stevens develops a unique (worthy) "trans(per)formative pedagogy" poststructuralist conception based around "radical hopelessness," see Maurice E. Stevens, *Troubling Beginnings: Trans(per)forming African-American History* (NY: Routledge, 2003).

52. Parker J. Palmer, *The Courage to Teach: Exploring the Inner Landscape of a Teacher's Life*. San Francisco, CA: Jossey-Bass, 1998), Chapter 2.

53. Parker J. Palmer, "Teaching in the Face of Fear," *NTLF, 6*(1997), n.p.

54. Parker J. Palmer (interviewed by Sarah, ed. *Green Money Journal*), "Making the Difference: Integral Life; Integral Teacher," Retrieved May 11, 2004 from http://www.greenmoneyjournal.com/article.mpl?newsletterid=17&articleid=142.

55. Parker J. Palmer, *A Hidden Wholeness: The Journey Toward an Undivided Life*. San Francisco, CA: Jossey-Bass, 2004), 105.

56. My guess is that his Westernized exoteric Christian ontological discourse (i.e., Quaker theology and practices of humbleness) are highly impacting him (and his FME) to this day with its rigid "dualism" (1st-tier perspective) re: human development. There is a rather non-creative complacency in Palmer's FME discourses, and that is likely due to a complacency within his spiritual/religious tradition. My discernment is not to make this 'wrong' or 'bad' but merely discern its location on the spectrum of FMSs, and to then utilize that in critique, in regard to how he or anyone applies such a FMS as part of FME practices.

57. I have studied the recent 2007 transcripts of Palmer (excerpts and interpretations of his interview) in the doctoral research of VanderWeil (2007). His FME discourse, like VanderWeil's, is primarily based in FMS-6 (some FMS-5, some FMS-2, and some FMS-8). They skip FMS-7 (critical integral) analysis of FME (recall, "spiritual by-pass," as I have called it earlier in this book), as do most all "fear-positivists." They believe they are "holistic," and are to some degree, but relative to the FMS-7 position, they are not, and their discourse is still embedded in 'fear'-based patterning itself. Thus, one could not classify their FME work as fully emancipatory, from a critical integral (e.g., Fisherian, Rosadoian, Wilberian) perspective.

58. Wilson N. Brisset, "Bibliographical essay on fear," *The Hedgehog Review: Critical Reflections on Contemporary Culture, 5*(2003), 115-123.

59. Rick Ginsberg, and Bruce S. Cooper, "Introduction: What's Fear Got to Do With It?," *Educational Policy, 22*(2008), 5-9. Rick Ginsberg, and Leif F. Lyche, "The Culture of Fear and the Politics of Education," *Educational Policy, 22*(2008), 10-27.

60. Rick Ginsberg, and Timothy G. Davies, *The Human Side of Leadership: Navigating Emotions at Work* (Greenwood, 2007), 114.

61. Lehr and Martin, 37.

62. Ginsberg and Lyche, 11. "Nearly 25 years later [post-*Nation At-Risk* report], this sense of risk and fear still pervades the media. Ignoring the fact that the United States today is unequivocally the worldwide leader in commerce, industry, science, and technological innovation—not to mention military superiority—the onslaught of sensational

press regarding education continues." I wonder what these authors would say in October-November of 2008, when the American economy and country is in grave crises in all those domains he mentions—and hardly, the "worldwide leader" in them all. This triumphalist chauvinistic Americanism in Ginsberg's discourse is FMS-4 (with a lot of FMS-3 "bravado" more than humble virtue of "courage" (FMS-5, 6). It is not close to "fearlessness" as in FMS-7). This is a further indicator to me of Ginsberg's questionable appropriation of Jiddu Krishnamurti in his FME teachings, as Krishnamurti (FMS-9) was the furthest thing from preaching 1st-tier triumphalist chauvinistic Americanism. Ginsberg is on "defense" in his discourse, and that is not 'right' or 'wrong' it is merely a developmental indicator of the centre of gravity of his dominant worldview and FMSs. There is nothing 'wrong' with his drawing on Krishnamurti's 3rd-tier discourse re: FME, but Ginsberg ought to (as ethical integrity demands) acknowledge he is not anywhere near operating in consciousness (i.e., FMSs) where Krishnamurti is (was). Mis-interpretation by an junior FMS of a senior FMS is the danger (subtle symbolic violence) I am pointing to. Thus, due caution is required (*via* self-critical reflection) on Ginsberg's part—which is not there in his writing (albeit, I like his "Epilogue" in the book with Davies which shows a willingness to risk and be vulnerable in sharing the conflict and processes of working through some fear issues self-reflectively—what I would call good humanistic FMS-6 fearwork). I have raised this appropriation of Krishnamurti with Ginsberg in correspondence but he did not respond to my 2008 e-mail to dialogue.

63. Ginsberg and Lyche, 10.

64. Mayes, Associate Professor, McKay School of Education, Brigham Young University in Utah, is one of the leading 2nd-tier (spiritual) curriculum theorists today, using the spectrum approach and integral theory (*a la* Wilber) with transpersonal theory (*a la* Jung). Albeit, he has not yet developed a systematic FME to accompany it. Clifford Mayes, "The Teacher as Shaman," *Curriculum Studies, 37*(2005), 329-348. See also Clifford Mayes, *Seven Curricular Landscapes: An Approach to the Holistic Curriculum* (Lanham, MD: University Press of America, 2003).

65. R. Michael Fisher, "A Movement Toward A Fearless Society: A Powerful Contradiction to Violence," Technical Paper No. 10 (Vancouver, BC: In Search of Fearlessness Research Institute, 2000), 6-9.

66. Excerpt from "Learning With Confidence" wrkshp. Retrieved March, 1, 2003, http://www.east.asu.edu/learning/Fall2002Reports/elearning_report_September2_2002.htm

67. Excerpt from Alan November, a leading international technology educator, used this term "Fearless Learning" at a major conference on education and the future. Retrieved December 3, 2005 from http://www.aberdeeneducation.org.uk/information/reports/sett2002keynote.htm.

68. For example: Iverna Tompkins, and Dianne McIntosh, *Fearless Parenting: Handle with Love* (Bridge-Logos, 1996); Helen Boehm, *Fearless Parenting for the New Millenium* (AuthorHouse, 2004).

69. R. Michael Fisher, "On Being a 'Fear' Critic," Technical Paper No. 14 (Vancouver, BC: In Search of Fearlessness Research Institute, 2002), 7.

70. Beck and Cowan (Spiral Dynamics theorists and practitioners), have a beginning outline of such an "Education" perspective in respect to the v-memes. Their model shows that the earliest levels (v-memes) of cultural development (individual and/or collective) are more or less "fearful" and once Yellow v-meme (my FMS-7) is reached "Life is learning; Intrigued by process; Freedom just to be; Rarely fearful." Donald E. Beck, and Christopher C. Cowan, *Spiral Dynamics: Mastering Values, Leadership and Change* (Cambridge, MA: Blackwell, 1996), n.p.

71. Arnow, *Teaching Peace*.

72. Gustavo Fischman, Peter McLaren, and Heinz Sunker, *Critical Theories, Radical Pedagogies, and Global Conflicts* (Lanham, MD: Rowman and Littlefield, 2005), 187.

73. See adult educator Robert Regnier, "Warrior as Pedagogue, Pedagogue as Warrior: Reflections on Aboriginal Anti-racist Pedagogy," in *Anti-racism, Feminism and Critical Approaches to Education*, eds. R. Ng, P. Staton, and J. Scane (Westport, CT: Bergin and Garvey, 1995), 67-86.

74. McLaren has recently written about these political leader/educators of revolution, and despite the male-bias, he recognized "King, Chavez, and Malcolm were all fearless warriors and men of great dignity, intelligence, and sensitivity." P. McLaren, *Che Guevara, Paulo Freire, and the Pedagogy of Revolution* (Lanham, MD: Rowman and Littlefield, 2000), 174. I note, and it seems significant, that Freire is not included in McLaren's select (elite) list of "fearless warriors" (pedagogues). I would agree, but that is a discussion for a much larger topic and debate around use of "violence" (contrasting with a pure notion of "non-violence") in revolutionary change and transformation, and the role of the educator in that. What would a fearless standpoint theory (FMS-9) say about that, and/or a FMS-7?

75. David R. Blumenthal, *The Banality of Evil: Moral Lessons from the Shoah and Jewish Tradition* (Georgetown University Press, 1999).

76. The notion of "existential capacity" is new in my thinking in the past couple years. It comes from, but transcends, the notion of "emotional capacity" (*a la* John Heron, and others). Existential capacity, is linked closely with Terror Management Theory (as discussed earlier in this book) and notions of how much "mortality salience" (as TMT people call it) can an individual, group, or organization handle effectively, without folding into a 'fear'-based patterning of dismissing (denying, dissociating, violating) 'Other.' A lot more work needs to go into this, but I see it as key in understanding what I mean by the "path of fearlessness" as a soul journey of development and evolution along the spectrum of consciousness toward higher and higher degrees of existential capacity (grossly, defined: ability to face death without fear)—not inconsistent with the best of FMS-6b existentialist research and philosophy. As well, educators, would do well to add Harvard educational psychologist, Howard Gardner's multiple intelligences into this discussion and theorizing (especially, what he has later called "existential intelligence," and now "spiritual intelligence" —which I suspect nicely follow the developmental shift ("by-pass") from FMS-6b to FMS-8, respectively). There are technical issues to be resolved (as Wilber would point out), because "existential" and "spiritual" as Gardner uses them (and Wilber, to some extent) are "lines" of development, not one continuous "stage" or "level." That thinking will have to wait for another publication in the future. See Howard Gardner's work on multiple intelligences in summary at http://www.infed. org/thinkers/gardner.htm.

77. Critical pedagogues David Gabbard and Karen Appleton in a recent article referred to Peter McLaren as "Socratic" and as an educator who "has always demonstrated a remarkable capacity for fearless speech = *parrhesia*." D. Gabbard, and K. A. Appleton, "Fearless Speech in Fearful Times: An Essay Review of *Capitalists and Conquerors, Teaching Against Global Capitalism and the New Imperialism* and *Teaching Peter McLaren*. Retrieved November 16, 2008 from http://mrzine.monthlyreview.org/ agm301005.html. See P. McLaren, *Capitalists and Conquerors: A Critical Pedagogy Against Empire* (Lanham, MD: Rowman and Littlefield, 2005). For a more in depth description of the idea of "fearless speech" (in classical Greek philosophy, *parrhesia*) see Michel Foucault, *Fearless Speech*, ed. J. Pearson (NY: Semiotext(e), 2001). In reading

McLaren's work for years, with great admiration, I would argue his work is FMS-6b (with a lot of FMS-3 and sometimes what sounds like a lot of (immature) masculinist Leftist *bravado* not fearlessness or fearless, as I use the latter terms in my model).

78. McLaren, *Che Guevara, Paulo Freire, and the Pedagogy of Revolution*, 174. Note, McLaren in this same book uses "fearlessness" to describe Che (p. 128), and thus he uses *fearless* (p. 174) and *fearlessness* loosely, without definition, and interchangeably. This tells me he has not utilized the best distinctions (FME) of which FMS-7 begins to make.

79. Hazel E. Barnes, "Sartre," (essay in a lost book source, I cannot find, 1989), 354.

80. Peter McLaren (with K. Gutierrez), "Pedagogies of Dissent and Transformation: A Dialogue with Kris Gutierrez," in *Critical Pedagogy and Predatory Culture: Oppositional Politics in a Postmodern Era*, ed. P. McLaren (NY: Routledge, 1995), 148.

5

UNIFYING THE FEARLESSNESS MOVEMENT:
Educational Implications for a New Activist Agenda

Introduction

From the beginning of this book I have expressed two major things: (1) underlying most all other problems humans have to overcome, the worst problem is the Fear Problem and, (2) my way of analyzing the Fear Problem is through using at least three major archetypal parts of myself, first the *integralist* theorist, which dominates the theoretical domain (first three chapters), second the *educationist*, which has been prominent throughout with the call for a unified new critical holistic-integral approach to fear management/education (FME) on the planet (applied specifically in Chapter Four) and, third the *activist*, ever alert to the real practical problems and challenges before us, while searching for the core healthy and developmental "right means" for taking action to bring about change and transformation (perhaps, even revolution), while under the forces of resistance to it.

Overshadowing my postmodern methodology is a more loosely constructed *feminist/spiritualist* lens, which continuously challenges the tendencies and domination of male-biased approaches to conceptualizing and managing fear ('fear'). I end with Chapter Five and an important woman's leadership 'voice' in Margaret Wheatley. I opened the book with important women's voices of the Fearlessness (R)evolution (Chapter One). If there are activists among you who doubt the value of my emphasis, or wish to read others who have likewise honored women as spiritual political activists and leaders of fearlessness in current times, I recommend reading *Daughters of Fearlessness* (1988) by Floating Eaglefeather. Of course, a critical holisitic-integral approach favors not merely one side or the other of the gender-biases, but rather seeks to integrate them for optimum Intelligence in solving our worst human problems.

A simple conclusion: *fearlessness* is a counter-revolution to *fear* and *visa versa* and in that interlink between them lies great power. Everyone with an activist interest wants more power to defend their cause. And if, as I've suggested in earlier chapters, fear and fearlessness are best seen as part of an evolutionary living systems Defense, then activists ought to be very interested in the way this book frames FME. How activists achieve power, for 'good' (activi*st* work) and 'bad' (ideological activi*sm*) is of great critical interest to me and anyone attempting to facilitate, lead and/or manage mobilizing social forces.

Chapter Five, with limited space, is dedicated to a quick glance at some of the ideas behind an educational platform for a new activist agenda based on unifying the Fearlessness Movement *via* the World's Fearlessness Teachings (WFTs). I have argued throughout that experts and others who talk, teach, and write about fear (and fearlessness) and how best to handle it, do not typically, get together and pool their resources and experience to make a stronger Fearlessness Movement. My 'call' then, is a futurist agenda. The 21st century has just begun and I envision an emancipatory imaginary that is not easy to grasp for those who are not futuristically oriented. The Fearlessness Movement or (R)evolution is a means to initiate an activist future 'prime cause' *for* the evolutionary Spiral. It is a cause *against* Fear's Empire and its devolutionary excesses. Without this, our intelligences will be limited, largely competing not cooperating, and thus, less likely will we solve any of our worst problems before Nature's call of 'extinction' presses in even harder than it is today.

My discourse positioning, for the cognitive written part of this book is 2nd-tier (integral vision logic). This discourse is not afraid to claim there is an 'enemy,' while understanding that 'enemy' is both within and without. The holistic-integral Fear Management Systems (FMS) model put forth in the various Figures throughout this book offer a vision (mapping) of our potential developmental intelligence and ethical trajectory across 'Fear' Barriers 1, 2, and 3. The way of that trajectory I have labeled the *path of fearlessness* or simply, *maturity*. For me, this kind of maturity (i.e., fearlessness) *is* an activist agenda.

The aim is to assist in developing a more mature and sustainable activist work on the planet, than what tends to dominate (i.e., in forms of immature activism based on fear and 'fear' = fearism *cum* terrorism). I have suggested that a 1st-tier Green (pluralist) Movement (as one example) has to begin to see its strengths and weaknesses, and from a larger context to examine what is next (i.e., potentially better)? I recommend a complementary 2nd-tier Yellow (integralist) Movement, of which activist-author David W. Korten has somewhat similarly implied in his developmental schema of *The Great Turning* (which I deal with later). Implicitly, from the beginning, I and the spirit of fearlessness have asked you—sometimes begged you—to *awaken* your inherent desire for mature liberation (some call "enlightenment"), not merely for yourself, but all Beings. You are offered here, in the context of a world over-ridden with fear, a 'choiceless choice' of fearlessness (FMS-7) and a perspective referent of fearless (FMS-9) (see Chapter Three). For those who know *The Matrix* film—you are offered the "red pill" and/or "blue pill" (hang on, that fascinating fearlessness narrative is coming later, below).

The articulation of the WFTs brought together into one volume is a first. It won't be the last. It's a baby-step on a long journey of more research, theorizing, and 'best practice' testing. Such a unification, while keeping all the glorious diversity of views of fear and fearlessness in the physicality of one volume, is powerful and potentially empowering for those pursuing a path of health, freedom, justice, peace, sustainable living and so on. Clearly, this is not a self-help manual for activists fighting for these 'good' causes, as much as it is a theoretical framework, model, and pointer to 'right means' for enacting change and transformative work ahead. And mostly, this book offers a route to a unique critical literacy of fearlessness.

The following is a performance of a few more applied FMS critiques on contemporary and important activist-leaders-writers in the organizational and political realms, such as Richard Moore, newly elected President Barack Obama (US), David W. Korten, Margaret Wheatley, and Francis Moore Lappé. I ask what kind of FME they promote and what are the alternatives? I have always intended this book as universal and international, albeit, I am most familiar with the North American scene, and thus I draw primarily on those examples but there could be others from other locations than the USA. However, let's face it, the USA is a current hotbed (and culture of fear)—undergoing major changes and crises, and thus, for heuristic purposes at this historical moment, it is a good place to examine FME.

And a final point is that my interest, although highly political in this chapter, is not for or against any particular political positioning either traditional or radical. My interest is to set an educational reference and to query its implications for political interests and ideologies along the spectrum. I cannot unhook from my educationist with an integralist view on politics and political movements. For some this will be disappointing, and others, perhaps it will be a refreshing approach to politics and governance that allows us to learn and grow from differences and similarities in various political positionings. Arguably, in the future the world will need many different perspectives politically. I still think some global universals and unifying aspects to political endeavors is useful. The WFTs are one source for this unifying direction. The source I draw on below is a critical integral perspective and a postmodern meta-narrative provided (in part) by *The Matrix* movie.

Critical Adult Education and the New Activist Agenda

> If you don't know fear in this kind of business [social action education], if you're playing on the cutting edge of social change, in conflict situations when the sides are lined up and there's violence all the time, then you'd better learn to know it (Horton, 1981).

Myles Horton, cited above,[1] an adult educator-leader who worked intimately with the dangerous Civil Rights Movement during the Martin Luther King Jr. era in American history, is right to foreground fear (and I would add fearlessness) in activist-educational work. Unfortunately, the Horton's of the world, like the Kings, are rare. My training is in both schooling and adult education. I have preferred the Hortonian critical sociopolitical dimension of adult education and its marvelous history in the workers' (union) movements of the late 19th century and its critical role in the postmodern civil rights, women's, peace, environmental and other activist movements. Schooling education (K-12) has been mostly 'silent' on these fronts because of its conservative control by the State. Adult educators were the first to call for "lifelong learning" (see Chapter Four) in the 1970s as a new concept in adult development and emancipation from the 'norms' of the past and tradition. However, critical transformative and radical adult educators, too many to mention, have been fighting against the appropriation of "lifelong learning" into the 1980-90s neo-liberal and neo-con functionalism paradigm, in order to create human/learning capital markets for profit. Critics, like black African-American adult educator Ian Baptiste, have argued that most of the latest 'lifelong learning' jargon and policy is "a most excellent ethical decoy" that avoids civic responsibility and the reality that our world is becoming increasingly unjust in the divide between the rich/learned and the poor/unlearned.[2] I agree fully.

My self,[3] and critics like Baptiste, Mindell,[4] and particularly Mike Newman,[5] have called for adult educators (and other educators) to critically re-look at the current dominant 'neutralizing' of the power of activist-led adult and continuing education from the emancipatory tradition. They argue "conflict" has been largely gutted and "critical thinking" or "dialogue" have replaced the important critical elements of a "pedagogy for the oppressed" (*a la* Freire). Newman observed,[6]

> I look at some currently fashionable adult education theories, concluding that a number mislead or are simply too nice, too unfocused, too inward-looking or too mechanical to help us help others learn in contexts of opposition [conflict] and hostility [e.g., in war zones or in Culture Wars]. And I look for some principles and processes that might help us help others learn how to identity, define, and then deal with their enemies.

Elsewhere, I have argued that Newman is a critical leader for future activist-adult education work (and conflictwork),[7] whereby his approach of "defining the enemy" is critical for groups learning how to do activist work, and being realistic as to their marginalized positioning re: hegemonic power and resistance by oppressor groups. Newman, of course, does not say we should fight to destroy the "enemy"[8] once defined; but rather, to act intelligently to defend our cause from corruption, evil, and to undermine the propagandist pedagogies of our 'enemies' through good critique. I have followed such an agenda throughout this book re: FME and I recommend likewise to other activist-adult education initiatives (not to exclude the more rare K-12 critical pedagogy initiatives). Promoters, conscious or unconscious, of Fear's Empire are my enemies and enemies of the work I do to undermine fearism (see *The Matrix* story where knowing your enemy is critical to everything emancipatory).

What I also appreciate about Newman's work and others who have elaborated distinctions between Old and New Social Movements (NSMs) in the 20th century,[9] is they have shown that new activist organizations (and coalitions) are typically loose and unstructured, contingent, and flexible to flow and shift as required. Individual expression is often the 'norm' rather than towing the 'party' line on all issues. NSMs may be revolutionary but often they do not have a such a broad agenda. They may have an issue-agenda and cause at any moment, which may shift somewhat as needed. For example, Left (and/or Marxist) movements are Old (modernist), while gays and lesbians, anti-globalism (e.g., WTO protests), environmentalists, Mothers Against Drunk Driving, etc. are New (postmodern).

The Fearlessness Movement/(R)evolution (see Chapter One), as I have conceived it (among some others) and argued for in this book is another, yet unrecognized form of the NSMs. More or less, all NSMs are intended to improve civil society, strong democracy, and engage conflicts that need to be engaged to improve quality of life (if not emancipation) for all. These social movements, Old or New, are important teaching and "learning sites" (*a la* Welton, Holford, Finger).[10] The downside of the postmodern NSMs is that they tend to like their independence and autonomy and may not be willing or able to unify under a larger cohesive and more powerful movement, as I am calling for here in regard to all these social movements joining in the Fearlessness Movement. But that is jumping ahead too quickly. I now turn to a postmodern meta-narrative which may serve to unify the social movements of the 21st century for the cause of fearlessness.

"Wake Up, Neo!"

Regardless of being a fan or critic, watching *The Matrix* sci-fi postmodern action film (1999), you'll recall the opening blistering and mysterious scenes: black screen and single blinking digital light with mysterious voice-overs, cops busting in to a room and harassing one tough beautiful women (named Trinity, played by Carrie-Ann Moss) sitting in front of her computer (hacking) in her tight black leathers, three mean suit-clad Agents of The Matrix (virtual program) wearing dark glasses and slick polished black identical shoes . . . and by Scene 12, barely a couple of minutes into the intense action of future urban *film noire*, we see and hear the Agents, frustrated by Trinity's sheroic escape in a spit-second phone booth dissolve, declare: "We have the name of their next target." "The name is Neo."[11] And he, little do we know at that point in the story, happens to be their nemesis and so-called "terrorist" enemy no. 1. For the rest of the film and the two sequels to follow (2003), Agents chasing and fighting the rebel Neo is a ubiquitous theme.

For those who have not seen this film, I highly recommend you watch it about now on DVD or VHS, and perhaps watch it a few times.[12] Contemporary American spiritual warrior and teacher Stuart Wilde wrote in 2001:[13] "Confused? Watch the film *The Matrix* again and again. I've seen it 56 times so far.

There are hundreds of symbols in the film. How they got there, I don't know. It's irrelevant. It's all there albeit as an allegory."

Referring to *The Matrix,* artist-mystic and cultural critic Jake Horsley, says this action film is for everyone; but the younger cyber-generation are the one's who most easily relate to it and often (not always) 'get it.' He reflects that,[14]

> Like all true myths, *The Matrix* is a journey of individuation, by which the soul, through trial and adversity, purges itself of all that is foreign to it and so comes to experience the totality of itself. This apotheosis of self [I call egocide, see Figure 5.1] . . . consists of a form of enlightenment [I call path of fearlessness] in which the world entirely becomes no more than a mirage ['fear'-based reality], a mirage by which the soul is tricked, tested and challenged. Once Neo [with a lot of help from his *companeros*] is able to 'read the code,' the game [of The Matrix] is over; or at least he has moved to the next level [see Figures 2.1, 3.1 and 'Fear' Barrier crossings]. . . . By seeing the world [of the 'Fear' Matrix or Fear's Empire] as it is he has transformed it from an adversary into an ally, perhaps even a lover: it is [more or less] subject to his *will*, to shape as he sees fit. This transcendental climax [of the first movie in 1999] makes *The Matrix*, the greatest and most popular action movie ever made, not just a modern myth but a metamyth: a myth about the eternal process by which myths, and humans, are made. It reveals the world itself as a myth, and Man, as both Messiah and Adversary [i.e., his Shadow], still torn between the two opposing sides of his nature. Since so many adolescents, and even older, viewers believe the movie to hold secrets that only they can decipher, secrets of empowerment, enlightenment, and emancipation [secular and/or sacred], it would be rash of us to dismiss this possibility without further investigation. . . . we owe it to them, and to ourselves, to at least entertain the possibility that *The Matrix* is something more than just a movie. . . . Movies are the ultimate art form, and a movie like *The Matrix* combines punk sensibility with philosophical insights, kung fu mysticism, conspiracy theory, occultism, mass destruction chic, psychedelic dream imagery and effects, paranoid awareness [I call life in a culture of fear], and, last but not least, a messianic [prophetic] message of redemption [Reversal]. As such, it is now, for younger generations at least, the holy book of our times.

The plethora of popular and scholarly articles and books written about this blockbuster film trilogy are too many to mention (most can be found on the Internet). Earlier in this book I mentioned a new religion "Matrixism" has begun and is growing worldwide. Radical scholars Ken Wilber and Dr. Cornel West (Princeton University) give their description of the entire film as a "feature" in *The Ultimate Matrix Collection* 10-DVD box set. The significance of these scholars valuing of the movie is unwarranted for pop cultural films anywhere, that I know of. Wilber, a friend of Larry Wachowski, dubbed *The Matrix* "the defining myth of our age."[15] Reynolds discussed in part the correlation between Wilber's concept of the "AQAL Matrix" (also called "AQAL Metatheory") and *The Matrix* film that Wilber has so admired and analyzed "through integral eyes."[16]

The Matrix metamythic ("fiction") narrative of the emancipatory journey of the soul and of the struggle of humanity in the 21st-22nd centuries, was featured in my Education doctoral dissertation *Fearless Leadership In And Out of the 'Fear' Matrix* (2003), as mentioned earlier in this book. I used this film's story (and characters) to depict the nature of group activist work in the future, within a postmodern traumatic (cyborgic and post-human) context (Matrix) of the *culture of fear* (see Chapter Two). I intended with the dissertation to create a first 21st century universal curriculum material for emancipatory education (i.e., for fearlessness).[17] In this chapter I'll show some very brief contours of the film's relevance to unifying the Fearlessness Movement (and potential for a real and virtual Fearlessness (R)evolution).

Now, back to Neo, the film's main protagonist and transformative heroic figure (played by Keanu Reeves). His everyday Matrix name is Mr. Anderson, but his underground Resistance name as hacker is coded to Neo (symbolically referring to "new, it means change" in humanity, according to Larry Wachowski). But Neo is not free from the 'Fear' Matrix (Figure 5.1).

Figure 5.1 Fear's Cousins: Suicide vs. Egocide

- R. Michael Fisher ©2008

"The world of the Matrix is a world of fear," says philosopher James Lawler.[18] Neo, an activist himself, is still stuck in the 'Fear' Matrix of the 1st-tier, plagued by panic, anxiety, fear(s), guilt and shame. The movie shows all of these, and their pervasive disabling aspects to Neo's growth (and of those he interacts with). He learns to develop bravery, and gets lost in bravado at times.[19] He learns to develop courage (a virtue) as part of his character. He doesn't stop there. He learns to develop through the FMSs all the way to fearless, as he encounters terror (and the ultimate egocide in the last scenes of the trilogy). This learning journey is a path of egocide in pursuit of escaping from the Matrix and individuating (*a la* Joseph Campbell, Abraham Maslow, etc.) and transformation, instead of suicide[20] (or "bad faith" *a la* Sartre, or "intellectual suicide" *a la* Camus[21])—a theme of choice we see as a deep pattern in much of the Western canon of existential literature and strategies within FMS-5 (and FMS-6b).

For our basic purposes here, Neo is not "awake," although he doesn't know that yet. This is depicted to us conspicuously at the beginning of the trilogy in Scene 12 (1st film), where we see him sleeping on his couch in his messy computer-geek apartment landscape. The Wachowski's original script describes this postmodern cyberworld/psyche well:[22]

> 12. INT. NEO'S APPARTMENT – It is a studio apartment that seems over-grown with technology. . . . At the center of this technological rat-nest is NEO, a [young 20s] man who knows more about living inside a computer than out-side one.

The point, is to depict and understand the contemporary world of media and technology—that is, a mediated world, one in which "increasingly people are living not from within the matrix of their own thought and action but vicariously, living through representations of life constructed by others" (*via* media, simulacrum *a la* Baudrillard).[23] The theme of the entire trilogy is revealed next: Trinity, off screen, is hacking into Neo's computer with a message typed onto his computer as he opens his eyes—"Wake up, Neo." He tries to type and erase it, frightened that his own computer is out of his control and then more typing occurs (*via* Trinity, yet unknown to Neo but she has been watching him for some time)—"The Matrix has you." The scene unfolds and Neo eventually meets Trinity and they exchange intimate and revealing questions and answers.

Ultimately, the quest of Neo, representing anyone who is still "plugged in" to The Matrix (System) but has become disturbed enough to ask questions that shouldn't be asked. He ends up with the pivotal question: "What is The Matrix?" Millions of viewers of the film were confronted with this same question in months of advertising before the first release of the movie in 1999, the end of the millenium, the *fin de siècle* question of contemporary human beings, at least as the Wachowski's wanted it to be. I took it seriously, as did a whole lot of other people on the planet. It made a lot of sense. In my unique narrative (dissertation), I turned it into the question "What is the 'Fear' Matrix?" Equivalently, this is what contemporary sociologists since the mid-1980s have been calling the "culture of fear," and what some populist radical thinkers have turned into a conspiracy theory of reality (e.g., David Icke[24]). I'll leave it up to readers to decide what conceptualizations are best to generalize about our human condition (context), especially in a postmodern 21st century.

So many themes could be discussed of value in *The Matrix* but with little space here, suffice it to focus on the awakening theme. I mean what activist agenda is not about increasing awareness—that is, about *waking people up* to something they should be paying more attention to and remembering to be so awake as to make some changes and support changes, as particular activists see fit? To 'wake up' is decidedly a change of perceptions, and with new perceptions, as William Blake would say,[25] we can actually become those changes of perception and see what our true desire is that we couldn't see (perceive) previous to waking up. What Neo cannot see, and Trinity (and the Resistance group, led by Morpheus, played by Laurence Fishburn) can see is that it is only fear, doubt, and disbelief that holds him back from his and humanity's emancipation (including human survival)—and holds back evolution along the spectrum of consciousness.

Many times Morpheus, as Resistance leader, tells Neo he is helping him "free his mind." What he means is *awaken his mind* from the socialization, education, and fear-conditioning (trance) Neo has identified himself with, as a member of 'normal' society in The Matrix (System, Program). The awakening however, is complex, as it also is an uncovering of the Shadow (individually and collectively)—that is, some awareness is "repressed" and "denied" in a pathological way during development. To face this, in the awakening, is deeply terrifying, as most spiritual initiates from around the world and through time have shared it. I know it myself. Both ignore-ance and arrogance ('fear' patterns) are involved in making us who we are 'normally' at any one time. I am not talking about fear(s) at FMS-4 but 'fear' (FMS-7 level).

During Scene 63 in Neo's training to be a fearless Sacred Warrior for the Resistance (and to take on Morpheus's prophecy of finding Neo as "The One" savior of humanity), Morpheus and Neo are walking along a typical Western downtown busy sidewalk of people rushing mindlessly to work. Morpheus says to Neo,[26]

> The Matrix is a system, Neo, and that system is our enemy. But when you are inside and look around, what do you see; businessmen, lawyers, teachers, carpenters. The minds of the very people we [from the "unplugged" Resistance movement] are trying to save. But until we do, these people are still a part of the system and that makes them our enemy. . . . You have to understand that most of these people are not ready to be unplugged [from The Matrix] and many of them are so inured, so hopelessly dependent on the system that they will fight to protect it. . . . anyone that we haven't unplugged is potentially an Agent.

Morpheus makes two teaching points, applicable to any social movement: (1) that people 'unawake' are not easy to "unplug" from their *status quo* illusions of 'normal' and that everything is 'fine' and doesn't need to change including themselves and, (2) that there are "programs" (i.e., discourses, FMSs) flowing inside all people not yet unplugged, not yet awakened, and when those are challenged with another truth or reality, they become vicious, and act as Agents to destroy those that may attempt to awaken them. Bottomline *rule* of the awakening process, as Morpheus tells Neo early on in the story (Scene 43) is that "we do not free a mind once it reaches a certain age. It is dangerous. They have trouble letting go. Their mind turns against them." Albeit, Morpheus admits he broke the rule himself because he felt Neo was special.[27]

The problem Morpheus points out in the awakening process, is the problem encountered in general by coercing people to develop faster than they are able— that is, asking them to be more aware (and free) than they can cope with (*a la* Erich Fromm's "Fear of Freedom" syndrome). Elsewhere I've written,[28]

On my own journey of awakening, seeming to 'unplug' on more than one level and at more than one life-juncture, I know the terror involved. I have seen it in others I have worked with as a therapist and educator, and a leader of a social movement. I relate to Stuart Hall's concept of the 'diasporic intellectual' as an analogy for being 'displaced' once you start to unplug and carry it out publicly, with real life, often delimiting, consequences.

Reynolds, paraphrasing Wilber on transformation (distinct from translation) in development, notes that the "intellectual challenge is to shake the ego out of its slumbering sleep of ignorance, to awaken it from its dualistic dilemmas [illusions] in order to transcend itself in the nondual consciousness of reality which is *always already*."[29] However, what Wilber's critical integral theory of development reminds us of continually, is that people have to "develop" (evolve) level-by-level (without skipping levels) in hierarchical fashion, in order to integrate healthily the shifting (expanding) awareness from dual to nondual reality/identity. Premature 'rejection' of the lower for the higher, usually doesn't work—or at least doesn't sustain, and the higher is going to fear the pull of the lower—and thus, becomes a pathological higher level of development with its own damages to follow. The explanation for that can be seen in part in Chapter Two, though reading Wilber's work is best to understand this principle of development and role of Phobos-Thanatos.

Activists in their zeal often coerce people (subtlely or grossly) to develop critical awareness faster than they are able because of the 'good cause' they fight for. They tell people they should take on more 'big problems' in the world than they currently are (or want to). Activists want to download their problems as perceived onto another person who does not yet perceive such problems—or doesn't want to. I see this collective problematic ('error') in the way the US (post-9/11) has tried to impose a Western industrialized FMS-5 (and some FMS-6) "democracy" and ideological pluralism onto FMS-1, 2, 3 in Afghanistan and Iraq. It is inappropriate development strategy and will not work. The bloodshed and costs are evidently tragic for all of us to witness today.

In retrospect, in smaller ways, I have done this myself as an emancipatory leader within the In Search of Fearlessness Movement. Activists (and their leadership) typically don't ask if people, and particular individuals, are developmentally ready to hear and know and live with what the activist/teacher wants to make them aware of. Little 'real' ground support is offered in activist movements for the people who they are trying to 'wake up' to some truth, crisis, emergency, or problem in the world that needs fixing—yesterday.

Prophets typically do the same thing. They rarely follow the rule Morpheus speaks of. I have recently critiqued Al Gore and his eco-warriors on Global Warming (with their mantra of "Inconvenient Truth"[30]) for doing this. I would critique the Fearlessness (R)evolution leaders in Chapter One likewise (with some rare and partial exceptions). Jennifer McMahon, a philosopher and critic, wrote,[31]

> In both *The Matrix* [Wachowski's] and *Nausea* [Camus], the main characters come to an awareness of the true nature of the human condition. As they illus-

trate, this awareness is unpleasant and met with resistance largely because the truth it reveals is terrifying. Morpheus acknowledges the burden of authenticity when he tells Neo, "I didn't say it would be easy, I just said it would be the truth." We see the [fear-based] desire to escape this burden evidenced not only in Cypher's choice to return to the Matrix, but also in Mouse's fascination with his virtual woman in red and Neo's nostalgia for the noodle soup shop when he first re-enters the Matrix. Importantly, both *The Matrix* and *Nausea* illustrate that authenticity [vision into 2nd-tier FMS-7 reality] is difficult not only because the truth it reveals is hard to stomach, but also because inauthenticity is the norm. Existentialists [i.e., FMS-6b view] agree that most people are inauthentic [controlled by fear, 'fear'] . . . existence contains numerous [terrifying] phenomena that we would prefer to deny. Death, suffering, and meaninglessness are three obvious examples. . . . people prefer to comfort themselves with a vast array of lies about life. . . . most people prefer to flee the facts and remain in a "dreamworld" of their own.

Arguably, that dream world is held in place by what Ernest Becker (Chapter Three) calls "cultural defenses." *Hope* is one of the biggest of those defenses and it can easily be subverted by 'fear'-based perception and actions (recall Overstreet's caution in Chapter One). I am more and more convinced that new FMS-6b or FMS-7 conceptualizations like (post-colonial) "radical hopelessness"[32] and/or "fearlessness," respectively, are much better ways to be in reality authentically but not desperately (i.e., not 'fear'-based).

If I were to add another level of terror to 'waking up' for human beings, beyond the existential analysis (and TMT), I would add Wilber's transpersonal (integral) analysis (FMS-9), and thus further examine all forms of repression/oppression dynamics (including the evolution of the self/Self conflictual dialectic) with its ontological source back to the "Atman Project" (see Wilber's earliest books). That's, however, beyond my intent here in this discussion.

In *The Matrix* film's 'waking up,' in regard to Neo especially, it turned out to be (apparently) the right decision which Morpheus made—accomplished with relatively skillful means. However, in the later films of the trilogy we see that this was not the case for other humans who were selected in previous cycles of the 'the game' as 'the One.' As well, it was not the case for Cypher (played by Joe Pantoliano), a member of the Resistance (i.e., unplugged), who actually turns effectively against the Resistance from the inside—that is, he's a terrorist from within and causes much destruction and death, as he bargains with the Agents to return him to "ignorance is bliss." Cypher's mind was not ready to awaken to the life/truth of living in and out of the Matrix like Morpheus and the crew of the Resistance. Cypher could not choose and develop fully toward a self-identity that was across 'Fear' Barrier 2—and instead of progressing, he eventually chose regression—an example of the danger Morpheus warns of.

Fear ('fear') is the main factor for that regressive vs. progressive choice. It was suicide that Cypher decided on, instead of egocide (as Neo chooses time and again *via* modeling Morpheus and loving Trinity). The worst part, is the Resistance completely didn't see the betrayal coming from Cypher, and that is most disturbing. The audience sees it right from the very first dialogue in the movie between Cypher and Trinity. And even more disturbing: the zealous and victorious warriors in the story are blinded to their own blindness, as philosopher and critic Thomas Hibbs wrote, "The lesson of Cypher seems to have been forgotten"[33] by the Resistance from beginning to end. No one ever talks in self-critical reflection of how their own organization 'blew it' and as to what they could do differently in the future. Apparently, in this way, Morpheus, as activist-leader-teacher, has not created a very good learning organization.[34]

Why were Morpheus (captain) and his crew oblivious to the needs of Cypher? I suggest it is because they were *too* concerned with their activist mission and objectives, to care about the (subjective) real challenge of a real developing and struggling person in their ranks. Close observation of the story indicates Morpheus et al. were *too* afraid of the failure of their mission (one of the flaws of FMS-3 to 6, and less so with FMS-7). Characteristically, my experience with activists, as an insider and outsider, is they objectify people for the most part as political 'bodies' needed (i.e., volunteers, and numbers count most to "win") for their ideological movements. I've seen far too many in activist movements burn out, get diseases and suffer mental health problems. Unfortunately, many of the movement's leaders are super-survivors ("Thrivers," see Figure 2.1) and may get very out-of-balance, addicted, distorted, pathological and violent themselves, even when their 'good cause' is one of non-violence, caring, love, justice and peace. Too many other activists fighting for green sustainability" are sometimes living lives themselves not sustaining of healthy intimate relationships. I wish I had not seen so many 'Cypher-programs' in activist movements and among leaders, but that is the reality I've seen and why I have spent this time writing about it in this chapter.

To really understand some of the dynamics of 'waking up,' as Neo experiences it as an initiate into an elite Resistance movement against the Matrix, one has to watch the film and watch the amount and kinds of fear (and its cousins) he experiences. He never really develops into FMS-7. This is a critique I have of most every activist movement I've known or read about. Thus, 'fear' as a pattern or Project, is under-theorized in such movements. The Wachowski's do not seem to fully utilize an integral model (*a la* Wilber), and thus add little to the development and revealing of FMS-7, at least not in the movie scenario. And that is why I wrote my own sequel during my dissertation to portray a FMS-7 integral analysis, in part.

The pivotal theme of awakening is most clearly depicted in the movie with the "red pill" vs. "blue pill" scene, in which Morpheus offers the pills (aka choice) to Neo early on in the story. I'll reveal nothing more than to say, to watch that scene as archetypal in the human imaginary of so many young people who "love" *The Matrix*. Oh, how we all wish we had someone like Morpheus offering to give us a conscious choice in life. Mostly, the choice to swallow the "blue pill" is unconscious/habitual (forced)—as we normatively follow what everyone else is doing. How to actually make that critical (transformative) decision to stay in the Matrix and relatively unawake ("blue pill" modality) OR to 'unplug' from it all ("red pill" modality) and enter the path of fearlessness and awakening to nondual reality ultimately (FMS-9), is a decision that must be made both individually and collectively. Clearly, Neo has a lot of excellent informed-mature-support to cross the 'Fear' Barriers and manifest his great potentials. The love (with fearlessness) he received from some devotional members of the Resistance is palpable and necessary for successful healing, development and evolution of consciousness. It is a community-based affair. Virtually every writer, fan or critic, misses this point—even Wilber and West focus on individual (spiritual) development of Neo, rather than a feminist perspective of the communal development at the base of individual development and Neo's success. Neo *is* what the community allows him to *be* and what they believe he can be. Sure, Neo puts in 50% of the effort but the other 50% is the group dynamic. I cannot emphasize this enough, as so much of the human potential and 'new age' rhetoric of the last 50+ years really misses this integral point in development and evolution—that is, they miss the *cultural context* and its powerful influence—of which, in general, the postmodernist sees more clearly than the modernist.

Unlike most commentators on *The Matrix,* secular activist-leader and populist political writer, Richard Moore (born in California, lives in Ireland) takes a decidedly community-based view, in his new book *Escaping The Matrix: How We the People Can Change the World* (2006). I was particularly excited to see Moore's Table of Contents with sections entitled "Imperialism and the Matrix," "9/11 and the New American Century," "Capitalism and the Matrix," and "Education Outside the Matrix." I bought the book right away. Although, I found it somewhat disappointing, if not reductionistic (i.e., FMS-6) in the superficial reading of *The Matrix* metamyth overall. Moore defines his "transformational paradigm" based on the red pill vs. blue pill metaphor from the movie:[35]

> The defining dramatic moment in the film *The Matrix* . . . occurs just after Morpheus invites Neo to choose between a red pill and a blue pill. The red pill promises 'the truth, nothing more' [says, Morpheus]. Neo takes the red pill and awakes to reality—a [horrifying] reality utterly different from anything he or the audience could have expected. . . . The story [after Plato's famous parable of shadows on the cave wall] is a kind of multi-level metaphor, and the parallels that drew my attention had to do with political reality. . . . [re: "post 9/11 hysteria] Our everyday media-consensus reality—like the Matrix in the film— turns out to be a fabricated collective illusion. . . . I began to see that consensus reality—as generated by official rhetoric and amplified by mass media—bears very little relationship to actual reality. *The Matrix* was a metaphor [myth(?)] I was ready for.

R. Moore describes his search for the truth behind the "elite blueprint for world order in the new millenium"[36] and it is not a pretty story. His way of handling this awakening from "Matrix reality" to an alternative and critical one is managed (apparently) by him through taking leadership action as an activist-researcher-writer-speaker on an international scale (The Cyberjournal Project). After reading his Chapter One synopsis/critique of our current state of affairs, his offering is for us all to merely learn more, analyze more ("gain some perspective")[37]—all very rational (i.e., FMS-5) in order to handle the horror of and crisis of our world today. This is a common intellectual (Western liberal) approach to 'waking up' that men and *transformational learning theory* (e.g., Giroux, Mezirow et al., etc.) tend to promote. He says his book is interested in "global transformation, not just the transformation of a single society"[38] What about individual/group and community transformation? What curricular and pedagogical emancipatory frameworks and praxis is required for the task? He has little to say in depth around these issues and/or the types of problems Neo or Cypher go through in a Resistance (activist) community—but he has a lot of logistics to offer for organizing communities, dialogue, etc. His calm rationalistic, pragmatic, functionalism is somewhat contradictory to his earlier point, where he concludes (with an 'apple pie' call for unification) in his Foreword:[39]

> Ultimately, social transformation depends on our ability, as human beings, members of an allegedly intelligent species, to get beyond our superficial differences and realize that we are all in this together. A better world for all of us is a better world for each of us!

Holistic (FMS-6, and FMS-8) as Moore sounds here, he virtually ignores the role of fear ('fear') and its cousins, and a more holistic-integral viewpoint (i.e., FMS-7). He also is not interested to dialogue with me on these issues (e-mail communication by him dropped off immediately after my initial critique of his book), which strikes me as insincere, if not unethical, in terms of his valuing of talking and sharing about different views, as promoted in his book. Despite these shortcomings, I give him full credit, at least for what he writes in attempting to get to core issues of common interest, underneath stereotypical conflicts and skepticism, between liberal and conservative agendas.[40] This sets his work onward, as I see it, towards a much needed integral political perspective.

As we leave the postmodern holy book, metamyth—*The Matrix* narrative—and metaphor of the soul's journey, I wish to at least point to alternative curricular and pedagogical work done on the dialectical relationship between "transformative learning" and "restorative learning," in the work of feminist and spiritually-focused authors/educators Elizabeth Lange[41] and Barbara Bickel.[42] In their work there is a humane and sensitive approach (i.e., FMS-2, 6, 6b, and some FMS-7 and 8) toward a more 'balanced' curricula, than what we normally see in activism (FMS 3, 5 and 6). They suggest that in order to wake people up it is important to first allow and create spaces to restore their basic ethical capacities prior to any transformational potentials. Busy fragmented lifestyles and pace tend to disorient people from their 'centers' of ethical sensibility. The message of Lange and Bickel is: *support* is key for people and transformation may or may not follow. The continual wounding in Fear's Empire and the pressures to conform to it are immense. To have a healthy and sustainable emergent global consciousness, in the face of crises and resistances to change, fear/terror needs to be given lots of attention in both restorative *and* transformative learning.

Some Important Contemporary American Activists

At this moment of writing President-elect **Barack Obama** has shaken, in a good way, the despair of most Americans, and particularly black African-Americans. It is a new era for American politics, with ripple-effects likely around the world during the next four year term. The press and magazines analyzing and celebrating his Democratic victory over Republicans in the USA has led me to include his approach to FME in this chapter. Of course, I am not talking about only Mr. Obama but his election team and advisors in general, of which he is the symbol (albeit, rather bright) leader. A recent photograph in my local newspaper[43] shows very happy Obama fans wearing t-shirts. They show four identical (differentially colored) images of Obama's portrait with the words under each portrait as follows: "HOPE, BELIEVE, YES WE CAN, CHANGE." This is "The Obama Code" as political linguist George Lakoff calls it.[44]

Obama knows the country (world) is in deep economic crisis and a lot of other problems are going to hamper progress for some time to come. He is being positive and his t-shirts reflect that. "Hope" is no. 1. This is primarily a Blue FMS-4 (with FMS-5 and 6 undertones) discourse, secular or sacred. Hope sells. It is the alternative to fear. A recent political cartoon (prior to the election) on my wall, given to me by a colleague the other day, reads with a title "The 2008 Fall Classic." There is an image of a happy Barack Obama in a baseball suit (white) with the large letters of the word "Hope" written across it like a team name. Beside Hope, is a smaller, sourer, dark baseball suit on McCain (his rival for President) with the letters "FEAR" (note: capital letters are used on the latter and capital and small letters on the former).[45]

In Obama's election victory speech in Grant Park, Chicago, he said many wonderful things, while the fearologist in me picked out the FME approach (excerpt) he offered as well as "hope":

> . . . who still wonders if the dream of our founders is alive in our time. . . . [not just Red and Blue States] we are, and always will be, the United States of America. Its the answer that led those who have been told for so long by so many to be cynical, and fearful, and doubtful of what we can achieve to put their hands on the arc of history and bend it once more toward the hope of a better day. . . . change has come to America.

Obama wrote this speech, more or less, by himself. Ever eloquent with words and ideas, he knows how to fire people up, coach, and inspire them to "hope of a better day" beyond fear and its cynical and doubtful attitudes. He tells the people 'the truth,' he often says, as well (paraphrasing) 'not what they want to hear, but what they need to hear' about the real challenges and problems ahead. He talks about the "not-so-young people who braved the bitter cold" and "we know there are brave Americans waking up in the deserts of Iraq and the mountains of Afghanistan to risk their lives for us" and "I have never been more hopeful than I am tonight," etc. He knows America is "the home of the brave," etc. All FMS-2, 3, 4 (especially "patriotism" as FMS-4). He draws on these early fear management systems to buttress a people and a nation living in a "culture of fear" and under many kinds of threats. One cannot help but see parallels in Obama's tone and FME discourse with his black brother Morpheus, in his assertion to his fellow warriors at one point in *The Matrix Reloaded* (2nd film in the trilogy):[46] "Some of you believe as I believe. Some of you do not. But those of you that do, know we are nearing the end of our struggle. The prophecy will be fulfilled soon."

Prophecy and hope (for a "Savior") is rooted in FMS-2 (with more complex aspects in FMS-4, 6 and 8). At a later point in the second film, the warrior (Lock) and councillor (Hamann) are discussing how much of the facts and threats (risks) the people of Zion should be told about. Everyone is rather conservative in not wanting to share much until Morpheus comes in on the conversation and declares it best to tell "The truth. No one will panic. Because there is nothing to fear. That army [Sentinels working for the Matrix machines] will never reach the gates of Zion." This proved untrue as the Sentinels did breach the walls. And so Morpheus's "truth" is not only inaccurate, because of his hope in Neo as Messiah (and sign of Hope), but it also shows Morpheus's zeal of vision and hope over-rides the fear and struggle of the people, who are not so convinced and advanced as Morpheus is as a leader-warrior. He comes across quite (bravado = twisted FMS-3) narcissistic at this point (an activist trait too often seen)—ignoring developmental and 'real' differences between himself and others.

Another example comes in Morpheus's dramatic (if not erotic) adrenalin-coaching-speech to the threatened people of Zion in the second film:[47]

> Zion! Hear Me! It is true, what many of you have heard. The machines have gathered an army, and as I speak that army is drawing nearer to our home. . . . Believe me when I say we have a difficult time ahead of us. But if we are to be prepared for it, we must first shed our fear of it! I stand here before you now, truthfully unafraid. Why? Because I believe something you do not? No! I stand here without fear because I remember. I remember that I am here not because of the path that lies before me, but because of the path that lies behind me! I remember that for 100 years we have fought these machines. I remember that for 100 years they have sent their armies to destroy us. And after a century of war, I remember that which matters most. We are still here! [crowd cheers and applauds].... This is Zion and we are not afraid!

Frankly, this speech, though I have heard it 15 times or more, still gives me the shivers. I like it on the one hand, and despise it on the other. Too complex to go into here, suffice it to say one ought to be cautious toward anyone who shouts in a mass gathering: "Believe me. . . . we are not afraid!" Basically, critical integral FMSs theory offers us a guide to not merely gobble-up anyone's total authority re: fear management—especially, when they try to tell you what you are, without asking you what you are—that is, afraid, or not afraid. At the same time, I love the spirit of fearlessness that arises in moments of great terror (as Zion, like America, faces today).

Obama, in his victory speech, calls on "us [to] resist the temptation . . . [and divisive] immaturity that has poisoned our politics for so long." And he quickly shows his basic (immature) masculinist (FMS-4) militaristic leadership discourse: "To those [terrorists] who would tear this world down [make it fearful]—we will defeat you . . . [by "might of our arms" and by] unyielding hope." The bravado quality of bravery (FMS-3) he asserts (not mentioning even the word "courage" of FMS-5, 6 in the entire speech) stuns with the militaristic words *"conquer fear"*—in terms of what the nation did during the 1930s. "Yes we can!" he rallies the call and excites his followers in majestic kingly style.

As fine as Obama's inaugural speech was, it lacks sophistication in its FME and the role of fear ('fear') and fearlessness in the deepest problems of American culture and so much of the world. At one level, it is quite an integral speech in that it includes a lot of different v-meme values (in 1st-tier especially), but it cannot get beyond FMS-6, and mostly it revolves around a bravado FMS-3 and FMS-4. I do not know if that is 'bad' or 'good'—time will tell. I will suggest that Obama could have learned a few lessons from another victorious American President in the Depression, that is, Franklin D. Roosevelt and his famous inaugural address March 4, 1933: "The only thing we have to fear is fear itself." For a State leader (FDR) to state such a claim to a whole nation (and Western world) without making so many ideal "promises," is profound. FDR's wisdom was, perhaps, much more useful in the long term than a lot of cheer-leading that bypasses the topic of fear and its management (as seen in Obama's inaugural speech and much of his 2006 book *The Audacity of Hope*).

I agree with Forrest Church re: FDR (and 25% of a nation unemployed), "What the new president did was to utter the hitherto unspoken word that lurked in everyone's heart—*fear*. . . . No other presidential address matches Roosevelt's . . . in directness and immediacy of its impact" (even though FDR's famous dictum on fear goes back centuries to many other sources).[48] Lest I not judge Obama prematurely for his over-positivity. I only want to point out how FMSs theory can be applied. But, that said, his FMS-4 is not a good sign if one is looking for him to immediately un-declare the "War on Terror"[49] (a fear of fear itself)—a misguided Bushian declaration that only feeds terrorism rather than defeats it—never mind to mention that such a war has cost trillions of dollars and is sinking the US economy by its unforgiving debt load. Unfortunately, Obama's FME discourse shows he is not yet capable of seeing beyond that problematic and reproduction of the culture of fear dynamic itself. He actually has the opportunity to use the discourse of fearlessness (FMS-7) and beyond, if he chooses and is able to do so. He is, rightfully, like so many of his followers and supporters (such as Al Gore)[50] fed up with American "politics of fear" and fear-mongering overall. His solution seems to be to go the other way to an extreme "politics of hope." I am not convinced that's wise either.[51]

David C. Korten, an important anti-globalism activist-writer and leader today, has brought forth a most important integral and developmentally-based model for his vision of "The Great Turning." He is President of People-Centered Development Forum and he co-founded in 1990 *Yes!: A Journal of Positive Futures*. He currently edits the magazine. As previously mentioned in earlier sections in this book (see Figure 2.1), Korten, much like Obama and R. Moore, believes in unification of humanity and its movements *via* a new holistic adult maturity. He wrote:[52]

> . . . I have grown in my understanding of the processes by which the world's people are awakening to the reality that we are one people with one destiny on a small planet and that we can and must accept adult responsibility to and for

one another and the web of life that sustains us all. . . . This awakening ["trans-formation," as he calls it, or "Great Turning"] gives us cause for hope.

Like R. Buckminster Fuller, the prophetic-economist E. F. Schumacher so-berly reminded us of this theme of a beautiful "small planet" and adult responsi-bility to live appropriately, some 40 years ago.[53] Yet, Korten's form of "hope" is quite extraordinary, (in part) beyond FMS-4 and 5 and 6. He is rather, more closely aligned, in part, with a FMS-7, 8 perspective—rare indeed, for any activ-ist movement and leader. His FME approach shows its maturity by embracing an evolutionary and millenial historical (feminist) perspective. He accomplishes this by using Riane Eisler's feminist work on Dominator vs. Partnership Cul-tures in the Western world. As well, he demarcates "Empire" (similar to R. Moore's "Matrix reality") as a kind of "cultural trance"[54] but one in which more and more people are taking the 'red pill' so to speak, and "making the choice to walk away from"[55] it (similar to R. Moore's "unplugging").

His (somewhat) FMS-7 integral perspective then notes the importance of a "spiritual awakening" as well as an economic, sociopolitical, cultural and psy-chological one. Korten utilizes developmental theorists, some of whom Wilber uses,[56] to 'map' out the evolutionary trajectory of human development/maturity. He then links, importantly, the premodern discourse of FME (ancient wisdom) of "Love vs. Fear," noting:[57]

> Love and fear are both integral to our human nature and necessary for our full development. Love is a binding spiritual force that opens our minds and hearts to life's creative possibilities. Fear alerts us to real dangers and focuses our at-tention to ensure that we do not neglect our own survival needs. However, when fear awakens our defenses, it also evokes our capacity for violence, in-cluding violence against those we love. How we resolve [manage] the tension between love and fear has major consequences for the course of our lives—and our politics. The deep democracy of egalitarian civic engagement that is inte-gral to Earth Community [vs. Empire] necessarily depends on a mature sense of mutual trust, responsibility, and caring.

"Fear is Empire's friend," writes Korten.[58] Fear is also constructed in a fear-positive way by Korten. He raises "hope" and he talks about "courage" a good deal, as ways to manage fear (FMS-5); but he also, unlike R. Moore, talks about real "emotional support" in helping people (activists) make the "Great Turning" (i.e., his idea of a "global Alcoholics Anonymous").[59] These are all good quali-ties of FMS-6b (emotionally-sensitive) political practice. The Great Turning is a shifting from immature levels of development/awareness to mature levels (see Figure 2.1)—that is, from 1st Order (Magical) and 2nd Order (Imperial) and 3rd Order (Socialized) across a kind of 'Fear' Barrier (as I would call it), toward the mature levels of development available—that is, 4th Order (Cultural) and 5th Order (Spiritual). Exciting for me as Korten's developmental (hierarchical) per-spective is within the activist discourse, he unfortunately doesn't have a very complicated theory of fear ('fear')—at least, not a postmodern one. And equally disappointing, and limiting, is his lack of use of the term "fearlessness" or "fear-less" throughout. As well, he uses "Culture of Empire" rather than "culture of fear"—and thus misses any engagement with a massive body of good sociological and anthropological literature (among other disciplines) on the latter. He does not cite my work. Some of these short-comings are (perhaps) because of his own "spiritual bypass"—stuckness in the Western cannon on "courage" (and concomitantly, fear-positivist camp)—and going from FMS-6 to FMS-8, without fine-tuning FMS-7 analysis in an integrated development way. These short-comings, however, ought not to discourage anyone from consulting his work as highly important FME in the 21st century.

Our penultimate social activist-leader worth looking at here is the famous **Frances Moore Lappé**. Author of some 16 books, she's probably best known for authoring the multi-million seller (translated in many languages) *Diet for a Small Planet* (1971) and her work on attempting to solve the world hunger problem and build a new democracy, with assistance from her daughter Anna (The Small Planet Institute). Frances and Anna wrote a popular sequel entitled *Hopes Edge: The Next Diet for a Small Planet* (2003). Not having read her work previously, my research interest in her FME discourse came with her 2004 book (with Jeffrey Perkins) entitled *You Have the Power: Choosing Courage in a Culture of Fear*. Like Noam Chomsky, Henry A. Giroux, and some others political activists/educators, "culture of fear" was directly fronted in the book. What did they say about it? Unusual among them, Lappé jumps into the "fear hype" problematic of our era and cites Barry Glassner's *The Culture of Fear*, however that's all the critics of the culture of fear (among several) she cites. And she only gives a few sentences to Glassner's pivotal work.[60] She also never defines "fear" with a lot of nuance or creativity, as one would expect in a FMS-7 fearlessness discourse. Fear is an inner biological feeling or emotion as far as she is concerned (i.e., FMS-5).

Quickly, as *hope, courage* and *empowerment* are obviously her key words, one sees she is operating in the traditional Western canon of FMS-5 and FMS-6 (1st-tier). In this sense she is not radical at all, as she is made out in most activist circles. She talks on the opening page about meeting many courageous people in the world: "we learned a lot about courage—we learned it doesn't mean fearlessness."[61] What is inconsistent is her co-author's praising of Buddhist nun Pema Chödrön's writing on fear as helping him "recognize that . . . uncomfortable feelings were potentially positive."[62] This is the fear-positivist's main interest, rather than in deconstructing and reconstructing our knowledge of fear ('fear'). The inconsistency is that Chödrön is one of the strongest spiritual advocates of the conception of "fearlessness" that I know of in the Western world.[63] It seems Lappé and Perkins are (as co-authors) at odds on FME. Upon reading further, I found they were not at odds totally because Frances in talking about "fear of conflict" in democracy as a problem, cites Burmese Nobel Peace Laureate Aung San Suu Kyi "for her pro-democracy heroism."[64] Likewise, Kyi is one of the strongest political activists I know of to endorse "fearlessness" (see Chapter One). It appears the co-authors read only what they want to read into Chödrön's and Kyi's teachings, but leave out central 2nd-tier and 3rd-tier Buddhist conceptions, like *fearlessness* (see Chapter Three).

I expect the co-authors would gain a lot more curiosity (and less fear) of fearlessness, if they were to take time to check out the WFTs overall. This bias against fearlessness is typical of FMS-5 and 6, at least in some circles (not all). There is really not much more to discuss in terms of Lappés rather reductionist (and partially true) view of FME, which is summarized so nicely in the following quote:[65]

> We've come to see that we don't have to pray for our fear to finally go away and leave us alone. Nor do we have to reach Reverend Njoya's level of self-mastery in order to recognize that yes, fear is *within* us, not an external force. We can, in our own way, harness the energy of fear and, like the lion taking aim, choose where and what we do with it. Instead of robbing us of power, fear can be a resource we use to create the world we want.

I disagree that "fear is *within* us, not an external force." Unitarian Universalist scholar and counselor Forrest Church wrote, "Fear doesn't only exist within us. It permeates the very institutions that contain our lives. Every one of them."[66]

Lappé's FME is an advice to take *action* even when in fear (echoes of Susan Jeffer's view of courage as "feel the fear and do it anyway" from the 1980s). It's roots as a discourse go well back in the Western (masculinist) world with variations, but more recently can be found in the bravado dictum of a Western film star cowboy. "John Wayne put it simply: 'Courage is being scared to death—and saddling up anyway.'"[67] This FMS-5 discourse I have found in many contemporary woman author's who are writing about fear and its management and even fearlessness (e.g., Arianna Huffington). This is too simplistic a view or teaching—that is, overly psychologistic, modernist, and non-developmentalist—at least, for the complex postmodern world of the culture of fear that they say they are addressing in a post-9/11 world. It is disappointing, from the point of view of FME, how un-holistic and non-integral Lappé's text comes across, when she is such a charismatic person/teacher/leader who promotes holistic values.

Our last but not least activist-leader and author is **Margaret Wheatley**, an internationally renowned organizational and leadership consultant, and co-founder and President of the Berkana Institute (since 1992). The Berkana Institute website reads:[68]

> The Berkana Institute serves people globally who are giving birth to the new forms, processes and leadership that will restore hope to the future. Since 1992, Berkana has gradually expanded its work to reach pioneering leaders and communities in all types of organizations and in dozens of nations. The need for new leaders is urgent. We need people who can work together to resolve the pressing issues of health, poverty, hunger, illiteracy, justice, environment, democracy. We need leaders who know how to nourish and rely on the innate creativity, freedom, generosity, and caring of people. We need leaders who are life-affirming rather than life-destroying. Unless we quickly figure out how to nurture and support this new leadership, we can't hope for peaceful change. We will, instead, be confronted by increasing anarchy and social and ecological meltdowns.

Readers, after studying this book, may do their own critical analysis of the FMSs used and FME discourse that Wheatley either writes of or endorses on the website. You may note one of her latest books entitled *Turning to One Another: Simple Conversations to Restore Hope to the Future* (2002). However, my focus of intrigue is Meg Wheatley's conversations with eminent spiritual teachers like Pema Chödrön and more particularly, her recent five-day seminars at the Shambhala Institute, Halifax, Nova Scotia, Canada. The recent ad for this from Wheatley reads: "I will be offering the course "Call to Fearlessness" with co-teachers Chris Grant and Jerry Granelli. This promises to be a deep inquiry into the sources of our courage and fearless action."[69] The combining of a text with *courage* and *fearless* easily integrated and yet worth naming as distinct, seems characteristic of Wheatley's unique and mature, if not holistic-integral, FME of late.

It is refreshing to listen to her and Chödrön talk about fear and then *bravery*, *courage*, being *courageous*, etc. in a long 1999 article but do not mention *fear-lessness* or *fearless*. Yet, interestingly, they use those 1st-tier forms of fearless-ness in a 2nd-tier perspective and *with* a transformative meaning frame, related to "the basis of awakening, of spiritual awakening," says Chödrön at one point.[70] These women leaders, uncharacteristically, are not against fearlessness or fear-less. And nowhere is that more obvious than in Wheatley's document "Eight Fearless Questions" that came from her address at the Shambhala Institute Core Program in June 2006,[71] when she began her "Call to Fearlessness" for world leaders of all kinds. I won't repeat her discussion of fear and the "way out of fearfulness" as she argues. In many ways it is FMS-5 and 6, with a positive spin on fear and its role as a basic Defense (which I have theorized in my model all along in this book). What is most interesting however, is her challenge to leaders in what they call themselves. She asks, "How do you identify yourself? And have you chosen a name for yourself that is big enough to hold your life's work?" I can relate to that, and that's why I call myself a *fearologist* (at times, I use "prophet of fearlessness" or "liberation educator"). Then Wheatley pushes her aim in poignant 2nd-tier fashion, asking leaders:

> *Are we choosing names that demand fearlessness?* You're a coach. You're an executive. You're a consultant. You're a teacher. You're a minister. You're a hospital administrator. You're a civil servant. Are those names demanding fear-lessness of us? I don't know what would create fearlessness, but I think this is a very important question.

Throughout this book I have offered archetypal examples of "Sacred War-rior," "Outlaw," "Lover," and "Royal Leader," among others (e.g., "fearolo-gist") to meet the demand Wheatley suggests. Indeed, Wheatley's thinking here shines with clarity and the "gift of fearlessness," even though it encircles the mysterious, unknown and uncertain. She does not bog down in traditional FME (Western masculinist) discourses of fear and courage, that is, trying to overcome and conquer. Rather, her deep feminine intuition cuts through so much of the popular rhetoric of our day and the labels of pc positivity or of simple function-alist 'neutrality.' She says that is not good enough anymore, as the world has become too fearful and horrifying. Leaders cannot simply carry on with 'normal' identities as if everything is the same, while hugging old ways as reliable to manage new territory.

I love this radical and reasonable questioning, and especially how it is 2nd-tier, across 'Fear' Barrier 2, as she challenges everyone: *"So, what is there to fear about fear?"* This echoes FDR perhaps, but more than he, Wheatley acutely guides us to "fearless questions," not settling for "hope" as the answer in a culture of fear. She remarks, "There's something very interesting to understand about hope. That is, that hope and fear are one." Sounds like radical hopelessness as FMS-7, 8, even some 9. Her eight fearless questions are:

1. Does the world need us to be fearless?
2. What if we can't save the world?
3. What is it like to live in the future now?
4. Why do we imprison ourselves?
5. Why are we so afraid?
6. Can we work beyond hope and fear?
7. What would it take for us to just deal with *what is*?
8. [What would it take] To not need to be always engaged in changing the world?

Wheatley's discussion on each of these questions is brief, and the point of them is more to create the FMS-7, 8, 9 dialogue, which she witnesses to be lacking among leadership theory and practices today. I agree. Her document ought to go down in history (herstory) (fearstory) as pivotal to a 21st century leadership 'call' in and out of the 'Fear' Matrix.

She has no doubt been greatly influenced as a Westerner by the Eastern teachings through her connection with the Shambhala Institute for Authentic Leadership in Nova Scotia, Canada (*a la* Trungpa). I love that her values and thinking have been altered to extend beyond the Western canon of FME, and are integrating (at least, questioning) the core assumptions she has been raised on about the nature of fear and fearlessness, and the very definition of *leadership* itself.

How validating it is for my own research to come across a 2007 article online entitled "Fearlessness: The Last Organizational Change Strategy" by Art Kleiner (interview with M. J. Wheatley). They talk about how "corporate courage has faltered in the wake of September 11, 2001."[72] They discuss how many leaders in those corporations, whom Wheatley had trained years before, had back-tracked, regressed ethically, and fallen prey to fear like most everyone else. This regress she saw awakened some part of her as a spiritually-focused organizational consultant. It brought her to question that maybe *courage (or love) is not enough*, and thus she has turned to *fearlessness* and *fearless per se*, in search of a new FME theory and set of strategies.

Although, I certainly don't agree with everything said by Wheatley on FME, her most recent discourse is one of the best examples of the WFTs, holistic-integral, from a contemporary and highly successful well-known leader today. May she, and the women leaders of the Fearlessness (R)evolution in Chapter One coalesce and unify the movement(s) of the spirit of fearlessness today. I have tried unifying leaders, and failed. I look forward to working with these women in the future, and/or with anyone with a FMS-7 vision! A new *fear education* is a comin.' It all depends on when we hear the 'call' and are truly developmentally (spiritually and politically) *ready*. In this book, with a lot of great help from the WFTs, I offer some new 'maps' for a postmodern universal FME initiative, and I am grateful to have been supported to offer them as a gift of fearlessness.

I end this book with Wheatley's 2006 speech to leaders—a 'call' in her own voice as a transpersonal 'voice' of the spirit of fearlessness itself:

> What is the name that is big enough to hold your fearlessness, that is big enough to *call* you into fearlessness? That is big enough to break your heart? To allow you to open to the suffering that is the world right now and to not become immobilized by fear and to not become immobilized by comfort? What is the way in which you can hold your work so that you *do* feel free from hope . . . and therefore free from fear?

Notes

1. Excerpt from Mike Newman, *The Third Contract: Theory and Practice in Trade Union Training* (Sydney, Australia: Stewart Victor, 1993)

2. Ian Baptiste, "Beyond Lifelong Learning: A Call to Civically Responsible Change," *International Journal of Lifelong Education, 18*(1999), 94-102.

3. R. Michael Fisher, "Toward a 'Conflict' Pedagogy: A Critical Discourse Analysis of 'Conflict' in Conflict Management Education," unpublished masters thesis (Vancouver, BC: The University of British Columbia, 2000). R. Michael Fisher, "Unveiling the Hidden Curriculum in Conflict Resolution and Peace Education: Future Directions Toward a Critical Conflict Education and 'Conflict' Pedagogy," Technical Paper No. 9 (Vancouver, BC: In Search of Fearlessness Research Institute, 2000). Note that I have brought in the work of Ken Wilber and his critical integral theory, in part, to these research projects on 'conflict' pedagogy and its importance in the world today.

4. Arnold Mindell, *The Leader as Martial Artist: An Introduction to Deep Democracy* (NY: HarperCollins, 1993); A. Mindell, *Sitting in the Fire: Large Group Transformation Using Conflict and Diversity* (Portland, OR: Lao Tse Press, 1995).

5. Mike Newman, *Defining the Enemy: Adult Education in Social Action* (Sydney, Australia: Stewart Victor, 1994); M. Newman, "Locating Learning in Social Action," ed. B. Brennan in Social Action and Emancipatory Learning [seminar], *UTS Seminar Papers* (Sydney, Australia: School of Education, 2005). M. Newman, "Response to 'An Open Letter,' *Australian Journal of Adult and Community Education, 37* (1997), 57-61.

6. Newman, *Defining the Enemy*, ix.

7. R. Michael Fisher, "How Are We Handling Conflict?: Newman's Challenge to Conceptualize and Deal With the *Enemy* in a Violent World," unpublished paper, 1999.

8. Baptiste and Newman, for example, promote appropriate forms of civil disobedience and use of coercion when needed by activists/educators in dealing with the enemy. Baptiste wrote: "People who freely and knowingly harm others are enemies and should be treated as such." He also is critical, like Newman, and myself, that the Western psychologism of "romantic humanism" tends to dominate the field of adult and higher education today and ends up denying "the inherence of evil" in the world of the powerful and dominant—this, is ethically unjustifiable and unprofessional. Ian Baptiste, "Educating

Amidst Intractable Conflicts: A Pedagogy for Disempowering the Enemy," unpublished paper, 1998. My point: 'conflict' is a critical site of learning.

9. See for example, Jürgen Habermas, "New Social Movements," *Telos, 49*(1981), 33-37.

10. Michael Welton, "Social Revolutionary Learning: The New Social Movements as Learning Sites," *Adult Education Quarterly, 43*(1993), 152-164; John Holford, "Why Social Movements Matter: Adult Education Theory, Cognitive Praxis, and the Creation of Knowledge," *Adult Education Quarterly, 45*(1995), 95-111; Matthias Finger, "New Social Movements and Their Implications for Adult Education," *Adult Education Quarterly, 40*(1989), 15-22.

11. Larry Wachowski, and Andy Wachowski, "The Matrix" Shooting Script, (August, 12, 1998), ed., Spencer Lamm, in *The Art of The Matrix* (NY: Newmarket Press, 2000), 281.

12. *The Matrix*, directed by the Wachowski Bros., produced by Joel Silver (Warner Bros., Inc. ©1999), rated R.

13. Stuart Wilde, *God's Gladiators* (Chattanooga, TN: Brookemark LLC, 2001), 12.

14. Jake Horsley, *Matrix Warrior, Being the One: The Unofficial Handbook* (London, UK: Gollancz, 2003), 6-8.

15. Excerpt taken November, 08, 2008 from http://integrallife.com/contributors/larry-wachowski.

16. Brad Reynolds, *Where's Wilber At?: Ken Wilber's Integral Vision in the New Millenium* (St. Paul, MN: Paragon House, 2006), 49-50. See "AQAL Metatheory" in Reynolds, 344.

17. R. Michael Fisher, *Fearless Leadership In and Out of the 'Fear' Matrix*, dissertation available online in pdf (Google "R. Michael Fisher"). Note, in the dissertation I wrote a screen play sequel to the first Matrix film, before the 2nd and 3rd sequels had come out. I researched and wrote this all without knowing Ken Wilber was interested in the film and that he knew Larry Wachowski. The coincidence is uncanny that my fav integral philosopher (KW) was 'onto' the same metamyth reading of the film as myself, albeit, we differ in those interpretations somewhat. The main point of my sequel dissertation script is to understand and work with *The Matrix* characters set in combination with Irish Republican Army young rebels in Ireland—all written through a cyber-feminist lens. The secular sociopolitical and cultural aspects of the metamyth interest me as much as the psychospiritual dimensions (the latter, which Wilber's interpretation tends to focus on).

18. Lawler wrote: "According to the belief-structure of the Matrix, we can never escape from fear." Neo's journey in the end, transcends this limitation but that is not the case for everyone else in the film. James Lawler, "We are (the) One!: Kant Explains How to Manipulate the Matrix," in *The Matrix and Philosophy: Welcome to the Desert of the Real*, ed. William Irwin (Chicago, IL: Open Court, 2002),147.

19. At the end of the first Matrix movie, philosopher Thomas Hibbs wrote, "Having won a crucial battle with the Agents of the Matrix, Neo [on a phone line to the Agents and all viewers watching the movie] warns them he will reveal all things to all people [*a la* Plato's cave allegory] and then they will enter an uncertain and unpredictable world. As he [Neo] puts it, 'I know you're out there. I can feel you now. I know that you're afraid [i.e., dualism]. You're afraid of us. You're afraid of change. I don't know the future. I didn't come to tell you how this is going to end. I came to tell you how it's going to begin... I'm going to show these people what you don't want them to see . . . a world without you, a world without rules and controls, without border or boundaries [i.e., nondual] . . . where anything is possible. Where we go from there is a choice I leave to you.'

Here Neo ignores all sorts of complications: he underestimates not so much the continued opposition of the Matrix as the likely resistance of complacent, still enslaved humans." I agree, in part, Neo is a very non-intellectual naive leader throughout the film. He is a populist leader, not unlike Jesus of Nazareth in Christianity. Thomas S. Hibbs, "Notes from Underground: Nihilism and *The Matrix*, in *The Matrix and Philosophy: Welcome to the Desert of the Real*, ed. William Irwin (Chicago, IL: Open Court, 2002), 164-165. For a thorough youthful, somewhat naive but positive Christian reading of *The Matrix* meta-myth, See Kristenea M. Lavelle, *The Reality within The Matrix* (Wisconsin Dells, WI: Saxco, 2000).

20. Tank, one of Neo's male ("true human") *companeros* on the 'ship' they work from, says: "Neo, this [sacrifice] is loco. They've [Agents] got Morpheus in a military-controlled building. Even if you somehow got inside, those are Agents holding him. Three of them! I want Morpheus back, too, but what you are talking about is suicide" (excerpt from Wachowski's, p. 366). I would call this egocide instead of suicide, as the journey is seen from a perspective larger than what Tank or most others might see in the actions Neo takes to save Morpheus from death. Such is the theme of any "hero's journey" (*a la* Joseph Campbell)—self-sacrifice is ego-sacrifice in its healthiest forms. The spectrum of choice between suicide and egocide came to me first from an article written on the futurist R. Buckminster Fuller by Smith: "Buckminster Fuller didn't want to be a hero. But in 1927, at age 32, he found himself at a crossroads, contemplating suicide after the death of his daughter, instead he committed 'egocide,' deciding to make his life an experiment to test the possibilities for living in a way as beneficial to humanity as possible." I am not sure if Fuller used the terms egocide and suicide this way himself. Stephanie Smith, "The Good Guide to R. Buckminster Fuller," *GoodMagazine, 2007*. Retrieved May 1, 2008 from http://goodmagazine.com. Another good source on this conception of egoicide vs. suicide as part of the transformative journey comes in the groundbreaking work of Jungian therapist and psychiatrist Rosen. See David H. Rosen, *Transforming Depression: Healing the Soul Through Creativity* (NY: Penguin Books, 1996). Transcending ego in development, in my words, is transcending the 'fear'-based structures of the self/psyche/ego/soul (and concomitantly, the socialized matrix of the "culture of fear" in which we develop a self).

21. Jennifer L. McMahon, "Popping a Bitter Pill: Existential Authenticity in *The Matrix* and *Nausea*, in *The Matrix and Philosophy: Welcome to the Desert of the Real*, ed. William Irwin (Chicago, IL: Open Court, 2002), 167.

22. Wachowski's, "The Matrix," 281.

23. Excerpt from David G. Smith, a Canadian educator and critic, who also wrote of the cultural interpreter Jerry Mander who suggested that American society is "the first in history of which it can be said that life has moved inside media." D. G. Smith, *Pedagon: Interdisciplinary Essays in the Human Sciences, Pedagogy and Culture* (NY: Peter Lang, 1999), 53.

24. David Icke, *Children of the Matrix: How an Interdimensional Race Has Controlled the World for Thousands of Years—and Still Does* (Wildwood, MO: Bridge of Love Publications, 2001).

25. "If the doors of perception were cleansed, every thing would appear to man [sic] as it is, infinite. . . . Man's desires are limited by his perceptions, none can desire what he has not perceiv'd", says William Blake, cited in Horsley, front matter page.

26. Excerpt from Wachowski's, 323-324.

27. Ibid., 314.

28. I have written about how Cypher was incredibly destructive in undermining the Resistance. He was ignored by his fellow rebels. It was his own fear (terror) that being

unplugged was not the way to freedom (i.e., "ignorance is bliss"). Arguably, Morpheus, Trinity and Neo, have their own terror in their pursuit of freedom, and would not look at what was happening under their nose with Cypher's betrayal. One can also watch the film to see how terrified Neo is at many points (especially in the first film)—literally he gets ill with the terror of the real. Fisher, R. Michael, "'Unplugging' as Real and Metaphoric: Emancipatory Dimensions to *The Matrix* Film Trilogy," Technical Paper No. 33 (Carbondale, IL: In Search of Fearlessness Research Institute, 2009), 11.

29. Reynolds, 345.

30. I am referring to Al Gore's book and DVD with this name. The DVD cover illustration of a hurricane image coming out of an industrial smoke stack, is a good example of manipulation of fear—of how to terrify people into 'waking up' to global warming as an activist issue of "truth" (a very controversial truth, at that). Al Gore, *An Inconvenient Truth: The Planetary Emergency of Global Warming and What We Can Do About it* (NY: Rodale Books, 2006); A. Gore, *An Inconvenient Truth: A Global Warning* (Hollywood, CA: Paramount Pictures,™and ©2006).

31. McMahon, 172-173.

32. The young black academic Maurice E. Stevens, offers a fascinating articulation of "radical hopelessness" (as he critiques Peggy Phelan and Henry A. Giroux's work on hope). Speaking mainly for black people (and other marginalized groups in the US and elsewhere), Stevens suggests "We must insist . . . on a kind of radical hopelessness, a sense that we cannot act under the sign of hope when history has repeatedly reversed the effect of that sign, making it a burden that stills social movement and personal responsibility. . . . Trans(per)formance strongly resists hope and calls for something more difficult. It calls for and necessitates an ambivalent facing of the everyday terrors that make one." Pres. Obama is not quite theorizing at this radical level, for sure. See Maurice E. Stevens, *Troubling Beginnings: Trans(per)forming African American History and Identity* (NY: Routledge, 2003), 174-175.

33. Hibbs, 165.

34. It ought to be noted that even the so-called 'good' learning organization can twist and exploit its learners/employees. Marsick and Watkins have found this in their studies. They wrote, "When the learning organization is used for purposes not originally intended, it can create a culture of fear, in which constant change has a negative impact and employee knowledge is inappropriately exploited." V. J. Marsick, and K. E. Watkins, "Looking Again at Learning in the Learning Organization: A Tool That Can Turn Into a Weapon!," *Learning Organization,* 6(1999), 207.

35. Richard Moore, *Escaping the Matrix: How We the People Can Change the World* (Redwood City, CA and Wexford, Ireland: The Cyberjournal Project, 2006).

36. Ibid., 33.

37. Ibid., 66.

38. Ibid., xv.

39. Ibid., xvii.

40. Ibid., xvi.

41. Elizabeth Lange, "Transformative and Restorative Learning: A Vital Dialectic for Sustainable Societies," *Adult Education Quarterly, 54*(2004), 121-139; E. Lange, "Re-enchantment to Escape Empire: Spirituality, Sustainability, and Critical Transformative Learning," paper presented at Thinking Beyond Borders: Global Ideas, Global Values," online *Proceedings of the Canadian Association for the Study of Adult Education,* 27th National Conference (Vancouver, BC: Canadian Association for the Study of Adult Education, 2008).

42. Barbara Bickel, "Living the Divine Spiritually and Politically: Art, Ritual, and Performative Pedagogy in Women's Multi-faith Leadership," unpublished dissertation (Vancouver, BC: The University of British Columbia, 2008).

43. Chris Wissmann, "Barack Obama: A Responsible, Progressive Future?," *Nightlife* (Carbondale, IL), Nov. 6-12, 2008, 6.

44. Retrieved February 28, 2009 from http://www.truthout.org/022409R.

45. From "Pen and Think" (Boulder Camera ©10/24/08, Creators Syndicate), *Southern Illinoisian*, October 26, 2008.

46. Excerpt from *"The Matrix Reloaded-* Transcript." Retrieved December 1, 2003 from http://www.pitt.edu/~bobhaus/reloaded2.txt.

47. Ibid.

48. Forrest Church, *"Freedom from Fear: Finding the Courage to Act, Love, and Be* (NY: St. Martin's Press, 2004), 4. The dictum FDR used in 1933 can be traced to Montaigne, Lord Willington, Henry David Thoreau and Francis Bacon (among others).

49. This is my own view of what Obama needs to do right now (and I have told him so on his website: http://www.change.gov/yourvision)—since then I have found at least five writers from around the Western hemisphere saying likewise, of which I recommend Jonathan Steele, "Now He Must Declare That the War on Terror is Over," *The Guardian*, Nov. 6, 2008.

50. See Chapter One, "The Politics of Fear," in Al Gore, *The Assault on Reason*. NY: The Penguin Press, 2007), 23-44.

51. The tendency Obama (and so many others) get trapped in, is to create simplistic ('false') dichotomies to rally upon (e.g., "fear" vs. "hope"). This over-determines the 'choices' (options) in which all people ought to think about. My alternative is that a "fearlessness" (at least) is the better way than both "fear" and "hope"—a point I make clear through the wisdom of Margaret Wheatley's writing at the end of this chapter. I don't set up "fearlessness" as an either/or choice, but as a growth and vision to aim for along the continuum 'fear,' 'hope,' and 'fearlessness'. . . or even beyond that to 'fearless.'

52. David C. Korten, *The Great Turning: From Empire to Earth Community* (San Francisco, CA/Bloomfield, CT: Berrett-Koehler/Kumarian Press, 2005), 16, 21.

53. E. F. Schumacher, *Small is Beautiful: A Study of Economics as if People Mattered* (London: Sphere Books, 1974).

54. Ibid., 18-20.

55. Ibid., 21.

56. Pivotal among them is developmental psychologist, Dr. Robert Kegan (The William and Miriam Meehan Professor in Adult Learning and Professional Development, Harvard University). Note, Korten does not cite Wilber, for some odd reason.

57. Korten, 34.

58. Ibid., 34.

59. Ibid., 54.

60. Frances Moore Lappé, and Jeffrey Perkins, *You Have the Power: Choosing Courage in a Culture of Fear* (NY: Jeremy P. Tarcher/Penguin, 2004), 12-13.

61. Ibid., 1.

62. Ibid., 62.

63. For example, see Pema Chödrön, *The Places That Scare You: A Guide to Fearlessness in Difficult Times* (Boston, MA: Shambhala, 2001). Chödrön has authored many spiritual books and is current director of Gampo Abbey in Cape Breton, Nova Scotia, Canada.

64. Lappé and Perkins, 85.

65. Ibid., 24.

66. Church, xv.

67. Ibid., xv. Forrest Church (p. xvii) also follows this Western (immature) masculinist (pragmatist) canon and defines three distinct kinds of *courage* to overcome five distinct kinds of fear. He rationalizes this FMS-5 courage-theory of fear management using the militarist governing philosophy of Winston Churchill, a man, says Church, who "considered courage the greatest of all virtues, since we can't exhibit the others without it. If we lack the courage to act (or to control our actions), justice, temperance, and prudence are impossible. Without the courage to love, love can never be sustained. Nor can faith or hope flourish apart from the courage to be." I for one, see partial truth in Churchill's FME theory but on its own it lacks the integration (holistic view) of the Eastern philosophies (and mystics), where fearlessness is pronounced as the greatest of all virtues. My model asks us to examine both East and West together, rather than avoiding the other exists, which I see in the FMS-5 (existential) Western discourses of FME (and less so in Eastern FME teachings overall). Understanding the WFTs requires a critical holistic-integral approach as I have taken in this book.

68. Excerpt retrieved November 13, 2008 from http://www.berkana.org/index.php?option=com_content&task=section&id=17&Itemid=136.

69. Retrieved March 11, 2008 from http://meg.c.topica.com/maafX70abwXIWb UnVQLeaehISF/.

70. Margaret Wheatley, and Pema Chödrön, "It Starts With Uncertainty," *Shambhala Sun,* November, 1999. Excerpt from p. 3 of a document retrieved December 2002 from http://www.margaretwheatley.com/articles/uncertainty.html.

71. Margaret Wheatley, "Eight Fearless Questions," Excerpt from "A Call to Fearlessness for Gentle Leaders," address at the Shambhala Institute Core Program, Halifax, June 2006. Published in *Fieldnotes,* September/October 2006 by The Shambhala Institute for Authentic Leadership. Retrieved June 8, 2007 from http://www.shambhalainstitute.org/contact.html.

72. Art Kleiner (interview with M. J. Wheatley), "Fearlessness: The Last Organizational Change Strategy." Retreived October 2, 2007 from http://www.strategy-business.com/li/leadingideas/li00044?pg=1.

References Cited

Adams, D. "Early History of the Culture of Peace: A Personal Memoir." Retrieved October 4, 2008 from http://www.culture-of-peace.info/history/introduction.html.

Ahmed, S. "Be Very Afraid!" *New Internationalist,* 376 (2005). Retrieved October 19, 2005 from http://www.newint.org/issue376/be-very-afraid.htm.

———. The Cultural Politics of Emotion. NY: Routledge, 2004.

———. "The Politics of Fear in the Making of Worlds." *Qualitative Studies in Education* 16 (2003): 377-98.

Allen, C. L. "How We Can Handle Our Fears." *Sign of the Times,* June (1985): 3-5.

Altheide, D. L. "Notes Towards a Politics of Fear." *Journal for Crime, Conflict and the Media* 1 (2003): 37-54.

———. "Mass Media, Crime, and the Discourse of Fear." *The Hedgehog Review:* Critical Reflections on Contemporary Culture 5 (2003): 9-25.

———. Creating Fear: News and the Construction of Crisis. NY: Aldine de Gruyter, 2002.

Amini, L. F. and R. Lannon, *A General Theory of Love.* NY: Random House, 2000.

Anderson, D. G. "Of Synthesis and Surprises: Toward a Critical Integral Theory." *Integral Review,* 3 (2006). Retrieved November, 1, 2008 from http://integralreview.org/current_issue/documents.

Anderson, K. H. R. "*La première Femme*: The Mother's Resurrection in the Work of Camus and Irigaray." *French Studies,* 55 (2002): 29-43.

Angelou, M. *Life Doesn't Frighten Me.* NY: Stewart, Tabori and Chang, 1993.

Anshen, R. N. "Epilogue: What World Perspectives Means." In *The Meaning of The* Twentieth Century: The Great Transition, K. E. Boulding. NY: Harper Colophon, 1965.

Ardrey, R. The Hunting Hypothesis: A Personal Conclusion Concerning the Evolutionary Nature of Man. NY: Atheneum, 1976.

———. African Genesis: A Personal Investigation into the Animal Origins and Nature of *Man.* NY: MacMillan, 1961.

Arendt, H. Eichmann in Jerusalem: A Report on the Banality of Evil. NY: Penguin, 1994.

Aronowitz, S., and Henry A. Giroux. Postmodern Education: Politics, Culture, and *Social Criticism.* Minneapolis, MN: University of Minnesota Press, 1991.

———. Education Under Siege: The Conservative, Liberal, and Radical Debate Over *Schooling.* South Hadley, Massachusetts: Bergin and Garvey, 1985.

Aronowitz, S. False Promises: The Shaping of American Working Class Consciousness. NY: McGraw-Hill, 1973.

Arnette, J. L., and M. C. Walsleben, Combating Fear and Restoring Safety in Schools. NCJ 167888. Washington, DC: Department of Justice, Office of Justice Programs, Office of Juvenile Justice and Delinquency Prevention, 1998.

Arnow, J. Teaching Peace: How to Raise Children to Live in Harmony—Without Fear, Without Prejudice, Without Violence. NY: A Perigree Book, 1995.

Azam, I. Sons of the Soil: Some Poems, Short Plays, Stories and Articles About War. London Book Co., 1974.

Baptiste, I. "Beyond Lifelong Learning: A Call to Civically Responsible Change." International Journal of Lifelong Education 18 (1999): 94-102.

———. "Educating Amidst Intractable Conflicts: A Pedagogy for Disempowering the Enemy." Unpublished paper, 1998.

Barber, B. R. Fear's Empire: War, Terrorism, and Democracy. NY: W. W. Norton, 2003.

Barnard, W. S. *Onsnuwe Wereld 10.* Miller, n.d.

Baudrillard, J. The Spirit of Terrorism and Requiem for the Twin Towers, trans. Chris Turner. London, UK: Verso, 2002.

Bauman, Z. *Liquid Fear.* Cambridge, UK: Polity Press, 2006.

———. Liquid Times: Living in an Age of Uncertainty. Cambridge, UK: Polity Press, 2006.

———. "Educational Challenges of the Liquid-Modern Era." *Diogenes* 50 (2003): 15-26.

———. Intimations of Postmodernity. NY: Routledge, 1992.

Beck, D. (interviewed by Jessica Roemischer) "The Never-ending Upward Quest." *What is Enlightenment?* Fall/Winter (2002): 105-26.

Beck, D., and C. Cowan, Spiral Dynamics: Mastering Values, Leadership and Change Cambridge, MA: Blackwell, 1996.

———. "V-Memes: A Self-Discovery Process" worksheet. Denton, TX: The National Values Center, Inc., 1994.

Beck, U. "An Interview [by J. Yates] with Ulrich Beck on Fear and Risk Society." *The Hedgehog Review: Critical Reflections on Contemporary Culture,* 5 (2003), 96-107.

———. *World Risk Society.* Cambridge, UK: Polity Press, 1999.

———. *Risk Society: Towards a New Modernity,* trans. Mark Ritter. London, UK: Sage, 1992.

Becker, E. *The Denial of Death.* NY: Simon and Schuster, 1997. [original published in 1973]

———. The Structure of Evil: An Essay on the Unification of the Science of Man. NY: The Free Press, 1976. [originally published in 1968]

Beittel, K. R. Alternatives for Art Education Research: Inquiry into the Making of Art. Dubuque, IO: Wm. C. Brown, 1973.

Bennis, W. G. On Becoming a Leader: The Leadership Classic. Da Capo Press, 2003.

Bernstein, P. Math Without Fear: A Concrete Approach to Mathematics. Philadelphia, PA: Lutheran Settlement House, 1992.

Berry, T. "Foreword." in Transformative Learning: Educational Vision for the 21st *Century.* E. O'Sullivan. Toronto, ON: Ontario Institute of Studies in Education/ University of Toronto Press (1999): x-xv.

Bhave, V. "The Intimate and the Ultimate," Excerpt from M. Hern, *Deschooling Our Lives.* Stoney Creek, CT: New Society Publishers, 1996. Retrieved June 2, 2006 from http://www.learningnet-india.org/Ini/data/publications/revive/vol1/v1-6b8.php.

Bickel, B. "Living the Divine Spiritually and Politically: Art, Ritual, and Performative Pedagogy in Women's Multi-faith Leadership." Unpublished dissertation. Vancouver, BC: The University of British Columbia, 2008.

――. "Embracing the Arational Through Art, Ritual and the Body," Paper presented at the 3rd International Conference on Imagination and Education, July 13-16. Burnaby, BC: Simon Fraser University, 2005.

――. "From Artist to A/r/tographer: An Autoethnographic Ritual Inquiry into Writing on the Body." *Journal of Curriculum and Pedagogy* 2 (2005): 8-17.

Bickford, S. The Dissonance of Democracy: Listening, Conflict, and Citizenship. Ithaca, NY: Cornell University Press, 1996.

Blum, R. *The Book of Runes*. NY: St. Martin's Press, 1982.

Blumenthal, D. R. *The Banality of Evil: Moral Lessons from the Shoah and Jewish Tradition*. Georgetown University Press, 1999.

Boehm, H. *Fearless Parenting for the New Millenium*. AuthorHouse, 2004.

Boler, M. *Feeling Power: Emotions and Education*. NY: Routledge, 1999.

Bondevac, D., W. Boon, and S. Phillips. *Beyond the Western Tradition; Readings in Moral and Political Philosophy*. London: Mayfield, 1992.

Bondurant, J. V. Conquest of Violence: The Gandhian Philosophy of Conflict. Berkeley, CA: University of California Press, 1965.

Boshier, R. *Introduction to Adult Education* (Adult Education 412). Vancouver, BC: The University of British Columbia, Continuing Studies and Technology, 1996.

Boulding, E. Cultures of Peace: The Hidden Side of History. NY: Syracuse University Press, 2000.

Bourke, J. *Fear: A Cultural History*. UK: Virago Press, 2005.

Boteach, S. Face Your Fear: Living With Courage in an Age of Caution. NY: St. Martin's Griffin, 2005.

Box, P. H. Three Master Builders and Another: Studies in Modern Revolutionary and *Liberal Statesmanship*. Freeport, NY: Books for Libraries Press, 1925.

Braden, G. *Awakening to Zero Point*, video, 1996. From http: www.lauralee.com.

Brady, M. E. "The Fearlessness of Courage." *Southern Journal of Philosophy* 43 (2005): 189-211.

Brisset, W. N. "Bibliographical Essay on Fear." *The Hedgehog Review: Critical* Reflections on Contemporary Culture 5 (2003): 115-23.

Britten, R. Fearless Living: Live Without Excuses and Love Without Regret. NY: Dutton/Penguin Group, 2001.

Brookfield, S. D. The Power of Critical Theory: Liberating Adult Learning and *Teaching*. San Francisco, CA: Jossey-Bass, 2005.

Campbell, J. (with B. Moyers). *The Power of Myth*, ed. Sue Flowers. NY: Doubleday, 1988.

――. *Myths to Live By*. NY: Bantam Book, 1978.

Campbell, K. *A Stoic Philosophy of Life*. Lanham, MD: University Press of America, 1986.

Camus, A. "Neither Victim Nor Executioner." *Combat* (1946). http://ww.ppu.org.uk/e_publications/camus1.html.

Carrington, H. *Psychic World*. Kessinger Publishing, 2003.

Cary, T. The Michael Jackson Story: Man in the Mirror. Directed by Tom Cary. IMAVision/Oasis International ©2004.

Cayce, H. L. *Faces of Fear*. Cambridge, MA: Harper and Row San Francisco, 1980.

Chambers, H. E., and R. Craft. No Fear Management: Rebuilding Trust, Performance and Commitment in the New American Workplace. Boston, MA: St. Lucie Press, 1998.

Chandiwala, B. K. C. A. *At the Feet of Bapu*. Navajivan Publishing House, 1954.

Chernus, I. "World War II and the Origins of the Cold War: Toward a Nonviolence History." In Nonviolence for the Third Millenium: Its Legacy and Future, ed. G. S. Harak. Mercer University Press (2000).

Chödrön, P. The Places That Scare You: A Guide to Fearlessness in Difficult Times. (Boston, MA: Shambhala, 2001.

Church, F. Freedom from Fear: Finding the Courage to Act, Love, and Be. NY: St. Martin's Press, 2004.

Clarkson, M. Intelligent Fear: How to Make Fear Work for You. Toronto, ON: Key Porter Books, 2002.

Clements, A. Instinct for Freedom: Finding Liberation Through Living. Novato, CA: New World Library, 2002.

———. "Editorial." Spirit in Action: WorldDharma Monthly Newsletter, Vol. 1 (1999).

———. "We are Still Prisoners in Our Own Country: An Interview with Aung San Suu Kyi." *The Humanist* 57 (1997): 15-21.

Cloeren, H. J. Language and Thought: German Approaches to Analytic Philosophy in the 18th and 19th Centuries. Walter de Gryter, 1988.

Collins, R. *Four Sociological Traditions.* NY: Oxford University Press, 1994.

Conway, D., and R. R. Verdugo. "Fear-free Education Zones." *Education and Urban Society* 31 (1999): 357-67.

Corradi, J. E., P. W. Fagen, and M. A. Garretón, eds., *Fear at the Edge: State Terror and Resistance in Latin America.* Berkeley, CA: University of California Press, 1992.

Corradi, J. E. "Toward Societies Without Fear." In J. E. Corradi, P. W. Fagen, M. A. Garretón, eds. Fear at the Edge: State Terror and Resistance in Latin America Berkeley, CA: University of California Press (1992): 267-92.

Crittenden, J. "Foreword: What is the Meaning of 'Integral.'" In *The Eye of Spirit: An Integral Vision for a World Gone Slightly Mad,* Ken Wilber. Boston, MA: Shambhala (1997): vii-xii.

Crush, J. *Power of Development.* NY: Routledge, 1995.

Davis, M. The Ecology of Fear: Los Angeles and the Imagination of Disaster. NY: Vintage, 1999.

Dawkins, R. "Design for a Faith-based Missile." *Free Inquiry,* 22 (2001-02): 7-8.

de Becker, G. Fear Less: Real Truth About Risk, Safety, and Security in a Time of *Terrorism.* Boston, MA: Little, Brown & Co., 2002.

———. The Gift of Fear: Survival Signals that Protect us from Violence. NY: Bantam Doubleday Dell, 1997.

Desai, M. *The Story of My Life.* Pergamon Press, 1979.

Descartes, R. "The Passions of the Soul." In *The Philosophical Works of Descartes,* trans. E. S. Haldane & G. R. T. Ross. London: Cambridge University Press, 1975. [original published c.1650]

Diego, X. "US Christian Leaders Apologize for Iraq War." February 25. Inter Press Service, 2006. Retrieved March 2006 from http://www.commondreams.org/ headlines06/0225-03.htm.

Dover, K. J. Greek Popular Morality: In the Time of Plato and Aristotle. Oxford, UK: Basil Blackwell, 1974.

Dozier, R. W. Jr. Fear Itself: The Origin and Nature of the Powerful Emotion that Shapes Our Lives and World. NY: St. Martin's Press, 1998.

Edwards, R. Changing Places?: Flexibility, Lifelong Learning and a Learning Society. London, UK: Routledge, 1997.

Edwards, T. L. Brazil: A Global Studies Handbook. ABC-CLIO, 2007.

Eisler, R. The Chalice and the Blade: Our History, Our Future. San Francisco, CA: Harper and Row, 1987.

Ellin, N. ed., *Architecture of Fear.* NY: Princeton Architectural Press, 1997.

Evrigenis, I. *Fear of Enemies and Collective Action.* NY: Cambridge University Press, 2008.

Fanon, F. *The Wretched of the Earth,* trans. C. Farrington. NY: Grove Press, 1965.

Farrell, K. Post-traumatic Culture: Injury and Interpretation in the Nineties. Baltimore, MA: John Hopkins University Press, 1998.

Felman, S. "Education and Crisis, or the Vicissitudes of Teaching." In *Testimony: Crises of Witnessing in Literature, Psychoanalysis, and History,* eds. S. Felman and D. Laub. NY: Routledge (1992): 1-56.

————. "Psychoanalysis and education: Teaching Terminable and Interminable." *Yale French Studies* 29 (1982): 21-44.

Ferguson, M. *Aquarius Now: Radical Common Sense and Reclaiming Our Personal Sovereignty.* Boston, MA: Weiser Books, 2005.

————. The Aquarian Conspiracy: Personal and Social Transformation in the 1980s. Los Angeles, CA: J. P. Tarcher, 1980.

Ferrer, J. N. Revisioning Transpersonal Theory: A Participatory Vision of Human *Spirituality.* Albany, NY: State University of New York Press, 2002.

Filliozat, J. Religion, Philosophy, Yoga: A Selection of Articles, trans. M. Shukla Motilal Banarsidass, 1991.

Floating Eaglefeather (Amalina Wallace). Daughters of Fearlessness: A Medicine Bundle of Interviews with Spiritual Activists (Australia: Friends of UNICEF and Greenpeace, 1988).

Finger, M. "New Social Movements and Their Implications for Adult Education." *Adult Education Quarterly* 40 (1989): 15-22.

Fischman, G., P. McLaren, P., and H. Sunker. *Critical Theories, Radical Pedagogies, and Global Conflicts.* Lanham, MD: Rowman and Littlefield, 2005.

Fields, R. The Code of the Warrior: In History, Myth, and Everyday Life. NY: Harper-Collins, 1991).

Fisher, R. M. "Postmodern Developmental Philosopher *Par Excellence*: Ken Wilber's Role in Education, Part I (Introducing Ken Wilber)." Paper submitted, *Interchange: A* Quarterly Journal of Education.

————. Encyclopedia of the World's Fearlessness Teachings. Ms. in progress.

————. "'Unplugging' as Real and Metaphoric: Emancipatory Dimensions to The *Matrix* Film Trilogy." Technical Paper No. 33 (Carbondale, IL: In Search of Fearlessness Research Institute, 2009).

————. "Fearless Standpoint Theory: Origins of FMS-9 in Ken Wilber's Work." Technical Paper No. 31. Vancouver, BC: In Search of Fearlessness Research Institute, 2008.

————. "History of the Fearlessness Movement: An Introduction." Technical Paper No. 22. Vancouver, BC: In Search of Fearlessness Research Institute, 2007.

————. "Culture of Fear and Education: An Annotated Bibliography." Technical Paper No. 28. Vancouver, BC: In Search of Fearlessness Research Institute, 2007.

————. "Conceptualizing a Fearlessness Philosophy: Existential Philosophy and a Genealogy of Fear Management System-5." Technical Paper No. 23. Vancouver, BC: In Search of Fearlessness Institute, 2007.

————. "Disappear Fear: Action Fearology for the 21st Century." Technical Paper No. 26. Vancouver, BC: In Search of Fearlessness Research Institute, 2007.

————. "Toward an Integral Terror Management Theory: Use of the Wilber-Combs Lattice." Technical Paper No. 24. Vancouver, BC: In Search of Fearlessness Research Institute, 2007.

————. "Ken Wilber and the Education Literature: Abridged Annotated Bibliography." 2007. http://ww.pathsoflearning.net/resources_writings_Ken_Wilber.pdf

————. "An Integral Fearlessness Paradigm." Technical Paper No. 20. Vancouver, BC: In Search of Fearlessness Research Institute, 2006.

————. "Invoking 'Fear' Studies." *Journal of Curriculum Theorizing* 22(4) (2006): 39-71.

————. "Wilber and Fear Management Theory." Technical Paper No. 17. Vancouver, BC: In Search of Fearlessness Research Institute, 2004.

————. "Capitalizing on Fear: A Baseline Study on the Culture of Fear for Leaders." Unpublished document. Minneapolis, MN: Intellectual Architects, Inc., 2004.

————. "Fear is...". Technical Paper No. 16. Vancouver, BC: In Search of Fearlessness Research Institute, 2003.

————. "Fearless Leadership In and Out of the 'Fear' Matrix." Unpublished dissertation. Vancouver, BC: The University of British Columbia, 2003. Available as a free pdf online http//: m1.cust.educ.ubc.ca/Artography/phd.php.

————. "Report on the Status of Fear Education." Technical Paper No. 15. Vancouver, BC: In Search of Fearlessness Research Institute, 2003.

————. "What is the 'Fear' Matrix? (Part 1: Failure of Cultural)." Technical Paper No.13. Vancouver, BC: In Search of Fearlessness Research Institute, 2002.

————. "On Being a 'Fear' Critic." Technical Paper No. 14. Vancouver, BC: In Search of Fearlessness Research Institute, 2002.

————. "Fearology: The Biography of an Idea." Technical Paper No. 12. Calgary, AB: In Search of Fearlessness Research Institute, 2001.

————. "Toward a 'Conflict' Pedagogy: A Critical Discourse Analysis of 'Conflict' in Conflict Management Education." Unpublished masters thesis. Vancouver, BC: The University of British Columbia, 2000.

————. "Unveiling the Hidden Curriculum in Conflict Resolution and Peace Education: Future Directions Toward a Critical Conflict Education and 'Conflict' Pedagogy." Technical Paper No. 9. Vancouver, BC: In Search of Fearlessness Research Institute, 2000.

————. "Toward a 'Conflict' Pedagogy: A Critical Discourse Analysis of 'Conflict' in Conflict Management Education" Unpublished masters thesis. Vancouver, BC: The University of British Columbia, 2000.

————. "The Movement Toward a Fearless Society: A Powerful Contradiction to Violence." Technical Paper No. 10. Vancouver, BC: In Search of Fearlessness Research Institute, 2000.

————. "How Are We Handling Conflict?: Newman's Challenge to Conceptualize and Deal With the *Enemy* in a Violent World." Unpublished paper, 1999.

————. "Defining the 'Enemy' of Fearlessness." Technical Paper No. 6. Calgary, AB: In Search of Fearlessness Research Institute, 1997.

————. "A Guide to Wilberland: Some Common Misunderstandings of the Critics of Ken Wilber and His Work on Transpersonal Theory Prior to 1995." *Journal of Humanistic Psychology* 37 (1997): 47-54.

————. *Spectrum of 'Fear.'* Unpublished ms, 1997.

————. "*Thanatos* and *Phobos*: 'Fear' and its Role in Ken Wilber's Transpersonal Theory." Unpublished paper, 1997.

————. "An Introduction to: An Epistemology of 'Fear': A Fearlessness Paradigm." Technical Paper No. 2. Calgary, AB: In Search of Fearlessness Research Institute, 1995.

————. "Coral-colored 'Flower'—An Anti-predator Adaptation," *Calgary Field- Naturalist*, 88 (1976): 148.

Fisher, V. D. "Beauty and the Experience of Women's Identity." *AQAL: Journal of* Integral Theory and Practice 3 (2008): 68-86.

Foucault, M. *Fearless Speech*, ed. J. Pearson. NY: Semiotext(e), 2001.

Foucault, M. Power and Knowledge: Selected Interviews and Other Writings, 1972-1977. NY: Pantheon Books, 1980.

Foundation for Inner Peace. *A Course in Miracle.* Tiburon, CA: Foundation for Inner Peace, 1975.

Fox, F. and I. Prilleltensky, *Critical Psychology: An Introduction.* London: Sage, 1997.

Francis, A. H. ed. Schools Without Fear. Proceedings of the 14th Annual International Alliance for Invitational Education Conference. Greensboro, CA: International Alliance for Invitational Education, 1996.

Francois, D. The Self-Destruction of the West: Critical Cultural Anthropology. Editions Publibook, 2007.

Freire, P. *Pedagogy of Hope; Reliving Pedagogy of the Oppressed,* trans. R. R. Barr. NY: Continuum, 1994.

Fuller, R. B. *Critical Path.* NY: St. Martin's Press, 1981.

Furedi, F. Culture of Fear Revisited: Risk-taking and the Morality of Low Expectation London, UK: Continuum, 2006.

———. *Politics of Fear.* London, UK: Continuum, 2005.

———. Therapy Culture: Cultivating Vulnerability in an Uncertain Age. London: Routledge, 2004.

———. Culture of Fear: Risk and the Morality of Low Expectation. London: Cassell, 1997.

Gabbard, D., and K. A. Appleton. "Fearless Speech in Fearful Times: An Essay Review of Capitalists and Conquerors, Teaching Against Global Capitalism and the New Imperialism and Teaching Peter McLaren. Retrieved November 16, 2008 from http://mrzine.monthlyreview.org/agm301005.html.

Gadon, E. W. The Once and Future Goddess: A Symbol for Our Time. NY: Harper and Row, 1989.

Gáleano, E. Upside Down: A Primer for the Looking-glass World. Trans. Mark Fried NY: Henry Holt, 2000.

Gard, R. A. ed. *Buddhism.* NY: George Braziller, 1962.

Geist, V. Life Strategies, Human Evolution, Environmental Design: Toward a Biological Theory of Health. NY: Springer-Verlag, 1978.

Gillian, S. N. The Beauty of Fear: How to Positively Enjoy Being Afraid. Bronx, NY: Phemore Press, 2002.

Gimbutas, M. *The Language of the Goddess.* NY: Harper San Francisco, 1991.

Ginsberg, R., and B. S. Cooper. "Introduction: What's Fear Got to Do With It?" Educational Policy, 22 (2008): 5-9.

———. and L. F. Lyche. "The Culture of Fear and the Politics of Education." Educational Policy 22 (2008):10-27.

———. and T. G. Davies. The Human Side of Leadership: Navigating Emotions at *Work.* Greenwood, 2007.

Giroux, H. A. Against the Terror of Neoliberalism: Politics Beyond the Age of Greed. Boulder, CO: Paradigm, 2008.

———. "What Might Education Mean After Abu Ghraib: Revisiting Adorno's Politics of Education." Comparative Studies of South Asia, Africa and the Middle East, 24 (2004): 3-22.

———. The Abandoned Generation: Democracy Beyond the Culture of Fear. NY: Palgrave/Macmillan, 2003.

———. "Mis/education and Zero Tolerance: Disposable Youth and the Politics of Domestic Militarization." Boundary: An International Journal of Literature and Culture 28 (2001): 1-92.

———. Theory and Resistance in Education: A Pedagogy for the Opposition. South Hadley, Massachusetts: Bergin and Garvey, 1983.

Goodey, J. Boys Don't Cry: Masculinities, Fear of Crime and Fearlessness, *The British Journal of Criminology* 37 (1997): 401-418.

Goodin, R. E., and D. Parker. "Introduction: Symposium on Martha Nussbaum's Political Philosophy." *Ethics* 111 (2000): 6-7.

Gore, A. *The Assault on Reason.* NY: The Penguin Press, 2007.

———. An Inconvenient Truth: The Planetary Emergency of Global Warming and What We Can Do About it. NY: Rodale Books, 2006.

———. An Inconvenient Truth: A Global Warning. Hollywood, CA: Paramount Pictures,™ and ©2006.

Green, T. A. D. Twelve Reasons Christians Don't Grow . . . Even in Good Churches! Xulon Press, 2007.

Griffin, S. "Fearlessness," *Yes! Magazine.* Summer (2003). Retrieved April 18, 2005 from http://www.futurenet.org/article.asp?id=604.

Gordon, M. T., and S. Riger. *The Female Fear.* NY: The Free Press, 1989.

Grahn, J. "Are Goddesses Metaformic Constructs?: An Application of Metaformic Theory to Menarche Celebrations and Goddess Rituals of Kerala and Contiguous States in South India." Unpublished dissertation. San Francisco, CA: California Institute of Integral Studies, 1999.

———. Blood, Bread, and Roses: How Menstruation Created the World. Boston, MA: Beacon Press, 1993.

Greer, G. *The Whole Woman.* NY: Alfred A. Knopf, 1999.

Griscom, C. The Healing of Emotion: Awakening the Fearless Self. NY: Simon and Schuster, 1990.

Guess, J. B. (Rev.) "Don't Ever Say What You're Never Going To Do," *United Church News* (Aug.-Sept. 2005). Retrieved April 2006 from http://www.ucc.org/ucnews/sept05 /leader.htm.

Guimón, J. *Art and Madness.* The Davies Group, 2006.

Habermas, J. "New Social Movements." *Telos* 49 (1981): 33-37.

Hahn, T. N. No Death, No Fear: Comforting Wisdom for Life. Riverhead Books, 2003.

Hare, R. D., D. J. Cooke, and S. D. Hart. "Psychopathy and Sadistic Personality Disorder." In *Oxford Textbook of Psychopathology*, eds. R. D. Davis, T. Millon, and P. H. Blaney. NY: Oxford University Press (1999): 555-84.

Harman, W., and H. Rheingold. Higher Creativity: Liberating the Unconscious for *Breakthrough Insights*. Los Angeles, CA: Jeremy P. Tarcher, 1984.

Hastings, J. ed. *Encyclopedia of Religion and Ethics* (Part 23). Kessinger Publications, 2003.

Hauerwas, S., and Charles Pinches. Christians Among the Virtues: Theological Conversations with Ancient and Modern Ethics. Notre Dame, IN: University of Notre Dame Press, 1997.

Hayward, J. *Sacred World; A Guide to Shambhala Warriorship in Daily Life.* NY: Bantam, 1995.

Heim, M. Theories of the Gift in South Asia: Hindu, Buddhist, and Jain Reflections on *Dāna*. NY: Routledge, 2004.

Heron, J. Co-operative Inquiry: Research into the Human Condition. London, UK: Sage, 1996.

———. Feeling and Personhood: Psychology in Another Key. London, UK: Sage, 1992.

Hibbets, M. "Saving Them From Yourself: An Inquiry into the South Asian Gift of Fearlessness." *Journal of Religious Ethics*, 27 (1999): 437-62.

Hibbs, T. S. "Notes from Underground: Nihilism and *The Matrix*. In *The Matrix and Philosophy: Welcome to the Desert of the Real*, ed. William Irwin. Chicago, IL: Open Court (2002): 155-65.

Holford, J. "Why Social Movements Matter: Adult Education Theory, Cognitive Praxis, and the Creation of Knowledge." *Adult Education Quarterly* 45 (1995): 95-111.

hooks, b. *All About Love.* NY: William Morrow, 2000.

Horsley, J. Matrix Warrior: Being the One (The Unofficial Handbook). London: Gollanz, 2003.

Howard, L. Introducing Ken Wilber: Concepts for an Evolving World. AuthorHouse, 2005.

Huber, C. *The Fear Book: Facing Fear Once and For All.* Zen Meditation Center, 1997.

Huffington, A. "Fear Watch '08: Keeping an Eye Out for GOP Fear-mongering," *The Huffington Post,* June 25, 2008, http://www.huffingtonpost.com/arianna-huffington/fearwatch-08-keeping-an-e_b_109262.html.

———. On Becoming Fearless in Love, Work, and Life. Boston, MA: Little, Brown and Co., 2007.

———. (in conversation with B. Patrick), "Becoming Fearless," 2006. Retrieved December 2, 2006 from http://coaches.aol.com/business-and- career/feature/_a/ interview-with-arianna-huffington/20060908145309990001.

———. (interviewed by L. Frum). "No More Fears: Arianna Huffington Was Once Terrified." *National Post,* September 30, 2006. Retrieved December 18, 2006 from http://www.canada.com/nationalpost/news/story.html.

Humphreys, C. *A Popular Dictionary of Buddhism.* London: Curzon Press, 1976.

Icke, D. Children of the Matrix: How an Interdimensional Race Has Controlled the World for Thousands of Years—and Still Does. Wildwood, MO: Bridge of Love Publications, 2001.

Jampolsky, G. *Teach Only Love; The Seven Principles of Attitudinal Healing.* NY: Bantam, 1983.

Jary, D., and J. Jary. *Collins Dictionary of Sociology.* Glasgow, Scotland: HarperCollins, 1995.

Jeffers, S. *Feel the Fear And Do It Anyway.* NY: Fawcett Columbine, 1988.

Johnson, R. "Neither Aristotle nor Nietzsche." In *Kierkegaard After MacIntyre: Essays on Freedom, Narrative, and Virtue,* eds. J. J. Davenport, and A. Rudd. Open Court (2001): 151-72.

Johnston, B. V. Pitrim A. Sorokin: An Intellectual Biography. Lawrence, KS: University Press of Kansas, 1995.

Johnston, C. The Creative Imperative: A Four-dimensional Theory of Human Growth and Planetary Evolution. Berkeley, CA: Celestial Arts, 1986.

Jon, T. Mindful Knitting: Inviting Contemplative Practice to the Craft. Tuttle Publications, 2004.

Jones, S., and J. Gosling, Nelson's Way: Leadership Lessons from the Great Commander Nicolas Brealey Publishing, 2005.

Kagan, J. *Three Seductive Ideas.* Cambridge, MA: Harvard University Press, 1998.

———. Galen's Prophecy: Temperament in Human Nature. Boulder, CO: Westview Press, 1997.

Kegan, R. In Over Our Heads: The Mental Demands of Modern Life (Cambridge, MA: Harvard University Press, 1998),

Keen, S. The Passionate Life: Stages of Loving. NY: Harper and Row, 1983.

Kent, F. Nothing to Fear: Coping with Phobias. NY: Harper and Row, 1979.

Khyentse, D. *Enlightened Courage.* Ithaca, NY: Snow Lion, 1993.

Kidder, R. M. *Moral Courage.* NY: William Morrow, 2005.

Kleiner, A. (interview with M. J. Wheatley). "Fearlessness: The Last Organizational Change Strategy." Retrieved October 2, 2007 from http://www.strategy- business.com/li/leadingideas/li00044?pg=1.

Kline, N. The Shock Doctrine: The Rise of Disaster Capitalism. Metropolitan Books/Henry Holt, 2007.

———. No Logo: No Space, No Choice, No Jobs. NY: Picador, 2002.

Kopp, S. *Raise Your Right Hand Against Fear; Extend the Other in Compassion.* Minneapolis, MN: Compcare, 1988.

Korten, D. C. The Great Turning: From Empire to Earth Community. San Francisco, CA/Bloomfield, CT: Berrett-Koehler/Kumarian Press, 2005.

Krishnamurti, J. *The Collected Works of J. Krishnamurti.* Krishnamurti Foundation of America, 1991.

Kyi, A. S. S. "Freedom from Fear." In Violence and its Alternatives: An Interdisciplinary *Reader,* eds. M. B. Steger and N. S. Lind. NY: St. Martin's Press (1999): 313-16.

———., and A. Clements. *The Voice of Hope.* NY: Seven Stories Press, 1997.

———. Freedom from Fear and Other Writings, ed. M. Aris. UK: Penguin, 1995. [original essay "Freedom from Fear," 1991]

Lamb, C. *Bridgid's Charge.* Corte Madera, CA: Bay Island Books, 1997.

Land, G. Grow or Die: The Unifying Principle of Transformation. Leadership 2000, Inc. [original published in 1973]

Lange, E. "Re-enchantment to Escape Empire: Spirituality, Sustainability, and Critical Transformative Learning." Paper presented at Thinking Beyond Borders: Global Ideas, Global Values," online Proceedings of the Canadian Association for the *Study of Adult Education,* 27th National Conference. Vancouver, BC: Canadian Association for the Study of Adult Education, 2008.

———. "Transformative and Restorative Learning: A Vital Dialectic for Sustainable Societies." *Adult Education Quarterly* 54 (2004): 121-39.

Lappé, F. M., and J. Perkins. You Have the Power: Choosing Courage in a Culture of *Fear.* NY: Jeremy P. Tarcher/Penguin, 2005.

Lavelle, K. M. *The Reality within The Matrix.* Wisconsin Dells, WI: Saxco, 2000.

Lawler, J. "We are (the) One!: Kant Explains How to Manipulate the Matrix." In *The Matrix and Philosophy: Welcome to the Desert of the Real,* ed. William Irwin. Chicago, IL: Open Court (2002): 138-52.

Lefebvre, H. Everyday Life in the Modern World. Transaction, 1984.

Lehr, J. B., and C. Martin. Schools Without Fear: Group Activities for Building *Community.* Minneapolis, MN: Educational Media Corporation, 1994.

Lerner, H. The Dance of Fear: Rising Above Anxiety, Fear, and Shame to be your Best and Bravest Self. NY: HarperCollins, 2005.

Lerner, M. *Spirit Matters.* Hampton Roads Publications, 2000.

Lindeman, C. E. *The Meaning of Adult Education.* Montreal, QB: Harvest House, 1961. [original published in 1926]

Lippe-Biesterfeld, I., and J. Van Tijn. Science, Soul, and the Spirit of Nature: Leading Thinkers on the Restoration of Man and Creation. Santa Fe, NM: Inner Traditions/ Bear and Co., 2005.

Lipton, B. *Biology of Belief* ("*Lite*"). Recorded in 2005 at "What the Bleep Do We Know! Conference, Berkeley, CA. Mephis, TN: Spirit 2000, Inc., ©2005.

Listerborn, C. "Understanding the Geography of Women's Fear: Toward a Reconceptualization of Fear and Space." In *Subjectivities, Knowledges, and* Feminist Geographies: The Subjects and Ethics of Social Research, eds. L. Bondi, H. Avis, and R. Bankey. Lanham, MD: Rowman and Littlefield (2002): 34-43.

Love, B. J., and K. J. Philips. "Ageism and Adultism Curriculum Design." In *Teaching for Diversity and Social Justice: A Source Book,* eds. M. Adams, L. E. Bell, and P. Griffin. CRC Press (2007): 359-80.

Luke, A. "Text and Discourse in Education: An Introduction to Critical Discourse Analysis." ed. M. W. Apple, In *Review of Research in Education* 21 (1995-96): 3-48.

Luther, M. "Sermons on the Gospel of St. John, Chapters 14-16. In *Luther's Works, Vol. 24,* ed. J. Pelikan, St. Louis, Missouri: Concordia Publishing House, 1961.

Lutz, C. A. *Unnatural Emotions; Everyday Sentiments on a Micronesian Atoll and their Challenges to Western Theory.* Chicago, IL: University of Chicago Press, 1988.

Mackie, F. *The Status of Everyday Life: A Sociological Excavation of the Prevailing Framework of Perception.* London: Routledge, 1985.

Mahaprajna, A. "Freedom From Fear: And the Freedom Must Be Total." Retrieved June 29, 2008 from http://www.greaterkasmir.com/full_story.asp?Date=27_6_2008&ItemID=7&cat=11.

Maidman, D. *Think Peace.* Directed by C. Ogilvie (©2007 DreamHouse, Creative, Inc. and Production, Inc. See http://www.thinkpeace.com.

Malin, B. "Be Afraid, Be Very Afraid: The Pedagogy of Fear." *Bad Subjects,* May-June, (2000). Retrieved October 17, 2002 from http://bad.eserver.org/issues/2000/50/ malin.html.

Margolis, D. R. *The Fabric of Self: A Theory of Ethics and Emotions.* New Haven, CN: Yale University Press, 1998.

Marsick, V. J., and Watkins, K. E. "Looking Again at Learning in the Learning Organization: A Tool That Can Turn Into a Weapon." *Learning Organization,* 6 (1999): 207-11.

Martin, S. Born Standing Up: A Comic's Life. NY: Scribner, 2007.

Maslow, A. *Toward a Psychology of Being.* NY: Van Nostrand Reinhold, 1968.

———. The Psychology of Science: A Reconnaissance. NY: Harper and Row, 1966.

Massumi, B. "Preface," In *The Politics of Everyday Fear,* ed. B. Massumi. Minneapolis, MN: University of Minnesota Press (1993): vii-x.

———. "Everywhere You Want to Be." In *The Politics of Everyday Fear,* ed. B. Massumi. Minneapolis, MN: University of Minnesota Press (1993): 3-37.

Masters, R. A. Truth Cannot be Rehearsed: Talks, Sessions, and Essays About the Art of *Being Fully Human.* Vancouver, BC: Xanthyros Foundation, 1990.

Matthen, M. "Biological Universals and the Nature of Fear." *The Journal of Philosophy* XCV (1998): 105-32.

Matustík, M. B. "Towards an Integral Critical Theory of the Present Age." *Integral* Review, 5 (2007): 227-239.

May, R. *Man's Search for Himself.* Toronto, ON: New American Library of Canada, 1967.

Mayes, C. "The Teacher as Shaman." *Curriculum Studies* 37 (2005): 329-48.

———. Seven Curricular Landscapes: An Approach to the Holistic Curriculum. Lanham, MD: University Press of America, 2003.

McHoul, A., and W. Grace. A Foucault Primer: Discourse, Power and the Subject Washington Square, NY: New York University Press, 1998.

McIntosh, S. Integral Consciousness and the Future of Evolution: How the Integral Worldview is Transforming Politics, Culture and Spirituality. St. Paul, MN: Paragon House, 2007.

McLaren, P. Capitalists and Conquerors: A Critical Pedagogy Against Empire. Lanham, MD: Rowman and Littlefield, 2005.

———. Che Guevara, Paulo Freire, and the Pedagogy of Revolution. Lanham, MD: Rowman and Littlefield, 2000.

———. (with K. Gutierrez). "Pedagogies of Dissent and Transformation: A Dialogue with Kris Gutierrez. In Critical Pedagogy and Predatory Culture: Oppositional *Politics in a Postmodern Era,* ed. P. McLaren. NY: Routledge (1995): 143-47.

McMahon, J. L. "Popping a Bitter Pill: Existential Authenticity in *The Matrix* and Nausea. In The Matrix and Philosophy: Welcome to the Desert of the Real, ed. William Irwin. Chicago, IL: Open Court (2002): 166-77.

Merton, T. *New Seeds of Contemplation.* New Directions, 1972.

———. "Faith and Violence," In *Thomas Merton on Peace*, ed. G. C. Zahn. NY: McCall, 1971.

Mezirow, J. Fostering Critical Reflection in Adulthood: A Guide to Transformative and *Emancipatory Learning.* San Francisco, CA: Jossey-Bass, 1990.

Miller, A. Thou Shalt Not Be Aware: Society's Betrayal of the Child, trans. H. and H. Hannum. NY: Farrar, Straus, Giroux, 1985.

Miller, J. One of the Guys: Girls, Gangs, and Gender. NY: Oxford University Press, 2001.

Miller, S., J. Brodine and T. Miller eds. Safe By Design: Planning for Peaceful School *Communities.* Seattle, WA: Committee for Children, 1996.

Miller, W. I. *The Mystery of Courage.* Cambridge, MA: Harvard University Press, 2000.

Mills, S. *Discourse.* NY: Routledge, 1997.

Mindell, A. Sitting in the Fire: Large Group Transformation Using Conflict and *Diversity.* Portland, OR: Lao Tse Press, 1995.

———. The Leader as Martial Artist: An Introduction to Deep Democracy. NY: Harper-Collins, 1993.

Moore, R. Escaping the Matrix: How We the People Can Change the World. Redwood City, CA and Wexford, Ireland: The Cyberjournal Project, 2006.

Moore, R., and D. Gillette, King, Warrior, Magician, Lover: Rediscovering the Archetypes of the Mature Masculine. NY: HarperCollins, 1991.

Nagle, B. A., and P. Pascareua. Leveraging People and Profit: The Hard Work of Soft Management. Elsevier, 1997.

Nathanson, D. L. Shame and Pride: Affect, Sex, and the Birth of the Self. NY: W. W. Norton, 1994.

———. *The Many Faces of Shame.* NY: The Guilford Press, 1987

Negri, A. with A. DuFourmantelle. Negri on Negri: In Conversation with Anne *DuFourmantelle*, trans. M. B. DeBevoise. NY: Routledge, 2004.

Newman, A. "Aestheticism, Feminism, and the Dynamics of Reversal." *Hypatia,* 5 (1990): 20-33.

Newman, M. "Locating Learning in Social Action," ed. B. Brennan in Social Action and Emancipatory Learning [seminar] *UTS Seminar Papers.* Sydney, Australia: School of Education, 2005.

———. "Response to 'An Open Letter,' Australian Journal of Adult and Community Education 37 (1997): 57-61.

———. Defining the Enemy: Adult Education in Social Action. Sydney, Australia: Stewart Victor, 1994.

———. The Third Contract: Theory and Practice in Trade Union Training. Sydney, Australia: Stewart Victor, 1993.

Nixon, G. "The Transformational Opportunity of Absolute Hopelessness and Non- Attainment." *Voices: The Journal of the American Academy of Psychotherapists,* Summer (2001): 55-66.

Noddings, N. *Women and Evil.* Berkeley, CA: University of California Press, 1989.

Norton, C. "Victory over Fear," n.d. Retrieved March 12, 2007 from http://www.anglefire.com.realm/csu/victory.htm

Nuemberger, P. Strong and Fearless: The Quest for Personal Power. Yes International, 2003.

Nuernberger, P. "The Structure of Mind and its Resources." In *Transcendence and Mature Thought in Adulthood*, eds. M. E. Miller, and S. R. Cook-Greuter. Lanham, MD: Rowman and Littlefield (1994): 89-116.

Obama, B. The Audacity of Hope: Thoughts on Reclaiming the American Dream. Crown, 2006.

Oden, M., and G. Dick-Read. Childbirth Without Fear: The Principles and Practice of Natural Childbirth. Pinter and Martin, 2005.

O'Hara, M. L. "'Let it Fly': The Legacy of Helen Bass Williams. Unpublished dissertation. Carbondale, IL: Southern University of Illinois Carbondale, 2004.

Olssen, M., J, A. Codd, and A-M. O'Neill. Education Policy: Globalization, Citizenship and Democracy. Thousand Oaks, CA: Sage, 2004.

O'Sullivan, E. Transformative Learning: Educational Vision for the 21st Century. Toronto, ON: Ontario Institute of Studies in Education/University of Toronto Press, 1999.

Overstreet, B. W. Understanding Fear in Ourselves and Others. NY: Harper and Row, 1971) [original published in 1951].

Palmer, P. J. A Hidden Wholeness: The Journey Toward an Undivided Life. San Francisco, CA: Jossey-Bass, 2004.

————. (interviewed by Sarah, ed. Green Money Journal). "Making the Difference: Integral Life; Integral Teacher." Retrieved May 11, 2004 from http://www.greenmoneyjournal.com/article.mpl?newsletterid=17&articleid=142.

————. The Courage to Teach: Exploring the Inner Landscape of a Teacher's Life. San Francisco, CA: Jossey-Bass, 1998.

————. "Teaching in the Face of Fear." NTLF, 6 (1997), n.p.

Pascal, F. Bad. NY: Simon Pulse, 2002.

Paul III, Pope J. Crossing the Threshold of Hope. Toronto, ON: A. A. Knopf, 1994.

Paulston, R. "From Paradigm Wars to Disputatious Community." Comparative Education Review, August (1990): 395-400.

Pérez-Gómez, A. Built Upon Love: Architectural Longing After Ethics and Aesthetics. Cambridge, MA: The MIT Press, 2006.

Peters, T. J., and Robert H. Waterman Jr. In Search of Excellence: Lessons from America's Best-Run Companies. NY: Harper and Row, 1982.

Pirsig, R. M. Zen and the Art of Motorcycle Maintenance. NY: Bantam Books, 1976,

Plato. The Dialogues of Plato, trans. Benjamin Jowett. NY: Scribner, Armstrong, 1874. [original may have been published nearly 2000 years ago]

Pöggler, F. "'Education After Auschwitz' as a Perspective of Adult Education." in Adult Education in Crisis Situations: Proceedings of the Third International Conference on the History of Adult Education, eds. F. Pöggler, and K. Yaron. Jerusalem: The Magnes Press, 1991.

Popkewitz, T. Struggling for the Soul: The Politics of Schooling and the Construction of the Teacher. NY: Teachers College Press, 1998.

————. A Political Sociology of Educational Reform: Power/Knowledge in Teaching, Teacher Education, and Research. NY: Teachers College Press, 1991.

Pritzker, B. M. A Native American Encyclopedia: History, Culture, and Peoples. NY: Oxford University Press, 2000.

Pyszczynski, T., S. Solomon, and J. Greenberg. In the Wake of 9/11: The Psychology of Terror. Washington, DC: American Psychological Association, 2002.

Quiñones Rosado, R. Consciousness-in-Action: Toward an Integral Psychology of Liberation and Transformation. Caguas, Puerto Rico: ilé Publications, 2007.

Rachman, S. J. Fear and Courage. NY: W. H. Freeman, 1990.

Ranganathananda. Eternal Values for a Changing Society. Bharatiya Vidya Bhavan, 1984.

Ray, P. H. "The Rise of Integral Culture," Noetic Science Review, #37 (1996). Retrieved August 11, 2007 from http://www.noetic.org/publications/review/issue37/r37_Ray. html.

Redfield, J. The Celestine Prophecy; An Adventure. NY: Warner Books, 1994.

Regnier, R. "Warrior as Pedagogue, Pedagogue as Warrior: Reflections on Aboriginal Anti-racist Pedagogy. In Anti-racism, Feminism and Critical Approaches to Educa-

tion, eds. R. Ng., P. Staton and J. Scane. Westport, CT: Bergin and Garvey (1995): 67-86.

Research and Forecasts, Inc., with A. Friedberg. *America Afraid: How Fear of Crime Changes the Way We Live* (based on the widely publicized Figgie Report). NY: New American Library, 1983.

Reynolds, B. Where's Wilber At?: Ken Wilber's Integral Vision in the New Millenium St. Paul, MN: Paragon House, 2006.

————. Embracing Reality: The Integral Vision of Ken Wilber: A Historical Survey and Chapter-by-Chapter Guide to Wilber's Major Works. NY: Jeremy P. Tarcher/ Penguin, 2004.

Ridley, F. A. *The Revolutionary Tradition in England*. National Labour Press, 1947.

Robin, C. *Fear: The History of a Political Idea*. NY: Oxford University Press, 2004.

Rodriguez, E. "Time to Be Fearless." Retrieved October 11, 2007 from http://evelynrodriguez.typepad.com/crossroads_dispatches/2006/12/the_time_has_c o.html.

Rosen, D. H. Transforming Depression: Healing the Soul Through Creativity. NY: Penguin Books, 1996.

Roth, G. (with J. Loudon). *Maps to Ecstasy; Teachings of an Urban Shaman*. San Rafael, CA: New World Library, 1989.

Rowe, D. *Beyond Fear*. London, UK: Fontana Paperbacks, 1987.

Ruhela, S. P. *Quotations from India*. M. D. Publications PVT, Ltd., 1997.

Sardello, R. *Freeing the Soul from Fear*. NY: Putnam Penguin, 1999.

Schneier, B. Beyond Fear: Thinking Sensibly About Security in an Uncertain World. NY: Copernicus Books, 2003.

Schumacher, E. F. Small is Beautiful: A Study of Economics as if People Mattered. London: Sphere Books, 1974.

Seaton, E. "The Commodification of Fear." Topia: Canadian Journal of Cultural Studies, 5 (2001): 1-18.

Segal, J. Living Beyond Fear: A Tool for Transformation. Hollywood, CA: Newcastle, 1984.

Seshagri Rao, K. L. Mahatma Gandhi and Comparative Religion. India: Motilal Banarsidass, 1978.

Sharp, H. "Why Spinoza Today?, or, 'a Strategy of Anti-Fear,' *Rethinking Marxism*, 17 (2005): 591-608.

Shen, P., and G. Bennick. Flight From Death: The Quest for Immortality, DVD narrated by Gabriel Byrne. Transcontinental Media ©2005.

Shikpo, R., F. Fremantle, and D. Hutchens. Never Turn Away: The Buddhist Path Beyond Hope and Fear. Wisdom Publications, 2007.

Shlapentokh, V., and E. Shiraev. *Fears in Post-communist Societies*. Macmillan, 2002.

Simon, J. Governing Through Crime: How the War on Crime Transformed American Democracy and Created a Culture of Fear. NY: Oxford University Press, 2007.

Slaughter, R. Futures Beyond Dystopia: Creating Social Foresight. London, UK: Routledge Farmer, 2004.

Small, J. *Transformers: The Therapists of the Future: Personal Transformation: The Way Through*. Marina Del Ray, CA: DeVorss and Co., 1984.

Smith, D. G. *Pedagon: Interdisciplinary Essays in the Human Sciences, Pedagogy and Culture*. NY: Peter Lang, 1999.

Smith, M. R., and E. T. Jones. "Neophobia, Ontological Insecurity, and the Existential Choice Following Trauma." *Journal of Humanistic Psychology*, 33 (1993): 89-109.

Smith, S. "The Good Guide to R. Buckminster Fuller." *GoodMagazine*, 2007. Retrieved May 1, 2008 from http://goodmagazine.com.

Stearns, P. N. American Fear: The Causes and Consequences of High Anxiety. NY: Routledge, 2006.

Steele, J. "Now He Must Declare That the War on Terror is Over." *The Guardian*, Nov. 6. (2008).

Stevens, M. E. Troubling Beginnings: Trans(per)forming African-American History. NY: Routledge, 2003.

Sumpton, J. *The Hundred Years' War*. University of Pennsylvania Press, 2001.

Sunstein, C. Laws of Fear: Beyond the Precautionary Principle. Cambridge, UK: Cambridge University Press, 2005.

Tatar, M. Off With Their Heads!: Fairy Tales and the Culture of Childhood. Princeton, NJ: Princeton University Press, 1993.

Taubman, P. "Teaching Without Hope: What is Really at Stake in the Standards Movement, High Stakes Testing, and the Drive for 'Practical Reforms.' *Journal of Curriculum Theorizing* 16 (2000): 19-33.

Taylor, S. E., L. C. Klein, B. P. Lewis, T. L. Gruenewald and et al., "Biobehavioral Responses to Stress in Females: Tend-and-Befriend, Not Fight-or-Flight." Psychological Review 107 (2000): 411-29.

Tikekar, I. B. Integral Revolution: An Analytical Study of Gandhian Thought. Sarva Seva Sangh Prakashan, 1970.

Tolle, E. "Women Embody Enlightenment" (excerpt from *The Power of Now*), Common Ground, March (2008).

Tompkins, I., and McIntosh, D. *Fearless Parenting: Handle with Love*. Bridge-Logos, 1996.

Torbert, W. R. The Power of Balance: Transforming Self, Society, and Scientific Inquiry. Newbury Park, CA: Sage, 1991.

Trungpa, C. Shambhala: The Sacred Path of the Warrior. Boston, MA: Shambhala, 2007. [original published in 1984]

———. (edited by C. R. Gimian). Shambhala: The Sacred Path of the Warrior Book and *Card Set*. Boston, MA: Shambhala, 2004.

———. *Cutting Through Spiritual Materialism*. Boulder, CO: Shambhala, 1973.

Tuan, Y-F. *Landscapes of Fear*. Minneapolis, MN: University of Minnesota Press, 1979.

Tudor, A. "A (Macro)Sociology of Fear?" *The Sociological Review* 51 (2003): 238-56.

Valles, C. G. *Let Go of Fear*. NY: Triumph, 1991.

VanderWeil, E. "Accepting a Ring of Fire: Stories of Engagement with Fear in Transformational Adult Learning." Unpublished dissertation. Spokane, WA: Gonzaga University, 2007.

Vanier, J. *Be Not Afraid*. Toronto, ON: Griffin House, 1975.

Vanzant, I. *Until Today!* NY: Simon and Schuster, 2000.

Verdugo, R. R., and J. M. Schneider. "Quality Schools, Safe Schools: A Theoretical and Empirical Discussion. *Education and Urban Society,* 31 (1999): 286-307.

Verma, V. The Emergence of Himachal Pradesh: A Survey of Constitutional Developments. Indus Publishing, 1995.

Vinobā, S. N. *Vinobā: His Life and Work,* Popular Prakashan, 1970.

Viscott, D. *Emotional Resilience; Simple Truths for Dealing with Unfinished Business of Your Past*. NY: Random House, 1996.

Von Mises, L. Planning for Freedom: And Other Essays and Addresses Libertarian Press, 1962,

Wachowski, L., and A. Wachowski. "The Matrix" Shooting Script, August, 12, 1998, In *The Art of The Matrix,* ed. S. Lamm. NY: Newmarket Press, 2000.

———. *The Matrix*. Directed by the Wachowski Bros., produced by Joel Silver. Warner Bros., Inc. ©1999.

War Resisters International Triennial Conference. *Liberation and Revolution: Gandhi's Challenge.* War Resisters International, 1969.

Webster's New Collegiate Dictionary. *New Collegiate Dictionary.* Toronto, ON: Thomas Allen and Sons, Ltd., 1981.

Welton, M. "Cunning Pedagogics: The Encounter between the Jesuits and the Amerindians of 17th Century New France. Canadian Association for the Study of Adult Education Proceedings, 2003. Retrieved March 12, 2004 from http://www.oise.utotoronto.ca/CASAE/cnf2003/2003_papers/mweltonCAS03a.pdf.

———. "Social Revolutionary Learning: The New Social Movements as Learning Sites." *Adult Education Quarterly* 43 (1993): 152-64.

Weor, S. A. Revolution of the Dialectic: A Practical Guide to Gnostic Psychology and Meditation. Thelema Press, 2007.

Wetton, N. *Schools Without Fear.* Forbes Publications, 1998.

Wheatley, M. "Eight Fearless Questions." Excerpt from "A Call to Fearlessness for Gentle Leaders." Address at the Shambhala Institute Core Program, Halifax, June 2006. Published in *Fieldnotes*, September/October (2006), The Shambhala Institute for Authentic Leadership. Retrieved June 8, 2007 from http://www.shambhala institute.org/contact.html.

———. and P. Chödrön. "It Starts With Uncertainty." *Shambhala Sun,* November (1999). Retrieved December 2002 from http://www.margaretwheatley.com /articles/uncertainty.html.

Wilber, K. Integral Spirituality: A Startling New Role for Religion in the Modern and *Postmodern World.* Boston, MA: Integral Books/Shambhala, 2006.

———. *Kosmic Consciousness.* DVD set from Sounds True, Inc., ©2003.

———. Boomeritis: A Novel That Will Set You Free. Boston, MA: Shambhala, 2002.

———. "Endnote 1" Chapter 10 in *Boomeritis.* Retrieved July 1, 2005 from http://wilber.shambhala.com/html/books/boomeritis/endnotes/ch10.cfm/.

———. Integral Psychology: Consciousness, Spirit, Psychology, Therapy. Boston, MA: Shambhala, 2000.

———. A Theory of Everything: An Integral Vision for Business, Politics, Science, and *Spirituality.* Boston, MA: Shambhala, 2000.

———. The Marriage of Sense and Soul: Integrating Science and Religion. NY: Random House, 1998.

———. *A Brief History of Everything.* Boston, MA: Shambhala, 1996.

———. Sex, Ecology, and Spirituality: The Spirit of Evolution (Vol. 1). Boston, MA: Shambhala, 1995.

———. Grace and Grit: Spirituality and Healing in the Life and Death of Treya Killam *Wilber.* Boston, MA: Shambhala, 2000. [original published in 1991]

———. Grace and Grit: Spirituality and Healing in the Life and Death of Treya Killam *Wilber.* Boston, MA: Shambhala, 1991/93.

———. "Paths Beyond Ego in the Coming Decades." *Paths Beyond Ego: The Transpersonal Vision,* eds. R. Walsh and F. Vaughan. Los Angeles, CA: Tarcher/Perigree, (1993): 256-65.

———. Eye to Eye: The Quest for the New Paradigm. Garden City, NY: Anchor Press/ Doubleday, 1983.

———. "Odyssey: A Personal Inquiry into Humanistic and Transpersonal Psychology." Journal of Humanistic Psychology 22 (1982): 57-90.

———. Up From Eden: A Transpersonal View of Human Evolution. Garden City, NY: Anchor Press/Doubleday, 1981.

———. No Boundary: Eastern and Western Approaches to Personal Growth. Boulder, CO: New Science Library, 1981. [original published in 1979]

———. The Atman Project: A Transpersonal View of Human Development. Wheaton, IL: The Theosophical Publishing House, 1982. [original published in 1980]

———. *Spectrum of Consciousness*. Wheaton, IL: The Theosophical Publishing House, 1977.

Wilde, S. *God's Gladiators*. Chattanooga, TN: Brookemark LLC, 2001.

Williamson, M. A Return to Love: Reflections on the Principles of a Course in Miracles NY: Harper Collins, 1992.

Willoughby, R. R. "Magic and Cognate Phenomena: An Hypothesis." In *A Handbook of Social Psychology, Vol. 1*, ed. C. Murchison. NY: Russell and Russell, 1935.

Wilson, C. *The Occult*. Watkins, 2006. [original published in 1971]

Wintle, J. *The Perfect Hostage*. Hutchinson, 2007.

Wissmann, C. "Barack Obama: A Responsible, Progressive Future?" *Nightlife* (Carbondale, IL), Nov. 6-12, 2008.

Yesudian, S. Self-reliance Through Yoga: Aspects of Yogic Wisdom Collected and Commented on by the Author. NY: Unwin Paperbacks, 1979.

Yin-Shun (Venerable). The Way of Buddhahood: Instructions from a Chinese Master, trans. W. H. Yeung. Wisdom Publication, 1998.

Zeldin, T. *An Intimate History of Humanity*. NY: HarperCollins, 1994.

Zimmerman, M. Contesting Earth's Future: Radical Ecology and Postmodernity. Berkeley, CA: University of California Press, 1997.

INDEX

('F)fear': 251, 271; arro-gance
(Phobos), 40; barrier (crossing), 49, 62, 64, 76, 166, 181,
231, 246, 250, 257; barrier
(phenomenology), 48; Barrier-
1, 48, 64, 85, 246, 251; Barrier-
2, 48, 50, 54, 61, 159-62, 166,
181, 226, 231, 246, 251, 255;
Barrier-3, 48, 76, 181, 251;
bar-riers, 47-9, 76, 154-5, 190,
246, 266; -based, 37-8, 64, 70,
75, 96, 126, 151, 156, 158-9,
161-4, 167-70, 177, 179, 189,
225, 230, 240, 242, 250, 255,
269; -based (not), 216, 255;
construction, xxxviii, 92, 101,
212; coping with (vs. healing),
99, 132; corrupts, xxix; cousins
(shame and guilt), 216; created
by knowledge, xxviii; creative
dynamic, xxxviii; crisis-focused (reality), xxxiv; critics (better), 230; cultural matrix of, 80;
culturally modified forms of,
xxviii, xxxiv, 70, 151, 228;
cycle, 98; define (how), 97;
defined (inverted commas), 3;
definition (multi-dimensional,
complex), 95; definitions (contradictory), 95; discourses,
xxxiv, 151, 215, 231, 233; disguises, xxxiv, 165; dissociated,
47; education and, 95, 221; education (postmodern), 221; emancipation from, 161, 226; Empire of, 161; evil, 95; Fall Redemption, 169; false, xxxiv;
Fear's Empire, xxxiv; FMSs
(managing), 37; fearism, 212;
fearism (equal to), 246; 'fearlessness' can dissolve, 156;
first-tier, 36-7; Flatland is, 188;
framing (beyond Wilber's), 92;
itself, xxxiv, 92, 95, 182, 194,
227, 232; itself (fear pattern),
xxxiv; knowledge of (deconstructing and reconstructing),
263; liberation from, 167 Love
vs., 37, 167; manage (better),
223; manufactured, 151;

masked (bravado systems),
133; Natural (not), 146; nature of,
227, 266; new (view of), 100; norm
(organizing motivation), 99; normalization of, 38, 154 pathological,
157; pattern (addiction), 156; pattern (discourse), 101; pattern
(Phobos-Thanatos), 169, 188;
pattern virus (FPV+), 42, 214;
patterning, xxxviii, 3, 118, 165,
169, 208, 212, 256; patterning
(repressive), 160; Thanatos: ignore-
ance), 208, 235, 253; Phobos-
Thanatos, 169, 188; postmodern
(conceptualization), 157, 233;
postmodern (theory of), 110
Projection, 208; projections
(ignore-ant and arrogant), 154;
projections (drop off at second-
tier), 154;; subjective definition
(meaning), 92; suffering, xxxvii;
symbolized fear, 64; systematic
study (lacking), 159; vaccine,
xxxvii, 29, 159, 222, 238; vaccines
(six), 204; violence, 95, 98, 163;
virus, 29, 42; vision (Setting Sun),
159; Wars, xvii, 95; Wilber
identifies (in Phobos-Thanatos),
188; won't dissolve 'fear,' 156
'Fear' Matrix: xxxi, 80, 97-100, 132,
141, 207, 215, 251; accumulation
(problem), 98; Agents (adults are
first), 234; Agents, xxxix, 164, 188;
architecture becomes interesting to
FMS-7, 71; architecture of fear, 99;
authorities, 154; break out of, 70;
cancerous growth, 100; cannot see
(to get beyond), 154; complex, 99;
constructed (re: fear-positivists'
philosophy), 101; construction seen
through, 153; corrections from
FMS-7 (and 8, 9), 99; Cultural, 98;
cultural trance-blindness (beyond,
FMS-7), 71; culture of fear and,
101, 252; defined, 98-9; denied,
101, 154; destructive, 150; detected
now by FMS-7 for first time, 71;
developmental continuum and
(FMS-7), 71; education and, 222;
eliminating, 99; embedded in, 227;
'fear' itself, xxxiv; fear pattern,

labeled, 105, 183; lacking normal fear response, 105; leader(s), 8, 51, 158, 183; leadership, xvii, xxx, 13, 157, 160, 251; learned, 105, 184; learning, 229; life, 10-1, 183; legitimate (discourse), 184; letting go, 11; literally interpreted,; living, 7; Living Challenge, 6; love, 10; love (beyond), 266; love (saturated with), 181; marketing (hype), 229; masculinism (juvenile), 18-9, 180; master warriors, 157; mastery, 11, 157-8; mature (most), 37, 181; meanings (many), 181; meditators, 180; men (narrow view), 19; metaphoric landscape, 182; meta-physical truth, 77; misogyny, 18; mistrusted, 191; most mature (intelligent) of the FMSs, 182; monks (self-emolation), 191; motivating (source for real change), 11; movements, 5; moving and, 11; mudra (abhaya), 15; mystical state, 77; mystics (nondual), 181-2; negative (view toward), 105; Neo (develops to), 251; never in fear, 182; no ego (self, fear, person), 181; no fan of, 226; no 'fear' (fear), 180, 182; no formula (FMS-9), 77; no need (for approval), 179; no need (to convince), 182; no need (to seek safety and security, FMS-9), 77; no one is 100%, 17; no self, 182; nondual (domain), 76, 181; non-violence (ultimate), 180; nondual 180-1; normalized, 105; not, 17-9, 243; not a need, 184; not against, 265; not all will (can), 190; not in favor of, 16; not inhibited (re: authories), 105; not mentioned, 222, 224; not natural or essential, 230; not used by existentialists, 234; not used by (Heron), 178; not used by (Noddings), 153; One, 30; One (path of), 180; ones (nondual), 7, 76; ones (abnormal), 180; ontology (false), 184; pain (less), 179-80; paradox, 184; parenting, 113, 229, 241; parents, 230; pathological, xxix, 133, 179, 229; patriarchy, 16; peace (state of), 21; pedagogical

architecture, 25; pedagogues, 242; people (natural), 179; perspective, 24 ; person, 76; persons (religious tradition or not), 181; personalities (beyond), 182-3; philosophical, 76; place, 22; plans, 216; play, 183; political pundit, 10; popular cultural (distortions), 133, 180; positive (vs. negative), 76, 139, 179; possibility, 226; powerful, 183; practice, 11, 147, 182, 184; pre/trans fallacy, 107; psycho-spiritual phenomenon, 77; philosophia (Treya), 187; problem itself, xxix; qualities, 183; quasi-, 223; Questions (Eight), 265-6; rarified state (stage), 181; receiving not striving, 184; reform, 216; rejected (if a need), 184; reported (by boys/men), 19; resistance to, 55, 190-1; resistance (fear-positivists), 191; revolution(s), 1, 5, 6, 8, 10, 216; rhetoric (popular culture), 133; role models, 11; Sacred Warrior (Neo), 253; sages, 181; saturated with love of God, 181; self, 18, 22, 113, 214; sexism, 18-9; shallow, 19, 98; shallowness, 184-86, 187-90, 209, 229; sheroes, 19; shocked by (disbelief), 179; sign to almost any behavior or product, 180; Sikhs (vs. Jains), 164; skeptical of, 18; social (political resistance), 180; social (worth), 139; socially unacceptable, 18-19; society, 5, 40-1, 232; speech, 232, 242-3; Spirit as, 76; spiritual, 76; stage (of development), 182; stage/state (rarified), 181; standpoint (FMS-7 and 9), 92, 232; standpoint theory, xxix, 77, 136, 188-90, 208; state of experience, 179, 186; suffering (beyond), 180; system (FMS-9), 77, 188; taken literally (West), 179; Tantric, 179; taught, 134; teachers, 231; teleclasses, 6; temperament (natural), 105, 179; terror and, 190-1, 251; terror and (not ontologically dependent), 190; threat to order and control, 229; time to be, 19; totally, 181; touched by it, 183-4; Treya

fourth, 48, 70, 229; fourth and fifth, 262; fifth, 48, 74; Left, 84

Organic paradigm, 170

organic, 63, 109-10, 129, 148, 220

organism(ic), 33, 62, 85, 98, 107, 109, 111, 120, 126, 128, 147

organization(s), xii, xiv-xv, xxvi, xxxi, xxxix, 3, 8, 21, 27, 34, 36, 39-40, 54, 60, 65-6, 69-70, 73, 95, 125-6, 133, 136-8, 145, 152, 154-5, 159-60, 166, 170-3, 221, 228, 239, 242, 249, 256, 270

organizational: 30, 37-8, 52, 62, 64, 85, 141, 247, 258; change (fear-lessness), 266; consultant, 264; development, xxxix, 21, 223; dy-namics, 170; framework, 99; prin-ciple, 224; reform (movement), 237; structures (new), 71; vacuums, 25, 33, 67

organized fear trade, xii, xxxiv,

orienting: 126, 135, 153, 174, 204; generalizations, 39, 77-8, 82

origin(ary): 114, 118; story (US and European vs. goddess), 115

Osho, 22, 142, 176, 207

O'Sullivan, Edmund, 26-8, 40

O(o)ther(ness): 47, 75, 86, 108-9, 128, 130, 178-9, 196-7, 203-4, 242, 260; Greater, 66, 119

other-worldly: vs. this-worldly, 187

Outlaw: 48-9, 88, 159, 161, 229, 234, 265; post-adult, 49;

outer vs. inner: *See also* inner, exter-iors vs. interiors

Outsider, 234

Overstreet, Bonaro Wilkins, xxvi, xxviii-xxix, 157, 255

P

pain(ful), 49, 66, 96, 101, 108, 124, 139, 162, 172, 179-80, 216-7

Pakistanian ideal, 5

Palmer, Parker J., 13, 212, 225-8

Pandora's Box, xxxii

panic: xxviii, xxxii-xxxiii, xli, 150, 237, 251; -free, 191; *See also* emergency, time, moral panic

panicology, xxvi

paradigm(s), x, xii, 55-6, 58, 69, 73,

83-4, 99, 152, 156, 161, 164, 167-71, 177, 184, 205, 212, 238, 248

paradigmatic (Love vs. fear), xiv, 167

paradisical, 108-10, 112

paradox(ical), 55, 77, 115, 118, 138, 141, 184, 239; FMS-6, 69-70

paranoia, 72, 80, 250

parent(s)(al), 12, 33, 105, 108, 113, 141, 211, 225, 230-1

Parks Daloz, Laurent A., 141

Parks, Rosa, 14, 176

parrhesia (fearless speech), 242-3

participation, 177-8

Partnership (model), xxxix, 170

Pascal, 86

Pascal, Francine, 19, 105

Pascareua, P. xviii

passion(s), xxvi, xl, 90, 134, 145, 157, 230; *See also* emotions

passionate, 150, 187, 225

passivism, 134

pastoral power, 141

paternalism, 18, 60, 66, 86, 141, 147,

pathological, x, xxv, xxix, 4, 17, 30, 34, 37, 47, 51-3, 57, 64-5, 67-9, 73, 75, 83, 85, 92, 98-101-2, 112, 118, 122, 124, 129-30, 132, 134, 136, 139, 142, 149, 154, 156, 162, 165, 179, 186, 188, 189, 199, 201, 207, 223, 229, 231-2, 253-4, 256, 260,

pathologize: 129, 134; Red (meme), 65

patriarch(al)(y), xi-xii, xxx, 16-8, 51, 101, 114-5, 141, 189

Patrick, Maven Bethanne, 11

patriotism, 259

pattern(s): 37, 109, 111-2, 118, 126, 130, 147, 150, 156, 160, 162, 165, 168-9, 177, 183, 187, 204, 207-8, 212-4, 228, 237, 240, 252-3; of existence, 34; that connect, 35; *See also* fear, 'fear'

Paul, Pope John: FMS-4, 67, 106

Paul (biblical), xxvii

Paulston, Roland, 236, 238

pawo (brave warrior), 158

peace(ful): xi, xviii, xxx, 2, 5, 9, 15, 21, 40, 60, 134, 150, 163-4, 165, 173, 213, 222, 230-1, 247-8, 256, 264; defined, 165; Green (vs. Yellow), 164; Movement, 176; Nobel prize for, 13, 263; *See also*

Vanier, Jean, 106
Vanzant, Iyania, 28
Vaughan, Francis, 75
Venus, 19
vertical: distinctions, 190; perspective
    (vision-logic, integral); vs. horiz-
    ontal, 184-5
vice: *See* cowardice, sin
Vicious Circle vs. Benign Circle, 169
vicious: when reality is challenged, 253
(V)victim(s): xiii, 8, 19, 48, 60, 69-70,
    89, 93-4, 100, 124, 144, 164, 202,
    222, 225, 231; *See also* abuse,
    crime, Green, hurt, oppression,
    postmodern, repression, trauma,
    violence
victimization, xxxii, 69, 74, 126
victimology, xxvi
victory, 130, 140, 181, 256, 258-9, 261
Vikings, 125
village life, 112, 121, 191, 196
violating, 242
violence: xi-xii, xvi, xxxii, xxxix-xl, 2-
    3, 7-8, 13, 18, 29, 30, 32, 34, 36,
    40, 46-7, 55, 62, 65-6, 69-70, 94-5,
    98-9, 108, 122, 126, 133, 135-6,
    145, 148-9, 154-5, 158, 161, 163-5,
    180, 192, 195, 202, 213, 230, 232,
    234, 238, 241-2, 247, 256, 262; *See
    also* DCFV, Defense, hurt, ideol-
    ogy, integration, non-violence, op-
    pression, suffering, trauma, vicious,
    war
virtual: 98, 255; and real (The Matrix),
    251
virtue(s): xxix, 47, 137-8, 140, 174,
    241, 251; ethical (fearless), 191;
    great(est), 222, 272; meta-, 143,
    156, 181; *See also* charity, courage,
    faith, fearlessness, hope, strength
virtuous character (citizen), 139
virus: xiii, 214, 223; 'fear,' 29; of fear,
    11, 42; *See* fear
Viscott, David, 104-05
vision(ing): x, xvi-xvii, 2, 22, 25-8, 45,
    55, 59, 77, 81, 97, 102, 116, 159,
    178, 185, 204-5, 208, 214, 216,
    224-5, 231-2, 246, 255, 260, 267;
    Setting Sun (vs. Great Eastern
    Sun), 158-60, 162, 166, 168; *See
    also* logic

visionar(y)(ies): 5, 94, 117, 172, 201;
    See also prophets
Vivekananda, Swami, 124
volition: *See* will
voluntary simplicity, 27
Voltaire, 87
Von Mises, L., 82
voting our fears, 12
vulnerability, 17, 47, 64, 85, 110, 119-
    20, 122, 133, 215, 241

W

Wachowski brothers: xxxix, 80, 95,
    168, 193, 250-2, 254, 256, 268; *See
    also* Matrix
waking up: xxxvi-xxxvii, 7, 137, 162-
    3, 168, 182, 252, 254-8; *See also*
    awakening
Walker, Alice, 20-1
walking, 119, 262
walls, 85, 220, 222-3
Walsh, Roger, 61
war(s): xi, xvi, xviii, 7-8, 20-1, 65, 73,
    123, 128, 137, 158, 164, 213, 230,
    232, 236, 238, 260-1; -based,
    xxxix, 212; culture, xii, xviii, 213;
    -like, 65; -making, xiii; -zone(s),
    xxxiii, 248; without end, 4, 93; *See
    also* Culture, fear, terror
War (Cold): xvii, xxxii, 223
War (Vietnam), 191
War of Fear, xvii, 75
War on Crime, xxxii, xl
War on Fear, xvii, 93
War on Iraq, 236
War on Terror, xvii, xxx, 4, 75, 93,
    95, 190, 261, 271; *See also* terro
War Studies, xxvii
(W)warrior(s): xxxix, 13, 17, 20-1,
    65-6, 85, 99, 119, 123, 125, 13
    152, 156-9, 162, 168, 175, 231
    233, 242, 249, 256, 259; *See (
    eco-, hero, leaders, sacred, Sl
    bhala
warriorship: 166, ; defined, 158
Waterman, Robert H. Jr., 237
Watts, Alan, 51, 75
waves, xiii; *See also* levels
Wayne, John, 264
We: 268; *See* Big Three

R. Michael Fisher, Ph. D.

Fisher, an artist, writer, teacher, counselor, human development consultant and public intellectual, completed his formal education in environmental biology, education, rehabilitation studies, adult education, curriculum and pedagogy. His latest work has examined the relationship between domination, conflict, fear and violence and how we learn and teach about this dynamic. He is particularly interested in advancing theories of leadership (second-tier).

Co-founder and Director of the In Search of Fearlessness Research Institute (since 1989), he has worked with various oppressed populations and facilitated holistic-integral workshops and courses on healing and liberation for nearly 30 years. Currently he serves as Principal and Liberation Educator for Grow & GO: Emotional-Based Learning consulting firm. A Canadian citizen, he is currently living with his life-partner in the United States.

See his website and blog:
http://www.feareducation.com
http://fearlessnessteach.blogspot.com